THIRD EDITION

LEARNING
AND
BEHAVIOR

Biological, Psychological,
and
Sociocultural Perspectives

LEWIS BARKER
Auburn University

Prentice
Hall

Upper Saddle River, New Jersey 07458

Library of Congress Cataloging-in-Publication Data

Barker, Lewis M.
  Learning and behavior : biological, psychological, and sociocultural perspectives /
Lewis Barker.—3rd ed.
    p.   cm.
  Includes bibliographical references and index.
  ISBN 0-13-032342-X
    1. Learning, Psychology of.   2. Psychobiology.   I. Title.

BF318 .B37 2001
153.1'5–dc21

00-059842

VP/Editorial Director: Laura Pearson
Acquisitions Editor: Jayme Heffler
Editorial Assistant: April Dawn Klemm
Managing Editor: Mary Rottino
Production Liaison: Fran Russello
Editorial/Production Supervision: Marianne Hutchinson (Pine Tree Composition, Inc.)
Prepress and Manufacturing Buyer: Tricia Kenny
Art Director: Jayne Conte
Director, Image Resource Center: Melinda Lee Reo
Manager, Rights & Permissions: Kay Dellosa
Image Specialist: Beth Boyd
Photo Researcher: Karen Pugliano
Marketing Manager: Sharon Cosgrove

This book was set in 10/12 New Aster by Pine Tree Composition, Inc., and was printed and bound by R.R. Donnelley & Sons Company. The cover was printed by Phoenix Color Corp.

©2001, 1997, 1994 by Prentice-Hall, Inc.
A Division of Pearson Education
Upper Saddle River, New Jersey 07458

Printed in the United States of America
10   9   8   7   6   5   4   3   2   1

ISBN 0-13-032342-X

Prentice-Hall International (UK) Limited, *London*
Prentice-Hall of Australia Pty. Limited, *Sydney*
Prentice-Hall Canada Inc., *Toronto*
Prentice-Hall Hispanoamericana, S.A., *Mexico*
Prentice-Hall of India Private Limited, *New Delhi*
Prentice-Hall of Japan, Inc., *Tokyo*
Pearson Education Asia Pte. Ltd, *Singapore*
Editora Prentice-Hall do Brasil, Ltda., *Rio de Janeiro*

*Dedicated to past and future genes and memes
that continue to shape an ever-expanding worldview.*

BRIEF CONTENTS

CONTENTS

CHAPTER 4   **CONTEMPORARY CONDITIONING METHODS
AND APPLICATIONS   102**

CHAPTER 6   INSTRUMENTAL LEARNING AND OPERANT
             CONDITIONING   192

CHAPTER 8   **PUNISHMENT AND THE AVERSIVE CONTROL
OF BEHAVIOR   275**

CHAPTER 10   APPLICATIONS OF LEARNING AND BEHAVIOR THEORY   333

CHAPTER 11   CONCEPTUAL LEARNING AND THINKING   365

PREFACE TO THE SECOND EDITION

Learning and Behavior: Biological, Psychological, and Sociocultural Perspectives has been written as a primary text for a college-level course in learning. This book will be of interest to students and instructors who recognize the broad, pervasive role that learning and behavior theory plays in our human lives. The subtitle reflects a range of interests that extends beyond typical treatments of "animal learning."

This revision is designed to be as thought-provoking, "user friendly," and as relevant to student interests as the first edition. Students want to know about themselves and the lives of others. A persistent theme in this text is that laboratory experiments using nonhuman animals can help us account for the behavioral complexity we encounter in our everyday lives. I offer students a deterministic, behavioral/biological perspective, to counterbalance the "softer" explanations they may encounter in other courses in their psychology major.

Learning is too important to be relegated to some esoteric subfield called "animal learning"—one that the majority of psychologists and students make jokes about. Humans are animals, too. Among our more interesting human behaviors is language. Language allows us a unique human culture, and written language has made civilization possible. Chapter 12 is concerned with how humans learn to use spoken and written language, how this is related to thinking and intelligence, and why we are the only civilized animals that have evolved.

Offended by *Far Side* cartoons in a scholarly book? Dislike "boxed" topics? Of the opinion that footnotes have no place in "modern" textbooks? This one has a sprinkling of all three, and I have included them because they allow me the illusion of keeping my informal classroom voice. My major professor pointed out to me years ago that there's no sense talking if no one's listening. A few disgressions and other surprises should reinforce page turning in the same way that some humor will make a fifty-minute class seem a little shorter.

PREFACE TO THE THIRD EDITION

Many who used the first two editions of this text joined with my own students in wanting more chapter-to-chapter predictability. So, in addition to updating the scholarship in learning and behavior, a specific objective of this third revision was to write chapters of more equal length. This was accomplished both by cutting some material and by regrouping the main ideas in twelve rather than 10 chapters. The result is three shorter chapters rather than two long chapters on classical conditioning, with one chapter featuring applications of classical theory. In addition, there are three shorter chapters rather than two long chapters on instrumental conditioning, with one of these also featuring real-life applications. On the advice of reviewers, the prose has been simplified, the number of key terms has been reduced by about 18%, and the popular feature *Discussion Starters* has been moved to the instructor's manual.

Allison Westlake, Assistant Psychology Editor at Prentice Hall, and the following reviewers: David K. Hogberg, Albion College; Etan Markus, University of Connecticut; and Michael J. Renner, West Chester University; Barbara Basden, California State University; Frederick Brown, Pennsylvania State University; Ron Ulm, Salisbury State University; and James King, University of Arizona shaped the manuscript. In addition, Dr. David Eckerman at the University of North Carolina, Chapel Hill, is acknowledged for his invaluable editing role in pointing out both errors in fact and in interpretation, and in furthering the text's thematic development. While acknowledging Dr. Eckerman's role in improving the text, the errors and dubious interpretations that remain are mine.

Less direct meme development that continues to shape the ideas in this text include the hundreds of scientists whose work is cited in the text, and long-time friends and mentors John Flynn, Herbert H. Reynolds, Jim Smith, and Chuck Weaver. Each continues to provide critical and personal mirrors for many of my ideas. My extended family includes Ronald, Beverly, Dick, and Marilyn, daughters Kristen, Melinda, Kira, and Jane, son-in-law David, and grandchildren Sarah and Benjamin. You will meet some of them in this book.

Early in an academic career, students are faced with many choices. This text is merely one path to explore. I hope that you find your formal education both enjoyable and profitable. Paraphrasing a Hindu expression, ". . . if the journey is not what you expected, don't be surprised."

Lewis M. Barker

CHAPTER 1

Issues in Learning and Behavior

The horses were already moving. He took the first one that broke and rolled his loop and forefooted the colt and it hit the ground with a tremendous thump. The other horses flared and bunched and looked back wildly. Before the colt could struggle up John Grady had squatted on its neck and pulled its head up and to one side and was holding the horse by the muzzle with the long bony head pressed against his chest and the hot sweet breath of it flooding up from the dark wells of its nostrils over his face . . . he cupped his hand over the horse's eyes and stroked them and he did not stop talking to the horse at all . . .

Cormac McCarthy, *All the Pretty Horses* (1992, pp. 103–104)

INTRODUCTION

This is a book about how humans and other animals learn and behave. In Cormac McCarthy's description of a young cowboy "breaking," or domesticating, a wild mustang, John Grady is behaving the way a human does, and, not surprisingly, the horse is behaving like a young colt. Both species behave in a manner that reflects their different genetic endowment and their past learning. Both are learning how to interact with each other—learning, among other things, what to expect from each other in the future.

What Is Learning?

For present purposes **learning**[1] is defined as a more or less permanent change in behavior resulting from personal experiences with an environment. Learning could be defined in other ways. For example, learning could be defined as an alteration in the way the brain works, or as a change in the way someone thinks. But over the years, psychologists have settled on a definition tied to a change in behavior. Why? One reason is that behavior is more easily observed. We can typically see and readily measure changes in behavior.

By contrast, even though we assume that learning experiences produce changes in brain chemistry, the science of the neurochemistry of learning and memory is in its infancy. At present, only the most basic neurochemical correlates of simple reflex learning in snails have been identified. Then why not define learning as "changed thinking"? Certainly thinking results from learning. But thinking is different from learning. What is normally called "thinking" depends on what a person says.

"What are you thinking?"

"I'm thinking about what I learned on my date last night."

---

[1]Boldface terms are defined as key terms at the end of each chapter and also in an appendix.

Since we know that babies and birds and horses can learn, but we can't get a verbal self-report about what they are thinking, it is best to begin our study by defining learning in terms of changes in observable behavior. Another reason is that people may or may not give accurate reports about their thoughts. In this case, for example, the person may not have been thinking about anything, but says something to be polite.

Finally, much of what we learn in life, as we will see throughout the text, may only marginally involve thinking. We drive our cars without much thought. Phobias, to take another example, are learned without "thinking." Finally, it is likely that the protagonist John Grady didn't consciously think about the early childhood experiences that led to his ability to expertly train the wild horse. It is also likely that the horse learned to respond to its new rider without giving it much thought.

What Is Behavior?

Behavior is what you do, the ways you act, how you respond to your environment. Much of your behavior has been learned, but behavior change by itself is not "learning." Your behavior is affected by other factors as well as by learning. Drugs can change behavior, but typically the alteration is temporary and behavior returns to normal. A child's fatigue, as every parent knows, can drastically alter his or her behavior. A night's rest restores behavior to normal. A horse's fear will cause it to behave wildly, but both the fear and wildness dissipate with time. By contrast, learning is relatively permanent. For example, once a child has learned the alphabet, under most circumstances it doesn't go away.

Learning and Behavior: Biological, Psychological, and Sociocultural Perspectives

Your human ability to learn widely varying tasks during a lifetime complements other behavioral tendencies you inherited at conception. The ability to run is part of your endowment, but you had to learn to dribble a soccer ball while running. Your behavior is highly dependent on the specific environment of the culture into which you were born. Learning to get around on the freeway system in Los Angeles does not prepare you to find your way around New York City on the subway system. The research of psychologists and other behavioral scientists enhances our understanding of the interplay of these innate and learned behaviors. Let us begin by looking at the more biological end of the spectrum.

Genes and Environment. Few readers would disagree with the observation that most of their behavior results from their personal interactions with their own, unique environments. Without any personal knowledge of each other, each of us can deduce that the other has learned a great deal in classroom settings. Classrooms provide a language-rich environment. Without extensive educational experiences in language-rich environments, humans cannot understand written language. Nor can they understand complex ideas. Though these skills do depend on our genes, they also critically depend on learning.

Another way of saying this is that there appears to be nothing in the human genotype (the sum of your genetic endowment) that has specifically prepared you to read and to write. As every schoolchild knows, while learning to talk is easy, learning to read and write requires a great deal of effort. Most humans can walk, run, and talk: Only a highly organized environment, however, affords humans the experiences necessary for competitive athletics, or to read and to write. Learning is an important way that genes interact with environment to determine behavior.

Human genes provide blueprints for brains that determine patterns of behavior in ways scientists are only now beginning to understand. A toddler does not learn to walk or to babble, and it is likely that horses do not learn to hang around in herds. Rather, these behaviors appear during the course of development, and each is an indication of the genetic endowment that an animal inherits at conception. An animal's genetic endowment provides inherited tendencies. But in the course of a lifetime what is learned and how it is learned determines an individual's unique behavior. And what is learned depends very much upon the specifics of the environment in which one's genes are being expressed. (Notice that these arguments are applicable to animals in general, not just to humans.)

Behavior Is Determined by Many Factors.   We are as interested in understanding behavior as we are in understanding how a person learns. What does it mean to "understand" an animal such as a human? The answer, unfortunately, is not simple. To fully understand an animal (such as yourself), you would need to know its evolutionary history, biology, psychology, and sociology. How does its brain work? How do its endocrine glands influence behavior? What does it eat? These "body" aspects in turn are related to questions of survival. What is its life cycle? In the niche it occupies, how does the animal's brain/behavior solve problems of reproduction and care of offspring? These complexities have led some scientists (Timberlake, 1994; Tinbergen, 1950) to develop models of an animal's "behavioral system" that incorporates ecology (environment), physiology, and learning.

What is the role of culture in human learning? A people's culture consists of all the ideas, objects, and ways of doing things created by the group. Culture includes arts, beliefs, customs, inventions, language, technology, and traditions. Cultures create complex environments within which human genotypes can interact. Here we can inquire about more complex roles of learning—in language, in art, and in the formation of beliefs, customs, and traditions. For example, what is the role of learning in the thinking that produces inventions and technology and in language? To summarize, the how and what of human and nonhuman animal learning and behavior can be analyzed from biological, psychological, and sociocultural perspectives.

Comparing Learning Theory and Behavior Theory

Behavior is a term that encompasses both learned (acquired behavior) and innate (instinctive behavior) components. Because genotypes must be expressed in a specific environment, most behaviors consist of both innate and acquired components. A specific environment constrains, or determines the behavior that can be expressed. For example, the genotype of a person born into an environment that contains literate caretakers and children's books is expressed differently than the same genotype born into a bookless, illiterate environment.

Were you to make a list of your behaviors, more than likely you would consider very few of them to be exclusively "innate" or "learned." In comparison with simpler animals, such as spiders and newts, human behavior is especially variable. As evidence, consider the multitude of cultural variations among humans. For this very reason, the science of psychology focuses on a systematic analysis of individual differences—what you have learned and how you have learned over the course of your lifetime. Learning psychologists are more interested in genotype-environment interactions—the specific experiences that have shaped you to be "you"—than they are in human behavior in general.

Learning Theory. Another way of saying this is that unless one knows your unique history—that is, all the environments that you have experienced since conception—one really doesn't know you. A science of behavior is an attempt to account for how your behavior has been shaped by your immediate environment—the people, places, relationships, and events you have experienced. A **learning theory** proposes that a limited number of general principles of learning can account for much of the observed variability in your behavior. What stimuli impinged on you, and what effect did these stimuli have? What were the outcomes of your unique encounters with your unique environment? It is likely that certain events had greater impact than others, including, as we will see in later chapters, stimuli that reward and punish and stimuli that afford predictability and control over the environment.

Language is yet another example of behavior. Most readers of this text first heard the unique sounds of the English language—an environment that influenced but did not totally determine their language behavior. Obviously, this same language environment does not produce language behavior among pet dogs and cats and other nonhuman animals. Your unique human genetic makeup allowed you to be receptive to and to learn from a particular language environment. So what you learned in part has been determined by your human genotype. A tentative first conclusion: Learning theory by itself cannot account for any given acquired behavior, such as language.

Behavior Theory.   By contrast, **behavior theory** encompasses the interplay of genes and environment (Halliday & Slater, 1983; Plomin, 1990).[2] As noted earlier, your total genetic endowment—that which you received from biological parents at conception—defines your genotype. The combination of these innate tendencies, plus the learned personal behaviors acquired in your lifetime, determines your unique physical and psychological nature—your **phenotype.** Do not confuse genotypes and phenotypes. Your genotype is the theoretical you, the potential "you" at the moment of conception. Your phenotype is the real you resulting from the special environment your genotype encountered in its lifetime. Another way of saying this? Phenotypes are genotypes expressed in an environment.

Phenotypes Are Unique.   You think and behave differently from others in your family, any of your friends, and even unknown others (a) because of your basic nature and (b) because you have had unique experiences. By definition each of us has a one-of-a-kind genotype, and each of us has been raised in a unique environment. Therefore, each of us, and every individual life form, is a unique phenotype.

Nature and Nurture.   Learning is an important part of "nurture" in the "nature-nurture argument." Learning is implicated in "environment" in questions relating to the role of environment in gene expression. Take as an example the feeding behavior of titmice (various species of birds) native to England. Some individual birds of the species have been observed to remove the paper caps and to eat the cream from the top of bottles of home-delivered milk (Fisher & Hinde, 1949). Neither this nor any other species has evolved in an *ecological niche* (i.e., an immediate environment) that contained bottles of milk as a food source. Such feeding behavior, therefore, is not an instinctive behavior. (This type of behavior is discussed in detail in the next chapter.)

These birds, however, have inherited eyes for seeing, a manipulative beak, an underlying physiology that regulates hunger, thirst, and so on. This basic equipment supports feeding in a variety of environments. Therefore, we can safely conclude that in their lifetime, birds learn to eat cow's milk from bottles. (In a behavioral analysis of this situation—as we'll see in Chapter 6—the cream is the *reinforcer* for the bottle-top pecking response. The process of *reinforcement* makes it more likely that the bird will return to the next milk bottle.)

Notice the parallel of this feeding bird to our earlier discussion of reading and writing language. Reading, writing, and removing bottle caps are not instinctive behaviors. Nevertheless, we use visual, auditory, and motor systems that are inherited and that serve other functions to get the job done.

Behavior Theory Is All-Encompassing.   Modern behavior theory is more global than learning theory. Reflect, for a moment, on why this is so. A "the-

---

[2]"Behavior theory" should not be confused with "Behaviorism" as defined by John B. Watson, B. F. Skinner, and others (see Chapter 6). As we will see, **behaviorism** embodies an extreme environmental determinism which, for the most part, ignores genetic differences in behavior.

Photo 1.1   A Bird Discovers a New Ecological Niche

Photo from J. Markham/Bruce Coleman, Inc.

ory of behavior"—a theory ostensibly aimed at understanding why humans behave as they do—would encompass all of personality theory (normal and abnormal), motivation theory, learning theory, behavioral genetics, anthropology, neurophysiology, sociology, literature and the fine arts, and other relevant enterprises. Learning theories help us understand why humans behave as they do. In and of themselves, however, learning theories do not provide complete accounts of behavior.

Why Study Learning?   If behavior theory is more all-encompassing than learning theory, why do psychologists emphasize learning? One answer has already been given. Behavioral scientists at present do not know enough to integrate all of personality theory, all of behavioral genetics, all of neurochemistry, all of sociology, and so on. Another reason, more important, is that learning theory is proving useful in understanding behavior. After a century of laboratory study, psychologists have begun to appreciate the complexities of learning and how learning theory can be applied to the study of behavior. Learning, then, is our focus. The results of experiments in this text represent progress in achieving the goal of an all-encompassing behavior theory.

Interim Summary

1. ***Learning*** is defined as a relatively permanent change in behavior resulting from experiences with the environment.

2. *Behavior* is what you do, the ways you act, and how you respond to your environment.

3. Inherited tendencies can be attributed to an organism's genes; learning determines unique behavioral tendencies.

4. Animal learning and behavior can be analyzed from biological, psychological, and sociocultural perspectives.

5. An individual organism comprises a phenotype (a genotype expressed in an environment).

6. Learning results from experience with the environment and contributes to nurture in the nature/nurture contrast.

7. *Learning theory* proposes that general principles of learning can account for much of the observed variability in animal behavior.

8. Learning is a subset of *behavior theory,* that the way animals behave reflects the interplay of their genetic predispositions within a particular environment.

Discussion Questions

1. You will likely find your future in your present. That is, your local, immediate environments of home/ apartment, school/work will in part determine your present and future friends, your career, and so on. In a nutshell, that is all that is meant by the phrase *environment shapes behavior.* I give my children much freedom, but I encourage them to "stay in school" rather than to "go to work." What likely reasons (other than completing their education) contribute to my concern for where they spend their time?

2. Do you agree with the assertion that "book learning" accounts for only a small (but important) portion of all the things we learn in our lifetime? If you disagree, are you prepared to explain to millions of illiterate humans how little they have learned in their lifetimes?

3. An accomplished pianist was asked how she came to play the piano so well. She replied that she chose her parents well. Have you contemplated your genetic endowment? Your early environmental experiences? Or do you think you are a free agent who can choose to make your own way in life irrespective of your specific nature and nurture? We will return to these questions in later chapters.

Underlying Issues in Learning and Behavior Theory

An issue that I frequently encounter in teaching a learning course occurs when students realize that the evidence underlying learning theory comes primarily from laboratory experiments using nonhuman animals. Questions— and challenges—arise. Reading entertaining horse stories is one thing. But why study rats, pigeons, and dogs to find out how humans learn? Doesn't the fact that we can speak, and our ability to reason—assuming these behaviors are lacking in nonhuman animals—make animal learning experiments both irrelevant and meaningless to an understanding of human behavior? This is but one issue that needs to be addressed at the beginning of this textbook. In this section, we'll preview other problem areas.

1. **Comparing human behavior with nonhuman animals.** How are humans the same as and how do they differ from other animals? Which other animals? What do we know of the genetic structure of different animals? Of their brains compared with ours? Of their behavior patterns compared to ours? Of how they are socialized compared to us? Answers to these questions are not simple. "Comparison" questions are entertained primarily in Chapter 2 and again in Chapters 9 and 10.

2. **Problems of extrapolation**. Another issue raised by experiments in this book is the problem of *extrapolation*. There are two types of extrapolation that present difficulty. One is that of applying experimental results from the laboratory to real life. How relevant can laboratory findings be to everyday living? Can results from one experiment (let's say an analysis of how one learns to play the guitar) be applied to another experiment (i.e., learning how to tie shoes, or to program a computer, or to gentle a horse)? The other problem of extrapolation is that of applying the findings from learning experiments with nonhuman animals to humans. There are no easy answers here; arguments for and against extrapolation of both types of experimental findings will appear throughout the text.

3. **Catalogs of behavior, or general principles of behavior.** To the extent that behavioral scientists are successful in extrapolating experimental results from nonhuman animals to other animals, including humans, then the goal of discovering general principles (as has been the case in chemistry and physics) of learning and behavior may be achieved and a science of behavioral analysis realized. The alternative is not too exciting—the mere cataloging of what each species is or is not capable of learning, with no general principles. Some may find such catalogs interesting, but I do not. Here we will search for general principles.

4. **Animal intelligence.** What evidence should we accept to support or refute claims of nonhuman animal intelligence? Do we know whether animals are capable of thinking or whether they are able to reason? (You might want to try out these questions by analyzing your pet dog, cat, or goldfish.) As we see in Chapter 9, a number of chimpanzees have been taught American Sign Language (ASL) and other ways to communicate with humans. Now that they have these skills, do they use them to communicate? For example, we might ask whether chimpanzees with admittedly primitive language skills learn other tasks differently from chimps lacking these communication skills. One conclusion we will reach is that humans are not the only animals capable of both conceptual learning and thinking, broadly defined.

5. **Cognitive processes.** By limiting the study of learning to observable behavior are we restricting the science of psychology? To anticipate this argument, some learning theorists have proposed that references to human and animal emotional states, to memory processes, and to "expectations," and other cognitive processes are unnecessary—indeed, are ill-advised. Take as an example the following instance of behavior. The sound of a can opener brings your cat running. Why? A behavioral explanation is that it has been conditioned to do so: The sound of the can opener has become associated with getting fed, and the sound now signals feeding. Such an explanation is a fairly simple description of the procedures that produced the behavior.

   By contrast, a cognitive explanation might be that the cat "expects" to be fed when the sound of the can opener is heard. Now such an "expectation" necessarily requires a memory system in which the cat's prior memory of the can opener and food have been stored. Frankly, we don't know if cats have either expectations or memory systems: Both are inferences based on the cat's behavior. In this sense, reference to a hypothetical "expectation" or a "memory" doesn't really explain the cat's behavior. The question remains as to whether the analysis of more complex human behavior is helped or hindered by strict reliance on behavioral explanations. For example, does the fact that humans have language that allows us to talk about our expectations make possible different explanations for humans compared to mute animals? We'll revisit this argument in the next section and in later chapters.

6. **Scientific and nonscientific views of humans.** Can the human mind and human behavior be understood by scientific methods? Rene Descartes, 350 years ago, divided the psychological world of humans and animals into two realms: (1) reflexes and instinct, that is shared with other animals, and (2) voluntary behavior, that is restricted to humans. In this Cartesian view, animals are reflexive machines that behave instinctively, in contrast to humans who can act voluntarily and are purposive. Lost in Descartes' dichotomous argument is the fact that he also thought that humans could be studied scientifically.

   Many people living within our "scientific" Western culture continue to hold prescientific views about human nature. Is it possible that ignorance about the human mind is desirable because it preserves its mystery? Many share with Descartes the belief in the division of humans from other animals. Some contemporary religious leaders, for example, continue to assert human preeminence over (as well as distinctiveness from) the animal world. Polling consistently finds that approximately 80% of Americans espouse a belief in the "special creation" of humans as distinct from other animals.

   To the extent that you agree that humans cannot be studied scientifically, the present study of animal learning and behavior may seem to be an esoteric exercise in trivial research findings, an exercise unrelated to the human condition. I sincerely hope this is not the case. Box 1.1 highlights three individuals who, in challenging us to think differently about ourselves, helped bring about a scientific conception of human experience.

This text accepts the challenge of trying to analyze and understand the human mind from within a scientific framework. You may be surprised to find that behavioral scientists now have answers to questions about humans and other animals that Descartes didn't know enough to ask. The challenge to view humans from a scientific perspective begins here and continues through each of the following chapters.

Psychology of Human Learning and Cognition Compared

Thinking, memorizing, reasoning, reading, knowing. These terms are part of the vocabulary and psychological constructs of *cognitive psychology* and the study of *cognition* (Jahnke & Nowaczyk, 1998). Historically, "learning psychologists" have been concerned with behavioral analyses, especially of labo-

BOX 1.1   THREE INTELLECTUAL GIANTS

What is a scientific understanding of human experience? Ask 10 people and get 10 answers. Most would agree that such a view would encompass mainstream findings and theory in chemistry and physics, including the Big Bang origin of the matter in the universe. Focusing more on the existence of life and that which constitutes human nature, here I offer my three candidates for "most influential thinkers," namely, Charles Darwin, Ivan Pavlov, and Sigmund Freud.

We will meet Darwin (in Chapter 2) and Pavlov (Chapters 3 and 4) in more detail. Sigmund Freud's ideas are not critically examined in this book, but his influence is ever-present. What are the similarities and differences of these three individuals? All are DWEMs (dead, white, European males). All were born in 19th-century Europe, and all had biological interests. While none was a psychologist per se, each profoundly influenced modern conceptions of the human mind and behavior. Darwin addressed our phyletic and behavioral continuities with other animals. Pavlov showed us that we shared with other animals both common reflexes and common processes of conditioning those reflexes. Freud pointed out to us that although we are not always conscious of what we have learned during our lifetime, our adult mind is continuous with and is in part determined by childhood experiences. Hence, all were materialists who espoused various forms of biological determinism.

ratory experiments on nonhuman animals. By contrast, cognitive psychologists tend to view learning as the acquisition of information into human memory. Thinking is interpreted from within an "information-processing" model of psychology.

Concepts of learning and memory are obviously related. Can you think of an instance of learning that does not presuppose a memory system or vice versa? Can you think of a concept of memory as other than the repository of that which has been learned? Seldom, however, do the terms learning and memory seem to interact in the minds of psychologists! Separate research journals report experiments on "animal learning" and on "human memory." Different courses using distinctive textbooks on "learning" or "cognition" (or "memory") are offered in our colleges and universities by psychologists with vastly different understandings of these two terms.

"Learning" or "Thinking"? For the sake of argument let us put aside questions of evolution and psychological continuity among animals for the moment. Let us accept the assumption that humans are sufficiently different from animals that separate rules, or principles, may guide their learning. Let's listen to one of many students over the years who doubts that animal learning experiments mirror her own learning experiences in the classroom:

> *I sit here, listening to you, trying to make sense, thinking, comparing, contrasting, trying to understand. Then I go to the library and read, read, read . . . trying to learn the material in the textbook. Some of it I memorize.*
>
> *My dog cannot do what I do; it does not learn in the same way. What good does it do to study animal learning experiments if animals don't think as I do?*

These are excellent observations, and you may likewise be entertaining similar reservations. But consider the following: This student's comments imply (a) that she fully understands the realms of human learning and cognition; of nonhuman animal learning and cognition; and that she intuitively knows that human learning is distinct from animal learning and cognition in all ways. Unfortunately, behavioral scientists recognize the importance of this student's reservations, but do not presently know enough to arrive at the same conclusions as she. A new organization of scientists formed in the 1990s to specifically study "comparative cognition" in an attempt to answer such questions.[3]

Since we don't have all the answers, isn't it preferable to adopt the behavioral scientists' strategy of (a) looking at the evidence, (b) noting that the evidence is incomplete, (c) engaging in research aimed at answering specific questions, and (d) coming to some tentative conclusions that will change as more data are gathered? The hard part for both scientists and students alike is to be content with less-than-perfect answers to such complex questions. We

---

[3]International Conference on Comparative Cognition.
http://web.psych.ualberta.ca/ ~mspetch/co3/foundingmembers.htm

must learn to be patient and accept the fact that more is unknown than known about both human and nonhuman animal minds.

Animals Have Minds?   Some evidence that bears on the "animal mind" may surprise you. For example, humans and nonhuman animals alike engage in "timing" behaviors; likewise, both often make similar choices when presented with similar alternatives. Nonhuman animals and humans seem to reason and to learn some tasks in a similar manner. Nonhuman animals not only make choices but also think and otherwise behave in quite complex ways reflecting sophisticated psychological properties. Many species, not just humans, learn concepts. Humans and other nonhuman animals engage in communication. And, not unlike humans, a number of animal species pass on knowledge from generation to generation.

Let us suspend judgment for the present, then, regarding the uniqueness of humans, and return later to a serious treatment of these questions. My hope is that you, like the other student who raised these questions, soon will have a better idea of just how complex the questions are, even if the answers are less than satisfying. For now, consider the following questions: What evidence would convince you that animals can tell time? That animals can think? That animals can make decisions? That animals can behave in a voluntary fashion? Scientists are in agreement that what we take as evidence is that which is gained from formal observations and experimentation.

The study of animal learning and behavior can help us better understand how humans learn and how they think. Likewise, many of the techniques used by cognitive psychologists to study human memory involve problem solving and list learning, to name but a few methods. Interpreting the results of these human experiments makes use of associative models that in part are based on the study of laboratory animals (Baddeley, 1998; Slameka, 1967). The study of association formation begins in Chapter 3, but for present purposes, it merely refers to how two stimuli, or a stimulus and a response, become connected. Saying "cat" (a response) to the stimulus CAT is an example. The point is that both animal learning and human cognitive approaches are complementary. Learning and memory theory for both animals and humans are increasingly seen to be interdependent.

Application of Theories of Learning

The psychology of learning also has an applied dimension. Our study of experiments in this text will help you better understand how to educate your children; why some people might have eating disorders and others a chemical dependency; and how each of us can learn to be sick and learn to be well. To the extent that your roommate or a close friend (or you) has problems with relationships, we better understand such problems by studying that person's learning history—the rewards and punishments that have shaped a maladaptive behavior. By applying learning theory to our skilled performances, to our use of language, to our emotional and rational behaviors—both dysfunctional and normal—we attain insight and the power to change behavior. Let us look at some of these applications.

Learning the Alphabet.   Most of us don't know when or how we learned the alphabet. Likely, the average reader has forgotten just how complex this is for a child. While there is general agreement that children must learn the alphabet before they can learn to read, little is known about this process. Some studies have shown that in middle-class homes, hundreds to thousands of hours are spent in pre-school reading-related activities (Adams, 1990). By the end of kindergarten these children know the names and sounds associated with the alphabet. Children from at-risk homes—who know little upon entering kindergarten—tend to not catch up. Estimates of literacy attainment in the 1st and 3rd grade—dependent upon alphabetic skills—are now predictive of whether a child will be a high school dropout (Snow, Burns, & Griffin, 1998).

Recent studies have demonstrated that children learn the alphabet by making simple associations, not unlike how other animals learn to make associations (Bus & van IJzendoorn, 1999; Metsala, 1999). But "hundreds to thousands" of hours to learn 26 letters of the alphabet? Actually, the problem is not as simple as it seems. An analysis shows that 26 lower- and uppercase letters = 52 visual symbols, each of which has a name, stands for a sound, and can be printed: 52 + 52 + 52 = 156 separate responses associated with these 52 visual symbols. (Add 10 digits of the number system, each visual stimulus having a name, and each printed.) The discrimination is made more difficult because some letters have more than one sound, and the names and sounds of each letter sometimes overlap and sometimes do not. Figure 1.1 shows other reasons that learning these alphabetic associations are difficult: Each letter can appear in a different size, a different font (including multiple variations of cursive writing), and a different color. Does the top row end in DL1 or D11? Does the bottom row include an O or a 0 (zero)?

The rules governing association formation, generalization, and discrimination have been derived from experiments with nonhuman animals. The application of these rules helps us to understand both the alphabetic learning process, and, as we'll see in a later chapter, the remediation of these skills in children. We'll study the basics of learning in several chapters before applying the rules.

Learning and Clinical Psychology.   I have a good friend who will only travel by car or train because he is afraid of flying. He is reluctant to seek out psychotherapy because he thinks that "talk therapy" never helped anyone, and he doesn't want to take medication. What do you think? Can he or any of the estimated 15% of Americans who suffer anxiety disorders benefit from psychotherapy?

FIGURE 1.1 Learning Letters and Numbers

The alphabet may be difficult to learn because 52 upper- and lowercase symbols must be differentiated from 10 number shapes (total = 62 symbols). Individual letters and numbers can vary in shape (font), size, and color, making the number of symbols to be discriminated far more than 62.

Many undergraduate majors studying psychology have professional aspirations. Their goal is to go to graduate school and then through course work, practicums, and internships to become licensed as clinical psychologists, as social workers, as professional counselors, or as professionals in other applied occupations. More often than not, these career-oriented students do not see the relevance of courses in animal learning (or, for that matter, courses in perception, physiology, or cognitive or quantitative psychology!). Rather, most students view the "applied" courses (personality, abnormal, social, developmental, testing) as the relevant preprofessional curriculum.

Allow me to offer a different perspective. The study of animal learning is as critically important to the practice of clinical psychology as it is to how children learn. The bulk of patients seeking therapy have emotional- and cognitive-based "lifestyle disorders." Most were not born that way. Many are presently dysfunctional because of a myriad of aversive learning experiences. As we will see in examples throughout this text, aversive conditioning is rapid, powerful, and long-lasting under a variety of circumstances in differing environments. Our understanding of phobic and panic disorders, post-traumatic stress disorders (PTSD), reactive depression, eating disorders, educational problems (learning disorders), sexual disorders, marital disorders, and psychophysiological disorders, to name but a few, depends on theories of learned behavior.

Likewise, the recommended therapy for these disorders are largely laboratory based. By that, I mean that associative models used in behavioral and cognitive-behavioral therapy are based on laboratory research with non-human animals. Increasingly, such therapeutic approaches are seen to be an effective (and cost-effective) alternative to drug therapy (Clay, 2000). In summary, students with aspirations in clinical psychology are well served by learning the empirical research basis for their chosen discipline.

We'll spend several chapters learning the rules before applying them.

Learning and Child Development: Parenting Skills. A psychology major attracts many students because they seek a better understanding of themselves, of friends, and of family members. Who am I? Why do I think, feel, and act as I do? To return to an earlier theme, a multifaceted behavior theory—including genetics, learning, sociology, and so on—addresses such questions. In many respects, each course in a psychology curriculum addresses one or more aspects of a broad "theory" (or "theories") of behavior.

Integral to a comprehensive theory of behavior are learning and the analysis of learned behavior that such theory affords. Beginning with your genetic endowment, you subsequently have learned to be who and what you presently are. Your present level of socialization reflects the total of your environmental experiences to date. Significant others, including parents, have guided you (or not); reinforced and punished you (or not); and arranged formal learning opportunities in schools, camps, churches (or not).

Many of you will in turn become parents during your lifetime and will be faced with making decisions about how you will raise your children. What do you want from them and for them, and how will you arrange their environment to maximize attaining your mutual goals? Over a half-century ago a famous learning psychologist named B. F. Skinner (1948) wrote *Walden Two* in which he proposed that a child's behavior could be trained in a programmed environment. In his utopia, illiteracy and criminal behavior were replaced by happy, productive people.

In this text you will read about the outcomes of experiments by Skinner and others that manipulate the environments of animals, including humans, for the purpose of changing and controlling their behavior. No guarantees, but your children might profit from your study of the experimental analysis of behavior. At a minimum you will likely become more interested in how you were raised, and more analytical about your role as a parent.

Learning and Culture.   Ethnic and cultural differences fit a nature/nurture framework. Ethnicity denotes "ancestry, culture, language, nationality . . . religion, or a combination of these things" (*World Book Encyclopedia*, 1991). Ancestry is nature; the remaining factors are nurture—they are environmentally determined. In the course of your lifetime, not only have you learned to speak the language peculiar to your culture, but also you have learned about religious practices, about cultural foods and clothes styles, about dating practices and other habits of interacting, and . . . just about everything else you can think of. This could be a long book.

Interim Summary

1. Issues throughout this text include those of comparing human behavior with nonhuman animals; problems of extrapolation from nonhuman animals to humans; the problem of explanation in terms restricted to behavior, or by reference to cognitive processes; questions of animal intelligence; whether scientists should catalog specific instances of behavior or seek general principles of behavior; and scientific versus nonscientific views of humans.

2. While recognizing the complexity of humans, it is assumed that the human mind and human behavior can be understood by scientific methods.

3. Laboratory-based learning theories can be shown to apply to how a child learns the alphabet, the development and treatment of anxiety disorders within clinical psychology, the socialization process, parenting skills, and the foundations of culture.

DISCUSSION QUESTIONS

4. My mother used to say that there are some things we will never know about people and other things we shouldn't even try to find out. I loved my mother and respected her opinions, but as a scientist, I respectfully disagree with her and think that an experimental analysis of human behavior is both desirable and possible. Do you think that human beings can and should be studied scientifically? How do you feel about being "an object of study"?

THE QUEST FOR A SCIENCE OF LEARNING

The study of learning is a formal science. As is the case in other areas in psychology, however, the methods used to study learning seem to be radically different from, say, those of chemistry, biology, or physics. In this section, we briefly look at the methods of inquiry into psychological processes and then focus on particulars in the science of learning. Here you will learn about operational definitions, the problem of reification, the learning-performance distinction, levels of analysis, and reductionism.

History of Science

Science is one of the more complex (and curious) activities in which humans engage. Those of us who enjoy Western culture take for granted the various methods by which science is accomplished, the knowledge attained, and the technology made possible by these findings. We may also value artistic and religious experiences, for example, that provide a type of knowledge that is independent of scientific criteria. An underlying premise of this text is that a scientific perspective provides an important understanding of human behavior.

Those who study the history of science and scientific thinking find precursors of "modern" science in Greek philosophers who lived several thousand years ago. These mathematicians, astronomers, logicians, and inventors—to name but a few of the behavioral activities of natural philosophers—formulated problems and discovered a variety of philosophical tools, including mathematics and logic. The activity of these ancient philosophers found fruition in modern Western European scientific thinking that dates from the 1600s. Our present focus is on the behavioral sciences, arguably only about 150 years old. Behavioral studies on laboratory animals have only a 100-year history.

Generations of students have found the activities of psychologists working with animals in laboratories to be a curious enterprise, indeed. As mentioned earlier, "What are you trying to prove?" and "What can we learn about humans from the study of rats?" are legitimate questions.

The Science of Learning.   A behavioral scientist's activities in the laboratory can be divided into two parts. First, a decision is made as to what will be studied, followed by the questions of how the investigation will continue. In the same way that our understanding of any phenomenon depends on the perspective from which we view it, the results of learning experiments are directly influenced by the way in which the experiment is performed, that is, the method used. For this reason it is important at the outset to understand some of the underlying theory and methods used to investigate learning and behavior both in real life and in the laboratory.

Learning as a Hypothetical Construct

Earlier, learning was defined as a relatively enduring change in behavior resulting from particular kinds of experiences. Unfortunately, it is presently impossible to directly observe the learning process. We simply cannot crawl into the brains of the people (or, for that matter, the brains of much simpler animals) and actually see or feel or hear learning. These processes are not currently observable.

How is it possible to have a science of learning if learning is unobservable? Terms like learning are not unusual in psychology; consider, for example, memory, motivation, fear, and intelligence. These words describing processes of the mind are generally referred to as **hypothetical constructs.** Intelligence, for example, is assumed to exist but cannot be observed directly. (It is not even clear what it means to suggest that "it" could be observed directly, other than to assert that "it" is composed of neurochemical changes or of patterns of neural activity).

Hypothetical is perhaps a poor term because it implies that processes such as learning and intelligence are nonexistent or even imaginary. Nothing could be further from the truth. As every school child knows, memory and intelligence are routinely measured as performance on paper and pencil tests.

Operational Definitions

To define intelligence as an IQ score is an operational definition. An **operational definition** means that the construct at hand is defined according to the operations that measure it. For example, performance on a final exam operationally defines what you have learned in the course. Typically, arguments to the effect that IQ tests do not measure "real" intelligence or that final exams do not measure what was really learned in a class are disagreements about operational definitions. Yes, other performance measures can be used to measure "intelligence" and to measure what was learned in a class. *But intelligence and learning do not exist independently of some measure of performance.* Arguments to the contrary run the risk of reification. To reify means to assert the existence of something without having independent evidence that "it" exists.

It doesn't help, for example, that everyone has a general idea of what intelligence is and that what intelligence is is something different from a score on a test. Likewise, to assert that you know more than what a test samples is at one and the same time true and begging the question. Tests are performance measures, and good tests are designed to allow you to express what you have learned. The futility of asserting that "intelligence cannot be measured" and that "there is no way to measure what I have learned" should be apparent. (If you disagree with this perspective—or don't understand it—discuss it with your professor.)

Learning-Performance Distinction

Note that behavioral scientists measure "performance" and infer learning, intelligence, memory, and so on from these observations. As noted before, learning and memory formations are currently unobservable processes. We infer such processes based on the changes in performance that can be measured. The difference between what is measured and what is inferred is known as the **learning-performance distinction.**

Consider, for example, a rat negotiating its way through a maze to obtain food. Often, the length of time it takes the rat from the start box to the goal box (where the food is) is operationally defined as a measure of learning. That is, rats that don't know the maze take longer to get through it than rats that have learned the proper sequence of turns. In this example, a rat might take 5 minutes on the first trial, do better on most subsequent trials, and by the 20th trial take only 15 sec from start box to goal box. From this change in performance we can conclude that the rat has learned the maze. For the next 10 trials we remove food from the goal box, and observe that it now takes longer, say 2 minutes, for the rat to go from the start box to the goal box. Did the rat forget the maze, or was its performance merely slowed because of the absence of food? After finding food on the next several trials, the rat once again negotiates the maze in 15 sec. We can conclude that the performance, but not the learning, was affected by removing the food from the goal box.

"Hard Science" and Psychology

The psychology of learning is characterized here as a science—that is, as a systematic, objective, analytical enterprise. Not everyone agrees that psychology is a science. Biologists, chemists, and physicists, for example, often object to the subject matter of psychology. How can one study learning (or motivation or memory), they ask, when these processes are unobservable? After all, the primary goal of a science is to observe and analyze objectively the various phenomena of nature. Are not physical phenomena, such as the chemical reactions of basic biological processes, more objectively measured? Would it perhaps be better to be looking for the biochemical determinants of the learning process and not merely analyzing the behaving animal?

Obviously, behavioral scientists think not. Behavioral scientists think that studying behavior is important in its own right. But let us analyze the hard science argument more carefully. What are the consequences of reducing the learning process to concrete physical and/or chemical entities? The argument is called reductionism.

Reductionism

As you well know, the world is described by several kinds of language. Artists and musicians and priests certainly see the world in different terms than engineers and politicians. Within the world of science there also exist levels of analysis.

While their activities vary widely, a communality of purpose and spirit exists among scientists. Some scientists investigate phenomena at a *molar level*. An example of a molar-level study is to analyze the behavior of a whole, intact organism. Others attempt to understand some aspect of behavior by determining which parts of the brain (anatomy) or which chemicals (biochemistry) are involved when a particular behavior occurs. They are pursuing a more molecular level of analysis. The tendency to explain a phenomenon by reference to a more *molecular level* of analysis, such as biochemistry, is called **reductionism.**

Chicken Example. Let us use as an example a scientist wanting to understand the sand-eating behavior of a newly hatched chicken. Jerry Hogan (1977) has accomplished such an analysis. He found that young chicks do, in fact, ingest sand. As far as is known, there are no more nutritive advantages for sand-eating chickens than there are for sand-eating kids. Over a period of time, sand eating drops off. At that time, when given a choice between seed and sand, chicks eat only seeds. It appears that young chicks learn to develop a discrimination between grains of sand and similarly shaped seeds.

It is certain that biochemical changes are occurring in the brain of the chick as it learns the sand-seed discrimination. Moreover, research that informs us as to which biochemicals change, when they change, and how they change, enhances our understanding of the learned sand-seed discrimination. Yet you should recognize that a complete knowledge of these biochemical changes does not in and of itself answer all questions that might be asked about the sand-seed behavioral discrimination. What interaction with the environment leads to these changes? In what feeding niche did it evolve, and how does that evolutionary history influence the present behavior? It is, after all, the behavior of the creature that we are attempting to account for. Are there social factors involved in learning the discrimination, and so on? A biochemical analysis might clarify how the animal is changed as it learns, furthering the understanding of the behavior in question. However, in no way does the biochemical analysis constitute a better explanation of the phenomenon by comparison with the molar analysis of learning as Hogan (1977) described. Together, the molar and molecular analyses provide a better understanding than either alone.

Molar analyses of a behavior are appropriate and necessary for a complete understanding of behavior. Reductionism alone constitutes neither a better explanation nor a better science.

Scientific Content and Method Compared

Science can be roughly divided into two components: methodology (how and what is done in an experiment) and content (what is found out). Students typically hate methodological considerations. ("I don't care who did what, when, or how! All I want to know is what was found out!") Unfortunately, content cannot be separated neatly from methodology. Indeed, as argued before, more often than not, methodology determines content. Consider, for example, learning researcher *X*, who is conducting a laboratory investigation of the determinants of "choice" behavior.

Let's say the researcher puts a rat in a cage and trains it to press a lever. The rat's "choice" is to press the lever or not, and this investigator's understanding of choice is restricted to answers gleaned from this simple methodology. By contrast, researcher *Z* might put a rat in a cage with two levers, and arrange conditions in which the rat presses one or the other. *Z*'s understanding of "choice"—of choosing between two alternatives—will likely differ because of the different method. (We'll return to clarify such experiments in a later chapter.)

Interim Summary

1. Scientific analyses and laboratory study yield knowledge about human behavior that complements our artistic and religious experiences.
2. Learning, memory, motivation, anger, and intelligence are alleged processes of the mind called ***hypothetical constructs;*** they are assumed to exist but are not directly observable.
3. "Performance on a multiple choice test" is an example of an ***operational definition*** of learning—a definition of learning based on a performance measure.
4. Performance is observed and measured, and from changes in performance, learning may or may not be inferred. The difference between the observed performance and the inferred (and invisible) process of learning is known as the ***learning-performance distinction.***
5. The error of *reification* is to assert the existence of a psychological process in the absence of a performance measure.
6. Learning can be studied at different levels of analysis, from *molecular* to *molar*. Explaining behavior by reference to a more molecular level (such as changes in brain biochemistry) is known as ***reductionism.*** Reduc-

tionistic explanations of behavior in physiological or chemical terms are neither better nor more scientific that molar observations.

7. The science of learning consists of both method (how an investigation was conducted) and content (what was discovered).

PSYCHOLOGICAL EXPERIMENTS IN LABORATORIES

No one would mistake McCarthy's John Grady for a psychologist training an animal in a laboratory learning experiment. But there are similarities. John Grady arranged a unique environment for his wild mustang. The horse learned new responses as a result of this experience. Here we look at ways in which laboratory experiments resemble real-life scenarios. You may be surprised to find that what John Grady did and how the horse responded can be profitably analyzed from a formal learning perspective.[4] Let us look, then, at psychological experiments in the laboratory.

Most of the experiments you come across in this text are designed to investigate cause-and-effect relationships. Certain precise experiences or manipulations are imposed on experimental subjects. Then the effects of these treatments are assessed in tests specifically designed to measure one or more aspects of the changed behavior. Laboratory studies in the behavioral sciences—in areas of learning and memory, in particular—have common features. Indeed, experiments on rats and college students (and horses) more often than not use a similar scientific method.

The Black Box Approach

When students ask why dogs, or rats, or pigeons are studied in the laboratory if the researcher is interested in human learning and memory processes, one answer is that each species can be considered an interchangeable "black box" in which stimuli go in one end and responses come out the other end (see Figure 1.2). In this view, any animal provides a model for similar processes in other animals. For some researchers, what might be inside the black box is often of less interest than whether there are similarities in differing species' responses to stimuli that go into the box.

Emphasis on Similarity Among Species.   One assumption underlying this black box approach is that the behavioral processes under study are the same (or are similar) from species to species. For example, all animals respond in similar ways to confinement, food, pain, stroking, and so forth. John Grady's horse responded to stroking and "gentling" by becoming calm. Humans, rats

---

[4]See Dougan & Dougan, (1999). This article, about a real life "horse whisperer" can also be viewed in its entirety at http://www.envmed.rochester.edu/wwwrap/behavior/jeab/jeabhome.htm.

Stimulus ⟶ [black box] ⟶ Response

FIGURE 1.2   The Black Box Approach to Behavior

In the black box model of behavior, stimuli impinge on an animal, and the animal responds. The S-R relationships can be investigated regardless of what happens—either physiologically or psychologically—inside the animal. Behaviorists attempt to build a science of behavior using this approach.

in laboratories, and most land-dwelling vertebrates respond in a similar manner.

Emphasis on Differences Among Species.   Yet other researchers justify the study of a particular species of animal, such as kangaroo rats, Japanese quail, or honey bees because they are interested in the peculiarities of that particular species' behavior. *Homo sapiens,* after all, is only one of thousands of species whose behavior we do not understand! A researcher I first met as a graduate student had a "thing" about snakes and continues to profitably study their behavior to this day. The point is that there are legitimate reasons to study the behavior of all animals.

Applying the Black Box Model.   Let us set up a laboratory learning experiment using college students as subjects that deals with a behavior characteristic of humans. English-speaking subjects are allowed to study Spanish-language vocabulary for several minutes. Sometime later they are asked to recall these words in a test of vocabulary retention. Referring again to the black box in Figure 1.2, note that the words may be considered the *stimulus variables* (i.e., the experimental treatment imposed on the subjects). The degree of retention—the number of words recalled or percentage of the list retained—is the *response variable.* This response or behavioral measure—specifically, the number of words recalled—is the evidence that learning has occurred in a subject. (In this example, then, the operational definition of learning is *the number of words recalled.*) For students familiar with scientific methodology, stimulus and response variables are also known as *independent* and *dependent variables.*

Stimulus, Response, and Intervening Variables

In this example, you can see the sequence of events typical of all psychological experiments. Response variables are systematically related to preceding stimulus variables, rendering the process of "learning" into an observable event. The stimulus variable imposed on the experimental subjects is the *cause*, and the *effect* is reflected in the response measure selected by the experimenter. Learning in humans and laboratory animals, then, is operationally defined as a change in behavior that can be related to specific events in the environment. When a behavioral scientist is able to make a reliable, law-like statement relating measured responses to preceding stimulus conditions, learning assumes the status of an **intervening variable.**

Independent and Dependent Variables

In all learning experiments, indeed, in all psychological experiments, the goal is to identify the cause-and-effect relationship under investigation. The treatment or manipulation of stimulus variables imposed by the experimenter on the experimental subject is referred to as the **independent variable.** In the previous example, presenting the list of Spanish words is the independent variable. In all experiments, the experimental manipulation is called the treatment, and the group of subjects that receive the experimental manipulation—the independent variable—is known as the **treatment group.** Typically these subjects are compared to other group(s) of subjects given a control treatment. A **control group,** therefore, is exposed to all the same conditions as the treatment group except for the independent variable. The response used to assess the treatment effects of the independent variable is known as the **dependent variable.** The measure of retention of Spanish words constitutes the dependent variable in the previous example. The dependent variable is so named because the response outcome *depends* on the treatment variable.

A Sample Learning Experiment

Experimental treatments are compared to control groups to determine whether an effect is real. What we learned from the "recall of foreign words" experiment is limited by the simple comparison of "before" and "after" performance and the absence of other comparison groups.

Hypotheses and Hypothesis Testing. An experiment involves hypothesis testing. A *hypothesis* is a hunch, idea, or theory that is formally tested in an experiment. For example, one might have a *working hypothesis* that more Spanish words will be recalled if a person studies more (which was implied but not specified in the example). Note that a working hypothesis is a simple statement of what you expect to happen if you run an experiment. Let us turn this example into a real experiment. First, identify 30 students enrolled in a first-year Spanish course. Each student is given the same list of 20 Spanish words to study. Next, divide the 30 students into 3 groups with 10 subjects in each group (i.e., $n = 10$/group), as follows:

Group 1: Subjects study for 60 seconds (enough to read the list one time). Then subjects are allowed to read a novel of their choosing for 59 minutes. Note that 60 minutes elapse from the beginning to the end of the treatment.

Group 2: Subjects study the Spanish words for 15 minutes and then read a novel of their choice for 45 minutes.

Group 3: Subjects study the Spanish words for 60 minutes.

Twenty-four hours later the students are given the English equivalents of the 20 words and are asked to make the Spanish translations. The mean number of correct responses is computed for each group. The results are displayed in Figure 1.3. Can you identify the treatment group(s) and the control group(s)? By interpreting the graph, can you verbalize the results before reading further? Another way to ask this question is: Can you label the x axis, the y axis, and the functional relationship that is depicted?

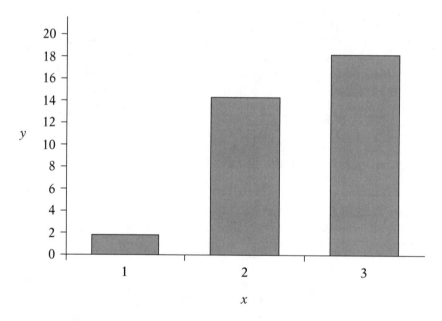

FIGURE 1.3   Bar Graph Depicting Results
of Spanish Vocabulary Experiment

Responses are plotted along the y axis as a function of conditions 1, 2, and 3, plotted along the x axis. (See text for description of the conditions identified as 1, 2, and 3.) Note the general form: Any response can be plotted as a function of any stimulus condition.

Experimental Design

Note in this experiment that the independent variable—the amount of time each group is allowed to study—is displayed along the x axis as a category. Each category (1, 2, or 3) represents a treatment condition selected by the experimenter. This experiment is an example of a **between-groups design** in that each group is assigned a different parameter (i.e., 1, 15, or 60 minutes) of the independent variable. (A parameter is one of the various levels that an independent variable can assume, usually variations in stimulus *duration, intensity, frequency, concentration,* and so forth.) The idea is to test the hypothesis that a systematic, or *functional relationship* exists between the independent variable and the dependent variable. The working hypothesis is that amount of study (1 minute, 15 minutes, or 60 minutes) influences the number of Spanish words recalled in a later test.

By contrast, a **within-subjects design** compares a pretreatment measure of the dependent variable with a post-treatment measure in the same subjects. For example, the investigator might give the 20 Spanish words to all three groups before allowing them to study. Their performance would constitute a pretest (or a baseline) from which to measure the effects of the treatment. After studying the Spanish words for 1, 15, or 60 minutes, they would then take a post-test. The post-test performance of each group would be compared with its respective pretest performance—hence, a within-groups design.

Consider Figure 1.3 once again. What parameter of the independent variable was manipulated?[5] Note that the dependent variable plotted on the y axis is the number of Spanish words recalled during the test. The mean values plotted are 1.8, 14.3, and 18.2 words, respectively, for Groups 1, 2, and 3.

Statistical Analysis. These experimental results could be subjected to a statistical analysis to see whether the **null hypothesis** could be rejected. The null hypothesis in this experiment is that the three groups do not differ from each other. That is, that the results observed in Figure 1.3 would have occurred even if study time had been equated for the three groups. Yet another way to state this counterintuitive argument (i.e., the null hypothesis) is that the amount of time spent studying had nothing to do with the number of successful Spanish translations.

A statistical procedure called an ANOVA (analysis of variance) of these data would compare both the means and the variance (how scores differed relative to each other) of the three groups. The size of the mean differences in Figure 1.3 appear to be sufficiently large that the results of the ANOVA would likely allow us to reject the null hypothesis. A statistically significant difference among the groups would allow us to tentatively conclude that the

---

[5]The parameter of *time*—the amount of time students were allowed to study the Spanish words—was manipulated.

"amount of time studying the Spanish words" was causally related to the re-call performance of these words. Based on these results, we therefore accept the working hypothesis. From the performance of these students, we can assert that "time spent studying" (practice? familiarity? trials? thinking?) is related to the learning process.

John Grady's treatment of the wild mustang in the chapter opening can be likened to a laboratory experiment. Confining, stroking, covering the animal's eyes, and whispering into its ear are stimulus variables. It is likely that such response variables as heart and respiration rate, dilation of the pupils, adrenal gland secretions, leg-kicks, and so on systematically changed as a function of the continued treatment. The "experimental" design was within-subjects: The horse's wild behavior in the presence of a human (a pre-test) became more gentle as a result of the treatment. Any of a number of behavioral response measures, such as rearing, whinnying, biting, pawing, or running, could have been quantified and compared with pretreatment measures. On the basis of these results, one could have concluded that there was a functional relationship between the treatment variables and the response outcome. But, because none of this was systematically measured, it was *not* an experiment.

Interim Summary

1. Molar behavior can be studied scientifically.
2. Learning is an inference made from observations of an animal's performance. Learning that has been operationally defined and investigated in experiments, and that bridges the gap between stimulus and response variables is an ***intervening variable.***
3. A simple analysis of behavior employs a black box model in which incoming *stimulus variable*s can be systematically related to *response variables*.
4. Researchers manipulate treatment conditions, or ***independent variables,*** and measure ***dependent variables*** (usually some form of behavioral response).
5. ***Treatment groups*** are compared to ***control groups*** in an experiment. The conditions of the control group are made as identical as possible to the treatment group except that the independent variable is not manipulated in the control group.
6. In a ***between-groups design,*** each group is assigned a level, or *parameter* value of an independent variable, and results are compared to a control group. In a ***within-subjects design,*** the effects of the independent variable are compared with a pretest measure.
7. The basic design of a learning experiment:
   a. State *working hypotheses* about what is expected to happen.
   b. Operationally define terms.

    c. Set up treatment and control conditions for comparison.

    d. Measure performance.

    e. Test **null hypothesis** (that there is no difference between groups) using statistics.

  8. One outcome of a successful experiment is the identification of a *functional relationship* in which a response measure is related to stimulus conditions.

DISCUSSION QUESTIONS

5. But what is the correct answer? I share the exasperation of students who ask questions that aren't yet answerable. (And as a psychology professor, I am well aware that there are more of those kinds of questions than any other!) However, consider the risks of not being able to live with tentative conclusions . . . the inability to live with indecision? How do you respond to someone who always has the "right" answer to your every question in comparison with a person who says "I'm not sure . . . here is a possible answer, based on this evidence."

6. In responding to the following questions, assume that the physiological mechanisms underlying learning are now known: (a) Would a behavioral analysis of learning any longer be necessary? (b) Can you make the case that a black box approach might still yield valuable information?

CHAPTER SUMMARY

1. Learning is defined as a relatively permanent change in observable behavior that results from experience.

2. Behavior theory includes both genetic and environmental components. Behavior theory can be thought of as the nature/nurture analysis of behavior.

3. Behavior is (a) what you do, (b) how you act, and (c) the way you respond to your environment. As a general rule, differences among humans result more from each individual's personal experience with a unique environment than from the particulars of their genotype.

4. Learning is a hypothetical construct. Like other psychological constructs, such as intelligence, memory, and personality, learning is inferred from observations of behavior. The learning process can be distinguished, then, from the performance of behavior.

5. Learning can be analyzed and explained at several different levels of analysis. Explaining learning by reference to biochemical changes in the brain is called reductionism.

6. Theories of learning attempt to account for behavior by noting the effects of immediate, local environments. Environments include both the *ecological niches* and laboratory where animals are studied. Human environments include interactions with other people in homes, classrooms, and rock concerts.

7. Issues in learning include questions regarding the universality of "laws of learning," the extrapolation of the results of animal experiments to humans,

humans as objects of scientific study, individual differences in learning, the role of volition and choice in learning, and the influence of human language and cognition on conditioning and learning.

8. Learning theory derived from studying animals can be applied to an understanding of health issues such as obesity and chemical dependency, to psychopathology, to parenting skills and child development, to the learning of skilled behavior (i.e., playing a musical instrument), to the learning of emotional behavior, to the socialization process, and to the learning of language and concepts.

9. Although other kinds of experience and knowledge—art, music, interpersonal relationships—inform the human condition, human behavior and human experience can also be understood from a scientific perspective.

10. Learning can be studied scientifically, both in humans and in laboratory animals.

11. The study of learning is critical to the scientific analysis of human behavior.

KEY TERMS

behavior   3

behavior theory   6

behaviorism   6

between-groups design   27

control group   25

dependent variable   25

hypothetical construct   19

independent variable   25

intervening variable   25

learning   2

learning-performance distinction   20

learning theory   5

null hypothesis   27

operational definition   19

phenotype   6

reductionism   21

treatment group   25

within-subjects design   27

CHAPTER 2

Biological Bases of Learning and Behavior

Each of us is a tiny being, permitted to ride on the outermost skin of one of the smaller planets for a few dozen trips around the local star . . . individual organisms see nothing of the overall pattern—continents, climate, evolution. They barely set forth on the world stage and are promptly snuffed out—yesterday a drop of semen, as the Roman Emperor Marcus Aurelius wrote, tomorrow a handful of ashes. If the earth were as old as a person, a typical organism would be born, live, and die in a sliver of a second. We are fleeting, transitional creatures, snowflakes fallen on the hearth fire. That we understand even a little of our origins is one of the great triumphs of human insight and courage.

Carl Sagan and Ann Druyan,
Shadows of Forgotten Ancestors, (1992, p. 30ff)

INTRODUCTION

To understand our behavior, we must entertain a longer perspective than the course of events in a lifetime. Another way to say this is that the determinants of each human's behavior begin before conception. How can this be so, you ask? Is human behavior predestined? Where did this counterintuitive notion of prebirth influences on behavior come from?

The publication of Charles Darwin's monumental theory of evolution allowed humans a new way to think about their behavior. At present, evolutionary theory is crucial to an understanding of the broad brush strokes of behavior and to learning and memory processes in particular. At an intuitive level, the logic and rationale for incorporating evolutionary theory into a textbook on learning may not be apparent. Consider, however, that learning and behavior are the activities of all living creatures, and, further, that evolution is the major scientific theory that addresses our biological origins. We'll see that it addresses our behavioral origins as well.

Humans and other animals are influenced by both their nature and their nurture. In this chapter we will begin to consider our human nature. Evolutionary theory provides a context in which to understand genetics, the design of our brain, and other basic processes of biological and behavioral motivation. In this chapter, we will ask how genes, the brain, and ecological niches help determine the way we learn and behave. Let us begin by considering learning and behavior in two broad categories of life: plants and animals.

EVOLUTION

"Live and learn" is a common figure of speech. Living and learning are not synonymous, however, because not all life forms learn. Few would disagree with the statement that plants do not learn, remember, or, for that matter, even behave much!

Plants.   What plants "do" is respond in curious and highly interesting ways to certain physical features in their immediate environment. The manner in which plants do this superficially resembles reflexive behavior in animals (see Chapter 3). For example, the tendency for some plants to open leaves in sunlight and to orient roots "down" and stems "up" are forms of tropistic behavior, or *tropisms*. Tropisms are movement adjustments that simple organisms make in response to changes in the environment. Since most plants are sessile (attached, relatively unmoving), they are capable of making only minor, usually local, movements. Compared to animals, plants sense their environment poorly and move very little. Lacking sensory and motor neurons, synapses, and a central nervous system, plant behavior is not characterized by learning and memory processes.

Animals.   Now contrast the behavior of plants just described with the behavior of animals. The animal kingdom is "full of life." Animals move. (Hence, the term animation). Because they move, animals come across much more variation in their environment than do plants. Among other *things* they encounter are other animals. Movement produces constantly changing environments with which the animal must interact. To test this theory, compare the amount of environment you would experience sitting for 5 minutes with that you would encounter walking around (or driving around) for 5 minutes.

The Role of Learning in Animal Behavior

The range of responses in animals is considerably beyond that of the blind tropisms of plants. Animals are able to adjust their reactions on the basis of the outcomes of previous actions. That is, animals can learn. Among the things they learn is that certain features of the environment are often associated with other features of the environment. For example, bears can remember that buzzing is associated with the stings of gold-and-black insects. These assorted stimuli also predict the nearby presence of honey. Humans and other land-dwelling vertebrates learn about and form memories of the environments they inhabit. For example, I have a memory of this particular stretch of muddy river. Last year I learned that this river floods over there when it rains; now I remember that it can be crossed where it narrows, by the large cottonwood tree.

Learning Is Adaptive.   What the bear and I have learned from such experiences will help us survive. That is, our ability to learn and to remember is adaptive. Such learning is neither frivolous nor random; rather, it tracks the environment and often promotes survival. Indeed, the ability to learn and to remember may be one of our most adaptive characteristics.

Learning in Simple and Complex Animals: A Preview

Animals with simple nervous systems behave in less complicated ways than those with complex nervous systems. For example, the common housefly feeds reflexively when taste cells on its legs are stimulated, causing its proboscis (trunk-like mouth) to lower (Dethier, 1978). It doesn't lower its proboscis unless certain chemicals stimulate the taste cells, initiating the reflex. Chickens, however, must learn how to eat. They initially peck at both grain and sand indiscriminately. Grain but not sand satisfies their hunger, and the chicks eventually learn to peck the grain and not to peck the sand (Hogan, 1977).

Should one surmise, therefore, that the housefly is born "knowing" what to eat? This is not a simple question. Humans cannot experience what a housefly "knows," since human brains do not allow the same qualities of mental life as that afforded by housefly brains. For our current discussion, let us simply say that feeding behavior in the housefly is reflexive and that learning plays a role in how a chicken eats.

In general, learning and memory formation play an increasingly important role in the behavior of complex animals as opposed to the tropisms of plants and reflexes of simpler animals. We might ask why some animals survive perfectly well by reflex while others must learn life's lessons. Further, we might challenge the notion that learning is always adaptive. If so, why is "maladaptive behavior" so prevalent—especially among humans? In Chapter 7, we consider maladaptive behavior in some detail.

Darwin's Theory of Evolution

Charles Darwin's theory of **evolution,** simply stated, is that existing species of life on Earth are the end result of a process of natural selection. We turn to Darwin's theory for the purpose of addressing behavioral processes of motivation and **adaptation.** An adaptation is any characteristic that improves an organism's chances of transmitting its genes to the next generation. To help direct your reading of this section on evolution, let us first consider the following questions:

- How are humans and animals related?
- What is "instinctive" behavior in animals?
- Do humans have instincts?
- What laws govern how and why each species behaves, learns, and remembers?
- Do humans follow the same laws of learning and behavior as other animals?

Charles Darwin (1809–1882) proposed a theory of organic evolution in his 1859 book, *On the Origin of Species by Means of Natural Selection*. Contemporary psychological theories of both learning and behavior are now based on evolutionary considerations. For example, all animals have a biological nature—in particular, a form of brain—that allows them to learn and to behave in a predictable fashion. Psychologists work from the assumption that the human mind and human behavior can be understood best by examining evidence from both nature (genes, brains) and nurture (environment, behavior).

Genetics. Our current view of evolution encompasses a number of distinct component theories (Mayr, 1991). For example, modern evolutionary theory is a synthesis of Darwin's theory of natural selection with the more recent science of *genetics*. **Genetics** is the study of patterns of heredity and variations in plants and animals. Four ideas that define current evolutionary theory that relate to learning and behavior theory are covered here: heredity, variability, reproduction, and natural selection.

Heredity

The most obvious feature of life forms is physical—how plants and animals appear. Early taxonomies (groupings or arrangements) were primarily based on the physical features of plants and animals. Offspring resemble parents. Chickens reproduce chickens and humans, humans. The term **heredity** refers to the transmission of like structure, of physical form, through sexual reproduction.

The basic unit of the process of heredity is the gene, and readers are referred to any of a number of modern biology books to fathom the complexities of gene functioning. The idea of how genes might evolve is also beyond the scope of this text (see Lewontin, 1983). For our discussion, human genes are the mechanism for making the next generation of humans, chicken genes for chickens. The related concepts of genotype and phenotype were discussed in Chapter 1. A genotype is the basic combination of genes that defines an individual. A phenotype is the genotype as expressed in the environment. Your genotype is the potential "you" at conception; the physical you, at conception through the present, is an example of a phenotype.

Phenotypes Learn. Phenotypes that have the same genotype (as in "identical" twins) vary because they live in and interact with different environments. For present purposes, we can consider that phenotypes learn and form memories following interactions with environments. "Learning" is a phenotypic characteristic. Is it also possible for the environment to influence the genotype? The answer is yes . . . and no. An understanding of "how yes" and "how no" will clarify the complex relationships of genotype, phenotype, heredity, and behavior.

Lamarckian Evolution.   Before Darwin, the noted French naturalist Jean
Baptiste Lamarck (1744–1849) proposed a different theory now known as
Lamarckian evolution. Lamarck believed that the environment caused
changes in the genotype. That is, he thought (a) that slight changes experienced during an animal's lifetime gradually modified an animal and (b) that
the next generation profited from the transmission of these acquired characteristics.

One ramification of this view is that children would benefit from the
musical, or mathematical, or bowling abilities of their parents who patiently
perfected these skills during their lifetime. What a great idea! Unfortunately
(or fortunately, for the children of murderers, car thieves, and other criminals), evidence supporting the theory of Lamarckian evolution is lacking.
Rather, the next generation's genotypes are relatively well protected from environmental influence. Specifically, the genes in sperm and eggs are well protected. They are *not* affected by the minute biochemical changes in the brain
that are known to underlie memory and other experiences acquired during a
lifetime. Therefore, the only environment that can influence one's genes
(genes that produce the next generation's genotypes) during the course of
one's lifetime consists of certain chromosome-damaging drugs, high levels of
ionizing radiation, and other agents known to be responsible for genetic mu-
tations.

Human Inheritance

Evolutionary theory and genetics become personal when you consider your
own human identity. As an individual, you have both a unique and a shared
inheritance. You are unique because of the one-of-a-kind DNA (deoxyribonucleic acid, a complex protein structure containing all genetic instructions)
contributed by your mother's and father's genes. Your behavior, in part, is determined by the unique interaction of the DNA you received from each
parent.

Genetic History Extends Beyond Parents.   Each of your parents likewise
was created by a unique combination of DNA making up approximately
20,000 genes on each of their parent's 23 chromosomes. (During fertilization,
each human male and female contributes 23 chromosomes to produce offspring with 46 chromosomes.) Like infinitely regressing mirrors, the process
continues backwards in time. Your shared inheritance refers to the process of
genetic transmission that has been ongoing in *Homo sapiens* for 100,000 or
more years.

Cranial endocasts (rubber castings taken from the inside of skulls, which
allow estimates of brain size and shape) suggest few brain differences among
Homo sapiens during the past 100,000 years. With the possible exception of the
elaboration of language (allowing higher levels of cognition?), our ancestors
may have lived, learned, laughed, and loved much as we currently do.

Humans Had Nonhuman Ancestors.   Beyond 200,000 years ago? Evolutionary theory is based on the assumption of continuity among species as well as relatedness within species. That is to say, humans and other animals have common ancestors with all other life forms. Understandably, we are most interested in humans. Both paleontological and microbiological findings continue to expand our understanding of our origins. Estimates of human lineage have been made using mitochondrial DNA (mDNA) techniques. Though these models are tentative (Hedges, Kuman, Tamura, & Stoneking, 1991), researchers postulate a common origin of African women, a "mother of Africa," designated "Eve," who lived approximately 200,000 years ago (Vigilant, Stoneking, Harpending, Hawkes, & Wilson, 1991).

Humans' closest living nonhuman relatives? The chimpanzee, with whom we share a common ancestor, living approximately 7 million years ago. Because of their genetic closeness to humans, we will stay focused on the chimpanzee throughout the text. From another perspective, we can ask *How apelike are humans?* Quite. See Box 2.1 for some comparisons.

Human Nature

Given our genetic relationships with other primates, the observation that all humans are related should come as no surprise. This shared inheritance is the physical basis for "human nature"—the tendency for humans to behave like humans and less like other species of animals. Human nature has three components: a collective **phylogenetic history** (the genetic history of life on earth), an **ontogenetic history** (an individual's ontogeny is defined as the total of life experiences from conception to death), and our collective **extragenetic history** (Sagan's, 1977, term for the cumulative oral and written experiences of individual humans). Among all species, only *Homo sapiens* have an extragenetic history.

Of course, it follows that there is also "tiger nature," "pigeon nature," "bee nature," and so forth. Each member of a *species* shares common genetic material and common inherited behavior patterns. Indeed, a **species** refers to a group of animals with common genetic material and common behavior patterns that are reproductively isolated from other animals. Do aspects of human behavior also resemble the behavior of other species of animals? Some, obviously, more than others. We behave more like other primates than chickens because we share more genetic material with primates (see Box 2.1 and Figure 2.1). Likewise, in many particulars we behave more like rats, dogs, and cats than like chickens or trout. Humans, rats, dogs, cats, and monkeys are mammals and as such share certain common, and important, biological and psychological characteristics.

Summary of Heredity.   Heredity refers to the transmission of physical structure from one generation to the next. A new genotype is formed at conception; the phenotype, but not the genotype, changes during a lifetime. Changes in the

BOX 2.1   CHIMPANZEES: SO CLOSE AND YET SO FAR AWAY

DNA, deoxyribonucleic acid, makes up the complex molecules from which each gene is constructed. Fifteen years ago, scientists Charles Sibley and John Ahlquist took chimpanzee DNA and human DNA, separated the double helix of each into two strands and allowed one strand from each species to recombine. Then they measured the resulting match of the DNA of one species to the other. Their technique resulted in a 98% match of the DNA of humans and chimpanzees, and a 97% match of human DNA with mountain gorilla DNA. These and other techniques allow scientists to estimate that humans diverged from chimpanzees about 7 million years ago, and from gorillas about 10 million years ago.

The figure (from Diamond, 1992) shows that humans are genetically closer to the pygmy chimpanzee, *Pan paniscus*, than to the common chimp, *Pan troglodyte*. The two chimps share 99.3% of their DNA, and we share 98.4% of our DNA with *Pan paniscus* (Sibley, Comstock, & Ahlquist, 1990). We are closer kin to *Pan paniscus* (see dashed lines connecting to ordinate) than chimps are to gorillas, and than mice are to rats. Put a somewhat different way, if you were a chimpanzee, your genetically closest non-chimp relative would be human, not a gorilla!

The chimpanzee has a brain size of only 450 cubic centimeters (cc) compared with humans' large, 1350 cc brain. Nevertheless, it is a trifle discomforting to realize that human civilization depends on less than 2% of our "essence."

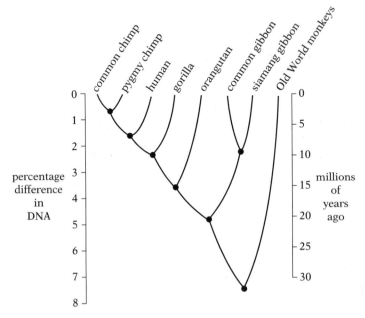

Family Tree of the Higher Primates

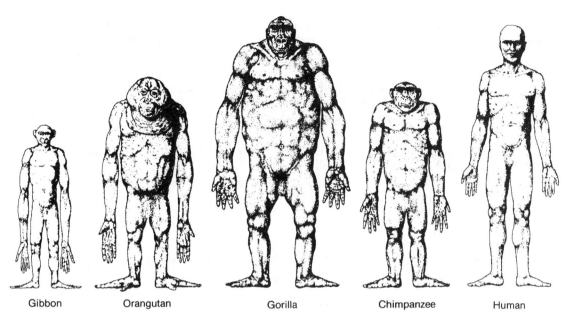

Gibbon   Orangutan   Gorilla   Chimpanzee   Human

FIGURE 2.1   Humans and Other Apes

The extant apes with all hair removed, showing proportions of adults, drawn to the same scale. The animals are arranged in terms of their similarity of genetic material relative to humans. (Modified from Strickberger, 1990.)

phenotype, such as learned behavior, do not change the genotype, and therefore such changes cannot be inherited by the next generation. Evidence from paleontology, comparative anatomy, and DNA-matching techniques reveals that humans share common genetic ancestry with each other, and with other living animals. Human nature differs from that of other animals because humans have unique phylogenetic, ontogenetic, and written histories.

Though we're all human, each of us dresses differently, and we prefer certain kinds of music, foods, and people rather than others. Another aspect of Darwin's theory allows insight into these differences. Let us turn our attention to individual differences.

Variability

A second major idea defining evolutionary theory is *variability*. **Variability** refers to the wide range of genetic variation *within* a species. When genetic material is transmitted through sexual reproduction from a parent generation to offspring, differences in structure are introduced. Unless you have an identical twin, you are an individual genetically different from all others. We need not concern ourselves here with the mechanisms of variability; the science of genetics points to both mutation and events during cell *meiosis* as contributing factors. Mutation is a permanent, random chemical change in the DNA molecule.

Many have observed that *variety* makes life interesting. According to Darwin, variety makes life possible. The slight differences introduced from generation to generation determine the course of evolution. Variability in part determines which individual organisms survive and which do not. Why? Because some of the differences are advantageous to living and others are not.

The significance of the concept of variability in Darwin's theory, therefore, is that some genotypes in interaction with environment (i.e., phenotypes) are more viable than others.

Sex and Reproduction

Sex and reproduction are often minimized in discussions of Darwin's theory. But heredity and variability are genetic mechanisms that can be expressed only as the result of a sexual act. In politics and the world of business, power lies with those who control the money. In biology, the name of the game is "who produces the next generation?"

Indeed, the reproductive urge appears to be central to the adult life of most animal species. We do not find it surprising that humans spend billions of dollars annually for perfumes and other odorants, the apparent purpose of which is to enhance opportunities for, and otherwise maximize, encounters that may lead to sexual reproduction (Stoddart, 1990). Nor does anyone find it surprising when a student passes on a study session for the opportunity to spend time with a potential mate.

Most psychologists view sex as a primary reinforcer and incentive (see Chapter 6 for a fuller discussion). Freud and Jung asserted that sexual energy and an innate "life force," respectively, motivated humans. What do you think? Is most (all?) of your motivation derived from the more primal motivations of sexual pleasure, that is, of your "selfish genes" (expression from Dawkins, 1976, discussed below)? Before even considering the ideas of reward and the process of reinforcement, would you suspect that the opportunity to engage in sexual behavior would be high on a list of satisfying events?

Natural Selection

Both heredity and variability can be accounted for by the science of genetics. Even in the absence of a theory of genetics, in Darwin's time animal breeders selectively bred dogs and horses for specified phenotypic characters—color, size, temperament. Changes introduced from generation to generation were accomplished by human-directed, or *artificial selection*.

Darwin postulated that similar selection factors occurred from one generation to the next under *natural* rather than artificial circumstances. He called this **natural selection.** He and others noted that too many offspring are reproduced in the course of a breeding lifetime and that typically there are insufficient resources to accommodate the abundance of new lives. Therefore, competition ensues for limited resources. The prize of winning this competition for nature's resources is life and the opportunity to live long enough to reproduce. The cost of losing is death or lessened opportunities to successfully produce the next generation.

Selective Pressures.   Darwin's theory of natural selection is as prone to misinterpretation as it is insightful and controversial. Essentially, he proposed that each species is best understood as a unique solution to specific problems of survival. Some individuals are better able than others to overcome the environmental obstacles they face in day-to-day living. Such obstacles, or impediments to survival, are called **selective pressures.** Not only might some birds have better protective coloration (i.e., camouflage), to use a popular example, but some may learn more quickly than others. That is, some individuals may be bigger, stronger, and faster, and some others may be slower but smarter. The environment blindly "selects" behavioral characters (such as the ability to learn) in the same way it selects adaptively colored individuals. It is not difficult to imagine many instances in which the ability to rapidly adjust behavior to a changing environment—that is, to learn—would be selected for.

Fitness and Inclusive Fitness.   Protective coloration, rapid learning, and other behavioral adaptations facilitate survival for "lucky" individuals (Gould, 1989). When environmental conditions change between generations (i.e., if and when selective pressures change), some individuals live and some die—the luck of the draw. Yet others among the varying offspring that do survive will have more of an advantage in reproducing their offspring—in which case, nature again selects the more advantageous characteristics to be reproduced. The measure of an animal's success in producing viable offspring is called **fitness.** Counting the number of one's offspring, and the number of *their* offspring, is a measure of *inclusive* (total) *fitness.*

Sometimes individuals (and species) that are perfectly adapted cannot adjust rapidly enough to a changed environment. When a large asteroid impacting the earth drastically disrupted their ecosystem 65 million years ago, dinosaurs and the majority of other plants and animals died. One estimate is that 95% of all species that have ever existed have become extinct because of changed environments.

Integrative Nature of Evolutionary Theory

Darwin's theory continues to offer a vital understanding of the natural history of life and of behaving animals. His conceptual framework has been remarkably successful in accounting for seemingly contradictory (and certainly puzzling) features of life on Earth. The result of evolution is a world populated by unique living organisms. So disparate in appearance and behavior are these plants and animals that Darwin's allegation that all are related, indeed, are continuous forms of life, sometimes seems bizarre. An yet, natural selection provides an accounts for the historical progression of certain living forms and the elimination of others. Little evidence supports the view that present conditions differ substantially from times past when the fossil record was accumulating. There is no good reason to suspect that humans are other than another end product of these processes.

Interim Summary

1. Plant behavior is best described by simple movement adjustments, called *tropisms*, to the sun, to gravity, and so on. Moving animals meet changing environments, and their nervous systems are adapted to adjust rapidly in reaction.

2. In his theory of **evolution**, Charles Darwin proposed that existing *species* of life on Earth are the end result of a process of *natural selection.* Four important components of evolution are heredity, variability, sex (reproduction), and natural selection.

3. An **adaptation** is any characteristic in a plant or animal that promote survival and yields a reproductive advantage. Typically, learning is adaptive.

4. Contemporary evolutionary theory weds the modern science of **genetics,** the study of patterns of heredity and variation in plants and animals, to reproduction and natural selection.

5. A *genotype* is the combination of genes that defines an individual. A *phenotype* is a genotype expressed in the environment.

6. **Heredity** refers to the transmission of like structure, of physical form, through sexual reproduction.

7. **Lamarckian evolution** is the discredited theory that experiences acquired during one's life can be transmitted to offspring.

8. Humans have been in their approximate present form for 100,000 to 200,000 years. Chimpanzees are the nearest living form of primate to humans. Our common ancestor with chimpanzees lived about 7 million years ago.

9. Each human is a unique being that combines his or her *phylogenetic, ontogenetic,* and *extragenetic history.*

10. A **species** refers to animals that are reproductively isolated from other animals.

11. **Variability** refers to the wide range of genetic variation *within* a species.

12. **Natural selection** is the theory that plants and animals that are better adapted to their environment (to nature) are selected for (that is, they produce more offspring that are successful).

13. Plants and animals that overcome impediments presented by nature, called **selective pressures,** breed the next generation. The resulting form of life reflects this adaptation to nature; luck accounts for many survivors.

14. **Fitness** refers to an animal's success in producing viable offspring; measuring reproductive success over several generations defines one's *inclusive fitness*.

DISCUSSION QUESTIONS

1. Are cats smarter than mice? If you answered yes, ask yourself why there are so many mice in the world.

EVOLUTIONARY-INFLUENCED RESEARCH STRATEGIES IN LEARNING AND BEHAVIOR

Not all behavioral scientists agree on what constitutes the most appropriate research strategy to study learning. We'll begin by introducing the main players, the psychologists whose work dominates this text. Among experimental psychologists, for example, some contemporary behaviorists take their lead from B. F. Skinner, while others continue to exploit the insights that physiologist Ivan Pavlov brought to basic learning processes. As we'll see in detail in later chapters, Skinner and his followers have been highly successful in describing and analyzing animal behavior from a laboratory-based, black box, stimulus-response-reinforcement perspective. Likewise, Pavlov's experiments continue to afford insight into basic conditioning, the conditioning of emotional responses, drug behavior, and so forth.

Skinner, Pavlov, and most contemporary psychologists in fact acknowledged that animals are the end result of evolutionary processes. However, they effectively side-stepped the comparative perspective by assuming that basic learning processes are common to all animals. To the extent they are right, it becomes possible to study one or a few species of animals and extrapolate the results to all others.

And so, the contemporary study of animal learning is not dominated, but rather is influenced by evolutionary thinking. In this section, we will briefly review evolutionary influences on the contemporary study of animal learning and animal behavior—namely, the disciplines of ethology, neuroethology, sociobiology, and evolutionary psychology.

Learning in General and Species-specific Learning

Current theories of learning take into account both general and highly specialized features of living organisms. Behaviors common to many animal species reflect genetic similarity. We humans in fact appear to learn some behaviors in the same manner that rats and pigeons do. Another way of saying this is that some types of learned behavior seem to be governed by *general processes.* Most of this textbook takes this position, and we will explore the implications of general process learning throughout.

Species-specific Behaviors.   At the same time, dissimilarity and diversity among life forms are apparent, and behaviors that are unique to a species reflect unique evolutionary strategies in meeting environmental obstacles. **Species-specific behaviors** are defined as innate perceptual and response patterns typical of a species. Fish swim, pigeons fly, and monkeys swing from limb to limb. Yet, when appropriately food-reinforced in a learning laboratory, all can learn to respond to a visual pattern. Taken together, the theoretical approaches of *species-specific behaviors* and of *general learning processes common to all animals* help us understand learning, the most adaptive of all behavior processes (Halliday & Slater, 1983).

Next we examine research strategies based on an evolutionary perspective that have been taken by different types of behavioral scientists. Some conduct field research (ethologists), some do laboratory research (comparative psychologists), and yet others do a combination of the two (various other specialty fields will be noted). Although these fields have distinct histories, their methods and theoretical orientations often overlap. In particular, the relationship of ethology to comparative psychology constitutes a long and controversial history. The interested reader is directed to Domjan (1987a, 1987b), Galef (1984), Gottlieb (1984), Hodos and Campbell (1969), and Jaynes (1969). While these fields are male-dominated, females have made significant research contributions. For a treatment of the role of women in the development of theory in ethology and comparative psychology, see Furumoto and Scarborough (1987).

Ethology

Ethologists study the role of learning within the context of species-specific behaviors: How do animals behave within their naturally occurring ecological niches? Ethologists study free-ranging behavior among various animals (as opposed to observation and manipulation of animal behavior in laboratories). Behavior, they propose, is best understood as instinctive. Particular behaviors are considered to be evolutionary adaptations that implement survival strategies. Classical European ethologists working in the middle part of the 20th century, therefore, heartily disagreed with the laboratory approach to animal learning and behavior taken by American psychologists.

Consummatory Behaviors.   Classical ethologists focused their studies on several species of birds and fish. Among various birds' behavioral repertoires are behaviors indispensable for survival: feeding, courting, mating, caretaking of offspring, and so forth. Collectively, these behaviors in birds and other animals are called **consummatory behaviors.** The idea of consummatory behaviors is often confused with feeding or ingestional behavior. The manner in which ethologists use the term is in the broader sense of *behaviors necessary for survival.*

Behavior as Adaptation.   How does one explain the remarkable diversity of animal behavior observed in nature? Ethologists suggest that we first ask what selective pressures are currently operative in the niche the animal occupies. Second, what selective pressures must have been present in the animal's evolutionary past? Then ethologists ask how a particular behavior functions to help the animal overcome a specific problem presented by the environment. The behavior is the adaptation; it is useful, and its ultimate purpose is to aid survival and to promote successful reproduction.

Imprinting.   One example of an ethological approach to study behavior is their analysis of the phenomenon of *imprinting.* **Imprinting** is a type of learning characterized by the rapid development of a genetically-programmed response to a specific stimulus at a particular stage of development. Under normal conditions, imprinting is adaptive in that it allows goslings to successfully engage in consummatory behaviors. Nobel-prize winner Konrad Lorenz found that geese behave in a peculiar manner if they are exposed to abnormal environments during a few critical hours shortly after hatching. If during this time period, goslings view a moving human (instead of a moving mother goose), for the remainder of their lives they tend to treat humans as geese. At maturity, they even court and attempt to mate with humans (see Box 2.2). Lorenz called this phenomenon imprinting, which is now considered to be a special type of rapid, long-lasting, instinctive-like learning.

Instinct.   The term instinct is a useful, but slippery one. We need a term to describe unlearned behaviors in animals. At its simplest, **instinct** refers to genetically predisposed, innately organized behavior. Unfortunately, however, the term is circularly defined and misleading. Consider the following: Why do squirrels bury nuts? Squirrels bury nuts because this behavior has "survival value." A squirrel's nut-burying "instinct" promotes survival in the niche into which the animal was born. According to this argument, those squirrel-like creatures in the past who did not instinctively bury nuts (or successfully engage in other consummatory behaviors) died. How do we know this? Because (completing the circle) the ones that are alive bury nuts. Because of its circular definition, calling it instinctive does not *explain* nut-burying behavior.

Likewise, chickens (are motivated to) scratch to secure food. The scratching behavior is adaptive—it is instrumental for survival. These kinds of behaviors appear in animals naturally, or innately, meaning without elaborate training. A strategy taken here is to use the term instinct sparingly. In place of instinct, for example, we will refer to consummatory behaviors. In other places, we'll refer to instinctive-like behaviors, or *fixed action patterns.*

BOX 2.2   CRITICAL PERIODS IN GEESE

With childlike curiosity, Konrad Lorenz played with hatchling geese and recorded his valuable observations. He and other European ethologists identified critical variables in the gosling's behavioral development, including the phenomenon of imprinting. Imprinting occurs only during a few critical posthatching hours, known as the **critical period,** when an animal is particularly sensitive to certain features in the environment. "Following" behavior is depicted in the photo. Birds must see the moving object (Lorenz) during their critical period, a few hours after hatching. They will then follow him for a lifetime. However, seeing Lorenz moving at 1 to 2 days of age (outside of their critical period) would have no greater effect on the birds' subsequent behavior than any other kind of visual stimulus. Imprinting to moving objects is an example of a species-specific behavior. Only a few species of birds exhibit this particular behavior (Lorenz, 1935).

Fixed Action Patterns.   Modern ethologists have recast the idea of an instinct as a **fixed action pattern** (**FAP**). A fixed action pattern is an orderly, relatively fixed series of movements, triggered by a biologically meaningful stimulus. To qualify as a FAP, a behavioral sequence must meet four specific criteria (Moltz, 1963). First, the behavior must be stereotyped—it must occur in about the same way each time. Second, once begun, this behavioral sequence should be difficult to disrupt and should continue to completion. A third characteristic of a FAP is that once completed, there is a latent period. That is, some time must pass before the FAP will occur again. Finally, a FAP must be innate, or unlearned. That is, the animal must perform the full integrated behavioral sequence of the FAP the first time it is elicited. An excellent example of a FAP is the analysis of egg-retrieving responses of the Graylag goose (Lorenz & Tinbergen, 1938; see Box 2.3).

Sign Stimuli.   A **sign stimulus** is a specific environmental stimulus that triggers innately organized behaviors such as fixed action patterns. An underlying brain mechanism called an **innate releasing mechanism (IRM)** is hypothesized to be particularly receptive to a sign stimulus. The IRM is the "lock" to which the sign stimulus "key" has been perfectly tailored. Encountering a particular stimulus unlocks the neural mechanism, releasing the FAP. (Compare this analysis of an FAP with the description of reflexive feeding in flies on p. 34.) For example, a moving goose is the sign stimulus that releases *following behavior*. A wandering egg is a sign stimulus that releases egg retrieval.

FAPs and Reflexes.   Except for the complexity of motor behavior exhibited by geese who are following their mother or retrieving eggs, in many particulars FAPs resemble reflexes. The idea of simple reflexes—such as salivation when food is placed on the tongue, or the constriction of a pupil in bright light—will be discussed in the next chapter. Reflexes, however, are modifiable in interaction with the environment while FAPs may be less modifiable. Nevertheless, we may consider FAPs to be reflex-like and the concept of FAPs a more sophisticated analysis of the slippery term, instinct. Let us look at a few more examples of complex behavioral reflexes.

Comparative Psychology

European researchers of how nonhuman animals learn (ethologists) used different methods and assumptions than those in the United States (psychologists and *comparative psychologists*). Comparative psychology is the study of the motivation and behavior of animals for the express purpose of identifying similarities and differences among them. Again, Charles Darwin's work was seminal. His publication *The Expression of Emotions in Man and Animals* in 1872 helped determine the direction of the study of emotion by psychologists and comparative psychologists alike.

BOX 2.3 "SMART" BIRDS OR "SMART" GENES?

It is not uncommon for a Graylag goose's egg to roll out of her nest, and for her to get up and approach it. Seeing and approaching the egg are called *appetitive behaviors* and are considered preliminary to engaging in consummatory behaviors. Appetitive behavior is modifiable; it is often followed by a fixed action pattern (FAP), which is not.

The egg is the sign stimulus (or sign-releasing stimulus—see text). The FAP consists of the goose placing the under-surface of her bill against the far side of the egg and systematically scooping it back towards the nest. If all goes well, the egg will be retrieved and the goose will sit on it. If the egg rolls off to the side once the retrieval sequence begins, however, something interesting occurs. The bird often simply continues the sequence to completion. She inefficiently scoops

the area where the egg should be, waddles back into her nest, and assumes her position on an imaginary egg.

The more frequently the egg rolls out, the less vigorous is the retrieval response. If the egg stays in the nest for a long period of time, the goose may well wind up retrieving an imaginary one anyway! In other words, she may perform the FAP in a *vacuum* (Lorenz's term) without the relevant sign stimulus.

What is really strange is that a particularly vigorous retrieval response can be elicited by an oversize egg. A goose will attempt to retrieve a bowling-ball-sized "egg" in preference to a real egg. Finally, fulfilling the requirements necessary to be classified as an FAP, a brooding goose will attempt to retrieve a "wandering egg" the first time it spots one.

The Roots of Comparative Psychology.   But an interest in animal learning and behavior antedates even Darwin. From before the beginning of written history, humans have lived with domesticated animals (Diamond, 1997). Since then, probably most cat and dog owners have at one time or another wondered what pets thought about. The first scientists interested in animal psychology, in the 1800s, were no different. What, they wondered, was the nature of a nonhuman animal mind?[1] One obvious clue to an animal's mind was the fact that animals showed evidence of learning. They readily learn to recognize other animals and caretakers, where and when food is presented, how to get around in their surroundings, how to respond to signals and cues, and so forth. Understandably, animal learning became the focus of a number of the early post-Darwinian scientists.

Domestication.   Compared with feral (wild) animals, the niche of domesticated animals contains human beings. Animals reared in environments containing humans learn different behaviors in comparison with nondomesticated animals. Feral animal niches, for example, better allow for the appearance of FAPs and other species-specific behaviors. The reason is they are born into environments that contain sign-releasing stimuli. Animals living with humans must adjust their behavior accordingly, because their evolutionary history did not prepare them to do this. Among the differences in the approaches of ethologists and comparative psychologists was the former's study of innately-disposed behavior of animals in the nature, and the latter's interest in how domesticated animals acquired new skills, studied in laboratories. The controlled environment of a laboratory became the domesticated animal's ecological niche.

Role of Environment in Controlling Behavior.   Studying domesticated animals raises other issues. How could a domesticated animal's environment be arranged to better control its behavior? This interest differed from the strategy of noninterventive observations of feral animals by ethologists. The manipulation and control of animal behavior are best accomplished in an artificial laboratory environment. It is no accident that early comparative psychologists worked with animals in zoos (Greenberg, 1987). (Note, however, that Konrad Lorenz also gained control over his domesticated goslings' *following behavior*. How? By his presence in their ecological niche during a critical period.)

Individual Differences Versus Species-typical Behavior.   Historically, comparative psychologists concentrated their research on just a few species

---

[1]Domjan (1987b) has identified the earliest scientists who specifically contributed to the field of comparative psychology as Charles Darwin (*The Descent of Man*, 1871); George Romanes (*Animal Intelligence*, 1884); C. Lloyd Morgan (*An Introduction to Comparative Psychology*, 1894); and Margaret Washburn, (*The Animal Mind: A Textbook of Comparative Psychology*, 1908).

of animals: primarily cats, dogs, pigeons, monkeys, and humans. Diamond (1997) has noted that all of these animals have been domesticated for thousands of years in various cultures. A classic criticism of comparative psychologists is that their selection of which animals to use for comparison with one another does not make good sense from an evolutionary perspective (Hodos & Campbell, 1969). Why? Because, if comparative psychologists were attempting to discover the "evolution of learning," the phylogenetic relationships among these animals made little sense. Evolution is not described by a simple progression of bird to rat to monkey to human.

Certainly the Hodos & Campbell (1969) argument has merit. But what if the behavior of animals with larger brain-to-body size ratios becomes "more organized" and "more versatile . . . due to enhanced perceptual, cognitive, learning, social, and/or motor skills" (Gottlieb, 1984, p. 454). There is, Gottlieb argues, a logic and an implicit theory, both in the range of animals selected for study and in the evolutionary strategy employed by comparative psychologists. Nevertheless, the selection of both the species of research animal and the type of behavior studied continues to divide ethologists from comparative psychologists (Domjan, 1987b).

Morgan's Canon and the Law of Parsimony. One of the earliest theoretical problems facing comparative psychologists persists to the present. It concerns how humans should be treated within a comparative psychology framework. Should the focus be on their species-specific characteristics—their uniqueness—or on basic learning processes they have in common with other animals? Conwyn Lloyd Morgan (1894) was among the first to address the issue when he wrote *An Introduction to Comparative Psychology:*

> *In no case may we interpret an action as the outcome of the exercise of a higher psychical faculty if it can be interpreted as the outcome of the exercise of one which stands lower in the psychological scale.*

This statement, now called **Morgan's Canon,** has been widely interpreted as a plea for *parsimony*—to use the simplest explanation possible in interpreting one's observations. Morgan's canon has also served as an admonishment for psychologists not to commit the sin of *anthropomorphism*—that is, of attributing human characteristics to animals. A closer inspection of Morgan's other writings, however, lends another interpretation. Morgan assumed *a priori* that humans have "higher psychical faculties" that could not be found in any nonhuman animal. A more parsimonious position would have been to assume *a priori* that humans are animals that share common genes and common psychological processes (Griffin, 1978; Dess, 1998).

Indeed, psychologists who have followed Morgan's Canon seem to have applied the law of parsimony in only one direction, that of *not* attributing psychological complexity to nonhuman animals. The argument should also be applied to humans; that is, we shouldn't assume cognitive complexity in humans if their behavior can be interpreted in terms of more basic processes that are common to all animals.

Zoomorphism. Is there a theoretical alternative to being guided by a fear of being too anthropomorphic? Consider that a Darwinian perspective emphasizes the continuity of life forms rather than a dichotomy of humans and other animals. Comparative psychologists should be comfortable with a *zoomorphic* position, one that attributes some nonhuman animal qualities to humans as well as some human qualities to nonhuman animals. **Zoomorphism** is consistent both with the evolutionary continuity of animal behavior and with parsimony. In addition to Morgan's admonishment to beware anthropomorphism, psychologists should also be cautioned to not attribute complexity to humans when their behavior can be explained in terms of general processes. Though Morgan was uncomfortable in acknowledging our animal nature, he nevertheless played an historic role in developing comparative psychology and in identifying both anthropomorphic and zoomorphic positions.

Animal Models. The primary interest of ethologists is an in-depth understanding of the behavior of a particular (nonhuman) species. By contrast, the application of animal research to better understand human behavior and/or to test general theories of learning and behavior sets psychologists apart from classical ethologists. To this end, psychologists and comparative psychologists often use **animal models** to better understand the behavior of humans. A model is a standard that can be used for comparison. Examples of animal model research includes the search for the determinants of alcoholism, the development of new antibiotics, an understanding of the determinants of appetite, emotional behavior, concept formation, and mental disorders, to name but a few. However, the largest use of animal models by psychologists who study learning processes is to test associative theory and other general process learning theories. The results from experiments using rats, dogs, pigeons, and monkeys used as models are deemed applicable to most all animals, including humans.

Comparative Psychologists and Ethologists Compared

The respective orientations of researchers in comparative psychology and in ethology continue to provide two windows into the minds and behavior of animals (Timberlake, 1993). Ethologists observe a particular species' behavior in the natural environment (i.e., in "nature"). For this reason ethologists study species-specific behavior. Comparative psychologists typically bring one or a few species of animals into laboratories to conduct behavioral experiments, sometimes studying how different animals learn the same task. More often, however, they ask questions about general processes of learning. How do different environments change the behavior of individual animals of the

same species? For example, we'll see in the next chapter that through training, some dogs begin to salivate when a bell rings, while others don't.

In no small measure, differing methodologies account for many of the
conceptual differences between ethology and comparative psychology. Psychologists who study learning prefer the more tightly controlled, contrived,
artificial setting of the laboratory. Many of the species-specific tendencies
that might otherwise intrude into an investigation of "pure" association formation are minimized in the laboratory. In turn, the laboratory environment
allows the researcher to seek general processes across species and situations,
including consummatory behaviors studied by ethologists (Domjan, 1983).
Table 2.1 summarizes the major differences between psychological and classical ethological approaches to the study of behavior.

Species-specific Defense Reactions

Many contemporary studies of animal learning blend the foregoing approaches of ethology and comparative psychology. Consider the following example of laboratory research into innately organized behavior in mammals
which has some similarity to FAPs described in birds (Bolles, 1970, 1971,
1972). An experimental psychologist, Bolles noted that rats respond to aversive stimulation in predictable, characteristic ways. For example, when given
painful electric shock, they jump and run; in the presence of moving stimuli,
they initially freeze and then run. By contrast, pigeons flap their wings and fly
when shocked rather than jumping and running.

Can animals learn new responses rather than merely exhibit innately organized behavior? Yes, but at a significant cost in time and energy. For exam-

TABLE 2.1   Two Methods Of Studying Behavior

Psychological Approaches	*Ethological Approaches*
1. Focus on individual differences within a species/across species	1. Focus on species-typical behavior across species
2. Interest in general processes among vertebrates	2. Interest in species-specific behaviors
3. Study domestic animals under laboratory conditions	3. Study feral animals within (natural) ecological niche
4. Interventive manipulation of behavior	4. Unobtrusive observations
5. Human manipulation and control of animal behavior	5. Observation of animal in niche; no interest in controlling behavior
6. Use of animal models; extrapolation to human behavior; tests of general theories	6. Animals do not "model" behavior; little/no interest in extrapolation to human condition or testing "general" models
7. Ultimate focus is human species and human behavior	7. Focus on nonhuman animal behavior

ple, rats required to press a bar to avoid electric shock took thousands of trials, and not all of them learned the task (D'Amato & Schiff, 1964). Running in response to pain, on the other hand, takes no training. Bolles called these innately patterned responses **species-specific defense reactions (SSDRs)**. How such defensive behaviors occur is invariant both for the particular environmental stimulus and for each species.

Sociobiology and Evolutionary Psychology

Complex human and nonhuman animal social interactions can be successfully analyzed from within an evolutionary perspective. The models and concepts of *sociobiology* (Wilson, 1975) and of *evolutionary psychology* (Barkow, Cosmides, & Tooby, 1992) have generated both excitement and controversy. Sociobiology is the study of the genetic determinants of social behavior. Evolutionary psychology is the study of human and animal minds and behavior from the perspective of evolutionary theory. Here we take a brief look at their respective proposals that the determinants of an animal's behavior exist before its conception.

Proximal and Distal Causation. Sociobiologists and evolutionary psychologists are responsible for a shift in thinking about the determinants of behavior from *proximal causes* (psychological and sociological) to *distal* (or *ultimate*) *causes*. Distal causes of behavior refer to genetic predispositions to behave, as suggested by Darwinian adaptation and the concept of instinct. A satirical expression attributed to Samuel Butler (1835–1902) captures the philosophy of evolutionary psychology in a clever way. Butler turned around a common expression that "An egg is a chicken's way of making another chicken." He quipped that "A chicken is an egg's way of making another egg," a statement that evolutionary psychologists would agree with. From their perspective, the phenotypic forms of life—adult frogs, chickens, and humans—are viewed as elaborately evolved devices that have one purpose only, the perpetuation of the species. Everything about the adult human form, including language and social behavior, is an elaborate adaptation to accomplish one purpose—to self-replicate (see Barkow and others, 1992; Dawkins, 1995; Dennett, 1995). It is for this reason that Dawkins (1976) proposed that humans and other animals have "selfish genes."

By contrast, other psychologists propose that learning and proximal causes determine important aspects of human behavior. Speaking and understanding language may be a species-specific behavior, but it can only be expressed in an immediate environment. The form of language one learns to speak and understand (French, Swahili, English) and the facility one has with that language is proximally caused. They propose that we can best understand behavior by analyzing the environmental influences on it.

Both types of thinking are correct: Behavior is determined by both distal and proximal causes.

Interim Summary

1. Ethologists study the adaptiveness of an animal's ***species-specific behavior*** within its ecological niche. The ultimate purpose of behavior is to survive and to reproduce.

2. ***Consummatory behaviors*** such as eating and drinking, courting and mating, and taking care of offspring are among the survival behaviors studied by ethologists.

3. Konrad Lorenz found that under certain conditions during a ***critical period,*** a young animal might experience a type of rapid, long-lasting learning called ***imprinting.***

4. ***Fixed action patterns (FAPs)*** are instinctive behaviors
   a. that are innate, or unlearned.
   b. that occur in the same way each time.
   c. that are difficult to disrupt (once started, they continue to completion).
   d. that are followed by a latent period during which the FAP cannot occur.

5. Fixed action patterns (FAPs) are released by ***sign stimuli*** that normally occur within an animal's ecological niche. Sign stimuli are detected by ***IRMs (innate releasing mechanisms)*** hypothesized to be in the animal's brain.

6. Comparative psychologists, neuroethologists, sociobiologists, and evolutionary psychologists all study animal behavior from an evolutionary perspective.

7. ***Morgan's canon*** admonishes comparative psychologists to not attribute complex psychological processes to nonhuman animals if their behavior can be explained by simple psychological processes.

8. Comparative psychologists adopt ***zoomorphism,*** the attribution of animal qualities to humans, in recognition that humans and nonhuman animals may share some psychological processes.

9. Comparative psychologists also use ***animal models*** to study general properties of behavior. The major differences between comparative psychology and classical ethology are summarized in Table 2.1.

10. ***Species-specific defense reactions (SSDRs)*** are innately patterned responses to pain.

11. Sociobiologists and evolutionary psychologists emphasize the distal causes (genetic, Darwinian) of behavior, while psychologists stress more the proximal causes (environment, nurture) of behavior.

Discussion Questions

2. According to Moltz's four criteria, is sleep a fixed action pattern? Is the human sex act?

3. When I was about 13 years old, I became fascinated with female breasts and since then have discovered that I was not alone. Why age 13, and why the near universal interest among males in female breasts?

4. Given our nonhuman ancestry, perhaps we have been too slow to extrapolate findings from research animals to ourselves. Do you agree that our culture, in not adopting a zoomorphic perspective, underestimates animal intelligence and overestimates human intelligence? Can you think of examples that do not involve Lassie?

Quest for General Processes and a Science of Behavior

Lever-pressing rats and key-pecking pigeons? If these laboratory scenarios seem to be unrelated to what most people think of as learning . . . your perception is correct. However, one reason that these arbitrary tasks are used is the belief that something quite fundamental and basic might be discovered about the learning process—independent of the animal's niche behaviors. In developing his now-famous experimental chamber, called the Skinner box, B. F. Skinner (1959) wanted to minimize the interference of FAPs, SSDRs, or other rat-specific or pigeon-specific behavior to interfere with the study of learning. He wanted to conduct an objective analysis of how new, non-instinctive responses, might be learned in the laboratory.

Assumptions Underlying General Process Learning Theory

A primary goal of **general process learning theory** is to find a set of laws that can adequately describe the learning process in all animals. General process learning is often contrasted with species-specific learning. Psychologists who accomplish laboratory learning experiments attempt to systematically and objectively identify and test these common process laws. Let us look at some other assumptions in animal learning.

Behavioral Flexibility. At the outset, most behavioral scientists acknowledge the importance of learning in the development of behavior. Biological influences (distal causes) on behavior are not ignored, but learning is viewed as the primary source of identifiable behavioral variability. Another way to state this is that instinctive behavior is important, but what is of most interest in the study of both human and animal behavior comes about through associative learning processes.

Lawfulness of Learning. A further assumption of behavioral scientists is that behavior is neither capricious, accidental, nor random. Rather, it changes in predictable, adaptive ways. A simple example: You get mad and kick at a jammed door and break a toe. More than likely you will not repeat that behavior. Why? Because you and most other animals change behavior that results in inflicting self-pain. Likewise, if a rich neighbor goes on vacation and gives you $200/day to housesit, you will likely tell that person how much you enjoy this work and that you are available "anytime." Most animals respond to rewards and punishments in predictable ways.

Generality of Learning.   General process learning theory implies that many of the phenomena of learning are general in two ways: across species and across situations. That is, general processes can be observed under comparable sets of conditions in a variety of species. The biological and behavioral continuities offered by Darwin's evolutionary theory provide the conceptual basis for assuming common psychological processes (see next section on common brain parts). Learning that is transituational means that the same stimuli conform in a lawlike manner at different times, in different experiments, in different individuals, and in different laboratories.

Replicability.   Scientists assume that the various phenomena of learning are reproducible—that they can be demonstrated in other laboratories under similar sets of circumstances. Both replicability and predictability of outcome, therefore, illustrate what is meant by the "lawfulness" of learning.

Benefits of Laboratory Analysis.   Comparative psychologists assume that a laboratory is the best place to study learning and behavior for the following reasons:

1. Laboratories allow for more careful measurement of the learning process than do observations made in natural settings.
2. Manipulation of one or more independent variables in laboratory research allows for the use of control procedures.
3. Control procedures in turn allow the experimenter to deduce with confidence the necessary and sufficient conditions for learning. For example, is temporal contiguity necessary for learning to occur? If not, is it a sufficient condition? A logical analysis of these questions requires scientists to control the experimental environment in which learning occurs.
4. Laboratories allow for the control of various nonlearning effects, or *confounded variables*. In the absence of specific control procedures, many experiences (such as light-dark cycles, changes in diet and sleep, sex and age of organism, to name a few confounded variables) contribute to changes in behavior that are easily mistaken for learning effects.

Why Rats and Pigeons?

A researcher named Small (1901) first used rats in tests of mental processes. Many psychologists continue to use laboratory rats or pigeons in laboratory studies of learning. We have seen that ethologists (and some psychologists) object to these laboratory experiments. So, why do psychologists continue to use so few other species in learning experiments?

Two opinions regarding the use of laboratory rats in psychology have emerged during the past 80 years; namely they definitely are, or definitely are not, worthy of study. On one hand, in addition to humans, laboratory rats continue to be one of the most commonly used experimental subjects in learning research. From this observation, it can be concluded that at least one large group of scientists continues to think their use is justified. Indeed, the majority of experiments cited in this text use rats as subjects.

Most students, many ethologists, and some psychologists, however, decry the use of these "loathsome" creatures because they are convinced that no good will come from their study—except the dubious goal of better understanding the behavior of rats. "The proper study of mankind is man" (and of womankind, woman?)—so the saying goes (and as modified). Indeed, a comparison of the mental mechanisms and capacities of rats and humans is no contest. (Their respective brains will be compared in the next section.)

Laboratory rats continue to be used because they are hardy, fecund, and relatively inexpensive. Fecundity refers to reproductive capability. They have large litters throughout their normal lifetime, allowing researchers to breed their own research subjects. Rats and pigeons are used because they are small, require minimal facilities and support personnel, and are resistant to infection. But are laboratory rats that have now been inbred for hundreds of generations still "normal"? Surprisingly, the answer seems to be "yes." Comparisons of the behavior of albino laboratory rats with *Rattus norvegicus* (the wild stock from which it was derived) finds quantitative rather than qualitative differences. For example, comparisons of food neophobia (wariness of novel foods) (Mitchell, 1976), of taste preference behavior (Shumake, Thompson, & Caudill, 1971), of burrowing behavior in climatic extremes (Boice, 1977), and of learning (Boice, 1973, 1981; Eibl-Eibesfeldt, 1970) reveal no major differences among strains of rats, including white lab rats.

As a result of a century of experimentation, we know much about the brain and behavior of rats and pigeons. Both are sufficiently complex to keep several generations and many thousands of scientists busy. The study of the tobacco mosaic virus and *Drosophilia* (a fruit fly) have allowed geneticists a better understanding of the general mechanisms of genetics. In the same way, the study of rats and pigeons have improved our understanding of both brain-behavior relationships and generalized animal learning processes.

Ethics of Animal Experimentation

The fact that most humans are not too fond of rats and mice raises some ethical concern. Two such questions will be touched on here; one regards the human food chain and the other concerns using animals in research. Because much has been written in serious treatments (Miller, 1985), and in the popular press regarding animal welfare, and because few minds will be changed regardless of the arguments presented here, I will be brief. Suffice it to say that some individuals and organizations would outlaw all animal experimentation.

Animal rights activists would outlaw all animal research on grounds of cruelty. At the risk of oversimplifying complex issues, the benefits accruing from the responsible use of animals in medical and neuroscience research would seem to outweigh nonhuman animal rights. The review process for all animal experimentation focuses on reducing distress and assuring that if there is distress the research must be demonstrably important. I for one am not interested in living in a prescience, or nonscience, culture. A cost-benefit analysis of this issue by a high school student is presented in Box 2.4.

Comparison of Representative Brains

Its only a slight oversimplification to say that learning takes place in the brain. The size of my human brain can be approximated by placing my two closed fists together. The rat and pigeon brains are no larger than the tip of my finger. How can these two brains be compared for their respective learning capabilities, you ask? More important, why assume that these brains accomplish learning in the same manner?

Vertebrate Plan. Many researchers have studied the brains of representative species of vertebrates. Two outcomes are noted here, beginning with observations by C. Judson Herrick. Common features of brain organization, that

---

Box 2.4 Ethical Issues of Animals in Research

Jan Hison, a senior at D. H. Conley High School (Pitt County, CA), captured first place at a National Health Occupations Students of America (HOSA) Research Persuasive Speaking Contest. Prior to researching the speech, Ms. Hinson was against the use of animals in research. Studying the issue changed her mind. Major points in her speech included these:

- Animal research has extended human life spans by 20 years.
- By law, research facilities provide animals with humane living conditions—that are less stressful than the struggle for survival in the wild.

- 90–95% of animals suffer no pain in research.
- The majority of 20th-century medical advances have depended on animal research, as follows: cardiac catheterization; organ transplant techniques; discovery of insulin and DNA; treatments for tetanus, rheumatoid arthritis, whooping cough, and leprosy; and development of the heart-lung machine, and Salk and Sabin vaccines.
- Animal research has resulted in millions of pets that are free of heart disease, leukemia, and kidney failure.
- Five million abandoned animals are destroyed at animal shelters each year—animals that could be productively used in medical research.

Herrick (1948) called the **vertebrate plan,** reflect the evolutionary related-ness and continuity of vertebrates. (Vertebrates include fish, amphibians, rep-tiles, birds, and mammals.) Relevant to how animals learn, humans have in common with other vertebrates a spinal cord containing similarly organized sensory and motor nerves, brain stem structures, a cerebellum, 12 paired cra-nial nerves and their attendant motor and sensory nuclei, a hypothalamus, and a thalamus. The structures that mediate learning are common to all ver-tebrate nervous systems.

Reptilian Brain. Further brain organization common to all vertebrates can be seen in Figures 2.2 and 2.3. MacLean (1970, 1977) describes "reptilian" features of the human brain common to all vertebrates, which are overlain by "old mammalian" and "new mammalian" features. Higher cognitive processes of humans, such as language, MacLean proposes, are among the functions of

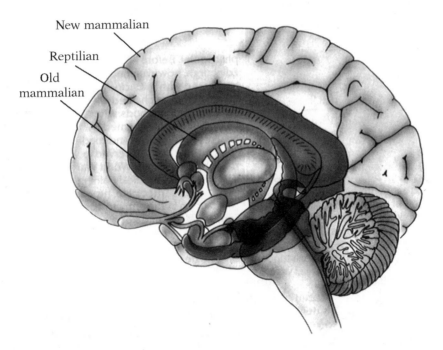

FIGURE 2.2 Common Brain Features Yield Common Learning Processes

The human brain as conceptualized by MacLean (1977) consists of a primi-tive "reptilian" brain, overlaid successively by "old" and "new" mammalian brains. Cerebral hemispheres are larger in the more recently evolved fore-brain of mammals, a process called *corticalization*.

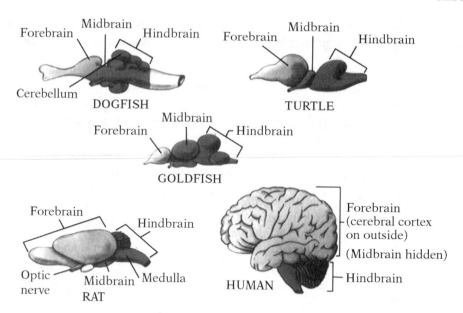

FIGURE 2.3   Vertebrate Brains Have a Common Plan

Note the three major divisions of hindbrain, midbrain, and forebrain in representative vertebrate brains (not to scale). (After Kalat, 1984.)

the cerebral hemispheres (new mammalian). However, neocortex, which is found in the cerebral hemispheres, is common to birds and mammals, not just to humans. Again, there is sufficient commonality of brain structure and function to support general processes learning theory.

Conclusions from Brain Comparisons

Rats, birds, monkeys, and humans certainly have old mammalian brain structures, conform to a vertebrate plan, and possess other features of physiological organization, including common neurotransmitters and neuroendocrine systems. Rat and pigeon brains are small, but their organization is sufficiently complex to allow these animals to perceive process and readily learn from interactions in its environment. Indeed, as we see in the next chapter, associative learning is easily investigated even in invertebrates (animals lacking central nervous systems) (Abramson, 1994).

Earlier, zoomorphism was presented as an alternative to Morgan's Canon, which serves to isolate humans from other animals. Here we have learned that humans have brains built on guidelines that are common with other vertebrates. Such brain organization provides a neuroanatomical basis for a common stimulus-response (S-R) psychology. These common brain features support the idea that many processes of learning and behavior may be general to all animals.

Species-specific behaviors are often accounted for by reference to special brain structures. During the course of evolution, for example, it is likely that a brain part found in the visual tectum of some goslings promoted better following behavior than in others. The behavior was adaptive, and these brains were selected for. Following behavior is species-specific to geese. By contrast, in exploiting their ecological niche, sparrows developed different brain mechanism, yielding their own species-specific behavior. At the same time, both species—indeed, most all animals—were also solving common problems. Hence, both species differences in behavior and similarities in behavior (general processes) can in part be accounted for by specific brain structures.

Anatomical and physiological similarities among all vertebrates support a black-box approach to the study of behavior. What about humans? Psychologists are finding that we learn like other animals, and we learn like no other animals. We'll revisit this idea throughout the following chapters.

Interim Summary

1. Many psychologists who conduct learning research try to avoid measuring species-specific behaviors. Alternatively, their goal is to investigate **general process learning theory** by studying a few species of animals and cautiously extrapolating results to other animals.

2. A laboratory approach to animal learning emphasizes an animal's *behavioral flexibility*—that learning accounts for most individual differences in behavior within a species.

3. Behavioral scientists assume that behavior is *lawful, orderly,* and *predictable,* and that experiments in animal learning are *replicable*.

4. General processes of learning are general in two ways: across species and across situations.

5. Rats and pigeons are commonly used in laboratory learning experiments because they are small and cheap, because much is known about brain-behavior relationships in these species, and because they are representative of other vertebrates.

6. All vertebrates and many invertebrates have sufficiently developed brains to support learning processes. Herrick's **vertebrate plan** is that common to all vertebrates are a spinal cord, brain stem, cerebellum, cranial nerves, hypothalamus, and thalamus.

7. McLean's *reptilian brain* addresses more recent changes in the vertebrate brain, including an *old* and *new mammalian* brain that now surrounds the brainstem.

8. Because of common brain parts, basic processes of animal learning can be studied from an S-R, black-box framework with rats and pigeons.

DISCUSSION QUESTIONS

5. The history of our species is a short, recent one. Our human brains are essentially mammalian, and they differ little from those of other primates. In particular, except for size, the human brain is remarkably similar to the chimpanzee brain. Assume that a goal of psychology and behavioral neuroscience is the complete understanding of the human mind and behavior. What are the implications of the fact that our brains have been nonhuman a great deal longer than they have been human?

CHAPTER SUMMARY

1. The ability to learn new behaviors complement more innately organized behaviors. Hence, learning is adaptive.

2. Darwin's theory of evolution provides an understanding of continuity among species as well as the basis for such concepts as species-specific behaviors, instinct, motivation, and learning as adaptation.

3. Contemporary evolutionary theory incorporates the modern science of genetics (genes and heredity) along with the concept of species resulting from the process of natural selection. Finess is a measure of reproductive success.

4. Humans share many physical and behavioral characteristics (and much DNA) with other species, especially other primates. Human nature is accounted for by a consideration of phylogenetic, ontogenetic, and extragenetic history.

5. Biologically oriented scientists seek the distal, or phylogenetic, determinants of behavior. These include an understanding of evolutionary processes, of how species are adapted to their environmental niches, of behavioral genetics, and of comparative brain structures.

6. Ethologists study species-specific, consummatory behaviors in the field. Lorenz described imprinting, a type of rapid, long-lasting learning, and fixed action patterns (FAPs) that are released by sign stimuli.

7. Behavioral scientists who study animal learning in laboratories are most concerned with an animal's ontogenetic history—the proximal events that describe how the environment influences behavior.

8. The zoomorphic perspective of comparative psychologists guides their search for common learning processes among all animals. They use animal models to study general properties of behavior.

9. General psychological processes exist across species in part because of similarities of brain structure, identified by Herrick as the vertebrate plan.

10. Rats and other laboratory animals are appropriate animal models for general physiological and behavioral studies, and for research guided by general process learning theory. *What* different animals learn is variable; *how* they learn has many features in common.

KEY TERMS

adaptation   34
animal model   51
consummatory behaviors   44
critical period   46
evolution   34
fitness   31
fixed action pattern (FAP)   47
general process learning theory   55
genetics   35
heredity   35
imprinting   45
innate releasing mechanism
   (IRM)   47

instinct   45
Lamarckian evolution   36
Morgan's canon   50
natural selection   41
selective pressure   41
sign stimulus   47
species   37
species-specific behaviors   44
species-specific defense reaction
   (SSDR)   53
variability   39
vertebrate plan   59
zoomorphism   51

CHAPTER 3

From Reflexes to Simple Conditioning

[An insect] . . . can see, walk, run, smell, taste, fly, mate, eat, excrete, lay eggs, metamorphose. It has internal programs for accomplishing these functions— contained in a brain of mass, perhaps, only a milligram—and specialized, dedicated organs for carrying the programs out. But is that all? Is there anyone in charge, anyone inside, anyone controlling all these functions? . . . Or is the insect just the sum of its functions, and nothing else, with no executive authority, no director of the organs, no insect soul?

Carl Sagan & Ann Druyan, *Shadows of Forgotten Ancestors* (1992, p. 167)

REFLEXES

Animals are born with innate, unlearned response tendencies. These responses, called **reflexes,** occur involuntarily when elicited by specific stimuli in the environment. Reflexes are simpler than fixed action patterns (FAPs). We now turn to the reflex and to reflexive behavior for three reasons: (a) reflexes are of interest to ethologists, physiologists, and psychologists alike; (b) reflexes provide the basis for simple conditioning; and (c) both reflexes and conditioned reflexes are important in understanding the complexities of human behavior.

A number of diverse reflexes and reflexlike behaviors are listed in Table 3.1. The survival value of each is self-evident. A human infant, for example, will draw up arms and legs reflexively in response to a sudden, loud noise or a loss of equilibrium—a response known as the Moro reflex. Further disturbance will elicit crying. Noise, the eliciting stimulus, triggers the reflexive-like response, crying, that in turn triggers the infant's caregiver to action. Thus, reflexes in humans and insects are, without exception, adaptive. Most of the reflexes listed in Table 3.1 are retained into adulthood.

Note that the "stimulus" in the simple stimulus-response (S-R) framework of the reflex are naturally occurring in the environment in which the animal lives. These stimuli make up Darwin's "nature"—the *nature* referred to in *natural selection*. Each response reflects the operation of an organism's inherited anatomy, physiology, and behavior as it meets with the environment. For example, nature has selected animals whose pupils dilate in bright light, and newborns that root and then suck in response to the stimulus of a warm nipple around its mouth. The environment is the source of reflexive behavior in that it places a selective pressure on evolving animals. Animals with adaptive reflexive tendencies were selected over those lacking them.

Sherringtonian Reflexes.   Not all reflexes have the underlying anatomical simplicity of the patellar (knee-jerk) or the eye-blink reflex. These two well-known reflexes are characterized by identifiable sensory neurons synapsing on identifiable motor neurons. Typically, one or more interneurons separate the direct sensory and motor component. For the patellar and eye-blink reflexes, the synapses occur in the spinal cord and medulla, respectively.

TABLE 3.1 Types of Reflexes

ELICITING STIMULUS (Stimuli originate in the environment; i.e., Darwin's "nature")	REFLEX (Reflexes are the DNA's programmed responses to stimuli)
1. "Motor" (touch) reflexes	
Patellar Tap ⟶	Knee Jerk
Pressure on the ⟶ Surface of the Eye	Eye Blink
2. Light and sound reflexes	
Loud Noise, Loss of Equilibrium ⟶	Moro Reflex
Decrease/Increase ⟶ in Light Intensity	Dilation/Constriction of the Pupil
3. Temperature reflexes	
Increase in Body Temperature ⟶	Sweating
Localized Intense Heat (Burn) ⟶	Blister
Match Burn on Arm ⟶	Arm Withdrawal
Sudden Drop in Body Temperature ⟶	Goose Bumps
4. Feeding/Ingestional reflexes	
Taste of Food ⟶	Salivation
Taste of Sour Lemon ⟶	Salivation
Finger, Food in Throat ⟶	Gag Reflex
Ingestion of Toxin ⟶	Nausea, Loss of Appetite, Vomiting
Salt Loss ⟶	Aldosterone Release
5. Immune system reflexes	
Cedar Pollen ⟶	Histamine Release
Antigens ⟶	T-Lymphocyte Release

Sensory-to-motor nerve activation completes what is known as a *reflex arc*. The motor component of the reflex was identified by Sherrington (1906) as the "final common pathway." Hence, simple reflexes are often called **Sherringtonian reflexes.**

Extending the Idea of Reflex. Look, however, at other reflexes listed in categories 3 through 5 in Table 3.1. Sweating and salivation are glandular responses, not skeletal muscle contractions, yet by convention both are considered reflexive. But what about blister formation to burns? Remember that in the patellar reflex, motor neurons compose the "final common pathway" causing the lower leg to jerk when the patella is tapped. What is the final common pathway that directs the histamine release and extracellular fluids that are secreted around injured cells? What about nausea response to toxins?

For present purposes let us simply observe that all reflexes are not Sherringtonian. The underlying physiology of nausea, of immune system functioning, of temperature regulation, of fluid and electrolyte regulation, and so on, though more complex, can be thought of as reflexlike. Recall the opening description of the reflexive life-cycle behaviors of insects—walking, eating, smelling, and so forth. Such complex reflexes raise the possibility that at least some components of functionally similar human behaviors may also be reflexive. Walking, for example, doesn't seem to be learned. Nor do chewing and swallowing. But learning does seem to be involved in the selection of spinach over ice cream.

Unlearned responses serve to protect the newborn and adult organism alike against any number of environmental dangers. However, this arsenal of reflexes falls woefully short of the complex responses (e.g., running, shouting, climbing) and the chains of responses (stalking prey, escaping predators, fighting, eating and drinking, communicating) required for survival. These seemingly more "voluntary" responses are acquired through learning.

Hardwiring Versus Plasticity

Reflexes are studied primarily by physiologists, and at present the brain organization underlying reflexive behavior is fairly well understood. Indeed, innately organized sensory and motor nerves are often referred to as the brain's hardwiring. By contrast, modification of brain physiology (which is presumed to underlie learned behavior) is often referred to as the brain's **plasticity.** Early research by Rosensweig, Krech, Bennett, & Diamond, (1962) had demonstrated that rats who were given an enriched environment (by being housed in groups) had neurons with more highly developed dendrites than animals housed individually in stark cages. Changes such as these provide evidence for the brain's *plasticity,* or ability to change, during a lifetime.

Our working assumption is that complex behavior is mediated by both hardwired and more plastic brain functioning. What is the importance of plasticity? In the previous chapter, we learned that variability within a species comes about through genetic mechanisms. Since most members of a species have similar behavioral tendencies, plasticity resulting from environmental differences is the basis for learned behavioral differences.

Neurogenesis. Recent research has shown that *neurogenesis*—the process of forming new neurons—occurs in the brains of senescent (old) mice who are moved from single housing to group housing (Kemperman, Kuhn, & Gage, 1998). This evidence of neurogenesis greatly extends the concept of the brain's plasticity. Not only can "old" neurons be modified in function, "new" neurons can be trained in adult animals.

Interim Summary

1. *Reflexes* are unlearned responses to environmental stimuli. Reflexive behavior can be best understood as involuntary, adaptive responses that have evolved because they promote survival and enhance reproductive success.

2. A reflex is composed of a sensory component (elicited by the appropriate environmental stimulus—Darwin's "nature") and a motor nerve component that adaptively completes a *reflex arc*.

3. The patellar and eye-blink reflexes are called **Sherringtonian reflexes.** A Sherrington reflex occurs when sensory nerve activity arrives at the brain or spinal cord, makes synapse with one or a few interneurons which in turn synapse with motor neurons, the final common pathway.

4. More complex reflexive-like tendencies involve more brain components. Immune system functioning and the physiology of ingestion are two examples.

5. Reflexes are considered to be hardwired, whereas learned behaviors result in *plasticity* in brain functioning.

6. Plasticity and *neurogenesis* allow an organism to adaptively respond to changing environments throughout a livetime. Learning involves a physical modification of inherited brain mechanisms.

NONASSOCIATIVE LEARNING

While riding with her father through a brief North Florida thunderstorm, 4-year-old Kristen fearfully watched bright flashes of lightning and heard the sharp cracks of thunder. Then, over the next 10–15 minutes, the storm began to dissipate.

> *"Where's the thunder?" she asked.*
> *Distracted, Dad pondered how to explain the physics of thunder and lightning to a 4-year-old.*
> *Far off in the distance where the storm had moved, another flash brightened the dark sky.*
> *Again Kristen asked, "Where'd the thunder go?"*
> *At this point Dad realized that she had apparently learned a lightning-thunder association. She could still see the flashes, but the low growl of accompanying thunder was too distant to be heard.*

Learning by association is what this book is about. But something called nonassociative learning also occurs. Before analyzing the association that Kristen had apparently learned, let us first see what happens when two common stimuli, thunder and lightning, impinge on our nervous systems. The stimulus events experienced by the 4-year-old can be depicted in a 2 × 2 table of possible outcomes (see Figure 3.1). The stimulus event of lightning (S_1) occurs or doesn't occur. The second stimulus event (S_2), thunder, also may or may not occur. The two stimuli may occur together (cell a), or neither may occur (cell d). The effect of one stimulus acting alone on an organism (cells b and c) is called a **single-stimulus effect.**

S₂—Thunder

Present   Absent

	Present	a	b
S₁—Lightning	Absent	c	d

FIGURE 3.1 An Association Matrix

> The joint occurrence of S_1 and S_2 occupies the upper-left cell, labeled a. Either stimulus may occur alone, for example, cell c, thunder alone, or cell b, lightning alone. Cell d indicates the absence of both stimulus events, and can be labeled *context* in that stimulus events always occur against a background of ambient conditions, or context.

Habituation

Direct your attention for a moment to an example of a single-stimulus effect. First consider "silent" lightning displays many miles away. The child might reflexively turn her head to see the lightning. In doing so, she orients (directs attention) to it. Over a period of time, faraway lightning would elicit less responsiveness from the child; she would orient less to each new occurrence. This reduced responsiveness of an organism to repeated stimulation is called **habituation.** Habituation is typically considered to be an example of **nonassociative learning** because it can be thought of as a single-stimulus effect, and because it is a relatively permanent change in behavior resulting from a single stimulus. In fact, it may be days before another flash of lightning again elicits as strong a response. (An alternative view that considers habituation from an associative perspective is presented in Chapter 4.)

Habituation is a basic property of behaving organisms. Stimuli that by themselves are not too meaningful tend to be ignored. If you asked the 4-year-old, she might say she quit looking at the lightning because it was boring. Habituation is the most basic form of learning, that is, learning not to respond to repetitious, meaningless stimuli. Other examples of habituation include not hearing the ticks of a clock, not feeling the clothes you are wearing, and not seeing the page numbers as you read this book—until your attention is directed to these stimuli.

Every waking minute we are exposed to thousands of stimuli (auditory, visual, cutaneous, chemical, etc.). Fortunately, we can't possibly attend to all of them. Only the most critical, meaningful stimuli that demand attention get it. The other stimuli must fade into the background stimulus conditions (cell d, Figure 3.1), or we would constantly be in sensory overload. Habituation is the process that allows this fading to occur. In a sense, we are learning what to respond to, and what not to attend to, and this seems to be a perfectly reasonable use of the term learning. Single-stimulus events that are repeatedly encountered become relatively permanently "habituated." Such stimuli, for example, less readily form new associations. (The reduced associability of familiar stimuli is a phenomenon called latent inhibition, discussed in the next chapter.)

Habituation Is Not Receptor Adaption. The process of habituation is often confused with the more peripheral processes of receptor adaptation and/or receptor fatigue. For example, rods and cones become less sensitive to light stimulation immediately after they are exposed to light. Following sound stimulation, hair cells in the cochlea of the ear likewise have refractory periods during which their responses are reduced. In the absence of further stimulation, these sensory adaption processes typically recover within a few seconds to a few minutes. By contrast, habituated responses may remain so for days, weeks, and months.

Remember the distinction made earlier between learning and performance? We infer learning from performance, but not all changes in performance constitute learning. The present example of sensory adaption is an excellent example of performance changes (i.e., reduced sensitivity to sights and sounds) that do not constitute learning.

How "General" Is Habituation? We have begun to entertain arguments to the effect that learning is a general process. A general process allows one to make meaningful behavioral comparisons across widely divergent species and in a variety of learning situations. Habituation is a general process. For example, let's compare the effects of rhythmically stroking the "arm" of a starfish and the arm of a human infant (i.e., an invertebrate and a vertebrate, respectively). Following repeated stimulation the initial reflexive movements of the arms of both species diminish. In both instances, we would say that the response is habituated. Because of dissimilar nervous systems, the neural mechanisms underlying these movement responses presumably differ (see Box 3.1).

Perhaps we should not be surprised at the similar outcomes of habituation experiments displayed in Box 3.1. Apparently, there are no exceptions to the generality of nonassociative processes throughout the animal kingdom. Razran (1971) points out the similarity of patterns of habituation in a variety of responses in planaria, worms, snails, goldfish, frogs, turtles, birds, and humans.

Sensitization

Repetitive stimulation, however, does not invariably lead to reduced responsiveness. Had Kristen, for example, experienced lightning flashes right next to her, she would not have habitutated to them. Intense visual, auditory,

BOX 3.1   HABITUATION: A GENERAL BEHAVIORAL PHENOMENON

The figure shows the similarity of the time course of decreased responsiveness to repeated stimulation in spinal rats, normal rats, and adult humans (Lehner, 1941).

a. Withdrawal response decreased for tail-pinched rats after 13 trials in the first "habituation cycle." (These rats had transected spinal cords, thereby eliminating the brain's control over the habituation response.) Fifteen sec later, the same tail-pinch stimulus habituated in seven trials (second habituation cycle). By the sixth cycle, habituation was accomplished in two trials.

b. "Startle," or jerking, reflex to a loud sound habituates more slowly in intact rats, compared with the tail-pinch reflex in spinal rats. Again, the interval between blocks of rapidly repeated stimulations is 15 sec. Note that half as many stimulations (approximately 15) are sufficient to habituate the response in the second cycle, compared with 30 stimulations in the first cycle.

c. The same pattern of habituation of the abdominal reflex (muscle twitch to touch) of adult humans, again with 15 sec between each block of response habituation.

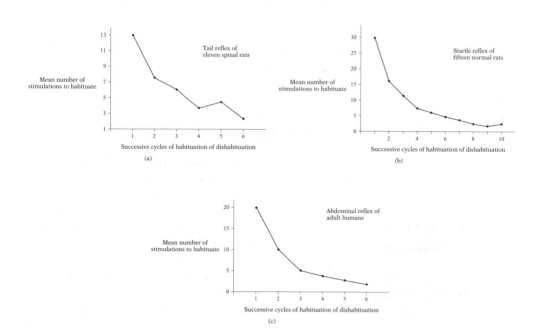

Source: Figures from Lehner, 1941.

cutaneous, and chemical stimuli do not habituate readily. In fact, often one or more presentations of a powerful stimulus can have the opposite effect. Rather than reduced responsiveness, animals can become yet more activated when the stimulus is presented again—a phenomenon called **sensitization.**

Nervous systems are constantly being attuned to the environment with which they interact. The stimulus effects of lightning and thunder are good examples of the nonassociative learning processes of sensitization and habituation. A sharp crack of thunder sensitizes 4-year-olds and adults alike. After one or more bone-jarring stimulus events, one's "nerves" are on edge, and other noises tend to elicit a greater-than-normal response. We await, we anticipate, the next crack of thunder. Such is the nature of sensitization. But the gentle rumbling of distant thunder has a different effect. In fact, low-intensity, rhythmic stimulation often has a calming effect (such as petting a cat, on both the stroker and the strokee).

Sensitization can also produce a relatively permanent change in a person's behavior. For several years after experiencing thunderstorms, the 4-year-old in question was aroused at their first approach. Her memory of close lightning strikes remains with her and has sensitized her to that particular class of auditory stimulus events. Unless a different set of associations are created, this learning may last throughout her lifetime. Note that being sensitized to thunderstorms is adaptive. Perhaps this is the stuff phobias are made of. (Are phobias adaptive? We address this question in a later chapter.)

Habituation and Sensitization Compared

To reiterate, some responses to repetitive stimuli tend to habituate, and others tend to sensitize. Both processes occur in all species of animals (Davis & File, 1984; Peeke & Petrinoviche, 1984). As a general rule, responses to regularly occurring presentations of stimuli of low to moderate intensity tend to habituate (Thompson & Spencer, 1966). High-intensity stimuli tend to sensitize the organism. To give you some idea of the complications that can arise in assessing nonassociative effects, consider an experiment by Davis (1974). In two groups of rats he compared the effects of presenting a loud noise of 110 decibels (dB) lasting only a fraction of a second. The rats differed only in the level of background noise in their experimental chamber, which was either 60 dB (relatively quiet) or 80 dB (relatively loud), respectively. Davis measured the rats' startle response to aperiodic presentations of the loud, 110-dB noise. The startle response decreased over trials in the group with low background noise (habituatrion) but increased in the group with the high background noise (sensitization). Depending on the level of background noise, the same 110-dB stimulus had two opposing effects—habituation and sensitization, respectively.

Simple-Systems Research: Neural Mechanisms
of Nonassociative Learning

Nonassociative learning (sensitization and habituation) has been studied in a California marine snail called *Aplysia*. The chemical events at synapse in sensory and motor neurons subserving a gill-withdrawal reflex have been described by Kandel and his associates (Carew, Hawkins, & Kandel, 1983; Kandel & Schwartz, 1982). This simple-systems approach to understanding the neural underpinnings of nonassociative learning is described in Box 3.2. Notice that this research provides one example of how a basic reflex—from sensory neuron, to interneuron, to motor neuron—can be modified by experience with the environment.

Sensitization and Habituation in Vertebrates:
LTP and LTD

Studies of *long-term potentiation (LTP)* and *long-term depression (LTD)* are examples of brain research that are providing insight into the neural substrates of nonassociative learning (Bliss & Lomo, 1973). **Long-term potentiation** is a lasting increase in the responses of neurons in the brain (mostly in the hippocampus) that serve sensory neurons. It may be that these relative permanent increases in nerve cell responses underlay learning. **Long-term depression** is a lasting *decrease* in these neuronal responses. In demonstrations of both LTP and LTD, neurons are rapidly stimulated with a train of high-frequency electrical impulses for a brief period of time. Such treatment facilitates these neurons to discharge more easily when further stimulated (LTP) or with more difficulty (LTD)—an effect that lasts for days and even weeks. Furthermore, stimulating several axons simultaneously produces more LTP than when only one neuron is stimulated. The neurochemistry of these synapses is now well understood (Rosenzweig, Leiman, & Breedlove, 1999). We will return to studies of long-term potentiation and long-term depression when the neural substrates of associative conditioning are considered.

Analysis of Nonassociative Learning

These examples readily illustrate the importance of the concepts of habituation and sensitization for understanding important changes in response patterns. There is irony in the fact that all psychologists cannot agree on the importance of single-stimulus events. This is true even to the point that some theorists ignore nonassociative phenomena. Why is this so? How has learning come to be defined "in terms of association" and single-stimulus effects relegated to other areas of psychology? Answers to these questions are not simple. Consider the following arguments.

Post-hoc Analyses of Nonassociative Effects. Single-stimulus effects are difficult both to conceptualize and to investigate in the laboratory. Ideally, a

BOX 3.2   NEURAL MECHANISM OF NONASSOCIATIVE LEARNING

MECHANISM OF HABITUATION

1. Repeatedly touching an *Aplysia*'s syphon produces the same number of action potentials...

2. ...but less neurotransmitter is released at synapse.

3. As a consequence, fewer action potentials are produced in the motor neuron...

4. ...and the gill-retractor muscle contracts less to each siphon touch.

MECHANISM OF SENSITIZATION

1. Shocking the *Aplysia*'s tail activates a sensory neuron.

2. The sensory neuron synapses upon a facilitatory neuron...

3. ...increasing the amount of neurotransmitter affecting...

4. ...and the number of action potentials produced by the motor neuron.

5. The gill-retractor muscle therefore contracts more to each siphon touch.

Source: Adapted from Pinel, 1993, p. 512.

scientist would like to be able to predict in advance the nature and direction of the outcome of an experimental treatment. This is difficult to do in investigations of single-stimulus effects. For example, very low to moderate intensity shocks can habituate; high-level shocks can sensitize; and very-high-intensity shocks (Overmier & Seligman, 1967) can produce a reduction in responsiveness that resembles habituation, a phenomenon that has been called "learned helplessness." And to complicate the matter, another test subject, or the same test subject on another day, or one in background conditions that are more intense, might give a different result.

What this means is that a researcher is restricted to a post-hoc analysis of the very thing that is being investigated: The experiment is done, results recorded, and then a hypothesis is formed. Not good science! This loss of predictability retards the scientist's search for lawlike relationships.

To summarize, predicting whether certain independent variables will act to sensitize, to habituate, or to have some other effect is problematic. The animal's response depends critically on the species under study, the nature of the physical stimulus, the background conditions, and the animal's prior history with the stimulus in question.

Single-stimulus Effects in Ethology, Physiology, and Psychology

Even though difficult to sort out, single-stimulus effects, including sensitization and habituation, are important for their inherent survival value. Recall that FAPs are released by a single type of stimulus, called a sign stimulus. One interpretation of the complex responses elicited by such a stimulus is that the infant goose's visual brain is preprogrammed to be sensitive to this type of movement during a critical period of development. Neurons allowing the perception of movement are tuned to whatever moving stimulus is experienced. In turn, the goose's following behavior is tied to activation of these neurons.

Specific neurons in the brain are preprogrammed to be sensitive to other complex stimuli, such as food, water, and drugs. Certain drugs have their complex effects to the extent that they can stimulate naturally occurring receptor sites on neurons. As indicated in Table 3.1, our brains and behavior have evolved to be especially sensitive to nature's stimuli that affect our survival. Such processes presumably are part of the "operating equipment" present at birth.

Ethology and comparative psychology are not the only sciences that are concerned with the nonassociative effects of stimuli. Psychologists who study processes of sensation and perception are very much interested in single-stimulus effects in humans and other animals. The discipline of psychophysics has given us methods for measuring response characteristics to a variety of stimuli. Other behavioral and biological scientists have traced physical stimuli through our sensory systems and throughout the central nervous system. Physiological psychologists and those in the neurosciences investigate the effects of complex stimuli such as foods, drugs, spoken words, and so on acting on the body.

Adaptiveness of Sensitization and Habituation. Sensitization and habituation are adaptive learned responses. Consider that living organisms that are either "drowsy" or "wired" are at less than their optimal arousal level for coping with environmental demands. Sleepy? Predators are watching. Wired? Potentially important stimuli are better perceived against a background of habituated stimuli, and nervous twitches may give away the position of a prey animal. Likewise, for a period of time following a "stronger" stimulus, the nervous system displays a greater than normal sensitivity. In large measure, a learned balance of habituation and sensitization is critical for optimal awareness.

Interim Summary

1. An association matrix summarizes the effects of two stimuli presented alone or in association. The effect of one stimulus acting alone on an organism is called a ***single-stimulus effect.***

2. ***Nonassociative learning*** is the concept that single stimuli acting alone can produce relatively permanent effects known as habituation and sensitization.

3. ***Habituation*** refers to a relatively permanent reduced responsiveness following repeated stimulation with low-intensity stimuli.

4. ***Sensitization*** is the term used to identify increased responsiveness for a time period following a relatively intense stimulus.

5. A stimulus can lie along a dimension (both physically and perceptually) from simple to complex. Simple stimuli have less of an effect on animals (both associative and nonassociative) than do complex stimuli.

6. The neural basis of sensitization and habituation has been studied in the gill-withdrawal reflex of *Aplysia*, a marine snail.

7. Relatively long-lasting increases in the sensitivity of individual neurons in vertebrates, called ***long-term potentiation (LTP),*** and long-lasting decreases in the sensitivity of individual neurons, called ***long-term depression (LTD),*** may underlie habituation and sensitization.

8. A single-stimulus effect is seen in initiating a reflex, in acting as a sign-stimulus, in initiating a sensory event, and in nonassociative effects such as sensitization and habituation. All are behaviorally adaptive.

DISCUSSION QUESTIONS

1. The Coolidge effect (Rosenzweig, et al, 1999) refers to the fact that males of some (most?) species of mammals and birds respond with more interest to a new sexual partner than to a familiar partner (i.e., one recently copulated with). Is this an example of habituation to familiar partners? Can you identify in this example a learning-performance distinction (see Chapter 2)?

The Association of Stimuli

Saint Ildefonso used to scold me and punish me lots of times. He would sit me on the bare floor and make me eat with the cats of the monastery. These cats were such rascals that they took advantage of my penitence. They drove me mad stealing my choicest morsels. It did no good to chase them away. But I found a way of coping with the beasts in order to enjoy my meals when I was being punished. I put them all in a sack, and on a pitch black night took them out under an arch. First I would cough and then immediately whale the daylights out of the cats. They whined and shrieked like an infernal pipe organ. I would pause for awhile and repeat the operation—first a cough, and then a thrashing. I finally noticed that even without beating them, the beasts moaned and yelped like the very devil whenever I coughed. I then let them loose. Thereafter, whenever I had to eat off the floor, I would cast a look around. If an animal approached my food, all I had to do was to cough, and how that cat did scat!

Lope de Vega, *El Capellan de la Vergen (The Chaplain of the Virgin)* (1615); trans. by J. H. Arjona, as cited in Bousfield (1955)

Most present-day investigations of learning are associative in nature. Even though sign stimuli can have unusually large effects on behavior, complex animals (including humans) meet comparatively few such innate-releasing stimuli in their lifetime. Rather, we solve many problems of adaptation and survival by learning to associate and to remember the important stimuli in our environment and responses to them. We learn by the reinforcing and punishing consequences of our behavior, also an associative process. And so it is to associative theory that we turn.

Modern learning theory is a form of philosophical associationism. The formal theory of *associationism*—that learning can be defined as the association of two or more sensory stimuli—can be traced to the writings of 17th-century philosophers now known as the British Empiricists. They include John Locke, Thomas Hobbes, George Berkeley, and others. Obviously, simple ideas of association have been around for a long time, as the protagonist in Lope de Vega's play indicated by his cat-conditioning experiment. Rather than cats, John Locke was more interested in how humans learned from their immediate environment. Our ideas, wrote Locke, result from the association of simple sensory events. These "raw sensations" became associated to produce complex associations:

All the ideas we have of particular distinct sorts of substances, are nothing but several combinations of simple ideas. . . . It is by such combinations of simple ideas, and nothing else, that we [mentally] represent particular sorts of substances to ourselves. . . .

Thus, the idea of the sun—what is it but an aggregate of those several simple ideas—bright, hot, roundish, having a constant regular motion (etc.)

John Locke, *An Essay Concerning Human Understanding* (1690)

Empiricism. The British associationists assumed that a primary source of knowledge about the world is based on experience with the world. Hence, knowledge is empirical, that is, guided by observation. Modern science uses empirical methods; laboratory study involves seeing, hearing, and otherwise observing, testing, and measuring. *Empiricism* is the main approach (and philosophy) that distinguishes science from other ways humans can get knowledge about the world (cf. spiritualism and intuitionism, which have no real-world referents).

The British empiricists did not do experiments in laboratories. Nevertheless, many of their ideas about associationism have proven to be remarkably insightful. Modern scientists retain the basic approach of these philosophers: The most simple learning processes are operationally defined as the association of two or more sensory experiences, a sensory experience with a response, and so forth.

Four Tenets of Association Theory

Association theory concerns the relationship (connection, union) that results when two or more stimuli are paired together in time. Beginning with the British associationists and elaborated by subsequent researchers, association theory may be summarized as follows:

1. *Temporal contiguity*. The process of association formation is integrally dependent on *temporal contiguity*. That is, for stimulus events to be associated, they must occur close together in time. For example, you learned the meaning of "watch out!" when someone yelled this at you—immediately followed by a near-miss. Vertebrate nervous systems readily make associations when stimuli sensed by them occur closely together in time. The **contiguity theory of association** is defined as a learned association between two stimuli that occur closely together in time.

2. *Intensity*. More intense stimuli are more associable than less intense stimuli. For reasons not well understood (but that TV advertisers know only too well), louder sounds and brighter lights are more quickly associated (in advertising, with brand-name products). In addition, larger rewards and punishers influence the rate of learning more than do smaller ones.

3. *Frequency*. The more frequently stimuli are presented together, the stronger is their association. A common example is the use of flash cards in which mastery depends on time spent studying. The more frequently you go through the cards (i.e., the more trials), the better the material is associated: $9 \times 7 = ?$

4. *Similarity*. The similarity of two events influences their associability. Some events seem to "belong" together, and, as a result, they are more easily associated. For example, assume that you visit a zoo. While there, you experience both new animal smells and you also hear a new song

played over the loudspeaker. Which association would be stronger two years later? Would the smell or the music most likely put you in mind of the zoo? We explore several hypotheses about similarity later in this chapter. Presumably, the role of similarity in association has something to do with hardwiring in the brain.

Association Theory: Example and Analysis

With these principles in mind and in the spirit of John Locke, let us return to the thunderstorm example that opened this chapter. Recall that Kristen wanted to know what had happened to the thunder. She could still see the lightning in the distance, and her question indicated that she had learned to associate the lightning stimulus with the thunder stimulus. At that point, she had an "idea" that a storm is composed of rain, thunder, and lightning (in the same way that Locke's idea of sun was warm, red, and round). After being experienced together, the elements belonged together. In the presence of only one element, the other was missed.

Learning About Causality.   In this 4-year-old's perceptual world, however, causality was probably not inferred from her observations. Because of the nature of thunderstorms, thunder sometimes seems to precede and sometimes to follow lightning. It is likely that Kristen learned that thunder and lightning were highly correlated, but she had not yet learned that lightning causes thunder. That is, she most likely had not learned that lightning is the antecedent condition, or cause, of the thunder. Having learned the thunder-lightning (or lightning-thunder) association, the absence of thunder was puzzling. Her still-not-quite-predictable world had become even less so.

Careful observation over a number of trials with a nearby storm might allow human observers to infer that thunder invariably follows lightning strikes. Unless one learns about (and remembers) the physics of lightning and thunder in a science class, however, one will not know that a lightning strike causes thunder by heating and expanding air molecules that "thunder" on contraction.

Contiguity and Contingency

Knowledge provided by correlation is incomplete, so how do animals learn about causality? Let us look in more detail at what is known as the *contingency theory of association* and see what it adds to the associationist theory of contiguity. The **contingency theory of association** is that stimulus-stimulus associations occur when an animal learns that one stimulus precedes and signals the occurrence of a second stimulus. According to Rescorla (1968), contingency theory focuses on the information value of one stimulus that signals the imminent occurrence of a second stimulus. Contiguity theory stresses the time relationship of two stimuli, while contingency theory emphasizes their order and probability of occurrence.

For simplicity, let us call the lightning stimulus S_1 and the thunder stimulus S_2. Contingency theory highlights an additional aspect of what an animal learns during an association, namely, the predictability of S_2 by S_1 because of the lightning $\rightarrow$ thunder sequence.

A *contingent* relationship exists between these two stimuli to the degree that one stimulus predicts the other. For example, if the contingency between S_1 and S_2 is perfect, the probability of S_2 given the occurrence of S_1 equals 1. In a perfect contingency, each and every time there is an instance of thunder, lightning has preceded it. Symbolically (where p means probability),

$$p(S_2/S_1) = 1.0 \qquad (3.1)$$

or, each and every time S_2 is presented S_1 does *not* occur.

$$p(S_2/ \text{ no } S_1) = 1.0 \qquad (3.2)$$

Equation 3.1 reads "the probability of S_2 given S_1 is equal to 1.0," and Equation 3.2 reads, "the probability of S_2 given no S_1 is equal to 1.0." These perfect relationships between thunder and lightning can be altered in several ways. For example, what if Kristen had heard thunder follow lightning on only half the occasions? There would not be a perfect contingency of $p(S_2/S_1)$ = 1.0. The equation reflecting this "half" predictability would be:

$$p(S_2/S_1) = 0.5 \qquad (3.3)$$

Would Kristen have learned the contingent relationship? If yes, would she have learned it as quickly? We analyze this question and other issues related to contingency theory in the next chapter. The important thing to remember here is that predictable sequences of two stimuli add more information than two stimuli merely occurring together.

Two-Stage Theory of Association. From the foregoing example, it seems likely that association formation has two distinct stages. In stage 1, two stimuli are perceived simply as being related to each other (that is, correlated), but one stimulus is not perceived as reliably preceding or causing the other. The association occurs by temporal contiguity—two events happening at about the same time. After a number of trials (that increase the frequency of association), one stimulus may be perceived to always precede the second stimulus. That is, the first stimulus is perceived as being the cause of the second. This more complex second stage is *association by contingency*. Together, contiguity and contingency constitute a **two-stage theory of association.**

Association Theory and S-R Theory

Behavioral science began when philosophers crawled out of their armchairs and began to work in their laboratories. The raw sensory experience of John Locke became the psychologist's stimulus. Since Locke's "ideas" are difficult to measure, the behavioral scientist instead concentrates on relating the organism's response to an incoming stimulus—both of which *are* measurable. Coughing and pain are readily associated by cats. Association theory easily becomes translated into the stimulus-response (S-R) theory of the laboratory. More often than not, S-R analyses do not refer to what is happening inside the organism, for example, the changes assumed to be taking place in the brain as learning occurs and as memories are formed. Recall that for this reason S-R psychology is also known as a black-box approach.

U.S. Laboratories.   Darwin's influence on the development of comparative psychology at the end of the 1800s has already been noted. At Columbia University in 1898, E. L. Thorndike moved the study of animal behavior into the laboratory. In a later chapter, we'll see that Thorndike placed hungry cats in boxes and measured how many trials it took for them to learn to escape. He then formulated basic general principles of instrumental learning, so named because the animals' responses were "instrumental" in escaping the box. In 1913, psychologist John B. Watson (1879–1958) promoted an objective science of behavior at Johns Hopkins University. Working within an S-R framework, Watson studied the effects of conditioning responses of both laboratory animals and humans. In later chapters we look more carefully at Watson's contributions to general process learning theory.

Russian Reflexology.   During this same time period, Ivan Pavlov in Russia was independently arriving at a philosophical position similar to Watson's. Pavlov studied both reflexive and conditioned reflexive, or learned, behavior. Both proposed that learning could be objectively measured by observing behavior.

Thorndike, Watson, Pavlov, and others influenced several generations of contemporary learning theorists. The result was that learning was studied in the laboratory as an observable change in behavior rather than as a mental process. Contemporary learning theory follows the lead of these early behaviorists. Ultimately, however, the elusive constructs we call "learning" and "memory" will be understood from a variety of perspectives, including biological, psychological, and sociocultural.

Interim Summary

1. Seventeenth-century philosophers now known as the British associationists proposed that knowledge was derived through the association of sensory stimuli.

2. ***Association theory*** is the relationship (the connection, or union) of two or more stimuli when they are paired together in time.

3. Four tenets, or rules, proposed by the British associationists that govern the formation of associations are (a) ***temporal contiguity***, (b) frequency, (c) intensity, and (d) similarity (or belongingness) of stimuli.

PHOTO 3.1 "Pavlov . . . Pavlov . . . That name rings a bell."

Cartoon by R.L. Zamorano

4. The ***contiguity theory of association*** is that the association of two stimuli occurs when they are presented close together in time.
5. The ***contingency theory of association*** is that the association of two stimuli occurs when when one stimulus reliably precedes and signals the occurrence of a second stimulus. The probability of one stimulus reliably predicting another can be manipulated in learning experiments.

6. A *two-stage theory of association* posits that events are first perceived as being correlated and second interpreted as being causally related. Causal relationships are inferred from contingent sequencing of two stimuli.

7. By the beginning of the 20th century, the study of learning moved into the laboratory. Learning was an inference made from observing changes in behavior in response to arranged stimulus events.

DISCUSSION QUESTIONS

2. In a recent survey, I found that many college students have forgotten the physics of thunder and lightning. Most thought that thunder and lightning occurred simultaneously and that lightning only seemed to occur before thunder "because light travels faster than sound in air." Why do you think that more people remembered the physics *of sound and light transmission in air* than the physics of *lightning heats air that causes thunder when the* *expanded air molecules collapse*? Do one or more of the British associationists' four rules (i.e., contiguity, intensity, frequency, and similarity) help explain this misattribution of causality? *Hint:* Which of these two rules of physics have you heard most often?

3. In terms of contingency and contiguity, why is it that flashing red and blue lights in rearview mirrors reliably elicit fear responses in some but not in all drivers?

PAVLOV'S SALIVARY CONDITIONING

Experiments that we now refer to as **Pavlovian conditioning** (also known as **classical conditioning**) were first reported at the turn of this century by a Russian physiologist, Ivan Pavlov.[1] His main work in this area, *Conditioned Reflexes*, was published in 1927.

Pavlov's research and that of his associates originally focused on the digestive process in dogs. In the course of his physiological studies, he described the *salivary reflex*; that is, he carefully measured the amount of salivation caused by precisely measured amounts of food placed on the dog's tongue. Not too interesting, perhaps, but these and other studies in digestion earned Pavlov a Nobel Prize in 1906.

---

[1] In 1902, an unpublished dissertation by E. B. Twitmyer, "A study of the Knee Jerk," was defended at the University of Pennsylvania. In his laboratory research, Twitmyer repeatedly sounded a bell a half-second before hitting the patellar tendon of students, thereby causing the patellar, or knee-jerk, reflex. The sound alone came to elicit the reflex (Twitmyer, 1974). Pavlov, not Lope de Vega, not Twitmyer, is credited with the "discovery" of conditioning because of the 30 years he devoted to its study.

Pavlov's other observations that we continue to study are more interesting. He noted that salivation occurred not only as a reflexive response to food being placed in the mouth. His dogs also salivated just prior to actual ingestion—almost as if the animal anticipated eating. Because this salivation occurred without real-world food, Pavlov called it a **psychic secretion.** Pavlov the physiologist knew that without the appropriate eliciting stimulus, reflexes weren't supposed to work this way. Could he understand the dog's higher mental faculties by investigating the role of the dog's cerebral hemispheres as new associations to the salivary reflex were learned? Pavlov took a chance and devoted 30 years of his life to a thorough examination of this question (Pavlov, 1927/1960).

Basic Observations.   On closer examination of the phenomenon, Pavlov found that the mere sight of food being prepared was sufficient to produce salivation in his dogs. The sight of food and the taste of food were always paired in time. Pavlov reasoned that the animal had learned to salivate to a broader range of stimuli because it had associated sight with taste (e.g., the sight of food preparation).

Pavlov tested his hypothesis of association by pairing the sound of a bell with the taste of food. (In addition to an electronic bell, Pavlov used the sounds of a metronome, "bubbling water," tuning forks, various pictures, vibration, and so on in pairings with food. For ease of illustration, most examples given refer to a bell.) Figure 3.2 shows a dog in a conditioning apparatus that Pavlov and his associates used to study association formation. To begin with, he noted that the dog pricked up its ears and turned its head to the source of the bell's sound—an *orienting reflex*—but did not salivate. That is, the orienting reflex to the bell is different from the salivary reflex to the food. After a number of paired presentations with food, the bell's sound elicited salivation even before food was tasted—a process Pavlov called *conditioning*, now known as Pavlovian conditioning or classical conditioning. He immediately grasped the adaptive nature of this type of learning:

> *It seems obvious that the whole activity of the organism should conform to definite laws. If the animal were not in exact correspondence with its environment, it would, sooner or later, cease to exist. To give a biological example: if, instead of being attracted to food, the animal were repelled by it, or if instead of running from fire the animal threw itself into the fire, then it would quickly perish. The animal must respond to changes in the environment in such a manner that its responsive activity is directed towards the preservation of its existence.* (Pavlov, 1927/1960, pp. 7–8)

Questions of adaptation aside, on the face of it, Pavlov's description of conditioning sounds like an esoteric laboratory exercise. Present-day behavioral scientists are not especially interested in the digestive processes of dogs, nor, as we will see later, in the lever-pressing or maze-running abilities of

FIGURE 3.2   Inside Pavlov's Laboratory

Pavlov (center) and his colleagues trained dogs to stand in a harness-like apparatus during experimental sessions. During experiments, the dogs would be isolated and could see and hear only the sights and sounds presented by the researchers.

rats. But we continue to study behavior in experiments such as these. They inform us about the process by which basic learning occurs in most species of animals in a variety of situations.

Application of Conditioning to Humans.   The general form of research in the remainder of this chapter begins with an inborn reflex. Through association, the original eliciting stimulus is replaced with a new, arbitrary stimulus. Are such simple conditioning processes determining factors in humans? Certainly. Consider, for example, the many domestic creatures who inhabit kitchens. The rattling of a box of dog biscuits or the lid of the cookie jar is sufficient to cause both orienting responses and conditioned salivation. For most of us, the mere mention of a thick, juicy steak or chicken fajitas sizzling over a bed of hot charcoal often have the same effect. But not for vegetarians. Why is that? A perfume or distinctive voice may bring to mind a particular individual and cause your stomach to flip-flop. Similarly, running toward an icy lake will raise goose bumps. The sight of a fast-approaching dust cloud (or fist) will produce an eye blink—not unlike the reflex elicited by touching the cornea. The appearance of a green sheen on a slice of turkey elicits a disgust response in adults but not in very young children. Why is that? The readers of this text can make appropriate responses (pronouncing, writing) to the letters *x*, *y*, and *z*, but most have not learned similar associative responses to, for example, the Cyrillic alphabet.

Remember Sherringtonian reflexes? It turns out that they can be modified by experience. The environment can come to control reflexes in new ways. One result is that each individual has a unique conditioning history; some have learned things that others have not.

Thought experiment: You now know how Pavlov brought the salivary reflex of a dog under the control of a neutral stimulus (i.e., the bell). Could you describe how it might be possible to condition a person to be disgusted at the sight of green meat? Or to sneeze when he or she merely sees a cat? Think about biting into a freshly cut lemon: Mouth water? You will have the basic mechanics of conditioning by the end of this chapter and should be able to make applications of learning to a better understanding of human behavior.

Elements of Pavlovian Conditioning

Simplicity in theory and method may not guarantee scientific success. Part of the reason we recognize Pavlov as the most important figure for this kind of conditioning is the simplicity of his analysis. Only four basic components (two stimuli, one response, and time) are involved. Let us now consider *excitatory conditioning* as initially demonstrated by Pavlov (see Figure 3.3). More specifically, the following preparation is an example of **appetitive conditioning** in that Pavlov elaborated a conditioned salivary response to a food stimulus (cf. appetite).

Two of the four components you already know—the food stimulus and reflexive salivation. Pavlov labeled these unlearned components the **unconditioned stimulus (US)** and the **unconditioned response (UR)**, respectively. For Pavlov's dogs, then, the taste of food is the unconditioned stimulus that automatically elicits the reflexive response of salivation, the unconditioned response.

To this basic reflex is added a learned, or conditioned, component. A new stimulus such as a bell is thrown into the mix. Before training, the bell has no special effect on the animal's appetitive behavior. That is to say, the bell initially is a *neutral stimulus* with respect to the salivation response. After training, a new response is learned. The animal now salivates to the bell. When the bell comes to control salivation, it is called the **conditioned stimulus (CS).** The newly learned response—salivation to the bell—is called the **conditioned response (CR).**

In summary, after repeated pairings of the CS (bell) with the US (taste of food), the bell is able to produce the learned, or conditioned, response of salivation. The basic elements of conditioning are the CS, the US, the time interval relating these two stimuli, and the new CR.

What About the Orienting Reflex?   As noted earlier, the bell doesn't initially cause salivation, but it does produce an orienting reflex. The dog makes head

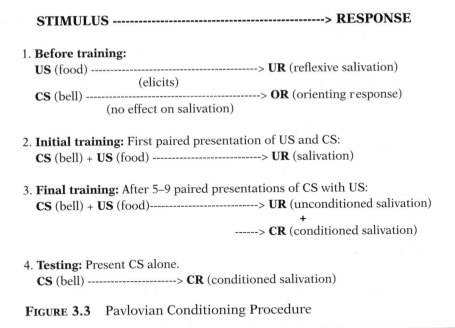

STIMULUS --> **RESPONSE**

1. **Before training:**
   US (food) --> **UR** (reflexive salivation)
                            (elicits)
   CS (bell) --> **OR** (orienting response)
                   (no effect on salivation)

2. **Initial training:** First paired presentation of US and CS:
   CS (bell) + **US** (food) ---------------------------> **UR** (salivation)

3. **Final training:** After 5–9 paired presentations of CS with US:
   CS (bell) + **US** (food)---------------------------> **UR** (unconditioned salivation)
                                                           +
                                         ------> **CR** (conditioned salivation)

4. **Testing:** Present CS alone.
   CS (bell) ----------------------> **CR** (conditioned salivation)

FIGURE 3.3   Pavlovian Conditioning Procedure

and ear adjustments in localizing the source of the sound. The orienting re-flex (OR) is not considered basic because with repeated trials the OR rapidly changes from a response to a "what is it?" stimulus to a response to a stimulus that signals food is available.

A Typical Pavlovian Conditioning Experiment

Let us conduct an idealized experiment along the lines that Pavlov reported. Our experiment can be characterized as appetitive excitatory conditioning (inhibitory conditioning is discussed later). Let us first set the CS, US, and time-interval parameters. Recall from Chapter 1 that the specification of intensity, frequency, amount, and duration of stimuli are parameters of the stimulus. As we shall see, conditioning outcomes critically depend on stimulus parameters.

Conditioning Parameters.   As experimenters, we set the parameters. Let the conditioned stimulus be a 500-hertz (Hz) frequency tone sounded at 70-dB loudness for 10 sec (think of a 10-sec-long doorbell). Let the unconditioned stimulus be 5.0 g (about 1/4 tsp) of powdered meat dropped onto the animal's tongue. The *CS-US interval* will be 30 sec. By convention, the **CS-US interval** is measured from stimulus onset to stimulus onset—in the present example, from the first sound of the tone to the first taste of the meat.

Next, let us set the *intertrial interval* at 3 min, where a **trial** consists of a CS-US pairing. The **intertrial interval** is the amount of time (typically a few minutes) between pairings of the CS and the US. We will condition the dog for a total of 20 trials but will measure every fifth trial to see how much conditioning has taken place.

To summarize our hypothetical experiment, the stimulus parameters are

CS = 10.0-sec, 500-Hz tone at 70 dB
US = 5.0-g meat powder
CS-US interval = 30.0 sec
Intertrial interval = 3.0 min
Trials: *n* (number) = 20

Recognize that if we changed any of these stimulus parameters (that enter the dog's brain through sensory channels), the conditioning outcome would be somewhat different. Another way to say this is that within a stimulus-response framework, the response depends on the stimulus.

Measuring Conditioning.   How do we know if and when conditioning is completed? The researcher can measure changes in salivation only if he or she has some idea of how much dogs salivate in the first place. Since an animal salivates when food is placed on its tongue, Pavlov was able to measure both unconditioned salivation (i.e., salivation to the food alone) as well as conditioned salivation when the tone was sounded (see Figure 3.3).

The first measure of salivation in the presence of the tone, prior to conditioning, is called a **baseline** measure of salivation. The baseline measure answers the question of how much saliva flows normally, and assures us that dogs don't salivate to this sound in the absence of food. In our experiment, let us measure the total amount of saliva during the 10-sec tone CS and, say, for 20 sec following (total = 30 sec). After five trials, on every fifth trial thereafter, we want to test to see how the conditioning process is proceeding. To do this, we measure salivation to the tone in the absence of the food.

Conditioning Results.   The results of our hypothetical experiment are shown in Figure 3.4. Note in this graph that only the conditioned responses to the tone when measured in the absence of food are plotted. How can we conclude that conditioning has occurred? Might not salivation have occurred even if the tone had been sounded repeatedly and no food presented? Perhaps sounding a tone for 30 sec every 3 min might drive the dog nuts, thereby increasing salivation!

Control Groups.   This is a conditioning experiment, and experiments need control groups or conditions. Pavlov's control group was a within-

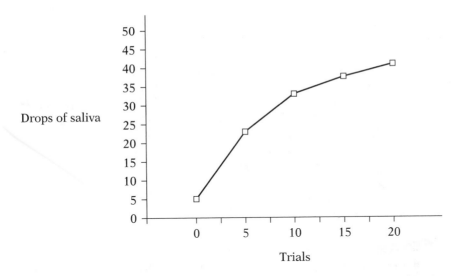

FIGURE 3.4   The Growth of Association

   Typical plot of an acquisition function. Only the CS is presented on trials 0,
   5, 10, 15, and 20. On all other trials, the tone and food are paired, and salivation to the food is not plotted.

subjects control. During pretesting, the dog's baseline salivation was
measured in the absence of either the CS or US. Note that this condition
closely resembles cell d in the association matrix (Figure 3.1, p. 69). To truly
conclude that conditioning occurs because of a tone-food association,
however, additional control groups are needed. Recall that several nonassociative control groups are possible. **A habituation control group** receives
only the CS, and a **sensitization control group** receives only the US (cells b
and c in Figure 3.1, respectively, assuming that lightning can be considered a
CS and thunder a US). The logic is to compare the effects of each stimulus
presented alone to both presented together. In our experiment, a dog in the
habituation control group would merely hear the bell. A dog in the sensitization control group would only be given food. Treatment effects attributed to
the *association* of two stimuli can then be separated from single-stimulus
effects.
      Control groups in learning experiments are often referred to as *sham-
treatment groups*. (Some researchers call the sensitization control group a
pseudoconditioning control.) Rescorla (1967) has suggested the inclusion of a
random control group in which both the CS and US are presented but never
together in time. A random control group precludes association of the CS and

US by not allowing them to be temporally contiguous.[2] We'll revisit these ideas in discussing other conditioning methods.

Context. To say that there is an absence of stimuli in cell d is not quite accurate. It turns out that the stimulus conditions in cell d constitute the background, or context, in which the stimuli are presented to the animal. The **context** is the background stimulus conditions of a learning experiment. For example, the context in Pavlov's laboratory might include the hum of fans, background lighting, distinctive odors, and so forth. We'll see that these context stimuli also enter into association during conditioning and affect the outcome of conditioning.

Experimental Extinction and Spontaneous Recovery

If, after conditioning, the CS continues to be presented without the US, the conditioned response diminishes. Because the CS is presented without the US, this procedure is also called **extinction** or **experimental extinction.**

The plotted decline in the conditioned response is called an *extinction curve* or *extinction gradient* (see Figure 3.5). In the example we have been considering, salivation during experimental extinction is our measure of the strength of conditioning. Learning is typically "measured in extinction."

Resistance-to-extinction. Recall the acquisition function in Figure 3.4, and the argument that the rate of conditioning is reflected by the slope of the line. We can also compare the slope of the extinction curve and measure the rate of extinction (see Figure 3.5). **Resistance-to-extinction** is measure of the strength of conditioning or learning based on a the number of extinction trials it takes to extinguish the response. Recall that the conditioned response depends on such conditioning variables as the nature of the CS and US and the number of previous conditioning trials. As a general rule, the conditioned response lasts longer, and the rate of extinction is slower, following many as opposed to a few conditioning trials.

Spontaneous Recovery. Suppose that the conditioned response has extinguished to the level depicted on the 14th extinction trial (solid line in Figure 3.5). Instead of conducting the next extinction trial in that session, we mercifully remove the dog from the conditioning laboratory and return it to its home cage. The next day we bring the dog back for the remaining extinction trials. We would measure a different outcome under these conditions (dashed line). The level of extinction is not as great after the 24-hour interruption. As Figure 3.5 indicates, the conditioned salivary response on the 16th trial is stronger than it would have been without the 24-hour interruption. Pavlov

[2]In another condition, called a *truly random control*, CSs and USs are presented randomly and can occur together by chance.

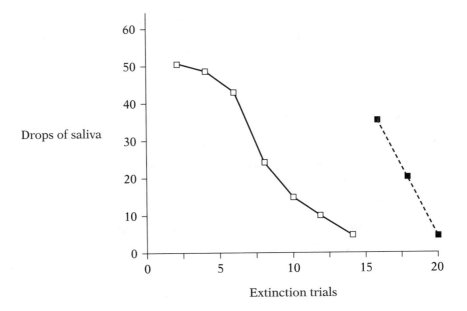

FIGURE 3.5 Extinction and Spontaneous Recovery

A salivary response to a CS has been previously conditioned. On extinction trials 1–14, the CS continues to be presented, but food is no longer forthcoming. The drops of saliva decline over trials (open squares). If time is allowed to pass (i.e., the animal is returned to its home cage overnight), and experimental extinction trials resume the next day (dotted lines), the animal salivates more than would be expected, a phenomenon called spontaneous recovery (dark squares).

called this reappearance of conditioning following a delay in the extinction process **spontaneous recovery.**

Internal and External Inhibition

Pavlov proposed that normal extinction is hastened by a process he called **internal inhibition.** He attributed internal inhibition to the dog's frustration at not receiving its expected food during the extinction trials. When the dog is removed from the experimental situation, its frustration dissipates with the passage of time. One way to understand spontaneous recovery is that the subsidence of internal inhibition allows the "true" extinction rate to be seen.

Internal inhibition should not be confused with another of Pavlov's concepts, that of *external inhibition*. **External inhibition** is the temporary disruption that occurs during either the acquisition or extinction of a conditioned response that is caused by an external stimulus. For example, if, during the conditioning experiment described earlier, someone had slammed a door in the lab during the 30 sec that the bell (CS) was being sounded, this distraction would have disrupted the process of conditioning the dog. Later we'll return to discussions of the different ways in which Pavlov developed his idea of inhibition.

Comparing Appetitive Conditioning with "Defense" (Aversive) Conditioning

In some of his experiments, Pavlov used a sour solution instead of food as the unconditioned stimulus. Dogs salivate unconditionally to sour tastes just as they do to tasty food. You might want to try dripping lemon juice on your tongue to test this.[3] In contrast to food-based appetitive conditioning, Pavlov used the term *defense conditioning* to describe experiments that used aversive unconditioned stimuli. In addition to a sour solution placed on the tongue, researchers in his laboratory used mild electric shock to condition a leg-withdrawal reflex. Conditioning experiments using aversive stimuli (as opposed to a food stimulus) are now referred to as **aversive conditioning.** The following chapter will introduce three contemporary aversive conditioning procedures: eyelid conditioning, conditioned suppression (cf. fear conditioning), and taste aversion conditioning.

The Relationship of Conditioning and Perception

When an optometrist asks which of two lenses makes your visual world clearer, or when an audiologist asks you to press a button when you can no longer hear a sound, your responses communicate your personal sensory experiences. The study of how your responses are related to incoming physical stimuli is called *psychophysics*. In the same manner, measuring a dog's responses to systematically presented stimuli allows insight into its perceptual world. The results of Pavlovian conditioning experiments have provided important windows into the perceptual worlds of dogs, nonverbal human infants, and other animals.

Pavlov's Sensory Analyzers.   Because a dog initially salivates to food placed on the tongue but does not salivate to a ringing bell, we can infer that the dog can discriminate between tasting and hearing. Pavlov reported that his dogs would salivate to the sight of the white lab coats worn by technicians, and learned to discriminate a black square from a triangle. These experiments allowed him to conclude that the dog could see shapes, and shades of black and

---

[3]If you have a good imagination, just the thought of lemon juice on your tongue will produce salivation. "Thinking" that produces a reflexive response sounds suspiciously like Pavlov's "psychic secretions." Throughout this text, we confront the fact that thoughts and words easily acquire conditioned stimulus properties.

white. Pavlov (1927/1960) referred to a dog's *sensory analyzers* as those portions of the brain responsible for different sensory perceptions. In his late-19th-century understanding of brain functioning, for example, the sound of the bell was perceived by the dog's "auditory analyzer," a picture by the "visual analyzer," touch by a "cutaneous analyzer," and so forth. Vision, audition, touch, taste, and smell, among other senses, define how animals discriminate their environment, and conditioning was viewed as a way to get one of these analyzers to signal another.

Likewise, Pavlov found that his dogs responded to similar stimuli in a similar manner. For example, a tone of 500 Hz heard by dogs (and humans) sounds more similar to a tone of 512 Hz than to one of 530 Hz. How do we know that? For humans, this is an easy experiment. Because we have learned to use language to track the environment (words denoting concepts such as greater than, more than, equal to, and so on are learned early in life), we can simply ask humans, "Which two of these stimuli are more alike?" German psychophysicists did these experiments with humans more than 100 years ago.

Generalization. But what about dogs and other animals? What do their psychophysical functions look like? Researchers this past century have measured the sensory functions of a variety of animals using Pavlovian methods. These animal psychophysicists have found that vertebrate nervous systems track the environment in a manner similar to the way humans do. For example, let's first condition a dog to respond to a 500-Hz tone. Then, let's measure salivation to various tones of differing frequencies. You would find that responses track the stimuli. That is, dogs respond most to the original CS (500 Hz), next most to closely related stimuli (for example, 490 and 510 Hz), and least to highly dissimilar stimuli (for example, 400 and 600 Hz). This tendency of animals to respond in a similar way to stimuli that are like the original stimulus is called **generalization.**

The Adaptiveness of Generalization. The innate, hardwired tendency of animals is to treat similar stimuli in a similar manner. This process is reflected in part by a brain organization honed by natural selection. Generalization has survival value. To recognize that a snake is a snake no matter whether it is an exact copy of the other snake that just bit you is adaptive. Screeching tires don't all sound exactly alike, but their signal value is equivalent.

The importance of the concept of generalization is that we can account for responses to stimuli that have never been experienced firsthand. There is economy in learning one response to a particular situation that then generalizes to others. Our language reflects these properties, which are characteristic of all animal nervous systems. Following a particular experience (such as getting a traffic ticket in a school zone), we "learn" about similar situations never before encountered. I slow down not only in that particular school zone but also in all school zones. That is, my learned response generalizes to other school zones, and also to hospital zones. I exhibit highly adaptive behavior generated from a limited but meaningful experience.

It is also adaptive that learning nuances between similar stimuli can be trained. Musicians, artists, writers, and scientists cannot afford to generalize all similar musical notes, all colors and forms, all words and grammatical rules, and all laws and axioms. In the next chapter, under the topic of conditioned discrimination, we see how fine discriminations between stimuli can be learned.

Pavlov's Second Signal System

You look up and notice that your psychology teacher is walking toward you. Too late to escape and worried about the exam you took from her a few days ago, you reluctantly make eye contact. She stops. You tense. "Congratulations," she says. "You made a high B on your last exam." "Yes!" you blurt out.

How can the words "congratulations" and "a high B" evoke elation? Pavlov extended the application of his association theory to an analysis of how humans learn some aspects of language. Specifically, how do humans learn to attach meaning to words? The process is so basic that it is included here, early in the text. My intention is to alert students to the power and importance of Pavlov's ideas in accounting for important aspects of human behavior. As we see here and in later chapters, classical conditioning involves much more than how Russian dogs salivate!

How Words Acquire Meaning. Pavlov described how words can become conditioned stimuli that control conditioned responses. First he reasoned that all words derive their meaning by association with sensory signals from the environment. For example, seeing an apple is a signal, which, in his terminology, stimulates the animal's "visual analyzer." Seeing the apple is the first signal of the real apple. The word "apple," Pavlov reasoned, is a conditioned stimulus that is associated with the perceived apple. Naming the perceived apple *apple* is the second signal of the real-world apple. Thus the word apple is the signal of signals; hence, the **second signal system** (Pavlov, 1927/1960).

Conditioning Language. Pavlov further avowed that conditioning in the second signal system was not different from other kinds of conditioning. All the rules governing the formation of conditioned responses applied equally to learning language. More often than not, repetitions (trials) of the word with the object are necessary. Additionally, more intense stimuli lead to more rapid learning.

A parent interacts with a child who is learning to talk. She presents to the child objects, relations, and actions and names them in close temporal contiguity—*apple* for apple and *hot* for a heated object. The word *good* may be accompanied by a loving embrace. *Good* is the CS, and the loving embrace that follows it is the US. The sight of a flame is a CS; the flame itself is a US. The words that signal the direct experience of the US—*hot, burn*—may be paired with the pain of the flame or the urgency of a parent's voice. The sight of the flame and words describing it are thus conditioned. Later the child learns that more complicated behavior can be signaled by the word *congratulations*. That word, and many others, have been conditioned to control emotional responses. The Japanese word for congratulations does not control the emotional responses of English speakers. "You made a high B" is a signal associated with academic success in a subset of our English-speaking culture.

Pavlov's observations are important for a number of reasons. Humans make only about 40 phonemic sounds, and cross-culturally, language patterns using these sounds vary widely. Languages as spoken sounds are meaningful only to the extent that particular sounds are associated with objects in the environment—a process described by Pavlovian conditioning. Words, we will see, are arguably the most important conditioned stimuli controlling human behavior.

Neural Basis of Association

Changes in the strength of connections between neurons parallel some associative conditioning phenomena. We have seen in long-term potentiation (LTP), for example, that stimulating neurons can produce effects that may last for weeks. This finding raises the possibility of long-lasting associative effects between neurons (Kelso, Ganong, & Brown, 1986). But extrapolating the measured effects of LTP or LTD on one or two "cooperating" neurons to the probable integration of hundreds of thousands of central nervous system (CNS) neurons in associative learning is a tremendous leap.

The question of neural substrates of behavior arises each time we look at different conditioning situations. Most contemporary conditioning preparations involve vertebrates, as we see in the next section, but a CNS isn't necessary for simple associative processes such as classical conditioning. Invertebrates, including *Aplysia* and insects, have ganglia rather than a CNS, yet can be conditioned. Let us take a closer look at these experiments.

Simple Animal Conditioning: Aplysia. Simple animals with simple nervous systems provide researchers with simple black boxes in which to poke around. We previously saw that the neural basis of nonassociative conditioning could be investigated in *Aplysia* (see Box 3.2). So has associative conditioning, as seen in Box 3.3. Using an aversive conditioning procedure, a light touch that signalled electric shock comes to elicit the gill-withdrawal reflex. It is assuredly the case, however, that "conditioning" the few neurons found in *Aplysia* is different from the neuronal changes subserving associative conditioning in vertebrate brains. Why? By contrast with invertebrates, the brains of dogs, humans, and even pigeons are large and highly organized. Vertebrate brains allow a richness of sensitivity to environmental change, of perceptual

BOX 3.3   SIMPLE SYSTEMS APPROACH TO ASSOCIATIVE LEARNING

In addition to sensitization and habituation, the gill-withdrawal reflex has been conditioned (Carew, Hawkins, & Kandel, 1983) by pairing a light touch (CS) of the siphon with electric shock to the tail (US). After several pairings, the CS elicits the CR of gill withdrawal. Shown is a discriminated Pavlovian conditioning preparation (also reported by Carew et al., 1983). In this preparation, lightly touching the mantle is the CS^- (not reinforced), whereas touching the siphon is the CS^+ (reinforced). The changes in synaptic activity are indicated.

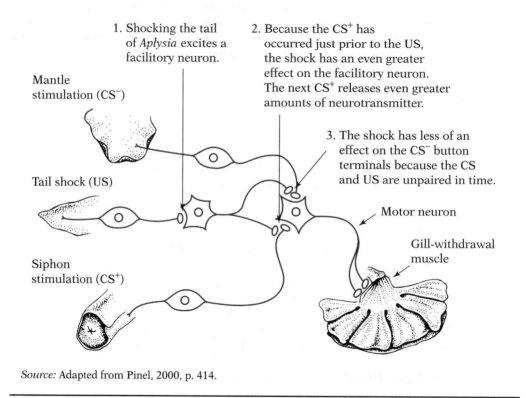

1. Shocking the tail of *Aplysia* excites a facilitory neuron.

2. Because the CS^+ has occurred just prior to the US, the shock has an even greater effect on the facilitory neuron. The next CS^+ releases even greater amounts of neurotransmitter.

3. The shock has less of an effect on the CS^- button terminals because the CS and US are unpaired in time.

Mantle stimulation (CS^-)

Tail shock (US)

Siphon stimulation (CS^+)

Motor neuron

Gill-withdrawal muscle

Source: Adapted from Pinel, 2000, p. 414.

knowledge of environment enhanced and mediated by memory, and of plasticity of responsiveness unknown to and unknowable by *Aplysia*'s brain.

Invertebrate Conditioning Preparations. This chapter was introduced with descriptions of insect behavior: They see, walk, run, smell, taste, fly, mate, eat, lay eggs, and so on. The inference was that their primitive brains are programmed to do these things innately and that they live without either conscious awareness or an "executive in charge." The fact of the matter is that insects and other invertebrates can also benefit from their experiences. They can adaptively adjust their behavior; they can learn. Associative processes are so general among animals that invertebrates can be used in learning experiments. You have already read about *Drosophilia*, a lowly invertebrate commonly used in studies of genetics (including behavioral genetics). The anatomy, physiology, and behavior of a close cousin, the common fly, have been investigated so thoroughly by Dethier (1978) and others that the functional significance of 280 of the animals 287 neurons is now known. Comparative psychologists who study learning in invertebrates recognize that simple animals account for 97% of all animal species. Lacking a CNS, they nonetheless learn in an associative manner (Abramson, 1994).

The honeybee also learns quickly, both in the field and in the laboratory (Batson, Hoban, & Bitterman, 1992). Classical conditioning in the honeybee has been accomplished (Bitterman, Menzel, Fietz, & Schäfer, 1983; Abramson, 1994). Brought into the laboratory, the bee's body is placed in a small metal tube with its head and antennae exposed. A sugar-water US is brought to the bee's mouth, and the reflexive response is proboscis extension. Since bees do not extend their proboscis in response to smelling cinnamon oil, this odor was used as a neutral CS. After 12 pairings of the cinnamon CS with the sugar water US, however, the smell of the cinnamon alone reliably produced proboscis extension. Appropriate control conditions established that associative learning had occurred.

Where in the Vertebrate Brain Is Conditioning? Several features of vertebrate brains were compared in Chapter 2. The purpose was to provide a neurological substrate for general processes of learning. Given the fact that so much of the brain is common among different vertebrates, learning can be compared readily from one species to another. Dogs and other mammals share homologous (genetically similar) parts of the brain with humans. In Box 3.4, some of the parts of the brain that must be involved in conditioning responses to sights and sounds in mammalian brains are indicated. Note that the schematic follows an S-R framework in tracing the auditory and taste stimulus in and the salivary response out. Other integral brain parts involved in food-based learning not indicated in Box 3.4 are the hippocampus, hypothalamus, limbic system, and cerebellum. We'll look at some details of the neural bases of other conditioning preparations in later chapters.

Interim Summary

1. ***Pavlovian conditioning*** involves modifying of the food-saliva reflex. Pavlov called food the ***unconditioned stimulus (US)*** and salivation to food the ***unconditioned response (UR).***

BOX 3.4 PEEKING INSIDE THE BLACK BOX: SPOTSKI'S BRAIN

Conditioning in a dog is initiated by stimulating nerve pathways in its brain. The *chorda tympani* (branch of Cranial Nerve VII) is the primary taste nerve in the dog. It synapses in the *solitary nucleus* in the medulla. Interneurons in an adjacent nucleus then stimulate other neurons that complete a Sherrington-like reflex of salivation. For sights and sounds to activate the salivation reflex, the thalamus gets involved. Stimulating the optic nerve, lateral geniculate nucleus (LGN), striate cortex, and other areas subserving vision can come to elicit the reflex. For sounds, the cochlear nucleus (and other nuclei) in the medulla, medial geniculate nucleus (MGN) of the thalamus, and primary and secondary projection areas of auditory cortex are involved. For all conditioning, a mid-brain structure called the hippocampus (not shown) is involved. The cerebellum is intimately involved in tone-shock conditioning. See Klopf (1988) for a neuronal model of classical conditioning of vertebrates.

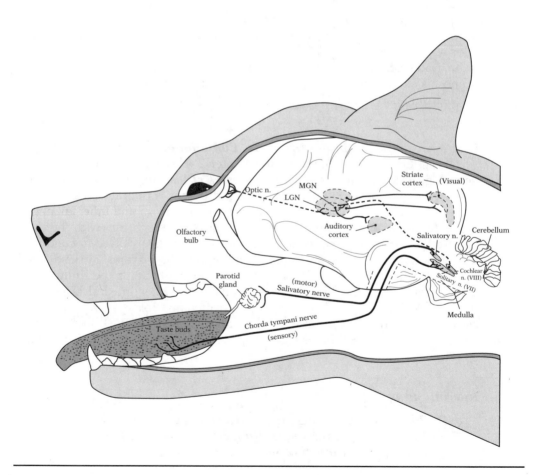

2. Stimuli that do not control the feeding reflex may instead produce *orienting responses*.

3. By pairing neutral sights and sounds—Pavlov's **conditioned stimuli (CSs)**—with food for a number of **trials,** CSs alone come to produce the **conditioned response (CR)** of salivation.

4. The **CS-US interval** is measured from the onset of the CS to the onset of the US. The **intertrial interval** is the time between conditioning trials.

5. Associative conditioning is inferred from comparisons of conditioning treatments results with one or more control groups, such as the **habituation control group** and the **sensitization control group.**

6. The **context,** or background stimulus conditions of a learning experiment influences the associative process.

7. The rate of conditioning and extinction is determined by the parameters of the CSs and USs.

8. In **extinction** (also called **experimental extinction**), the CS is presented in the absence of the US. Following extinction, and subsequent rest, recovery of the conditioned response to a higher level is known as **spontaneous recovery.**

9. **Internal inhibition** is Pavlov's term to account for the diminution of a conditioned response during an extinction procedure. **External inhibition** is a temporary disruption in conditioning or extinction due to an extraneous, disrupting stimulus.

10. Using food as the US defines **appetitive conditioning;** using aversive stimulation defines defense, or **aversive conditioning.**

11. **Generalization** is the nonassociative process by which similar stimuli produce similar responses.

12. Pavlov's **second signal system** describes how words can become CSs that control emotional responses. Words are among the most important CSs controlling human behavior.

13. The associative process is mediated by brain mechanisms such as long-term potentiation (LTP) and long-term depression (LTD).

14. Bees and *Aplysia*—two invertebrates lacking CNSs—can be conditioned.

15. Vertebrates have CNSs with many common features. It is likely that some similarly conditioned responses in different species use homologous parts of the brain.

DISCUSSION QUESTIONS

4. Manual stimulation of the genitals typically produces sexual arousal. Erotic daydreams and looking at sexy pictures can also produce sexual arousal. Can you identify unconditioned and conditioned reflexes in these examples?

5. Note in Box 3.1 that successive blocks of habituation and "rehabituation"

eventually produce near zero responding to a stimulus. Imagine that you are the human subject depicted in the lower figure and that you no longer respond to the stimulation after the sixth block of trials in a given session. What do you think would happen if you were to be stimulated the next day or a week later? Is it likely that your "fully habituated" response would return? Is this similar to the phenomenon of spontaneous recovery?

6. Is it likely that a human suffering cortical damage in an automobile accident would no longer be able to be classically conditioned? Why or why not?

CHAPTER SUMMARY

1. Reflexes are involuntary, adaptive responses. Most learned behaviors involve a modification of these inherited response tendencies.

2. Single stimuli acting alone can produce relatively permanent nonassociative learning effects known as habituation and sensitization.

3. Habituation refers to reduced responsiveness to a stimulus following repeated stimulation by that stimulus.

4. Sensitization refers to increased responsiveness for a time period following a relatively intense stimulus.

5. The two-stage theory of association describes how animals first learn that two events are correlated (occur close together in time—the contiguity theory of association) and second, that one event appears to cause the other (the contingency theory of association).

6. General process learning focuses on association formation that is common to all animals.

7. Reflexive behavior can be modified by simple conditioning procedures developed by Ivan Pavlov and others.

8. Pavlovian, or classical, conditioning involves modification of a reflex by pairing it with a neutral stimulus, which eventually comes to control the reflex.

9. Pavlovian salivary conditioning involves modification of the food-saliva reflex. Food, the unconditioned stimulus (US), causes reflexive salivation (the UR). A bell (or other conditioned stimulus, or CS) paired with food soon produces salivation, the conditioned response (CR).

10. Control groups for associative conditioning include habituation controls, sensitization controls, and random controls.

11. Learning is typically measured in extinction. During extinction, Pavlov proposed that internal inhibition occurred, hastening the process. Spontaneous recovery—the reappearance of an extinguished response—he explained as the dissipation of internal inhibition with the passage of time.

12. Pavlov's external inhibition is the temporary disruption of conditioning or extinction due to an extraneous stimulus.

13. Pavlov's second signal system describes how the sounds making up words can act as CSs that signal objects and actions in the environment. The meaning of words is acquired by associative processes.

14. Simple systems approaches include measurement of individual neurons in the invertebrate *Aplysia* and classical conditioning in invertebrates such as the bee.

KEY TERMS

appetitive conditioning   86

association theory   78

aversive conditioning   92

baseline   88

classical conditioning   83

conditioned response (CR)   86

conditioned stimulus (CS)   86

context   90

contiguity theory of association   78

contingency theory of association   79

CS-US Interval   87

excitatory conditioning   91

extinction (experimental
    extinction)   90

generalization   93

habituation   69

habituation control group   89

internal inhibition   91

intertrial interval   88

long-term depression (LTD)   73

long-term potentiation (LTP)   73

nonassociative learning   69

Pavlovian conditioning   83

plasticity   67

psychic secretion   84

reflex   65

resistance-to-extinction   90

second signal system   94

sensitization   72

sensitization control group   89

Sherringtonian reflexes   66

single-stimulus effect   68

spontaneous recovery   91

trial   88

two-stage theory of association   80

unconditioned response (UR)   86

unconditioned stimulus (US)   86

CHAPTER 4

Contemporary Conditioning Methods and Applications

CONTEMPORARY CONDITIONING METHODS

A hypnotic trance was induced in a young male subject, and then deepened over the next few minutes. After sufficient preparation, the hypnotist showed the audience a piece of chalk, told the subject "I'm now going to burn you with a lighted cigarette." He placed the chalk on an exposed forearm. The subject's arm jerked away.

"Did it hurt?" the hypnotist asked.

"Yes, it did," the subject replied.

The camera focused on the arm. First there was a discoloration of the skin where the chalk had been placed, and, within minutes, a blister appeared.

A hypnotist and his subject performed the demonstration.[1] How is this phenomenon to be explained? We could focus upon the hypnotic state, still poorly understood from either a behavioral or neuroscience perspective. We might posit subconscious (or unconscious) mechanisms, but neither constitute an explanation. Perhaps "cognitive" processes mediated the behavior? Again, that does not constitute an answer to the cause of the blister. A more parsimonious Pavlovian explanation might focus instead on reflexes and about how "normal" blisters are formed. Could the arm jerk and blister formation be some type of conditioned response, similar to salivation to a bell?

In this chapter we will first look at classical conditioning experiments—many of them based on avoidance conditioning—that have extended Pavlov's basic concept of salivary conditioning. We'll see that the various methods used and results obtained from these procedures can be used interchangeably to build and expand on a general theory of conditioning. Finally, we will explore applications of conditioning theory in the realm of psychosomatic disorders, the immune system, asthma, and drugs. We'll return to the "hypnotic blister" example: After reading this next section, you may have already figured it out by the time blisters are further discussed.

Fear Conditioning

Any of a number of intense environmental stimuli produce pain or fear-inducing responses in animals. For example, loud noises, electric shocks, and poisons disrupt normal homeostatic functioning in animals. Such stimuli induce changes in the nervous system that in turn activate us to action. When a normally neutral stimulus (such as a tone CS) is repeatedly paired with a disruptive stimulus (such as an electric shock US), conditioned fear to the tone results. An example of fear conditioning in humans is presented in Box 4.1.

---

[1] I saw this demonstration on "The Paul Coates Show," truly live television, without interruptions or gimmicks, in the early 1950s in Los Angeles. Blister formation under hypnosis has also been accomplished in the laboratory (Spanos & Chaves, 1989).

BOX 4.1   AN UNUSUAL EXAMPLE OF FEAR CONDITIONING

During the 1960s I was one of a number of paid U.S. Air Force volunteers who rode "impact sleds." In one phase of this research, airmen tested space suits that eventually were worn by Apollo astronauts. Would the suits tear on impact, or would critical helmet fittings fail during takeoffs, landings, EVAs (space walks), moon walks, and so on? Short on money, we volunteered to be strapped to a sled that was propelled along rails. Impacts were varied to simulate the various angles and *g* forces astronauts would experience in emergency situations. (Notice the bent nose and lips in this photo,

taken with high speed film at the point of impact.

A 40-second countdown preceded the sled acceleration and final impact. During these 40 seconds, a European-style emergency vehicle horn ("dee doo, dee doo") reverberated throughout the test site. This distinctive signal accompanied the anticipation and high autonomic nervous system arousal of being strapped to a sled soon to be slammed into a barrier. To this day, emergency vehicles in Paris and London cause heart palpitations and sphincter-control problems for at least one of these now aging airmen.

Conditioned Emotional Responses. One way to measure a **conditioned emotional response** in the laboratory is to sound a tone (CS) that has been paired with electric shock (US) while a rat is pressing a lever to obtain food (Estes & Skinner, 1941). The intensity of the shock is adjusted just high enough to cause the rat to momentarily stop the lever-pressing response when it is shocked. After a number of tone-shock pairings, the rat learns (is conditioned) to interrupt lever pressing when the tone is sounded. Because the lever-pressing response is disrupted in the presence of the tone, this method is called **conditioned suppression.**

Suppression Ratios. How is conditioned suppression measured? A *suppression ratio* is used to quantify the change in responding to the tone from a pre-CS condition (during which the tone has no effect on how a rat presses a lever) to post-conditioning (during which the rat no longer presses the lever when the tone is sounded). The suppression ratio is computed in the form $b/(a+b)$, where b is the number of responses, say, in a 30-sec period when the tone is sounded, and a is the 30-sec pre-CS period before the tone is sounded. Note in this simple formula that if the tone has no effect on responding, then the number of responses in both time periods a and b would be approximately equal. Let's assume the rat makes approximately 10 responses in both of the two 30-sec periods. The suppression ratio would be computed as 10/10 + 10 = 10/20 = 0.50. So, preconditioning (baseline) suppression ratios would be about 0.5. Now assume that the rat has been conditioned to fear the tone, and suppresses responding when the tone is sounded. Let's say the rat again makes 10 lever presses in the baseline period, and only one response in the presence of the tone. The suppression ratio would be 1/10 + 1 = 1/11 = 0.09. From these two examples we see that the suppression ratio extends from ~ 0.5 (no suppression) to ~0.0 (complete suppresssion).

Using Conditioned Suppression. The conditioned suppression technique is one of the most popular methods used in the contemporary study of classical conditioning. For example, in a series of experiments, Leon Kamin and his students have tested a number of Pavlov's assumptions about the laws governing the acquisition of conditioning. Pavlov had proposed three such laws, now collectively known as *Law of Strength*. Simply stated the **Law of Strength** is that higher intensity USs, higher intensity CSs, and shorter CS-US interstimulus intervals produce better conditioning. Some of Kamin's conditioned suppression experiments that used tone-shock pairings in rats tested these ideas, and the results are shown in Figure 4.1.

    The upper panel shows that low-, medium-, and high-level shocks produce no conditioning, intermediate conditioning, and rapid acquisition of the conditioned response, respectively. (Remember that lower suppression ratios reflect better conditioned responses.) The lower panel shows that as the interstimulus interval increases, conditioning worsens. These results of fear conditioning, using the conditioned suppression procedure in rats, produced

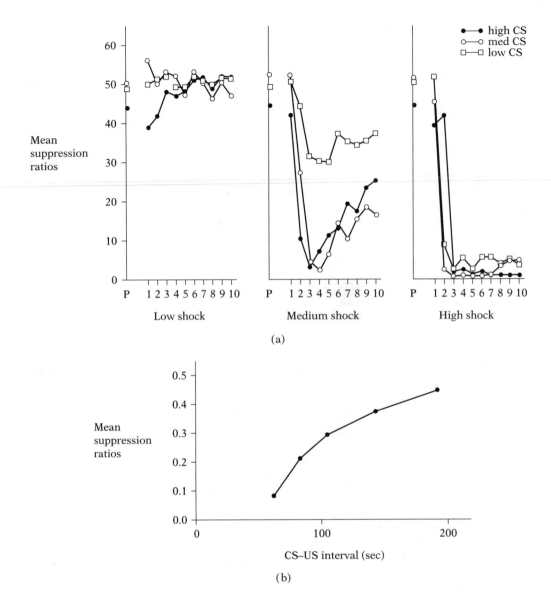

FIGURE 4.1 Testing the Law of Strength

Conditioned suppression tests of Pavlov's Law of Strength are reported by Annau and Kamin (1961). Upper panel: Note that increasing CS intensity (low, medium, and high) and US intensity (left, middle, and right panels, respectively) generally leads to both faster acquisition and lower suppression ratios (better conditioning). The baseline levels of suppression (labeled "P," for preconditioning) are ~0.50. In the lower panel (redrawn from Kamin, 1965), the mean suppression ratios for independent groups are plotted as a function of the interval between a 1.5-sec tone CS and a brief electric shock US. Data are means for acquisition days 2 through 5. Shorter CS-US intervals produces better conditioning, but notice that rats are able to make tone-shock associations even with 100 sec between the onset of the tone and the electric shock.

results similar to Pavlov's findings using salivary conditioning in dogs. General process theory is supported by these experiments.

Rabbit, Rat, and Human Eyeblink Conditioning

Classical eyeblink conditioning is another important conditioning methodology. A puff of air (the US) to a human, rabbit, or rat's eye elicits a reflexive blinking response (the UR). When a tone (CS) is presented immediately prior to the air puff (US), an animal can be conditioned to blink to the sound of the tone. A number of investigators have used this classical preparation for many years. How eyeblink conditioning relates to other general process learning methods has been addressed by Gormezano, Kehoe, and Marshall (1983).

Three examples of the outcome of conditioning eyeblink responses in rabbits and humans can be found in Figure 4.2. Rabbit conditioning is shown in the top panel. The percentage of conditioned responses (out of 82 conditioning trials per day) is plotted for 8 acquisition days. Note the relative lack of conditioning in the early trials. There is a regular growth of response (as indicated by the percentage of conditioned responses on each day) throughout the 600-plus acquisition trials. The middle panel of Figure 4.2 shows the outcomes of conditioning eyeblink responses in humans (Hartman & Grant, 1960). In general, there is a slow growth of association of the eyeblink to the tone over 10 to 15 trials, but human conditioning occurrs much more rapidly than in rabbits.

But, you might be wondering, humans are not stupid. Surely the college students who volunteer as subjects in a classical conditioning experiment are aware of the fact that a tone sounds a second or so before an airpuff hits their eye! Why, then, should it take so many trials? The bottom panel of Figure 4.2 addresses these issues. It turns out that subjects who are *aware* that the tone and airpuff are related within the first 10 trials learn more quickly than those who do not pick up on their association (Woodruff-Pak, 1999). In fact the response *is* learned (see middle panel in Figure 4.2) with repeated conditioning trials, and the learning may *not* always involve awareness.

Salivary and Eyeblink Conditioning Compared. Compare the acquisition functions for eyeblink conditioning in Figure 4.2 with salivary conditioning in dogs (see Figure 3.4, p. 89). Both rabbits and humans (and rats; Schmajuk & Christiansen, 1990) require more trials to condition an eyeblink response. A dog requires 5 to 9 trials for salivary conditioning, yet humans took 15 to 40 trials (middle panel), and rabbits several hundred trials in eyeblink conditioning.[2] A literature review by Lennartz and Weinberger (1992) found that acquisition during conditioning could be characterized as being either fast or slow. Fast acquisition was found for salivary conditioning in dogs, the conditioned

---

[2]This statement is not meant to imply that dogs condition quickly because they are aware of the CS-US contingencies. The question of awareness arises only in the conditioning of humans who can speak to the issue.

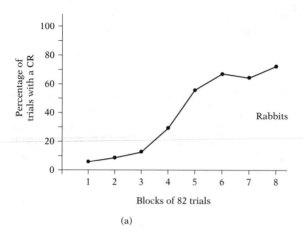

(a)

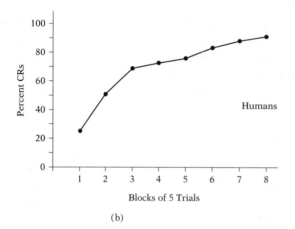

(b)

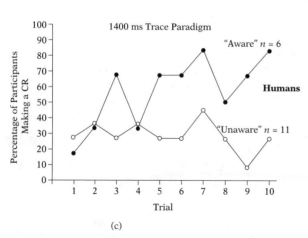

(c)

FIGURE 4.2 A Comparison of Human and Rabbit Eyelid Conditioning

The increase in percentage of conditioned eyeblink responses is plotted as a function of training days in rabbits (top panel) and humans (middle panel). The bottom panel shows that humans who later said they were "aware" that the tone and air puff were associated learned the conditioned eyeblink response more quickly (filled circles) than those who were unaware of the contingency (open circles). Data from Gormezano, Kehoe, & Marshall, 1983, (top panel); Hartman & Grant, 1960, (middle panel) and Woodruff-Pak, 1999, (lower panel).

suppression procedure in rats, and conditioned changes in blood pressure, respiration, pupil size, and heart rate measured in a number of different species. Reflex systems that were conditioned more lowly included eyelid and flexion responses. Why this is the case is not known. But the finding that awareness during eyelid conditioning facilitates the acquisition of the response (see Clark & Squire, 1998, 1999) may be part of the reason for these differences. Let's look at some more experiments.

Neural Basis for Classical Eyelid Conditioning. Many neuroscientists in this century assumed as did Pavlov that the cerebral hemispheres mediated learning. This is not the case. Several neuronal models for eyelid conditioning have been proposed (Clark & Squire, 1998, 1999; Lavond, Kim, & Thompson, 1993; Steinmetz, 1996; Thompson, 1986). In all, neurons in a discrete area of the cerebellum (called the *lateral interpositus nucleus*) have been found to underlie the tone-air puff conditioning of the rabbit's nictitating membrane (McCormick & Thompson, 1984). These neurons may be responsible for the timing arrangement of the tone and shock necessary for classical conditioning (Green, Ivry, & Woodruff-Pak, 1999). The neural story that is emerging is that certain brain areas underlie salivary conditioning and others eyeblink conditioning. These examples of appetitive and defense conditioning, though behaviorally similar, involve different parts of the brain.

Taste Aversion Conditioning

Several thousand experiments on a variety of different species over the past 30 years have made *taste aversion conditioning* another popular method of studying classical conditioning (Barker, Best, & Domjan, 1977; also see Riley & Tuck, 1985, for a bibliography of many of these experiments). In a typical **conditioned taste aversion** procedure, rats are allowed to drink a novel-flavored solution (the CS) and then are made sick by an illness-inducing toxin (the US).[3] A conditioned taste aversion to the novel flavor results. That is, in comparison with rats in a control group that were not made sick, the conditioned rats no longer prefer the target flavor.

Humans have an intuitive grasp of this kind of conditioning because in our lifetimes, many of us have become sick after eating or drinking (Bernstein & Webster, 1980; Garb & Stunkard, 1974). Often a particular flavor or food item is tagged as the culprit. A personal vignette: At the age of 6, I became sick after eating warm, overripe fresh pineapple. I disliked pineapple for many years afterward, and even today I remember the incident all too vividly.

Humans can also have taste aversions conditioned through Pavlov's second signal system. A student related that her grandfather lived with her fam-

---

[3]Many treatments have been used to induce illness in rats, including one of the first demonstrations that used ionizing radiation (Garcia, Kimeldorf, & Koelling, 1955). Other methods included drugs, nausea-inducing rotation, magnetism, surgery, lesions, and tumors.

ily, and she grew up listening to his complaints about lamb. It seems while stationed overseas during the Korean War that for weeks at a time he had nothing to eat except lamb, and, a result, he hated it. Years later, this student relates that she first encountered lamb when the host at a formal meal announced that they were having a leg of lamb. She was overcome with cold sweats, a churning stomach, and nausea. She poked the food around as long as she could and then took a bite and gagged. The taste, she related, was OK. It was the idea of it—an expectation associatively conditioned through her grandfather's complaints about lamb—that made her nauseous.

One-Trial, Long-Delay Learning. Taste aversion learning by humans and animals takes place rapidly—often in a single trial. In addition, under certain circumstances conditioning can result even over a long delay between a taste and an illness (Garcia, Hankins, & Rusiniak, 1974). Figure 4.3 shows the results of a one-trial taste aversion conditioning procedure in different groups of rats that

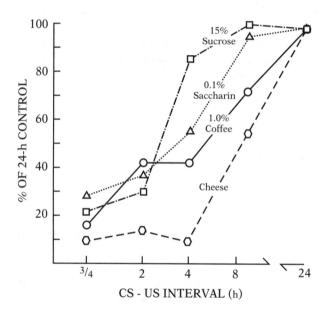

FIGURE 4.3   One-trial, Long-delay, Taste Aversion Conditioning

> The figure shows the results of a post-conditioning test of taste aversion to either sucrose, saccharin, coffee, or cheese. The animals that were made ill soon after tasting these flavors (3/4 and 2.0 h) show greater aversion than those that had 4 and 8 h delays between the taste and the illness. In addition, the cheese and coffee flavors were conditioned over longer delays than were the saccharin and sucrose flavors. Note that the values are plotted as a percent of the control groups' values for each flavor, whose flavor and illness were separated by 24 h. (from Barker, 1982).

tasted one of four flavors. The interval of time between tasting the flavor and becoming sick was varied from 3/4 hour to 2, 4, 8, or 24 hours. The figure shows a clear functional relationship of both the flavor effect (some tastes condition more easily than others) and the CS-US interval effect (Barker, 1982).

Because tastes and illness can be associated over a long delay in a single trial, this conditioning methodology has proven to be a popular one. For example, taste aversion methodology is now used to condition immune system functioning (Ader, 1985; Husband, 1992), as we see later in this chapter. The apparent simplicity of this preparation also makes it a favorite for those researchers attempting to find the neural basis of conditioned taste aversions (see Chambers, 1990).

Summary of Contemporary Conditioning Methods

Table 4.1 summarizes the contemporary conditioning methods discussed to this point. Conditioned suppression, eyeblink conditioning, and taste aversion conditioning are compared with Pavlov's appetitive and defense salivary conditioning preparations. Again, we owe to Pavlov this simple way of describing association formation: A neutral conditioned stimulus that through repeated association with biologically meaningful reflex, comes to control the

TABLE 4.1   A Comparison of Contemporary Conditioning Methodologies

Name of Procedure	US	UR	CS	CR
Pavlov's appetitive salivatory conditioning (dogs)	Food	Salivation	Bell, metronome, pictures, cutaneous stimuli	Salivation
Pavlov's defensive (aversive) conditioning (dogs)	Sour flavor	Salivation	Bell, metronome, pictures, cutaneous stimuli	Salivation
Proboscis extension (bees and other insects)	Sweet flavor	Proboscis extension	Cinnamon odor	Proboscis extension
Rabbit eyelid conditioning (rabbits, humans)	Air puff to eye	Eye blink	Tone, lightflash	Eye blink
Conditioned suppression (*Conditioned fear*) (rats, pigeons)	Electric shock	Stops lever-pressing response	Tone, lightflash	Stop lever-pressing response
Conditioned taste aversion (rats, humans)	Toxin	Sickness, loss of appetite	Flavored fluid	Loss of appetite

reflex. The similiarity of these procedures and results form one basis of general process learning theory.

Interim Summary

1. A ***conditioned emotional response*** can be conditioning in laboratory animals. In ***conditioned suppression,*** a tone or light (CS) is paired with electric shock (the US). Conditioning is measured by the degree to which the tone or light CS suppresses lever-pressing responses (the CR) in rats. Conditioned suppression is measured by computing a *suppression ratio* that varies from ~0.50 (no conditioning) to 0.0 (complete suppression, excellent conditioning).

2. Pavlov proposed that three laws, or functional relationships, governed how much conditioning would occur: the ***Law of Strength*** is that higher intensity USs, higher intensity CSs, and shorter CS-US interstimulus intervals produce better conditioning.

3. When tones or lights (CSs) signal an aversive air puff to the eye (US), the procedure is known as ***classical eyeblink conditioning.*** Eyeblink conditioning is typically conducted on rabbits and humans. After conditioning, the CS can evoke a reflexive eyeblink CR.

4. ***Conditioned taste aversions*** are studied in rats, humans, and other animals. A flavor (the CS) is paired with toxin (the US), and the conditioned response takes the form of a learned aversion to the target flavors.

5. One-trial, long-delay learning can be studied using the taste aversion conditioning methodology.

DISCUSSION QUESTIONS

1. Can you relate the outcome of a conditioned suppression procedure to the fact that so few people volunteer to speak out in the classroom?

2. After reading this chapter, which group in the lower panel of Figure 4.2 would best predict the results of an eyeblink conditioning experiment in which *you* were a subject? Why?

3. Why do you think it is so hard to convince someone with a conditioned taste aversion to a specific alcoholic beverage that it really *tastes* OK, that the *taste* didn't make them sick, but rather that they drank too much and suffered alcohol poisoning? Why, in this case, is reasoning overridden by conditioning?

VARIABLES THAT AFFECT CONDITIONING

As indicated by his Law of Strength, Pavlov was interested in discovering what events, or variables, control the conditioning process. Why did some of his dogs learn more quickly than others? Why were some CSs more effective in producing conditioned salivation than others? Why is it that conditioning tended to last longer following some conditioning procedures compared to others? Here we look more systematically at the variables that control conditioning.

Resistance to Extinction.   The most common way of comparing both the effectiveness of conditioning, and variables that affect conditioning is by measuring its *resistance to extinction*. The simplest way to measure **resistance to extinction** is, following conditioning, to count the trials until a criterion level of extinction is reached, allowing us to compare extinction gradients for two or more procedures. For example, Pavlov found that dogs would salivate more after 20 conditioning trials than 10 trials, and also that the conditioned response lasted longer in extinction. That is, there is more resistance to extinction of the conditioned response after many conditioning trials compared to extinction following a few conditioning trials. Using this measure, what predictions can we make about good conditioning procedures?

Five Rules of Conditioning

Let's begin by listing five rules that Pavlov and other experimenters have discovered that govern how rapidly associations are formed, and how much resistance to extinction can be measured:

1. Number of trials rule.
2. CS intensity rule.
3. US intensity rule.
4. CS-US interval rule.
5. CS-US, or US-CS sequencing rule.

1. Number of trials rule.   Pavlov was the first laboratory scientist to measure how conditioning systematically improves as more trials are conducted. Figure 3.4 (p. 89) shows that more salivation is evident on the 10th than the 5th trial, and more on the 15th than on the 10th trial. As a general rule, the magnitude and persistence of the conditioned response are directly related to the number of conditioning trials. Is one-trial taste aversion conditioning an exception to this rule? No. (Details will follow in a later chapter.) Intuitively obvious though it may be, why more than one trial is typically necessary for conditioning is a matter of speculation. The questions of *how many trials* and *why more than one trial* continue to be raised by learning theorists.

What else leads to faster acquisition and greater resistance to extinction of the conditioned response? In addition to the number of trials, we've already noted that Pavlov found three other interrelated factors of conditioning. Collectively, these next three rules are known as Pavlov's Law of Strength (where strength refers to the magnitude, or amount of, conditioning).

2. CS intensity rule. The intensity of the signalling stimuli in conditioning is an important variable. In Pavlov's experiments, louder sounds conditioned the dogs faster and the training lasted longer. In taste aversion conditioning, more concentrated flavors produce better conditioning. Finally, rats learn to suppress lever press responses more quickly if louder tones are paired with electric shock.

These findings are not as intuitively obvious as the number of trials variable. Perhaps it is the case that an animal's attention is better captured during conditioning by more intense CSs. We know from many experiments that attentional factors are as important in conditioning experiments as they are in other learning situations. For example, most of us must pay attention to what we are reading if we want to learn and remember the material. One theory is that the CS "signals" that the next few seconds (minutes?) are important, that is, that something important is about to happen. More intense signals also activate more of the nervous system that in some way may enhance the associative process. The quality of the CS is as important as the intensity: Notice in Figure 4.3 that some flavor qualities (such as cheese) produce better conditioning than sweet sucrose.

3. US intensity rule. If more food is used in the conditioning situation (i.e., a more intense US is used), dogs condition more rapidly and the training lasts longer. Higher doses of poisons, and higher levels of electric shock, respectively, condition taste aversions and fear responses more quickly. Figure 4.1 shows that higher intensities of shock produce more rapid acquisition and longer-lasting conditioned fear responses.

4. CS-US interval rule. Temporal contiguity is an important factor in conditioning. When the interval between the bell and the food is short (i.e., when the CS-US interval is measured in seconds), dogs condition faster and the training persists longer than if, during conditioning, the bell and food are separated by minutes. Likewise, the tone-to-shock interval in conditioned suppression, and tone-to-airpuff interval in classical eyeblink conditioning are critically important variables in learning fear responses. (Eyeblink conditioning in particular becomes much more difficult to accomplish if several seconds intervene between the onset of the tone and the eyeblink: the optimal conditioning interval is 0.5 sec). In general, the longer the interval between CS and US, the less conditioning is likely to occur.

5. CS-US, or US-CS sequencing rule. The fifth rule of Pavlovian conditioning is that the sequencing of stimuli determines the nature, or direction, of the response to be learned. Let us do another thought experiment. Assume that you are a rat trapped in an experimental test chamber. Every time you hear a tone, within 5 sec you are shocked. More than likely, after 10 or fewer trials you would use the time following the tone to prepare yourself for the shock—perhaps by adjusting your posture—to minimize the effects of the shock. (In fact, rats do just that.)

Now imagine a slightly different conditioning situation: You are first shocked, and then 5 sec later you hear the brief tone. The tone no longer predicts the shock; rather, the shock predicts the tone. The tone is an "all-clear" signal; it predicts a safe period, the intertrial interval, during which no shocks will occur. Question: Would your responses to the tone differ in the two instances? Obviously, yes. Just as the tone acquires fear-inducing properties in the first situation, in the second situation, after 10 conditioning trials, you can begin to relax when you hear the tone. The tone predicts that the ordeal is over; hence, the tone has become a safety signal.

What have we learned from our thought experiment? The CS → US sequence gives one response, and the US → CS sequence gives an opposite one. Merely knowing the first four rules of conditioning described in the preceding section does not allow us to predict the experimental outcome unless we know the direction of the stimulus sequencing.

Summary of Five Rules of Conditioning. To summarize, five main factors determine the rate of acquisition of conditioning, the magnitude of the conditioned response, and the persistence of conditioning as measured by resistance to extinction. Rule 1 is that the number of conditioning trials determines how much conditioning occurs. Rules 2, 3, and 4 compose Pavlov's Law of Strength: Other factors held constant, the magnitude of a conditioned response varies as direct functions of CS and US intensity and as an indirect function of the CS-US interval. Rule 5 states that the order of the CS and US determines the nature, or direction, of the response to be learned.

Other dimensions of stimuli that play an important role in conditioning are qualitative parameters (whether the stimuli are sights, sounds, foods, etc.) and other quantitative parameters (including how long a stimulus lasts). More is said about these latter variables in the next chapter dealing with more complex conditioning situations.

Temporal Factors in Conditioning

Our preceding thought experiment did not begin to exhaust the many possible ways in which two stimuli can be related in time. Several of the more important of these temporal relationships between the CS and US are diagrammed in Figure 4.4. This type of diagram emphasizes the quantitative parameters of onset, duration, and offset of the stimuli, as well as their relationship to each other in time. Not depicted are other dimensions of stimuli that play an important role in conditioning: quantitative parameters such as stimulus intensity (brighter, quieter, etc.) and qualitative dimensions (sights, sounds, tastes, etc.).

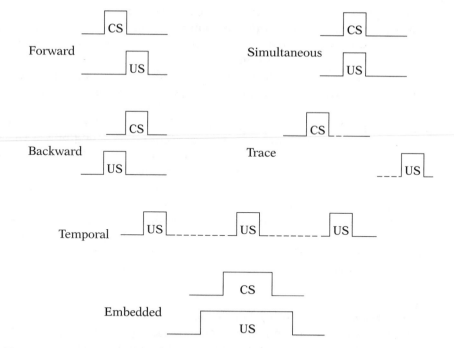

FIGURE 4.4 Six Temporal Patterns of Pavlovian Conditioning

In Pavlovian conditioning, stimulus events with measurable onsets, durations, and offsets are arranged in time. Different time arrangements produce very different outcomes. In temporal conditioning, the US events are presented on a regular schedule without an explicit CS.

Forward and Trace Conditioning. Let us begin by more formally defining the now familiar instances of Pavlovian conditioning that have already been introduced, namely, *forward conditioning* and *trace conditioning*. In **forward conditioning,** the CS onset precedes the US onset, and both stimuli overlap in time. (Because of this overlap, the procedure is sometimes referred to as *delay conditioning*). Compare the stimulus arrangements of both types of conditioning in Figure 4.4. Note that **trace conditioning** is a special example of forward conditioning in that both the CS onset and offset precede the US onset.

Remember that Pavlov's Law of Strength describes how conditioning diminishes if the CS and US are separated in time. Hence, in trace conditioning there are limits as to how much gap can exist between the CS and US.[4] If the

---

[4]Historically, the term trace in trace conditioning refers to a memory trace theory. In this theory, when the conditioned stimulus is presented, it is conceptualized as being entered into memory. At stimulus offset, it persists as a memory trace just long enough to be associated with the US when it is presented.

interval is too long, the two stimuli cannot be associated. For example, imagine being the rat that is conditioned with a tone CS and shock US. The tone sounds for 10 sec, and the shock is presented 30 sec from the tone's onset (hence the CS-US interval is 30 sec). After a number of trace-conditioning trials such as these, the rat will learn a conditioned suppression response. If, however, the CS-US interval were 3 h rather than 30 sec, the rat would not be conditioned.

Simultaneous and Embedded Conditioning. You would be mistaken if you were led to conclude from this example that conditioning results when stimuli are perfectly contiguous in time and never results when stimuli are far removed in time. As Figure 4.4 illustrates, among the most contiguous of stimulus relationships is one called **simultaneous conditioning,** in which the CS and US have identical onsets, durations, and offsets. Most demonstrations of simultaneous conditioning typically involve relatively brief conditioned stimuli (tones and lights lasting only a second or two) paired with short duration unconditioned stimuli (a tiny amount of food or a brief electric shock). Under these circumstances, very little conditioning occurs, even after many trials, in both conditioned suppression (Kamin, 1965) and salivary conditioning (Pavlov, 1927/1960). Contiguity of stimuli is not a sufficient condition for association to occur in these preparations; rather, the CS must precede the US by a fraction of a second or so.

Embedded conditioning is a variation of simultaneous conditioning in which the onset and offset of one of the stimulus elements occur sometime during the other element (Heth, 1976; see also Figure 4.4). Embedded conditioning often occurs during the pairing of longer duration stimuli. For example, in taste aversion conditioning, a flavor might be experienced for several minutes in the middle of an illness episode lasting several hours. The flavor (CS) is said to be embedded in illness (US). Conditioned flavor aversions reliably occur in these situations, which is surprising since it represents a type of backward conditioning (Barker, Smith, & Suarez, 1977).

The differentiation of embedded conditioning from simultaneous conditioning is important for another reason. Outside of the laboratory, timing arrangements encountered by animals are not as neat as they are when arranged by laboratory researchers. Most stimuli encountered in natural contexts are of longer duration than 1 sec, and the relationship of these stimuli with other stimuli often varies across trials. Yet conditioning occurs despite the lack of precision in timing. Successful embedded conditioning includes (but is not restricted to) conditioning situations using drugs, while ingesting flavors and foods, experiencing toxins, recovering from illness, and in other long-duration stimulus complexes.

Backward Conditioning. In **backward conditioning,** the US onset precedes the CS onset. The outcome of this temporal sequencing confused even Pavlov! Again, contiguity predicts that stimulus association should occur, and it does. The direction of conditioning, however, is less predictable. That is, many such stimulus arrangements produce what is called *inhibitory conditioning*, the opposite of excitatory conditioning, especially after many conditioning trials have been conducted.

Recall our previous discussion of stimulus sequencing. In forward conditioning with dogs, the animal salivates to the tone CS. In backward conditioning, the dog suppresses salivation to the tone. In conditioned suppression experiments with rats, tone-shock (forward) sequences condition fear responses while shock-tone (backward) sequences condition "relief" responses. We have much more to say about excitatory and inhibitory conditioning in the next chapter.

Temporal Conditioning. Pavlov noted that following regularly spaced placements of food on the dog's tongue, salivation eventually began to occur just prior to food delivery. In **temporal conditioning,** precise time intervals act as the CS that controls the dog's salivation response. The passage of time can be measured, but it has no physical properties.

Again, Pavlov's observation is an important one. Time schedules are principal ways that humans organize events and responses in their world, and the passage of time can and does act as a signal to control these responses. We often eat whether we are hungry or not at noon because 12 o'clock signals lunchtime. Moreover, in laboratory experiments, the passage of time can be a confounding factor. That is, animals (like humans) may anticipate when certain treatments are likely to occur and adjust their responses accordingly. Another way to say this is that "time of day" and "time between treatments" provide the animal important contextual cues. That these cues affect their responses must be taken into account in the interpretation of treatment effects.

Interim Summary

1. ***Resistance to extinction***—the number of extinction trials to a criterion level of extinction—is the most common way of measuring strength of conditioning.

2. Five rules that govern conditioning are the number of conditioning trials, CS and US intensity, the duration of the CS-US interval, and whether the CS is presented before or after the US.

3. ***Forward conditioning*** and (short) ***trace conditioning*** stimulus sequences are the best for conditioning most stimuli. In forward conditioning the CS onset precedes the US onset, and both occur together. In trace conditioning, an interval of time separates the CS from the US.

4. The ***simultaneous conditioning*** and ***embedded conditioning*** timing relationships work for intense, long-duration stimuli but typically not for brief stimuli. Unless the CS onset precedes the US onset, even after

many trials, contiguous stimuli lasting only 1 to 2 sec are not sufficient for conditioning

5. In ***backward conditioning*** the US onset precedes the CS onset. The conditioned response following a few backward conditioning trials may reflect excitatory conditioning, but after more trials usually reflects inhibitory conditioning, opposite to what is obtained in forward conditioning.

6. ***Temporal conditioning*** results from regularly scheduled unconditioned stimuli; the passage of time can act as a conditioned stimulus.

DISCUSSION QUESTIONS

4. Can you relate the *number of trials* rule governing conditioning to the idea that more intelligent people learn things more quickly than less intelligent people?

5. Can you relate the *CS-US,* or *US-CS sequencing rule* to the *two-stage theory of association* discussed in Chapter 3?

CONDITIONING MORE COMPLEX PHYSIOLOGICAL SYSTEMS

> *"The biological sciences have become compartmentalized and bureaucratized—and that simply reflects our ignorance. I'm a psychologist, you're a biochemist, (or) a pharmacologist, (or) an immunologist. We've divided the pie into manageable pieces. But this division has no bearing on the biology. The biology doesn't recognize these disciplines. There is only one organism, and the nature of the relationships among systems is every bit as important, functionally, as the relationships within a system.*
>
> *"The mind and the body (are) the same thing . . . they are inseparable components of the whole . . . You see, we have a funny language. To talk about mind and body is to set up a dichotomy . . . We have a one-dimensional language for a three-dimensional problem."*

(Robert Ader, 1993, in Bill Moyer's *Healing and the Mind,* p. 245)

We have seen that simple reflexes and simple motor responses can be easily conditioned. Can more complex physiological systems—such as immune system functioning—be conditioned? We'll soon see that the answer is yes. But first we will revisit some issues that provide a conceptual framework for what is involved in the conditioning of more complex physiological systems. In this next section, we'll try to understand what Robert Ader means when he says that mind and body are the same thing, inseparable components of the whole.

We begin by comparing the reflex-like behaviors found in Table 4.2 with the simple reflexes listed in Table 3.1 (p. 66). These reflex-like responses are

TABLE 4.2 Types of Complex Reflex-like Behaviors
with Their Eliciting Stimuli

ELICITING STIMULUS (Source: Environment Darwin's "Nature")	REFLEX (Source: genetically programmed response)
Ingestion of toxin	Nausea, loss of appetite, vomiting
Salt loss	Aldosterone release, salt appetite
Morphine	Pupillary dilation, warming
Cedar pollen	Histamine release
Antigens	T-lymphocyte release
Stimulation of genitalia	Erection (M), vaginal lubrication (F)
Tissue damage	Pain, crying, clenching teeth
Localized heat	Tissue damage, pain, blister
Strange food	Wariness, caution (neophobia)
Strange human, animal	Wariness, caution (neophobia)
Death of a loved one	Weeping, wailing, sadness, depression

also elicited by stimuli that animals encounter in their immediate environment. But the responses are more complicated. These stimuli trigger highly integrated response systems that involve the brain, immune and neuroendocrine systems. Consider pain, eating and drinking, and sexual behavior. Are these merely reflexive behaviors, or is more "mind" involved.

Food on an animal's tongue causes salivation, a Sherringtonian reflex. But what about the wariness an animal exhibits when it encounters strange food. Is this reflexive also, even though it is not a Sherringtonian reflex? Humans weep and become depressed when a loved one dies. Is this reflexive? Are we "reflexive machines," or is will and volition involved in the experience of pain and pleasure, in what we eat and drink, and in how we make love and select mates? These are among the issues to be considered next.

Voluntary and Involuntary Behavior

The concepts of voluntary and involuntary behavior have a long history. Aristotle and Descartes proposed that humans alone are capable of voluntary behavior. Not everyone agrees with this position. (Voluntary behavior has been attributed to the higher cortical functioning of humans. However, other big-brained animals have similarly organized brain structures.) Aristotle, Descartes, and others propose that there are both voluntary and involuntary aspects of human behavior. Walking and talking are examples of what is meant by voluntary behavior; digestion, breathing, and the regulation of fluids are examples of involuntary behavior.

CNS and ANS. Historically, the central nervous system (CNS) was presumed to provide the physiological basis for voluntary behavior, while the autonomic nervous system (ANS) was assumed to control involuntary behavior. This partitioning of behavior has permeated learning theory. B. F. Skinner, among others, proposed that Pavlovian conditioning of the salivary reflex was ANS mediated, and that the conditioning of skeletal muscles (such as those used in running a maze, or pressing a lever, or talking) was controlled by the CNS (Skinner, 1938).

Are CNS and ANS Separate?

Psychologists, we'll see in later chapters, still think the distinction of Skinner's two kinds of conditioning and learning is a meaningful one. But they are currently less certain about what underlies these differences. One reason is that there is now evidence of remarkable interactions among what were once thought to be relatively isolated physiological systems. What is of interest now is *which* physiological systems, in *what* ways, can, through conditioning, be controlled by the environment. If, as was alluded to above, the immune system can be classically conditioning, distinctions between ANS and CNS, and between types of conditioning become less important. (Keep in mind that resolving this issue may have implications for questions of voluntary and involuntary behavior.)

Studies of neuroendocrine, immune system, CNS and ANS functioning in the past decade have led to a new integration and redefinition of these systems (Booth & Ashbridge, 1992; Dantzer & Kelly, 1989). Evidence from a wide variety of studies (Husband, 1992) now attest to the fact that these systems are interconnected: One such holistic configuration is diagrammed in Figure 4.5.

What can we conclude from Figure 4.5? (1) The central nervous system and the autonomic nervous system are more interconnected than they are conceptually separate. (2) Because of this interconnection, a distinction between voluntary and involuntary behavior may have become blurred. (3) There may be any number of ways that conditioning and learning can occur; it is less likely that learning can be divided into two "types" based on brain organization.

In the remainder of this chapter, we will explore conditioning and learning research that impacts health and physiological functioning. We will see that physiology and behavior are interactive. Among the health and physiological systems that can be conditioned are:

- Various components of the *immune system*, including asthma
- Temperature, and pain reactions when drugs are used as unconditioned stimuli
- Drug tolerance
- Physiology relating to sickness and wellness behavior

This is an impressive list. We begin our analysis of conditioning complex physiological systems by examining psychosomatic interactions.

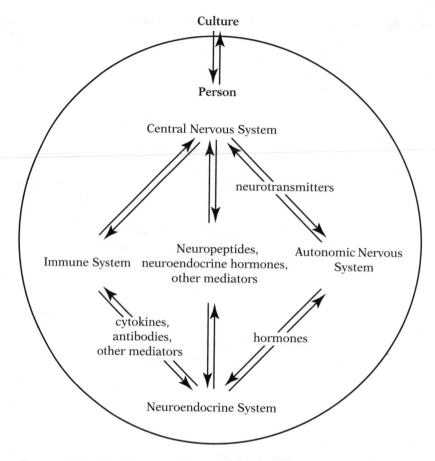

FIGURE 4.5   Psychoneuroimmunology: Mind-body Interactions

A person influences and is influenced by culture. Systems making up a person—including the CNS, ANS, and the neuroendocrine and immune systems—are in intimate interactive communication with each other via neurotransmitters, hormones, cytokinines, and so forth. (After Booth & Ashbridge, 1992).

Psychosomatic Interactions

With his simple demonstrations of psychic secretions at the turn of the century, Pavlov (1927) began the experimental study of *psychosomatic interactions* (psyche = mind; soma = body). From this perspective, consider that a dog's perception of a ringing bell can fool it into salivating. Pavlov could not have foreseen that his conditioning experiments would become the primary research methodology for contemporary studies of behavioral medicine.

When psychosomatic interactions produce deleterious effects in either the anatomy or physiology, they are called **psychosomatic disorders.**

This chapter was introduced with the story of a hypnotist who caused a pain response and blister to form in a hypnotized subject merely by touching him with chalk. Can this blister can be considered a psychosomatic disorder? Have you formed an idea yet of how it was produced?

The "Blister Reflex"

Earlier it was suggested that the arm jerk and blister formation might be conditioned responses. From Table 4.2 indicates that blister formation can be thought of as a reflexive-like response to localized heat: In Pavlovian terms, localized heat is the US, while the blister (and tissue damage, pain, etc.) is the UR. The physiology is somewhat more complicated. Capillaries become increasingly permeable when skin is heated (the eliciting stimulus), and plasma loss produces the localized edema called a blister (the reflexive response). Can we construct a conditioning scenario that might have preceded the televised demonstration?

Analysis of Blisters as CRs.   If the phenomenon in question is a conditioned response, what might the CS, or CS-complex be? Three possible CSs are (1) the chalk, (2) touching the forearm, and (3) the hypnotist's words. The placement of the chalk on the forearm informed the brain where to place the blister. The operative CS, however, was the word "burn." Had the hypnotist done everything the same except substitute a different word in place of "burn" (such as, "I'm now going to *murph* you with a lighted cigarette"), it is unlikely that the blister would have formed.

Using Pavlov's Second Signal System.   Given the foregoing analysis, what the TV camera did not show were the conditioning trials preceding the demonstration. More than likely the subject had previously experienced burns (including cigarette burns) and consequent blister formation. Most humans have had such experiences. Is it likely that the word "burn" functions as a CS in this and other situations? As we saw in an earlier section, Pavlov's (1927) analysis of the *second signal system* detailed how our language can be considered the "signal of signals," a representation of reality one level removed from incoming first-order sensory signals. To the extent that language is learned, many of our nouns and verbs have been *associated* with objects and actions in the environment. A lighted cigarette is an object that burns. It is likely that the words "burn" and "lighted cigarette" signaled the reflex, thereby eliciting blister formation.

Differences in Conditioning Humans and Nonhumans

Does the foregoing conditioning analysis completely explain the phenomenon in question? No. Too many questions remain. Blisters and warts can be readily conditioned in a hypnotic state (Spanos & Chaves, 1989), while other demonstrations of conditioning in humans and nonhuman animals occur during "normal" consciousness.[5] One estimate is that ten to thirty percent of adult humans could make conditioned blisters (Hilgard, 1979). A similar demonstration involving nonhuman animals has not been reported. Is this an argument against general process learning theory? Not necessarily. To redirect this argument, blister formation is merely a reflex, and reflexes are readily conditioned in all animals. Perhaps it hasn't been reported because it hasn't been tried.

However, if one maintains that *only* humans can make conditioned blisters, because humans alone have higher cognitive processes, the law of parsimony would be violated. If a blister *were* to appear on the skin of a human (in the absence of heat) psychological malfunctioning would be suspected. The fake blister would likely be seen as a psychosomatic disorder.

It is more parsimonious to ask if evidence exists that complex physiological responses can be conditioned in humans and animals. The answer to this question is a resounding yes. Does conditioning provide a good model for psychosomatic disorders in general? Again the answer is yes, as we will see throughout the remainder of this chapter (see also Ader, Weiner, and Baum, 1988).

Interim Summary

1. Historically, the physiology and reflexive behavior of humans has been viewed as being continuous with that of other animals.

2. Voluntary behavior in humans is attributed to their alleged higher cortical functioning. However, other complicated animals have similar brain structures and brain functioning.

3. The distinction between voluntary and involuntary physiological systems—mediated by the CNS and ANS, respectively—has been blurred by evidence of their interdependence.

4. Because of their interactions, the CNS, ANS, neuroendocrine, and immune systems are now better thought of as components of an integrative system.

5. Behavior mediated by the CNS, ANS, and neuroendocrine and immune system provides the basis for psychosomatic interactions. A *psychosomatic disorder* is defined as a somatic, or physiological problem, caused by a conditioned response that has been elicited by conditioned stimuli.

6. Blisters are reflex-like, and can be conditioned under a state of hypnosis in some people.

[5]While non-hypnotized subjects can, in theory, be conditioned to blister, I am not aware of controlled demonstrations to this effect. (See, however, the related example of "hive" formation in this chapter.)

7. Pavlovian conditioning provides a defensible account of psychosomatic disorders, and is one of the primary research methodologies of contemporary behavioral medicine.

Discussion Questions

6. Do you agree with Aristotle and Descartes that only humans engage in voluntary behavior?

7. Table 4.2, on p. 120, suggests that stimulation of genitalia causes erections in males and vaginal lubrication in females. Can you describe a conditioning scenario (Pictures? Words?) in which CSs could come to control these responses?

8. Is conscious awareness necessary for a person to exhibit voluntary behavior? Must a person be aware of the response being made for that response to be conditioned?

9. If a blister can form in absence of heat, is it possible that a blister can be prevented under conditions that it *should* form? Know any firewalkers you could ask?

10. *Pseudopregnancy* is a psychosomatic condition more commonly known as *false pregnancy*. In a *pseudopregnancy*, there is no fetus. Yet, the menstrual cycle stops, breasts swell, morning sickness develops, colostrum appears (a clear, sweet fluid that precedes breast milk), labor begins, and the cervix dilates in preparation for delivery. Women who experience most of these symptoms have previously had a child or have read about the sequences of symptoms. Most such women want to be pregnant and grieve when they find that they have merely experienced some of the signs of pregnancy. Can you make the case that normal pregnancy is an elaborate 9-month "reflex" and that pseudopregnancy is a conditioned reflex? What triggers it?

The Immune System and Psychoneuroimmunology

Psychoneuroimmunology is an area of research that studies the interconnectedness of the immune system, brain, mind, and behavior—a relationship suggested by Figure 4.5. A number of researchers have developed human and nonhuman animal models that demonstrate how various components of the immune system can be conditioned. Let's begin by looking at how the immune system functions *without* the complications of conditioning.

Immune System Functioning

Many volumes of text would be necessary to describe the full functioning of the immune system. Its basic functioning in mammals is to resist toxins and infectious organisms that might cause damage to tissues and organs.

Acquired immunity describes the process whereby antibodies and sensitized lymphocytes (white blood cells) destroy invading organisms and toxins.

T-lymphocytes play an integral role in the immune system. Present at birth, T-lymphocytes directly bind to the membranes of invading cells (such as a foreign protein, a cancer cell, or the transplanted cells that comprise someone else's heart). T-lymphocytes then release both *lysomal enzymes* (that directly attack the cell's integrity), and a *macrophage chemotaxic factor* (that attracts other killer cells to the site). From a Pavlovian reflex perspective, invading cells can be thought of as the US, and T-lymphocyte production and functioning as the UR.

Conditioning the Immune System: T-lymphocytes

Robert Ader and his associates demonstrated that the number of T-lymphocytes present in rats could be manipulated by a simple conditioning experiment (Ader, 1985; Ader and Cohen, 1982; Ader, Cohen, & Bovbjerg, 1982). First, they injected rats with a drug called Cytoxan® (the US). Cytoxan® is a drug—known generically as cyclophosphamide—that mimics some of the properties of ionizing radiation. It is routinely used as chemotherapy to suppress immune system functioning, including the lowering of T-lymphocyte production. The next day, the researchers recorded a reduced T-lymphocyte count, an unconditioned response to the drug treatment.

Ader and associates then conditioned the rats by allowing them to drink a saccharin solution (the CS), followed by the Cytoxan® injection (the US). A control group received saccharin and Cytoxan® a day apart to preclude their association. After several trials, one per day, they recorded the number of T-lymphocytes when these two groups of rats drank saccharin. The post-conditioning drinking of saccharin in the absence of the drug is an extinction test. Relative to controls who drank saccharin but had not been conditioned, Ader found fewer T-lymphocytes in the rats in the treatment group.

Conditioned Immunosuppression. The reduction of T-lymphocytes following this conditioning procedure is called *conditioned immunosuppression*. Presumably the saccharin had become associated with the drug's effects, and components of the immune system responded to the saccharin flavor in the same way that it had to the drug. It is likely that the mechanisms that allows conditioning of the immune system are recently discovered CNS nerve fibers serving immune system cells (Felten, 1993).

Conditioned Facilitation of Immune Response. Ader's demonstration of conditioned immunosuppression was the first of many investigations in the psychoneuroimmunology research area. *Conditioned facilitation* of the immune response has since been reported, using exteroceptive stimuli as CSs (Krank & MacQueen, 1988; Gorczynski, Macrae, & Kennedy, 1982; Bovbjerg, Cohen, & Ader, 1987). In research by Krank and MacQueen (1988), for example, *increases* in antibody production were conditioned. They injected mice with cyclophosphamide while the mice drank water in a distinctive environment (a novel room in which 80-dB music was played). Mice exposed to this distinctive room and music in extinction produced higher levels of antibodies compared to groups of mice in which there was no prior pairing of these stimuli with the drug. Possible reasons for the differences between this study and Ader's finding of *suppression* of antibodies are discussed later (see *Conditioned Compensatory Responses*, p. 138).

Importance of Psychoneuroimmunology. Why is psychoneuroimmunology important? These experiments demonstrate that elements of the immune system can function in the absence of stimuli that normally trigger it. We should not be surprised by these findings. Earlier we learned that a dog's salivary response could also be brought under the control of an arbitrary stimulus, such as a bell. The present findings are more important. Salivation, and changes in salivation via conditioning, have implications for the preliminary stages of digestion. By contrast, the integrity of the immune system is vitally important for health—for the optimal functioning of all physiological systems and behavior. The immune system is critically important for health and longevity. An understanding of how the immune system can be conditioned may allow us to *learn* to be healthier.

Thoughts Affect Immune Systems. That the immune system can be conditioned using an arbitrary taste stimulus such as saccharin opens the door to other kinds of control. Is it possible that words, thoughts, and beliefs, acting as CSs, can become associated with immune system functioning? What do you think? Can thought processes, such as the perception of stressors, affect your health?

Several studies using both rats and humans provide supportive evidence that psychological variables can affect the immune system. In one study, for example, two groups of rats received the same number of shocks. One of the groups was given the opportunity to escape shock, but received some they were unsuccessful in escaping. These rats had normal immune functioning. The other, called a *yoked-control group*, received the same number of shocks, but were unable to make a response to escape them. Rats in the yoked-control group were immunosuppressed (Laudenslager, Ryan, Drugan, Hyson, & Maier, 1983). The *perception* of the stressor, and not the stressor alone, produced these changes in the immune system.

NK (Natural Killer) Lymphocytes. Other aspects of the immune system may also be affected by psychological stress. One study measured NK (natural killer) lymphocytes during a 12-min period of stress. Paid male volunteers merely waited, knowing that when the 12 min was up they would receive a painful electric shock. Relative to a control group, worrying suppressed the immune system of these subjects as measured by reduced NK activity (Breznitz & others, 1998).

Expectations Affect Immune System Functioning. These and other aspects of the immune system that are affected by fear, worry, and stress are also responsible for slower and more complicated postoperative recovery from surgery. There is growing evidence that a patient's expectations influences the course of recovery, and that both perceived pain and worrying delay surgical wound healing (Kiecold-Glaser, Page, Marucha, MacCallum, & Glaser, 1998). Finally, personality variables have also been found to affect immune function. Both perceived stress and immunosuppression during test-taking were found to differ as a function of students' personality profiles (Jemmott, et al, 1990). There is converging evidence, then, that the conditioned perception of stressors can affect one's immune system—hence, one's health (Jemmott & Magloire, 1988; Jemmott, Hellman, McClelland, Locke, Krause, Williams, & Valeri, 1990).

Asthma

Nine million Americans suffer from a baffling condition called asthma. Although these people come from every walk of life, and range in age from infants to the very old, they have one thing in common—difficulty in breathing, alternatively described as "hungry for air." Sometimes an asthma attack can be fatal.

The sign in the allergist's office summarizes what the allergy suffer already knows: Asthma attacks occur under a variety of conditions. Figure 4.6 summarizes the Rule of E's: Asthma is aggravated by environment, exertion, and emotion. One implication of this observation is that the same amount of external stimulus (cedar pollen, for example) doesn't always produce an identical asthmatic response, as would be the case if asthma were a simple reflex. Let us look more closely at this physiological condition.

Environment	Provides antigen (allergen) and irritant (harsh, dry, cold)
Exertion	Causes irritation of mucous membranes
Emotion	Always heightens symptoms with any combination of the above, or may induce asthma even in the absence of these factors

FIGURE 4.6 The Rule of E's

The "Rule of E's" summarizes three of the most important variables that contribute to asthma attacks.

Physiology of Asthma. Asthma is a type of allergy involving yet another component of the immune system. In normal people, certain stimuli that invade the body, called *antigens,* activate immune responses. The presence of large quantities of *reagins,* or sensitizing antibodies, cause some individuals to overreact to certain types of antigens known as *allergens.* When this occurs in allergic or asthmatic individuals, an allergic response called an *allergen-reagin reaction* takes place.

Serious health problems may result from such overly sensitive immune systems, and asthma can be thought of as a disorder involving overly sensitive airways. Allergen-reagin reactions involve attaching antibodies to and thereby damaging cells throughout the body. If a sufficient number of cells are damaged in this *anaphylactoid* reaction, death can ensue.

The allergen-reagin reaction can therefore be understood as a US-UR reflex. Is it possible to condition an asthmatic reaction? That is, can asthmatic and allergic responses be brought under the control of neutral stimuli? A related question is the role emotion plays in the Rule of E's. How can emotion be a facilitating factor in this reflex? We begin by looking at asthma in animals.

Asthma in Guinea Pigs. Guinea pigs have overly sensitive airways, making them good animal subjects upon which to do asthma research. Guinea pigs can be made asthmatic by first injecting them with a foreign protein, such as egg albumin.[6] The albumin acts as a US. Their immune system responds by making sensitizing antibodies (reagins) to the invading protein (a UR). Upon subsequent encounters with the allergen, an allergen-reagin reaction occurs in the bronchioles of the lungs. There, mast cells release a *slow-reacting substance of anaphylaxis* causing the bronchial smooth muscle to spasm. Breathing difficulties follow. The response of the guinea pig following one sensitizing treatment is so severe that unless a vasoconstrictor (such as Isuprel®) is immediately administered, the guinea pig will die. The breathing difficulty is another UR to the US.

Conditioning Asthma in Guinea Pigs. Asthma in guinea pigs has been conditioned (Justesen, Braun, Garrison, & Pendleton, 1970). The foregoing sensitizing treatment makes the pig asthmatic. Breathing is measured by a pressure transducer in a sealed environment (see Figure 4.7). Recordings are made of slight changes in air pressure as the animal breaths normally. Figure 4.7 shows that when aerosol egg albumin (the US) is administered into the air stream serving the chamber, breathing is disrupted (the UR).

A hissing nebulizer squirts the egg albumin (the US) into the airstream in an aerosol form. A conditioning trial thus consists of the hissing sound (the CS), the aerosol egg albumin (the US), and disrupted breathing (the UR).

---

[6]Any protein that is not "self" is foreign. The exception would be the interchangablility of body parts of identical twins. Somone else's transplanted liver is a "foreign protein."

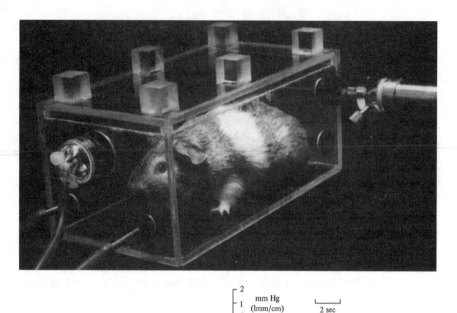

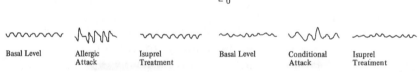

| Basal Level | Allergic | Isuprel | Basal Level | Conditional | Isuprel |
| | Attack | Treatment | | Attack | Treatment |

FIGURE 4.7 Conditioning Asthma in Guinea Pigs

The guinea pig shown weighs about 850 g. The nebulizer is attached at the back of the box. Whole-body breathing records (*plethysomograms*) are recorded from fluctuations in air pressure within the sealed chamber. Shown are baseline breathing (*basal level*), disrupted breathing to the egg albumin (*allergic attack*), recovery of breathing following Isuprel® treatment, and the disrupted breathing to the sound of the nebulizer alone (*conditional attack*). (From Justesen, et al. 1970).

Isuprel® restores breathing to baseline levels. In the research by Justeson, et al. (1970), *all* guinea pigs showed conditioned disruptions in breathing to the sound of the nebulizer alone after 6 to 12 trials. That is, the hissing sound, acting as a CS, caused the asthma attack.

This demonstration of conditioned asthma raises several important issues. Would it be possible, for example, to maximize conditioning (more trials, more salient CSs, etc.) and fatally disrupt breathing using only a CS? Isuprel® was used to recover baseline breathing following a conditioned asthma attack. Here is another experiment to consider: Could a discrimination be trained between the sound of the aerosol egg albumin and a different sound for the aerosol Isuprel® such that the CS associated with the latter could be shown to relieve breathing disruptions to the former? That is, induce psychosomatic asthma, and recover breathing with another conditioned stimulus!

Conditioning Asthma in Humans. The behavioral conditioning of asthma has also been reported in humans. For example, in a design similar to the guinea pig study just noted, two allergic individuals were first exposed to allergens when using a breathing apparatus. After several trials, they produced allergic symptoms when asked to use the breathing apparatus alone, in the absence of allergens.[7] Within the clinical literature on the treatment of asthma are numerous reports of psychosomatic (i.e., conditioned) asthma. Included is an allergic reaction to an artificial rose in a patient allergic to the smell of roses (reported by Gauci, Husband, & King, 1992). Apparently the visual features of the real rose acted as a CS, and the fragrance was the US. After a lifetime of pairings, the visual features of the plastic rose was a CS that controlled this patient's asthma.

Allergic rhinitis (hay fever) is related to asthma. It has also been conditioned in humans, using both mast-cell mediators and a "subjective symptom score" as dependent variables (Gauci, Husband, & King, 1992). In this research, a number of asthma suffers were recruited to participate in a study concerned with "alternative" treatments for hay fever and allergic rhinitis. Divided into three groups, they were given water, a "medicine," (actually an inert soft drink), or nothing. Each treatment was conceptualized as the "conditioned stimulus." Immediately thereafter, each subject was challenged with an allergen (the US). Both "subject symptom scores" (a self-report measure) and mast-cell activity were measured. Two days later, the treatment was repeated. The CSs were given, but not the allergen. These researchers reported that the "medicine" treatment diminished mast-cell activity relative to the other two groups.

The Placebo Effect

These results of experiments that show recovery when "treated" with a conditioned stimulus are known as a *placebo effect*. A **placebo effect** is a conditioned response that mimics the effects of a drug treatment (the unconditioned stimulus). In humans, via the second signal system, a placebo effect may reflect the expectation of drug or other treatment effect. Interestingly, in

---

[7]After hearing a lecture on asthmatic conditioning, a student reported to me that he had replaced the Isuprel® in his asthmatic roommate's nebulizer with water, and for one week watched symptomatic relief obtained from the water placebo (*placebo*, from the Greek, "I will please"). Ethics aside, the point is that drug administration is *always* accompanied by environmental CSs that may act as conditioned stimuli. See *conditioning drug responses* later in this chapter.

the present study, Gauci, et al, (1992) hypothesized that these subject's *expectations* regarding treatment was a confounding variable. They apparently did not expect the "medicine" treatment to exert placebo properties. These researchers concluded that the entire experimental treatment had CS properties, and that one-trial conditioning had been effected.

Asthma and Emotionality

Conditioned allergic reactions are likely to be experienced by all asthma sufferers. These occasions also provide excellent opportunities for a variety of conditioning situations. For example, have you ever had your breathing forcibly disrupted for any length of time? Without special training most people panic. That suffocation produces such extreme emotional responses is adaptive. Oxygen is our most critical homeostatic need, and its availability demands our immediate attention. The point is that the emotional components of allergic responses are also excellent USs, available for conditioning to a variety of environmental cues. It is no wonder that allergists have long recognized the inherent circularity of this medical condition; emotion causes the asthma causes the emotion.

In one study, for example, using 30 healthy female college students, breathing changes were induced by having them perform either a stressful arithmetic task or a non-stressful control task. Differently colored lights projected on a screen while they performed one or the other task served as conditioned stimuli. After a number of trials, the color alone produced changes in both respiration rate and respiratory resistance (Miller & Kotses, 1995).

Is it unreasonable to suggest that guinea pigs as well as humans suffer emotional responses as they gasp for air? Concurrent with disruptions in breathing, these emotional responses readily enter into association with the nebulizer sounds. After several pairings, the sound of the nebulizer alone would produce a "panic" response, further disrupting normal breathing. In any case, both the Justeson, et al. (1970) and Gauci, et al. (1992) experiments provide compelling demonstrations of human psychosomatic disorders. Treatments for panic disorders will be considered in a later chapter.

Conditioning Hives

Uticaria is an immune system response commonly known as *hives*. Though not well understood, hives result when antigens enter specific skin areas and cause histamine release. Among other actions, histamine produces a local vascular dilation and capillary permeability. Within a few minutes of its release, it causes a "red flare" and swelling (a hive). Many individuals produce hives in situations where the antigen is either not present, or is present but is not causing a reaction. Consider the following example:

A woman in her mid-thirties is stressed by the presence of visiting in-laws. After several hours she is overheard saying that she must get away or she will "go crazy." A few minutes later the first hive appears on her upper arm. She retires to her bedroom, saying she will be OK "...if left alone." Within the next fifteen minutes, several six-inch diameter, one-half-inch raised welts appeared on her arms, legs, and torso. An hour later, all hives had disappeared without leaving a mark.[8]

It is tempting to speculate that the presence of in-laws acted as a conditioned stimulus, setting the occasion for the emotional/stress response. Given the time course of the appearance and disappearance of the hives, it is likely that histamine was released locally as a conditioned rather than as an unconditioned response. Another common example of an emotionally induced change in the skin is blushing. "Blushing" is caused by localized vasodilation of the face and neck, most noticeably the cheeks. Which particular conditioned stimuli control your "blushing reflex"? Certain people? Certain words?

Interim Summary

1. **Psychoneuroimmunology** is a research area that integrates physiology and behavior. Pavlovian conditioning is the primary methodology used in psychoneuroimmunology.

2. The *immune system's* function in animals is to recognize and to resist toxins and infectious organisms. *T-lymphocytes* attack and destroy invading cells.

3. The immune system can be conditioned to respond to CSs. In Ader's research rats drank saccharin (the CS) followed by Cytoxan® (the US), a drug that suppresses immune functioning (the UR).

4. This conditioning procedure produced **conditioned immunosuppression:** Tasting the CS (saccharin) reduced the rat's *T-lymphocyte* count (the CR). An opposite effect, **conditioned** *immunofacilitation* has also been demonstrated.

5. The perception, or interpretation, of stressors has been demonstrated to have immune system consequences in rats and humans.

6. Asthma has been classically conditioned in guinea pigs in which the sound of a nebulizer (the CS) produced an asthma attack, following pairings of the sound and a US, egg albumin. Disrupted breathing has been conditioned in humans as well. The emotional consequences of disrupted breathing are potential USs available for association with environmental cues.

7. A **placebo effect** is a conditioned response that mimics real treatment effects (that is, it mimics the response to the unconditioned stimulus).

---

[8]Personal observation by the author.

8. Hives and blushing can be interpreted as conditioned responses triggered by specifically learned CSs.

DISCUSSION QUESTIONS

11. Charged with buying illegal amounts of valium, Jennifer Whitt, a 24-year-old college student from Austin, Texas, spent almost 10 months in a prison in Reynosa, Mexico. She survived this time period without her asthma medication. Two hours after her release in September 1992, Jennifer suffered an asthma attack while her parents drove her across the border into southern Texas. A lifelong asthma sufferer, she died a few hours later in a U.S. hospital. Can you think of some reasons that her attack might have been so severe the day she reentered the United States?

12. Use the Rule of E's to identify factors that are responsible for "exercise-induced asthma" among competitive athletes.

13. Drugs prescribed for treatment of a physical condition are often ineffective and often have aversive side effects. Conduct a cost-benefit analysis of prescribing placebos in place of "real" drugs.

DRUGS, DRUG EFFECTS, AND CONDITIONED DRUG EFFECTS

> *An elderly man in the terminal stages of cancer, suffering acute, chronic pain, was being maintained on a high dosage of morphine. Bedridden, the patient was administered the morphine on a strict schedule by a relative. On one occasion the relative was late, and the patient crawled into the next room where he administered the drug to himself. Though the drug dosage was equivalent to what he had been taking, the patient died of an "overdose"* (Siegel, Hinson, Krank, & McCully, 1982).

Drugs act upon humans and other animals alike. Using animal models of drug effects for several decades, pharmacologists have identified both physical addiction and tolerance to certain drugs. But pharmacologists cannot tell us why humans abuse drugs while other animals, for the most part, do not. By applying Pavlovian conditioning theory to the study of drug effects during the past two decades, behavioral scientists have provided insight into both drug-taking behavior and drug-tolerance effects.

Drugs as Stimuli

Tones and lights of short duration are "simple" conditioned stimuli. They produce definable afferent neuronal responses of limited duration that project to easily defined areas of the brain. By contrast, Pavlov's USs ("biologically meaningful stimuli,") are more complex. USs evoke motivational and emotional responses from more diverse areas of the brain, as well as from neuroendocrine and immune systems.

Drugs are USs. Drug are complex stimuli. Drugs not only have sensory properties, but each drug also has one or more sites of action in the brain and other parts of the body. The pharmacological effects of a drug constitute its unconditioned stimulus properties. Given the complexity of drugs as stimuli, should we anticipate that conditioning using drugs as USs will differ from salivary conditioning in dogs? Surprisingly, simple associative models work quite well. The overdose story introducing this section provides questions that research has answered. The main question is, How can the same dosage of a drug have two different effects? Fortunately, animal research on the development of drug tolerance provides a conceptual framework to help us understand how a "normal" drug dosage can sometimes be an "overdose." We begin by first looking at various aspects of drugs and drug-taking behavior, and then we will return to the question of drug effects.

Drug-taking Behavior

On the surface, taking drugs seems to be an example of a voluntary behavior. Addictive drugs, however, are often craved like air, food, and water. Both food and drug cravings can be analyzed as resulting from physiological need states. After a thorough literature review, Tiffany (1990) concluded that drug-seeking behavior of habitual drug users may largely be determined by "automatic" (involuntary) processes, rather than as the result of voluntary processes.

Drugs are powerful unconditioned stimuli, and addictive drugs are potent reinforcers. Each drug-taking episode can be considered a conditioning trial in which environmental stimuli (CSs) are paired with drug effects (USs). Smoking a cigarette and drinking a beer are drug-taking behaviors that take place within a stimulus context.

As is the case with many other stimuli used in conditioning, both the effectiveness and the associability of drugs change with repeated trials. The reduced effectiveness of drugs repeatedly taken, called drug tolerance, is especially true of "addictive drugs." An example of an addictive drug that loses its effectiveness over time is morphine.

Conditioning and Drug Tolerance

Morphine is an alkaloid derivative of opium primarily used by humans at analgesic (pain-relieving) dosages. Its primary effect is on the central nervous system. Complex, endogenous opioid receptors (such as endorphins) are activated by morphine, producing a number of changes in CNS functioning and physiological systems. Among the easily measured "unconditioned responses" to morphine are respiratory depression (at high doses), and analgesia, euphoria, and increased body temperature (at moderate doses).

Simple Conditioning with Morphine. Pavlov (1927) reported some of the first conditioning experiments using injections of morphine in dogs. The appearance of the white-coated researcher who would inject a dog with morphine eventually became the CS that produced drug-like responses (see Box 4.2). Pavlov's observations of conditioning using morphine as a US and sights and sounds as CSs produced results similar to his other preparations. But we now know that "drug effects" are more complicated than his simple picture suggests. Let's next consider questions about drug tolerance.

Tolerance = Pharmacological Tolerance Plus Behavioral Tolerance

Tolerance is defined as a reduction in the intensity of the effect of a dose of a drug over repeated trials. Tolerance has been likened to habituation (Baker & Tiffany, 1985). Another way of assessing tolerance is to note the increasing requirement of a larger dose to achieve the same level of drug effect over trials.

Pharmacological Tolerance. Mechanisms of tolerance vary from drug to drug. For example, *metabolic tolerance* to the daily ingestion of alcohol is characterized by compensatory changes in biochemicals (such as increased levels of alcohol dehydrogenase) that inactivate (metabolize) the drug. Be-

---

BOX 4.2   CONDITIONING DRUG RESPONSES IN DOGS

Drugs are such powerful USs we should not be surprised at their control over human behavior. Pavlov was among the first researchers to document the intensity of conditioned responses using morphine as a US:

"...It is well known that the first effect of a hypodermic injection of morphine is to produce nausea with profuse secretion of saliva, followed by vomiting, and then profound sleep.

"...when the injections were repeated regularly...after five or six days the preliminaries of injection were in themselves sufficient to produce all these symptoms—nausea, secretion of saliva, vomiting and sleep.

"...in the most striking cases all the symptoms could be produced by the dogs simply seeing the experimenter. Where such a stimulus was insufficient, it was necessary to open the box containing the syringe, to crop the fur over a small area of skin and wipe with alcohol, and perhaps even to inject some harmless fluid before the symptoms could be obtained. The greater number of previous injections of morphine the less preparation had to be performed in order to evoke a reaction simulating that produced by the drug." (Pavlov, 1927, p. 35 ff.).

Is it obvious that what Pavlov referred to as a "harmless fluid" is what is now called a placebo, and the responses he observed to the CSs were the placebo effect?

---

cause it is metabolized, less of the drug is available to reach receptor sites in the brain. *Physiological tolerance* to alcohol occurs when the presumed receptive sites on (as yet unspecified) neurons change, such that the effects of the drug at these sites are reduced.[9] These, and other biological mechanisms for other drugs characterize the many ways in which *pharmacological tolerance* for a drug develops. **Pharmacological tolerance** is the portion of total drug tolerance that can be attributed to pharmacological properties of drugs.

Behavioral Tolerance. It is also the case that in addition to the development of pharmacological tolerance over trials, animals experience a *behavioral tolerance*. **Behavioral tolerance** is the portion of total drug tolerance that can be attributed to learned or environmental variables as opposed to pharmacological variables. It helps animals cope with the effects that drugs have on the ability to both sense and move about the environment. For example, given enough trials in a drug state, rats under the influence of alcohol can learn to balance better while traversing a narrow ledge (Wenger, Tiffany, Bombardier, Nicholls, & Woods, 1981). This sensory-motor adjustment is a form of behavioral tolerance. Indeed, demonstrations of tolerance to stimuli other than drugs suggests a general mechanism. Homeostatic adjustments occur to repetitive stimuli. For example, tolerance develops to a variety of physical circumstances such as heat, cold, and delivery of electric shocks, exercise (the *training effect*), and even to the effects of brain lesions. Studying drug tolerance processes is an example of how animals learn to tolerate, or adjust, to repetitive stimuli.

Conditioning Morphine Tolerance

How much tolerance can a person develop to morphine? A great deal. An initial dose of 100 to 200 mg produces sedation and respiratory depression to the point of death. After repeated administrations, tolerant subjects can take 20–40 times this dosage (as much as 4.0 gm) without adverse effect (Baker & Tiffany, 1985). The question becomes one of determining how much tolerance is pharmacological, and how much is behavioral tolerance.

   We are now ready to consider an elegant demonstration of how Siegel (1975; 1977) partitioned morphine tolerance into *behavioral* and *pharmacological* components. He began by injecting rats with 5.0 mg/kg morphine sulfate, subcutaneously (under the skin) on a daily basis. This dosage of morphine produced several unconditioned responses—increased body temperature (hyperthermia), decreased heart rate (bradycardia), and decreased sensitivity to pain (analgesia). How was the response to pain measured? Rats without morphine will immediately withdraw and lick their paw when it is

---

[9]"Physiological tolerance" is far more complicated than indicated here. In addition to changes in receptor number and receptor sensitivity, changes to morphine, for example, probably occur in intracellular second-messenger systems to which opiate receptors couple.

placed upon a hot plate. (The temperature of the hot plate made it uncomfortable, but did not damage tissue.) Morphine's effects reduces their sensitivity to pain, and they may wait 20 to 30 sec before removing their paw from the hot surface.

Effects of Environment on Tolerance.   Drug administration took place in a room in which 60-dB white noise provided a constant background. (White noise is the sound parents make when "shushing" a child). This *distinctive environment,* we will see, provided the contextual cues that eventually controlled some of the responses to the morphine.

As tolerance to the morphine accrued (about 6 days), each injection produced less analgesia and less hyperthermia. The question Siegel wanted to answer was how much of the reduction in analgesia and hyperthermia was caused by decreases in the drug's pharmacological action, and how much was caused by behavioral tolerance. To find out, he interrupted the schedule of drug administration by taking the rats to a room having different background cues. The morphine administered in this new environment again became effective. That is, the morphine once again produced analgesia (less pronounced pain) and again warmed the animals (see Figure 4.8a and b, respectively).

Conditioned Compensatory Responses.   Siegel concluded that the context of the familiar room (in which the rats had been injected daily with morphine) had become a conditioned stimulus. The rat's tolerance to the morphine was in part because the drug was being administered *in this environment*. The familiar environment, Siegel reasoned, contained CSs that had come to control **conditioned compensatory responses.** How so? The rats normal physiology, he argues, allows homeostatic mechanisms to counteract the effects of drugs. That is, the ANS responds to counteract the warming effects of morphine by cooling the body, and by increasing heart rate (tachycardia) to counteract the bradycardia produced by morphine. Less intuitively, he also proposed that an increased sensitivity to pain counteracts the analgesia produced by morphine. Behavioral tolerance is caused by these conditioned compensatory responses.

The Drug-Overdose Case.   Let us return to the case study of apparent morphine overdose given at the beginning of this section. Recall that the sickly individual was given daily morphine injections in his *familiar* bedroom by another individual. The fatal dose was self-administered in a *different* room. Self-administering the drug in a novel room bypassed the familiar environmental stimuli that would have elicited the conditioned compensatory responses. The effectiveness of the high dosage of morphine was thereby increased, unfortunately, to a fatal level (Siegel and others, 1982).

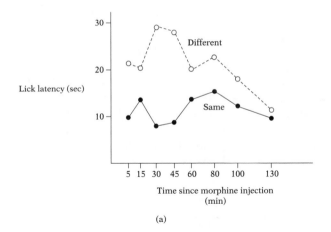

(a)

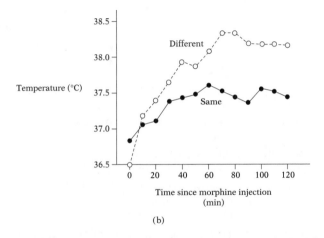

(b)

FIGURE 4.8 Conditioning Pain and Temperature Responses

(a) The figure shows the reaction time of two groups of rats that withdraw their paw from a hot surface and lick it following 6 trials with morphine. The groups of rats tested in a different environment leave their paws on the hot surface two to three times as long—indicating the morphine is effective in blocking their pain response. The same dosage of morphine is much less effective when administered in the same environment. Rats with no morphine would lift their paw and lick it immediately.

(b) The figure shows the body temperatures of two groups of rats administered the same dosage of morphine in the same environment in which tolerance developed, or a *different* environment. The warming effect reoccurs in a different environment that lacks environmental cues controlling conditioned compensatory responses. (After Siegel, 1977.)

Conditioning Withdrawal Responses in Humans

Other drug-conditioning phenomena have been demonstrated in humans. One study used the drug naloxone. Naloxone mimics a host of heroin withdrawal effects, including subjective components (craving, nausea, and cramps); behavioral components (blinking, yawning, restlessness); and ANS components (decreased skin temperature, increased heart rate, tears from the eyes). In this study, addicts volunteered to be studied during drug withdrawal in methadone-maintenance programs (O'Brien, 1975). Naloxone was paired with a conditioned stimulus complex of tone/odor. After 7 to 10 trials the CS complex reliably produced conditioned responses similar to the naloxone treatment.

Street addicts coming into the treatment centers carry their drug-conditioning history with them. When asked to perform a "cook-up" ritual under laboratory conditions, the detoxified addicts' pupils dilate and skin temperature decreases prior to any drug action (O'Brien, Testa, Ternes, & Greenstein, 1978). The conditioned stimuli controlling the response is a complex including the sight of a bag of heroin, the odor of the cooker, and anticipation of shooting up. Such sights, smells, and physiological changes easily become conditioned stimuli (Ternes, O'Brien, Grabowski, Wellerstein, & Jordan-Hays, 1980).

Conditioning Alcohol Tolerance

Few readers of this text are either heroin addicts or morphine users. If it turns out that if conditioned compensatory responses are specific only to conditioning with opiates, their application to humans, while interesting, is limited. But what of alcohol, a commonly used drug? Ethanol, found in beer, wine, and distilled spirits has a different pharmacological action from the opiates. The research conducted by Le, Poulos, & Cappell (1979) is important, then, in extending the generality of Siegel's framework to a commonly used drug, ethanol. Their research, and that of others, now provides a conditioning model of alcohol tolerance that has important treatment implications (Melchior & Tabakoff, 1984).

Among its more interesting pharmacological actions, ethyl alcohol has a cooling effect on the body.[10] Le, et al. (1979) injected rats intraperitoneally with 2.5 g/kg for nine trials in a distinctive environment. The first dose produces substantial motor impairment (rats appear drunk) and also drops the body temperature from 98.6° to about 95° Fahrenheit. Figure 4.9 shows the change in the hypothermic unconditioned response from the 1st to the 9th trial. By the 9th trial, alcohol has lost much of its cooling effect.

On the 10th trial alcohol was administered in the rat's home cage rather than in the distinctive (familiar) environment. Figure 4.9 shows that the cooling effect reappeared. Le, et al. (1979) interpreted this finding within Siegel's framework: conditioned *hyper*thermic compensatory responses were interfering with the normal pharmacological action of ethanol. The environmental cues controlled at least a portion of the temperature changes to alcohol. Therefore, not all of the observed tolerance could be due to loss of pharmacological action at a receptor site.

---

[10]St. Bernards carrying brandy kegs provide a substance to stranded mountaineers that may burn the throat and stomach (and thereby arouse the RAS). Nevertheless, the end result is to further cool the body—unless the person has an extensive history with ethanol consumption in cold climates—see text.

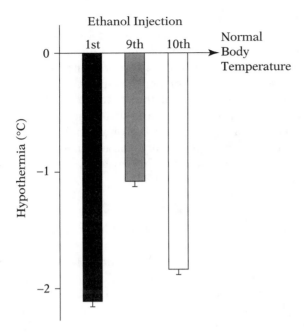

FIGURE 4.9 Alcohol, Tolerance, and Body Temperature

> The first time a rat is injected with alcohol (2.5 g/kg, i.p.) its body tempera-
> ture plummets ~2°C (to ~ 95–96°F). After 9 injections (1 per day), the body
> temperature of the now alcohol-tolerant rat does not decrease as much.
> However, if it is injected in a novel environment (10th injection), its body
> temperature again plummets. (After Le et al., 1979.)

Conditioning Changes in Body Temperature

Because body temperature itself is a factor in how well the immune system
functions, there is increasing interest in demonstrating that body temperature
changes can also be conditioned (Bull, Brown, King, Husband, & Pfister, 1992).
In this research, novel-flavored fluids (CSs) were paired with either pyretics or
anti-pyretics (USs). (A pyretic is any drug, toxin, or treatment that increases
body temperature. Aspirin and Tylenol® are common antipyretics.) They found
conditioned temperature changes to the CS of about the same magnitude reported by Le et al. (1979) to ethanol (Bull, Brown, King, & Husband, 1991).
Body temperature, therefore, can be conditioned by a variety of means.

CSs Trigger Drug Craving? Humans are creatures of habit, making it important to understand habitual alcohol-drinking behavior. When people are

asked why they drink alcohol, many simply respond "I crave it." Others drink alcohol but do not report consciously "craving" it (Kassel & Shiffman, 1992). Le et al. (1979) speculated that periodic drinking in familiar environments would produce both time and place cues for the conditioned compensatory responses, including hyperthermia. They further reasoned that a slight warming effect could provide the somatic basis for the "psychological craving" for alcohol, and conscious awareness of the warming would not be necessary to trigger the response of seeking alcohol. Treatment of alcoholism should take into effect this learning component. Specifically, the treatment of alcoholics should include the extinction of conditioned compensatory responses as well as alcohol abstinence (Melchior & Tabakoff, 1984).

Conditioning of Food Allergies.   The finding that both morphine and alcohol tolerance are determined in part by whether they are experienced in novel or familiar places raises questions about other environmentally-sensitive conditioning phenomena. For example, consider that *food allergies* occur in 8% of children. The role of environment in conditioning allergic responses to flavors of foods, however, has not been investigated. In a recent report of 13 children who had life-threatening food allergy incidents, 5 of the 6 fatal cases occurred outside of the home (novel environment), whereas the remaining 7 non-fatal reactions occurred at home (Sampson, Mendelson, & Rosen, 1992). Of the non-fatal reactions to foods, 2 of the children who came closest to dying were visiting in other people's homes. The report focused on somewhat longer delays in the administration of epinephrine in the fatal vs. non-fatal incidents. However, the role of increased allergic responses triggered by a novel environment should not be ruled out.

Interim Summary

1. A drug's pharmacological effects are its unconditioned stimulus properties.
2. Drug-taking behavior is influenced by both the pharmacological properties of the drug, and by the conditioned responses to the environment in which the drug effects were experienced.
3. Early experiments with morphine demonstrated that conditioned stimuli could produce morphine-like effects in the animal.
4. ***Tolerance*** is a reduction in the intensity of the effect of a dose of a drug over repeated trials.
5. ***Pharmacological tolerance*** is attributed to changes in the physical response to pharmacological properties of drugs over time.
6. ***Behavioral tolerance*** of a drug's effect is attributed to learned or environmental variables as opposed to pharmacological variables.

7. Siegel's research showed that morphine tolerance has two components: *behavioral tolerance* and *pharmacological tolerance*.

8. ***Conditioned compensatory responses*** are understood as homeostatic adjustments elicited by drug-predictive cues of familiar environments. When rats and humans experience the drug in a novel environment (one that does *not* contain drug-predictive cues), tolerance disappears and the drug again becomes more effective.

9. Conditioned compensatory responses have been shown to be a factor in tolerance to ethyl alcohol.

10. Drugs affect the immune system that partly controls body temperature. Drug tolerance conditioning models have been successfully applied to conditioning body temperature changes.

11. The expression of food allergies is likely controlled in part by conditioned stimuli in novel and familiar environments.

DISCUSSION QUESTIONS

14. Ted drinks five beers at a party while his twin brother Ned consumes the same amount of alcohol going to different bars. Given equal histories with alcohol (and, hence, equivalent amounts of alcohol tolerance), which twin would you predict would be the most wasted after five drinks? Why? Under what conditions might they be similarly affected?

15. What might a person do to enhance the effectiveness of *any* drug they are taking?

CHAPTER SUMMARY

1. Conditioned suppression, typically involving tone-shock pairings, is a common way of measuring conditioned emotional responses. In conditioned suppression, a suppression ratio can vary from ~0.50 (no conditioning) to 0.0 (complete suppression, excellent conditioning).

2. Pavlov's *Law of Strength* is that higher intensity USs, higher intensity CSs, and shorter CS-US interstimulus intervals produce better conditioning.

3. In classical eyeblink conditioning of rats, rabbits, and humans, tones or lights (CSs) signal an aversive air puff to the eye (US), and a conditioned eyeblink response (CR) results.

4. In conditioned taste aversions in rats, humans, and other animals, a flavor (the CS) is paired with toxin (the US), and a learned aversion to the flavor is the conditioned response. Taste aversions conditioning is characterized by one-trial, long-delay learning.

5. The most common way of assessing how much conditioning has occurred is to measure resistance to extinction by counting the number of extinction trials it takes to extinguish the response.

6. Five rules that govern conditioning are the number of conditioning trials, CS and US intensity, the duration of the CS-US interval, and whether the CS is presented before or after the US.

7. CSs and USs can be paired in six ways: forward conditioning, trace conditioning, simultaneous conditioning, embedded conditioning, backward conditioning, and temporal conditioning.

8. Based on differences in higher cortical functioning, humans have been alleged to be the only animals that exhibit voluntary behavior.

9. Due to their interactions, the CNS, ANS, neuroendocrine, and immune systems are now thought of as components of an integrative system, thereby blurring the traditional distinction between voluntary and involuntary physiological systems.

10. A psychosomatic disorder is defined as a somatic, or physiological problem, caused by a conditioned response that has been elicited by conditioned stimuli. Pavlovian conditioning provides a defensible account of psychosomatic disorders.

11. Psychoneuroimmunology is a research area that integrates physiology and behavior.

12. The T-lymphocytes in an animal's *immune system* recognize and resist toxins and infectious organisms by attacking and destroying foreign protein.

13. Ader showed that saccharin could act as a CS that could be used to condition the immune system, producing either conditioned immunosuppression or conditioned immunofacilitation.

14. Asthma can be classically conditioned in guinea pigs and humans.

15. A placebo effect is a conditioned response that mimics real treatment effects.

16. Drugs are unconditioned stimuli that when taken in various environments provide the occasion for conditioning.

17. Tolerance, a reduction in the intensity of the effect of a dose of a drug over repeated trials can be broken down into pharmacological tolerance and behavioral tolerance.

18. Drugs (including morphine and alcohol) taken in familiar environments result in conditioned compensatory responses that reduce the effectiveness of the drug.

19. Body temperature and food allergies can be conditioned.

KEY TERMS

CHAPTER 5

Complexities of Conditioning

Sometime in late March, after the Indian violets had come, we would be gathering [acorns] on the mountain and the wind, raw and mean, would change for just a second. It would touch your face as soft as a feather. It had an earth smell. You knew springtime was on the way. . . .

Then the yellow dandelions poked up everywhere along the lower hollow, and we picked them for greens—which are good when you mix them with fireweed greens, poke salat, and nettles. Nettles make the best greens, but have little tiny hairs on them that sting you all over when you're picking. . . .

Everything growing wild is a hundred times stronger than tame ones. We pulled the wild onions from the ground and just a handful would carry more flavor than a bushel of tame onions. . . . Bitterroot has big lavender-pink faces with yellow centers that hug the ground, while moonflowers are hidden deep in the hollow, long-stemmed and swaying like willows with pink-red fringes on top.

Forrest Carter, *The Education of Little Tree* (1976, p. 100)

We have seen that simple conditioned responses may result when one CS enters into association with one US. It is in fact the case, however, that environments seldom present us with such solitary, "simple" stimulus events as seen in the laboratory. Nature, as a Cherokee Indian named Little Tree learned in his first few years of life, is complicated. Unlike laboratory experiments, knowing seasons and where to find plants and how they taste and whether they are poisonous is not an easy subject matter to master. Nature doesn't often break down stimuli into discrete elements.

Does predictability disappear under these conditions? That is, when, outside of a controlled laboratory environment, *several* stimuli are placed in contiguous and/or contingent arrangements, does conditioning occur? How about when a stimulus is one that the animal is already familiar with? Let's take some of these questions in turn.

Ecological Validity. We saw in the previous chapter that laboratory learning experiments *can* be designed to investigate real-world problems, such as conditioning taste aversions, asthma, the immune system, and drug responses. And yet, experimenting on the learning abilities of caged animals raises a number of problems. This research appears to lack ecological validity. To be ecologically valid, an experiment should ask an animal to learn a task that it is likely to encounter in its ecological niche. Learning about foods, the location of predators, and the context in which they occur are examples of ecologically valid tasks.

How Does an Animal's Prior Learning Affect New Learning? Most of what we learn in the real world is an accumulation of a lifetime's experiences. Yet most laboratory learning experiments use young *naïve* animals—ones that haven't experienced any of the conditions to which they will be exposed. This is to keep what animals have previously learned from biasing the experiment's outcome. However, the problem of how prior learning affects subsequent learning is an important one with practical implications. College algebra teachers, for example, are often heard complaining about the way their students were taught algebra in high school. What students previously learned, they argue, often interferes with performance in college classrooms. What is needed is research that specifically addresses how prior learning affects new learning. Many of the experiments described in this chapter address the question of how prior learning affects new learning.

Why Are There Apparent Failures of Conditioning? Why are some species more easily conditioned in certain environments than others, and what are we to make of apparent failures of conditioning and learning. For example, without a spell-checker on my computer I now fear that I'll go to my grave forever misspelling certain "problem words." How is it possible that humans are able to remember a face over a period of many years even after a brief meeting while an acquaintance's name may escape them even as they interact? Why is it that we can conjure up a face by merely hearing the person's voice on the phone yet have a hard time making name-face associations? Some non-human animal experiments point to similar problems. To what extent do these observations present a problem for learning theory?

Let's now turn to some complexities of conditioning.

LEARNING AND RELEARNING: EFFECTS OF PRIOR EXPERIENCE ON CONDITIONING NEW RESPONSES

We begin by looking at an example of complex human behavior in Box 5.1. Throughout this chapter we return for further analysis to this example of taste aversion conditioning. After reading it you will likely have several hypotheses for Tracy's, Candace's, and Carlos's behavior. (You may want to take a minute to jot down in the margins your best guesses for their differently learned responses.) Their behavior can be explained by applying the results of laboratory animal experiments. Unless you already have a good background in learning theory, you will probably be surprised by the range and sophistication of arguments that can be brought to bear on their human behavior based on laboratory animal experiments. By the end of the chapter, you will have a better idea why Candace, Tracy, and Carlos learned, remembered, and behaved as they did.

Latent Inhibition: The CS Preexposure Effect and the US Preexposure Effect

Pavlov was the first experimenter to observe that a novel CS was more easily conditioned than a familiar one. He found that a dog that had previously heard a bell, whistle, or metronome of a particular timbre and intensity re-

BOX 5.1   LEARNING ABOUT PIZZA

Three years ago, Candace and Tracy, identical twins living in a rural part of Nebraska, came to Miami, Florida, to visit their cousin Carlos. All three had previously eaten pepperoni pizza and were hungry for it, so Carlos took them to his favorite restaurant, Momma Rollo's. Neither Candace nor Tracy had eaten at Momma Rollo's before this occasion.

In addition to the pepperoni pizza, Candace and Carlos each ordered a can of Dr. Spicey while Tracy drank only water. Since Dr. Spicey was unavailable in rural Nebraska, neither Candace nor Tracy had ever before experienced its distinctive taste. All ate three slices of the pepperoni pizza.

Hours later, the twins became sick, experiencing both nausea and vomiting. Carlos felt okay and a phone call home confirmed that the twins' mother was sick with the same symptoms. Because Carlos did not get sick but their mother was, Candace and Tracy reluctantly concluded that their meal at Momma Rollo's did *not* make them sick. They probably had a stomach virus they had brought from Nebraska.

After this incident the following changes in their behaviors were noted:

1. For several months after returning to Nebraska, neither Candace nor Tracy had any desire to eat pizza. Why?*

2. Carlos returned to Momma Rollo's three weeks later and ate pepperoni pizza. Why the difference between Carlos's and the twins' behavior?

3. (Assume that prior to their experience at Momma Rollo's, the twins had had identical taste preferences.) After several months elapsed, the twins once again began to eat pizza. Candace ordered a cheese topping only, and Tracy, a sausage pizza. Why did neither order pepperoni? What is your hypothesis as to why Candace ordered a cheese topping rather than sausage?

4. Two days after the illness incident (while still in Florida), Tracy drank a Dr. Spicey at Tom's apartment and loved it. Candace still dislikes the taste of Dr. Spicey three years later. Why the difference?

5. Candace dislikes Dr. Spicey more than she dislikes pepperoni pizza. Why the difference?

6. Candace and Tracy visited Carlos a year after the illness episode. Candace says she will eat pizza but would rather not go back to Momma Rollo's; Tracy also says she will eat pizza and, furthermore, is indifferent about the choice of restaurant. Why do the twins respond to Momma Rollo's restaurant differently?

7. Candace says, "Just mentioning Dr. Spicey or seeing the Dr. Spicey can makes me ill." Why does Candace not want to talk about her taste aversion?

*You probably know the answer to this question already since taste aversion conditioning was discussed in Chapter 4. Other experiments presented in this chapter will help you answer the remaining questions.

quired more CS-US trials to acquire a conditioned response to that stimulus. The question is, why are novel stimuli more easily conditioned?

Many experimenters have since tried to answer this question, including those who called the phenomenon **latent inhibition** (Lubow, 1989; Lubow & Moore, 1959) and others (Albert & Ayers, 1989) who called it the **CS preexposure effect.**[1] Both terms are defined the same, as a reduction in conditioning caused by familiarity of the conditioned stimulus. Similar differences are also found to exist between novel and familiar unconditioned stimuli. Previous exposure to a drug, or an electric shock, or food make them less effective in conditioning experiments. This phenomenon is called the **US preexposure effect** (Baker, Mercier, Gabel, & Baker, 1981; Randich & LoLordo, 1979).

The procedures that produce both the CS preexposure effect and the US preexposure effect are diagrammed in Figure 5.1. A no-preexposure group (top) serves as a control group; it has a CS-US pairing that results in a conditioned response of a given magnitude. The CS preposure group receives several CS preexposures prior to the CS-US pairing, producing a smaller CR than the control group. The same is true for the US preexposure treatment (bottom). As a general rule, more preexposure to either a CS or US produces a larger preexposure effect.

Why Are Familiar Stimuli Less Easily Conditioned?   Hypotheses abound as to why novel stimuli are more easily conditioned than familiar stimuli. The question is an important one. With apologies to Pavlov, the adage "you can't teach an old dog new tricks" comes to mind. (Probably the saying refers more to "being set in one's ways" than it does to the inability of an aging brain to learn new tasks.) Nevertheless, prior experience does influence later learning, and the latent inhibition phenomenon may be the most elementary demonstration of this point.

Nonassociative Theory of Latent Inhibition

Students often confuse habituation with latent inhibition, and for good reason. The two phenomena are similar. Habituation refers to response diminution following repeated presentations of a stimulus, while latent inhibition refers to lowered associability when a familiar stimulus is used in conditioning. The orienting response is diminished in both cases; humans and animals so habituated appear to pay less attention to the familiar stimulus.

---

[1]Unfortunately there are often two terms for the same phenomenon. We've already seen conditioned emotional responses and conditioned suppression. Both conditioned suppression, and the CS preexposure effect are descriptive of procedures, while "latent inhibition," and "emotion" refer to unobservable events.

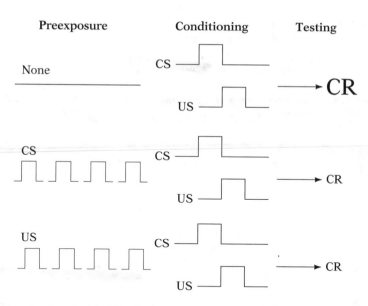

FIGURE 5.1 Latent Inhibition

Preexposure to either a CS (middle) or US (bottom) reduces the association of these stimuli during conditioning relative to the association of novel stimuli that have not been preexposed (top). For illustrative purposes, four preexposures, and one-trial conditioning, are shown.

One theory proposed to account for the latent inhibition effect, then, is a nonassociative one. A stimulus that has become habituated and that captures less attention during conditioning is less associable than novel stimuli to which attention is directed. Novel stimuli are more *surprising* (Wagner, 1976). The habituation hypothesis has a particularly difficult time accounting for the US preexposure effect, though. By definition, USs are less susceptible to habituation and are more "attention-getting" than are CSs. And yet preexposed USs, including electric shock (Baker & Macintosh, 1977) and illness-inducing chemicals (Suarez & Barker, 1976) do not work as well in conditioning as do novel shock and novel toxins. Both CS and US preexposure effects seem to be better accounted for by associative theories.

Associative Theories of Latent Inhibition

A nonassociative theory involving reduced attention-capturing properties of familiar stimuli has been discussed. Let's next look at two associative theories of latent inhibition:

THE FAR SIDE   By GARY LARSON

High above the hushed crowd, Rex tried to remain
focused. Still, he couldn't shake one nagging
thought: He was an old dog and this was a new trick.

1. *Interference Theory of Latent Inhibition.* In this theory, presenting the CS alone allows the CS to become associated with background contextual cues. The CS thereby effectively becomes part of the context. By merging into the context, the signal-to-noise ratio of the CS is diminished. The now-familiar CS is less a signal and more a part of the background, thereby reducing its associative potential (Grahame, Barnet, Gunther, & Miller, 1994; Rudy, 1994; Wagner, 1976).

   One prediction from this theory is that the more preexposure to the CS, the more associations would be made and the greater would be the latent inhibition effect. Just such a finding has been reported (Ayres et al., 1992). These researchers preexposed different groups of rats to the CS for varying time periods in conditioned suppression experiments and found predictably varying amounts of latent inhibition. Habituation of the context cues also increased the signal value of the CS. In summary, prior associations of the CS with other contextual cues are presumed to interfere with the formation of new associations.

2. *Learned Irrelevance Theory of Latent Inhibition.* A second associative theory also posits that associations are made when the CS is presented alone. The animal learns that the CS does not predict anything new; hence, an "association" is made between the CS and "nothing new." According to this theory, to an information-processing animal, the CS signals safety (Kalat, 1977; Kalat & Rozin, 1973), or becomes irrelevant (Baker & Macintosh, 1977; Best & Gemberling, 1977).

An implication of this theory of latent inhibition is that animals have expectations. For example, rats and other animals are hesitant the first time they taste a novel flavor. This **neophobia** (fear of the new) reflects a built-in expectation "to be wary of novel flavors." Given this biological predisposition to expect aversive consequences, when nothing bad happens, the rat associates the flavor with "nothing bad happening" and learns that the new flavor is safe (Kalat, 1977; Kalat & Rozin, 1973).

3. *Retrieval Failure Hypothesis of Latent Inhibition.* An animal that is preexposed to a stimulus forms a memory of that stimulus within a particular context. Conditioning occurs with that same stimulus in a *different* context. If you change contextual cues either during preexposure, conditioning, or testing, latent inhibition is disrupted. Such experiments have led to a *retrieval failure* hypothesis of latent inhibition (Baker & Mercier, 1982; Bouton, 1993, 1994; Rosas & Bouton, 1997). This hypothesis proposes that latent inhibition is not a deficit in acquisition, but rather a deficit in retrieval from memory. That is, whatever associations are learned about the CS during preexposure do not interfere with acquisition of CS-US associations during conditioning. However, performance during the extinction testing may be based on associations from preexposure or from conditioning, depending on which memory is retrieved.

Another line of evidence supports the retrieval failure hypothesis. A long time delay between preexposure and conditioning (or between conditioning and extinction testing) disrupts latent inhibition (Ackil, Carmen, Bakner & Riccio, 1992). The idea here is that with longer intervals the preexposure memory becomes more difficult to retrieve, and therefore interfere less.

A Case Study of Latent Inhibition

The first day of class in a new school, you are awash in a sea of new faces, new desks, smells, and sounds. Alert and excited, you are processing your environment at an incredible rate. You make many orienting responses to rapidly changing stimuli. If you are a new student in a new country, the amount of new information may be overwhelming. The college classroom context in which you find yourself is composed of a combination of new and old experiences. That is, classrooms have features in common with most institutional buildings. In this classroom, you may notice windows (if most other classrooms you sat in did not have them) or not notice windows (if most other classrooms you have experienced did have them). Notice padded seats? Amphitheatre style room? The signaling strength of any stimulus in this new classroom is related to its novelty as well as to its intensity.

Algebra, Algebra, and More Algebra.   This new algebra classroom signals other previously learned associations as well. For example, you experienced algebra failures in the high school classroom: the word algebra written on the blackboard and textbook, formulas, and other students who by their verbal and nonverbal behavior expressed the anxiety you now feel. The instructor writes on the board a "familiar" equation:

$$y = ax + b$$

You recognize the equation as one you have seen before but were unable to master in a previous class. Your heart sinks, as does your performance.

Skip to the end of the semester. You now realize that only with great difficulty were you able to understand this particular equation, $y = ax + b$. By way of comparison, you more easily learned several new equations (i.e., novel ones that you had not previously seen). Why? Which of the following theories best accounts for your behavior?

Habituation Hypothesis.   According to the habituation hypothesis, you would be less likely to learn new associations to familiar stimuli because familiar stimuli are attended to less than novel stimuli. I doubt it. Evidence to the contrary would be the sinking feeling you had when that equation was written on the board. No lack of orienting response there! Rather, the evidence presented here leads to the conclusion that the difficulty of forming new associations to the equation $y = ax + b$ was not caused by habituation to the stimulus.

Learned Irrelevance Hypothesis.   According to the learned irrelevance hypothesis, you had more trouble learning $y = ax + b$ because the equation had been previously associated with other events and no longer predicted anything new when reencountered in the college classroom. Hardly! We've already determined that you associated the formula $y = ax + b$ with anxiety and feelings of failure. Nothing irrelevant about this particular equation. In this particular example, the learned irrelevance hypothesis does not apply.[2]

---

[2]You could make the case that for some individuals, $y = ax + b$ is both familiar and is "irrelevant" in the sense that the student verbalizes no interest in math (i.e., "math is irrelevant to what I want to do with my life"). The *learned irrelevance hypothesis* does not address this cognitive usage of the term *irrelevance*.

Associative Interference and Retrieval Failure Hypotheses. One clue to understanding how prior associations with a stimulus can influence new associations with that stimulus is readily evident in this example. Stimuli in previous algebra classrooms shared common contextual features with the equation $y = ax + b$. Presumably, the equation, blackboards, textbooks, and anxiety became associated together to form a context (we see how later). The "new" classroom is a complex CS eliciting both anxiety and "feelings of failure." The new teacher's job, moreover, is somehow to extricate the latently inhibited $y = ax + b$ stimulus from the "math phobia stimulus context" in which it occurs. Until that is done, new associations to the equation will be learned only with great difficulty. At test time, it is important that the right memories be retrieved; ideally, the ones learned in the college classroom should not have to compete with ones learned in high school.

Are you able to further apply what you have learned about latent inhibition? Box 5.1 (Question 5) asks you to provide a hypothesis to account for the fact that after a sickness experience Candace dislikes Dr. Spicey more than she dislikes pepperoni pizza. Reread the account of conditioning and see if you can relate latent inhibition to Candace's observed behavior. Again, for future reference, you might want to jot down your hypothesis in the margin.

Sensory Preconditioning

In the preceding example, the observant reader may have wondered how blackboards, the word algebra, formulas, textbooks, and faces can become associated together in a college classroom. All are stimuli, but where are the unconditioned stimuli (such as food, electric shock, illness-inducing toxin, and so forth) that we have noted in previous examples of conditioning? How can CSs become associated with each other in the absence of USs? Is a CS_1-CS_2 association possible?

An honest answer is that our theories of association are not adequate to answer this question. Recall that John Locke merely asserted that the sun was an associative complex of warm, round, and red stimulus characteristics. When this problem is brought into the laboratory, we typically measure CS-CS associations only indirectly. One method called *sensory preconditioning* is outlined in Figure 5.2.

The sensory preconditioning groups (top left) pairs two CSs (CS_1-CS_2) before a CS-US conditioning trial. The control treatment for this sensory preconditioning treatment is to present both CS_1 and CS_2 separately (bottom left). Then both groups are conditioned to CS_1 in the same way. Finally, during testing, both CS_1 and CS_2 are presented in extinction, and responses measured. The sensory preconditioning treatment produces a CR to both CS_1 and CS_2 (top right). In the control group there is a CR to the CS_1 but not CS_2. We

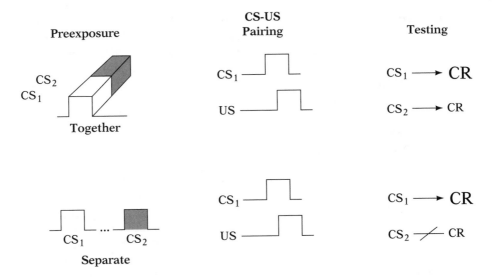

FIGURE 5.2   Sensory Preconditioning

Preexposure to CS₁ and CS₂ simultaneously presented together (top left) constitutes the sensory preconditioning treatment. The control for this treatment is to present CS₁ and CS₂ separately (bottom left). Following a CS-US pairing in both groups (middle panels), during testing (right panels) the sensory preconditioning treatment produces a CR to both CS₁ and CS₂ (top right), and a CR to the CS₁ but not CS₂ in the control group (bottom right).

can conclude that CS_1 and CS_2 had become associated during sensory preconditioning, such that conditioning to CS_1 had in some way transferred to CS_2.

Sensory Preconditioning and Background Context.   The importance of sensory preconditioning lies in the fact that it helps us better understand "background context." Context can be thought of as a stimulus complex of associated elements—associated because they are experienced together. (See Figure 3.1, cell d, on page 69.) When we attempt to condition a CS with a CS, a CS with a US, or a US with a US, the contextual background, held together in associative fashion, is always present. The context in which conditioning occurs is also conditioned (Archer & Sjoden, 1982; Bouton & Swartzentruber, 1986).

Let us return to the algebra classroom. It is unlikely that a student can ever "start over" or follow an instructor's advice to "forget everything you have learned [meaning mislearned] up to now." Too many contextual stimuli with prior aversive associations are present. Though relearning is possible, one can't merely wipe the slate clean and start over. From what we have learned in Chapter 3, one form of remediation would be to extinguish aversive conditioned responses by presenting the stimuli ($y = ax + b$, the blackboard, etc.) without the negative USs. This procedure would begin to extinguish the emotional responses that were previously conditioned to these stimuli (Bouton & Bolles, 1979a, 1979b). Sounds like therapy, and we talk about that in a later chapter.

Higher-Order Conditioning

In the preceding college classroom example, blackboards, formulas, textbooks, and the student's anxiety were identified as stimuli that had become associated together. "Anxiety" and "fear" are not neutral stimuli. But anxiety and fear are part of math phobia. Given that algebra-related stimuli are initially neutral, by what process can students form fear associations to them?

In the previous chapter, we saw that when a tone is paired with an electric shock in rats (and, in Box 4.1, when a "dee-doo" sound is associated with a nasty sled ride), the auditory stimulus comes to produce a conditioned fear response, or conditioned emotional response. In the college classroom, fear of failure is best understood as such a response. Next we show how a conditioned fear response can, in turn, be used to condition associations with new CSs.

Higher-order conditioning, first described by Pavlov, is a conditioning process in which a CS acquires unconditioned stimulus properties. The procedures differ, but the outcome of higher-order conditioning resembles sensory preconditioning in one respect: Both are associative processes in which conditioning occurs in the absence of an unconditioned stimulus.

Figure 5.3. illustrates a three-step process that produces two levels of higher-order conditioning. We'll use an experiment reported by Pavlov (1927/1960) to illustrate the procedure. In Step 1, a dog was conditioned to salivate to the sound of a metronome (CS_1) in pairings with food (the US). Then, to demonstrate *second-order conditioning*, "a black square [CS_2] is held in front of the dog for 10 seconds, and after an interval of 15 seconds the metronome is sounded during 30 seconds" (Pavlov, 1927, p. 34). This same sequence was repeated for 10 trials. On the 10th trial Pavlov reported that the dog salivated 5.5 drops to the black square, compared to a range of 9.5 to 13.5 drops of conditioned salivation to the sound of the metronome. Note that the black square had never been directly associated with food, yet a response had been conditioned to it.

Pavlov (1927) then reported the results of another researcher in his laboratory named Foursikov, who reported *conditioning of the third order*, shown in the bottom panel of Figure 5.3. Foursikov elaborated a leg-withdrawal conditioned response (CS_1 = touching the hind paw, US = briefly shocking the front paw, CR = withdrawing the front paw when the hind paw is touched). He then presented the sound of bubbling water (CS_2) followed by touching

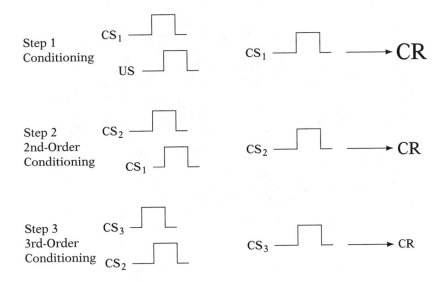

FIGURE 5.3   Higher-Order Conditioning

A stimulus associated with the US in Step 1 acquires US-like properties. Note that even in the absence of a US in Steps 2 and 3, conditioning nevertheless occurs because the CSs have acquired US-like properties. The CR become progressively smaller.

the hind paw (CS₁). As shown in Figure 5.3, second-order conditioning was measured. Finally, Foursikov presented a tone (CS₃), which he paired with the sound of bubbling water (CS₂). After a number of pairings, CS₃ (the tone), when sounded alone, produced the conditioned response of leg withdrawal. Such conditioning of the third order, shown in Figure 5.3, and the more common second-order conditioning are collectively known as higher-order conditioning.

Significance of Higher-Order Conditioning.   The significance of higher-order conditioning is twofold. First, the process allows conditioning in the absence of an unconditioned stimulus. Second, higher-order conditioning is another demonstration that prior conditioning experiences can continue to influence the present. After "neutral" stimuli have been conditioned, they, in turn, can be used to condition other responses. Box 5.2 contains several examples.

Let's return to the examples of words as CSs. Most humans inhabit language-rich environments. We know that language attains meaning through associative processes, so let's look at the possibilities presented by the higher-order conditioning of language. Referring back to Step 1 in Figure

Box 5.2 How Symbols Acquire Meaning

Is money an important part of your ecological niche? A fistful of $100 bills gets the attention of most of us. What about a ¥100 (Japanese yen) or £100 (English pounds)? Obviously, the value of any given currency is relative to the values of other currencies. If you have specific knowledge of exchange rates (that *associate* the value of one currency with the value of other currencies), you may already know whether $100 is more or less than £100 or ¥100.*

How does money attain value? Aside from international macroeconomic considerations that fine tune each currency's value, if you have lived much of your life in the United States, a $1 bill is a CS (a symbolic token) that has been associated with "biologically meaningful" events (USs) in one's niche. As a child you learned the value

of money by its association with candy, toys, and clothes and later with food, beverages, perfume and other cosmetics, sex, music, shelter, tuition, automobiles, and other stimuli and activities that can be purchased in our culture.

In a later chapter, we'll learn that *secondary reinforcers* attain value through Pavlov's process of *higher-order conditioning*. Money is one of the most important *secondary reinforcers*. Language is the most important secondary reinforcer governing human behavior. Just talking about money makes me salivate. Can you identify any conditioning of the third order in your past? Using the concept of higher-order conditioning, can you describe why someone might "fall in love with a car"? Finally, can you explain why not all people feel the same about the following artificial symbols?

*¥100 = approximately 7¢; £100 = approximately $150.

HIV+   BMW   ♱

158

5.3, let CS_1 be the word *no* and the "biologically meaningful" US be a stimulus complex represented by a parental figure. The parental figure's voice (intonation, intensity, etc.) or the parent's withdrawal of affection (or physical punishment or a "time-out") is a potentially aversive US that enters into association with the word *no*. In Step 1, then, the word *no* acquires punishing/ fear-inducing properties not unlike what a tone acquires in tone-shock conditioning.

CS_1, the word *no*, can now be used in association with other neutral stimuli in second-order conditioning during Phase 2. Among other stimuli that can be conditioned by the word *no* are other words such as *don't, wrong, incorrect, stop,* and *yuk*. More to the point, the conditioned emotional responses associated with the word *no* can now attach to other neutral stimuli.

The word *algebra* was conditioned through the process of higher-order conditioning. *No, wrong,* and *incorrect* with attendant conditioned emotional responses became associated with the formulas and equations found in a book labeled *algebra*.

Overshadowing

What would happen if two novel CSs were presented simultaneously? Would both become conditioned, or would only one be attended to, the other merging into the background? Pavlov and others have done these experiments using an *overshadowing* procedure (Pavlov, 1927/1960, p. 269ff). **Overshadowing** occurs when two CSs are conditioned simultaneously and one of them acquires more *associative strength* than the other. The CS that conditions best is said to overshadow the other CS. What is meant by the associative strength, or associative potential, of a stimulus? Simply put, the concept refers to how well one stimulus enters into association with another stimulus.

The basic design to demonstrate overshadowing is shown in Figure 5.4. The result of conditioning the two stimuli simultaneously (top) is compared with the results of conditioning each stimulus separately (middle and bottom). In the example given, CS_1 competes with and captures more of the associative potential of the US than does CS_2. Notice in Figure 5.4 that the CRs are greater to both CSs when they are conditioned separately compared to when they are conditioned together. In the overshadowing group, a fixed amount of associative strength of the US is shared by both CSs; hence, the CRs are of less magnitude than when they are conditioned separately.

Salience. Because in this experiment CS_1 was more easily conditioned than CS_2, CS_1 is said to be more *salient* than CS_2. The **salience** of a stimulus refers to its relative associability—its associative potential. The salience of a stimulus depends on many factors, including the quality and intensity of the stimulus, the context in which the animal experiences the stimulus, and peculiarities of the evolved nervous system of the animal. Let's look at some details.

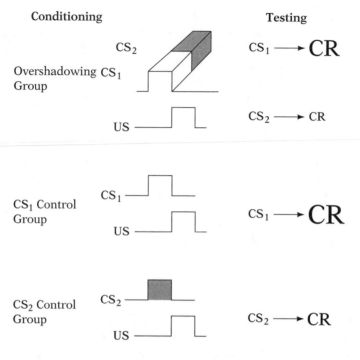

FIGURE 5.4   Overshadowing

In the overshadowing group CS_1 and CS_2 are presented simultaneously during conditioning, while two control groups present each CS separately. In the overshadowing group CS_1 is said to overshadow CS_2 because the CR is larger to CS_1 than to CS_2. The CR is also greater to CS_1 than to CS_2 when CS_1 and CS_2 are conditioned separately (compare middle and lower control groups). Hence, CS_1 is more *salient* than CS_2.

When two or more CSs are presented simultaneously, which stimulus will overshadow and which will be overshadowed are best predicted by Pavlov's Law of Strength. That is, the most intense conditioned stimulus captures most of the *associative potential* of the US. (Likewise, more intense USs have more associative potential than less intense USs). Between-species differences in the perception of visual, auditory, taste, and smell stimuli also play an important role in which stimuli overshadow and which get overshadowed. Pavlov (1927/1960), for example, reported that in salivary conditioning, dogs associated food better with auditory than with visual CSs (i.e., sounds rather than sights were more easily learned). Equating stimulus intensity across modalities is problematic. This makes it difficult to judge whether any given auditory stimulus is more intense than a given visual stimulus. We re-

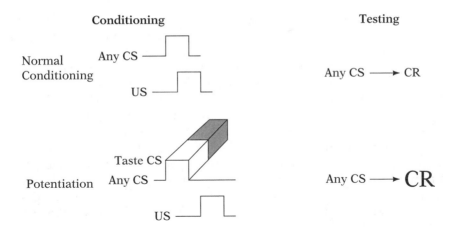

FIGURE 5.5   Potentiation

> The conditioned response to any conditioned stimulus (a sight, sound, or
> odor) can be enhanced if it is accompanied by a taste stimulus. The taste
> stimulus is said to potentiate the CR to another stimulus.

turn to this question and the possibility of cross-modality differences in overshadowing later in this chapter.[3]

Potentiation

Overshadowing demonstrates that not all stimuli are equally associable with
a given US. If two flavor stimuli (for example, a pepperoni pizza and Dr.
Spicey) were tasted during the same meal, likely one would overshadow the
other in association with an aversive event. But flavors have other unique
properties not shared by other stimuli. For reasons that are not readily apparent, when a flavor stimulus is simultaneously presented to an animal with another stimulus (e.g., a sight, sound, or odor), *potentiation* rather than
overshadowing is the outcome. **Potentiation** refers to a phenomenon that a
sight, or sound, or odor is conditioned better in the presence of a taste stimulus than by itself (see Figure 5.5).

    Rat experiments by Mark Bouton and his colleagues (Bouton, Dunlap, &
Swartzentruber, 1987) and by Michael Best and his colleagues (Best, Best, &

---

[3]Assume that the complex stimulus is a fruit salad composed of grapes, pineapple, banana
chunks, nuts, marshmellows, and Jello. If you were to get sick after eating the fruit salad, would
you be likely to attribute more of the sickness to one of the elements—let's say the pineapple
chunks—than to another component part? If so, why? This example pinpoints the problems of
trying to equate stimulus intensity both within (i.e., flavor) and across modalities.

Mickley, 1973; Best, Brown, & Sowell, 1984) have revealed the special power of flavors to potentiate the conditioning of background environments. In Best's experiments, some rats drink a novel saccharin flavor in a distinctive environment. They were then made ill, as well as other rats that hadn't tasted the saccharin. Following recovery, when the rats were put back in, those that had previously experienced the saccharin there drank less water in that environment than did the control rats. Associations with the environmental cues had been made stronger (potentiated) by the presence of saccharin.

Return with me to Momma Rollo's (Box 5.1, page 148). Many flavors were experienced there, and some were conditioned aversively. Did any of the flavors potentiate the conditioning of other stimuli? Hint: Based on the phenomenon of potentiation, can you come up with a hypothesis explaining why Candace was more hesitant than Tracy to return to Momma Rollo's?

Blocking

We have seen that stimulus intensity best predicts which stimulus will overshadow and which will be overshadowed when both are paired with a US. What would happen if CS_1 were familiar and CS_2 novel? Will CS_2 overshadow CS_1 or vice versa? The theory of latent inhibition would lead us to predict that when both are presented simultaneously, a novel stimulus will overshadow a familiar stimulus.

Let's test this hypothesis by first conditioning an association to CS_1. Then we'll simultaneously pair CS_1 with CS_2 in an second stage, as shown in Figure 5.6. Kamin (1968), for example, used a conditioned suppression design in which he first conditioned rats to fear a tone (CS_1) using electric shock (US). Then he simultaneously presented the tone (CS_1) with a novel light (CS_2) followed by electric shock. Remember that our prediction is that the novel light will capture most of the associative strength of the shock (US).

The results may surprise you. We predicted that a novel stimulus would overshadow the familiar stimulus. Kamin found just the opposite—**blocking**—that prior conditioning to CS_1 blocks conditioning to CS_2 when CS_1 and CS_2 are conditioned in compound (Kamin, 1968, 1969).

Why did the novel light fail to be conditioned? One hypothesis is that the novel light is a redundant stimulus, not useful in predicting the occurrence of electric shock. That is, the tone already predicts shock, and the rat may simply ignore the light when it occurs. Why is the CR to CS_1 larger in the blocking group than in the control treatment? Because CS_1 captures all the associative potential of the US in the blocking group, while in the control treatment the associative potential of the US was split between the two CSs.

Let us return to the algebra classroom. The college teacher says that she will use a different (new) method to help you learn a familiar (previously conditioned) mathematical equation. For the sake of the argument, let us assume that the previous CS (the equation in question) was aversively conditioned by association with anxiety-inducing stimuli ("wrong," "no," "incorrect," and a

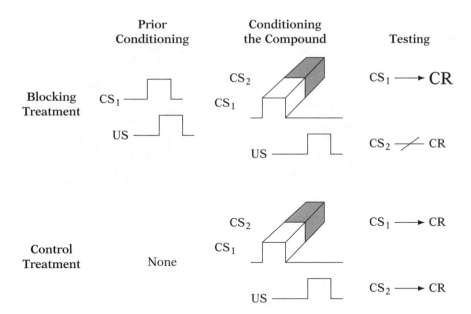

FIGURE 5.6   Blocking

A blocking procedure begins by conditioning a response to CS$_1$ (top left). A control group (bottom left) has no prior conditioning treatment. Then, CS$_1$ and CS$_2$ are conditioned in a compound in both groups (middle panels). When tested separately (right panels), both elements of the compound (that is, both CS$_1$ and CS$_2$) show conditioning (bottom right). Prior conditioning to CS$_1$, however, blocked the association to CS$_2$ (top right).

grade of D). Given Kamin's findings about blocking, what is your prediction concerning the success of new conditioning? This is one more reason that it is difficult for an old dog to learn new tricks.

Blocking or Augmentation?   Before concluding that prior conditioning always blocks new conditioning, we should look beyond Kamin's experiments. For example, recent studies using blocking designs in taste aversion conditioning have produced surprising results. Focus on Research 5.1 briefly describes experiments (Batsell & Batson, 1999; Batson & Batsell, in press) that have led these researchers to propose a new phenomenon called *augmentation*. Augmentation appears to be the opposite of blocking. More will be said later in this chapter about how the results of experiments can change when stimuli with very different properties are used in conditioning experiments.

FOCUS ON RESEARCH 5.1

Dr. Robert Batsell   *Dr. John Batson*
Kalamazoo College   *Furman University*

Historically, research in taste-aversion learning has produced outcomes that challenge the findings observed in more traditional forms of classical conditioning. For example, Garcia and Koelling's "bright, noisy, tasty water" experiment (1967) demonstrated that certain conditioned stimuli are better associated with one type of unconditioned stimulus than another. Even though research in taste-aversion learning has been conducted for almost 50 years, new studies continue to show differences across conditioning paradigms. For example, recent experiments from our labs that use procedures similar to Kamin's "blocking" design have produced results that are opposite of what you would expect.

In our initial experiments, we examined the effects of first preconditioning an aversion to an odor: the treatment rats drank a water solution scented with almond odor while the control rats drank unscented water. Both groups were made ill immediately after consuming these fluids. During the second conditioning phase, both groups drank a compound solution containing a bitter taste (denatonium saccharide) along with the almond odor. During testing, all rats were given the opportunity to drink the bitter denatonium. Although the control rats weren't especially fond of the bitter taste, they drank a little of it. The treatment rats drank almost none.

If Kamin's blocking had occurred, prior conditioning to the odor should block the formation of an aversion to the "irrelevant" stimulus, the bitter denatonium. That is not what happened. Thus, in the treatment group, odor preconditioning did not block learning the taste; instead, it produced a profound taste aversion. We have labeled this strong aversion conditioning within the traditional blocking design as augmentation (Batsell & Batson, 1999; Batson & Batsell, in press).

As a final word, it is important to note that both of us teach and do research in undergraduate institutions, rather than large research universities. The paper we publish are the result of collaborative research with many undergraduate students who work in our laboratories.

Interim Summary

1. Familiar stimuli are less easily conditioned than novel stimuli. This phenomenon is known as **latent inhibition**, the **CS preexposure effect**, and the **US preexposure effect**.

2. Both nonassociative and associative theories help account for latent inhibition. These include habituation, interference, learned irrelevance theories, and retrieval failure. Latent inhibition is best explained by the ideas of associative interference and retrieval failure.

3. **Sensory preconditioning** is a demonstration that two CSs can become associated with each other. In this procedure, CS_1 and CS_2 are presented together. Then, following conditioning of CS_1 with a US, the transfer of associative effects from CS_1 to CS_2 is seen by measuring the CR to CS_2.

4. **Higher-order conditioning** is a procedure in which CS_1 acquires US-like properties and can then be used to condition CS_2. CS_1 is first conditioned with a US. Then CS_2 is paired with CS_1 until a CR can be measured to CS_2.

5. **Overshadowing** results when two CSs of unequal salience simultaneously enter into association with a US. The more salient CS acquires more associative strength (i.e., conditions the better of the other). That CS is said to overshadow the other CS.

6. **Salience** refers to the characteristics of a stimulus, such as its intensity and quality, that allow it to enter into association more easily relative to another stimulus.

7. **Potentiation** describes a phenomenon in which the presence of a taste stimulus allows sights, sounds, and odors to acquire more associative strength in a pairing with a US.

8. If CS_1 has already entered into association with a US and CS_1 is then presented simultaneously with CS_2, followed by a US, CS_2 does not acquire associative strength (i.e., does not condition). CS_1 is said to have blocked conditioning to CS2. This procedure, called **blocking,** may be complete or partial.

9. In taste aversion conditioning, some experiments using blocking designs have found an opposite result, increased conditioning rather than blocking, a phenomenon called *augmentation*.

DISCUSSION QUESTIONS

1. An early reader of this text thought that I had overstated the power of taste aversion conditioning. Specifically, he said that he shared with me an aversion to pineapple but "didn't get sick at the thought of it." Furthermore, he "doubted that the sight of the can of Dr. Spicey [see Box 5.1] would make a person ill." What do you think? Is the thought of an aver-

sive learning experience sufficient to produce a conditioned response?

2. What do you suppose Dr. Spicey tastes like? What concepts account for the fact that you think you know what a fictitious drink tastes like?

3. The twins became sick after eating pizza, but they also had found out that they probably had a stomach virus. Why do you think that this

(cognitive) knowledge doesn't override the conditioning of their food aversion?

4. Can you incorporate (a) Pavlov's *second-signal system conditioning*, (b) the process of *higher-order conditioning*, and (c) *generalization* to show how failure experiences in an algebra classroom might contribute to problems in other school subjects.

INHIBITORY CONDITIONING

Latent inhibition, sensory preconditioning, higher-order conditioning, potentiation, and blocking so far have revealed the extent to which prior learning experiences can affect the conditioning of new responses. Conditioned inhibition is the last and one of the most important of this set of phenomena. We see that many of Pavlov's experiments dealt with what he considered to be "inhibitory properties" of the nervous system. His experiments helped to illuminate processes that contribute to the inhibition of behavior. Following Pavlov's studies, Konorski (1948); Rescorla (1969) and Baker & Baker (1985) have made some of the most important contributions to the study of *conditioned inhibition*. In simple terms, **conditioned inhibition** in some ways is the opposite of conditioned excitation. Let us begin by looking at the many ways in which the term inhibition has been used.

Excitatory and Inhibitory Conditioning Compared

You have already learned several ways in which the terms inhibitory and inhibition have been used. For example, inhibitory conditioning was identified as the outcome of backward conditioning procedures. The result is that performance of the conditioned response is opposite in direction to the unconditioned response. For example, if tone → shock sequences predict conditioned fear, shock → tone sequences produce conditioned "safety." Tone → shock sequences define forward, excitatory conditioning. Shock → tone sequences define backward, inhibitory conditioning. Excitatory conditioning produces more salivation in Pavlov's dogs, and inhibitory conditioning produces less-than-normal salivation. Let's look more closely at inhibitory conditioning.

Negative, or US-CS, Contingencies Procedure

Using the conditioned suppression procedure, Heth (1976) conditioned rats using forward and backward pairings. One group was exposed to 60 US-CS (i.e., backward or shock → tone) pairings. A backward pairing sets up a *negative contingency* of CS and US. By measuring their rate of lever-pressing responses, Heth inferred first that the rats initially feared the tone and only in later trials did the tone become a safety signal. (Remember that in forward conditioning, rats ostensibly fearing the tone suppress their lever-pressing responses during the tone; rats that treat the tone as a safety signal increase their rate of response following backward pairings.)

Given what we now have learned about conditioned inhibition, the reader should not be surprised at Heth's (1976) finding that excitatory (fear) conditioning to the tone preceded the appearance of inhibitory (safety) conditioning. You be the rat, trapped again in the scientist's box. If at the beginning of the experiment tones and shocks were introduced into your environment—no matter which came first—wouldn't you be fearful? Only later, after quite a few conditioning trials in which you were first shocked and then heard the tone, would you interpret the tone as a signal that no shock would be forthcoming for a given time period (i.e., a "safe period"). Heth found that even after 20 trials, the rats feared the tone. Inhibitory conditioning (accelerated responding in the presence of the tone) took 60 trials to form.

Excitors and Inhibitors. Is it obvious that the tone became a safety signal only in the context of fear? That is, that merely presenting the tone without shock would not make the tone a safety signal? We'll find that inhibitory conditioning always and only occurs within an excitatory context. Following excitatory and inhibitory conditioning, these CSs become capable of supporting additional, independent conditioning, a process described earlier as higher-order conditioning. CSs that signal excitatory conditioning are called **conditioned excitors,** or merely *excitors*. Likewise, CSs that signal inhibitory conditioning are called **conditioned inhibitors,** or *inhibitors*. After conditioning, these CSs alone can set up an excitatory or inhibitory state in an animal, influencing how the animal responds to other stimuli.

Inhibitory Conditioning of Flavors. In a standard taste aversion conditioning experiment, rats first drink a flavored fluid and then are made sick by exposure to an illness-inducing agent, such as a drug or toxin. Flavor → illness contingencies make rats (and humans) dislike the target flavor. What if we reversed the contingency? On several occasions make the animal sick and each time allow it to drink a novel flavor while it recovers from sickness? The rat comes to prefer the flavor it tastes while recovering from the illness—a phenomenon known as the *medicine effect* (Green & Garcia, 1971). Is the flavor initially aversive, only later becoming preferred, as is the case in other measures of inhibitory conditioning? Yes. Rats tasting a coffee flavor find it aversive after two illness–flavor trials (backward conditioning) but show a preference for the flavor after eight such trials (Barker & Weaver, 1991). In both shock → tone and illness → flavor pairings, an initial excitatory conditioning component (fear of tone and avoidance of flavor, respectively) is followed by the development of conditioned inhibition (tone = safety signal and flavor is preferred, respectively). In both examples, the inhibitory conditioning took place only in the context of an initial excitatory state.

Conditioned Discrimination

We've already seen that Pavlov used the term inhibition in several contexts. First, he identified as *external inhibition* the temporary disruption in conditioned salivation that occurs when a dog's attention is distracted either during conditioning or extinction. He used the term *internal inhibition* to explain spontaneous recovery following extinction. Pavlov likened this inhibitory process during extinction to frustration at not getting food, and spontaneous recovery to the dissipation of this frustration.

Pavlov also thought that the inhibitory process was basic to discrimination training. A procedure he used to train an animal to respond differently to two stimuli is now called **conditioned discrimination.** In a classic experiment that demonstrated both generalization and conditioned discrimination, a black circle served as the conditioned stimulus (see Figure 5.7). A dog was trained to reliably salivate in the presence of the circle (top panel). Then an

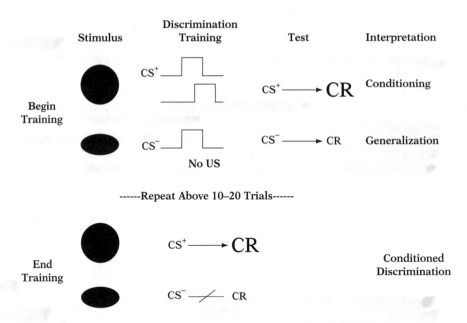

FIGURE 5.7   The Relationship of Generalization to Conditioned Discrimination

> To begin training, a circle (CS⁺) is paired with food (the US) until a CR occurs. Then an ellipse (CS⁻) is presented, and the dog salivates because of *generalization* to the circle. After repeated trials of circle → food, ellipse → no food, generalization disappears. At end training, conditioned discrimination of the circle from the ellipse occurs.

ellipse was substituted (2nd panel). Initially, the dog salivated to both the circle (top right) and also, in lesser amounts, to the ellipse. We can infer that the dog perceived the ellipse and the circle as being similar—that the dog *generalized* its response from the circle to the ellipse.

The circle continued to be paired with food. On alternate trials, the ellipse was shown to the dog, but it was never followed by food. By convention, presenting a CS with food is designated as a CS^+ *trial*, and presenting a CS^- without food is designated as a CS^- *trial*. (These are simply read as CS plus and CS minus trials.) A conditioned discrimination is said to develop when the dog reliably salivates to the CS^+ but not to the CS^-. (To do this in the present experiment, the dog had to overcome an innate tendency to generalize from the circle to the ellipse.) Test trials are shown at the bottom of Figure 5.7, in which the dog now shows a strong CR to the circle (CS^+) and no salivation to the ellipse (CS^-). Discrimination training is completed, and generalization no longer occurs (see Bush & Mosteller, 1951, for a theoretical account).

Experimental Neurosis.   Why did Pavlov think that conditioning discriminations involved an inhibitory process? Where in the preceding example is there evidence of an active inhibitory process, akin to the "frustration" he saw in his dogs during extinction? Pavlov found evidence of an active process of inhibition as he continued to train the dog, forcing it to make finer and finer discriminations between the circle and an almost circular ellipse. When the dog could no longer tell the difference between the CS^+ and CS^-, the discrimination broke down. And so, apparently, did the dog. In Pavlov's words:

> At the same time the whole behavior of the animal underwent an abrupt change. The hitherto quiet dog began to squeal in its stand, kept wriggling about, tore off with its teeth the apparatus for mechanical stimulation of the skin, and bit through the tubes connecting the animal's room with the observer, a behavior which never happened before ... the animal now barked violently ... in short, it displayed all the symptoms of acute neurosis [for several weeks]. (Pavlov, 1927/1960, p. 291)

Neurosis? From a discrimination training procedure? Pavlov thought that the combination of excitatory and inhibitory processes put the dog into an extreme emotional state that took weeks to dissipate. The outcome of this experiment aside for the moment, it seems clear that learning to discriminate is an adaptive process. After two meals at my favorite restaurant—a bad experience with catfish but a delightful flounder dinner—it is important that I discriminate (differentiate) between the two stimuli. One bad experience with catfish should not be overgeneralized to all fish. But all of us have been in this situation. The balance is precarious. In making fine discriminations for which there are important consequences, animals seem to incur a psychological cost. Let us look more closely at this interesting dynamic.

What Accounts for "Inhibition"?

> *Hurry, hurry, hurry. In another 10 minutes you'll be late for your appointment, and your destination is still many blocks away.*
> *Damn. The light turned red as you approach the next intersection.*
> *In our culture, a red light sets up an expectancy to respond in a certain way. Hit the brakes, and start an internal timer. Since you've come this way often, you know to within a few seconds how long the cycle of green to yellow to red to green should take.*
> *The signal doesn't change. You impatiently wait. The horn behind you honks. Decision time. Is it broken? Should I go? Look for cops.*

Here, as in Pavlov's laboratory, the inhibitory context is also the passage of time, conditioned by our prior (excitatory conditioning) experiences. We have a conditioning history in which a red traffic light means "stop and wait a fixed period of time." The long time delay due to a broken traffic light can be interpreted as an inhibitory stimulus, which has signal value only in relation to prior excitatory conditioning of traffic lights that change at regular intervals.

The Role of Excitatory Context. Conditioned inhibition on the surface appears to be no more than the mirror image of conditioned excitation in that the conditioned response changes direction when the CS-US relationship is reversed. Conditioned inhibition is more complex than conditioned excitation, however, because inhibition requires an excitatory context in which to be expressed (Baker, Singh, & Bindra, 1985; Rescorla, 1969, 1985). Excitation must both precede and set the stage for inhibition. A light not turning green is irritating only in the context that after a lengthy excitatory state it *does* turn green. From this and other examples, we see that demonstrations of conditioned inhibition require that

1. The animal have a prior history of conditioned excitation.
2. The animal be in an excitatory state when the inhibitory CS is present.

Stuck at the traffic light that won't change, the additional time delay can be identified as a conditioned inhibitor. The red light is the excitor. The red light (excitor) controlled your "foot-on-the-brake" response. The combination of the excitor and time passing (inhibitor) produced the "go" response, opposite to the "stop" response to the red light alone.

Explaining Internal Inhibition. Let us briefly review Pavlov's several demonstrations of internal inhibition to see whether these criteria were met. First the dog is conditioned in an excitatory manner (tone → food). Now, during extinction, the tone is presented, setting up an excitatory state. Trial after trial, food is not forthcoming in the presence of the tone. The extended passage of time (with the tone and without food) becomes an inhibitory stimulus. The conditioned discrimination procedure using a circle and ellipse, and other CS⁺, CS⁻ discrimination procedures are also tested in extinction. The apparent buildup of inhibition takes place over a lengthy work session of alternating states of excitation and inhibition. Let us look more closely at the inhibitory effect of the passage of time.

Inhibition of Delay Procedures

Boring. Absolutely boring. Is this prof ever going to say something interesting? This 50 minutes seems like 50 hours. If only I could lay my head down. I'm gonna break my neck jerking awake like this.

Pavlov was fascinated that procedures that produced inhibitory processes had the effect of inducing sleepiness in animals. One of his experiments—illustrating a procedure he called **inhibition of delay**—demonstrates the phenomenon. Inhibition of delay produces a suppression of responding in the early part of an ongoing response. First a dog was conditioned to salivate to a tactile CS (stroking its paw for 30 sec). Salivation was measured in 5-sec time intervals during the 30 sec CS. Figure 5.8 shows the results after many conditioning trials; salivation was inhibited during the first part of the interval. (Note that in the figure most of the salivation occurred just before delivery of food. Such timely salivation is highly adaptive in that it helps the

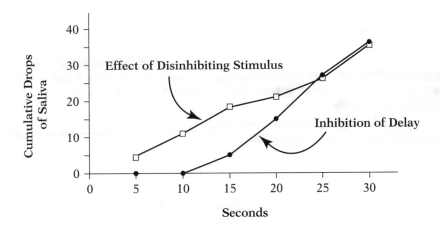

FIGURE 5.8   Inhibition of Delay, and Disinhibition

A dog conditioned to a 30-second tactile stimulus does not salivate evenly throughout the 30-sec period; rather, salivation is inhibited during the first 10–15 sec (closed circles), what Pavlov called *inhibition of delay*. Adding the sound of a metronome to the tactile CS has the effect of *disinhibiting* the inhibited salivation, freeing the dog to salivate earlier in the 30-sec period (open squares).

animal begin the digestive process.) The experiment also tells us that dogs, like humans, are sensitive to the passage of time.

How do we know that salivation is being actively inhibited during the initial 15-sec period? Pavlov used two lines of evidence to argue his case. First he noted that many of his dogs became drowsy—some even fell asleep—during conditioning over long delays. Drowsiness is a response that is opposite attentiveness and demonstrates the inhibition. Second, Pavlov ran a test in which he introduced another stimulus—the sound of a metronome—during the 30-sec tactile stimulus. The results are also shown in Figure 5.8. The metronome plus tactile stimulus released the animal from the process of inhibition, causing the dog to again salivate throughout the 30-sec interval (open squares). Pavlov called the process *inhibition of inhibition* (awkward) or **disinhibition** (better). In this example, the metronome is a disinhibiting stimulus, or *disinhibitor*.

Can you make the case that a boring lecture is one in which there are no disinhibitors? What would you advise your professor to do to help students not sleep? (Vary the drone.) Still stuck at the red light? Perhaps your mind has wandered (become drowsy during the wait) and you haven't noticed that the light has changed to green. A honking horn is a pretty fair disinhibitor, isn't it?

Comparing Inhibition Procedures. Remember Pavlov's phenomenon of external inhibition? His assistant Igor slammed the door during an acquisition trial in which the tone CS was providing an excitatory context. The door slam could be considered a disexcitor (Pavlov did not use the term). The door slam violated the animal's food expectancy, thereby acting as a stimulus that inhibited the excitatory conditioned response. Pavlov's internal and external inhibition are temporary phenomena; both dissipate with the passage of relatively brief periods of time. They are best understood, therefore, as nonassociative in nature.

By contrast, both latent inhibition and conditioned inhibition are long-lasting associative phenomena. One conclusion is that we've used the same word, inhibition, to describe very different processes. Table 5.1 summarizes the various uses of the term inhibition. Conditioned inhibitors *are* long-lasting, and they have been produced from a variety of other conditioned discrimination procedures (Hearst, 1972). For example, it is highly likely that conditioned inhibitors, among their other effects, produce measurable stress responses in the form of stress hormones (Dantzer, Arnone, & Mormede, 1980). Let's look at more examples of conditioned inhibition.

Induction Method of Producing Conditioned Inhibition

Presents. Presents. Presents. The expression on young Melinda's face reveals all too clearly her disappointment on opening her next present, the book *Black Beauty*. Her father is equally dismayed that he has apparently been un-

TABLE 5.1 Conditioning Procedures Using the Term *Inhibition*

Name	Description of Phenomenon
Latent inhibition (*Lubow and others*)	Reduced associability of familiar stimuli relative to novel stimuli
External inhibition (*Pavlov*)	Temporary disruption of conditioned excitatory process due to presentation of extraneous stimulus during conditioning
Internal inhibition (*Pavlov*)	Process occurs during extinction of conditioned excitatory response; dissipates with time, as evidenced by spontaneous recovery
Conditioned inhibition (*Rescorla and others*)	A state opposite to that of conditioned excitation; a process that produces a stimulus with conditioned inhibitory properties
Conditioned discrimination (*Pavlov and others*)	Begins with conditioning an excitatory response (CS⁺), followed by alternating trials with a CS⁻, ends with responding to one but not the other stimulus
Inhibition of delay (*Pavlov*)	Reduced responding and drowsiness during the first part of a long CS presented in extinction
Disinhibition (*Pavlov*)	The disruption of inhibition caused by introducing another stimulus

successful in instilling good manners in her. How can she be so unappreciative of this beautiful book? (Not to mention her lack of courtesy in not hiding her displeasure.) After all, she likes horses. And she likes to read. Why the adverse reaction to the book? Indeed, why is it the case that normally well-behaved children—and adults—all too often look a gift horse in the mouth and find it lacking?

The answer may be found by applying the results of experiments on inhibition conditioned by the *induction method*. The induction method is a procedure used to condition an inhibitory response by presenting an excitor with a neutral stimulus on occasions when it is *not* followed by food. Let's first examine the animal model before returning to the example. An excitatory context is created in Step 1 of Figure 5.9 by normal excitatory conditioning. (As an example, we'll condition a fear response to a tone—CS$_1$—as measured in a conditioned suppression experiment.) In Step 2, the tone—now a conditioned excitor—is presented simultaneously with a neutral stimulus (CS$_2$), such as a light, and the rat is not shocked. Finally, the light is tested alone. The animal's response to the light is opposite to that of the tone—here designated CR⁻. In the induction method, the light enters into association with (is induced by) the inhibitory process accompanying extinction of the excitatory tone. In the presence of the light, an animal would increase, not suppress, responding.

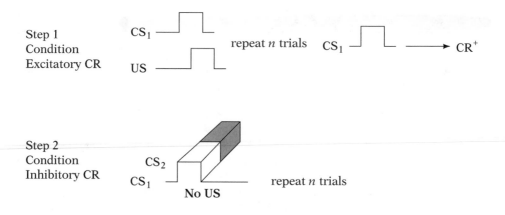

FIGURE 5.9   Induction Method

In Step 1, CS_1 is conditioned to produce an excitatory CR. Then, in Step 2, CS_1 is presented in compound with CS_2 and is *not* paired with a US. In Step 3, the CR to CS_2 is demonstrated to have acquired inhibitory properties.

Notice the similarity of this "induction method" to simple extinction. An inhibitory process was previously implicated in extinction; one explanation for spontaneous recovery was the dissipation of inhibition. Returning to the birthday party, did I mention that before opening *Black Beauty*, the first present Melinda unwrapped was a small color TV for her bedroom? Let the TV be an excitor, setting up an excitatory state in the form of BIG expectations. Let the book *Black Beauty* be a pleasant but comparatively neutral stimulus that occurs during the excitatory state. Are the conditions right for the book to become a conditioned inhibitor? If so, what effect will the book have on Melinda's excitatory state? What should you do, as a representative of the next generation of parents, to ensure that your child won't be a monster at her own party?[4]

[4]   a. Not celebrate birthdays.
      b. Celebrate birthdays but not give gifts.
      c. Punish the child by taking back any gift the child is not thankful for.
      d. Arrange for your child to open the gifts in an ascending order of perceived value (i.e., save the best for last).*

Indirect Methods of Measuring Conditioned Inhibition

In addition to the induction method, three other methods of producing conditioned inhibition have already been presented: backward contingencies, conditioned discrimination, and inhibition of delay. All these procedures are important because they demonstrate many of the subtleties and interactions of excitatory and inhibitory processes during conditioning. We've also entertained a couple of examples of how our mood swings can be modulated by conditioned stimuli in the environment—through extinction, and the sequence of receiving presents.

In addition to methods where inhibition is demonstrated by an opposite response, two *indirect* methods of measuring conditioned inhibition, *summation* and *retardation,* have been devised (described below). Why are they important? Because these methods provide demonstration experiments showing that inhibitors and excitors combine algebraically to modulate emotional behavior (Rescorla, 1971). Are the summation and retardation procedures necessary to demonstrate conditioned inhibition? No (see Williams, Overmier, & LoLordo, 1992). As we have already seen, conditioned inhibitory properties can be demonstrated using any of a number of methodologies.

Inhibitory Processes in Using Language.   Let us look at how these processes work in reading this text and in listening to a lecture in the classroom. Both activities involve responding to words. Words and combinations of words in sentences were initially learned in an excitatory conditioning context. Understandable words—words with meaning—act as excitors. They keep your attention from wandering as you read. In a lecture, understandable words and sentences are interesting. Get it! By contrast, words and sentences that are not understood (or are not too repetitive) act as inhibitors. In the preceding sentence, if you do not understand how the word *inhibitors* was used, you did not understand the sentence. The frustration of not understanding the sentence is evidence of an inhibitory process. If too many of the sentences you read are not understandable, or if you do not understand the point of a lecture, your attention wanders. Long sentences in long paragraphs strain your attention. You become drowsy—further evidence of the inhibition that accrues under these conditions. To get the full benefit of a reading or from a lecture, the momentary excitatory processes must outweigh the momentary inhibitory processes. An occasional disinhibitor, such as "Get it!" does wonders in both lectures and in reading. Let's look at an animal model.

Summation Test.   As the name implies, the **summation test** refers to a procedure in which CS_2 (a conditioned inhibitor) is presented with (added to) CS_1 (a conditioned excitor). The outcome is a conditioned response that reflects the sum of these two processes. For example, a tone excitor is conditioned by tone $\rightarrow$ shock sequences. The excitor suppresses lever-pressing.

Recall that in backwards conditioning, the electric shock US precedes a light CS and inhibitory conditioning results. The inhibitory conditioning produces enhanced lever-press responding. What would you predict would happen if, following this training, the excitor and inhibitor were presented simultaneously to the animal? Adding the light (inhibitor) to the tone (excitor) produces less suppression than would be expected to the excitor alone. The CR to the combined stimuli suggests that the CR to each stimulus summates algebraically (Bull & Overmier, 1968). In the conditioned suppression example, adding the light diminishes the ability of the excitor to suppress lever-press responses (Solomon, Brennan, & Moore, 1974).

The speed at which you drive a car in traffic is an illustration of the summation of excitatory and inhibitory elements. You approach a green traffic signal in a 35-mph zone. What stimulus elements contribute to your constantly adjusted speed? It is raining (inhibitor); the traffic is flowing smoothly (excitor); a police car is in the next lane (inhibitor); you are late for an appointment (excitor); you hear a siren (major inhibitor); the cop turns, and your rearview mirror is clear (major excitor). Your speed reflects the summation of these various elements.

The interaction of excitatory and inhibitory processes can be seen in driving a car, playing a basketball game, and reading the preceding paragraph. Eyes drowsy? Too many unexplained ideas (i.e., too many inhibitory, partially understood sentences)? Get up and walk around, and allow some of the inhibitory process accompanying a long session of processing difficult material to dissipate. To accomplish the same end it might be a good idea if your professor allowed a 2 to 3 min break in the middle of a long lecture.

Retardation Test. A final procedure that allows experimenters to indirectly measure conditioned inhibition is called the **retardation test.** Simply put, once a stimulus has been made a conditioned inhibitor, it is more difficult to turn that stimulus into an excitor. Let us return to the algebra classroom: In high school, you read too many words and too many formulas that you did not understand. Inhibitory processes built up to each CS⁻. These inhibitory processes interfere with trying to learn similar material. To the laboratory:

Using as an example flavor preference and aversion conditioning, we first condition a preference to a flavor using a backward contingency. This procedure produces the *medicine effect*: The flavor becomes preferred (a conditioned inhibitor). Next, this flavor inhibitor is paired with illness in an excitatory framework. A conditioned inhibitor can become a conditioned excitor—the flavor can be made aversive—but more trials are required relative to a control group. (Hence the name *retardation*.) Conditioned inhibition procedures have also been shown to affect second-order conditioning (Yin, Barnet, & Miller, 1994) and extinction and spontaneous recovery (Fiori, Barnet, & Miller, 1994).

In college, you can learn new responses to algebra symbols and formulas to which inhibitory processes were attached in high school, but it will be more difficult. Likewise, if you decide on the first day that your prof is a nerd, his presence becomes a conditioned inhibitor. The prof's presence will likely retard the learning of new material. A summary of ways by which inhibitors are conditioned and the indirect tests for conditioned inhibition are presented in Table 5.2.

We've previously discussed the questions of ecological validity and extrapolation of results to humans of conditioning experiments on animals in laboratories. Ultimately, you, the reader, must be the judge of these issues. From your reading so far, have you derived any insight into your personal behavior in:

Classrooms (bored and sleepy, waiting for the bell, or hopeless in the face of algebra)?

Your reaction to gifts?

Automobiles (how fast you drive or how your attention wanders while you are waiting at red lights)?

Your personal interactions with others?

Your attitudes toward foods and restaurants?

The effects the words of this text have on you (aroused or bored)?

Interim Summary

1. Pavlov identified two types of inhibition that directly affected excitatory salivary conditioning. The first type, *external inhibition,* occurs when an

TABLE 5.2   Additional Methods of Producing and Measuring Conditioned Inhibition

Methods of Production	
Method	*Description*
Backward conditioning	A US-CS procedure that produces a CR opposite in direction to the unconditioned response
Induction procedure	A neutral stimulus is added to an excitatory CS in extinction; the neutral stimulus acquires inhibitory properties.
Indirect Methods of Testing	
Method	*Description*
Retardation procedure	An inhibitory conditioned stimulus is slower to acquire excitatory properties during excitatory conditioning.
Summation procedure	An inhibitory conditioned stimulus is placed in compound with a novel CS, thereby slowing excitatory conditioning to the novel CS.

extraneous stimulus such as a sudden noise disrupts either conditioning or extinction of a salivary response. Pavlov proposed that a second type, that he called *internal inhibition*, occurred during extinction, as evidenced by spontaneous recovery.

2. **Conditioned inhibition** is the opposite of conditioned excitation.

3. Evidence of an inhibitory process occurs during a **conditioned discrimination** procedure. In this procedure excitatory conditioning (CS⁺) is alternated with inhibitory conditioning (CS⁻). The animal learns to respond to CS⁺ and not to respond to CS⁻. Under these conditions, emotional responses may be evident in the presence of CS⁻.

3. Pavlov used an **inhibition of delay** procedure in which he presented a long CS in extinction. The dog became drowsy, and its salivary response during the first part of the interval was reduced.

4. Conditioned inhibition can be produced by a negative contingency (backwards conditioning) procedure and by an *induction procedure*. In both the CS acquires conditioned inhibitory properties and is called a *conditioned inhibitor*.

5. Two indirect methods of measuring conditioned inhibition are the **retardation test** and the **summation test**. The retardation procedure shows that an inhibitor acquires excitatory properties more slowly than a normal CS during excitatory conditioning. In summation, an inhibitor is placed in compound with a novel CS, thereby slowing excitatory conditioning to the novel CS.

DISCUSSION QUESTIONS

5. Don't you just love it that U.S. idiom embodies animal learning theory as well as human behavior? Based on what you have learned in this chapter, what evidence can you use to dispute the saying that "you can't teach an old dog new tricks" while at the same time acknowledging the wisdom of the saying? How about "practice makes perfect"? Also, in what way are professors who are *so boring they put me to sleep* like Pavlov's dogs during *inhibition of delay*? If I belabor this issue, I risk making you *sick to your stomach*—but one individual has already suggested that this isn't possible by words alone! Come up with some other examples of idiom that reflect learning principles and send them to me (barkele@auburn.edu). I'll acknowledge you by name if your example is included in the next revision of this text.

6. Some people can't study with the TV on or in the presence of other distracting sounds; others can't study in a room that is too quiet. Pavlov and his successors were interested in individual differences such as these, and you can read about them in a book entitled *Pavlov's Typology* by J. A. B. Gray (1964). Can you use Pavlov's concept of *external inhibition* to account for the psychological dimen-

sion of noise, defined as *unwanted sound?*

7. Unable to release my foot from the accelerator, I recently wrecked my car. A wild dog in a rural environment was attempting to get in the passenger-side door, and I was attempting to get my family and myself out of danger. My superexcitatory state seemed to prevent me (a) from taking my foot off the gas and (b) placing it on the brake. I crashed into another car. Can you help explain to my insurance company what went wrong in terms of excitatory and inhibitory processes controlling my erratic driving behavior?

8. Given what you have learned so far, what do you think of general associative models of learning? Do learning experiments using laboratory animals tell you anything about yourself?

GENERAL PROCESSES AND PREPAREDNESS

Two views of behavior were presented in Chapter 2. On the one hand, ethologists focus on phyletic relationships among animals, and species differences of animals living within distinctive ethological niches. Animal behavior in these niches is adaptive: Animals engage in those behaviors that promote survival, and that produce the next generation.

On the other hand, comparative psychologists and other neuroscientists who study behavior focus more on behavioral plasticity. They ask how relatively large-brained vertebrates respond to changes in their immediate environment. How do animals learn and remember from their interactions with stimuli they encounter in the environment, and, in the case of humans, the environment that they also create?

Reexamining the Issues.   In this concluding section, we reexamine several issues raised earlier. Are there species differences in learning? Does each animal bring genetically predisposed behavior and innate reaction patterns to the laboratory? Is general process learning theory sufficient to account for most instances of animal learning? Why are certain stimuli and certain responses in certain animals conditioned relatively easily, but others conditioned with great difficulty? We start with the nature of the stimulus.

Can Any Stimulus Become a Conditioned Stimulus?

Earlier we asked whether the laboratory is a valid ecological niche in which to study learning. One question raised about laboratory research has to do with the use of "artificial" stimuli in conditioning animals. Where can electric shock be found in nature? Or, for that matter, carefully timed bells, whistles, and metronomes? Given the divergent evolutionary histories of animals and the different niches they presently occupy, is it reasonable to think that any stimulus is arbitrarily interchangeable with another? If some animals rely primarily on taste and smell to negotiate their niche, for example, isn't it reasonable to expect that they would learn differently using these stimuli than, for example, a visual or an auditory stimulus? Can learning measured in laboratories using arbitrary stimuli and arbitrary responses (such as lever-pressing) ever reflect real-life learning?

Pavlov's assertion was a qualified "Yes." After studying the issue for 30 years, he concluded:

> We must now take some account of the agencies which can be transformed into conditioned stimuli. This is not so easy a problem as appears at first sight. Of course to give a general answer is very simple; any agent in nature which acts on any adequate receptor apparatus of an organism can be made into a conditioned stimulus for that organism. This general statement, however, needs both amplification and restriction. (Pavlov, 1927/1960, p 38; italics added)

Among the "amplification and restriction" were pages and pages of experiments in his classic book, *Conditioned Reflexes*. He found that some CSs could be used to condition dogs easily, and others with difficulty. The law of strength held for a wide range of stimulus intensities, but if a stimulus was *too* intense, it could not be used effectively as a CS. Another troubling example is that of temporal conditioning. The mere passage of time (for which there is no apparent "receptor apparatus"!) can become an effective conditioned stimulus. In yet other experiments, Pavlov found that the *cessation of* a stimulus could become a conditioned stimulus. In his words,

> A metronome is sounded continuously in the experimental laboratory when the dog is brought in. The sound of the metronome is now cut out, and immediately an unconditioned stimulus . . . is introduced. After several repetitions of this procedure it is found that the disappearance of the sound has become the stimulus to a new conditioned reflex. (Pavlov, 1927/1960, p. 39).

Growth of General Process Learning Theory

Laboratory researchers took Pavlov at his word and by the mid-1960s had developed a general process learning philosophy with the following assumptions:

1. Choice of research animal is relatively arbitrary.
2. Choice of stimuli used in experiments is relatively arbitrary.
3. Choice of reflexes and types of responses by which to measure learning is relatively arbitrary.

Results from the study of a variety of animals in different conditioning situations from many different laboratories all seemed to support a general process approach to learning. A sampling of the relevant parameters of these experiments is presented in Table 5.3. Notice both the similarities and the differences in these experiments. For example, four different species (albeit all mammals) were used: dogs, a human infant, rats, and rabbits. Three sounds

TABLE 5.3 General Process Learning: A Comparison
of Conditioning Parameters

Researcher (Subject)	CS (Duration)	US (Duration)	CS-US Interval	Number of Trials
Pavlov (1927) (dog)	Metronome (30 s)	Food (~10 s)	30 s	5–9
Watson and Rayner (1920) (human)	White rat (~5 s)	Loud clang (~2 s)	~2–3 s	7
Kamin (1965) (rat)	81-dB white noise (2.0 min)	0.85-mA shock (0.5 s)	3.0 min	6–8
Gormezano (1965) (rabbit)	800-hz tone, 72 dB (0.6 s)	Air puff (0.5 s)	0.5 s	~200

(a metronome, white noise, a pure tone) and one visual stimulus (the sight of
a moving white rat) were used as CSs. Four different USs (three aversive, one
appetitive) were used: electric shock, a loud clang, an air puff, and food. CSs
were a half second to 2 minutes in duration; USs ranged from less than a second to a few seconds in duration. Interestingly enough, the number of trials
to accomplish conditioning (with the exception of eye-blink conditioning)
ranged from five to nine trials even in these highly diverse situations. The
basis of a general process position, then, is that conditioning outcomes are
predictable in a variety of animals and in a variety of stimulus situations.

Challenge to General Process Learning Theory

Several experiments were published—one in 1955, others in the mid-1960s—
that didn't seem to fit general process learning theory. One used ionizing radiation. Among its other effects, ionizing radiation disrupts eating and drinking
patterns. An important paper published in the journal *Science* suggested that
some of these disruptions had been conditioned (Garcia, Kimeldorf, &
Koelling, 1955). If so, the conditioning was unlike anything Pavlov had previously reported. Rats had been allowed to drink a 0.1% saccharin solution during a 6-h low-level ionizing radiation exposure. Several days later in the
absence of radiation they avoided the saccharin. John Garcia and colleagues
reasoned that the saccharin had functioned as a CS and the radiation acted as
a US. The aversion to saccharin was interpreted as a conditioned response,
and the rats' increasing acceptance of the saccharin-flavored water with repeated testing was interpreted as extinction of the CR.

Compared to the methods and results of experiments in Table 5.3, the
Garcia et al. (1955) finding raised several problems for traditional learning
theory:

1. The CS and the US each lasted 6 h rather than a few seconds or minutes.
2. Conditioning was accomplished in one trial.
3. Stimulus contiguity was apparently unnecessary: Assuming that the rats tasted saccharin early in the 6-h interval and that the response to radiation (radiation sickness?) occurred some time after the 6-h interval, the taste-to-illness interval could be interpreted to be more than 6 h in duration.

Such rapid, one-trial, long-delay learning was unprecedented. Was it unique? Was it outside the pale of general process theory? Many thought so. General process learning theorists frankly did not know what to do with John Garcia's experiments.

The "Bright, Noisy, Tasty Water" Experiment

After a number of rejections by the editors of journals of animal learning research, Garcia eventually published the results of yet another controversial experiment (Garcia & Koelling, 1966) Garcia and Koelling's "bright, noisy, tasty water" experiment is now considered a classic. Rats were placed in an experimental chamber and allowed to lick a tube containing water. By adding saccharin, the water could be made "tasty." Every time the animal licked the water tube, an electric circuit was completed to briefly flash a ("bright") light in the rat's environment. The same circuit also produced a brief click ("noisy"); hence, the water had bright, noisy, and tasty (as well as wet) conditioned stimulus properties.

Figure 5.10 shows that half the rats were trained to drink the bright, noisy, tasty water, following which they were exposed to ionizing radiation (the US). The other half were briefly exposed to electric shock after licking the fluid for a short time. To test whether the audiovisual (noisy, bright) or the taste component of the water conditioned best with the electric shock or with the radiation US, the bright, noisy, tasty water was separated into component parts during extinction tests. Rats had the choice of drinking either bright, noisy water or tasty water (bottom panels of Figure 5.10). They associated the audiovisual components of the compound stimulus with electric shock and the taste component with the radiation exposure.

Garcia and Koelling (1966) interpreted these results to mean that not all stimuli were capable of entering into association; rather, there was **stimulus specificity** in conditioning. Taste and sickness were easily associated together, Garcia argued, because rats were evolutionarily prepared to associate flavors with the normal consequences of eating. Likewise, the sights and sounds of predators were more likely to be conditioned with pain rather than with gut sickness. This experiment, he argued, provided evidence for two quite different learning systems, a telereceptor-cutaneous system and a gustatory-visceral system (Garcia, Hankins, & Rusiniak, 1974).

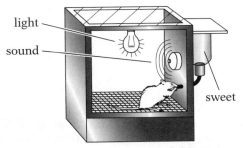

All rats drink bright, noisy, tasty water (the CS)

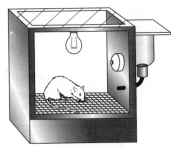

Half receive mild electric
shock (a US)

Half receive x-rays (a US)

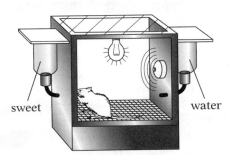

Rats that had the shock-US
avoid the bright, noisy
components of the CS, and
drink the sweetened water

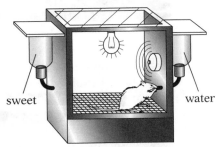

Rats that had the X-ray-US
avoid the sweetened water, ignore
the bright, noisy components of
the CS, and drink water

FIGURE 5.10 John Garcia's Bright, Noisy,
Tasty, Water Experiment

Preparedness: An Evolutionary Learning Theory

Following the publication of Garcia's work several other learning theorists (i.e., Rozin & Kalat, 1971; Seligman, 1970) agreed with his analysis. They broadened the evolutionary argument. In developing a theory of **preparedness,** for example, Rozin & Kalat (1971) proposed that animals are (evolutionarily) prepared to readily make some associations and are *unprepared,* or even *contraprepared,* to make others. What it learns is due both to the contingencies it faces in its lifetime and to the contingencies this species faced in its evolutionary past.

Preparedness and Neophobia. The rapid learning about flavors found in experiments by Garcia and others complements other behavioral tendencies in rats that increase their feeding success. Rats display neophobia (fear of new) when they confront unfamiliar flavors (tastes and smells) of foods and fluids.[5] Their innately organized feeding behavior prepares even hungry rats to approach new foods cautiously. Rats sniff, retreat, approach, sniff and nibble (taste), and retreat. On their next approach, they sniff, nibble, and ingest a small amount (the exact amount depending on hunger and the taste, smell, and temperature characteristics of the food). After minimal ingestion, again they retreat. On subsequent encounters they eat increasingly more (Barnett, 1963; Rzoska, 1953). One theory is that if rats experience no immediate ill-effects from what they ate, they shortly return to eat more. Given this innate wariness, or "bait shyness," about new foods, complemented by the rats' ability to form flavor-illness associations in only one trial, it is easy to see why "rats as pests" are so difficult to poison (Rzoska, 1953). Let us look more closely at the "number of trials to learn" evidence for preparedness.

Preparedness and Number of Trials. Rozin and Kalat (1971) used the "number of trials to learn" metric to support evolutionary arguments. For example, learning taste aversions in one trial, they argued, constituted evidence of preparedness in learning. Animals possessing brain structures that were able to learn rapidly about poisoned food sources lived; those that didn't died. Why? Because more than one poisoning trial increases the likelihood of a fatal encounter with poison. They further proposed that behaviors that are difficult to learn (that take many trials to learn) reflect unspecialized learning.

Unprepared and Contraprepared Learning. Pavlov's dogs, the argument continues, took five to nine trials to learn that sights and sounds predicted

---

[5]Including, of course, rug rats. Neophobic tendencies in humans are so strong that children attribute draconian motivations to parents who attempt to introduce new foods. Indeed, more than one of my children, even at 10 years of age, have accused me of trying to poison them.

food. The dogs were **unprepared,** or, at best, neutral regarding these stimuli; the intermediate number of trials necessary for conditioning to occur is evidence for their unpreparedness. Using similar reasoning, rabbits and humans are apparently **contraprepared** to learn that sights and sounds predict air puffs to the cornea of the eye. Such conditioning is not ever likely to happen in any animal's ecological niche. That such conditioning can occur at all attests to the inherent plasticity of mammalian brains, and is evidence for general process learning.

Birds Associate Color, Not Taste, with Poison? Given the diversity of life forms and of the niches they occupy, what predictions can be made concerning cross-species comparisons? Unless animals occupy very similar niches, the preparedness argument goes, one should not expect them to associate stimuli in the same way. Birds, for example, conduct visual rather than olfactory searches for food, so they should learn better about foods using visual rather than taste cues (i.e., the reverse of rats). This hypothesis was tested by Wilcoxson, Dragoin, and Kral (1971). They allowed both laboratory rats and Japanese quail to drink blue (food coloring) or sour (slightly acidic) water and then poisoned the animals with Cytoxan®. The entire procedure was accomplished in one trial. As in the bright, noisy, tasty water experiment, the compound CS was separated during extinction testing. The rats and quail were tested with a choice of drinking either blue or sour water. Rats, they reported, chose blue and declined the sour water. Quail rejected the blue-colored water but drank the sour water. Again, these results constitute evidence for stimulus specificity in conditioning. These researchers concluded that quail and rats are evolutionarily prepared to make selective associations.

Preparedness Versus General Processes

The preceding experiments present problems for general process learning theory on several counts: First, one trial learning over very long delays is possible for taste paired with illness-inducing stimuli. Second, specific stimuli appear to enter into association, and others not, depending on species of animal. The preparedness challenge to general process theory is an important one because most humans consider themselves to be truly unique among species. If special rules of association formation are found to hold for some species, it may be the case that learning accomplished by humans will be found to be quite different.

Analysis of Conditioning Failures. Why did rats fail to associate the audio-visual stimulus with the radiation stimulus? Is the rat really unable to make flavor-electric shock associations in the bright, noisy, tasty water experiment? Why are quail apparently unable to form a sour taste-sickness association? Let us take a closer look at the conditioning failures noted in these two experiments. For ease of comparison, the conditioning parameters used in these

experiments are summarized in Table 5.4. A number of methodological problems in Garcia and Koelling's (1966) classic experiment made their results
difficult to interpret. However, a replication of the bright, noisy, tasty water
experiment by Domjan and Wilson (1972) used a between-groups design that
both simplified the methods and clarified the theoretical issues. For this reason, their experiment rather than Garcia's will be the basis for further discussion. Domjan and Wilson used lithium chloride to induce sickness and
conditioned a taste aversion. The taste cue failed to become associated with
electric shock. Likewise, a "pulsed buzzer" was associated with electric shock
but not with lithium. Like Garcia, these researchers also concluded that not
all cues are equally associable with all consequences.

In comparison with the experiments in Table 5.3, there are fewer conditioning trials in the quail experiment (1 trial) and in Domjan & Wilson's (3 trials). Notice that the general process experiments listed in Table 5.3 all used
more trials. Perhaps conditioning failed in the quail experiment and in the
bright, noisy, tasty water experiment because not enough conditioning trials
were conducted. Would we conclude that salivary conditioning was impossible if Pavlov had conducted a single bell-food trial and found no conditioning? No. So a first response to the stimulus specificity theory is that these
experiments were not designed to test the hypothesis that some stimuli *cannot* be conditioned, but rather to show that some are *more easily* conditioned.

Is it easier to condition a taste with illness in rats and a visual cue with
illness in Japanese quail? Yes. Is it *possible* to condition a taste with illness in
quail and visual cues with illness in rats? The answer for quail is probably
"yes," and for rats, definitely "yes." Many such experiments were described
earlier in this chapter in which contextual cues (sight and sounds in the laboratory) entered into association with illness-inducing USs. It also is the case
that there are species differences among birds. Hawks, for example, *require*
taste cues to make visual associations. Hawks poisoned after eating black
mice learned not to eat them only if the mice were also made bitter flavored;

TABLE 5.4   Conditioning Failures?

Researcher	CS (Duration)	US (Quantity, Duration)	CS-US Interval	Number of Trials
Domjan and Wilson (1972)	Pulsed buzzer (35 s)	Lithium chloride (~20 ml/kg, ip)	35 s	3
	0.2% saccharin (35 s)	Electric shock (140V, 0.5 s)	35 s	3
Wilcoxson, Dragoin, and Kral (1971)	Blue water (30 min)	Cytoxan® (66 mg/kg)	30 min	1

only after the black-bitter-poison association was made did they quit eating black mice and continue eating white mice (Brett, Hankins, & Garcia, 1976).[6]

Taste-shock Associations. Given the research findings that visual cues can be associated with poisons, is there comparable evidence that taste can be associated with electric shock? Yes. An interesting experiment reported by Krane and Wagner (1975) indicated that an important variable in making taste-shock conditioning effective was to delay the shock. Saccharin has a relatively long-lasting aftertaste. Krane and Wagner compared taste-shock conditioning at various intervals and found that associations formed only if the taste's duration did not extend past delivery of the electric shock. [A student once suggested that if the electric shock were made intense enough, it presumably would take on some of the same characteristics of an "illness-inducing agent" (e.g., nausea). Why is this an important observation?]

Further Analysis of Preparedness Conditioning. The earlier conditioning "failures" were accounted for by simply noting that stimulus-stimulus associations cannot be expected to form in 1–3 trials. Were associations found to be impossible after many trials, the specificity in conditioning position could be considered a more serious challenge to a general process learning position. But, you may argue, taste aversions *do* form in one trial over long CS-US delays. Doesn't that observation by itself violate general process learning theory? Maybe, maybe not. Consider the following arguments:

1. Within a sensory modality, both intensity and duration effects are important factors in conditioning (see Pavlov's Law of Strength).
2. Although beginning with Pavlov, many have tried, but no one has yet solved the problem of equating stimulus intensities across modalities.
3. Regarding "tastes" and "poisons," general process learning theory predicts that both intensity and duration effects are important factors that predict ease of conditioning.

Preparedness or Stimulus Intensity Effects? Most demonstrations of one-trial taste aversion conditioning over delays of several hours have used very intense taste stimuli, that is, strongly flavored solutions consumed for several minutes (Barker & Smith, 1974; Smith & Roll, 1967) or over hours (Garcia et al., 1955), followed by long-lasting illnesses induced by such potent stimuli as radiation or lithium. What would happen if taste aversion conditioning parameters were altered so that they more closely resembled other general process procedures? That is, would you still find one trial conditioning over a 30-min delay if a very brief flavor (lasting only a few seconds) was paired with

[6]Why did the taste cue allow the hawk to begin to associate the visual cue with poison? (Why, in Box 5.1, was Candace reluctant to return to Mamma Rollo's?) See potentiation.

a tiny amount of toxin that produced only a mild illness? Such brief, less potent stimulus presentations are more comparable to the conditioning parameters reported in Table 5.3.

One-trial taste aversion conditioning has been found to be impossible under these conditions (Monroe & Barker, 1979). Rather, a mild conditioned aversion to the taste of saccharin was found only after eight such trials. These researchers concluded that the Law of Strength and general process learning theory better accounted for these results than did preparedness theory. Other theorists (Domjan, 1983; Logue, 1979) have come to similar conclusions.

General Process Learning Versus Preparedness: Tentative Conclusions

Animals bring not only specialized sensory and motor capabilities to the laboratory but also a brain that supports the ability to associate stimuli. As Pavlov first noted, each animal's nervous system apparently makes certain stimulus and response contingencies easier to learn than others; some stimuli are conditioned in a few trials, and others require many trials. Pavlov's observations became even more apparent when Garcia-like experiments were conducted. What can we conclude from these experiments?

Role of Stimulus Salience in Conditioning. The number of trials it takes for a stimulus to become a CS defines the salience of that stimulus. Among other variables, the best predictor of salience is stimulus intensity. As a general rule, more intense stimuli are more salient in that they require fewer trials to be associated. That stimulus intensity is the best predictor of stimulus salience seems to be invariant across species.

Role of Stimulus Specificity in Conditioning. Evidence for stimulus specificity in conditioning across species is not as compelling as evidence for stimulus intensity in conditioning across species. For example, Pavlov noted that his dogs associated sounds better than visual stimuli with food during excitatory conditioning and sights better than sounds with food during inhibitory conditioning over a delay. But the general rule he formulated still holds, namely, that any stimulus can be made into a conditioned stimulus.

General Process Learning Can Incorporate Preparedness. In accommodating the results of preparedness experiments, general process learning theory has been put to the test. While some researchers disagree (see Timberlake, 1994), it now seems that most observations of how and what animals learn can be incorporated into general process learning theory (Domjan, 1983; Logue, 1979). The end result is a synthesis, an evolutionarily based general process theory that accounts for many hundreds of behavioral observations in the field and in the laboratory. Humans are not rats or quail. And rats and quail learn some things differently (more or less rapidly) than humans. But evidence for a general process associative mechanism among animals remains convincing.

Interim Summary

1. Most stimuli can be made into conditioned stimuli, but both stimulus intensity and stimulus quality affect the ease of stimulus associability.

2. A number of experiments have demonstrated that some stimulus-stimulus associations are easy and others are difficult. This has been interpreted to mean that there is ***stimulus specificity*** in association.

3. ***Preparedness*** theory argues that some animals are evolutionarily predisposed to learn more quickly those tasks that promote survival.

4. Animals are said to be prepared, ***unprepared,*** or ***contraprepared*** to learn certain tasks if it takes few trials, an intermediate number of trials, or many trials, respectively.

5. Rapid learning about the consequences of ingestion is aided by innately organized feeding behavior. ***Neophobia*** toward new foods and reduced neophobia with continued exposure to these foods are adaptive in that poisoning is minimized.

6. The *bright, noisy, tasty water experiment* provides evidence of stimulus specificity in conditioning. Garcia and others have shown that flavors are easily associated with illness-inducing toxins and less easily associated with electric shock.

7. With optimal stimulus parameters, flavors and toxin effects can become associated in one trial over a delay of several hours. Garcia and others also suggested that visual and auditory stimuli were easily associated with pain but were contraprepared to be associated with illness.

8. Stimuli in "prepared" experiments often vary in modality, intensity, duration, and number of conditioning trials compared to stimuli in "contraprepared" experiments.

9. Matching shock intensity with illness intensity, intensity and duration of taste stimuli with audiovisual stimuli, and number of conditioning trials has not been accomplished, making comparisons across these experiments most difficult. Appealing to evolutionary arguments to account for different conditioning outcomes is confounded by these procedural differences.

10. Conditioning rats with brief tastes and illnesses cannot be accomplished in one trial over a long delay.

11. General process learning complements prepared learning. The former remains the best account of observed plasticity in animal behavior, including complex human behavior.

DISCUSSION QUESTIONS

9. A later chapter deals with language behavior. Given what you know about the concept of preparedness, can you guess which of the following aspects of language behavior is (are) *prepared* and which is (are) *unprepared?* Babbling? Speaking? Reading? Writing? Spelling? Which should take the most trials to learn?

10. This chapter was introduced with a passage from *The Education of Little Tree.* This sample of the cultural knowledge of Cherokee Indians in this century illustrates how much can be learned merely from noting the associations between stimuli. Is language necessary to acquire this knowledge? Is language necessary to transmit this knowledge to the next generation?

CHAPTER SUMMARY

1. Conditioning procedures accomplished in laboratories can account for complex behavior in laboratories as well as in nature.

2. Among the procedures that have been developed to measure the effects of prior experience on subsequent learning are latent inhibition, sensory preconditioning, higher-order conditioning, overshadowing, potentiation, blocking, and inhibitory conditioning.

3. Compared to novel stimuli, conditioned responses to familiar stimuli take longer to develop, a phenomenon called *latent inhibition*. Both CSs (*CS preexposure effect*) and USs (*US preexposure effect*) can be latently inhibited.

4. Two CSs can become associated together without the benefit of an unconditioned stimulus, a phenomenon known as *sensory preconditioning*. If one of the two CSs is then made a conditioned excitor, the other when tested also shows conditioned excitor properties.

5. When CS_1 is paired with a US, it becomes an excitor. Pairing CS_2 with the CS_1 makes CS_2 an excitor also. This phenomenon is called *higher-order conditioning*.

6. When two CSs are simultaneously conditioned, one is typically conditioned better than the other. One CS is therefore said to *overshadow* the other CS. The *overshadowing* stimulus also is said to be the more *salient* of the two CSs.

7. If taste is added to another CS in a conditioning situation, the CS conditions better than it would by itself. Taste is said to *potentiate* the conditioning of other stimuli.

8. In *blocking* CS_1 is first conditioned as an excitor and then put in a compound with CS_2. Both are conditioned with a US. Under these conditions, CS_2 does *not* become an excitor. CS_1 is said to have *blocked* CS_2 by this *blocking* procedure.

9. In addition to *latent* inhibition, Pavlov identified *internal* inhibition, *external* inhibition, and *conditioned* inhibition, inhibition of delay, and conditioned discrimination procedures. In all examples of inhibition, or inhibitory conditioning, the CR is opposite in direction to the excitatory CR.

10. Conditioned inhibitors can be produced by four methods: (a) by *negative,* or *US–CS, contingencies;* (b) in a *condi-*

tioned discrimination procedure in which a CS⁻ becomes an inhibitor in contrast with CS⁺ excitor; (c) by the *induction method* in which a neutral CS becomes an inhibitor after having been simultaneously paired with an excitor in extinction; and (d) through an *inhibition of delay* procedure in which the early portion of a long duration CS becomes inhibitory.

11. Two *indirect* methods of measuring conditioned inhibition are the *summation test* and the *retardation test*. Inhibitors and excitors algebraically *summate* when added together in extinction. When inhibitors are put into an excitatory conditioning context, the acquisition of excitation is slowed (*retarded*).

12. Any stimulus can be made into a conditioned stimulus, but the species of animal and stimulus intensity and quality affect the associability with a US.

13. A number of experiments demonstrate that some stimulus-stimulus associations are easily learned and others are difficult—that there is *stimulus specificity of association*.

14. *Preparedness* theory argues that some animals are evolutionarily predisposed to make some associations and to learn some tasks more easily than others. If many trials are required for learning, the animal is said to be *contraprepared;* for an intermediate number of trials, the animal is *unprepared*.

15. Rapid learning about the consequences of ingestion is aided by innately organized feeding behavior. *Neophobia* toward new foods and reduced neophobia with continued exposure to them minimizes poisonings.

16. Flavors are easily associated with illness-inducing toxins and less easily associated with electric shock. With optimal stimulus parameters, flavors and toxin-effects can become associated in one trial over a delay of several hours.

17. Matching shock intensity with illness intensity and intensity and duration of taste stimuli with audiovisual stimuli has been difficult to accomplish.

18. Preparedness arguments are confounded by procedural differences among experiments, including failure to equate stimulus intensity and number of conditioning trials.

19. *General process learning* remains the best theory to account for observed plasticity in animal behavior.

KEY TERMS

CHAPTER 6

Instrumental Learning and Operant Conditioning

Granpa told me that frogs can feel the ground shake when you walk. He showed me how the Cherokee walks, not heel down, but toe down, slipping the moccasins on the ground. Then I could come right up and set down beside a frog.

There is a way to run up a mountain.... Granpa showed me the way Cherokees do it. You don't run straight up, you run along the side and angle up as you go. But you don't hardly run on the ground; this is because you place your feet on the high side of brush and tree trunks and roots, which gives you good footing, so you'll never slip.

Granpa taught me how to hand fish.... This is when you lay down on the creek bank and ease your hands into the water and feel for the fish holes. When you find one, you bring your hands in easy and slow, until you feel the fish. If you are patient, you can rub your hands along the sides of the fish and he will lie in the water while you rub him. Then you take one hold behind his head, the other on his tail, and lift him out of the water. It takes some time to learn.

Carter, *The Education of Little Tree* (1976, pp. 58, 73, 94)

Up to now, the lens we have used to study learning has focused somewhat narrowly. In Chapters 3 to 5 we examined basic ways in which animals make associations between stimuli—namely, through the process of classical conditioning. In classical conditioning, environmental stimuli impinge on animals. In turn, animals respond in reflexive ways. Ultimately, through a process Pavlov called *conditioning*, modified reflexes may result from these reflexive interactions with the environment.

In describing classical conditioning as "the modification of basic reflexes," we seem to be relegating animals to automatons—highly interesting but nevertheless robotlike creatures programmed to sense and to respond in certain ways. Humans and other animals are not robots, but a great deal of evidence suggests that, indeed, we are programmed to sense and to respond in identifiable patterns. Our reflexes and other innately disposed behavior patterns have evolved in ways that guarantee matches with the environments we are likely to encounter during our lifetimes. That is, our reflexes are adaptive, and their modification, no matter how mechanical the process may be, also tends to increase our fitness with the environment. Animals engage in a variety of behaviors that seem to be initiated from *within* (i.e, from the internal environment, including the brain) rather than being triggered from *without* (the external environment). Humans and other complex animals seem to exhibit volition and will; they seem to engage in spontaneous voluntary behavior as well as involuntary reflexive behavior.[1]

In addition to our reflexes and innately prepared behavior, people behave in idiosyncratic ways. Genetic arguments aside for the moment, the existence of individual differences has been interpreted here as the result of

---

[1]Questions regarding "voluntary" and "involuntary" behavior are posed here and in following chapters. For present purposes, based on common language usage, accept the distinction as meaningful.

particular learning experiences. In Little Tree's culture, certain patterns of movement and skilled behavior have direct survival value. In Western urban cultures some individuals drive automobiles, program computers, play soccer and guitars, talk on the phone, and read books. People in all cultures learn to like particular foods, songs, dances, books, people—and to dislike others. Some of us excel, some are average, and others never quite get the hang of these learned behaviors. We can account for the many observed differences in human behavior by analyzing the *learning histories* of individuals.

INSTRUMENTAL AND THORNDIKEAN CONDITIONING

In this chapter we expand the study of learning by considering changes in such *nonreflexive* behaviors. How do animals learn as they move and act on the environments they occupy? That is, how do we learn when we *do* something, as opposed to having something done to us? Acquiring and modifying "voluntary" or nonreflexive behavior has historically been called **instrumental learning** or **instrumental conditioning.** "Benjamin's driving skills were *instrumental* in getting him to Miami safely" and "Sarah's assertive behavior is *instrumental* in getting her teacher's attention." The learning of instrumental behavior allows us to construct "new" behavioral units rather than being restricted to modifying reflexive behavior.

A question raised throughout this chapter and the next is the extent to which classical conditioning and instrumental conditioning result from different processes. As a first consideration, however, note that reflexive and instrumental behaviors more often than not work together. Thus, a woman caught walking in a dust storm blinks as the swirling cloud approaches her face (a reflexive response), turns her head, pulls her hat brim lower, and wraps a scarf about her face (all *instrumental responses*) to avoid the full brunt of the blast. Her eye-blink response is acquired through classical conditioning (taking advantage of a reflex) while the instrumental responses of bowing her head and making other shielding gestures are learned through instrumental conditioning (by escaping the aversiveness of blowing dust).

Shooting Free Throws and Kicking Soccer Balls.   We learn to aim a basketball shot toward a hoop by taking advantage of sensory-motor reflexes as well as by making skeletal-muscle adjustments. The eye involuntarily accommodates (the lens becomes thinner) while viewing the moving ball as it approaches the hoop. We shift weight, make minor adjustments in body posture via skeletal muscle flexion and extension, and perhaps change our timing from the previous shot. Some of these adjustments are under voluntary control; others are not. If the next shot is successful, the previous posture (composed of both reflexive and voluntary components) is reproduced on succeeding shots. As we will see, instrumental conditioning of new behaviors, such as making a successful hook shot or kicking a soccer ball with accuracy, are strengthened or weakened, depending on whether the ball goes where it is supposed to go. These skills take many thousands of trials to develop (see Figure 6.1).

FIGURE 6.1   Learning Skilled Behavior

Learning to play soccer requires hours of practice. Reinforcement theory plays a role in our understanding of how skilled performance is acquired and maintained. We begin by recognizing that movement is intrinsically reinforcing. Running around feels good to a child. Second, humans and other animals learn some skilled behavior through imitation; they watch a ball being kicked, for example, and then they model the behavior they see (Bandura, 1962). Reinforcement theory helps account for the way in which players acquire and maintain these skilled motor behaviors. Reinforcers include the praise of others (peers, parents, coaches), self-satisfaction for good play, meeting goals, and learning not to make mistakes (i.e, learning via negative reinforcement—to be covered in the next chapter).

Stimulus Contingencies and Response Contingencies

Instrumental conditioning differs from classical conditioning in other ways. One distinction described earlier, that of contrasting "reflexes" with "voluntary behavior," is not as simple as it seems. Not everyone agrees on what constitutes "voluntary behavior." A distinction between classical and instrumental conditioning that *can* be agreed on has to do with the requirement of a *response contingency* in instrumental conditioning.

Tail Wagging and Saliva Flow.   During salivary conditioning, an experimenter arranges stimulus elements to be presented to the dog. The dog is given food on a certain schedule in relation to a signaling stimulus. The dog does not have to make any particular response to attain the food. Another way to say this is that a stimulus-stimulus (i.e., CS-US) contingency is in effect in classical conditioning. Salivation is measured as the reflexive response to the US and as the conditioned reflex to the CS.

Dogs invariably make other responses, however, during conditioning situations. For example, they look around, they wag their tails, and they pant as they are about to be fed. Are these other responses also reflexive? Are they voluntary or involuntary? What if the experimenter arranged conditions such that the dog was *required* to wag its tail or otherwise to "beg" for its food? That is, rather than merely pairing a ringing bell with food (a stimulus-stimulus contingency), the experimenter required tail wagging before giving food to the dog (a response-stimulus contingency). Would tail wagging increase under these circumstances? Would salivation also increase?

S-S Versus R-S Conditioning.   A shorthand designation for classical conditioning is stimulus-stimulus conditioning, or **S-S conditioning.** By contrast, an instrumental contingency requiring a response before presenting food is called response-stimulus conditioning, or **R-S conditioning.** The most straightforward distinction that can be made, then, between classical and instrumental conditioning is the S-S versus R-S contingency.

Why is this distinction important? What does it matter if an experimenter requires a dog to wag its tail for food (R-S contingency) rather than merely pair the food with the sound of a bell (S-S contingency)? The example may appear trivial, but let us consider the *range of behaviors* that may be conditioned using either S-S or R-S contingencies. Instead of having the dog wag its tail, let's require it to climb stairs, or to sit quietly "on command," or to "point" a bird while hunting, or to race other dogs around a track, or to sniff out explosives hidden in airport luggage. Do such accomplishments seem on the surface to be more complicated, more impressive, than being conditioned to salivate to the sound of a bell? Why? What is the difference?

Range of Possible Responses.   One answer to the question of differences between S-S and R-S conditioning is that *what* animals can learn by S-S contingencies is limited to the range of reflexive responses the animal can make. That is, only inborn response tendencies can be conditioned. By contrast, animals can make a wide range of responses using their skeletal muscles to physically move within their niche. Risking oversimplification, to successfully operate in their environment requires the integration of both sensory and motor aspects of the animal's brain and body. Relative to reflexive responding, animal behavior becomes both more complicated and more interesting as it operates on a much wider environment. Think you could learn to catch a fish by hand like Little Tree did? What if your life depended on it?

Thorndike's Experiments

E. L. Thorndike (1874–1949) was among the first of behavioral scientists to describe how laboratory animals learn to make instrumental responses. Hence, another name for instrumental learning is *Thorndikean conditioning* (or *Thorndikean learning*).[2] In his famous *puzzle box* studies, Thorndike (1898) constructed an experimental chamber with a latching door that could be opened by animals trapped inside (see Box 6.1). Placed in the box for the first time, hungry cats "moved." Their movement included scratching, climbing, and bumping against the walls in a frenzied reaction both to the confinement and to the sight and smell of food available just outside the box. Eventually, by chance movement, the animal might bump against or claw at the simple latching mechanism. The door would release, allowing the cat to escape from the box.

Some time later the cat was returned to the puzzle box for second and third trials. Thorndike found that it took the cat less time to successfully locate and operate the latch. Following many more trials, on being put in the box the cat performed the specific behavior required to unlatch the door without hesitation. Thorndike's measure of learning was "time to escape from the puzzle box as a function of trials" (see Box 6.1). He also observed how dogs and chickens operated in other box environments.

Rats in Mazes

Following Thorndike's use of the puzzle box, many thousands of laboratory animals were conditioned and have learned instrumental responses based on food rewards. (The aversive control of behavior in laboratory animals—typically through the use of annoyers such as electric shock—is discussed in Chapter 7.) By the early part of the 20th century, studying rats in mazes was "in" and Thorndike's puzzle boxes were "out." Rats were placed in a *start box*,

---

[2]In conventional usage, *instrumental conditioning* is often contrasted with *classical conditioning*, and, likewise, comparisons are made between *Pavlovian* and *Thorndikean* conditioning.

BOX 6.1   THORNDIKE'S PUZZLE BOXES

Edward L. Thorndike (1874–1949) confined cats, dogs, and chickens in a variety of boxes to study their associative processes. Some boxes were easier to escape from than others. Pictured is Box K in which a lever had to be depressed and a rope pulled to unlock the door.

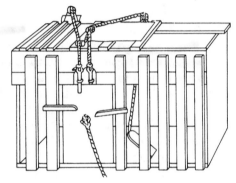

allowed to negotiate a variety of different kinds of turns in *runways* and given a food reward in the *goal box*. (See Figure 6.2.) A variety of mazes have been used, from complicated ones based on the famous human maze at Hampton Court, England, to simple straight runways and T-mazes. How many trials did it take before the rat made no errors (such as turning right when it was supposed to turn left)? How many seconds (or minutes) did the rat take to get from the start box to the goal box? Did it improve from the first trial (slow responding) such that after many trials it responded quickly?

Thorndike's Law of Effect

Thorndike (1911, 1932) postulated an elementary principle governing *all* behavior, namely, the *law of effect*. The **law of effect** simply states that a *response that is followed by a pleasant consequence will tend to be repeated and a response followed by an unpleasant consequence will tend to decrease in fre-*

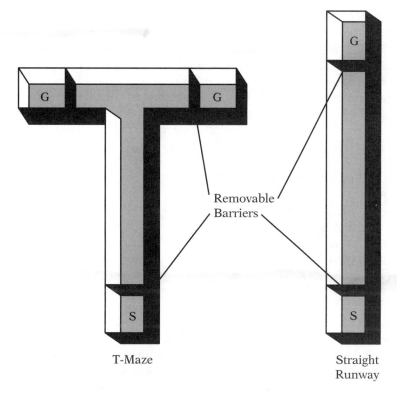

FIGURE 6.2   Types of Mazes

Two simple mazes, a straight runway, and a T-maze are shown. Removable barriers are used to confine rats in start boxes and goal boxes at the beginning and end of each trial, respectively. Mazes have walls that prevent the rat from climbing out.

quency. He called such pleasant and unpleasant consequences **satisfiers** and **annoyers,** respectively. In Thorndike's terms, instrumental movements (responses) that led to the hungry cat's escape from the goal box are "stamped in." "Stamping in" can be likened to "writing" on John Locke's (1690) *tabula rasa* (blank slate); both are metaphors for hypothesized changes in the brain when learning occurs. Unsuccessful movements by the cat (i.e., those that did not allow escape, thereby maintaining both hunger and the annoying confinement) tended to drop out. Wrong turns in mazes dropped out. The end result of the law of effect? Successful responses increase, and unsuccessful responses decrease; animals learn to be more efficient and more effective in operating on the environment.

Hedonism.   Another way to describe the law of effect is to note that all organisms are born with hedonistic tendencies. **Hedonism**—seeking pleasure and avoiding pain—is both adaptive and "normal" for us. Note that Thorndike neither discovered nor invented the law of effect; rather, he recognized the importance of this commonly known general rule governing behavior.[3] Most animals most of the time engage in behaviors that produce pleasure and discontinue behaviors that produce pain. Among the best understood incentives for hedonistic tendencies are the taste and olfactory components of palatable foods.

The Law of Effect, and General Process Learning Theory

The law of effect is a deceptively simple concept. Asserting that satisfiers increase and that annoyers decrease the probability of occurrence of all kinds of preceding behaviors, in *all* animals, however, covers a lot of ground! The law of effect complements classical conditioning in providing support for *general process learning theory*.

Both hedonism and the law of effect are compatible with an evolutionary account. Each can be accounted for as evolutionary adaptations. Risking a tautology, most pleasurable activities in life promote fitness, survival, and reproduction. Food, shelter, and mating (examples of Thorndike's satisfiers) are all pleasurable and adaptive, but the opposite is true of annoyers in the form of hunger, pain, and adverse climate. For most animals in their ecological niches, therefore, the very behaviors they engage in are instrumental in producing food; securing shelter and mates; and avoiding predators, toxins, and reproductive extinction. In summary, the law of effect embodies adaptive responses to selective pressures.

Dan Dennett (1975) beautifully describes both the adaptive nature of hedonism and the law of effect. He argues that the law of effect is an inevitable outcome of natural selection. Box 6.2 presents his theory of human cognitive behavior based on these innate response tendencies in interaction with environments.

Determinism and the Law of Effect

How well does the law of effect account for human learning and behavior? Again, the reader must ultimately be the judge. Most of us are aware that environment at a minimum influences our behavior even if we might disagree that it *determines* our behavior. Indeed, differences in philosophical theory and in learning theory hinge on this very distinction.

---

[3]My grandmother (and Little Tree's) understood and applied basic *carrot and stick* psychology without the benefit of exposure to Thorndike's theory. Carrots (dangled in front) and sticks (applied to the rear) were traditionally used as incentives to motivate donkeys to move in accordance with their human owners' wishes.

Box 6.2   "Thinking Good Thoughts and Making Good Choices"

Why do reinforcer's reinforce? Why does the presentation of food to a hungry animal (or water to a thirsty animal) allow responses that preceded these reinforcers to be so readily learned and repeated on future occasions? Dennett (1975), in an article entitled "Why the Law of Effect Will Not Go Away," argues that the role of reinforcement is to "select" behaviors and responses much the same way that the environment in Darwin's theory of natural selection "chooses" which organisms are to live and which will die. (A similar position has been advanced by Shettleworth, 1975.)

According to Dennett, those animals in past times who were *not* sensitive to "positive reinforcers" or "punishers" (i.e., those aspects of the environment that promote survival), would have gone extinct. Therefore, all extant animals were selected to obey the *law of effect*. The analogy of learning and natural selection has also been put forth by Dawkins (1995). He argues that pain is the analogue of death; learning to avoid pain is learning to survive.

Dennett further argues that "good ideas" are also selected by the same general mechanism. In response to a complicated stimulus environment (i.e., one in which simple reflexive responses are not elicited), all humans *generate* hypotheses, or ideas. The generation of such hypotheses is accomplished by brain structures that have also been selected through evolution; some genotypes underlying some brain structures are better than others at generating likely hypotheses. Intelligent humans *select* those ideas that provide the most optimal consequences (in the same way reinforcement selects appropriate responses). Therefore, according to Dennett, a Darwinian *natural selection* of intelligent behavior, mediated by the law of effect, ensues.

In light of Dennett's arguments, under what conditions is behavior "maladaptive?" Does the *law of effect* provide an ethic of "right" and "wrong?"

A position of *hard determinism* asserts that all human behavior could be accounted for by combining **biological determinism** with **environmental determinism.** A *biological determinist* asserts that genes expressed in a given environment severely restrict alternative response outcomes. Hardwired reflexive behavior, FAPs, instincts, and so on are examples of biologically determined behavior. Such behaviors are typically seen as being more or less "involuntary." An *environmental determinist* asserts that responses are affected by what they produce (i.e., the law of effect). In Thorndike's terms, such learned behavior is (involuntarily) "stamped in" by satisfiers. A *hard determinist* position, then, proposes that humans and other animals do not have "free choice." As we'll see in the following sections, John B. Watson and B. F. Skinner are famous advocates of a hard determinist position.

By contrast, a philosophy of *soft determinism* asserts that both genes and environments influence but do not determine human behavior. Genes and environment limit response alternatives but do not prohibit choice (i.e., truly voluntary behavior) from among these alternatives. To test your understanding of the distinction between hard and soft determinism, review Dennett's position in Box 6.2. Is Dennett a hard or soft determinist?[4]

John B. Watson's Behaviorism

> *Give me a dozen healthy infants, well-formed, and my own specified world to bring them up in and I'll guarantee to take anyone at random and train him to become any type of specialist I might select—doctor, lawyer, artist, merchant-chief, and yes, even beggarman and thief, regardless of his talents, penchants, tendencies, abilities, vocations, and race of his ancestors.* (Watson, 1924, p. 30)

One of the first psychologists to espouse a position of hard environmental determinism was also one of the more amazing characters in the history of psychology, John B. Watson (1878–1958). (See Box 6.3.) Watson's belief that human behavior is directly, inevitably determined by the environment is evident in his famous statement that opens this section. This clarion call announced a philosophy he called **behaviorism.**

The term *behaviorism* is unfortunate: Characterizing Watson's position as *environmentalism* is better. Why? Because genetic predispositions are ignored in Watson's theory, and, as we saw in Chapter 1, a general theory of behavior must include both innate and environmental components.

We may be generous and forgive Watson's trumpeting of environment over biology since in 1920 there was a paucity of evidence for behavioral genetics but a great surplus of empty speculation about human "instincts." The fact is that he offered little experimental evidence to support his environmental claims. He never trained a lawyer, physician, or thief. Watson's laboratory investigations bearing on the preceding quoted assertion consisted of only a few published papers. One was a classic that dealt with conditioning a fear response in a child (Watson & Rayner, 1920). Nevertheless, Watson's influence was profound. Behaviorism dominated academic psychology for the next 40 years and influenced both U.S. educators and popular culture (Buckley, 1989). Among those in the behaviorist movement was a young experimental psychologist just embarking on a 50-year research career. B. F. Skinner (1904–1990) and his many students *were* successful in accomplishing laboratory research on which a formal experimental analysis of learned behavior could be built.

Interim Summary

1. Behavior has both reflexive and nonreflexive (voluntary and involuntary) components.

---

[4]Hard.

BOX 6. 3 JOHN B. WATSON AND THE HISTORY OF BEHAVIORISM

John B. Watson during his student days at Furman University, circa 1899.

In his 1989 book *Mechanical Man: John Broadus Watson and the Beginnings of Behaviorism,* Kerry W. Buckley asserts that Watson's *behaviorism* played a major role in the modernization of American society. At the turn of the century, Watson left the South Carolina farm where he had been reared in poverty. After taking his doctorate at the University of Chicago, he moved to Johns Hopkins University, where, within a few short years, he founded the behaviorist movement and became one of America's most influential psychologists.

At the pinnacle of his academic career, Watson and his graduate student, Rosalie Rayner, published the infa-mous "Little Albert" experiment in which an eleven-month-old child was classically conditioned to fear a white rat. Their point? Not unlike other animals, Watson argued, humans are buffeted by nature on the one hand and an all-controlling environment on the other. We are programmed throughout our childhoods. According to Watson, human minds, consciousness, and will are illusions.

Watson's academic successes came crashing down in 1920 following a scandalous divorce (his extramarital escapades made the front pages of the *New York Times*). Forced to resign his academic position at the age of 42, Watson married Rayner and headed for a more lucrative job with the J. Walter Thompson advertising agency. There Watson promoted his behaviorist philosophy to a far wider audience than would have been the case had he remained a university professor. Together John and Rosalie wrote popular magazine articles, published books, and gave radio interviews, on, among other topics, their bizarre philosophy of child rearing. Fathers should be remote and inaccessible, they asserted. And even mothers should severely limit the amount of affection they give their children.

Buckley points out that the behaviorist philosophy fit well with the emerging urban culture of the "roaring '20s." A *New York Times* review of Watson's *Behaviorism,* published in 1924, called it "perhaps the most important book ever written."

2. Nonreflexive behavior can be modified by a process called ***instrumental conditioning*** or ***instrumental learning.*** Also known as *Thorndikean conditioning,* instrumental conditioning complements *classical conditioning* (the modification of reflexive behavior).

3. Researchers who condition animals by **S-S conditioning,** or classical conditioning procedures, arrange *stimulus-stimulus contingencies:* A CS is followed by a US.

4. Researchers conditioning animals by ***R-S conditoning,*** or instrumental procedures, arrange *response contingencies:* A response is followed by a positive reinforcer or a punishing stimulus.

5. Instrumental learning has been studied in the laboratory by measuring how long it took animals confined to puzzle boxes to escape (Thorndike), and by placing rats in mazes and measuring both wrong turns and time to complete the maze over repeated trials.

6. E. L. Thorndike proposed that behavior is modifiable by the ***law of effect:*** Responses followed by ***satisfiers*** (pleasant stimuli) will be repeated and responses followed by ***annoyers*** (aversive stimuli) will not be.

7. Both ***hedonism*** and the law of effect are adaptive: Both are the result of evolutionary selective pressures that select adaptive behavior by the effect it has on the environment.

8. Instrumental learning based on the law of effect addresses how *all* animals learn in *all* circumstances and is therefore a *general process learning theory.*

9. ***Biological determinism*** is the philosophical position that behavior is caused by genetic mechanisms. By contrast, John B. Watson's philosophy of ***behaviorism*** espouses a hard ***environmental determinism*** in which the expression of behavior is controlled by reinforcers and punishers. Modern determinists combine these two positions.

DISCUSSION QUESTIONS

1. Little Tree is learning adaptive survival skills in both passages from *The Education of Little Tree* that begin Chapters 5 and 6. What is different about the learning that is described from the kinds of learning we studied in earlier chapters?

OPERANT CONDITIONING

As a graduate student, B. F. Skinner objected to the way animal learning experiments were conducted in the laboratory. By his own account (Skinner, 1959), he decided to automate the runway procedure (see Figure 6.3). First he attached a feeder to the runway; the weight of the moving rat was *instrumental* in tilting the runway, mechanically activating the feeder. Skinner eventu-

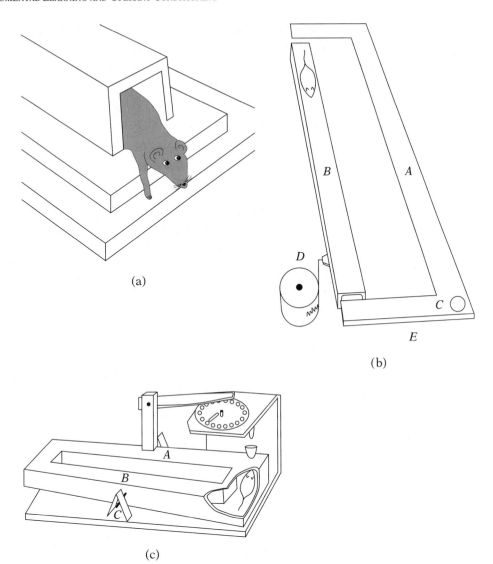

(a)

(b)

(c)

FIGURE 6.3 The Evolution of the Skinner Box

B. F. Skinner describes the evolution of the Skinner box in a tongue-in-cheek article decrying formal scientific method (Skinner, 1959). He claims that being personally lazy (which he wasn't) led him to design the Skinner box to automate the collection of data rather than continue the labor-intensive use of runways (a), of circular runways (b), and of a circular runway with an automated feeding device (c).

ally did away with the runway altogether. He next simplified the apparatus so that the rat merely pushed open a door to get food:

> *The behavior of the rat in pushing open the door...was obviously learned, but its status as part of the final performance was not clear. It seemed wise to add an initial conditioned response connected with ingestion in a quite arbitrary way. I chose the first device that came to hand—a horizontal bar or lever placed where it could be conveniently depressed by the rat to close a switch that operated a [feeder].* (Skinner, 1959, p. 366)

The Experimental Environment of the Skinner Box

With the invention of what became known as a *Skinner box*, Skinner's research strategy for many years focused on analyzing how food rewards influenced key pecking by pigeons and lever pressing by rats and other animals. The primary dependent variables that can be measured in this experimental environment are (a) rate of lever pressing, (b) control of response patterning under different conditions of reinforcement, and (c) "choice" behavior (in boxes with more than one response key).

Skinner's Research Strategy.   Skinner was aware of the criticism of ethologists regarding the study of animal behavior in laboratories. He was also sensitive to the ethologists' concept of innately organized behavior (Skinner, 1966). How did he justify his use of the conditioning box methodology?

1. Skinner intentionally removed animals from their natural environments to better identify and isolate independent variables controlling the animals' responses.
2. Skinner chose what he thought were arbitrary responses (key pecking and lever pressing) that were presumably *not* akin to FAPs or other biologically prepared responses (Skinner, 1963).
3. Skinner designed a convenient, economical, and reliable way to automate how a stimulus was delivered to the animal, and to measure its responses. In doing so he provided a standardized methodology that investigators adopted in laboratories around the world.

Figure 6.4 shows Skinner and his Skinner box. The small chamber consists of four walls, a ceiling, and a grid floor. From one wall a lever (sometimes called a *manipulandum*) protrudes. A rat or other small mammal is trained to press the lever. Depressing the lever activates an electrical switch, allowing responses to be recorded. In another version of the chamber, the manipulandum is a backlit panel or disc, called a *key*. Positioned on the wall at an optimal height for a pigeon to peck, the key is also connected to a *microswitch* allowing the pigeon's responses to be electrically recorded. Food or water can be delivered into a small container attached to the wall for the rats.

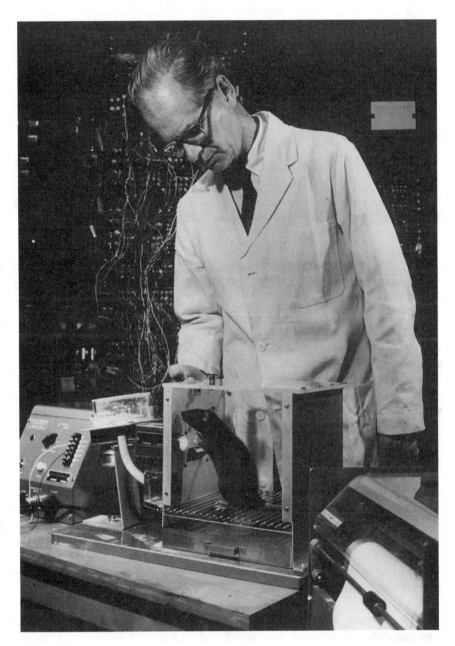

FIGURE 6.4   B. F. Skinner (1904–1990)

For pigeons, a movable "grain hopper" from which food can be pecked is made available for a few seconds, and then withdrawn from the chamber. The chamber may also be fitted with a speaker over which background masking noise (or any other auditory stimulus) can be introduced and with lights for both illumination and signaling purposes. Finally, aversive control of behavior can be investigated by applying electric current to the grid floor.

The Study of Operant Conditioning

How did Skinner begin the experimental analysis of behavior? Starting in the 1930s and continuing for 50 years, he and his many students systematically studied **operant conditioning** in these experimental chambers. Operant conditioning is best understood as a variant of instrumental learning.

Operant Responses.   First, Skinner defined the terms he would use to analyze behavior. He defined an **operant** as any response that "operated" on the environment (cf. *instrumental response*). Because a lever-pressing response is an easily repeated operant, Skinner's **free operant** method can be contrasted with the *discrete trial* methods characteristic of other types of behavioral analysis. Examples of discrete trials are classical conditioning, escaping from a puzzle box, and negotiating a maze. Each trial in these procedures has a discrete beginning, duration, and end. This sequence defines a *trial.* By contrast, in operant conditioning, one lever-pressing response is *not* called a trial. Rather, the individual makes responses at any time within an extrended session (typically lasting 30 to 60 min).

The power of the law of effect can be seen in operant conditioning. Naive rats can be easily trained to lever press and pigeons to peck at a lighted disc on the wall of a Skinner box. A hungry rat when placed in the chamber will explore the new environment for several minutes by sniffing, rearing on its hind legs, and touching objects with its front paws. The rat's exploratory behavior appears to be both voluntary and purposive rather than reflexive. For this reason, the rat's behavior is said to be *emitted* rather than *elicited.* An examples of *elicited behavior* from earlier chapters is reflexive salivation; food placed on the dog's tongue involuntarily *elicited* a salivation response. By contrast, instrumental responses—including arbitrary operants such as pressing a lever—are examples of what Skinner called *emitted behavior.*

Operant Level.   Every emitted behavior has an **operant level,** or *baseline,* of occurrence. For example, the likelihood that the rat will sniff floors and walls on first entering the box is high and that it will deftly depress the lever in the box is low. Operant conditioning, then, involves selecting a low-level operant and, through reinforcement, making the target response more probable.

Magazine Training.   During the rat's initial exploration, the experimenter initiates the first phase of training, called **magazine training.** Approaches to the food cup (cf. *magazine*, where military provisions are kept) are *reinforced* when the rat finds food in the cup. That is, behavior is reinforced by providing food immediately following the desired response. The food is called a **positive reinforcer** (cf. Thorndike would call it a *satisfier*).

Secondary Reinforcers. What has the rat learned up to now? *Where* the food is located. An electrical feeder is activated by the experimenter, delivering more food to the cup. (The feeder noise may initially produce a startle response that quickly disappears.) After a few trials the sound of the electrically activated feeder becomes a *conditioned stimulus* signaling food. Furthermore, after the feeder sound has been paired several times with food delivery, the feeder sound becomes a **secondary reinforcer** via the process of higher-order conditioning (discussed in Chapter 4). (Indeed, another term for a secondary reinforcer is conditioned reinforcer.) The sound of the feeder has become associated with food, and animals will work merely to hear the sound. The process by which a secondary reinforcer has its effect is called *secondary reinforcement*, or *conditioned reinforcement*. We return later to the secondary reinforcing effects of the feeder in another context. For now you might consider what secondary reinforcers control your behavior.

What has the rat or pigeon learned up to now? *Where* the food is located and *when* food becomes available (signaled by the feeder's sound). When the individual has learned these things, the magazine training is complete.

Shaping Behavior. Shortly after magazine training, the rat initially is given food for merely approaching the lever, usually located next to the food cup. (Likewise, the pigeon's illuminated key is placed head high on the wall for easy pecking, and it is located next to the feeder.) This intermediate procedure is necessary because the rat has yet to learn how to press the lever. For example, should the animal retreat to the rear of the cage and then turn its head back in the direction of the lever or make any movement toward the lever, the orientation behavior is reinforced by delivery of a positive reinforcer. Next, only the intermediate behavior of approaching and touching the lever is reinforced. After the animal is fully trained, the experimenter will reinforce only the **target response** or *target behavior*. In this instance, the target response is depressing the lever or key with sufficient force to close an electrical contact. This method of training responses that are approximately like the target behavior is called **shaping by successive approximation.** Eventually, only the target response (i.e., lever pressing) will earn the food reward.

Positive Reinforcement. The process by which selected operants are altered by the application of positive reinforcers is called **positive reinforcement.** The process of positive reinforcement (or, more simply, reinforcement) may be compared to Pavlov's conditioning. What has the rat or pigeon learned? *Where* the food is located, *when* food is delivered to the food cup, and, most important, the response contingency—*which* operant response is associated with the positive reinforcer, food. This last factor is what makes conditioning *operant* or *instrumental* rather than classical.

The Home Environment as a Skinner Box

Can human behavior be shaped? From his earliest writings, Skinner asserted that human behavior could be systematically changed by judiciously applying reinforcers and punishers. For example, his famous utopian novel *Walden Two* (Skinner, 1948) created a carefully controlled community. Adult "planners" and "programmers" shaped appropriate behaviors in both children and adults by carefully reinforcing only certain behaviors. Likewise, the programmers modified unwanted behaviors either by extinction or punishment or by rewarding alternative behaviors. Let's next look at a few examples of similarities in the methods by which rats, pigeons, and humans acquire new patterns of responding in Skinner boxes and home environments.

A Game of "Hot and Cold."   A favorite game played by children (and some adults) resembles experimenters with their rats. The task of the person that is selected to be "it" is to determine a *target behavior*—to find a particular object that has been hidden or to guess a secret word. The experimenters *shape* the behavior (moving around in the environment or guessing categories of words) by saying "you're hot" (for getting close) or "you're cold" for unwanted responses. For example, if a marble has been hidden in a vase on a shelf, movements toward that side of the room would be reinforced with the words "you're getting hot." Likewise, adults lead small children to Easter eggs by *successive approximation.* The words "hot" and "cold" can be construed as *secondary* reinforcers and punishers. These words have acquired meaning through the process of higher-order conditioning.)

Interim Summary

1. B. F. Skinner's research strategy is called ***operant conditioning.*** He picked an arbitrary response, called an ***operant*** (such as lever pressing), and analyzed how reinforcement modified and controlled that response in animals placed in an experimental chamber called a *Skinner box.* Because the response can be made repeatedly by the animal, it is called a ***free operant.***

2. The sequence of training operant responses is (a) to measure the baseline, or ***operant level,*** prior to reinforcement; (b) to initiate ***magazine training*** in which the sound of a feeder becomes a ***secondary reinforcer*** *(or conditioned reinforcer)* through its association with the ***positive reinforcer*** of food.

3. The ***target response*** of lever pressing is obtained by a procedure called ***shaping by successive approximation,*** or more simply, *shaping.* In this process, partial responses that approximate the target behavior are initially reinforced until, at the end stage, only the target response is reinforced.

4. The process of training a specific response using a reinforcer is called ***positive reinforcement,*** or, more simply, *reinforcement.* When a secondary reinforcer (conditioned reinforcer) is used, the process is called *secondary reinforcement,* or *conditioned reinforcement.*

5. Operant conditioning can be accomplished outside the Skinner box. Conditioning the desired target behavior requires both attention to detail and specific training skills.

DISCUSSION QUESTIONS

2. Can you verbalize the difference between a reinforcer and the concept of *reinforcement?*

3. Depending on the child's age and other circumstances, might one get better performance if a small piece of candy was used in place of the words "you're hot"? Why or why not?

4. Skinner's distinction between elicited and emitted behavior is controversial. The first time a hungry rat is placed in a Skinner box, it will explore the new environment for several minutes by sniffing, rearing on its hind legs, and touching objects with its front paws. A familiar environment does not elicit such behavior. Why does such behavior occur in a novel environment? Is such behavior elicited or emitted (or both)? Is it reflexive? Is it adaptive?

5. Eating good foods, drinking safe water, breathing clean air, living in safe homes and apartments, staying disease free, meeting sexual needs, and attaining other human consummatory behaviors are reinforcing experiences, as are such experiences as earning college degrees, receiving promotions, and buying new homes and BMWs. Which are primary, and which secondary, reinforcers? Which of these experiences are most likely to reinforce you and maintain your behavior? Could you make a reinforcement hierarchy?

6. Remember learning to ride a bike? Can you identify individual operants of this acquired skill? If anyone helped you to learn, did that person use successive approximation? Remember painstakingly printing the alphabet? Learning to play a musical instrument? Does the concept of successive approximation capture these processes as well?

7. We trained the professor of our graduate learning class to write only at the very top of the blackboard, an uncomfortable position that he could reach only by stretching. He never knew what his students were up to. We took advantage of his behavior of writing on the board while at the same time attempting to make eye contact with students. Before class we got together, made two little marks on each side of the blackboard about one-third down

from the top, and reinforced the professor only when he wrote above but not below the imaginary line connecting our marks. What is reinforcing to a professor? Eye contact. Expressions of interest in students' eyes. When he wrote below the line, we looked away. When he wrote above the line, we smiled, nodded sagely, and paid rapt attention. By successive approximation we inched him up, class by class. After several weeks he was on his tiptoes. Get together with other students before class and...

INSTINCTIVE BEHAVIOR AND OPERANT CONDITIONING

To this point, we have contrasted instrumental learning with the modification of innate reflexes by classical conditioning. But remember that behavior has more influences than just environmental contingencies. A complete behavioral analysis involves the interplay of species-specific behavior and learned responses. Consider the following observation by Thorndike. He used a puzzle box called Box Z that required a cat to perform a response selected by the experimenter. For example, he required one cat to scratch its belly. Thorndike would open the door and allow the cat to escape to its food when the cat performed that target behavior. Thorndike reported response degradations when he tried to reinforce responses such as scratching. With repeated trials the cat merely made swiping motions at its underside rather than effectively scratching itself. Other researchers, we will see, have also reported "response degradations." In this section, we'll look at experiments on rats, pigeons, and raccoons as well as humans that bear on the interaction of species-specific behaviors and learned responses.

Foraging and Learning in Mazes

Recall that Skinner chose the lever-pressing response by rats and key pecking by pigeons because he reasoned they were relatively arbitrary operants. That is, in his analysis, these responses were neutral with respect to the innately determined consummatory behaviors that animals brought with them to the laboratory. In particular, he was concerned that rats brought innate behavior patterns to the maze learning task. Let's look at an experiment that raised serious questions about the role of reinforcement in learning in part because of what rats do "naturally."

How Do Rats Learn to Run Mazes?   Classic experiments by Tolman and Honzik (1930a; 1930b) studied how three groups of rats learned their way through a complex maze. This particular maze had more than a dozen choice points prior to arrival in a goal box. On each trial, the number of errors (turning back toward the start box and entries into blind alleys) was counted along the way to the goal box. Once there, one group of rats was rewarded with food in the goal box. For the first 10 trials, two other groups were simply removed and put back in their home cages without being fed. The prediction of traditional reinforcement theorists is that the food reinforcement allows the first group to learn the maze more quickly than the other two study (Tolman & Honzik, 1930b). And, as Figure 6.5 illustrates, for the first 10 trials the number of errors decreased by over 60% for the food-reinforced group. Notice, however, that even in the absence of a food reward, the other two groups showed a more modest but still substantial 35% improvement in their error rate.

In addition to the obvious question concerning the role of food reinforcement in learning, several more basic questions are raised by the Tolman and Honzik (1930b) experiment. In order of behavioral complexity: Why do rats move in a maze in the first place? Why do rats find their way to the goal

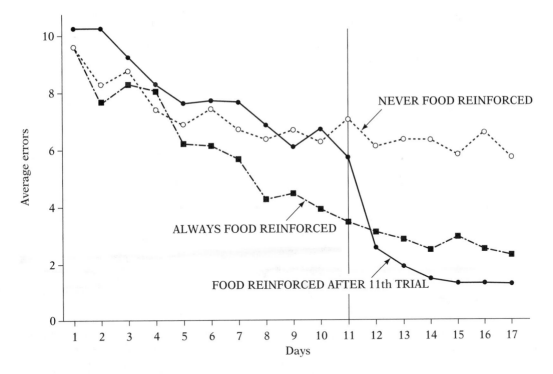

FIGURE 6.5 Tolman's Latent Learning Experiment

In Tolman and Honzik's latent learning experiment, the performance of rats labeled NEVER FOOD REINFORCED is compared with those labeled FOOD REINFORCED AFTER 11th TRIAL. Note the latter group's rapid improvement in performance relative to the group labeled ALWAYS FOOD REINFORCED, evidence for the phenomenon of latent learning. (Tolman & Honzik, 1930b)

boxes in mazes? Why do rats reduce the number of wrong turns on their way to the goal box in a maze?

Species-Specific Foraging Behavior. We only can try to make educated guesses as to a rat's motivation. Here we note that food deprivation increases movement in rats and that increasing movement is adaptive because active rats are more likely than inactive rats to encounter food. So the fact that all rats in the Tolman and Honzik (1930b) experiment were food deprived provides them basic motivation to forage within a novel environment. The answer to the second question is not unrelated to the first; rats also have species-specific foraging tendencies that allow them to rapidly and efficiently "map" the environment they traverse (see Olton, Collison, & Werz, 1977; Olton & Samuelson, 1976). These *cognitive maps* allow rats to become increasingly efficient at getting to a place where sometimes there has been food. Once there, one of two events takes place: Either the rats are fed (which is reinforcing) or they are removed from a place in which there is no food to a place where there is food (also reinforcing). The better performance of rats finding food in the goal box suggests that food is more reinforcing than merely being removed from the goal box and placed in a home cage in which the rat has a history of being fed.

Latent Learning

The second part of Tolman and Honzik's (1930b) experiment is not so easily explained, however. Note that in Figure 6.5 on the 11th trial, after traversing the maze, one group of rats that had never been food reinforced found food in the goal box. The effect of this single food-reinforced trial was dramatic; on the very next trial, these rats' performance equaled that of rats who had been food reinforced from the beginning. The remaining group of rats (that never experienced food reward in the goal box) continued to make the same number of errors as before. Tolman reasoned that the dramatic improvement in one trial reflected a change in performance rather than learning; that is, he assumed that all groups had learned the maze more or less equally after 10 trials. According to Tolman, more experience with the maze in the absence of food reinforcement was sufficient for learning to occur. Adding a food reward increased the animal's performance only. Tolman used the term **latent learning** to describe the learning that occurred in the absence of food reward.

Interpreting Latent Learning. Tolman admitted to the possibility that some form of weak, nonfood reinforcement is responsible for the improved performance of all rats over the first 10 trials. How do we now interpret the relatively more rapid learning of the rats that were food reinforced beginning on trial 11? These rats experienced the following cumulative reinforcement: (1) learning where food wasn't while foraging on trials 1 to 10, (2) being taken out of a nonfood environment and placed in a home cage, one that had acquired secondary reinforcing properties because of prior feedings there, and (3) after trial 10, discovering food in the goal box. So it is incorrect to say that this group learned the maze in the absence of reinforcement.

So much for the latent learning of this group. How about the food-reinforced group? During trials 1 to 10, the food-reinforced rats learned where food wasn't (early part of maze) and where it was (end of maze). Both the latent learning group and the food-reinforced group of rats, then, had a sufficient number of foraging trials to map the maze. The addition of the food incentive determined their terminal level of performance.[5]

A traditional interpretation of Tolman and Honzik's (1930b) concept of latent learning is that learning can occur in the absence of food reinforcement and that other sources of reinforcement cannot be ruled out. Why are there fewer errors across the first few trials for all groups in Figure 6.5? Making fewer errors means that the rat arrives at the goal box sooner, either to eat food (reinforced group) or to be taken out of the goal box and returned to the home cage more quickly (other two groups). Animals in the nonfood reward groups had a history of being fed in the home cage and a history of never being fed in the maze; therefore, the home cage would have more secondary reinforcing cues associated with it.

Latent Learning or Foraging?   An alternative interpretation of Tolman and Honzik's (1930b) experiment stresses the rats' innate behavioral predispositions: Making fewer errors in a maze makes a rat more efficient in that it expends less energy in locating the source(s) of food. Innate feeding tendencies are further played out in differentially reinforcing environments (i.e., food found in the goal box or food found in the home cage). In this view, hungry rats are disposed to systematic foraging, and these foraging experiences, whether successful or not in finding food in the maze, *are remembered* (Olton et al., 1977; Olton & Samuelson, 1976).

Purposive Behavior.   Ironically, Tolman would be in complete agreement with this alternative interpretation in that he was among the first learning psychologists to propose that behavior is purposive (Tolman, 1932). In Tolman's view, rats ran in order to secure food incentives rather than food acting to mechanically stamp in faster running speeds. For this and other reasons, as we see again in Chapter 9, Tolman is one of the first animal learning theorists who attributed cognitive processes to infrahumans.

---

[5]On examining Figure 6.5, the reader should not assume that the terminal performance of the two food-rewarded groups differed significantly. The mean number of errors of one group was less than the mean number of errors of the other, but no statistical analysis was reported in this study. In addition, the terminal level of performance theoretically could be shifted by either increasing or decreasing the rat's hunger level, by increasing or decreasing the palatability of the food reinforcer, and so forth.

Reinforcing Innate Feeding Tendencies in Humans.   Let's move from hungry rats seeking food in a maze to a human neonate seeking food from her immediate environment. Are there similarities? Human babies innately *root* (search for the nipple) when hungry. Environmental stimulation (tactile stimulation around her mouth) provides feedback as to her progress in finding a food source. (Not here. Not there. What's that smell? Here it is!) Sweet, warm milk from a nipple is a powerful reinforcer that both elicits and then reinforces the consummatory behaviors of sucking and swallowing. That learning occurs and that memories of this learned behavior are formed are evidenced by the increased sucking proficiency of older, more experienced nursers.

Skinner's Quest for Pure, Arbitrary Operant Responses

Skinner was aware of Tolman's experiments and agreed with him that rats brought innate tendencies into the laboratory. Skinner stopped using alleys and mazes and designed an arbitrary operant response, lever-pressing, to study the effects of reinforcement. He reasoned that rats might have evolved foraging behaviors but not lever-pressing ones. Lever-pressing, therefore, like a pigeon pecking a lighted key, was a more arbitrary response. Free from innate behavioral tendencies, the effects of reinforcement could more easily be determined. Why did Skinner think that the distinction between "arbitrary responses" and "innate feeding responses" was important? Simply because the range of possible behaviors that can be "arbitrarily" conditioned is greater than innately organized responses. Humans in fact write poetry and play the piano as well as ingest food. Writing poetry and playing the piano did not evolve in response to selective pressures, and neither is as important as the *consummatory behavior* of eating. This is the sense in which Skinner thought of lever pressing and key pecking as arbitrary.

Key Pecking Is Not Arbitrary.   But look closely at the photos in Figure 6.6. A pigeon is reinforced with water (top photos) or with food (bottom photos) for pecking at a backlit key. The difference is obvious. Water-reinforced pecking responses produce closed-mouth drinking postures (top), and food-reinforced pecking responses model those made by pigeons eating grain, closed mouth (Jenkins & Moore, 1973). At least in this instance, the operant is not as arbitrary as Skinner had hoped.

Preparedness and Instrumental Behavior

Should we be surprised that an analysis of operant responses reveals a certain degree of "innate" organization? Certainly not. Skinner's assertion that instrumental responses are "emitted" does not change the fact that animals have evolved to behave in specific ways. Their innately organized behavior patterns match the niches they have occupied over many years (Skinner, 1966). Evidence for *innately organized behavior*, *species-specific behaviors*, *preparedness*,

FIGURE 6.6 Birds' Beaks: Eating and Drinking Positions

Pigeons peck keys differently, depending on whether they are water-reinforced (top panels) or food-reinforced (bottom panels). Apparently, closed beaks facilitate drinking, and open beaks facilitate picking up grain. The response topography is not as arbitrary as Skinner thought operant responding should be (photos courtesy of Dr. Herbert Jenkins).

and *stimulus specificity* was presented earlier. What is known about the interactions of instinctive behavior and operantly conditioned responses? We begin with an example of complex human courtship behavior, and then present an animal model that helps to account for it.

Human Courtship Patterns. Have you ever found yourself wandering back to a place where you had a chance encounter with a person you found attractive? Imagine that you're driving around one day and see this magnificent person whose smile seems to be just for you. Over the next few days you begin to go out of your way to attempt to locate your goal—let's call this person Tracey. For the sake of argument, let us consider this complex behavior of "I'm attracted to you and want to see you/please notice me" a form of innately organized human courtship behavior.

Assume two things: first, that merely seeing Tracey is a positive reinforcer and, second, that your presence has no effect on whether or not Tracey appears. You learn that Tracey can be seen leaving at 8:15 A.M. and arriving at 5:30 P.M. You continue checking at other times even though you are seldom reinforced. As a matter of fact, you shower, change your clothes, and brush your hair before driving by at various times during the day and night. To your embarrassment, you find yourself parking nearby on the off-chance...

Further assume that Tracey finds out about you, considers you a pest (who *is* this strange person always smiling at me?), and without your knowledge begins to punish your behavior. Noticing your ever-present car, Tracey uses a different entrance and exit to the apartment complex. No reinforcement for this strange person. Aware that you no longer see Tracey with the same frequency, you nevertheless continue your pattern of behavior. Unaware that your behavior keeps you from seeing Tracey as often as you might, you nonetheless manage to encounter your "satisfier" at least some of the time.

How can we account for this pattern of behavior? What maintains your persistence? Recognizing that much of our sexual behavior defies rational analysis, should we suspect that some innate patterns of human courtship behavior are involved? Is it possible that associative reinforcement theory may also help explain what is going on? We begin our analysis by observing a pigeon in a (marginally) similar situation.

Autoshaping and Automaintenance

Place a pigeon in a Skinner box and on the average of once a minute light the bird's pecking key for 8 sec. After 8 sec, turn off the light and raise the grain hopper to allow the hungry pigeon to eat for several seconds. Simple enough. All the bird has to do is walk over to the grain hopper when it notices the light is on, wait for the food reinforcer to appear a few seconds later, and then eat. This procedure resembles classical conditioning: The light is the CS and the food is the US, and no response contingency is required. (Compare: Tracey's apartment is the CS; the sight of Tracey is the US; and no response on your part is required to make Tracey appear.)

Of the 36 birds trained in this manner by Brown and Jenkins (1968), *all* of them began to peck at the lighted key, even though pecking had nothing to do either with the light coming on or the food becoming available. Note that these researchers did not use the method of successive approximation to shape the naive birds' key-pecking behavior. Rather, they set automatic timers for the lights to come on and food to be delivered, and then walked away. Hence, the Brown and Jenkins training procedure came to be known as **autoshaping** (also called *sign tracking*—can you guess why?).

Analysis of Autoshaping.   On the surface, autoshaping appears to be procedurally more like classical conditioning than instrumental conditioning.

However, classical conditioning does not tell us why the first key-peck occurs. Food elicits reflexive digestive responses. Why does the light induce pecking behavior? The size of the backlit key is presumably too large to elicit generalized feeding responses (see Hogan, 1973). Since the bird doesn't merely confuse the large spot of light with food, most researchers concur that the light-food (S-S) sequence is learned quite quickly by classical conditioning. Because food and the light appear together in time, the pigeon begins to peck the light "as if" it were food.

Thought question: Would you predict that Tracey's apartment complex becomes "hot" by its association with Tracey? Is our hero courting the apartment complex as well as courting the person?

Automaintenance. Why does the pigeon continue pecking the key? Probably because the unnecessary pecking is being reinforced both by the food (primary reinforcer) and by the light (a secondary reinforcer established by higher-order conditioning). First, and most important, for the pecking response to continue, the availability of food must be positively correlated with the light being on. That is, pigeons will *not* peck at lighted keys if food is predicted less than 50% of the time that the light is on (Gamzu & Williams, 1971, 1973). Moreover, if grain availability continues to be associated with the light, pigeons maintain their (unnecessary) key-pecking responses indefinitely. Gamzu and Schwartz (1973) called this phenomenon **automaintenance.** What else is known about the phenomena of autoshaping and automaintenance? Perhaps the most striking finding is that pigeons seem to be relatively insensitive to the consequences of these key-pecking responses. This is quite ironic. Reinforcement theory demands that animals be exquisitely sensitive to the consequences of their responses, and, indeed, the subtle patternings of key-pecking and bar-pressing can be produced in the laboratory. These patterns show that in some ways they are exquisitely sensitive to consequences. But if the experimenter changes the reinforcement rules for pigeons on automaintenance schedules, another surprising finding emerges. That outcome shows that key-pecking is also in some ways innately tied to the food.

Maladaptive Key-Pecking Responses? Suppose that key pecking *delays* reinforcement. That is, arrange the contingency so that key pecks to the lighted key turn the light off and are *not* reinforced with food. (Note in this arrangement that both the *primary* and *secondary reinforcers* have been removed. In the human example, your presence drives off Tracey.) On the other hand, if the bird makes *no* key-peck responses while the light is on, food *is* forthcoming. Therefore, it pays the bird *not* to key peck because key pecking is punished by not getting the expected food reinforcement. However, after several hundred such trials of not pecking → food, pecking → no food, birds continued to peck the lighted key about one-third of the time (Williams & Williams, 1969). This procedure, called *negative automaintenance,* produces birds that frequently miss the opportunity to eat due to their persistent pecking.

The nonreinforced key-pecking behavior seen on negative automaintenance schedules is troublesome for reinforcement theory. Such behavior seems to be both maladaptive (expending energy without payoff) and contrary to the law of effect (engaging in behavior that delays reinforcement).

But is it?

Significance of Autoshaping and Automaintenance

What is the theoretical significance of autoshaping and automaintenance phenomena? These experimental results require us to analyze behavior within both innate and "arbitrary" categories and see how each is affected by positive reinforcers. We begin with a question: Why do pigeons continue to expend energy to key-peck in these situations? If we can answer this question, we may gain some insight into the human courtship pattern described earlier.

Pigeons Know How to Peck. First, the pigeons. Pigeons know how to peck at backlit keys without special training, and, as Figure 6.6 indicates, their pecking responses reflect innately organized behavior patterns for eating and drinking. Innately organized feeding responses of birds are not restricted to pecking. Mature hens, for example, visually search for food, peck at a variety of nonfood objects (which may move them, revealing food), make clucking noises to their chicks, and pick up and drop pieces of food near their chicks (Wickler, 1973).

Even though laboratory researchers are interested only in "operant key-pecking responses," the pigeons have no alternative but to bring their species-specific behaviors into laboratory settings. Other behavior, such as cocking the head and visually orienting to a lighted key that predicts food are also reinforced along with the key-peck response. We can safely conclude that autoshaping and automaintenance procedures result in the partial reinforcement of a variety of innately organized feeding responses (see Timberlake & Grant, 1975).

Reinforcement of Innate Feeding Responses. It turns out that the pecking responses of hungry pigeons are neither arbitrary nor trivial. Success in finding and ingesting food helps define their adaptive fitness. Recall that during automaintenance, when more than half of pigeon key-pecking responses went unreinforced, the pigeons would stop pecking the lighted key. Thus, these pigeons *were* adaptively responding to reinforcement contingencies. Earlier it was noted that during a negative automaintenance procedure (Williams & Williams, 1969) about one-third of the pigeons' key-pecking responses were ineffective in striking the key and were therefore "wasted." The focus on unreinforced responses clouds the fact, however, that on *two-thirds* of the trials key pecks that struck short of the key or just beside it were partially reinforced.

Furthermore, "wasted" or "inefficient" pecking at a lighted key parallels other niche behaviors that are *not* considered maladaptive. Birds peck for other reasons than to secure food. While most pecking responses *do* result in food ingestion, other pecking responses—at nonfood objects and dropping food near offspring are two examples—do not result in food ingestion. It may be that when all pecking responses are considered within the bird's niche, producing food two-thirds of the time may be *very* efficient.

Pigeon's Light Becomes Secondary Reinforcer.

In the Skinner box, visual orientation and non–food-pecking responses are components of these innately organized feeding patterns. This visual orientation is *also* reinforced by food. Because of the light/food association, the light becomes a secondary reinforcer. Both the appearance of the light and the partial reinforcement with food appear to maintain these component behaviors (orientation and pecking) indefinitely. Conclusion? The behavior of a pigeon on an automaintenance schedule in a Skinner box is neither maladaptive nor contrary to the law of effect. Indeed, predictions derived from associative reinforcement theory complement innate feeding behavior analyses. Together these theories provide an adequate account of the observed pecking behavior.

Automaintenance of Human Courtship Patterns.

The outcome of feeding strategies may determine life or death. Likewise, courting patterns of sexually mature humans that bear on reproductive success are neither arbitrary nor trivial. To the extent that we were successful in analyzing the pigeon's feeding behavior, can we identify innate behavior patterns, reinforced responses, and their interactions in our example of human courtship behavior? Needless to say, human courting behavior appears to be far more complicated than the manner in which pigeons secure food. But common elements can be identified. Both feeding and courting require a visual search. (Where is the positive reinforcer located?) Both require locomotor responses (approach behaviors) and other instrumental responses (preening?) necessary to secure the reinforcer.

Driving by Tracey's apartment can be likened to the pigeon's orienting responses to the light. Both the apartment complex and the light have something to do with reinforcement (i.e., both have been previously associated with reinforcement). Pecking is a component behavior of an innately organized feeding response. *Grooming* and "notice-me" behaviors are components of innately organized human courting responses. While on automaintenance, pecks at a lighted key are not instrumental in producing food. Likewise, grooming and "notice-me" behaviors are not instrumental in producing Tracey. In both cases, however, these innately organized behaviors are being maintained by partial reinforcement (i.e., both responses are associated with food and Tracey's appearance, respectively).

Under certain conditions, both pecking responses and "notice-me" behaviors may be punished. Food reinforcement can be made contingent on not
pecking, and Tracey can disappear contingent on your persistent responses.
Both pigeon and human responses will continue, however, as long as some
reinforcement is ultimately forthcoming (i.e., persistence pays).

Misbehavior of Organisms

Marion and Keller Breland were students of B. F. Skinner. They applied behavioral methodologies developed in laboratory research with pigeons and
rats to other animals. Specifically, they trained chickens, pigs, raccoons, and
other animals to perform cute circus acts for sideshows. If you have ever attempted to train an animal to do a trick, you already know how difficult it is
to achieve a consistent and reliable performance. In 1960, the Brelands wrote
The Misbehavior of Organisms, an article describing their animal training difficulties.[6] Their research is important because it calls for nothing less than
modifying the law of effect.

Among their other trained animal acts, the Brelands reinforced pigs and
raccoons for chains of responses that ended with the animal depositing a coin
in a bank. For example, a raccoon would work to earn a coin and would then
pick it up and drop it into the bank. Depositing the coin was the operant response that resulted in food reinforcement. The law of effect predicts that reinforced operant behavior such as dropping a coin would be learned
efficiently. After a sufficient number of trials, the hungry animal should
rapidly and effectively perform the operant and eat the food reinforcer. Some
of the Breland's trained animals did something else, however. Instead of depositing the coin, they played with it, delaying reinforcement.

Listen to the Brelands describe a raccoon required to drop *two* coins in
the bank to secure reinforcement: "Not only [would] he not let go of the
coins, but he spent seconds, even minutes, rubbing them together...and dip-
ping them into the [bank]....The rubbing behavior became worse as time
went on, in spite of non-reinforcement" (Breland & Breland, 1961).

Likewise, pigs would repeatedly push coins along the floor with their
snouts (cf. "rooting behavior") rather than deposit them in the bank as they had
been trained to do. Observations of the pigs' rooting behavior corroborated that
of raccoons' "washing" behavior in two ways; namely, both patterns of behavior
delayed reinforcement, and both patterns of behavior became worse with repeated trials. Do you recognize parallels in the behavior patterns of these pigs
and raccoons with previously encountered pigeons on automaintenance schedules that engaged in behaviors that delayed reinforcement?

Instinctive Drift. How did the Brelands explain such instances of "misbehavior"? First, they reasoned that in their respective niches, raccoons routinely wash their food before eating, and pigs routinely root with their snouts.

---

[6]The title is a parody of Skinner's *Behavior of Organisms* (1938).

These innate patterns of feeding appear to intrude on newly learned, highly arbitrary operants maintained by food reinforcement. The Brelands' term **instinctive drift** captures the most important aspect of the misbehavior they observed, namely, that arbitrarily established responses erode (drift) in the face of more innately organized behavior (instinct).

Comparing Instinctive Drift and Preparedness. Earlier we learned that rats have an innate tendency to be wary of novel foods, a phenomenon called neophobia. A rat's phobic response to new foods appears to *complement* its rapid (evolutionarily prepared) learning of flavor-toxin associations. By contrast, the Brelands' formulation of instinctive drift suggests that rather than working together, innate feeding patterns can also conflict with the learning of new associations. To the extent that instinctive drift works against prepared learning, it would seem to be an example of contraprepared learning. However, let's look more closely at details of the Brelands' experiments.

What Controls Instinctive Drift? What would happen if, instead of using small coins, food reinforcement were made contingent on the operant response of rolling a large, heavy bowling ball into the bank? Or if reinforcement were contingent on the operant response of pushing a wheelbarrow through a door in the bank? Would you expect to see instinctive drift in these circumstances? Or is it likely that instinctive drift is restricted to instances in which components of the animal's normal feeding niche are incorporated into the "arbitrary" operant?

The question being asked is whether the raccoon and pig are treating the coin as a *substitute* for food in the same way pigeons pecked the light "as if" it were food. Consider that the coin, or token, is a conditioned stimulus associated with the unconditioned stimulus of food (see Wolfe, 1934, for an account of chimps hoarding tokens that had been associated with food reinforcement). Note that unlike bowling balls and wheelbarrows, these coins are similar in size to the foods eaten by raccoons and pigs. After many trials, feeding responses may have become associated with the sight of the coin, and responses to the coins may have generalized from their responses to foods (Timberlake, Wahl, & King, 1982). Such a theory of **stimulus substitution** was proposed initially by Pavlov (1927/1960).

Associations can be made between a wheelbarrow and food, but can bowling balls and wheelbarrows also be *substitutes* for food? To the extent that these objects fall outside the stimulus generalization gradient of "food objects," substitution is highly unlikely. If they *were* on the generalization gradient, we would expect to see raccoons attempting to "wash" bowling balls, and pigs "root" at wheelbarrows. (You would likely attach positive feelings to Tracey's apartment complex by association but, being off the generalization gradient, would not "court" it. On the other hand, you might wash Tracey's car.)

Reconciling "Misbehavior" and the Law of Effect. Among other researchers, Shettleworth (1975) has studied the behavioral complexities of hungry animals. She has found that reinforcement worked to increase responding of some innately organized behaviors of the golden hamster (digging, rearing, pawing a wall). She found, however, that reinforcement minimally affected other behaviors, such as face washing, body scratching, and scent marking. (Scent marking involves marking one's territory by urinating on its boundaries. The urine contains pheromones.)

Are these truly failures of reinforcement? Her analysis emphasized the fact that reinforced or not, the first three behaviors increased during food deprivation. Hungry animals dig, rear, and paw as they search for food; they do not expend energy face washing, scent marking, or scratching. All six behaviors increased when reinforced. The behaviors that are innately instrumental in securing food increased the most, the others minimally.

Do the findings from automaintenance studies, from Shettleworth (1975) and the Brelands' account of misbehavior support the Brelands' conclusion that instinctive behavior is more powerful than acquired, or reinforced, behavior? I don't think so. A more parsimonious explanation is that primary and secondary reinforcement helped to maintain the behaviors that the Brelands attributed to instinct. In automaintenance, innate response tendencies and reinforcement principles interact in intricate ways to cloud even a "simple" key-pecking response. Likewise, a rat's foraging tendencies interact with food reinforcement to determine how it negotiates a maze. General process learning theory aids our understanding of these animals' interesting innate feeding tendencies.

Studies of Generalization Using Operant Conditioning

We are seeing that reinforcement modifies innate predispositions to respond. Another example involves changes in generalization. For example, a dog that is trained to salivate to a tone of 1500 Hz will also respond to tones of 1490 and 1510 Hz. Presumably, the tones sounded similar to the dog. My voice command for my dog Sadie to "Stay!" does not generalize well when my children use this word. First, their high-frequency voices do not sound like my voice. Second, because they have repeatedly used the word *stay* without appropriately reinforcing (or punishing) Sadie, their "stay" has been conditioned to mean something entirely different from my "stay!"

Not surprisingly, experiments using operant conditioning methodology have demonstrated similar findings concerning generalization. In a classic study, Guttman and Kalish (1956) reinforced pigeons with food when they pecked at a yellow lighted key (wavelength = 580 nanometers, or nm).[7] After training, the wavelength of light was changed on successive test trials, and the number of responses to a variety of wavelengths around the original wavelength were measured. During the test trials only the responses to one wave-

[7]Recognize that the "yellow" experienced by humans is likely to be perceived differently by a pigeon's brain.

length were reinforced; pigeons continued to respond during extinction as the light was changed to other wavelengths.

As you might expect, more responses were made to the most similar wavelengths and the least responses to the most different (most easily discriminated) wavelengths. Figure 6.7 shows this orderly pattern of responses,

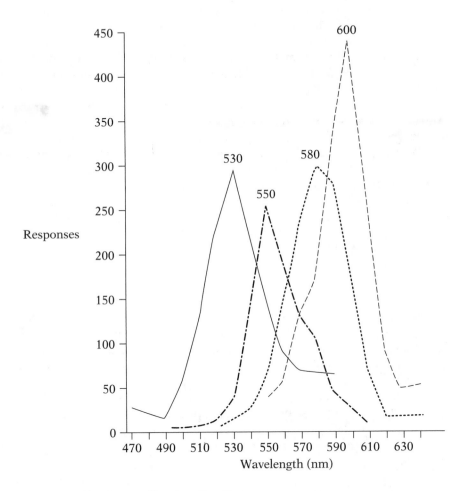

FIGURE 6.7 Generalization Gradients

Pigeons were food-reinforced to peck at backlit discs illuminated with wavelengths of either 530, 550, 580, or 600 nanometers (to humans these wavelengths appear green, greenish yellow, yellowish orange, and red, respectively). Each bird was then put on extinction. Pecking responses to the wavelength it was trained with and immediately neighboring wavelengths were measured. Each pigeon's pecking responses distributed around the peak of the original training wavelength. The pattern of responses is called a *generalization gradient* (after Guttman & Kalish, 1956).

called a **stimulus generalization gradient.** The peak of the pigeons key-peck responding is to the exact stimulus that was trained.

Invariant Stimuli?   What is the real-world applicability of these findings? It is that in the real world seldom is a "pure" stimulus—invariant 580-nm "yellow"—repeatedly presented and consistently reinforced. In nonlaboratory niches, one could argue, a predator sees form and movement as well as color in locating prey. The color may change as the prey moves from light to shadow and back. Movement also guarantees different patterns on the predator's retina from moment to moment. Does the learning that occurs under these stimulus conditions resemble learning using static stimuli in the laboratory?

The Guttman and Kalish (1956) findings demonstrate that a stimulus does not have to be perfectly reproduced on each occasion to control responding. Presumably, views of shapes and movements that differ from those initially reinforced also come to control responses. Generalization across varying stimuli produces meaningful, predictable, patterns of responses. I can recognize the difference in each of my children's voices, yet I recognize the words they speak as having the same signal value. An Episcopal service generalizes to a Methodist service. A meal in England is similar to one in Texas. We don't have to relearn each new environment as long as it is somewhere on our generalization gradient.

The Peak Shift Phenomenon

Guttman and Kalish's (1956) pigeons did *not* initially learn that pecking nonyellow stimuli failed to produced food. During training, the birds only saw one stimulus, the 580-nm light that was always reinforced. What would happen if the pigeon initially learns that one stimulus is associated with reinforcement and that another is not? Recall that Pavlov's dog learned to salivate to a circle (CS^+) and not to salivate to an ellipse (CS^-). One experiment used a similar procedure but used pigeons. Hanson (1959) asked what differences result when pecking at one color (S^+) produces food, and pecking at another color (S^-) doesn't. He used the following three groups:

Group 1: S^+ = 550 nm ; S^- = 590 nm (difference = 40 nm)
Group 2: S^+ = 550 nm ; S^- = 555 nm (difference = 5 nm)
Group 3: S^+ = 550 nm ; no S^-; (difference = ∞)

Notice that all three groups of pigeons were trained with the same reinforced stimulus, a light of 550 nm. The groups differed by having a very similar S^- condition (i.e., 555 nm), a highly dissimilar S^- condition (i.e., 590 nm), or no S^- during training.

Stimulus Generalization of Operant Responses.   After training, all pigeons were tested for stimulus generalization. Figure 6.8 shows the results. Pigeons in Group 3 produced a familiar generalization gradient around 550 nm similar to that found by Guttman and Kalish (1956; see Figure 6.7). Note that the peak of responding is precisely at 550 nm, the reinforced wavelength.

But look at the generalization gradients of the pigeons in which nonreinforced discriminations had been trained. Even though pigeons in all three groups were reinforced for responding to an S$^+$ of the same wavelength, the peaks of the gradients of the discrimination training groups were *shifted to the left*, a phenomenon called **peak shift.** The question is: Why would a pigeon make more responses to wavelengths of light for which their responses had never been reinforced? And, perhaps more important, why should the peak of responding be shifted *further* when, during training, the S$^-$ is closer to

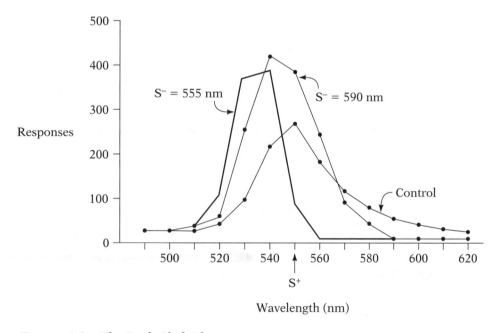

FIGURE 6.8   The Peak-Shift Phenomenon

Three groups of pigeons were food-reinforced to peck at a backlit key (wavelength = 550 nanometers), the S$^+$ condition. One of the three groups was also trained with an S$^-$ = 555 nm, another with S$^-$ = 590 nm, and the third group with no S$^-$ (a control condition). The generalization gradients for all three groups responding in extinction to different wavelengths are plotted. Note that the gradients for both groups trained with S$^-$ are shifted to the left of the peak wavelength of 550 nm (after Hanson, 1959).

the S^+ ? The answer is that the peak of responding to the S^+ is shifted *away* from the S^- experienced during training. The closer the S^- is to the S^+, the greater the shift. Another difference that arises during discrimination training is that the generalization gradients are *narrower* than for the S^+-only group, indeed, narrowest for the most similar S^- condition (i.e., 555 nm).

What is the importance of these findings? First, the presence of a nonreinforced stimulus, the S^- , appears to *sharpen* the discrimination of the reinforced stimulus. Furthermore, the closer the stimulus characteristics of the two stimuli, the more discriminating the pigeon becomes. It is as if the bird is forced to pay more attention to the *exact* attributes of a stimulus that provide information about reinforcement. Two human examples: When playing the piano, a G7 major chord *is* subtly different from a G7 chord. Only by repeatedly comparing two stimuli having highly similar attributes can a person distinguish one from the other. The same is true for wine tasters who after many trials can discriminate one red wine from another.

The second finding of importance is that when one stimulus is reinforced while a related stimulus is *not* reinforced, reactions to the whole range of stimuli are changed. In Hanson's (1959) research, the presence of a nonreinforced wavelength during training changed the bird's response tendencies to all other wavelengths. Another way to say this is that what the bird learned in the presence of the nonreinforced stimulus was measurable, but only indirectly. The effect could be assessed only in the presence of other stimuli.

The Inhibitory Nature of Discrimination Training. The necessity of measuring the effects of nonreinforced stimuli indirectly by the peak shift phenomenon is reminiscent of conditioned inhibition. Remember that *conditioned inhibition* was also measured indirectly via summation and retardation tests, and then only in the presence of a conditioned excitor (see p. 167). In the present situation, the S^+ can be construed as an excitor and the S^- as an inhibitor. The peak response to the excitatory S^+ is shifted, indirectly reflecting the role of S^-. Can the responses to S^- also generalize in the same way that responses to S^+ generalize? Yes, *inhibitory* generalization gradients have been reported by Honig, Boneau, Burstein, & Pennypacker (1963).

Interim Summary

1. Behavior involves the interplay of species-specific behavior and learned responses. Innate behavioral tendencies can modify the law of effect in the same way that the law of effect can influence species-specific behaviors.

2. Tolman showed that finding a food reinforcer in the goal box was not necessary for a rat to learn a maze, a phenomenon he called **latent learning.** Rats engage in species-specific foraging behavior in mazes, and learn where food is and isn't. They are reinforced by being removed

from a foodless environment and being returned to a home cage that has secondary reinforcing properties.

3. Contrary to B. F. Skinner's assertion that a pigeon's key peck is an "arbitrary" response, several lines of evidence reveal pecking to be a niche-specific feeding behavior.

4. ***Autoshaping*** and ***automaintenance*** describe pigeon-in-the-box methodologies that seem to produce nonreinforced responding. In autoshaping, presentation of a lighted key followed by food elicits unnecessary pecking at the lighted key. If food is paired with the light on at least half of the occasions that the key is lit, key-pecking responses will be maintained indefinitely (automaintenance), even in the absence of a response contingency.

5. The Brelands trained circus acts and reported what they believed to be *misbehavior of organisms* because of the failure of the law of effect.

6. Because the Brelands' pigs and raccoons delayed the food-reinforced terminal response of "dropping coins," and instead "washed" and "rooted" them, the animals' behavior was said to be caused by ***instinctive drift.***

7. Analysis of the "misbehaving" animals revealed that they were under the behavioral control of the coins for two reasons: (a) The coins were on the food reinforcer's generalization gradient and had become associated through Pavlov's theory of ***stimulus substitution;*** (b) the coins had also become secondary reinforcers that maintained the washing and rooting behavior.

8. Shettleworth's findings that a given reinforcer affects some responses more than others is similar to Garcia's stimulus specificity in conditioning. In both instances, our understanding of each experimental outcome is enhanced by a knowledge of each animal's innately predisposed eating and drinking behavior.

9. Human courting behavior and pigeon-feeding behavior can both be analyzed from the perspective of how reinforced behavior interacts with innate response tendencies.

10. Key-pecking in the absence of a food reinforcement contingency occurs because (a) species-specific key-pecking is emitted for reasons other than feeding, (b) the global feeding response involves orientation and approach behaviors (such as to the lighted key) as well as pecking behaviors, (c) the lighted key has become a secondary reinforcer (because of pairings with food) that reinforces both approach and pecking, and (d) responding is maintained by partial reinforcement with food (a primary reinforcer).

11. Pigeons trained to peck at a lighted key of one wavelength will also peck to keys of similar wavelengths, producing a ***stimulus generalization gradient*** around the target wavelength.

12. Pigeons trained to peck at one wavelength for food reinforcement (S$^+$), and to other wavelengths that are not food reinforced (S$^-$), sharpens their discrimination of the two wavelengths. The presence of the S$^-$ causes the response (which normally peaks to the S$^+$) to shift in a direction opposite the S$^-$, a phenomenon called **peak shift.**

DISCUSSION QUESTIONS

8. Do you learn anything in the absence of reinforcement?

9. Does pigeon behavior on an automaintenance schedule successfully model the example of human courtship behavior? Why or why not?

10. Those of you who have been horseback riding know what happens at the end of your ride when you and your horse are on the way back to the stable. It takes off like a shot. Why?

CHAPTER SUMMARY

1. Both classical conditioning and instrumental learning are responsible for behavioral changes. In instrumental learning a response is learned or modified when it is followed by a positive reinforcer or a punishing stimulus. The association is made between the response and the reinforcer or punisher.

2. Classical conditioning is described as learning stimulus-stimulus (S-S) contingencies, and instrumental learning as response-stimulus (R-S) contingencies.

3. E. L. Thorndike's law of effect states that responses followed by satisfiers (Skinner's positive reinforcers) will increase in frequency, and responses followed by annoyers (Skinner's punishers) will decrease in frequency. The law of effect reflects the hedonistic nature of animals. Reinforcement typically selects adaptive responses.

4. John B. Watson's and B. F. Skinner's behaviorism is best understood as a strict environmental determinism that contrasts with biological determinism.

5. B. F. Skinner's operant conditioning method experimentally analyzes behavior in terms of how reinforcement contingencies control operant responses. He chose lever-pressing, a free operant procedure, to analyze how reinforcers affect responses of animals.

6. Animals are operantly conditioned in Skinner boxes. After magazine training, new responses such as lever-pressing (rats) and key-pecking (pigeons) can be shaped by successive approximation. Both food, a positive reinforcer, and secondary reinforcers associated with food are part of the process of reinforcement.

7. Instrumental conditioning methods interact with inborn response tendencies. Rats bring foraging tendencies to mazes by that allow them to learn it without receiving food in the goal box, called latent learning. They escape the maze more quickly by learning where food isn't, and are reinforced by secondary reinforcement.

8. Key-pecking by pigeons isn't the arbitrary response that Skinner thought it was. Innate pecking tendencies produce the phenomena of autoshaping and automaintenance–key-pecking in the absence of a response-food contingency. Autoshaping and automaintenance entail procedures include both classical and instrumental conditioning components.

9. Marion and Keller Breland reported instances of the misbehavior of organisms that they thought violated the law of effect. They proposed that this misbehavior was due to instinctive drift. "Misbehavior" can be understood in terms of both innate feeding niche behaviors and the secondary and primary reinforcing stimuli maintaining the behavior.

10. Pigeons produce stimulus generalization gradients after being reinforced for pecking a key of a given wavelength. Peak shift occurs when an a S^- condition is trained concurrently with a S^+ condition. The peak shift phenomenon is evidence that inhibition can influences how a pigeon innately generalizes responses from one stimulus to another.

KEY TERMS

annoyers   199

automaintenance   219

autoshaping   218

behaviorism   202

biological determinism   201

environmental determinism   201

free operant   208

hedonism   200

instinctive drift   223

instrumental conditioning   194

instrumental learning   194

latent learning   214

law of effect   198

magazine training   208

operant (or **operant response**)   208

operant conditioning   208

operant level   208

peak shift   227

positive reinforcement   209

positive reinforcer   209

R-S conditioning   196

R-S contingency   196

satisfiers   199

secondary reinforcers   209

shaping by successive approximation   209

S-S conditioning   196

stimulus generalization gradient   226

stimulus substitution   223

target response   209

CHAPTER 7

Reinforcement and Behavior Control

Everyone knows the person who doesn't try, who isn't motivated, and hence, doesn't learn. In academics, athletics and other skilled performances we recognize that "motivation" separates the haves from the have nots. Some individuals "are hungrier" than others. Some achieve more because "they want it more." In a word, our understanding of how learning affects behavior seems to be intimately connected to our understanding of what *motivates* our behavior.

In this chapter, we enter the realm of motivated behavior: We focus on concepts of reinforcers and punishers, of reinforcement and punishment. Questions as to "*what* do we learn" and "*how* do we learn" shift ever so subtly to "*why* do we learn." In this chapter and the next, we'll attempt to analyze behavior both from the perspective of motivation, and the control that reinforcers and punishers exert over our behavior. For example, a question of the Las Vegas gambler who hour after hour, day after day, feeds silver dollars into a machine can be framed both in terms of motivation, and the control of behavior by processes of reinforcement.

> "*Beat me! Beat me!*" *said the masochist.*
> "*No!*" *said the sadist.*

> (Anonymous)

Maladaptive learned behaviors—as illustrated by the addictive behavior of a compulsive gambler, and by the hypothetical verbal exchange of the sadist and the masochist—intrigue us all. What motivates these individuals? Is their pleasure and pain learned? How is it that pain can become pleasure, and inflicting pain can give some people so much pleasure? One way to address this question is to ask why some events bring us pleasure and others are so aversive. More interesting questions cannot be asked than those that concern the wellsprings of human motivation and behavior. In courts of law and in personal relationships, we ask questions and puzzle over answers:

> ". . . what motivated you to leave me for her?"
> ". . . why did you try to kill yourself?"
> ". . . do you still love me?"

These questions go to the very heart of human nature; in this chapter we seek answers at the theoretical level. What determines whether a given stimulus is a reinforcer or punisher? What do food, sex, water, some drugs, electrical stimulation of a part of the brain, and an "A" on a test have in common?

TRADITIONAL THEORIES OF REINFORCEMENT

In previous chapters, we have seen that learned changes in behavior result from either stimulus-stimulus associations (classical conditioning) or response-stimulus associations (instrumental learning). In both conditioning procedures, learning occurs when the consequences of a behavior are either *satisfying* (i.e., tasty food, a smile) or are *annoying* (i.e., a painful electric shock, or a disproving glance). Up to now, we've only indirectly raised the issue of *why* associations are formed in both Pavlovian and instrumental conditioning. The similarities of procedures and results suggest that both types of learning are related, and that underlying brain mechanisms may be common to them.

A Brief Review of Pavlov and Thorndike.   For about one hundred years, learning theorists have struggled with the complexities of learning. Humans and other animals not only are born with, but also in the course of their lifetimes acquire motivated behaviors. Pavlov (1927) focused upon "biologically meaningful stimuli" in the environment that produce reflexes in animals. For Pavlov:

1. Animals (including humans) are biologically motivated to survive.
2. Reflexes are physiological adaptations that promote survival.
3. Neutral stimuli paired with these innate reflexes alter the brain's connections, such that conditioned reflexes may eventually occur to formerly neutral stimuli.
4. More often than not the conditioned reflexes are also adaptive in that they promote well-being and survival.

Thorndike (1898, 1932) also provided an early theory of human motivation. Some stimuli that animals encounter are *satisfiers*, others are *annoyers*, and yet others are "neutral." Behaviors that produce satisfiers are *stamped in*. Therefore, innately satisfying and annoying events provide motivation for learning. Learned responses, as governed by the *law of effect*, are the inevitable results of associations with satisfiers and annoyers.

Clark L. Hull's Drive Theory of Behavior

In the previous chapter, B. F. Skinner's method of analyzing behavior from an operant conditioning perspective introduced the behaviorist's understanding of reinforcers and reinforcement. Before reviewing and extending Skinner's findings, however, Clark L. Hull's drive theory of behavior will first be discussed. The reason is that Skinner's analysis is best understood as a reaction to other learning theorists with whom he was contemporary.

S-O-R Theory.   Hull self-consciously described himself as a *neo-behaviorist* to contrast his position with that of other behaviorists. He deviated from a pure stimulus-response (S-R) framework by specifically including *intervening variables* between the "S" and the "R." Hence, his position is characterized not as S-R, but rather as **S-O-R theory,** where "O" stands for such *organismic* *variables* as thirst and hunger. Given our knowledge of physiology (even in 1943!), he queried, why continue to treat the organism as a *black box?* His reasoning is even more valid today.

Drive Reduction Theory. Hull characterized animal behavior as a complex of physiological *drives* and *need states* that could in part be met through learning experiences. Writing in *Principals of Behavior* (1943), learning is "driven" (motivated) by the necessity of meeting these physiological demands. Hull therefore proposed a **drive reduction theory** of behavior as an alternative to descriptive behaviorism (Hull, 1943, 1952). This theory proposes that an animal has physiological needs for water and food. These needs are translated into motivated behavior by specific drives, or *drive states.* When these drives result in behavior that fulfills the needs, restoring the organism's homeostatic balance, the drive was said to be *reduced*—hence, drive reduction theory. Reducing drives by eating and drinking has the effect of reinforcing those behaviors that are instrumental in securing food and water.

Hull's System of Quantification. Hull's (1952) system represents a monumental attempt to construct a theory of learning built upon observations of behavior and assumptions about their causes. From these observations he derived corollaries, postulates and theorems. His drive reduction theory of learning, stated in the form of a mathematical equation, follows:

$$_sE_R = {_sH_R} \times D \times V \times K - (IR + {_sI_R}) \qquad 7.1$$

Though imposing, Equation 7.1 is not that difficult to understand. What is Hull attempting to model with this equation? The notation "$_sE_R$" refers to *reaction potential*—a probability that the *performance* of a learned behavioral response (R) has the potential (E) to occur under certain stimulus conditions (S). In other words, Hull is writing a learning equation that attempts to predict the probability of a learned response in a given situation—such as how quickly a rat can learn a maze using food reinforcement. What factors *are* important in how rapidly a rat learns to negotiate straight alley and T-shaped runways?

Here we are not going to elaborate all of the intervening variables he postulated, but begin by noting that the terms in the equation are merely being added, subtracted, or multiplied. Among the variables included in Hull's equation are $_sH_R$ (*habit strength,* or how much has already been learned); D (*drive*); V (*stimulus intensity dynamism*—a variable akin to intensity in Pavlov's *Law of Strength*); K (*incentive motivation*—both innate and acquired motivation to satisfy needs—see below); I_R (*reactive inhibition*—a variable that includes fatigue effects); and $_sI_R$ (*conditioned inhibition*). These variables are in turn operationally defined. For example, *drive* is defined in terms of "hours of food or water deprivation." Other terms in Hull's equation (not shown) are defined by reference to such variables as *Ng, Mg,* and *Tg*—the nature, amount, and delay of food reinforcement, respectively. The quality and amount of a reinforcer in part determines the degree of *incentive motivation* underlying behavior. Larger amounts, or tastier food provide greater (primary, or innate) incentive motivation for hungry animals.

Acquired Incentives. In Hull's analysis, stimuli paired with innate incentives such as food and water become acquired incentives. Acquired incentives in Hull's theory are Skinner's secondary, or conditioned reinforcers. (Both are acquired by the process of higher order conditioning.) Hull also proposed the concept of acquired motivation—to be distinguished from the primary motivation of hunger and thirst—to account for why animals are motivated by acquired incentive. The physical characteristics of the goal box in which a rat is fed are examples of acquired incentives.

Hull recognized the many human activities normally give pleasure, but do not involve drive-reduction. Earlier, a player who performed better than another was described as being "hungrier" than the other. A person's competitiveness can be understood as a combination of innate and acquired motivation. Finally, can you look at the equation and determine why Hull's is a drive reduction theory? Note that without *drive* (in the equation, let $D = 0$), there can be no performance, and, hence, the right side of the equation when multiplied by a zero goes to zero. Solving the equation, when $D = 0$, $_sE_R$ also is zero. No drive (no hunger), no motivation, no performance, no learning.[1]

Drive-stimulus Reduction Theory. Hull was forced to modify his drive-reduction theory in favor of a **drive-stimulus reduction** theory because of an experiment by Scheffield & Roby (1950). These researchers showed that non-hungry rats could learn an instrumental response that had been reinforced by a non-nutritive saccharin solution. They reasoned that neither a hunger drive or a thirst drive was reduced, and that the stimulus properties of saccharin was a sufficient incentive for learning to occur. Hull reasoned that reducing the drive caused by the stimulus itself was reinforcing; hence the (unfortunate) name, *drive stimulus reduction*.

Once the implications of Scheffield and Roby's simple demonstration sunk in, other examples of non-drive-reducing reinforcement appeared in the literature. The concept of reinforcement changed rapidly. For example, Sheffield and his colleagues next demonstrated that rather than reducing a drive, engaging in a behavior that presumably *increased* a drive (or at least increased the level of excitement) could also act as a reinforcer. These experiments (Sheffield, Wulff, & Backer, 1951) demonstrated that male rats learned to run quickly to a female in estrous to engage in copulatory behavior. Drive reduction theory predicts that achieving orgasm would *reduce* the sex drive, and that the resulting reinforcing effects of orgasm would enable the rat to

---

[1]The same is also true if there is no reward. When $K = 0$, $_sE_R$ also is zero.

effectively learn the preceding instrumental behaviors. However, in this experiment, the rats were separated *before* achieving orgasm. The male rats learned despite the lack of drive reduction, they reasoned, because sexual excitement is itself reinforcing (Sheffield, et al, 1951).

Analysis of Hull's Theory. Hull had a profound impact on both behavior analysis and learning and behavior theory. First, he recognized the complexity of behavior. He insightfully differentiated *learning* variables from *performance* variables. He developed a *hypothetico-deductive model* of how data can be used to generate a formal theory of behavior. Despite drive-theory's incompleteness, both drive-reduction theory and the prominent role played by acquired incentives remain as his legacy. Although both premature and too ambitious, Hull's attempt to integrate biological and psychological variables into a general theory of behavior is commendable. The reason is that contemporary investigations in behavioral neuroscience proceed from adaptive-evolutionary premises, and use integrated physiological and behavioral methodologies. Modern neuroscience may one day embrace an updated version of Hull's theory.

Skinner's Behavioral Theory

Following Pavlov's lead, in his theory of behavior Hull emphasized physiological variables critical for survival. B. F. Skinner did not. In his 1938 book *Behavior of Organisms*, "behavior" became descriptions of the effects of reinforcement and punishment on relatively simple operant responses. While aware of genetic predispositions (Skinner, 1957), by adopting a position of *environmental determinism*, he deemphasized biological determinants of behavior.

[Skinner acknowledged biology: He has stated "Where inherited behavior leaves off, the inherited modifiability of the process of learning takes over" (Skinner, 1953, p. 83). In another article he wrote: "Behavior analysts leave what is inside the black box to those who have the instruments and methods needed to study it properly. There are two unavoidable gaps in any behavioral account: one between the stimulating action of the environment and the response of the organism, and one between consequences and the resulting change in behavior. Only brain science can fill those gaps. In doing so it completes the account; it doesn't not give a different account of the same thing. Human behavior will eventually be explained (as it can only be explained) by the cooperative action of ethology, brain science, and behavior analysis. (Skinner, 1989, p. 18).]

Skinner (1950) insisted that his positions on questions of reinforcement, learning, and motivated human behavior were *atheoretical*—a most interesting theoretical position to take! A strict behaviorist who followed the lead of John B. Watson, Skinner proposed that questions relating to motivation were both unnecessary and undesirable. For the strict behaviorist, the use of terms such as *motivation, incentive, learning,* and *memory* adds nothing to observations of behavior. These terms allude to unobservable events, and each is an additional step removed from the reality of the observations of performance changes.

Skinner's Definition of a Reinforcer.   Skinner's atheoretical position had the intended effect of making behavioral analysis more rigorous and scientific. At present most behavioral scientists follow his lead in operationally defining reinforcers according to the effect a stimulus has upon the preceding response. Skinner's reinforcer is, therefore, defined as any stimulus whose application following a response has the effect of increasing the probability of that response. How does Skinner's definition differ from what you've previously learned? With their respective concepts of unconditioned stimuli and satisfiers, both Pavlov and Thorndike clearly had in mind that such stimuli *innately* elicited pleasure. Skinner, by way of contrast, doesn't require a reinforcer to be pleasing, because as a behaviorist, he has no way of knowing what pleases a non-speaking animal. If the effect of the stimulus is to increase the rate of emission of the preceding response, by definition the stimulus is a reinforcer, and the process is called reinforcement.[2]

Skinner's Definition of a Punisher.   The same distinctions hold for aversive stimuli. For Pavlov and Thorndike, such stimuli were *inherently* aversive. By contrast, Skinner also defined punishment operationally. If the effect of the stimulus is to decrease the rate of emission of the preceding response, by definition the stimulus is a **punisher,** and the process is called **punishment.** We'll see in the next chapter that responses can also have the effect of removing a stimulus, or preventing a stimulus from occurring. Withholding one of Thorndike's satisfiers is punishment. Parents more often punish teenagers by *preventing* them from driving a car or watching television than by "spanking" or applying some other aversive stimulus. Likewise, withholding one of Thorndike's annoyers can be a reinforcing event (it feels good when you stop hitting yourself in the head).

Figure 7.1 provides a descriptive summary of how, thanks to Skinner, reinforcers and punishers, and reinforcement and punishment, are currently defined. Responses can be strengthened or weakened by the effects they have in producing or preventing either positive and negative environmental stimuli. Processes of negative reinforcement and punishment will be dealt with in the following chapter. In the remainder of this chapter our focus will be on the process of reinforcement depicted in the upper left-hand cell.

---

[2]Yes, this is a circular definition. "Why is a given stimulus reinforcing? Because by increasing the rate of the preceding response, it acts as a reinforcer." In a later discussion, we will find a way out of this circularity by noting other defining properties shared by all reinforcers.

Effect of Stimulus on Preceding Response

	↑ Probability, or rate, of response	↓ Probability, or rate, of response
Response **produces** stimulus	*Process is* **Reinforcement** *Stimulus is a* **Reinforcer**	*Process is* **Punishment** *Stimulus is a* **Punisher**
Response **prevents** stimulus	*Process is* **Negative Reinforcement** *Absence of an Aversive stimulus is a* **Reinforcer**	*Process is* **Punishment** *Absence of stimulus is a* **Punisher**

FIGURE 7.1   Diagram of Reinforcement and Punishment

Summary of B. F. Skinner's operationally defined concepts of *reinforcement* and *punishment*, and the operational labeling of *reinforcers* and *punishers*.

Interim Summary

1. Pavlov's theory of behavior was that biologically meaningful stimuli elicit survival-promoting reflexes that can be modified through conditioning.

2. Thorndike proposed the *law of effect,* a simple statement that satisfiers increase responses that produce them, and that responses followed by annoyers tend to decrease in frequency.

3. Clark L. Hull's **drive-reduction theory** of behavior attempted to predict performance in a learning task by specifying physiological and psychological variables that set up need states, that in turn produced drives. Behavior that allows the animal to meet (reduce) these drives is reinforced.

4. In Hull's analysis, food and water are innate incentives. A stimulus paired with an innate incentive can become an **acquired incentive.**

5. Hull proposed the concept of **acquired motivation**—behavior motivated by secondary, or conditioned reinforcers.

6. Hull's approach to behavior is characterized as an **S-O-R model** (rather than a S-R model) because he postulates organismic variable such as hunger and thirst, and other intervening variables such as needs and drives, within the black box.

7. The theory of **drive-stimulus reduction** was proposed to account for observations that some effective reinforcers not only failed to reduce drive, but sometimes induced behavior. Drinking a saccharin-flavored solution empty of calories is an example of a reinforcing event that does not reduce a hunger or thirst drive.

8. B. F. Skinner rejected intervening variables, and operationally defined reinforcement as the process of increasing the probability of response by the application of a reinforcer. He defined a *reinforcer* (in a circular manner) as any stimulus that increased the rate of the preceding response.

9. Likewise, a **punisher** is any stimulus that when applied decreases the rate of the preceding response through a process called **punishment**.

DISCUSSION QUESTIONS

1. Why is "kissing" not considered to be a *drive-reducing* reinforcer? Why is "kissing" reinforcing in some contexts but not in others?
2. Why can Skinner's "atheoretical" position be considered "theoretical."
3. What criteria might one use to evaluate the respective learning approaches of Skinner and Hull?

SKINNER'S SCHEDULES OF REINFORCEMENT

With the possible exception of Ivan Pavlov, Skinner's study of reinforcers and the process of reinforcement have come to define general process learning theory as well as to provide the basis for an experimental analysis of behavior. Next we'll return to the Skinner box to examine in more detail what he did and what he found.

Measuring Operant Responses

We learned earlier that B. F. Skinner quickly discovered that measuring animal learning in a runway is difficult and tedious to accomplish, so he automated the measurement of operant responses (Skinner, 1959). At present, computer-control equipment is used to program the experimental animal's environment and to record its behavior. A popular and relatively simple way to visualize behavioral effects of reinforcement uses an instrument called a *cumulative recorder*, a device that generates a *cumulative record* (See Figure 7.2). The oper-

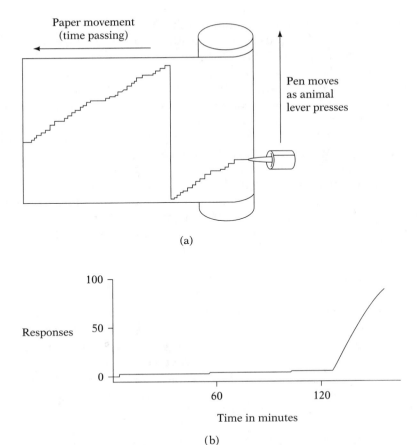

(a)

(b)

FIGURE 7.2 Measuring Operant Responses

Operant responses distributed in time are easily visualized on a *cumulative recorder*. A motor turns the drum of the instrument, pulling the paper though at a constant speed. A pen resting on the paper writes on the passing paper (7.2a). When the animal makes a lever-pressing or key-pecking response, a ratchet moves the pen sideways. The passage of time is indicated by the direction of the moving paper, and responses by upwards pen movements. In Figure 7.2b, only a few responses have been made in the first 2 h, as indicated by the flat line indicating the passage of time. You can see several upwards excursions of the pen during the first 2 h, and the rapid increase in lever-pressing after 2 h (after Skinner, 1938).

ation of a cumulative recorder is quite simple. Paper is unrolled onto a drum, and ink-writing pens (fixed in position) resting against the drum write on the paper as it unrolls at a constant rate.

Cumulative Records. Notice in Figure 7.2 how responses are plotted as time unfolds. An inked line is made horizontally (*x*-axis) with the passage of time. The pen is also connected to a pulley, and each lever press sends the pen up, vertically, one notch. If the lever is not depressed, the line continues horizontally. In other words, lever presses are displayed vertically, and the passage of time is displayed horizontally. The *slope* of the ink-drawn line shows the *rate* of lever-pressing (number of responses per unit time). The cumulative record is a visual shorthand allowing the experimenter to quickly and surely analyze the effects of reinforcement on operant behavior. Why is it called a cumulative record? The reason is that in a work session each response is added to previous responses, and the record shows this accumulation.

Schedules of Reinforcement

Skinner discovered that highly distinctive patterns of lever pressing result when animals are subjected to different **schedules of reinforcement** (Ferster & Skinner, 1957; Reynolds, 1968). Obviously, behavioral scientists are interested in patterns of the complex behavior of humans, not just the lever-pressing responses of rats. Before applying reinforcement theory to complex human behavior, let's first understand the effects of scheduling reinforcement on lever-pressing in the Skinner box.

Continuous Reinforcement. The simplest schedule of reinforcement is **continuous reinforcement** (abbreviated **CRF**). In continuous reinforcement each emitted response produces a positive reinforcer. Simply stated, animals appear to learn an "if-then" contingency; *if* I turn left in the maze, or *if* I peck the key, *then* a food pellet (or drink of water) magically appears. A strict behaviorist account, of course, merely describes the effects of this schedule of reinforcement on responses. During acquisition, CRF schedules characteristically produce *positively accelerated* patterns of response. This same pattern was seen in classical conditioning. A positively accelerated slope on a graph shows that increasing numbers of responses are made as time passes, and that less time is taken between each response.

After training, lever-pressing proceeds at a rate dictated by the quantity and quality of the reinforcer, the presence or absence of secondary reinforcers, how hungry the animal is, how hard or easy it is to press the lever, how rapidly the animal eats (or drinks) the positive reinforcer, and so forth.

Partial, or Intermittent Reinforcement. Using continuous reinforcement makes early training proceed more quickly. After this initial training, however, responding proceeds quite well even if a reinforcer is not given for each

"Oh, not bad. The light comes on, I press the bar, they write me a check. How about you?"

response, called **partial reinforcement** (or *intermittent reinforcement*). Having reinforcers only follow some responses is called *scheduling reinforcement* or *arranging an intermittent schedule of reinforcement*.

When reinforcement is given intermittently, two outcomes can be observed: (1) more responses are typically emitted each minute (faster responding) because not so much time is taken up consuming the reinforcer, and (2) the responding shows greater *resistance to extinction* when reinforcers are no longer given. Let's take in turn four schedules of reinforcement that have been most intensively studied: fixed ratio (FR), variable ratio (VR), fixed interval (FI), and variable interval (VI).

Fixed Ratio Schedule

In a **fixed ratio (FR)** schedule, reinforcement is contingent upon the completion of a fixed number of operants, such as lever-pressing or key-pecking responses. (A lever-pressing response in a Skinner box is sometimes referred to as bar-pressing.) For example, if every tenth response is reinforced, the schedule is designated "FR-10." The animal can lever-press fast or slow in making the ten responses. In a given session more positive reinforcers can be earned if the animal presses the bar more quickly.

The Post-reinforcement Pause on FR Schedules.   When the ratio of unreinforced to reinforced responses is relatively small (such as FR-5, when every

5th response is reinforced), the overall response rate is determined by how quickly the animal eats (or drinks) the positive reinforcer. As the ratio becomes larger (e.g., FR-100, every 100th response produces a positive reinforcer), the response that produces food is typically followed by a long pause, called the **post-reinforcement pause** (see Figure 7.3). The duration of the pause before responding resumes is directly related to the size of the ratio. Because the rat is either not responding at all during the post-reinforcement pause, or is steadily bar pressing (thereby producing a straight line), the off-on response pattern of an FR schedule is sometimes referred to as *break-and-run* responding.

Variable Ratio Schedule

As is the case with *fixed ratio* schedules of reinforcement, the **variable ratio (VR)** schedule requires a specified number of responses before a reinforcer is delivered. A pigeon responding on a VR-20, for example, is reinforced, on the

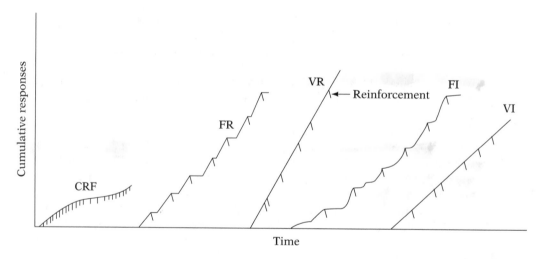

FIGURE 7.3 Cumulative Records of Common Schedules of Reinforcement

Cumulative records of CRF (continuous reinforcement), FI (fixed interval), FR (fixed ratio), VR (variable ratio), and VI (variable interval) schedules of reinforcement. The slope (steepness) of each line reflects the *rate* of response. The FR-schedule is characterized by break-and-run behavior, rapid responding and long post-reinforcement pauses. The FI schedule is characterized by "scallops"—low response rates immediately following reinforcement followed by increasing rates of response as reinforcement become imminent. The VR schedule produces a higher rate of response than the VI, and both schedules produce stable, evenly-spaced responding (straighter lines) than CRF, FR, and FI schedules.

average, for every 20th response. But the number of responses required for a particular positive reinforcer is varied from one reinforcement to the next. Computer programs determine that the subject is reinforced randomly, for example, after 1 or 2 responses or after 30 or 40 responses. Likewise, on a VR-50 schedule, on the average every 50th response is reinforced.

The post-reinforcement pauses on variable ratio schedules are shorter than for an animal working on a fixed ratio schedule of reinforcement (see Figure 7.3). Why? Put yourself in the rat or pigeon's place. First, can you come up with a *cognitive hypothesis* involving "expectancies"? Again, this time as a hungry rat, can you come up with a *behavioral hypothesis* that involves maximizing responses to get the most reinforcers per unit time?[3] Lacking the post-reinforcement pause, VR schedules generally produce high, steady rates of operant responding. Can you think of an example of human behavior that resembles that of rats working on a VR schedule of reinforcement? If you owned a gambling casino in Las Vegas, and you could program the slot-machines that your customers would play, what pay-off schedules (reinforcement schedules) would *you* use to maximize your profits? CRF? FR-50? VR-50?

Fixed Interval Schedule

An animal on a **fixed interval (FI)** schedule is reinforced for its first response following a specified time interval. Another way of saying this is that *interval* schedules of reinforcement make the positive reinforcer available after a programmed amount of time passes. Time-based interval schedules are in contrast with fixed or variable *ratio* schedules in which reinforcement is dependent upon *amount* and *rate* of work, irrespective of time. For example, an animal performing on a fixed interval 60-sec schedule of reinforcement (abbreviated FI-60), receives a reinforcer on the first response after sixty seconds has elapsed. (The interval is measured from the time of delivery of the preceding reinforced response.) Note that even though a time contingency has been added, the delivery of the food reinforcement is still *response* contingent: The animal *must* respond to get the food.

You be the hungry pigeon. Would you rather earn food for the first response you make after 10 sec (FI-10) or for the first response you make after 45 sec (FI-45)? After experiencing these two pay-off schedules for several sessions, would you respond the same on each? That is, can you predict what your post-reinforcement pause would look like on these two FI schedules? (After receiving a food pellet, what are your chances of getting another one any time soon? Better on the FI-10. On the other schedule, 45 sec must elapse before food is available again.)

---

[3]On a VR schedule, the very next response might be reinforced. To pause might delay immediate gratification.

Scalloping. Fixed interval schedules of many seconds duration preclude back-to-back reinforcers. These schedules typically produce cumulative response curves showing an extended pause (zero or near zero response rate) immediately following reinforcement. As the end of the fixed interval approaches, a gradual increase in rate occurs. Figure 7.3 shows this distinctive pattern, called *scalloping,* as it appears on the cumulative record. Such "scallops" are seen only following extensive training on longer FI schedules. Can you visualize the shape of the respective scallops on FI-30 and FI-120 schedules of reinforcement?

Do we see scallops in human behavior? Might employees visit their mailboxes more often on payday than on other days? Box 7.1 describes a remarkable example of the patterning of responses leading to the self-administration of morphine on an FI schedule.

Variable-Interval Schedule

Rather than being fixed, in a **variable interval (VI)** schedule the interval of time between positive reinforcer availability varies from a few to many seconds. Compare a FI-45 schedule that makes reinforcement available every 45

BOX 7.1   SCHEDULING EFFECTS IN THE SELF-ADMINISTERING OF MORPHINE

While visiting a friend in his hospital room where he was recovering from surgery, I had the opportunity to observe him self-administer morphine to control pain. An automated pump dispensed the morphine through an indwelling intravenous catheter. His physician determined both the amount of morphine available, and the interval of time between dosages. My friend could administer the morphine to himself by pressing a button once every 2 h (i.e., delivery of the drug was response-contingent on a FI-2 h schedule of reinforcement).

By watching his wristwatch this patient learned to accurately time the 2-h interval. After a number of such trials, his response pattern emerged clearly and predictably. As the 2-h period wound down, his button-pressing responses increased in frequency. During the final 30 sec (as best he could estimate by his wristwatch), he made responses every few seconds until morphine was delivered. A clear scalloping pattern had emerged.

Was this response pattern inevitable? Other drug studies investigating the use of morphine to control pain (Melzac, 1990) report individual differences in drug-seeking (cf. *sensation-seeking*) behavior. Not all individuals crave the pleasurable effects of morphine like this patient; rather, their behavior (including verbal reports) indicate that they fear the addictive properties of morphine. Although they experience pain, most individuals do not self-administer the drug as described above even when placed on the same schedule of reinforcement.

sec with a VI-45 schedule: A computer-generated VI-45 sec schedule might deliver response-contingent reinforcement after 1 sec or after 100 sec, or at other times in between. In a given work session the inter-reinforcement interval *averages* 45 sec. What is the effect of scheduling reinforcement availability such that it averages 45 sec rather than being exactly 45 sec? Again, the post-reinforcement pause is eliminated. Figure 7.3 shows that both variable interval (VI) and variable-ratio (VR) schedules generate little post-reinforcement pause, while both long fixed ratio (FR) and long fixed interval (FI) schedules do. Why? Because in both "variable" schedules, following the last reinforced response, reinforcement is possible with the very next response.

Stable Responding. The passage of time rather than the number of responses determines the availability of reinforcement on VI schedules. As a result VI schedules produce highly stable, moment to moment operant responses throughout a given work session. VRs and FRs produce the highest rates of response; the variable interval (VI) schedule produces the most evenly spaced, or stable rate of responding. Another way of describing the effects of VI schedules is to note that they produce the least variation in inter-response intervals.

Response-reinforcement Relationship. What in general can be said about how response patterns are related to the availability of reinforcement? Figure 7.4 shows that Peter Killeen (1975; Killeen & Bizo, 1998) found a direct relationship between both arousal (inferred) and pecking responses (measured) of pigeons as a function of their rate of reinforcement as averaged from different partial reinforcement schedules. We'll have more to say about the response-reinforcement relationship, and how it affects choice behavior, in a later chapter.

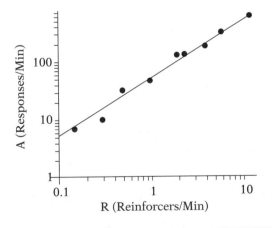

FIGURE 7.4 More Food Availability = More Responses

There is a direct relationship between averaged pigeons' response rates and the availability of food per unit time. The data are averaged from different experiments in which different partial schedules of reinforcement were used. (From Killeen and Bizo, 1998, Figure 1)

VI and VR Schedules of Reinforcement in Everyday Life

Assume that positive reinforcers can be identified in our daily lives, and that reinforcement maintains patterns of behavior. We have already noted two examples of the outcomes of scheduling reinforcement on human behavior—how people continue to play slot machines with little payoff (VR schedules) and (at least in one individual) how the periodic availability of morphine determined a distinctive pattern of responses. Let us look at one or two other examples:

Maintaining Behavior over Long Periods. For most people, courteous behavior is typically ignored and only occasionally reinforced. Drivers who reduce their speed to allow other cars to merge into traffic, or who allow left-hand turns in front of them only rarely get a smile or wave acknowledging (reinforcing) their behavior. More typically, all forms of courteous behavior are "in extinction"—that is, they are not being reinforced. (Have you recently been reinforced for saying "please?") Courteous behavior, rather, is maintained on a partial schedule of reinforcement. As another example, consider a third-grade schoolteacher who wants to praise her children for working independently. She contracts to make two or three response-contingent positive comments per week to each student who works independently. How would you characterize this schedule of reinforcement? In your estimation, would this plan have the desired effect of increasing the desired target behavior?

As students progress from elementary to secondary schools to college, parents and teachers alike pay less daily attention to both courteous behavior and to scholastic performance. Tests and course grades at variable intervals serve as opportunities for reinforcement. Furthermore, these opportunities are only loosely attached to complex behaviors such as reading, writing, comprehending, memorizing, and so forth, behaviors that characterize academic performance. Only rarely does one hear "good answer!" in the college classroom. So what maintains behavior over the long haul?

Surprising Reinforcers. Especially in the absence of continuous reinforcement, responding can be maintained at high levels on partial reinforcement schedules. One simple reason is that pigeons and rats don't get as full consuming their reinforcers if they get one only every now and then, so they work longer. Another characteristic of variable schedules of reinforcement that may increase their power to reinforce and thereby maintain behavior is that each aperiodic reinforcement is unexpected—that is, it is surprising (Kamin, 1969; Rescorla and Wagner, 1972; Terry & Wagner, 1975). Unexpected events capture attention. The response that produces an unexpected positive reinforcement stands out more than the rest ("What did I do to deserve *this*?"). The occasional reinforcement therefore selects a particular instance from a welter of ongoing behavior and makes it noteworthy. ("A little reinforcement can go a long way!") Surprising reinforcers undoubtedly capture attention. But they likely are not the main reason that operant behavior persists in the absence of reinforcement.

Extinction and the Partial Reinforcement Effect (PRE)

Animals responding on CRF show little *resistance to extinction*. By contrast, animals with a history of responding for long periods of time in the absence of reinforcement (i.e., FR-100, VR-50, FI-60, VI-45, etc.) are highly resistant to extinction. Remember from our study of Pavlovian conditioning that resistance to extinction is an important measure of the success of conditioning. Here, however, is the conundrum. Partial reinforcement by definition results in *fewer* reinforced responses. How can partial reinforcement result in better conditioning (as measured by resistance to extinction) than continuous reinforcement?

The Partial Reinforcement Effect(PRE). The tendency for animals maintained on partial reinforcement schedules to be highly resistant to extinction is called the **partial reinforcement effect,** or **PRE.** Why it occurs is not simple, but we'll entertain several hypotheses. First, is what the rat learns during acquisition reflected in extinction? If, for example, the animal experiences partial reinforcement while being trained to lever press, it may not perceive a difference when put on an extinction schedule. Therefore, it continues to respond longer than an animal trained and maintained on continuous reinforcement.

Frustration Theory. Pavlov proposed from experiments showing spontaneous recovery, and from conditioned discrimination experiments, that extinction procedures produced inhibitory conditioning. Likewise, Amsel (1958, 1992) has pointed out that following a history of continuous reinforcement, one consequence of extinction is a state of negative emotions such as frustration. Amsel's **frustration theory** can be interpreted to include a cognitive as well as emotional component.[4] That is, one can be frustrated if one has expectations concerning what the consequences of responding *should* be. From this analysis, animals carefully trained on partial reinforcement schedules treat non-reinforcement in a different way than animals continuously reinforced. An example: Imagine living in Italy where local phone systems are unpredictable at best. In using public phones over the years, Italians have lost many coins. That is, their telephoning operants have never been consistently reinforced. Sometimes they connect on the first coin; other times they must try

---

[4]A symposium devoted to a multi-faceted discussion Amsel's frustration theory can be found in the Vol 1(3), September, 1994 issue of *Psychonomic Bulletin & Review*.

several times (and lose coins) before connecting. North Americans, however, seldom lose a coin. In which country would non-reinforcement be more frustrating? Italians would persist in unreinforced responding (i.e., would show the partial reinforcement effect) because of their training. Given this understanding, can you explain why Italians are surprised when North Americans "become angry at telephones."

To summarize, different expectations are set up when animals are trained on partial reinforcement and continuous reinforcement. If trained on partial reinforcement, the animal may not even become aware of the difference when it is put into an extinction period. By contrast, animals trained on continuous reinforcement immediately become aware of its absence of reinforcment, and will stop responding. Frustration may result from thwarted expectations.

Extinction on Cumulative Records. Extinction as measured on a cumulative record is easy to detect. Remember that each lever-press sends the line up, vertically, a notch. If the lever is not pressed, the cumulative record continues horizontally (to the right). Therefore, when the rat or pigeon quits responding—as in an extinction phase of training—the plot continues horizontally rather than stepping up the record.

DRH and DRL Schedules of Reinforcement

Two schedules of reinforcement have been designed to reinforce *local rates of responding*. A **differential reinforcement of *h*igh rate** of responding **(DRH)** schedule reinforces bursts of lever pressing. A computer program monitors local rates of lever pressing and defines the response contingencies. A burst, for example, may be defined as 5 or more lever-presses by a rat (or 10 or more pecks by a pigeon on a lighted key) in a 2-sec time period. Only when the target level of responding is reached is a food reinforcer made available.

Instead of speed, what if the desired target behavior is very slow, accurately timed responding? A researcher might use a **DRL** schedule of reinforcement, where DRL stands for **differential *r*einforcement of *l*ow rate** of responding. For example, an animal on a DRL-30 second schedule must wait at least thirty seconds since the prior response before a response will produce a reinforcer. Each response made before the thirty seconds has elapsed resets a clock, and the animal must wait an additional thirty seconds before reinforcement is again available. The training and terminal performance of rhesus monkeys on a DRL schedule of reinforcement is discussed in Box 7.2.

Of what practical use are schedules of reinforcement that by their operation produce fine control over local rates of response? Absolutely none that I can think of.[5]

[5]Actually, a lot. For example, *all* behavior requiring rhythm and pacing—*all* skilled movement requiring precise local control over rate of response, including the artist's brush strokes, playing a piano, and reading and writing.

BOX 7.2   TRAINING PATIENCE IN MONKEYS

While stationed at an USAF research laboratory in the mid-1960s, I had the opportunity to train Rhesus monkeys on a DRL schedule of reinforcement. Eventually the monkeys were to be administered an experimental drug, that, among other effects, was likely to impair their timing behavior. I selected a DRL-15 sec schedule of reinforcement to help assess the drug's effects. On the DRL-15 schedule, a monkey withholds a lever-press response for 15 sec. Pressing the lever during the 15-sec period resets the clock: the first response after not responding for 15 sec is reinforced with a sugar pellet.

How do you train animals to be patient? Reinforcement by definition tends to *increase* the rate of response, which in this case resets the clock, preventing further reinforcement!

With the first animal I carefully followed a progression of time intervals that were gradually lengthened until the monkey was pausing for 15 sec between responses. After establishing responding to CRF, on successive days I put the monkey on a DRL-3, then a DRL-5, then a DRL-10 schedule of reinforcement. Progress was slow, because each time the schedule was changed, the monkey responded too much, delaying reinforcement. Each nonreinforced response was accompanied by vocalized frustration.

I sought and accepted the advice of another psychologist. He suggested that in training the next naive animal, I first establish minimal responding on CRF, set the timer on DRL-15 sec, and walk away. His reasoning was that

too-fast responding would extinguish, but that spontaneous recovery of responding would be immediately reinforced. The monkey's behavior? Initially, and predictably, a burst of responding following reinforcement, then many minutes of not responding, followed by a (spontaneous recovery) response that produced reinforcement. Ultimately this schedule produced a patient animal.

How efficient do Rhesus monkeys become after many hours practice on a DRL-15? Unbelievably so. In one representative session, Rhesus # 079 produced inter-response latencies (time between responses) measured to the hundredth of a second, as follows: 15.04; 15.08; 15.02; 15.04; 15.04; 14.97 (not-reinforced); 15.14; 15.07, 15:04 . . . and so-on, with no further misses during a 4-min session.

How are monkeys able to tell time with such accuracy? As we'll see in more detail in Chapter 11, one theory is that animals have an *internal clock* (Church, 1978, 1984). Other researchers have proposed a *behavioral theory of timing* (Killeen & Fetterman, 1988). A feature of the latter theory is the prediction that monkeys in the present study "did things" to help them keep track of time. Indeed, one monkey was observed to rhythmically strike her fist against the performance panel during the 15-sec interval between food availability. Her behavior, described in more detail in Chapter 11, helped her keep track of time. *One-thousand one, one-thousand two* . . .

Importance of Schedules of Reinforcement

Why have we spent so much time on schedules of reinforcement? Why should we care how a pigeon or rat responds when reinforcement is scheduled contingent upon time and rate of key-pecking and lever-pressing? Consider the following arguments. First, these laboratory investigations have produced a body of findings that has considerable application to the human condition. Humans, in fact, respond in ways predicted by these studies. For a wide variety of human behaviors, reinforcement, especially partial reinforcement, determines both the vigor and the pattern of responding—be it morphine administration, gambling behavior, piano playing, assembly-line production (see discussion question 6, below), or being courteous to one another. And, schedules of reinforcement point the way to a true science of behavior—the analysis and prediction of human behavior that is a goal of behavioral scientists. One might criticize the narrowing of behavior demanded by the Skinner box procedures. Yet at the same time one can recognize the power of prediction and elegance of behavioral control afforded by this simple methodology. As we'll see in the next chapter, these scheduling procedures are now effectively used in parenting and teaching, and in programs involving behavioral therapy and behavioral modification.

Interim Summary

1. **Schedules of reinforcement** describe the manner in which reinforcement delivery is patterned, or scheduled following operant responses.

2. The delivery of a reinforcer for each response is called **continuous reinforcement (CRF).** If each response is not reinforced, the animal is said to be on a **partial,** or **intermittent reinforcement** schedule.

3. Schedules delivering reinforcers based upon the number of responses an animal makes are called ratio schedules, including **fixed ratio (FR)** and **variable ratio (VR)** schedules.

4. Schedules delivering reinforcement based upon time between reinforcement are called interval schedules. These include **fixed interval (FI)** and **variable interval (VI)** schedules.

5. In general, longer FI and FR schedules produce **post-reinforcement pauses;** FI schedules produce *scalloping* patterns; VI schedules produce stable responding, and ratio schedules produce faster responding.

6. In general terms, a direct relationship exists between response rates and the availability of reinforcement on partial reinforcement schedules.

7. Responding given continuous reinforcement extinguishes quickly. Responding given intermittent reinforcement, on the other hand, extinguishes more slowly; the **partial reinforcement effect (PRE).**

8. Bursts of responses can be maintained on a **differential reinforcement of high rate (DRH)** schedule, and pauses between responses on a **differential reinforcement of low rate (DRH)** schedule.

9. An animal's behavior on different schedules of reinforcement can be compared with respect to acquisition, rate and patterning of responses, stability, and resistance to extinction.

10. Behavior in the real world is under the control of schedules of reinforcement.

DISCUSSION QUESTIONS

4. "Post-reinforcement pauses" are seen in everyday life in a variety of situations, and some bear little resemblance to lever-pressing and the presence or absence of food. For example, longer periods of study, and daily class attendance are usual responses immediately prior to an exam. What pattern of behavior is typically found in the class period following an exam? Another example: We seldom hear from politicians until just before election time. Why then? What is the "availability of reinforcement" in both examples?

5. As a gambling casino owner you want to maximize your profits. A machine that pays off on the average for every 100 plays makes more money than one that pays off every 50 plays. Likewise, one that pays out $1000 for every 100 plays makes you less money than one that pays out $500 /100 average plays. As a casino owner how would you determine the best way to maximize your long-term profit? HINT: Now that you know how to maximize resistance to extinction, how might you go about minimizing the frustration of non-reinforcement in your customers? Can you conceptualize a trade-off between customer frustration and customer satisfaction?

6. In automobile production, vehicles being assembled move past stationary workers at a fixed rate. Each worker must make one or more operant responses that add components to the autos. What schedule of reinforcement best describes this activity? Why do unions that represent workers negotiate with management the speed of the assembly line?

7. Observe two people having a conversation, and note the subtle cues controlling speaking and listening. Can you reconstruct the likely reinforcement history of individuals who lack conversational skills—who have not learned when to inhibit responding? Could you design a behavioral treatment that uses a DRL schedule to change the offending behavior?

CONTEMPORARY THEORIES OF REINFORCEMENT

We should not be too surprised by the fact that saccharin and sexual foreplay can act as reinforcers in both rats and humans. Many activities we engage in are pleasurable in spite of the fact our survival doesn't depend upon them. People ski, flirt, ride bicycles, take pleasure-inducing drugs, play (pianos, soccer, and computer games), read, worship, swim, sweet-talk, watch TV, invest money, spend hours cooking gourmet meals, high-five, listen to CDs, celebrate holidays, tell jokes, sunbathe, talk on telephones and the 'net, soak in a tub, brush hair, rub backs and receive paychecks. What an impressive list! Let us modify an earlier statement to propose that after primary needs are met, *most* activities humans engage in are pleasurable in spite of the fact our immediate survival doesn't depend upon them. These activities give pleasure, but many do not involve drive-reduction. A paycheck is a common example of a reinforcing, but not drive-reducing stimulus.

Bandura's Theories of Imitation and Social Reinforcement Theory

Art and music teachers, swimming and tennis coaches, as well as psychologists have long recognized the ability of humans to learn by observing and imitating (Skinner, 1953; Baer, Peterson, and Sherman, 1967). Bandura has written about imitation in terms of *observational learning* (Bandura, 1971). Bandura (1971) proposes as an alternative **social reinforcement theory.**

Bandura's theories contain non-learning accounts of human behavior. As did Skinner, he proposes that imitating someone else's behavior is a genetically predisposed behavior. An action that is first imitated can then become an instrumental or operant response that can be manipulated by reinforcement or punishment. The model (parent, teacher, or coach) provides the reinforcement or punishment for the imitated response. Under these conditions, Bandura refers to smiling and saying "good" as *social reinforcers*. Bandura's social reinforcers are considered secondary reinforcers by Skinner and acquired incentives by Hull. Bandura thinks that the satisfaction of *social approval* may be among the items at the top of the list of effective social reinforcers for both children and adults (Bandura & Walters, 1963). We will have more to say about modeling and social learning in the next chapter on applications of learning.

Premack's Theory of Reinforcement

Pavlov's *unconditioned stimulus*, Thorndike's *satisfier*, Hull's drive-reducing food are examples of reinforcers as stimulus objects. David Premack (1962) deemphasized reinforcement as an object, and reinforcement as *drive-reduction* and *drive-stimulus reduction*. Instead, he proposed that a reinforcing event is the behavior of "engaging in pleasurable activities." That is, for Premack, *eating* the food, rather than the food itself, was the reinforcing event. He then designed experiments to demonstrate that not all behavioral activities are equally reinforcing; rather, for an individual certain behaviors are more or less reinforcing at different times.

Drinking and Running Rats. How did Premack demonstrate these ideas? In an early experiment, he deprived rats of water for twenty three hours, then measured how much time they spent either drinking water or running in a running wheel (Premack, 1962). (Running in a running wheel is reinforcing to caged rats in the same way that access to physical activity is reinforcing to a confined human.) On another day, he allowed rats unlimited access to water in their home cages to establish baseline drinking. Then, allowing simultaneous access to these activities in a 1-h test session, he measured how much time they spent both running and drinking. Using these procedures, he found, not surprisingly, that thirsty rats would rather drink than run, and non-thirsty, but running-deprived rats would rather run than drink water.

Having established these baselines of behavioral activity, Premack next demonstrated that under certain conditions the activity of running would reinforce drinking behavior. He again began by restricting running and allowing rats water *ad lib*. During the next day's one hour test, running was more a more probable response than drinking. But rather than let them run freely, Premack made the opportunity to run contingent on drinking. He found that non-thirsty rats drink if such overdrinking was reinforced by the opportunity to run. In another experiment, he found that tired rats but thirsty rats would continue to run for the opportunity to drink.

The Premack Principle.   In a series of similar experiments, Premack and his students consistently found that the more probable of two responses would always reinforce the less probable response, a relationship now known as the **Premack principle.** This reinforcement relationship is *reversible*. By restricting one activity, the other is made more probable. By restricting both drinking or eating (as is normally done in most animal learning experiments) the opportunity to eat and drink will reinforce most other behaviors. Why? Because in a given testing session, most other behaviors are less likely to occur than eating (if the animal is hungry) or drinking (if the animal is thirsty) or running (if the animal has been confined).

Eating Candy or Playing Pinball.   In a clever experiment Premack (1962) showed that more probable behaviors of children will reinforce their less probable behaviors. First, he measured two behavioral baselines for each child in the study. Given the choice of playing a pinball machine, or of eating candy, which activity does each child prefer? Having established that some children preferred candy over pinball, and that other children preferred playing pinball over eating candy, Premack then determined under what conditions candy would reinforce pinball playing, and under what conditions pinball playing would reinforce candy eating. Remember that the Premack principle predicts that playing pinball would reinforce candy eating only for those children who preferred pinball to candy during the baseline measurement (and that eating candy would reinforce pinball playing only for those children who preferred eating candy to playing pinball during the baseline measurement). These predictions held true (Premack, 1962). A candy-preferring child would play pinball for the opportunity to eat candy, and a pinball preferring child would eat candy for the opportunity to play pinball. And even though both were pleasurable activities, the less probable behavior would *not* reinforce the more probable behavior.

Analysis of Premack's Principle. At the time Premack was proposing his theory, "reinforcers" were "things" that behavior produced or avoided, and the process of reinforcement was the effect that such "things" had upon the preceding responses. By extending the concept of reinforcement to "the opportunity to engage in (pleasurable) behavior," and by providing a method that demonstrated that reinforcement relationships were reversible as conditions changed, Premack shifted the focus of analysis away from "things," and back to behavior. The Premack principle remains just one of many ways to conceptualize reinforcement, however. Consider the following criticisms:

1. Reinforcers do not disappear merely because one chooses to measure "engaging in behavior." When rats "engage in drinking behavior," rats drink *water*. Likewise, children eat *candy*. Put bitter quinine in water and candy, and the behaviors involved in their consumption cease. The point is that the process of reinforcement in part is determined by properties of "things," and the behavior being measured is determined by these properties.

2. Running in a running wheel, playing pinball, skiing, and riding bicycles are reinforcing events that presumably share with candy and water the activation of pleasurable brain sites (see below). The Premack principle does not address the pleasure derived from engaging in certain behaviors.

3. "Engaging in reinforcing behavior" varies during the course of the day, and, for that matter, in the course of a lifetime. All traditional theories of reinforcement recognize that the reinforcing properties of food and water are conditional upon hunger and thirst, respectively. To take another example, the opportunity for a 15-year-old to drive a car is a highly probable behavior, while taking out the trash is not. New drivers will move mountains of trash for a spin around the block. After driving for a year or so, however, the suggestion that "I'll let you drive around the block if you take out the trash" does not seem like such a good deal. Likewise, given the alternative of purchasing either a new car or a face-lift, the choice can be expected to vary as a function of a person's age, sex, and so forth.

The power of reinforcers to reinforce follows many rules.

Inside the Black Box: The Brain's Basis for Reinforcement

Let us entertain the possibility that most *all* behaviors that humans repeatedly engage in are being maintained by a common process of reinforcement. Skinner's objections aside, "pleasure" certainly seems to be a common element in soaking in a warm tub, and receiving some unexpected money for your birthday. What is the nature of this alleged "common reinforcer?" Could it be other than pleasure? We might look inside the black box for an answer.

Serendipity. Over and above being a pleasant-sounding word, "serendipity" plays an important role in the conduct of science. Horace Walpole coined the word to describe a mythical faculty possessed by scientists that allowed them to make important discoveries—by accident. Others have noted that a successful discovery is often best attributed to "being in the right place at the right time." Indeed, B. F. Skinner, in eschewing the role of theory in this research, asserted that *serendipity* (including equipment breakdowns!) best accounted for both the direction and the successes of his behavioral discoveries (Skinner, 1959). As it turns out, serendipity also played a crucial role in a classic experiment that opened a window in the black box. For the first time researchers glimpsed the brain's mechanisms of reinforcement (Olds & Milner, 1954).

Electrical Stimulation of the Brain (ESB). Two psychologists, James Olds and Peter Milner, implanted electrodes deeply into subcortical areas near the hypothalamus of rats. Assessing the effects of **electrical stimulation of the brain (ESB)** in a conscious, free-ranging rat, they passed minute amounts of electric current through an implanted electrode. The current stimulated neurons at the electrode tip. By chance, Olds and Milner noted that some of the rats returned to the particular place in the open field apparatus where they had received the ESB on previous trials. They recognized that the ESB in these rats seemed to be acting as a reinforcer. They reasoned that the rats were learning an instrumental response because of the effects of the ESB (Olds & Milner, 1954).

To test their hypothesis, they programmed a Skinner box in a way that made ESB contingent upon lever pressing. They reasoned that if ESB acted the same as food and water reinforcers did in deprived rats, then rats should press the lever to secure ESB (Olds, 1962). Their hypothesis proved correct; ESB acted as a reinforcer. Rats would "self-stimulate" by pressing a lever that delivered electrical stimulation to certain nerve pathways in the brain (see Figure 7.5).

In the ensuing 40 years since Olds' and Milners' original observations, neuroscience research has illuminated the brain's basis for reinforcement to a level that goes well beyond the scope of this book (see Pinel, 2000, for a readable overview). A summary of some of the more important findings of this diverse research follows:

1. ESB has been demonstrated to have reinforcing properties for all species tested, including humans (Heath, 1963).
2. A factor common to many successful electrode placements (i.e., those that yield reinforcing effects) is that a structure called the *medial forebrain bundle (MFB)* is activated (Milner, 1976) as is the *mesotelen-*

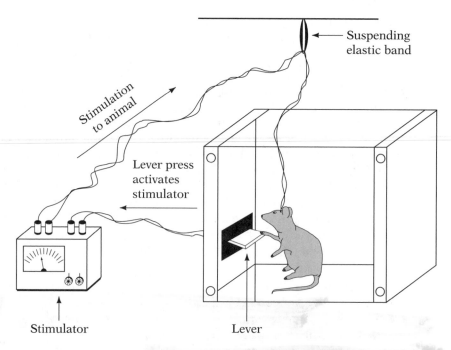

FIGURE 7.5   Electrical Stimulation of the Brain (ESB)

Rats will press a lever that activates the delivery of electrical stimulation to a rewarding site in its brain (after Pinel, 2000).

cephalic dopamine system (Wise, Bauco, Carlezon, & Trojniar, 1992). Brain structures other than the MFB, and neurotransmitters other than dopamine have also been implicated in the reinforcing effects of ESB (see Vaccarino, Schiff, & Glickman, 1989, for a review).

3. ESB can have motivational effects as well as reinforcing effects. Rats that are neither food, water, nor sex-deprived can nevertheless be induced to eat or drink (Valenstein, Cox, and Kakolewski, 1967), or initiate sexual behaviors (Caggiula & Hoebel, 1966) when ESB is delivered in the presence of food, water, or a sexual partner, respectively.

Comparison of ESB with Traditional Reinforcers

How effective is ESB? How does ESB (from a positive electrode placement—one that "works") compare with a traditional reinforcer such as food? One way to answer this question is to arrange for rats to choose between one of two levers—pressing one produces ESB reinforcement, while the other produces food. Routtenberg & Lindy (1965) conducted such an experiment using daily, 1-h trials. The rats chose ESB reinforcement rather than food. Since the rats had only the 1-h to eat during the course of this experiment, by choosing ESB they died of starvation within a few days. It can be concluded that ESB is an extremely effective reinforcer.

FR-10 Schedules Comparing ESB with Food Reinforcement.   An elegant experiment by Anderson, Ferland, and Williams (1992) provides another demonstration of the relative effectiveness of food and ESB reinforcement. Rats were first trained on an FR-10 schedule for food reinforcement until stable responding ensued throughout a 90-sec time period. Each FR-10 segment (signaled by a light) alternated with 30 sec of forced non-responding produced by using a DRL-30 sec (signaled by a tone). In order to return to the FR 10 for food, recall that there had to be a response-free thirty second period. Diabolically, the more the rat responds during the DRL-30 sec, the longer the delay in accessing food available on the FR-10 schedule. Figure 7.6a shows the results: After many sessions a representative rat's rate of response on the FR-10 is high, and is low on the DRL-30 sec.

Anderson et al. (1992) then began alternating two kinds of reinforcement available on the FR segments; namely, food and ESB. The same light signaled both the food and ESB schedules; the DRL-30 sec segment effectively separated them. The way in which this rat responded on alternating FR segments with either food or ESB reinforcement provided a way to compare each reinforcers ability to control responding. First, note in Figure 7.6b that the first ESB experience disrupted the pattern of non-responding on the DRL. The rat responded vigorously following the first ESB presentation and this responding continued for a long time. (Remember that responding on the DRL resets the timer, delaying entry into the next food-reinforced segment.) At this point, we do not know if the ESB has merely induced (excited) the lever-pressing, or if the ESB has acted as a different kind of reinforcer and changed the pattern of responding during extinction.

Negative Contrast.   After several more iterations of FR (for food), DRL, FR (for ESB), DRL, etc., a new phenomenon emerged. By session four, (see Figure 7.6b), even though hungry, the rat's lever pressing for food virtually stopped. At the same time, the rat had learned to inhibit responses on the DRL segment and gain entry into the FR segment, where it responded rapidly for ESB reinforcement. Having experienced both forms of reinforcement, apparently food reinforcement is now perceived as being *less* reinforcing to the rat—a phenomenon called **negative contrast.** Negative contrast is an example of **behavioral contrast** in which reinforcement and punishment effects are determined in part by the context in which they are delivered (see Flaherty, 1982 1991; for reviews).[6] In this study, we can use evidence of *negative contrast* to conclude that ESB is a more powerful reinforcer than food.

---

[6]A human example of *behavioral contrast:* When you make Cs on several tests throughout the semester, and a B on the final exam, you are pleased. When you make As throughout the semester and the same B on the final, you are disappointed.

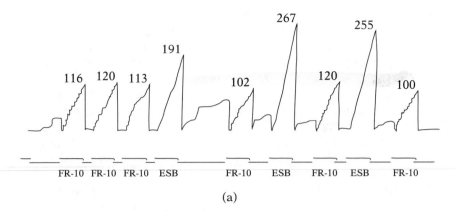

(a)

FIGURE 7.6A   Rats Prefer ESB to Food

Rats were trained to bar-press on multiple schedules of reinforcement, beginning with FR-10 for food, alternating with DRL-30 (not labeled) for the first three segments (Anderson et al, 1992). The DRL-30 was reinforced by reentry into the FR-10 segment. Then (fourth cycle from left), for the first time the rat's FR-10 was reinforced with ESB rather than food. Note how the rat responds at a higher rate, and continues lever pressing through the DRL portion of the schedule, thereby resetting the timer, delaying reentry to the next FR-10 portion of the schedule.

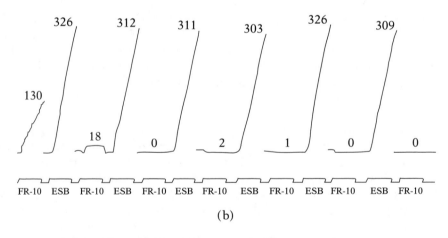

(b)

FIGURE 7.6B   Negative Contrast

After the last session depicted in Figure 7.4a, the hungry rat stops responding entirely for food while continuing to bar press at a high rate for ESB stimulation. Numbers reflect responses during each segment. Compared to ESB, food is apparently irrelevant to a hungry rat. This research by Anderson et al. (1992) provides a very powerful demonstration of *negative contrast*.

Choosing Between Two Reinforcers.   While the results of the Anderson et al. (1992) and Routtenberg & Lindy (1965) studies attest to the power and efficacy of ESB as a reinforcer, they also raise questions concerning reinforcers and adaptiveness. Rats who died because they chose the pleasures of ESB reinforcement over food (Routtenberg & Lindy, 1965) might invite a sermon about the evils of hedonism and the perils of succumbing to immediate gratification. An alternative is to pose the following serious questions: (1) about the relationship of reinforcement to adaptive and maladaptive behavior, and (2) about the relative value of two reinforcing events at a given moment in time.

Most examples of the effects of reinforcement on behavior are adaptive, which is why the law of effect is so pervasive. Ironically, we take for granted that humans often behave maladaptively. It is an interesting commentary that we are truly surprised when other animals seem to behave so. The fact that humans are the only animals who exhibit masochistic and sadistic behavior does not rule out the possibility that infrahumans might exhibit maladaptive behavior. Let us look more closely at the relationship of the law of effect to maladaptive behavior.

Reinforcers and Maladaptive Behavior

The Routtenberg and Lindy (1965) finding that rats chose the pleasures of ESB reinforcement over live-giving food parallels an experiment on adrenalectomized rats (Harriman, 1955). The adrenalectomized rats had a daily one-hour choice between a salt solution and a sucrose solution. Because adrenalectomized rats do not secrete aldosterone, they excrete too much salt in their urine. Unless salt is replaced, these rats will die within about ten days. Yet, when given the opportunity to select a life-affording salt solution, some (but not all) adrenalectomized rats instead drank the sucrose solution and died of salt-depletion (Harriman, 1955).

In the two experiments being compared, both the sucrose and ESB were more reinforcing than the salt-solution and food, respectively. Why? Using Skinner's ideas, sucrose and ESB were more reinforcing because each stimulus better controlled the animals' responses in the two-choice situation. But also by definition, selecting sucrose and ESB appears to be *maladaptive* because each behavior resulted in death. How can we account for this apparent violation of the *law of effect*? We can begin by asking what is reinforcing for normal rats. Normal rats prefer sucrose solutions to salt solutions, presumably because during the course of evolution "sweet" predicts calories within the feeding niches in which rats evolved (Richter, 1942). What about salt? In normal rats, a host of physiological mechanisms serve to conserve salt. Destruction of the adrenal glands is certainly a rare, most likely lethal, event, one that would not be a selective factor during evolution. Furthermore, except in laboratories, rats feed throughout the nighttime, and not during one hour in the middle of the day. They aren't prepared by evolution to deal with such limited access.

Conclusion? It is normal for rats to select sucrose over salt. To expect otherwise in a one-hour feeding period merely because a rat's adrenal glands have been removed would be wishful thinking. Rats have been naturally selected to be sensitive to calories, but not to survive removal of their adrenal glands. The fact that several rats *did* choose salt over sucrose is more an example of the remarkable redundancy of salt-conserving mechanisms than it is *maladaptive* behavior on the part of those who selected sucrose.

Is ESB Like Food?   So much for salt and sucrose. Why was ESB selected over food in the Routtenberg and Lindy (1965) and Anderson et al. (1992) experiments? Again, Routtenberg and Lindy's 1-h daily feeding periods demand tremendous feeding plasticity on the part of the rat. The question is why a starving rat would select ESB (that presumably it has little experience with) over eating food (an innately predisposed behavior). One suggestion is that the sensations attendant with ESB are both highly pleasurable and in some sense "reminiscent" of the pleasures of eating palatable foods (Pfaffman, 1960). In this scenario, lacking the cognitive abilities of humans to talk about "what the sensation of ESB *is like*," rats might simply confuse ESB sensations with eating sensations.

We have a lot to learn about brain mechanisms underlying reinforcement. The artificial stimulation of drugs, ESB, and perhaps the "normal" stimulation of other very powerful reinforcers and punishers (cf. post-traumatic stress disorders, p. 354) can apparently override the correspondence normally seen between adaptive behavior and the law of effect.

Integrating Brain Mechanisms with Reinforcement Theory

What are the implications of the finding that vertebrate brains have "reinforcement" areas, that, when stimulated, can either induce or reinforce behaviors? In the first place, recall that Hull's drive theory had to be modified to a drive-stimulus theory because of research showing that both non-nutritive saccharin, and non-orgasmic sex had reinforcing properties. Both instances are arguably pleasurable. The reported effects of recreational drugs such as cocaine and marijuana can be added to the list. It is likely that activities are reinforcing because they involve activation of the MFB and the mesotelencephalic dopamine system. Given that activation of these areas both induce and reinforce behavior, the necessary and sufficient conditions for reinforcement seems to be the activation of these and other brain areas.

Another possibility? Perhaps ESB is more pleasurable than eating tasty food because ESB elicits more palatable feeding sensations than the real food alternative. For example, the ESB might produce a chocolate-chip cookie sensation, compared to the bland Purina rat chow alternative. In fact, many humans report a preference for the pleasures of a cocaine high over that of sexual orgasm. Our understanding of this phenomenon is that the cocaine molecule is a more or less perfect key to activate locks on the endorphin receptor mechanism. And, as was noted above, it is likely that ESB also works on these same receptor mechanisms (Phillips & Fibiger, 1989).

Interim Summary

1. Bandura (1971) proposed ***social reinforcement theory*** as an alternative to Skinner's ideas of reinforcment. Bandura thinks that human children learn by imitating models (parents, teachers) who in turn use *social reinforcers* (smiling, nodding) for correctly modeled behavior.

2. Premack's theory of reinforcement focuses upon *behaving* rather than on reinforcers as pleasing stimuli. The ***Premack principle*** states that more probable behaviors will reinforce less probable behaviors, and that this reinforcement relationship is reversible.

3. A contemporary theory of (brain) reinforcement is based upon studies using ***electrical stimulation of the brain (ESB)*** in traditional learning situations and on observations regarding addictive drugs such as crack cocaine.

4. ESB reinforcers are so potent that animals choose them in preference to food, water, and other life-giving reinforcers. ***Negative contrast*** is an example of ***behavioral contrast:*** It describes the process of reduced interest in a reinforcer because it compares unfavorably with another reinforcer.

5. Preferring ESB to food is a seeming maladaptive behavior that can be understood as the artificial stimulation of selected neurons normally stimulated by life-giving reinforcers.

6. Reinforcers as either "pleasing events" or "engaging in pleasing behaviors" appear to have common brain bases; current candidates are the medial forebrain bundle and the mesotelencephalic dopamine system.

DISCUSSION QUESTIONS

8. Can you recapitulate the argument that using the concept of reinforcement as an explanation of why behavior increases is circular? One way out of the circle is to note that reinforcing events are more often than not *transituational.* That is, reinforcers will "work" in a variety of situations. Do observations of the effects of ESB and addictive drugs on the MFB constitute further evidence of the transituational nature of reinforcers?

9. What does "keeping up with the Jones" have to do with negative contrast?

ISSUES OF BEHAVIORAL CONTROL

Let's go to the supermarket. The whining is non-stop as you stand in line waiting to be checked out. You join other uncomfortable shoppers watching the battle of wills: Every time mom says "No, you can't have it," little Joey's hand in the candy rack clutches his choice more tightly. He turns up the volume: "Why not?" he whines. "I want this one. Pleeeease . . .? You said if I was good . . ."

After several more iterations, mom's "No, and that's final!" is followed by loud crying. Mom counters with "If you'll be a good boy and not cry, you can have it, but this is the last time." Joey nods contritely, quits crying and tears open the wrapper. Both mother and son (and everyone within earshot) appear content.

Let us begin our analysis of this behavioral encounter by answering the following question:

(1) In the scenario described above:
    (a) Is Mom controlling Joey's behavior?
    (b) Is Joey controlling Mom's behavior?
    (c) Are both a and b correct?
    (d) Is neither person in control of the other?
    (e) Are both out of control?

Answers (d) and (e) are both appealing. As a figure-of-speech answer (e) seems to be self-evident, but it is incorrect when we analyze the problem as a behaviorist might. The problem is one of semantics: A behaviorist analyzes behavior in terms of stimulus and reinforcement contingencies, thereby using the word "control" somewhat differently than the lay public. For a behaviorist, *all* behavior is controlled, or determined, by the environment. Therefore, Mom is controlling Joey, and Joey is controlling Mom. Answer (c) covers both of these possibilities.

In what way is Mom controlling Joey, and Joey controlling Mom? Can you identify the reinforcement contingencies at work in this example? Is it possible that Joey's persistence in responding is being maintained by some sort of partial reinforcement schedule?

The Concept of Behavioral Control

The manner in which the environment comes to control human and animal behavior has been a continuing theme in B. F. Skinner's writings.[7] His behaviorist philosophy, like John B. Watson's, has already been identified as an extreme form of environmental determinism. The method of behaviorism is to

___

[7]*Behavior of Organisms* (1938); *Walden Two* (1948); *Verbal Behavior* (1957); *Beyond Freedom & Dignity* (1971).

identify and analyze the way in which environmental stimuli exert control over an individual's behavior. The success of the method is measured (a) by how effectively reinforcement manipulates and controls ongoing behavior, and (b) given a knowledge of past reinforcement history, how accurate are predictions of future behavior. An individual's behavior is said to be under control at that point in training when an experimenter can make a highly accurate, reliable prediction that a particular response will occur in a particular situation. Before analyzing the respective behaviors of mom and Joey, let's again detour by the Skinner box.

Why does a pigeon peck a lighted key, or a rat press a lever? One answer is that deprivation motivates an animal to move (autoshaping is an interesting exception). Stimulus-cues of hunger motivate an animal to move instrumentally, seeking food within it's ecological niche. Prior learning in the Skinner box now allows specific responses to operate on the environment to secure food.

Stimulus Context in the Skinner Box.   Placing trained, hungry animals in a Skinner box provides the animal an occasion for specific operants to occur. The sights, sounds, and smells of the box are environmental stimuli (i.e., the context) that come to *control* the specific response of bar pressing. Changing the stimulus context, for example, by moving the lever to a different wall, or changing background noises in the box will disrupt the operant response. From this example, we see that stimuli comprising an environmental context is a major controlling factor in whether or not an operant response will occur.

The importance of context in the control and prediction of behavior is currently being investigated using a number of methodologies (see Bouton, 1984; 1991; Balsom & Tomie, 1985; Miller & Schactman, 1985a, 1985b). One we explored earlier was how familiar and novel environments controlled drug tolerance. Most procedures measure performance decrements when animals are preexposed, or conditioned, or tested in same or different contexts. Consider a real-life example: imagine that you first learned to drive one particular car over a one year period of time. Then you are asked to drive a different car that has some of the same operating features (steering wheel, brake and gas pedals, shifter, etc.) but the positions of these manipulanda, and the attendant sights, sounds, and smells differ (i.e., the context differs). Your driving ability (operant responses) would initially suffer because of these contextual differences.

Getting Control of Responses.   One way to demonstrate how a stimulus in the animal's environment can come to control operant responding is to arrange for a specific stimulus to be present when a response-food contingency is in effect. For example, the rat or bird can be trained to bar press or key peck when the houselights are on, and to not make these operant responses when the houselights are off. How? By having a response-food contingency in effect only when the houselights are on. When the houselights are turned off, the lever can be electrically disconnected from the feeder mechanism. With the lights off, the operants are no longer instrumental in securing food; the response-food contingency has been broken.

After several sessions of lights on/responses produce food, and lights off/responses do *not* produce food, the animal learns to respond in the presence of the lights, and to not respond in darkness. (The opposite can easily be trained, where responses in the dark are reinforced, but not those made in the light).

Discriminative Stimuli. Skinner called a stimulus (such as a house light) that signals that a response-food contingency is in effect a **discriminative stimulus (S⁺).** Therefore, a discriminative stimulus sets the occasion in which trained operant responses become highly probable. Typically an S⁺ controls high rates of operant responding because the responses are reinforced. Conversely, a S⁻ is a stimulus that signals that response-food contingencies are *not* in effect. There being no payoff when the S⁻ stimulus is in effect, the responses drop out.[8]

Stimulus Control. We are now able to formally define the stimulus control of behavior. When trained animals reliably make operant responses in the presence of S⁺ and do *not* respond in the presence of S⁻, the animal is said to be under **stimulus control.** In a Skinner box environment, an S⁺ (such as a tone) sets the occasion for a high rate of response, and an S⁻ (no tone, or perhaps a light or a tone of a different frequency) sets the occasion for a low rate of response. Responses in the presence of the S⁺ are reinforced, but not in the S⁻ condition.

An animal reliably lever pressing in the presence of one stimulus and not another is "under stimulus control." In the experiment by Anderson et al. (1992) described earlier, in the presence of the light rats bar pressed for either food or ESB, and didn't press during the tone that signaled a DRL-15 sec. The light was an S⁺ and the tone was an S⁻. Likewise, my dog Sadie will crawl up on the couch in the presence of my children, but not when I'm in the room. She begs for food from them, but not from me. My children are S⁺s for her crawling on furniture and begging at the table, and my presence is a S⁻ for engaging in these behaviors. Note that Sadie is under stimulus control in the presence of both me and my children: She has been differentially reinforced, and responds predictably depending upon the stimulus context.

Losing Stimulus Control. An S⁺- S⁻ discrimination is not unlike Pavlov's CS⁺- CS⁻ conditioned discrimination procedure (see Figure 5.7, p. 168). The difference is that S⁺s control *operant* responding and CS⁺s control *reflexive* responding. Recall that Pavlov trained dogs to salivate in the presence of a

---

[8]An S⁺ is similar in function to a CS⁺, and an S⁻ is similar in function to a CS⁻.

circle and to *not* salivate to an ellipse—that is, he required that the dog discriminate a circle from an ellipse. When the ellipse had become too circular (beyond the dog's capacity of visual resolution), the dog began to salivate to both stimuli indiscriminately. In Skinner's terms, Pavlov had "lost stimulus control" over the animal. Likewise, after successfully training an S⁺- S⁻ discrimination, if for whatever reason operant responses are no longer reliably controlled by the S⁺ and S⁻, the trainer (or parent) is said to have lost stimulus control.

Red and Green Traffic Lights. Consider another example: When you reliably stop your automobile at a red light, and go on green, Skinner would say that you are under stimulus control. The red and green traffic lights are S⁺s that control the operant responses of *foot pressure on the brake,* and *foot pressure on the accelerator,* respectively. The same red and green traffic lights are S⁻s for *foot pressure* off *the accelerator,* and *foot pressure* off *the brake,* respectively (that is, to *not* press the accelerator or brake, respectively). The stimulus control properties of red and green lights on driving an automobile are relatively simple. Can you identify the control characteristics of the yellow caution light?

Controlling Human Verbal Behavior

You may or may not be impressed with the behaviorist's analysis of your behavior at a traffic signal. More than likely you conceptualize human behavior as being far more complicated than a mere succession of operants controlled by discriminative stimuli. What role, for example, does language and thought play in controlling behavior? Skinner and others have pointed out that language usage can also be analyzed from a behavioral perspective (Skinner, 1957). Let's use the concept of stimulus control to analyze how a child learns her multiplication tables. Discriminative stimuli (S⁺s, the multiplication problems) control responses (verbal or written answers) that are reinforced (correct) or not (incorrect). In this example of a learned behavior, and in other examples of skilled performance, the subject learns which responses are reinforced and at the same time which are *not* reinforced. "Four-times-four = sixteen" (correct); "four-times-four = fifteen" (incorrect). Shooting the basketball "this way" is reinforced; shooting the ball "that way" is not reinforced.

Discriminated Operants. Back at the supermarket we left Mom and Joey exchanging words at the checkout counter. At that time, Mom was characterized as being in control of Joey's behavior, and Joey, Mom's. Can we bring the behaviorist concept of stimulus control to each person's behavior, including their verbal behavior? The bright candy wrappers in the checkout lane are CSs that have been associated with the chocolate USs they contain. In addition to these learned associations, Joey's past reinforcement history includes a sequence of operant behaviors that have been positively reinforced.

"Reaching for candy" is a **discriminated operant** that reflects the stimulus control the candy has over Joey's behavior. That is, on previous occasions these particular operants of reaching, grabbing, removing wrapper (the wrapper is the S^+) have produced response-contingent reinforcement.

Mom and Mom's words are part of this stimulus complex. On past occasions her words were S^+s controlling Joey's behavior. "No, you can't have it" was part of the stimulus complex in the presence of which Joey's operant behavior was ultimately reinforced by the candy. The word "no" in this stimulus context is an S^+ for Joey to turn up the volume of his cry, and to hold onto the candy even more tightly. Why? Because in the past that response in this context produced reinforcement. In turn, Joey's vocalizations (and the caustic looks of other shoppers) are the S^+s for Mom to respond verbally ". . . if you'll be a good boy and not cry, you can have the candy . . . but this is the last time." Joey stops crying, which reinforces Mom's verbal behavior, just as it did the last time it occurred. (This is an example of a kind of reinforcer we'll study in the next chapter under the topic of aversive control of behavior.) Recognize the controlling role of context in this example. The presence of a second parent (as part of the context) would likely have changed Joey's exchanges with his mother. Table 7.1 summarizes the S^+s and S^-s, and the discriminated operant responses characterizing this human interaction.

TABLE 7.1   Who's in Control?

	Joey
S⁺s Controlling Behavior	*Discriminated Operants*
Supermarket stimuli	Search for candy
Sight of candy	(a) approach candy; (b) reach for candy; (c)"Mom, I want this piece" (verbal behavior)
"No, you can't have it"	Louder vocalizations
"O.K., but this is the last time"	Tears off wrapper and eats candy
	Mom
S⁻s Controlling Behavior	*Discriminated Operants*
Sight of Joey moving towards candy	"No candy" (verbal behavior)
Joey says "please"	"No, you can't have it"
Louder vocalizations; others stare.	"O.K. but this is the last time"
Joey eats candy	Mom resumes shopping

Occasion Setting

Many laboratory experiments have investigated the features of how context control S⁺- S⁻discrimination learning (Holland, 1986). If a stimulus context, such as a room, comes to control discriminated responding, that stimulus is called an *occasion setter*. To the extent that Mom's and Joey's behavior occurred at the supermarket, this example mirrors **occasion setting** experiments in which features in this environment set the occasion for another stimulus to be reinforced or not. Ross & Holland (1981), for example, trained rats to use a light to give meaning to a tone. The presence of the light meant that a tone sounded a few seconds later would be an S⁺; the light set the occasion for the tone to be followed by reinforcement. If *not* signaled by the light, the tone would be an S⁻. The light set the occasion for discriminated learning, in the same way that the supermarket context set the occasion for Mom and Joey's verbal behavior.

Several points are worth emphasizing from the foregoing example of Mom and Joey in the supermarket:

1. Speaking words (using language) can be understood as an *operant* behavior which, like any other operant, can result in reinforcement or punishment. Reinforcing and punishing an individual's words increases and decreases, respectively, the probability they will be used in the future.

2. Words can and do function as *discriminative stimuli*. Words in some contexts mean different things than those same words in other contexts.

3. In all human interactions, the operant responses of one individual have stimulus properties that set the occasion for operant responses of the other person. From this example it is easy to see how Joey's behavior is controlling mom's, and vice versa.[9]

4. Behavior always occurs in a context, and the context can become an occasion setter. Among humans, occasion-setters can control when to argue, and when to make love.

Analyzing Complex Behavior as Chained Operants

Another point to be made from Table 7.1 is that seemingly complex human interactions can be more simply analyzed as behavioral sequences that are "chained" together. In these *stimulus-response chains*, each response has stimulus features that control the next response. Thus, Joey's verbal response "please" is the stimulus for Mom's "No, you can't have it."

---

[9]If you routinely argue with someone, both of you know which buttons to hit to keep it going. Also, a co-dependency relationship is an example from clinical psychology that profits from this analysis.

The concept of *chained operants* also allows us to better analyze Joey's behavior. A **chained operant** is a behavioral sequence analyzed in terms of a succession of discriminative stimuli with each setting the occasion for a different operant response, eventually ending in the delivery of a reinforcer. Joey sees candy at distance (S^+); approaches candy (operant); sees candy up close (S^+); reaches for candy (operant); sensory input as fingers touch candy (S^+); candy is picked up (operant); candy in hand is stimulus (S^+); for "Mom, I want this piece" (verbal operant). Joey puts the candy in his mouth and bites off a piece (operants). The taste of candy (positive reinforcer) reinforces all preceding operants.

Thought question: Can you describe student-teacher interactions in the classroom in terms of stimulus-response chains? What are the discriminative stimuli controlling the behavior of student and teacher? Hint: Identify the operant responses of both students and teachers. Note the stimulus characteristics of students' operants that control the teacher, and vice versa. (See discussion question 12.)

Behavioral Analysis of "Volition" and "Will"

Earlier Mom and Joey's interaction was described as a "battle of wills." John B. Watson and B. F. Skinner objected to the use of language such as "volition" and "will" to describe presumptive cognitive events. They both thought that the concept of cognitive processes added little to analyses of behavior, Watson denied the premise of human consciousness, and Skinner merely ignored it. In many of his writings, Skinner also downplayed the concept of free will. He proposed that analyses of observed behavior were more productive and that one's behavior was better predicted by knowledge of past reinforcement histories—by stimulus control—than by hypothetical personality characteristics, including that of "free will."

What do you, the reader think? Which terminology lends itself best to a scientific analysis of human behavior? What, if anything, is added to an understanding of Joey's behavior by describing him as a "brat," or as a "strong-willed individual"? In this instance, might not the label be inappropriate, given that Joey's mother is controlling his behavior?

Rules for Learning Complex Chains

Complex sequences of operant behavior are learned with difficulty. Remember learning to swim, to ride a bike, or to painstakingly print the alphabet? Pianists take many years to learn hand and finger movements, and months of intense practice for recitals. In all these examples, operants must be performed in sequence. Each operant can only be performed if the preceding operant has been successfully accomplished. Whether it be driving a car, writing your name, tying your shoe, or whistling a tune, all complex chains require the successful completion of individual operants.

In working with children, for example, parents, teachers, and coaches should be sensitive to individual differences in sensory-motor development (don't ask fingers to do what they are not yet capable of doing). Consider the "simple" task of a child learning to tie shoes. To expedite learning, parents should break it into component tasks for their child, as follows:

1. Separate each component response (separating the strings, crossing the strings, holding one bow, looping a string around the bow), and have the child practice each operant separately.
2. Initially reinforce the child for accomplishing the simple operants as they are performed separately.
3. After the child is capable of accomplishing each component, practice each operant in the *reverse* order of the shoe-lacing sequence. That is, form both bows for the child, and allow the child to pull it tight as the *first* skill they learn. Why reverse order?

Errors in Mazes. Why should the sequence of operant responses by reinforced in *reverse* order? An analysis of the errors that rats make while learning a maze indicates that they make fewer errors at the end of the chains than at the beginning (Hull, 1932). That is, the last response (for example, a final left turn before entering the goal box) is learned first, presumable because it is the last response that is reinforced with food. Then rats learn the next to last response, the third from last response, and so forth. For this reason, after helping the child practice all individual operants involved in lacing shoes, the child should be allowed to accomplish the last operant (pulling the bow tight), followed by a reinforcer. After several trials, allow the child to work alone on making the bow, then tying it. These last two operants will be chained together by the terminal reinforcement (as well as by the verbal reinforcement—secondary reinforcement—of the caretaker at each step).

So much for tying shoes. Now, let's consider how one learns to play a piano concerto . . .

Interim Summary

1. ***Behavior control*** is a concept that a stimulus in the environment (called a ***discriminative stimulus,*** or **S⁺**) becomes associated with reinforced responses, while another stimulus, a S^-, is not associated with reinforced responses.
2. The animal is said to be under ***stimulus control*** if, after S^+- S^- training, the response reliably occurs to the S^+ but not to the S^-. The discriminative stimulus is said to control the response.
3. A response that is controlled by a S^+ is called a ***discriminated operant.***
4. Introducing the S^- condition (in S^+- S^- discrimination training) produces results similar to the CS^- in the CS^+- CS^- discrimination.

5. Human interactions, including verbal behavior, can be analyzed from the perspective of reinforced operant responding under stimulus control.

6. Laboratory demonstrations of stimulus control have recently focused on the way in which the context in which the experiment is conducted controls responding.

7. Contextual stimuli can come to control the occasions during which a stimulus can be a S$^+$ or S$^-$. These stimuli are called *occasion-setters*, and the event, **occasion setting**.

8. Learning complex behaviors can be analyzed as the acquisition of **chained operants**—a sequence of individual operants that end with reinforcement.

DISCUSSION QUESTIONS

10. Should parents-to-be seek training in applied behavioral analysis, in which they would learn about Skinner's concept of stimulus control?

11. Student: Among other demonstrations of my *freedom to choose*, Dr. Skinner, are the very clothes I selected to wear this morning.

    Skinner: Were you free to wear your roommate's clothes?

    Student: No. But I'm free to choose to wear anything I own.

    Skinner: So some people have more freedom to choose than others because they have more alternatives—either more resources to buy clothes, or less scruples about wearing the clothes of others?

    Student: I suppose so, but that is not the point. I am free to choose to wear anything I own.

    Skinner: Did you choose to wear your clean, stylish clothes, as opposed to dirty, nonstylish clothes?

    Student: Of course I chose to wear clean, stylish clothes. However, I *could* choose to wear dirty or nonstylish clothes.

    Skinner: What determines your choice?

    (. . . continue the dialogue. Can you hypothesize an early family environment that made the "choice" of wearing clean, stylish clothes more likely? Could advertisers condition you to choose other stylish clothes? Can you also hypothesize environmental determinants of a student who "rebels" and "chooses" to wear dirty, nonstylish clothes?)

12. My major professor was James C. Smith of Florida State University. Among the many valuable things I learned from him was his analysis of behavioral control in the classroom. It only seems, he reasoned, that teachers are in control of their students. *Good* teachers are as much *controlled by* their students as they are *in control* in the classroom. What do you think Smith means by this analysis?

13. Remember learning to ride a bike? Painfully printing the alphabet? A musical instrument . . . ? Can you identify chained, component operants of these acquired skills? If anyone helped you to learn, did they use successive approximation? Reinforcement?

CHAPTER SUMMARY

1. Theories of reinforcement have been proposed by Pavlov (biologically meaningful USs), Thorndike (satisfiers), and Hull (drive reduction; drive stimulus reduction). All three recognized the adaptive/ evolutionary significance of reinforcers.

2. Clark L. Hull initially proposed a formal drive-reduction theory of behavior, later modified to a drive-stimulus reduction theory. He proposed that physiological needs induced drives, and his S-O-R model of behavior posited organismic variables (such as hunger) that intervened between the stimulus and response. For Hull, a reinforcer satisfied an animal's need.

3. Hull proposed that humans and other animals are motivated by innate incentives (food and water) and acquired incentives (such as money and other conditioned reinforcers).

4. B. F. Skinner's descriptive behaviorism rejected intervening variables. He defined a reinforcer as any stimulus that increased the probability of the response that preceded it. Adaptive-evolutionary considerations aside, Skinner defined reinforcement as the process of strengthening responses.

5. Skinner's operant conditioning method experimentally analyzes behavior in terms of how reinforcement contingencies control response tendencies. Operant behavior in the laboratory is measured in computer-programmed Skinner boxes.

6. Control of responding is analyzed by measuring the effects of schedules of reinforcement on responding, including continuous reinforcement (CRF) and partial, or intermittent reinforcement.

7. Partial reinforcement schedules include Fixed Ratio (FR); Variable-Ratio (VR); Fixed Interval (FI); Variable Interval (VI); Differential reinforcement of high (DRH) and low (DRL) schedules of reinforcement.

8. Differences in acquisition, rate and patterning of responses, stability, and resistance to extinction are generated by different schedules of reinforcement.

9. CRF extinguishes quickly, and by comparison partial reinforcement schedules show resistance to extinction— called the partial reinforcement effect (PRE).

10. Social reinforcement theory (Bandura) proposes that a child (the observer) learns by imitating models (parents, teachers). These models use social reinforcers (smiling, nodding) to reinforce correctly modeled behavior.

11. The Premack principle states that highly probable behaviors (such as eating) will reinforce less probable behaviors (such as pressing a lever). This reinforcement relationship is often reversed when the relative probabilities of occurrence of the two behaviors are reversed.

12. Electrical stimulation of the brain (ESB) can have reinforcing properties. Rats will bar-press to stimulate the medial forebrain bundle and mesotelencephalic dopamine system.

13. ESB can make food lose its reinforcement properties through a process called negative contrast.

14. Behavior control is a theory that specific stimuli in the environment that predict reinforcers can come to control behavior. An animal is said to be under stimulus control if a response reliably occurs in the presence of one but not another stimulus.

15. A discriminative stimulus (S⁺) sets the occasion for reinforced responses, while a S⁻ predicts non-reinforcement.

16. In occasion-setting, contextual stimuli can become occasion setters that predict when a stimulus acts as a S⁺ or S⁻.

17. Chained operants are sequences of individual operants that end with reinforcement.

18. Reinforcement theory and the analysis of stimulus control enhance our understanding of various aspects of human verbal behavior, of how complex behaviors are learned, and of how social interactions are maintained.

KEY TERMS

behavioral contrast   259
behavioral control   264
chained operant   270
continuous reinforcement   242
differential reinforcement of high
    rates (DRH)   250
differential reinforcement of low rates
    (DRL)   250
discriminated operant   268
discriminative stimulus (S⁺)   266
drive reduction theory   235
drive-stimulus reduction   236
electrical stimulation of the brain
    (ESB)   257
fixed interval (FI)   245
fixed ratio s (FR)   243
frustration theory   249
incentive motivation   235
intermittent reinforcement   243

negative contrast   259
occasion setting   269
partial reinforcement   243
partial reinforcement effect (PRE)
    249
post-reinforcement pause   244
Premack Principle   255
punisher   238
punishment   238
S⁻   266
S⁺   266
schedule of reinforcement   242
social reinforcement theory   254
S-O-R Theory   234
stimulus control   266
variable interval schedule (VI)   246
variable ratio schedule (VR)   244

CHAPTER 8

Punishment and the Aversive Control of Behavior

If you think nobody cares if you're alive, try missing a couple of car payments.

As the Jack Hand-like one-liner suggests, human behavior seems to be controlled as much by aversive events as by the reinforcement process described in the previous chapter. We try, but we cannot avoid all the bad things that can happen to us throughout a lifetime. In this chapter we look at processes of punishment and how aversive stimuli can come to control the behavior of animals (including people, of course).

PUNISHMENT

Anyone who has ever received a speeding ticket can appreciate the complexity of emotional responses accompanying punishment. First, a sinking feeling when you notice the flashing blue lights in your rearview mirror. Not quite fear, perhaps, unless there is an open container of alcohol in the car, or your probationary period from the last ticket hasn't yet expired. But definitely confusion and anxiety as you anticipate the unknown. The fear may soon give way to denial and anger as you review the unjust contingencies you have been subjected to. (No way could I have been going that fast. Why didn't you ticket the one that had just passed me? Lousy cops should be out catching the *real* criminals. Cruel and unusual punishment because this is going to cost me far more than it should. I drive fast, but safely.)

Punishment: A Single Process Defined by Two Procedures

Figure 8.1 shows that **punishment** is defined in terms of a reduced tendency to make the response that has previously produced an aversive consequence. Getting a traffic ticket is an example of the first kind of punishment because a response (speeding) has produced an aversive consequence (a ticket and a fine). Does getting a single speeding ticket result in less speeding? Not necessarily. We will look at the *effectiveness* of various punishment procedures below.

Withholding a Positive Stimulus. Another type of punishment is depicted in the bottom-right cell of Figure 8.1: An animal can be punished by not receiving an expected reinforcer—that is, one that it has a history of occuring in this situation. A dog that is routinely petted when its master arrives from work can be punished for having chewed up a houseslipper by *not* being petted. Another common example of this type of punishment is the "time-out" procedure used by parents and educators. By removing a child from a social environment ("No telephone calls 'till I say so!"), the child is prevented from receiving a reinforcer.

Effect of Stimulus on Preceding Response

	↑ **Probability, or rate of response**	↓ **Probability, or rate of response**
Response *produces* stimulus	*Process is* **Reinforcement** *Stimulus is a* **Reinforcer**	*Process is* **Punishment** *Stimulus is a* **Punisher**
Response *prevents* stimulus	*Process is* **Negative Reinforcement** *Absence of an Aversive stimulus is a* **Reinforcer**	*Process is* **Punishment** *Absence of stimulus is a* **Punisher**

FIGURE 8.1   Punishment

Summary of operationally defined concept of *punishment*, and the operational labeling of *two types of punishing* events.

Consider one last example that combines both the application of a punisher, and the withholding of an expected reinforcer. Your exam is returned with a "77" scrawled beside your name. You vaguely remember that you had two other exams on that day and instead of studying all the material in the assigned chapters, you only read the chapter outlines. But you thought you'd done better than the 77 would indicate. So, you were punished for studying too little with a low grade, and you were punished by *not* producing an expected consequence—a high grade. To summarize, the process of punishment can be effected by either applying a response contingent aversive stimulus, or by withholding an expected positive stimulus.[1]

Don't squat with your spurs on.

---

[1]Punishment is a singular process described by two procedures. Some theorists use the term "positive punishment" to describe responses that *produce an aversive consequence* and "negative punishment" to describe responses that *do not produce expected rewards*. The adjectives "positive" and "negative" are confusing in this context and will not be used here. ("Positive punishment" is an oxymoron, and "negative punishment" is redundant.)

Primary and Secondary Punishers

Innate, or Primary Punishers.   What Thorndike labeled as an "annoyer" Skinner simply described as an aversive, or punishing stimulus. For humans and most other animals, common aversive stimuli include cold, heat, hunger and thirst, loud noises, and a host of environmental stimuli that can cause pain, nausea, illness, etc. A stimulus that is inherently aversive is called **primary punisher.** The pain induced by spanking a child is an example of a "physical" or primary punisher.

Acquired, or Secondary Punishers.   A neutral stimulus can become a **secondary punisher** by acquiring secondary punishing properties through association with one of these primary aversive stimuli (Hake & Azrin 1965). In a method described in an earlier chapter, a rat heard a neutral tone followed by a painful electric shock. In this *conditioned suppression* procedure, the tone had several effects. It acted to suppress lever-pressing, and it may have caused an emotional response in the rat not unlike what you feel when you see police lights flashing in a rearview mirror. Punishing properties of stimuli, then, can come from both innate predispositions and can be acquired through conditioning. "Spanking" (physical pain) is a *primary* punisher, whereas the threat of a spanking is a *secondary* punisher. Secondary punishers include social disapproval (nasty glances), ridicule, and other violated expectancies.

[Another term for the "psychological pain" that accompanies the expectation of pain is *learned* pain. In non-human animals, including non-speaking humans, what is the experience of physical pain and what is the experience of learned pain, is unknown. For that matter, how two different adults experience either physical or learned pain is also indeterminant! For this reason, as indicated in Figure 8.1, we accept Skinner's behaviorist definition of an aversive stimulus—a punisher—in terms of its ability to suppress the responses that produce it, rather than its presumed physical or psychological aversiveness.]

Separating Innate from Acquired Punishers.   Characterizing punishment as innate or acquired can be difficult. Consider, for example, the punishing effects of isolation. Solitary confinement in prison is considered to be one of the worst punishments a human can experience. Why is isolation so punishing? It may be that mammals (especially primates) are by nature gregarious, or that they have a freedom reflex (as Pavlov thought). Or it may be that a human acquires expectancies of social contact during a lifetime, and that isolation violates these learned expectancies. All are reasonable explanations.

Another example of the difficulty of separating innate and acquired aspects of punishment can be found in how we use language. Consider the parent who uses abusive language to control a child's behavior. The abusive language may acquire some of its punishing properties by being paired with physical punishment. In addition, because loud noise by itself is punishing, innate aspects of loud abusive language cannot be ruled out. (Men are often accused of arguing unfairly because their voices are typically louder and arguably more innately punishing than women's voices. Certainly the secondary punishing properties of abusive language are confounded by a "scolding" or "bullying" delivery.)

Combining Punishments. In real life situations types of punishments are often combined. For example, having your phone service disconnected due to late payment combines several kinds of punishment. Disconnection violates your expectancies and also deprives you of convenience (*removes* you from Thorndike's pleasing state of affairs). The cost in dollars (a penalty) to reconnect is the application of a punishing stimulus. A penalty is defined as ". . . an imposed punishment for violating a rule." Simple penalties run the gamut from a yellow hanky thrown for being offside, to not being invited to a party. More serious punishment includes expulsion from school for low grades, fines, imprisonment, and capital punishment.

Reviewing the Nature and Procedures of Punishment. Before considering whether punishment is effective in controlling behavior, let us briefly summarize and review what we have learned to this point by having you sort the following examples of punishment into four categories: the punishment is either (1) innate or (2) acquired, and is produced by (3) applying a negative stimulus or (4) withholding an expected positive stimulus.

(a) having one's driver's license revoked following a serious driving infraction

(b) not feeding a hungry baby

(c) spanking a crying baby

(d) removing a hockey player to the penalty box for fighting

(e) confining a child to her room for lying

(f) reducing rank or salary of an employee for incompetent behavior

(g) making a child sit quietly in a classroom that is 90° F

(h) getting sick after eating a meal

(j) quietly informing your lover you have found another[2]

Gauging the Effectiveness of Punishment. On the basis of limited observations, both Thorndike (1932) and Skinner (1953) independently decided that punishment was relatively ineffective in controlling behavior. In one experi-

---

[2](a) acquired, withhold; (b) innate, withhold; (c) innate, apply; (d) acquired, withhold; (e) mixed, withhold; (f) mixed, withhold; (g) mixed, applied; (h) innate, applied; (j) acquired, applied.

ment Skinner used a low-intensity aversive stimulus—a spring-loaded lever that "slapped" the rat as it lever-pressed for food (Skinner, 1938). After "punishing" lever pressing responses with this slapping device, Skinner next demonstrated that following this punishment training, response suppression continued in extinction for a short period of time. But it quickly recovered. Because responding recovered to baseline levels relatively quickly under these conditions, Skinner concluded that punishment was ineffective in permanently altering behavior.

During the past 40 years, new observations have led behavioral scientists to different conclusions; namely, that under the right conditions, punishment can have specific and relatively permanent effects on behavior. What determines if punishment is effective?

Rules of Punishment

Table 8.1 compares the rules of punishment with the rules of both classical and operant conditioning. Here we see that punishment can be made more or less effective depending on the specifics of punishment training.

Punishment is Associative. A quick comparison of the rules in Table 8.1 shows a considerable degree of overlap among them. Both punishment training and classical and operant conditioning are in part determined (a) by the intensity of the punisher or the US; (b) by the number of conditioning trials; (c) by the interval of time between the response and the punisher (or between CS and US, and between response and reinforcer); and (d) by the sequence (response → punisher; CS → US; and response → reinforcer). The similarities in predicted outcome supports general process associative learning theory. In addition to the similarities of outcomes shown in Table 8.1, both punishment procedures and classical and operant conditioning procedures share the common effects of extinction, latent inhibition, generalization, and so forth. Let's look at some experiments on punishment.

Effects of Punishment Intensity Rule

The effect of punishment on responses is *directly related to the intensity of the pain-inducing stimulus*. Because it is easy both to quantify and control, electric shock is used in many animal experiments. Severity of electric shock affects how rats run in the alley of a maze (Karsh, 1962) and lever press in a Skinner box (Storms, Boroczi, & Broen, 1962). Intensity of electric shock also affects how quickly humans learn to *not* open a cigarette case when they are punished for opening it (Powell & Azrin, 1968). Other commonly used punishing stimuli are aversive chemicals and toxins that, by their sickness-inducing properties, punish eating, drinking, and other consummatory responses. In conditioning a taste aversion, for example, predictable dose-response curves showing higher drug concentrations (Gamzu, 1977) and

TABLE 8.1 A Comparison of Rules for Effective Punishment with Rules for Effective Classical and Operant Conditioning

Classical and Operant Conditioning	*Punishment*
(1) US/Reinforcer intensity rule *More intense USs and more potent reinforcers produce better conditioning*	**(1) Punishment intensity rule** *More intense punishers produce better conditioning*
(2) Number of trials rule *More CS-US trials, and more reinforced responses yield better conditioning during acquisition*	**(2) Number of trials rule** *More response-punishment trials produce better conditioning with qualification: Intensity of punishment must be relatively high.*
(3) CS-US, or response-to-reinforcement interval rule *Shorter CS-US ISIs and shorter response-to-reinforcement intervals yield better conditioning*	**(3) Response-to-punishment interval rule** *Shorter response-to-punishment intervals produce better conditioning*
(4) CS-US, or response-to-reinforcement sequencing rule *CS→US sequences yield excitatory conditioning; US→CS sequences typically produce inhibitory conditioning; a reinforcer must follow a response for learning to occur.*	**(4) Response-punishment sequencing rule** *Response contingent punishment produces better conditioning than non-contingent punishment. A punishment→ response sequence defines an escape paradigm*
(5) CS intensity rule *More intense CSs yield better conditioning; no known relationship between strength of S^d and better conditioning*	**(5)** *No comparable finding; no known relationship between response strength (effort?) and effectiveness of punishment*

higher radiation levels (Barker & Smith, 1974) better suppress drinking a saccharin solution. Animals learn more rapidly when higher shock intensities, higher levels of poisoning, and greater intensities of other punishers are used.

Skinner's Experiment Revisited. Why did Skinner (1953) conclude that punishment was ineffective in permanently altering behavior? A simple conclusion is that Skinner's "slapping" stimulus was too weak. From other experiments with other levels of punishers, by consistently applying a relatively intense punishing stimulus rats can be permanently trained to *not* lever-press. His conclusion regarding punishment is suspect for an additional reason: Following both reinforcement and punishment procedures, responses *normally* diminish in extinction. That is, extinction has the same effect on reinforced behavior as he observed for the "slapped" lever-pressing. A more parsimonious conclusion, then, is that punished behavior is neither more nor less permanent than food-based behavioral change when intensity of stimuli are equated. The benefits of a punishment procedure are that with sufficiently intense punishers, response suppression is adaptively rapid.

The Effects of Low-Intensity Punishers

When low-intensity USs and weak reinforcers are used in conditioning, acquisition is slower than with higher-intensity stimuli, but nevertheless these trials produce a predictable, cumulative effect. That is, it might take more trials to acquire a CR or operant response using weak stimuli, but learning does occur. By contrast, if the intensity of the punishing stimulus is too low on the first few trials, this low-intensity punishment has the effect of *diminishing* the punishing properties of later trials that use higher-intensity aversive stimuli (Azrin, 1966; Azrin & Holz, 1966). In this experiment, animals reinforced with food for bar-pressing were punished in extinction with different levels of shock. The animals acted as if they become habituated to the effects of weak electric shock, and the result was that even a higher shock intensity became ineffective in suppressing responses.

Performance Masks Punishment Effects? Was this habituation to the shock? Or, was something else going on? An alternative explanation to shock habituation is that hunger-motivated lever-pressing was sufficiently strong to mask the effects of a weak punisher. The question then becomes one of performance rather than learning. A human example illustrates this point quite well. Both children and adults can train themselves to self-administer insulin by painfully sticking a needle into their thigh muscle. "Needle-sticking" behavior should diminish because the response produces immediate pain. However, out of necessity some people stick themselves daily over many years, this behavior reinforced by a strong secondary motivation. The effect of pain was masked by the effects of the benefits.

Several years ago, following a surgery, an elderly acquaintance of mine hired a home nurse. The nurse afforded the opportunity of having someone else administer his daily insulin, and, not surprisingly, he was more than content to let the nurse do the honors. Why? The needle-stick had been self-punishing over many years, and the response was clearly aversive. Like the hunger-motivated rats, performing the response had been a necessity that prevented the aversive learning from showing. If they had the alternative of *not* being hungry, the punishing properties of low-intensity shock would no doubt have suppressed a lever pressing response. The point is that the *performance level* of a response is not always a reliable indicator that a response has (or has not) been learned.

Number of Punishment Trials Rule

When an aversive stimulus is of sufficient intensity is used (rather than one of too low intensity), punishment shows a trials effect. The more frequently that a response is punished, the lower is the subsequent response rate. A common way of measuring the effects of punishment is to shock the lever-pressing responses of an animal working on a food-based schedule of reinforcement. Each response followed by shock is a trial. Using a moderately high intensity shock, if every response in a work session is punished, rats stop lever pressing altogether. By contrast, rats shocked on every 100th or 500th response merely slow their rate of response. The rate of response is proportional to the number of punished responses (Azrin, Holz, & Hake, 1963).

Results of Continued Punishment Training

Once animals have learned the response-punishment contingency, their long term behavior may change as they continue to be shocked. Figure 8.2 shows the results of an experiment in which a pigeon has learned to peck a key for food on a VI-1 minute schedule of reinforcement. Then (first dashed vertical line in the figure), each key peck is punished by delivering electric shock to an electrode implanted under the skin. The response rate drops precipitously,

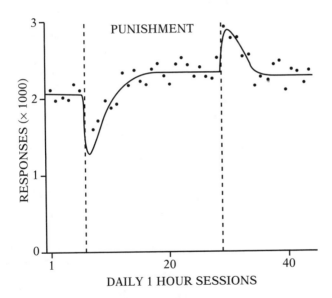

FIGURE 8.2 Punished Responses Interfere with Food-Reinforced Responses

A pigeon that is food-reinforced on a VI-1 minute schedule makes about 2000 key-peck responses in daily 1-h sessions. The introduction of a punishment contingency (left dashed vertical line), in which each key-peck is shocked, decreases the total key-pecks in the next few sessions. But the animal recovers to baseline, and exceeds baseline when the punishment contingency is removed (right dashed vertical line). (Figure from Azrin, 1966.)

but over ensuing sessions returns to baseline levels and above. When the punishment schedule is stopped (2nd dashed vertical line), the response rate increases above baseline for a few sessions. In this example, the effects of punishment were immediate, and the punisher lost its effectiveness with repeated training. These results have been replicated in similar experiments (Camp, Raymond, & Church, 1962).[3] As seen earlier, low-intensity painful stimuli habituate, and as a result responses are not as effectively punished by the shock. Such habituation seems to act as if it "immunizes" the animal against experiencing higher levels of pain. For high-intensity shocks, however, responses may remain suppressed indefinitely.

Response-to-Punishment Interval Rule

Punishment is an adaptive process that changes behavior. A key to effective punishment is to mimic the rapidly conducting sensory and motor fibers of the nervous system. How? By quickly applying an aversive stimulus to the desired response. The shorter the response-to-punishment interval, the more effective is the punishment treatment.

Punishment no less than reinforcement guides behavior by helping select from alternative responses those that produce the most pleasure and/or avoid the most pain. The CNS is designed to accomplish this selection of behavior optimally under certain conditions. For example, some pain fibers are especially fast-conducting. Both bee stings and touching a hot curling iron (and squatting with your spurs on) produce rapid reflexive responses, and equally rapid association formation. The new associations help identify where bees are, and the effects of touching a hot iron.

Likewise, a 77 grade on a test paper might punish the reading of Chapter Summaries in lieu of studying the text more thoroughly. In other cases a grade of 77 might not change studying behavior, in the same way that a traffic ticket is ineffective in slowing down some drivers. One reason why a 77 might be ineffective in changing this student's behavior is that it was delivered 3 weeks after the test-taking response. In this example, a number of non-target responses are being punished by a secondary punisher delivered 3 weeks too late! The adverse effects of delaying the punishing properties of electric shock following a lever-pressing response are detailed in Box 8.1.

Response-to-Punishment Contingency

A 77 on a test paper delivered *3 weeks* after the examination is arguably non-contingent. Such treatment resembles the non-contingent punishment group described in Box 6.3. The non-contingent group violates the response-to-

---

[3]Compare these results of repeated shock trials with the results of repeated morphine trials in Siegal's experiments in Ch 5.

Box 8.1   FAR SIDE: "Catch him in the act"

THE FAR SIDE   By GARY LARSON

© 1984 FarWorks, Inc./Dist. by Universal Press Syndicate   9-26

"Harold! The dog's trying to blow up the house again! Catch him in the act or he'll never learn."

Gary Larson's cartoon captures the behavioral law relating to the ineffectiveness of delayed punishment. The effects of delaying the interval of time between a response and an electric shock is clearly seen in an experiment by Camp et al. (1967). In different groups the response-to-shock delays were 2.0, 7.5, and 30.0 seconds. The results of these different delays in punishment were compared with a zero second delay (i.e., immediate punishment), a non-contingent punishment group (NC), and an unshocked group (control). The figure shows that immediate shock is best, both in faster acquisition (asymptotic during the second training session) and in maintaining suppressed responding for the duration of the experiment. Note also that 2.0-sec and 7.5-sec groups yield better suppression of responses than does the 30 sec delay group.

The *non-contingent* punishment group was shocked during the session, but not when it lever-pressed. Relative to the control group there is both an initial suppression and a long term "dampening" effect on the behavior of the non-contingently punished group. One interpretation is that the NC group found the Skinner-box environment to be more aversive than did the control group. (Figure from Camp, Raymond, & Church, 1967).

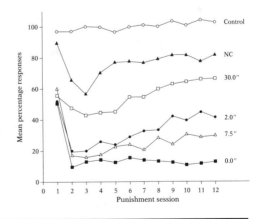

punishment *sequence* common to the other treatment groups (groups that in turn varied only by the response-to-punishment *interval*).

Why did we see a suppression of responses by this non-contingent punishment group? First, a few lever-pressing responses might have been paired with punishment in the same way that a *truly-random control group* produces chance pairings. Second, we can speculate about non-associative punishment effects. Third, punishment effects can be attributed to associations of aversive stimuli with the *context* in which they occurred rather than with specific responses. A general wariness about the testing environment might develop, that in turn would affect the *performance* of the learned response. Is it possible that a general disdain for school in part reflects non-contingent punishment rather than punishment of specific performances? Whether the response in question is lever pressing or writing the answer to a question, an immediate response-punishment contingency is the most effective way in which to change the desired response.

Another way to analyze the sequencing effects of aversive stimulation is to note that by definition, punishment only works to suppress behavior when the events occur in one direction. A response that terminates an aversive stimulus (that is, the aversive stimulus precedes rather than follows a response) defines an *escape* procedure, to be discussed in a later section.

Latent Inhibition of Punishment

Recall that prior exposure to a CS or a US makes these stimuli familiar, and that familiar stimuli do not condition as readily as novel stimuli. The phenomenon, known as *latent inhibition*, includes the US preexposure effect (see p. 149). One explanation for the finding that a low intensity punisher "habituates" and is no longer effective in controlling behavior is that punishers can also be latently inhibited. A number of laboratory demonstrations using a variety of stimuli have shown this to be the case. For example, shock is not as effective in punishing lever pressing when rats are familiar with it. In addition, a prior history with injections of lithium (producing gastric distress) make it less effective in punishing saccharin drinking (Suarez & Barker, 1976). Punishers, then, can be latently inhibited in the same manner as CSs and USs.

Interim Summary

1. **Punishment** is a process by which the application of an aversive stimulus, or the omission of an expected reinforcer, decreases the frequency of response that precedes the aversive stimulus.

2. A **primary punisher** is inherently aversive. A **secondary punisher** acquires its properties through association with a primary punisher.

3. Punishment is an associative process. Punishment is affected by latent inhibition, extinction, generalization, and so forth.

4. The process of punishment is most effective when the punisher is intense, when the response-punishment interval is minimal; when more trials are effected, and when the response-punisher contingency is not degraded.

5. With continued trials, a punisher may lose its effectiveness.

6. The effect of low intensity punishment is to habituate, and to latently inhibit the punishing properties of more intense punishers.

7. Non-contingent effects of punishment include a general response suppression. The response suppression may be due to the associative conditioning of aversive stimuli with environmental cues, such that an adverse emotional state causes a performance decrement.

DISCUSSION QUESTIONS

1. What is more punishing for you, pain, or learned pain?

2. Most parents attempt to use the secondary punishing properties of language to control their children's behavior. "No" (delivered in a stern voice, sometimes accompanied by a spanking hand) is understood by most English-speaking eighteen-month-olds. Under what conditions will the word "no" alone become a punishing stimulus? Why does "no" not work for some parents?

3. Gauging the appropriate intensity of secondary punishment is highly problematical. An interaction I had with a 4-year-old daughter made me acutely aware of my overreliance on (and ineffectiveness of) parental scolding and bullying. My goal was to teach her to say "please" and "thank you." My method was to constantly scold her for omissions and to reinforce her (praise her) for correct language usage. Leaving a restaurant one evening (after having scolded her during the meal), we happened upon a window display of sides of beef hanging in a butcher's shop. Curious as to what a 4-year-old thought about the display, I asked her why she thought they were hanging there.

   "Because they didn't say please?" she offered.

   What have you learned about the nature of punishment that makes her response understandable? Why should parents use punishment more sparingly than most of us do? Assuming that you will want your children to say "please" and "thank you," what reinforcement (and punishment?) contingencies will *you* use.

AVOIDANCE BEHAVIOR

In an earlier discussion, the hedonistic tendencies of animals to seek pleasure and to avoid pain were described as being adaptive. Indeed, a behavior that produces a reinforcer typically *is* adaptive, as is the process of reinforcement. Likewise, punishment has been described as adaptive, in that responses that produce pain tend to drop out. So we should not be surprised that most animals most of the time engage in behaviors that produce pleasure and that avoid pain.

Each animal does this differently in its ecological niche. In Chapter 2, we learned about species-specific defense reactions (SSDR's), genetically predisposed defense response that allow animals to avoid pain. Rats freeze or run away or attack when challenged; birds fly away or peck when challenged. Humans bring both innate responses (the activity of the sympathetic nervous system in preparing fight or flight responses is an example) as well as learned responses (dialing 911). Here we take a closer look at the aversive control of behavior by examining general processes that allow an animal to avoid pain in laboratory settings.

Negative Reinforcement

Figure 8.3 shows that **negative reinforcement** is the process by which a response that prevents or avoids an aversive stimulus increases in frequency. Students and researchers (Kimble, 1992) alike dislike Skinner's term "nega-

Effect of Stimulus on Preceding Response

	↑ Probability, or rate of response	↓ Probability, or rate of response
Response *produces* stimulus	*Process is* **Reinforcement** *Stimulus is a* **Reinforcer**	*Process is* **Punishment** *Stimulus is a* **Punisher**
Response *prevents* stimulus	*Process is* **Negative Reinforcement** *Absence of an Aversive stimulus is a* **Reinforcer**	*Process is* **Punishment** *Absence of stimulus is a* **Punisher**

FIGURE 8.3   Negative Reinforcement

Summary of operationally defined concept of negative reinforcement and that a response that prevents or avoids an aversive stimulus is reinforcing.

tive reinforcement"—probably for the same reason that no one enjoys reading a sentence in which "alike" and "dislike" appear side-by-side. "Negative reinforcement" seems to be an oxymoron. If reinforcement is a process that *increases* the rate of response, then *negative* reinforcement should *decrease* it. Instead we've learned that procedures that decrease the rate of response are called punishment (see Figure 8.1).

You will likely be asked an examination question to find out if you know the difference between the processes of negative reinforcement and punishment. For present purposes students should simply memorize the traditional distinction between them: reinforcement *of any kind*, including negative reinforcement, increases the rate of the preceding response. Punishment of any kind decreases the same the rate of the preceding response.

Negative Reinforcement Procedures

Imagine being trapped barefooted in a dimly illuminated Skinner-box with a steel grid floor, and a lever sticking out of one wall. Unable to escape, and just as you decide to relax and make the best of it, you feel electric shock on the soles of your feet. Aroused, you begin hopping around, and accidentally bump up against the lever. The shock stops. About the time you start to relax, the scenario repeats itself. Again, by hitting the lever, you escape the shock. The third time the shock occurs, you make a beeline for the lever, hit it, and terminate the shock.

(By Jove, I think I've got it! This lever, and my response, and electric shock seem to be associated together. Can I verbalize the contingencies after a few trials? It seems that my lever-pressing response allows me to escape, or remove myself, from the punishing stimulus called electric shock. Whether I can verbalize it or not, I think I'll hang around this lever.)

Escape and Avoidance Procedures. An experiment such as this was accomplished with rats by Murray Sidman (1953). Not only did Sidman's rats learn an **escape procedure,** that is, they learned to make a response that terminated an aversive stimulus, but with additional training another behavior emerged. Sidman reprogrammed his apparatus such that a lever-pressing response would both terminate a shock and also delay the onset of the next shock. Not surprisingly, in this **avoidance procedure** the rats eventually learned to respond *before* the onset of the shock, thereby avoiding the shock altogether. After several sessions, as indicated in Figure 8.4, a rat lever-pressing on this unsignaled *Sidman avoidance* task soon begins to respond at a relatively high rate—even continuing over a period of many hours. *Sidman avoidance* is also known as *free-operant avoidance* because to avoid shock the operant responses must be repeated by the animal during a work session. In this procedure, Sidman's rats learn to make avoidance responses to aversive stimuli by the process of *negative reinforcement*.

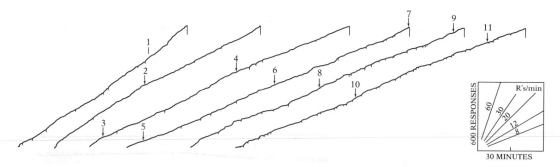

FIGURE 8.4   Rats Lever-Press to Avoid Shock on a Sidman
Avoidance Task

The performance of one rat on a continuous avoidance task is shown in this cumulative record of its responses during an 11-h session. Continuous lever-pressing allowed the rat to avoid most shocks. Numbers indicate hours during the session. Note that this rat was successful in avoiding most shocks (indicated by a tiny oblique mark on the record). (From Verhave, 1966, p. 22.)

Determinants of Avoidance Response Rates

Beside the cage and lever or key that the experimental animal performs on, what other stimuli control responding in a Sidman avoidance task? Certainly the intensity of shock the animal experiences will influence its rate of response. We've already seen in the use of aversive stimuli in punishment procedures that low-intensity shock doesn't work well. As might be expected from classical conditioning experiments, lever-pressing response rates have been found to vary as a direct function of shock intensity (see Theios, Lynch, & Lowe, 1966 for relevant experiments). But a shock level that is *too* high is likely to condition the passivity of *learned helplessness* rather than responses that are instrumental in avoiding pain.

Role of the Passage of Time.   In the unsignalled Sidman avoidance task the animal must respond at least often enough to avoid shock. That they learn this schedule (and learn it well—Box 8.2) attests to the ability of birds, rats, dogs, monkeys, and humans to effectively use the passage of time as a cue. Earlier we saw that Pavlov reliably conditioned salivary responses in dogs using only regularly spaced food USs and no CS (see *temporal conditioning,* p. 118). Monkeys also exhibit an exquisite sense of timing of their lever-pressing responses on a DRL schedule (p. 250). Regularly spaced responses on a Sidman avoidance schedule can be similarly interpreted as reflecting the rat's sensitivity to the passage of time.

BOX 8.2   HIGH PERFORMANCE MOTIVATED BY AVOIDANCE SCHEDULES

(a)

(b)

The Apollo expeditions to the moon in the 1960s to 1970s were supported by animal research. In response to Russia's first animal in space (a dog named *Latvia*), America launched two trained chimpanzees, *Ham* and *Enos,* into space (Rohles, Grunzke, & Reynolds, 1963). Ham was sent on a suborbital trajectory, and in a later flight, Enos circled the earth twice before a successful reentry.

In subsequent space simulations that mimicked some of the performance requirements of astronauts in a spacecraft, chimpanzees were trained on signaled Sidman avoidance and other discrete avoidance schedules (Koestler & Barker, 1965). In these experiments, a work session involved both food-based reinforcement and aversive schedules of reinforcement. Why use aversive schedules? Because both the animals' appetite and appetitively-based performances are hindered under conditions of high stress, including, for example, a rocket launch

(Rohles et al, 1963), stressful drug effects (Dews, 1958), and suffocation following loss of breathable atmosphere (Koestler & Barker, 1965).

During a work session a red light located above one lever was the discriminative stimulus (S^d) for the Sidman avoidance task. When the red light was on, lever-pressing delayed (avoided) electric shock (see panel a). Both the response-to-shock interval (*r-s interval*), and the shock-to-shock interval (*s-s interval*) were set at 5 sec. That is, the chimp had to make one response every five seconds (*r-s interval* = 5 sec) to avoid electric shock. If it did not respond, it received a one-second shock every five seconds (*s-s interval* = 5 sec) throughout the work session.

Discriminative stimuli (S^ds) for the *discrete avoidance* tasks were back-lit stimulus-response keys on the animal's performance panel. Each was illuminated in turn for 1 sec. After 1 sec the light terminated, and electric foot

(continued)

BOX 8.2   HIGH PERFORMANCE MOTIVATED BY AVOIDANCE SCHEDULES (*continued*)

shock was applied to the chimp's foot. The shock could be avoided if the chimp pushed the key (depressing a micro switch) before one second elapsed. A tone served as the S^d for another unlit key, that, when depressed within 1 sec, allowed the shock to be avoided (see panel b). Even with the low levels of electric shock used in these studies, chimpanzees rarely failed to respond to the negative reinforcement contingencies. Most per-

formed flawlessly session after session, day after day, without receiving an electric shock.

As a historical note, this experiment could no longer be accomplished. For ethical reasons, chimpanzees cannot be subjected to restraints (such as being confined to sitting in a chair) nor electrically shocked, or otherwise insulted. An unfortunate exception is their use in AIDS research.

Discrete-Trial Avoidance

When a *specific* discriminative stimulus is added to the experimental environment, even more precise stimulus control of avoidance responding can be achieved. Figure 8.5 shows a commonly used apparatus called a *shuttle-box*. Some shuttle-boxes connect two compartments via a hole through a wall that separates them; the one shown has two compartments separated by a low barrier wall. A *signaled* **discrete trial** avoidance procedure was reported by Solomon & Wynne (1953). They placed a dog in a shuttle-box having two compartments separated by a low barrier wall. When a tone was sounded, escape/avoidance contingencies were put into effect. During each discrete trial, signaled by a tone, the dog was allowed to first *escape* and with further training to *avoid* electric shock. It did this by jumping across the barrier from the electrified compartment of the shuttle-box to the shock-free side. When the researcher electrified this side, the dog could escape by reversing and jumping back across the barrier into the now-safe compartment. Soon the dog learned to avoid electric shock entirely by jumping from one compartment to the other at the onset of the tone, a task known as shuttle avoidance.

Learned Helplessness

The intensity of shock is an important consideration in all laboratory demonstrations of avoidance and escape procedures. Shock levels that "tickle" rather than produce pain do not produce reductions in responses. Shock levels that are excessive have some unpredictable effects. One example is research that produced an effect now popularly known as learned helplessness. *Learned help-*

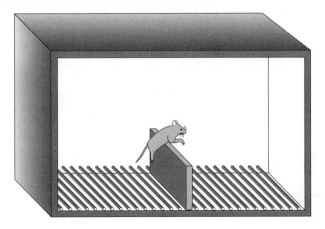

FIGURE 8.5 A Shuttle-box Used in Avoidance Training

Electric shock can be delivered through the grid floor to the animal (rats and dogs have been used) in either compartment. The animal can avoid or escape the shock by jumping to the other non-electrified compartment. With repeated training, the animal can avoid shock entirely by shuttling (moving) from side to side.

lessness is a maladaptive behavior pattern initially described by Maier & Seligman (1976). (See also Seligman & Maier, 1967, and Minor, Dess, & Overmeir, 1991.) In research with dogs, these researchers found that if dogs were exposed to intense electric shocks during pretraining, two of every three dogs failed to respond adaptively thereafter: After pretraining, dogs place in a shuttle avoidance apparatus for conditioning (using normal levels of shock) did not learn the avoidance response. Such dogs, described as helpless, were immobile. Though unrestrained, they whined and defecated but do not try to escape by moving from the shocked to the unshocked compartment.

Why the responses to intense aversive stimuli are so unpredictable is unknown. One theory is that animals learn that the shock occurs independent of their behavior—that is, it is uncontrollable (Maier & Seligman, 1976). We'll review this theory in the next chapter in the context of treating people who display symptoms similar to animals in learned helplessness experiments.

Discriminative Stimuli to Control Avoidance Responding

The use of discriminative stimuli (S^ds) to control responding allows different types of avoidance schedules to be combined. Box 8.2 describes two types of concurrent avoidance behavior in chimpanzees trained to respond to each of three different S^ds. Does it matter if an avoidance task is signalled or unsignalled? Sidman avoidance is "unsignalled" in that only the lever and other cues of the Skinner box set the occasion for the lever-pressing response. Since levers and electric shocks do not exist in the rat's world outside of the Skinner box, in reality the box and the lever are highly distinctive signals. The rat has no way of knowing that a distinctive cue such as a tone or a light may be important to the experimenter! The point is that we should not make too much of any alleged differences between unsignalled and the signaled avoidance tasks.

Shock as an S^d.   Painful electric shock can also be a discriminative stimulus that controls avoidance responses. In one experiment, rats were taught to run quickly down an electrified runway to a non-electrified goal box. In this *escape* procedure, the rats are reinforced by the termination of electric shock upon entry into the goal box. After learning this response, they were divided into two groups. For half the rats, the shock was turned off, and they no longer were required to make escape responses. For the other half, a section of the runway nearest the goal box remained electrified. You be the rat. What would you do under these circumstances? First consider how you would respond in extinction in the group with the non-electrified runway. For the first few trials, you might run quickly even though you are not being shocked. (Recall that the experimenter interprets your running speed to be a measure of resistance to extinction of the learned escape response. The more slowly you run, the more your learned escape response has extinguished.) Eventually you might learn, as the rats did in this group, that you could take your time getting to the goal box, there to be removed and returned to your home cage.

What about the group encountering the electrified runway near the goal box? One might argue that the electric shock punishes entry into the last part of the alley next to the goal box. Since punished responses normally decrease in frequency, you might predict that rats would stay in the first part of the alley where they are not punished. The interesting finding in this situation is that punishment *increased* the speed of running relative to the non-shocked rats (Brown & Cunningham, 1981). This is a strange finding. By not entering the last part of the alley, an animal could escape shock altogether. It could have stopped, for which there is no penalty. (It would eventually be removed and returned to their home cage even though it hadn't made it to the goal box.) However, these rats run in pain through the electrified portion into the goal box. Apparently, the shock acted as a signal that the escape contingency was still in effect.

Interim Summary

1. **Negative reinforcement** is a process in which a response that is instrumental in either escaping or avoiding an aversive event is strengthened.

2. In an ***escape procedure,*** a response is instrumental in removing or terminating an aversive stimulus. Opening an umbrella in a torrential downpour is an example.

3. In an ***avoidance procedure,*** a response is instrumental in preventing, or avoiding, an aversive stimulus. Opening an umbrella *before* walking out into a rain storm is an example.

4. Common laboratory investigations of negative reinforcement include *continuous,* or *free operant avoidance* (*Sidman avoidance*).

5. On a Sidman avoidance task an animal must respond on a lever repeatedly to delay (avoid) an electric foot shock. If this free operant avoidance task is "unsignalled," both the lever (and other stimuli within the Skinner box) and time cues act as discriminative stimuli that control the response rate.

6. A ***discrete trial*** avoidance task requires an animal to make one response when signalled to do so. An example is the *shuttle avoidance* task in which a dog is placed in a *shuttle box* and is required to escape or avoid electric shock by jumping from one chamber to the next.

7. Electric shock, and the pain of electric shock, can become a discriminative stimulus that controls responding.

8. Skilled human behavior is maintained by negative reinforcement. Examples include piano playing, operating word processors and automobiles, and following directions in filling out forms.

DISCUSSION QUESTIONS

4. Many skiers look for increasingly difficult downhill runs, perhaps to experience the pleasure of conquering fear as well as to experience the exhilaration of speed and control. Many skiers also think that falling down is a signal that they are sufficiently challenging themselves, and that only through such challenges will they become better skiers. Why is "no pain, no gain" too simple to account for a skier's motivation?

5. What motivates you to study for your exams? Why do so many people watch so much TV? Can you identify positive and/or negative reinforcement contingencies for each behavior?

6. Think about collisions in intersections as events to be avoided. Can you verbalize parallels between pushing a key on a performance panel (such as the example in Box 8.2), or jumping a barrier in a shuttle-box, and hitting the brakes as your automobile approaches an intersection? What are the discriminative stimuli (S^ds) controlling each of these responses? What motivates each response?

7. Assume that you could train someone to "hit the brakes," and that you could explain how such signaled, discrete trial avoidance behavior illustrates the concept of *negative reinforcement.*

THEORIES OF THE AVERSIVE CONTROL OF BEHAVIOR

"Beat me,! Beat me!" said the masochist.
"No!" said the sadist.

Questions about *acquired motivation* were raised in an earlier chapter. We now have several conceptual tools that may allow us to shed light on the intriguing bit of human behavior captured by the verbal interchange of these two maladjusted individuals. What reinforcement contingencies maintain the quite different roles that pain plays in the lives of the sadist and masochist? What are the theories of punishment and reinforcement that proposed to account for the aversive control of behavior?

Theories of Punishment

Thorndike's "theory" of punishment is an adaptive/evolutionary one: It is adaptive for an animal to avoid annoyers, and for responses that produce annoyers to decrease in frequency. Skinner's description of the effects of punishing stimuli on responding provides a contemporary *behavioral definition* rather than a theory of punishment.

Two-Factor Theory of Punishment. Another, more formal theory of punishment developed by Mowrer (1947, 1960) and elaborated by Dinsmoor (1954, 1977) is the **two-factor theory of punishment.** The first factor consists of classical conditioning. Cues in the environment, including the stimuli produced by the animals while responding, are classically conditioned to the aversive punishing stimulus. As a result of this conditioning, in Mower's terms, rats and humans *fear* or are wary of situations in which punishment has previously been meted out. The second factor is an instrumental conditioning component. Rats and humans can escape from their fear by engaging in some other behavior than the responses that have been punished (Dinsmoor, 1954). When faced with stimuli predicting punishment, rats suppress lever-pressing (measured) presumably by engaging in other behaviors (unmeasured). That is, punishment, like reinforcement, can be conditionally signalled (Holz & Azrin, 1961). A dog that has been punished crouches when a menacing hand approaches it. Similarly, a human can change study habits that produced punishing consequences and driving patterns that produce tickets. In summary, the two-factor theory of punishment entails both a classical and an instrumental component.

Where is the Reinforcement in "Negative" Reinforcement?

Theories of reinforcement were discussed in the previous chapter. But what theory accounts for the phenomenon of negative reinforcement? Referring once again to Figure 8.2, the lower-left cell shows that the process of negative reinforcement is accomplished in the *absence* of a reinforcing stimulus. The question learning theorists have raised for half a century is how the *absence* of a stimulus can reinforce behavior (Mowrer & Lamoreaux, 1942; Mowrer, 1960). Interestingly, negative reinforcement does not seem to be counter-intuitive. For example, we are initially motivated to keep our balance in riding a bicycle because it hurts to fall down. After sufficient avoidance training, people can ride bicycles for years on end without ever falling. Likewise, when asked the question: "Why are you skiing so cautiously?" a predictable answer is "Because I don't want to fall." We can't ask rats, monkeys, and dogs why they keep responding even though they are no longer being shocked. But we can put ourselves in their place, and their behavior seems reasonable enough.

What Persists Following Aversive Training?   One analysis of the persistence of avoidance behavior is that some aspect of the reinforcer is never totally absent: The negative reinforcer is present in the form of a memory. For example, we *remember* the pain of falling off bikes and skis. When a skier says, "I ski slowly because I don't want to fall" is it possible that we are not hearing a dispassionate statement of fact, but rather a disguised fear (or wariness) of falling. Perhaps the lessons learned during avoidance training remain with us in terms of memories of a painful experience, translated into fear that it might again recur.

Two-Factor Theory of Avoidance

Such an analysis, known as **two-factor theory,** was first proposed by Mowrer (1947, 1960). According to this theory, the two-factors underlying avoidance behavior are classically-conditioned emotional behavior and instrumentally conditioned motor (skeletal) responses. (Sound familiar?) Two-factor theory posits that fear is conditioned first by the pairing of pain with stimuli in the avoidance training environment. The stimuli may be easily specified, such as the presence of a lever in a Skinner box, or a tone or light signaling that shock-induced pain is imminent. Or the conditioned stimulus can be more subtle, such as the sensations of losing balance afforded by our vestibular apparatus. Vestibular sensations as well as the visual stimuli of skis and bikes have been associated with the pain of falling down.

   According to two-factor theory, after the fear response is conditioned, the second step involves conditioning instrumental responses—such as lever-pressing or jumping a barrier to avoid shock, or maintaining one's balance by turning a handlebar. Mowrer assumed that conditioned fear was present at all times during avoidance training. The (negative) reinforcement for such instrumental responses, he asserted, was the termination of the fear response. He reasoned that alleviation of fear is a positive experience, and that it is this positive experience that acts as the reinforcer for the preceding instrumental response.

Evaluation of the Two-Factor Theory of Avoidance

Are people who ride bikes, who ski, and who study their books to avoid failing classes really motivated by fear? Or is it more a feeling of *uneasiness* that is elicited when confronted with cues that have been associated with the training of the avoidance response? For example, on a Sidman avoidance schedule as well as in shuttle boxes, animal response are distributed in time. Is the *fear* of electric shock ever-present during a 1-h session, day in and day out? Or is it more likely that rats, dogs, and humans are merely wary and uneasy when faced with cues that predict aversive consequences unless they do something? Is *fear* reduced with each response, or is it more likely that responding becomes automatic, and animals are less conscious of the response-shock contingency?

The Kamin, Brimer, and Black (1963) Experiment. An experiment by Kamin, Brimer, and Black (1963) provides some insight into these complicated issues. In phase one rats were trained to lever press for food. In phase two they were placed into a shuttle box where a tone S^d set the occasion for shuttle-avoidance behavior. Four groups were trained to avoid electric shock on 1, 3, 9, or 27 consecutive trials. All rats were then returned to the Skinner box where they continued lever pressing for food. The tone was sounded while they lever pressed, and the effect this tone had on their response rate was measured. Kamin et al. (1963) found that following shuttle-aversion training, the tone produced different levels of suppressed responding in each group. The groups that reached the shuttle-avoidance criterion of being successful on three and nine consecutive shock avoidance trials apparently were more fearful of the tone to which they had been conditioned (i.e., the tone suppressed more responding than in the one-trial group). However, those rats with extensive experience on the shuttle-avoidance task, who in the presence of the tone reached the criterion of 27 consecutive avoidance responses, showed a very different pattern. The somewhat surprising finding was that the tone did *not* suppress lever-pressing responses in this group.

Vigilance Replaces Fear. One interpretation of this experiment is that fear first increases then diminishes with increasing experience (and increasing success) in successfully making avoidance responses. A history of making car payments on time avoids the aversiveness of its repossession, and of having a bad credit record. We humans have no way of knowing if the rats in the foregoing studies were fearful or merely "uneasy"—as we would be. Because their avoidance behavior was maintained at a high level of proficiency, we know they were motivated to respond even though they were independently assessed as being less fearful (see Mineka, 1979 for a fuller discussion of the independence of fear measures and avoidance responding). Humans monitoring radar screens in submarines and in air control terminals report high levels of *vigilance,* and autonomic nervous system measures tell us they are physiologically aroused. But until and unless there is an emergency (a particularly configured pattern on the radar screen), fear is *not* ever present during these stressful avoidance tasks. However, don't miss a blip, or a car payment.

As a final consideration, review in Box 8.2 the continuous and discrete avoidance tasks required of chimpanzees. While maintaining a relatively high rate of lever-pressing in the presence of a red light (the S^d), 1-sec duration discrete avoidance visual and auditory stimuli were presented as well. These stimuli elicited successful avoidance responses within a fraction of a second of their onset. Again, both from how the animals appeared and from performance measures, a state of vigilance rather than fear better describes them. Think of a human playing a computer game.

Cognitive Analysis of Avoidance Behavior

Of the following two possibilities, which is more likely? Is the behavior of "playing computer games" maintained more by positive or by negative reinforcement contingencies? That is, is the attraction of playing games reinforcing because skilled responses produce positive consequences, or because skilled responses prevent disaster? Another example: In playing a melody on the piano, depressing middle C on the keyboard is reinforced by the sound of middle C at the right time and in the right sequence in relation to other sounds. Pressing the middle-C key when middle C is called for is positively reinforcing. Is it not also the case that the very same response is reinforcing because making the response *avoids* violating the expectation that the note should be there? That is, appropriate responses to middle C avoid disharmony and prevent violation of the expected tempo. Usually things can be described equally well from these two opposite perspectives.

Do animals show an awareness of the occurrence and non-occurrence of events, and can they become vigilant? Apparently so. Characterizing an animal's avoidance behavior in these terms provides a cognitive perspective to questions inherent in avoidance behavior (see Seligman & Johnston, 1973). For example, consider again Sidman's unsignalled avoidance task. Responding by rats to avoid shock has been demonstrated even when time cues predicting the shock-shock and response-shock interval were masked (Herrnstein & Hineline, 1966; Herrnstein, 1969). Instead of fear reduction, these researchers argued, rats merely learn that a contingency exists between their responses and shock reduction.

The One-Factor Theory of Avoidance. Sometimes called a *one-factor theory of avoidance,* this theory stresses that rats are sensitive to rates of shock, and their lever-pressing patterns change in response to the shock schedule. While the simplicity of this one-factor theory is appealing, a criticism is that it does not adequately address *why* the rat responds to avoid shock in the first place.

Merely detecting a response-shock reduction contingency is not adequate motivation for a rat to bother to respond. Pain, fear, and vigilance are likely the underlying motivation for animals trained with electric shock.

Persistence of Avoidance Responses

The above analysis helps us understand why avoidance responding is so slow to extinguish. Each avoidance response is at one and the same time *being reinforced* and *not being punished*. First, a response is reinforced because it produces the desired outcome (avoiding shock; avoiding falling on the ski slopes; avoiding an F on a test; avoiding hitting keyboard D when you wanted C; avoiding GAME OVER on the video screen, and so forth.) In addition, the response prevents an undesirable, punishing outcome (electric shock, falling, failing, fumbling, choking, etc.). Finally, a response is reinforced because *not responding* is punished. In learning avoidance responses, humans and animals are punished for not responding appropriately. Hitting keyboard D instead of C is punishing to an ear expecting C. As is falling, failing, fumbling, choking, etc.

Avoidance responses extinguish slowly, therefore, because the consequences of responding is reinforcement, and the consequence of not responding is punishment.

Sadism and Masochism Revisited

An Analysis of Sadistic Behavior. Both sharp tongues, and the playground bully's fists produce small victories in the sadist's complex social interactions. Children reared in competitive environments are reinforced for being aggressively stronger, faster, and smarter, and along other dimensions by which individual differences vary. Sadists are reinforced for their behavior in part by not being punished for it. "Winners" deliver the punishment to "losers." Behavior learned in competition, however, does not always translate well in social interactions calling for cooperation. Furthermore, in social interactions, the sadist becomes a *discriminative stimulus* predicting punishment. Most humans will both be wary of and will suppress ongoing behavior in the sadist's presence.

An Analysis of Masochistic Behavior. Can pain become reinforcing? Do masochists learn to use pain to give themselves pleasure? (Our theories of reinforcement and punishment require that masochistic behavior be reinforcing because if it were punishing, masochistic responses would be suppressed.) Several psychologists have attempted to model this behavior using laboratory animals and have been surprisingly successful. Assuming that a low-intensity punisher can be used to signal as well as to punish, Holz & Azrin (1961) first trained pigeons to peck a key on a VI schedule for food. With the VI schedule still in effect, each pecking response was then punished with mild electric shock, similar to the procedure seen in Figure 8.2. In this experiment, the result was to halve the rate of key-pecking. Alternating with these food reinforced sessions in which each peck was also punished were sessions that were not food reinforced. From the hungry pigeon's perspective, only electric shock predicted food availability. Therefore, the pigeon had to engage in "masochistic" behavior (self-induced pain) in order to find out if food was available. Pain in this situation acted as an S^d that signaled the presence of food. The pigeons eventually learned to continue pecking for food *only if their key-pecks were punished,* and they stopped pecking if their key-pecking responses were *not* punished!

Abusive Relationships. Perhaps like these pigeons, a person who displays masochistic tendencies seek out punishment that, when terminated, is reinforcing. In other words, pain may become an S^d that is reinforced by its termination. For example, after being beaten by an abusive husband, a women might leave him, only to cyclically return to him again and again. Such behavior appears to be maladaptive, and such women are often criticized for intentionally putting themselves in harm's way. What is maintaining their behavior? A number of reinforcement and punishment contingencies can be identified. In addition to financial pressures of "going it alone," and learned social pressures "to keep the family together," such women often have a learning history that includes feelings of affection for the husband. In addition, beatings can have signal value other than the pain induced. In abusive relationships, beatings are often followed by pleasurable sexual relationships with the same man who a few minutes earlier was inflicting pain. In these situations, then, pain signals are reinforced in two ways; first, by their cessation, and secondly, by pleasurable sensations of sex. It is no wonder that the cycle continues.

Interim Summary

1. Mowrer's ***two-factor theory of punishment*** proposes that punishment is effected by two processes; classically conditioned emotions controlled by environmental cues, and relief from aversive emotional states by making instrumentally learned responses that minimize or remove these cues.

2. Mowrer's ***two-factor theory*** of avoidance behavior proposes that instrumentally conditioned operant responses are learned *after* emotional response to painful stimuli have been classically conditioned.

3. Vigilance rather than fear seems to better characterize long-term avoidance behavior of humans and other animals.

4. Avoidance responses are highly resistant-to-extinction because these responses have been reinforced in two different ways—responding is reinforced, and not responding is punished.

5. Masochistic behavior can be understood by recognizing that the cessation of pain is reinforcing; that the presence of pain becomes positive in that it signals that relief from pain is imminent; and that putting oneself into painful situations often reflects a past reinforcement history of pleasure derived from pain cessation.

DISCUSSION QUESTIONS

8. High-school coaches and aerobic instructors alike talk about "no pain, no gain." The long-distance runner is exhorted to "push through the pain barrier." In what way that athletes "use pain" to perform better similar to the way a person in an abusive relationship "uses pain" to achieve pleasure? Differences?

9. Small children learning to play soccer often turn their heads and bodies when an opposing player kicks the ball in their direction. What motivates this behavior?

10. Both skiing and riding a bicycle require a person to make small behavioral adjustments collectively known as "maintaining your balance." After learning both skilled acts, (a) why do people seldom fall, and (b) under what conditions do they fall? HINT: You might want to consider both skiing and riding a bicycle as *free operants*.

CHAPTER SUMMARY

1. Punishment is an associative process that produces reduced responding, because the target response produces an undesirable outcome (such as pain) or because the response is not followed by an expected reinforcer. Punishment is affected by latent inhibition, extinction, generalization, and so forth.

2. Primary punishers are innately aversive, and secondary punishers acquires their properties through association. More intense punishers that closely follow the response to be punished are most effective. Up to a point, more punished trials produce better response suppression, but with continued trials, a punisher may lose its effectiveness.

3. Using a low-intensity punisher tends to habituate the punishment process, making more intense punishers less effective. The process of punishment tends to produce a general response suppression.

4. Mowrer's two-factor theory of punishment proposes that the pain of a punisher is conditioned such that environmental cues associated with it produce fear. The second factor is that fear can be alleviated by making instrumentally learned responses.

5. Negative reinforcement is totally different from punishment. Like all reinforcement processes, it increases the rate of response. A response that either escapes or avoids an aversive event is strengthened through the process of negative reinforcement.

6. Laboratory studies of negative reinforcement include pecking or lever-pressing (free operant responses) to ei-

ther escape or avoid electric shock. An example is a Sidman avoidance task in which an animal makes repeated responses to delay and avoid electric shock.

7. Avoidance responding can be brought under stimulus control by introducing a discriminative stimulus, such as a light or tone, that signals when responses can avoid shock. An example is a discrete trial avoidance (press a panel to avoid a shock, or shuttle over a barrier to avoid shock. Shock itself can become a discriminative stimulus that controls responding.

8. Skilled human behavior—music, fine arts, athletic performance, operating computers are examples—is controlled by negative reinforcement.

9. A two-factor theory of avoidance behavior proposes that fear is learned in response to the pain of an aversive stimulus, and that operant responses that prevent the pain and alleviate the fear are thereby reinforced. Over time, humans and other animals become vigilant in making response that avoid pain.

10. Avoidance responses are highly resistant-to-extinction because responding is reinforced, and not responding is punished.

KEY TERMS

CHAPTER 9

Choice Behavior

Science has probably never demanded a more sweeping change in a traditional way of thinking about . . . (what it means to be an individual). In the traditional picture a person perceives the world around him, selects features to be perceived, discriminates among them, judges them good or bad, changes them to make them better (or, if he is careless, worse), and may be held responsible for his action and justly rewarded or punished for its consequences. In the scientific picture, a person is a member of a species shaped by evolutionary contingencies of survival, displaying behavioral processes which bring him under the control of the environment in which he lives, and largely under the control of a social environment which he and millions of others like him have constructed and maintained during the evolution of a culture. The direction of the controlling relation is reversed: a person does not act upon the world, the world acts upon him.

B. F. Skinner, *Beyond Freedom and Dignity* (1971, p. 211)

ARE WE FREE TO CHOOSE?

Decisions, decisions. Two tests tomorrow: Do I study psychology or Spanish? Gaining weight: Should I eat dessert or not? Call Margaret or mom first? Watch the soaps or listen to my newest CD? Study now, or sleep and get up early tomorrow morning? Sleep in, or make my nine o' clock class? Blue jeans or slacks? Is this person I've been seeing significant or not?

Daily, hourly, and by the minute, people engage in decision making. Making choices of one kind or another is characteristic of all animal life. As an animal you make the basic decision to move, to engage in voluntary behavior, or not. The simplest voluntary responses of animals involve choice.

What is known about this process? Are many processes involved? How do we make choices? How do we choose from among alternatives? Are there rules or laws governing our behavior? For example, are we born knowing how to make the best decisions, or do we simply make decisions based on the moment?

Free Will and Determinism. As we saw in an earlier chapter, one way to approach the question of choice is to raise the issue of free choice. Are we truly autonomous individuals—free agents, so to speak—who are the masters of our destiny? Or are our decisions the product of past reinforcement history —in which case our "choices" are based on maximizing reinforcers and minimizing punishers. In the opening quotation, Skinner says that we are controlled by a wisdom of our species as well as by our personal reinforcement histories. If, over millions of years, animals who consistently made bad choices became extinct, then those of us who remain are offspring of animals who consistently made good choices.

Can we even agree on how to use the term *choice?* Let us put a recently fed and watered hamster in its cage and attach a water bottle to it. Can we say that the hamster is free to choose to drink from the bottle—or not? Let us now repeat the experiment but not let the hamster drink water for 48 hours before allowing it water access. Is the hamster free to choose to drink from the bottle? Less free?

Consider another incident. You choose to go to Momma Rollo's and select pepperoni pizza from the menu. Later you get sick. You attribute your sickness to Momma Rollo's pepperoni pizza. Are you as free to choose this restaurant and this food item after getting sick? Can you see that the first example is what Skinner alludes to when he talks about how our evolutionary history constrains choice and that the second example shows how the environment acting on us constrains what we choose?

Choice Behavior and Economics

How people make choices is of as much interest to the marketing divisions of businesses around the world as it is to philosophers and psychologists. When more people choose to buy widgets than whatnots or imported rather than domestic automobiles, investors will line up behind the preferred choice. The tasks of the marketing divisions of companies making whatnots and domestic cars is to influence the decisions of purchasers to buy their products. Notice in this example that neither the purchaser nor the marketer much cares whether humans are *free to choose* from among alternatives. Philosophical positions of determinism versus free will do not allow us to predict *how* individuals make choices. Here we are interested in choice behavior, not the philosophy of choice. The question of widgets or whatnots focuses our observations: (a) selecting one object rather than another is a common human behavior and (b) choices are influenced (even if not entirely determined) by environment.

Evaluating Decision Making

Assume that widgets are better made than whatnots. Will everyone choose widgets? Highly unlikely. This question goes to the heart of individual differences in choice behavior; there are no simple answers to why people make the choices they do.

Choices are multivariably determined, and all humans make questionable decisions at one time or another. A questionable decision is one with which someone else disagrees. Indeed, some of us are more notorious than others for the consistency of our bad judgment. For example, what are some circumstances in which whatnots rather than widgets might be purchased? Whatnots are available nearby, and widgets are across town; whatnots are one dollar cheaper; whatnots are a more pleasing color of purple. You prefer widgets, however, but they are sold out, and a whatnot will do. No one in your family would be caught dead buying a widget; your ex-boyfriend flaunts his widget, and you can't wait to buy a whatnot out of spite.

Value.   One word can be used to summarize the reasons people choose between widgets or whatnots, namely the object's value. **Value** is the relative worth, merit, or importance of an object or activity. The value of whatnots in this example was determined by its *perceived utility*—your perception of its worth. Among the variables that influence its perceived utility are the way it looks and sounds (*esthetics*), how useful it is (*utility*), what its price is (*cost*), how near it is (*availability*). To give you a flavor of the complexity of this situation, let us note just a few of the choice determinants in this example: A five-dollar difference in purchase price is *everything* to a person with only a few dollars to his or her name, is *nothing* to a millionaire, and is *something* to the rest of us, depending on how near it is to payday. Likewise, taking a half-hour drive across town to buy a widget rather than a whatnot is nothing to a person with plenty of free time and an automobile at his or her disposal, but is everything to someone with no time to spare. (Let's not even consider the cost of the gasoline it takes to make that drive relative to what a person "saves.") The color purple? Wonderful, or unimportant, unless you have a conditioned emotional response to that particular shade because your ex was partial to it.[1]

Limitations of Theory.   Now the astute reader should have antennae out. If we can't predict something as unimportant as whether a person will buy a widget or a whatnot, then we're not going to be able to do a very good job of either predicting the outcome of, or helping advise someone on, the choice of a career, a marriage partner, or the advantages of leasing versus buying a car. This being the case, perhaps we should fold our tent and cut to Chapter 10, because in reality the analysis of choice behavior is even more complex than choosing between two items that are matched on most dimensions, such as whatnots and widgets. As is the case with all such human enigmas, we have more than one model, more than one law, and many observations about choice behavior for which we have neither models nor laws.

Retrospective and Chapter Preview

No matter how deficient our state of knowledge is, the issue of choice behavior is too important to ignore. From health decisions at the personal level, to political decisions at the social level, and to environmental decisions at the world level, good and bad choices are made daily. Indeed, a prominent learning theorist (Tolman, 1938) proposed that all behavior can be analyzed as choice behavior, and that a science of behavior would be greatly advanced if we could understand and predict the behavior of a rat at a choice point in a maze!

---

[1]That perceived utility is learned is illustrated by a recent experience I had helping a friend with a garage sale. We were setting the price of items for sale. I noticed that some items that he valued for sentimental reasons were overpriced relative to those to which he had less emotional attachment. For example, his memories of a certain dish his mother had used caused him to place an inflated dollar value on it.

In this chapter, we begin our inquiry into the origins of choice behavior with an overview of utility theory. Can we mathematically model the factors leading to choice decisions? From utility theory we turn to an in-depth examination of a model of choice based on adaptive-evolutionary considerations. Is there a genetic basis for making decisions? We then turn to a variety of animal models of choice behavior and examine several interesting laws that have come from laboratory experimentation. Can we design meaningful animal models to help us predict the choices that humans make? In the last section, we attempt to apply what we have learned to educational settings, to behavioral therapy, and to how people might make better decisions in their personal lives.

Utility Theory

Assume that an eccentric uncle has died. His will is being read, and you are to be a beneficiary. Among the conditions of his will are that you have to make a choice between these two alternatives: (a) You can choose to receive $3,000 outright, or (b) you can gamble to win $4,000 by spinning a wheel-of-inherited-fortune. You can land on one of 10 slots on the wheel. Eight of 10 slots will earn you $4,000, but two of the slots read $0. You are assured that the game is not fixed and that the two probabilities are correct: $3,000 with the probability of 1.0; $4,000 with a probability of 0.8. What do you choose to do?

When a study outlining this proposition was conducted in the late 1970s, more than 80% of the people responded that they would take the $3,000; only 20% were willing to gamble at even these high (80% chance of winning) odds (Kahneman & Tversky, 1979). I would be very surprised if the findings would be any different today; the old axiom to the effect that a bird in the hand is worth two in the bush is a timeless, accurate prediction concerning human behavior. But why do people make this choice?

Expected Utility

A model that came to be known as *expected utility* was proposed in the 18th century by Bernoulli, a mathematician, who described, among other mathematical functions, the probabilities associated with gambling. **Expected utility** is the expected gain from a decision made about a wager or transaction involving money or other tangible valuable. In this century, Bernoulli's work was incorporated into both economic gaming theory (von Neuman & Morganstern, 1944) and decision theory (French, 1986). Bernoulli's analysis of humans making decisions that didn't match the odds of winning bets was that people preferred to focus on the risk of losing and of the perceived value of the money involved rather than on winning and the absolute value of the money involved.

In some ways, the concept of expected utility is similar to the findings of traditional psychophysics formulated by the 19th-century German mathematician (and early psychologist) Gustav Fechner. The study of psychophysics described the mathematical relationship of the responses of the senses to the physical stimulus energy landing on them. *Brightness* and *loudness*, for example, are psychological terms referring to (and mapping) the intensity of visual and auditory stimuli, respectively. Likewise, the expected utility or expected gain from a decision made about money is a psychological function related to the real-world value of money.

Assume that such decisions must be made repeatedly about a given wager (*X*). Equation (9.1) describes this relationship mathematically. Note that the perceived or expected utility (*EU*) of an amount of money (*X*) is a function of expected gain (*G*), the mean value of *X* (μ_x), and the standard deviation of *x* (s^2_x).

$$EU\ (X) = G\ (\mu_x, s^2_x) \tag{9.1}$$

The important thing to remember about this equation is that human and animal judgments about gains (*G*) in money, food, or anything of value depend in part on how much money we're talking about (that is, μ_x) and how variable it is (s^2_x). In a wager, only under certain conditions is the risk of losing worth taking.

Interim Summary

1. Humans and other animals make choices throughout their lifetimes regardless of whether their behavior is determined or whether they have "free will."
2. A theory of choice behavior must take into account both adaptive-evolutionary considerations and personal reinforcement history.
3. People decide between two or more alternatives based on their perceived *value.* Factors that influence perceived value include esthetics, cost, utility, and availability.
4. *Expected utility* is the expected gain from a wager (gambling).
5. People who gamble focus on the risk of losing and of the perceived value of the money involved rather than on winning and the absolute value of the money involved.

DISCUSSION QUESTIONS

1. America, the land of the free, espouses in its Bill of Rights the freedom of religious expression. Yet more than 90% of Americans choose the same religion as their parents. Is this an example of the distinction between having a philosophy of choice and of choice behavior? Are you, the reader, free to choose your religion?

2. Carley Brock, from Silverton, Oregon, is the 61-year-old father of three children. He was recently ticketed by

local police and eventually fined $100 for "improperly supervising" his 16-year-old son Michael. Michael was caught smoking at school—his latest run-in with school officials and juvenile authorities. The elder Brock was one of 13 parents cited following the enactment of a new "parental responsibility" law. A number of states have enacted similar laws.[2] What do you suspect that Skinner would have thought about such laws?

ADAPTIVE-EVOLUTIONARY CONSIDERATIONS IN CHOICE BEHAVIOR

Equation (9.1) has been used to analyze decisions that people and animals make relating to their perception of the real world. As stated earlier, because most humans are risk averse, their *expected utility* does not match the actual values of their transactions. That is, because humans are risk averse, they do not maximize the gains available to them. What their expected utility *does* reflect are the multitudinous psychological variables that govern their decisions: Buying a whatnot because an ex-boyfriend has a widget is one example. For this reason, a number of researchers have decided to investigate choice behavior in nonhuman animals. Presumably, the learned psychological complexity that motivates animals is less than that found in humans. In the next section, we begin with a simple model of the choice behavior of honeybees. The question raised by Real's (1991) investigation seems simple enough: What is the biological and evolutionary basis of expected utility?

Economics of Choice in Animals

Yes, honeybees. Your presumed question as to the ecological validity of studying the behavior of honeybees as a model for human choice behavior is a legitimate one. Having raised questions regarding the extrapolation of research results from animals to humans throughout the text, I would be remiss to not comment here about the use of honeybees as a model of choice behavior. First, Real's (1991) investigation of choice behavior in honeybees succeeds at several levels; he does not conceptualize his research regarding how bees make decisions to be an exact model of how humans make choices. Second, the abilities of bees are quite remarkable (see Box 9.1), and their decision making is orderly with respect to the expected utility model described earlier. Finally, as we'll see, some remarkable consistencies of choice behavior exist whether bees, rats, pigeons, or humans are studied. Let us take an in-depth look, then, at the decisions of which bees are capable. (The superskeptical among you might want to take an extended look at Box 9.1 before proceeding. Call it consciousness raising or whatever. I think you will find that these insect brains are not what you thought they were.)

[2]Cox News Service release, January 8, 1996.

BOX 9.1   ARE BEE BRAINS SMART ENOUGH TO MAKE DECISIONS?

Sejnowski and Churchland (1992a, 1992b) are intrigued by the parallels of both organization and performance of computers and living brains. They start by comparing what a small honeybee can do that powerful computers can't. A honeybee brain has only 1 million neurons compared to a human's 100 billion. The honeybee brain operates at about 10 TFLOPS (10,000 GFLOPS), while powerful computers approach speeds of only 10 GFLOPS (i.e., 1 billion operations per second).

Honeybees share a number of sensory and motor abilities with vertebrates: They can see, sense vibration, smell, fly, walk, and maintain their balance. They are able to navigate long distances, recognize high-energy nectar sites, and remember those flowers they have already visited. Returning to the hive, they can communicate the location of nectar sources to other bees.

In the hive, they recognize and attack intruders. Their housekeeping abilities include removing garbage and dead bees from the hive. When the hive becomes crowded, responding to cues not yet understood, some bees will swarm and establish a new hive.

Whereas supercomputers need the constant care of humans, honeybees manage their activities independently of humans.

Foraging in Honeybees

What kinds of decisions do foraging honeybees make? Simply put, bees must determine which nearby flowers contain the most nectar. Energy is expended in foraging, and the return (gain in nectar) must always be balanced against this energy loss. Real (1991) studied how bees adjust their behavior (make their next decision about which flowers to visit) as a function of the reinforcement value of previously visited flowers. His method is to allow wild bumblebees to search a large, netted enclosure in which they can sample artificial cardboard flowers of different colors. Let us look at the details.

Colored Flowers Predict Reinforcement.   In the middle of each cardboard flower is a well containing a specified amount and concentration of diluted honey ("nectar"). That bees rapidly associate the color of the flower with the nectar has long been known. That is, bees learn to return to the color of flowers that have the most nectar. In one experiment Real allowed single bees to visit a patch containing 100 blue and 100 yellow flowers randomly spaced. All of the blue flowers contained 2 μl (microliter) and one-third of the yellow flowers contained 6 μl nectar. A foraging bee, by Real's analysis, could therefore sample each color equally often and receive an average 2 μl nectar per trip (6 μl divided across visits to three yellow flowers equals an average of 2 μl per visit). Remember, however, the bird-in-hand concept. Even though bees choosing blue flowers will never experience the 6 µl nectar jackpot of some yellow flowers, the blue flowers always have some nectar. What is your prediction of what bees would do in Real's (1991) experiment?

Bees Avoid Risk, Favor Consistency.   Figure 9.1 shows the results of this experiment (using the average performance of five bees) after allowing these bees a 40-visit foraging bout. We presume that the bees learned what the reinforcement contingencies were during these first 40 visits. Over the first 16 trials (see Figure 9.1), bees chose to visit the 2 µl-rewarded blue flowers approximately 84% of the time. On trials 17 to 31, the colors of the flowers were reversed: Yellow flowers always contained 2 µl, one-third of the blue flowers had 6µl, and two-thirds contained nothing. Again, the solid line after trial 17 shows a major reversal of preference mirroring the switch in reinforcement contingencies; now only about 23% of the visits were made to blue flowers.

Computing Risky Choices

How good are bees at adjusting their behavior as a function of even more subtle changes in reinforcement contingencies? That is, what if the problem were not quite so simple as having bees decide between consistent reinforcement and low probability reinforcement? In another experiment, Real (1991) continued to reinforce blue with 2 µl nectar, one-third of the yellow flowers with 5 µl nectar, and the remaining two-thirds of the yellow flowers with 0.5 µl. In this case, choosing half yellow and half blue flowers over the long run will continue to provide equivalent amounts of nectar (i.e., the reinforcement contingencies of blue and yellow flowers are equal). *All* choices will be reinforced. Again, for bees, the *expected utility* of these two conditions are *not* equivalent: Apparently, bees (and probably humans in a similar situation) prefer the less risky proposition of consistent reward. The dashed lines in Figure 9.1 indicate that the consistently reinforced blue flowers on trials 1 to 16 were visited 62% of the time, on average, and following a color switch, the now consistently reinforced yellow flowers were visited approximately 63% of the time. Real (1991) speculates that because the variance in expected reward was narrower in the second experiment (5% vs. 0.5% compared to 6% vs. 0.0% in the first experiment), the bees' preference for consistently rewarded colors was commensurably less in the second experiment (62% vs. 84% in the first experiment).

Raising the Stakes.   Let us return to our initial gamble to better compare what bees do relative to humans. Few of us would turn down $3,000 cash for an 80% chance at $4,000. Let us up the ante. Would you take $3,000 cash or an 80% chance at $10,000? Or $100,000? Or $1,000,000? An 80% probability means that four out of five times you are going to win the bet: Try getting those odds out of Las Vegas for any athletic contest! The point is that the ex-

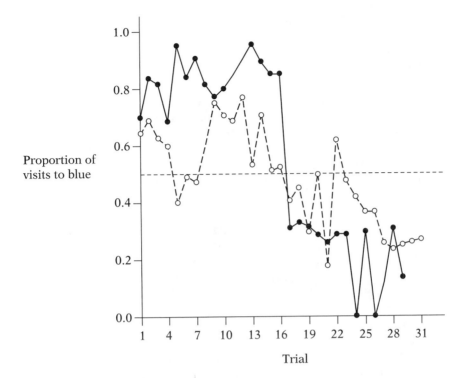

FIGURE 9.1   Efficiency in Time and Effort

Two separate experiments are plotted in the figure. The solid line shows that bees prefer blue to yellow flowers when blue flowers are consistently paired with 2 μl reinforcing nectar and when only one-third of the yellow flowers are reinforced (with 6 μl nectar; the remaining two-thirds with no nectar). After 16 trials, the reinforcement contingencies of the blue and yellow colors are switched, and bees continue to prefer the consistently reinforced color. The dashed lines are the result of a second experiment in which blue flowers continued to be reinforced with 2 μi nectar, one-third of the yellow flowers with 5 μl nectar, and two-thirds of the yellow flowers with 0.5 μl. The consistently reinforced blue flowers on trials 1 to 16 (dashed lines) were visited 62% of the time on average. Following a color switch (trials 17 to 31), visits to blue flowers dropped to 27%.

pected utility function Equation (9.1) predicts that risk taking will increase—that uncertainty can be compensated for—by increasing expectation. The prediction is that bees (and humans) will take more risks for higher than average expected rewards. In a second experiment, Real (1991) covaried the probability of finding a reward with the size of the reward and found just that: greater risk taking. As predicted in our human example, he reported a linear relationship connecting risk taking and reward size; specifically, he concluded from his studies that uncertainty can be compensated for by increasing the amount of the expected reward.

Maximizing Energy Gain

At several places in the text (typically within an adaptive-evolutionary context), reference has been made to the concept of *maximizing reinforcement opportunities*. Never well specified, the general idea being proposed was that behavior is neither trivial nor random. To behave entails costs. To *behave* means to *expend energy*. In a previous chapter, the Brelands' pigs and raccoons engaged in behaviors that delayed reinforcement (i.e., washing or rooting tokens rather than trading them for food). Such behaviors were viewed as being maladaptive. Choosing larger rewards over smaller ones is viewed as adaptive. Why? Because of an implicit awareness that energy well expended is more adaptive than energy wasted. Getting out of an empty maze more quickly by running faster is seen as adaptive because of a higher probability of encountering food elsewhere. Engaging in behavior incurs an energy cost, and the benefit should at a minimum equal that cost.

Biomechanics of Utility

As you might expect from reading about bees in Box 9.1, expected utility theory can be profitably applied to the problems faced by bees in meeting energy needs (Harder & Real, 1987). Bees, indeed, maximize their net energy gain by the decisions they make about which flowers to visit during foraging. Equation (9.2) is introduced with the following cautions: The student is not expected to either memorize or solve it (unless your prof. wants you to, in which case I sincerely apologize). Rather, the equation is introduced for two reasons. The first is to draw parallels with Hull's formidable equation—Equation (7.1), p. 235—that attempted to predict the likelihood of occurrence of a learned response based on both physiology and learned performance. The second is to to address risk aversion (a psychological construct) by examining niche behaviors.

Equation (9.2) (from Real, 1991) predicts that the rate of net energy uptake (E) for each flower visited by a bee equals

$$E = \frac{epSV - W(K_p(T_a + V/I) + K_f T_f)}{T_f + T_a + (V/I)} \tag{9.2}$$

in which e = the energy content of the nectar (15.48 Joules/per mg sucrose); p = the nectar density (mg/μl); S = nectar concentration; V = nectar volume; W = the bee's mass in grams; K_p and K_f = the energy costs of probing and flying, respectively; T = the total time duration of the visit to the flower; T_f = flight time between flowers; T_a = total time at a flower; and I = ingestion time, in seconds.

Equation (9.2) predicts that the costs associated with foraging are real and that because of these costs, the rate of energy intake is a deceleration, rather than a linear function, of nectar volume (Harder & Real, 1987). Such a function predicts that smaller, consistent rewards are more energy efficient than foraging for more variable rewards that include some larger ones. (Going to a yellow flower that has little or no nectar is a high energy cost.) At least in this simple animal, a cognitive function called *choosing* can be modeled and predicted merely by measuring simple biomechanical factors of energy expenditure and energy intake! *Choosing* is italicized here because the term implies a level of consciousness that bees and other nonhuman animals likely do not share with humans. Bees and birds in the following example presumably respond to the results of a concluded foraging experience and adjust their foraging behavior involuntarily, that is, without being aware of what they are doing. A model incorporating neurobiological and behavior data for how bees make their choices has been proposed (Montague, Dayan, & Sejnowski, 1993).

Take one last look at Equation (9.2). Would you say that the science of behavioral analysis has been successful in delving into the *black box?* Certainly, the analytical model proposed by Hull, which was maligned in his lifetime, was on the right track.

The question of animal awareness aside for the moment, effectively choosing from among foraging alternatives has Darwinian, life-and-death implications. When foraging involves feeding hungry offspring, the importance of making good decisions is paramount. Here we look at two additional examples. In the first, laboratory rats were offered two different water patches from which to choose. The effort involved to attain water was manipulated by requiring the rats to bar press on schedules that produced different amounts of water. Rats solved the problem in a way that reduced their overall energy costs relative to the costs associated with random sampling (Collier, Johnson, Borin, & Mathis, 1994). We return to another example of Collier's research later in this chapter.

So Much for Rats and Bees. How Do Birds Do It?

To take another example, the manner in which mountain chickadees (*Parus gambeli*) located in the mountains of northern California go about poking insects into voracious mouths in their nests has recently been reported by Grundel (1992). His results can be summarized in the form of decision trees regarding whether to return to a previous foraging location and what type of prey to take from there. In essence, his findings parallel what we now know about the decisions that bees make in foraging.

Beginning with a successful foraging expedition and having fed their offspring, chickadees typically adopt a *win-stay* strategy. (If prey is found, that is, if they *win*, then they *stay* with that location.) But not always. Grundel (1992) found that the proximity of the foraging location to the nest was important. If it took too long to get there on the previous flight, the chickadee would shift to another location. The operative rule was that if the time to get there was approximately 30% longer than the shortest successful foraging distance, even though prey was found at the more distant site, the chickadee was unlikely to return—a *win-shift* strategy.

Once at a site, which prey do they take? Grundel reported three rules that account for most of the variance in his observations of chickadee foraging patterns. The best predictor was *number* of prey; chickadees appear to take *whatever* size insect that was available in the largest numbers. In other words, number of insects was a better predictor of prey selection than *size* of prey. Size was, however the second-best predictor, with larger prey being preferred. Mixed with both of these factors, Grundel (1992) noticed a trend that if the foraging time was sufficiently short (i.e., if the location was a very short distance from the nest), chickadees would be even less selective of prey and would be more likely to select the same as last time. These strategies, presumably inborn response tendencies honed by experience, serve both bees and birds and do not seem to be unreasonable for humans.

Interim Summary

1. Bees and other animals are risk averse; the axiom "a bird in the hand is worth two in the bush" is descriptive of the behavior of many animals.

2. Given a choice of alternatives in which work expended varies with energy attained, bees, rats, and birds maximize their net energy gain by making adaptive choices.

3. Smaller, consistent rewards are more energy efficient than foraging for more variable rewards that include some large one.

DISCUSSION QUESTION

3. A friend of mine is about to buy an off-road vehicle. Living in a small town with a single dealership, he compares vehicles and prices available there with those in a large town 100 miles away. He has one decision to make from three choices: (a) He can buy outright a locally available vehicle he likes—except for an automatic transmission (he prefers a manual transmission); (b) he can buy the model he wants with a manual transmission from a town 100 miles away; or (c) he can order his choice of model and features from the factory, deliverable after 30 days. He is leaning toward buying the car locally. Why?

THE MATCHING LAW

You are a hungry pigeon trapped in a Skinner box in Richard Herrnstein's laboratory. Two keys in front of you seem to have something to do with food because you have learned to peck at the red key on the left-hand side and the

white key on the right-hand side and the grain hopper has sometimes magically appeared. Now, however, you find that you must peck more often yet receive less food. If you were able to understand English, you might have heard
a lab assistant mumble something about putting you on a *partial schedule of
reinforcement*. And, if you could read, you might notice that one piece of apparatus used to schedule your reinforcement on the left-hand key is labeled
VI-135, and the schedule of reinforcement on the right-hand key is a VI-270
seconds. These are lean schedules; you are reinforced for pecking on these
keys on the average of only every 2 minutes (plus) and every 4.5 minutes.
These **concurrent schedules** of reinforcement run simultaneously, and each
is independent of the other.

   Thought Question: How would you distribute your responses? As a hungry bee would in a way that *minimizes* risk? Recall that bees distributed more
than 80% of their responses to the color of flower that was consistently reinforced (and less than 20% of their responses to a color that was not consistently reinforced). Or would you distribute your responses in a way that
maximizes reinforcement?

The Matching Law in Pigeons

Herrnstein (1961) found that pigeons made twice as many responses to the
VI-135 as they did to the VI-270. That is, they matched their responses to the
available reinforcement. In a 1-h work session, for example, pigeons working
on the VI-135 averaged approximately 3,100 responses to earn 27 reinforcements and concurrently responded approximately 1,600 times, earning 13 reinforcements on the VI-270. Herrnstein then continued working his pigeons
on different combinations of concurrent VI schedules to see whether the percentage of key-pecking responses would consistently match the percentage of
available reinforcement on each schedule. As can be seen in Figure 9.2, pigeons match their responses to available reinforcement almost flawlessly—a
behavioral regularity called the **matching law.** Equation (9.3) mathematically describes the relationship of responses made and reinforcement earned
(Baum, 1974).

$$\frac{R_A}{R_B} = b \left(\frac{r_A}{r_B} \right)^a \qquad\qquad (9.3)$$

R_A and R_B refer to the *rates* of responding on keys A and B (i.e., left and right),
and r_A and r_B refer to the rates of reinforcement on those keys. When the
value of the exponent a is equal to 1.0, a simple matching relation occurs
where the ratio of responses perfectly match the ratio of reinforcers obtained.
The variable b is used to adjust for response effort differences between A and

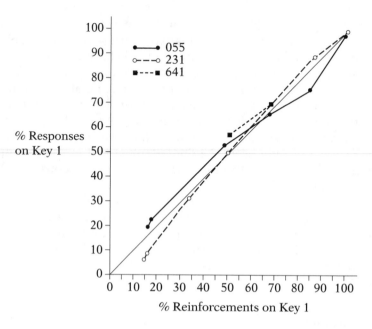

% Responses on Key 1

% Reinforcements on Key 1

FIGURE 9.2   The Matching Law

A perfect match between percentage of responses and percentage of reinforcements is indicated by the diagonal line. Depicted are the performances
of three birds on several different concurrent schedules (see text). These behavioral data lie on top of the predicted line, the basis for what Herrnstein
(1961) has called the *matching law*.

B when they are unequal. (Variable *b* might also be used if the reinforcers obtained for *A* and *B* were unequal.)

Although the derivation of the matching law from the expected utility
function expressed in Equation (9.1) is beyond the scope of this text, these
two functions are related. The regularity (low variability) of Herrnstein's data
is reminiscent of Real's bee-foraging data (Figure 9.1). Prediction of behavior
is high for both the bees and pigeons under the circumstances of these experiments. The observed functions typically lie very close to the predicted values.
There are circumstances, however, in which pigeons do *not* simply match the
ratios of responses to reinforcements. By way of illustrating these exceptions,
consider the following scenario.

Undermatching

You talk on the phone with your two best friends several times daily. Assume
that they both work odd hours, make other phone calls, and the longer you
delay your respective calls to them, the higher is the probability that they will be

home to take them. Friend A is home more than Friend B, and so the probability of Friend A answering when you call is twice that of Friend B. Not surprising, you match these reinforcement contingencies by calling Friend A twice as often as Friend B. At this stage, your phone calling/hit rate would fall somewhere along the diagonal of Figure 9.2, demonstrating a simple matching.

Undermatching Phone Calls. Further assume that over a period of time, you consistently call Friend A first, thereby introducing a delay in calling Friend B. Your strategy thereby *increases* the likelihood of being reinforced when you call Friend B. Under these conditions your phone-calling responses no longer match the reinforcement contingencies of getting through; by delaying, you increase your hit rate for Friend B. Reinforcement theory predicts that you would increase the rate of phone calling to Friend B relative to Friend A. If in fact you respond by calling Friend B more than predicted by the matching law, you are *undermatching* the predicted 2:1 ratio of phone calls. **Undermatching** refers to responding that is *less* than predicted for the available reinforcement. This is, by calling Friend B more, your ratio might come closer to a 50–50 match (i.e., 1:1), undermatching the predicted 2:1 ratio. Such undermatching has been observed under a variety of conditions, and several alternative explanations for undermatching have been proposed (Baum, 1974, 1979, 1981; Myers & Myers, 1977).

Changeover Delays. The hit rates for phone calls to Friend A and Friend B are similar to pigeons pecking on key A and key B for food reinforcement in Herrnstein's (1961) experiment. Recall that key A was reinforced twice as often as key B (VI-135 vs. VI-270). In fact, Herrnstein's pigeons initially *undermatched* by getting more reinforcements/pecks on the VI-270 than predicted by the matching law. Why? First, they learned that key A delivered the most reinforcement. Then, primarily by responding to key A (VI-135) for a long period of time, key B (VI-270) was more likely to deliver reinforcement on the pigeon's first peck on key B. These changeover responses would have the highest probability of being reinforced than any other responses in the session. So, shifting between the two keys was highly reinforced. To keep this reinforcement of shifting from happening, Herrnstein introduced a very brief **changeover delay (COD)** to separate the two components of the concurrent schedules. Whenever a pigeon switched from the left to right or from the right to left key, no reinforcement was available for 1.5 sec. Herrnstein viewed this 1.5-sec changeover delay as a punishment contingency for switching (see also Davison, 1991).

The Matching Law and Human Behavior: An Example

When you are among a group of friends, do you find yourself talking to one or two individuals more than the others? Do you tend to talk more with people who agree with you than with those who don't? A clever experiment reported by Conger and Killeen (1976) examined the effect that concurrent schedules of reinforcement had on how individuals distributed their responses (talking to one or another person). The test subject was introduced into a videotaped four-way discussion under false pretenses. The other three individuals involved were trained as confederates by the experimenter. One discussed an agreed-upon-topic with the test subject while the other two reinforced statements made by the test subject on a concurrent schedule. Reinforcement consisted of comments such as "I agree" or "Good point" or a simple head nod with a yes.

In the first phase of the experiment, one person reinforced about 80% of the subject's comments (the other reinforced far fewer comments). During a final 15-minute period the two confederates switched roles: The previously quiet person reinforced about 40% of the test subject's statements, while the previously supportive person reinforced none. The dependent variable was how much time the test subject spent talking to the confederates. After studying five individuals in this situation, Conger and Killeen (1976) reported good matches between talking and being reinforced: About 80% of responses were directed to the individual delivering reinforcement 80% of the time. When the source of reinforcement shifted from one to the other confederate, the responses followed reliably (the match was ~30% responses for a 40% reinforcement schedule).

Melioration

Herrnstein and Vaughan (1980) and Vaughan (1981, 1985) proposed another interpretation of matching and undermatching. Their analysis of pigeons responding on concurrent schedules is that the pigeons' response strategy is continually changing within a session. After gaining experience with the two VI schedules, within each session a pigeon shifts from one key to the other, always shifting toward the apparently better payoff until the rates of reinforcement per time spent pecking become equal. Accounts of matching that propose the pigeon is ideally maximizing reinforcement rely on the pigeon to keep track of an overall (daily) rate of pay on the two alternatives. The **melioration** account places more emphasis on a pigeon's short-term memory and key-to-key shifts depending on the most recently obtained reinforcer.

The issue of molar versus molecular strategies is far from settled (see Williams, 1991). Bees, it is argued, are short-term energy maximizers, perhaps because of constraints on their memory systems that do not allow them to keep daily running totals of the results of their choices (Real, 1991). By contrast, humans balance both short-term and long-term memories. You may remember that Friend B answered the phone each of the last three times you called and at the same time know that in the long run of events, Friend A is usually easier to contact.

Overmatching

Recall the rats that had electrodes implanted in their brains and had learned to bar press for ESB. Anderson et al. (1992) reported that when these hungry rats were allowed sequential access to either food or ESB reinforcement, after experience with both schedules they quit responding for food entirely. He called the phenomenon absolute *negative contrast*, a special case of *incentive contrast*. In general, when rewards of different value are repeatedly experienced, the better one becomes even better, and by comparison the lesser one sinks even further in value (see Flaherty, 1991).

Similar behavior observed on concurrent schedules of reinforcement has been called *overmatching*. In **overmatching,** a rat or pigeon spends too much time responding on the better of the two VI schedules; it does not distribute enough responses to the less reinforced lever to match the available reinforcement. In one study, for example, switching between levers was punished by electric shock, and pigeons restricted a higher proportion of their responses (than predicted by matching theory) to the richer schedule—hence, *overmatching* (Todorov, 1971). (Recall that the COD also acted as a punisher, yet it improved the match between responses and available reinforcement on two VI schedules.) The increment of food available on the lesser VI schedule apparently did *not* offset the painful cost of switching. Another way to interpret the phenomenon is that the introduction of shock magnified the contrast between the two schedules.

Overmatching in Play. Have you ever watched two young children playing with toys? During a play session, both children play with a variety of toys. Each toy has a particular value, as reflected by the amount of time a child plays with it. It is often the case that in the midst of plenty both zero in on one particular toy, Toy X. If Child A then asserts ownership of Toy X, a wary game of who plays with what ensues. The cost of choosing Toy X by Child B now includes the penalty of being harassed for attempting to play with it. One outcome is that when Toy X becomes available (when Child A shifts interest to other toys), Child B is less likely to choose it. The reinforcement is now available, but Child B does not respond commensurate with the toy's availability—behavior similar to pigeons that overmatch on concurrent schedules.

Labor, Leisure, Wages, and the Matching Law

Regularities of behavior indicate adaptive-evolutionary mechanisms, that is, responses that fit (match) the environment. Perhaps this is the reason that a pigeon's behavior on concurrent schedules is not especially surprising. Indeed, the matching law has an intuitive ring to it. Two common colloquialisms are "dogs [or people] respond to the way they are treated" and "hard work will be rewarded." Both sayings suggest that behavioral responses match (agree with) the reinforcement and punishment contingencies that have shaped and that maintain behavior.

We are puzzled by misbehaving pigs and raccoons precisely because for the most part our personal behavioral experiences conform closely to the matching law. In this section we continue with more examples demonstrating that work output typically matches the reinforcement contingencies. Most animal research on choice uses the concurrent schedules of reinforcement methodology (see Williams, 1988, for a review), making the studies that follow exceptional.

Matching Law in an Ecological Niche

Searching and Working for Food. Collier and his students (Collier, 1983; Collier, Hirsch, & Hamlin, 1972) built a controlled ecological system for rats in which he could more precisely measure the relationship of energy expended in work (pumping iron) and energy attained through such work (securing food). Rats were trained to press one lever (called the *search bar*) and were reinforced by the onset of different lights that signaled various work requirements. Energy expended in work was varied on each lever by adjusting both the weight and the number of repetitions of the lever press. If an S^+ associated with an additional low-work requirement was illuminated (an FR-10 with little added weight, for example), the rat could complete the work requirement and then eat. Other S^+s, however, indicated that the rat was required to complete more repetitions at higher weights in order to eat. Rats could choose *not* to work on a particular schedule by returning to the search bar. There the rat could search for other S^+s that required less work. [Note that like Real's (1991) foraging bees, the energy that these rats expended shopping around for an easier schedule on the search bar, called *procurement cost* is "real" energy that must be made up. That is, searching for an easier job takes time and energy, and these costs must at some point be recovered.]

What did Collier (1983) find? Rats entered into a trade-off between minimizing search time by working on high-energy-expending schedules and increasing search time if the costs were *too* high. That is, if the energy costs associated with pumping iron were too high, rats would spend more time searching for a low-energy-expending schedule leading to food. As has been found with other species, then, given a variety of options, rats are able to adjust their work schedules to maximize calories from food relative to calories expended in earning it. And they bring this strategy with them to the workplace, rather than learning it there.

Matching Law in the Workplace

How much is one's labor worth? The answer usually lies somewhere between what the worker thinks is fair and what the boss thinks is adequate. Typically, the workplace constitutes a large part of the ecological niche for many humans. Is there any evidence that the matching law applies to the work output of laborers and the money expended by owners? That is, do people work harder if they are paid more? Economists have analyzed this problem and have modeled this relationship as a **labor supply curve,** one version of which is depicted in Figure 9.3. Let us analyze this function and then see whether human economics conforms to the matching law studied in animals.

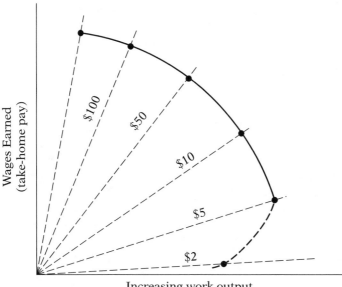

FIGURE 9.3 A Labor Supply Curve

Wages earned are plotted as a function of work output for wage rates between $2 and $100 per hour. For the medium and high wage rates, people work to maximize total wages earned; however, at the lowest wage rate, individuals appear to give up and no longer work as hard. At this lowest wage rate of $2 per hour, the tiny increment in wages attainable by additional work is apparently not worth the expended energy. The reversal in the function at this lowest wage level gives the standard labor supply curve its backward-bending character—presumably reflecting a work-leisure trade-off.

Working for Wages.   Note in Figure 9.3 that a person making $100 per hour works less (fewer hours) to earn a relatively high wage in contrast with a person making $50 per hour who works more hours to earn less money. This relationship holds for the intermediate wage levels: An individual's effort (hours worked) can be conceptualized as an attempt to maximize total wages earned. Such are the workings of a free enterprise economy, and most readers are familiar with this reality.

As the wage rate drops even more precipitously, however, to $2 per hour (considerably less than the minimum wage) an interesting thing happens; most individuals no longer work longer hours to make more money. The flat slope of the $2 per hour wage rate in Figure 9.3 indicates that very little is gained in wages even when many more hours are worked. In the vernacular, "The juice isn't worth the squeeze" (i.e., the extra money isn't worth the effort).

Labor Supply Curves and the Matching Law.   Does this backward-bending curve in Figure 9.3 indicate a breakdown in the matching law? Probably not. Among the differences between our animal models and the human experience is that (at least in some experiments) animals are very hungry and their work efforts result directly in eating and alleviating hunger. Humans earn wages that are traded for other amenities of life as well as for food.

The Labor-Leisure Trade-Off.   Look again at the idealized performance in Figure 9.3. It shows the behavior of individuals working during a typical workweek. Even working 40 hours per week, humans have much discretionary time in which to spend the wages they have accrued. Leisure time is valuable; much of the wage not spent on meeting energy needs (food) and in meeting other consummatory response needs (clothing, shelter, family needs, and so forth.) is spent on leisure. Not working costs and is considered worth the cost by many humans. One interpretation of the $2 per hour wage earner who limits total work is that this individual's leisure time has become more valuable relative to the benefits of working. Once basic energy needs are met, humans have earned the choice of not working.

Do we have an animal model for the work/leisure trade-off? It has been noted that when work requirements become too high for the payoff (i.e., when it appears that the juice isn't worth the squeeze), having met their energy needs, animals also quit responding for discretionary pleasure. For example, rats love sucrose solutions and will work (press a lever) for the sweet taste. (Assume in this study that the rat's energy needs have been met independently of this sucrose option.) What happens if you continue to increase the number of lever presses a rat must make just for the taste of sucrose? Given the option of not doing anything or working for a brief pleasure, rats eventually chose to do nothing (Kelsey & Allison, 1976), and, likewise, pigeons quit rather than work hard for nominal rewards (Green, Kagel, & Battalio, 1987). Not unlike the $2 wage earner, these animals chose to work less with two consequent results: (a) They do without the few extra reinforcements they might have earned, and (b) they have more time for doing nothing (leisure) as opposed to expending energy on work. The animal model seems adequate on all accounts.

Interim Summary

1. Choice is conveniently studied in laboratory animals using ***concurrent schedules*** of reinforcement.

2. Using concurrent schedules of reinforcement, Herrnstein (1961) found that the rate of key pecking in pigeons matched the reinforcement that was available on the two schedules, a phenomenon he called the ***matching law.***

3. *A **changeover delay (COD)*** discourages animals on concurrent schedules from switching to the alternate schedule to pick up an easy rein-

forcer. Without a COD, animals tend to exhibit ***undermatching,*** responding less than predicted for the available reinforcement.

4. ***Melioration*** describes short-term shifts from one key to the other (while on a current schedule), presumably due to the most recently obtained reinforcement. By contrast, matching describes a session-long strategy the end result of which is to maximize reinforcement.

5. ***Overmatching*** describes an animal that responds too much on the better of the two VI schedules, thereby not maximizing reinforcement available on the other schedule.

6. Collier (1983) found that by giving rats a search key by which they could sample other schedules, rats adjusted their work in a way that maximized the intake of calories relative to calories expended.

7. A backward-bending ***labor supply curve*** can be understood as another example of matching (work to wages) and is influenced by the reinforcement value of leisure.

DISCUSSION QUESTIONS

4. The NCAA has ruled that an athlete transferring to a new school is typically ineligible to play the first year at the new school. What is this rule attempting to influence/control?

SELF-CONTROL

Put yourself in the following two situations:

> *Scenario A.* You have stopped in the middle of a hectic day to have a bite of lunch and are reviewing your schedule. You see that you have a psychology exam the next day for which you *must* study. At that moment your best friend calls and begs you to go to a show tonight at 8:00 P.M. The show you've both been dying to see is playing, and you're torn between two alternatives: go to the show or study for the exam. You tell your friend that you have to study. Your friend counters that you can study before and after the show, but you are skeptical; you have been down that road before. After another 15 minutes of agonizing indecision, you say a final *no*; you reluctantly choose to study.
>
> *Scenario B.* You have a psychology exam tomorrow for which you *must* study. You finish a bite to eat, and at 7:00 P.M. you open your book. At that moment your best friend calls and begs you to go to the show. It starts at 7:20. You tell your friend that you have to study. Your friend counters that you can study after the show. You have a moment of self-doubt. Your friend says, "Let's get going or we'll be late." You look at your watch, at your psychology textbook, and hear yourself say "okay." You can always study after the show.

Immediate and Delayed Gratification. Which scenario is more likely? If you answer that both choices are likely, what are the circumstances that account for these two different courses of action? Assume that studying for the exam was a better decision: Is it the case that we make better decisions earlier in the day (i.e., noon as opposed to supper time)? Likely the person *was* more tired when the decision was made to go to the show. Do people consistently make bad decisions when they are tired? Not too likely. What we can agree on is that the decision to go to the show was made more impulsively. Deciding on a moment's notice allows less time for reflecting on the consequences of one's actions. We can also make a value judgment. Deciding to go to the show rather than study showed a lack of self-control. Let us begin with this issue.

Immediate Gratification and Self-Control

One very useful application of animal research on choice behavior is in the area of self-control. **Self-control** is defined as the ability to delay immediate gratification, usually with the goal of attaining a larger reinforcer at a later time. Achieving self-control is viewed as a defining feature of civilized behavior. Certainly self-control is conceptualized as being learned; we accept as normal the selfish behavior of infants and small children. A counselor would likely label as immature the person (and the behavior) who fails to graduate from school due to bad decisions about when and how much to study.

Is Self-control Adaptive?   On a daily basis we make decisions that reflect a conflict between achieving an immediate pleasure at the expense of a delayed reinforcer. Many decisions that affect a person's health fall into these categories. Choosing to drink alcohol may lead to the immediate pleasure of mild euphoria at the expense of incurring less favorable, more delayed outcomes (such as automobile injuries and hangovers). Choosing not to drink balances the loss of immediate pleasure with the long-term outcome of avoiding accidents and hangovers. The same can be said for impulsive sexual encounters that may lead to unwanted pregnancies, diseases, and heartaches. Likewise, choosing not to smoke (immediate) increases longevity (delayed). Choosing not to eat the double banana fudge sundae (immediate) allows for the reinforcement of reduced obesity/increased longevity (delayed). And so, learning self-control can be seen as an adaptive behavior. On the other hand, it is also likely that more individuals are conceived as a result of impulsive behavior than of calculations. So self-control in and of itself does not define adaptiveness. In this section, we explore what is known about how self-control is trained in both animals and humans.

Training Self-Control in Pigeons

Hungry again, you find yourself in a Skinner box. One peck at key A raises the grain hopper immediately, allowing you to feed a short while. One peck at key B raises the grain hopper for a longer period of time, allowing you to eat more food—but a 4-sec delay has been imposed between your pecking response and food availability. Your choices are, then, a small immediate reward versus a large delayed reward. You more often than not choose the key producing the immediate small reward. (Why should I delay gratification? I'm only a bird!)

Time Delays and Self-Control. Rachlin and Green (1972) tried to encourage self-control in pigeons given this choice between small/immediate versus large/delayed rewards. To accomplish this shift, they gradually increased the time interval between making the choice and receiving the reinforcement (see Figure 9.4). Using a *concurrent chain* procedure, a single response to key A

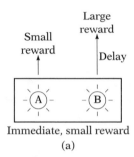

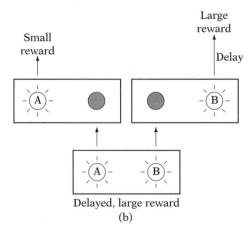

FIGURE 9.4   Teaching Patience to Pigeons

In (a), pigeons are first taught that their choice of the left or right key produces either a small reward immediately or a larger reward after a delay. After this training (b), responding to key A leads to an FR-10 requirement (on key A), followed by a small reinforcement delivered immediately. Responding to key B (b) leads to an FR-10 requirement, followed by a 4-sec delay, followed by a larger reinforcer. Pigeons choose the small reward in (a) and the larger reward in (b).

put the pigeon into a second schedule, an FR-10 on key A. Likewise, a response to key B put the pigeon in a FR-10 on key B. Completing the 10 pecks on key A produced the small immediate reward; completing the 10 pecks on key B produced a 4-sec delay and then the large (delayed) reward. Under these circumstances, pigeons began to peck key B, leading to the large delayed reward. They delayed immediate gratification, overcame their impulsive behavior, and (to the extent a pigeon can be a "self"), they exhibited self-control. Why? Rachlin (1974) developed a theory of self-control expanded on by Logue (1988). These researchers propose that the results of many other experiments using both humans and animals can be interpreted showing that self-control can be explained *as shifts in reward value over time*. Let's analyze their reasoning.

Self-Control, Immediate Gratification, and Expected Utility

Figure 9.5 shows the relationship of the value of a reward (that is, its expected utility) as a function of time prior to experiencing the reward. Note that if a choice between a large and small reward is made just prior to the small reward becoming available (i.e., point T_1 on the time line), the reward

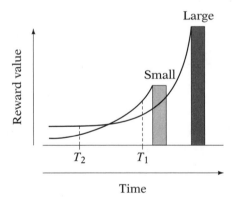

FIGURE 9.5   Expected Value of Large and Small Rewards

A reward's expected utility changes as a function of time. The value of a reward increases as the experience of the reward approaches. At time T_2, the expected values of two rewards are more in synchrony with their actual values. At time T_1, the expected value of the small reward exceeds the expected value of the large reward because the small reward is imminent. Choices for small rewards made at time T_1 reflect the fulfilling of immediate gratification; those made for large rewards at time T_2 reflect self-control.

value of the small reward is greater than the reward value of the large reward. As we saw in Equations (9.1) and (9.2), expected utility theory describes the relative value of rewards. The value of an item or action is in part determined by its ready availability; for example, your inheritance is of limited value if you can't get to it for 30 years. "A bird in the hand is worth two in the bush" is as much a statement about *time* (*now* versus the *future*) as it is about certainty and uncertainty.

Do you want to go to the show, or do you want to study? The relative value of studying versus going to the show varies as a function of when the question is asked and when the decision is made. If, for example, the question is posed and the decision is made at time T_2 (hours, weeks, days before the event), the relative values following from activity A (2 hours of pleasure enjoying a movie) versus the values following from activity B (studying to pass a class, earn a degree, and so forth.) can be more fairly weighed.[3] If the question is posed at time T_1, however, the immediate anticipation of activity A may outweigh that of activity B. The moral of the story is that if you celebrate Christmas, decide with your children in early December, not on Christmas Eve, that their presents will be opened on the morning of December 25.

Training Self-Control in Children

Earlier it was asserted that learning self-control is culturally based. Several studies have demonstrated that children learn to tolerate delays and thereby to make better choices. For example, 6-year-old children and older ones select large delayed rewards from two alternatives, while the 4-year-olds typically choose smaller, immediate rewards (Sonuga-Barke, Lea, & Webley, 1989). In another study, impulsive children were first allowed direct, immediate experience with both small and large rewards. A delay interval was gradually lengthened for access to the larger reward while the smaller reward continued to be immediately available. Several hyperactive children learned to choose the larger, delayed reward with this training, thereby demonstrating increased self-control (Schwitzer & Sulzer-Azaroff, 1988). Finally, children have been found to imitate adults who verbalize the benefits of delayed rewards as being "worth the wait" (Mischel, 1966). It is as likely that children who model on impulsive parents exhibit less desirable outcomes.

Concluding Thoughts. This chapter began with a quote from Skinner pondering whether an individual should "be held responsible for his [or her] action and justly rewarded or punished for its consequences." Skinner argues that your decisions and choices have been determined by your genes and by your unique reinforcement history. Because you are not a free agent, the envi-

---

[3]Note in the time prior to T_2 in Figure 9.5 that the expected reward values are in agreement with the "real" values of small and large rewards. This may not always be clear in real life, when disagreements often exist about the relative values of events and activities.

ronment is responsible for your actions. In this chapter, we have seen that there is some truth in Skinner's analysis: Certainly, for simple organisms such as bees and even some small-brained vertebrates—birds and rats—choices are constrained by innate strategies that minimize energy expenditure and maximize energy consumption. Likewise, our responses seem to be keenly tuned to the available reinforcement contingencies. Yet, some of these contingencies are subtle. Only with special training can we learn the patience of self-control—delaying immediate gratification for the goal of a larger anticipated award.

Interim Summary

1. ***Self-control*** is the ability to delay immediate gratification. It can be demonstrated in experiments by showing that animals will respond in a way that delays immediate gratification for a small reinforcer by choosing a larger reinforcer that is delayed.
2. Exhibiting self-control can be adaptive, but so can impulsiveness.
3. Self-control can be explained as shifts in reward value over time.
4. A small reward that is immediately available is more reinforcing than when it is delayed. Animals (including humans) can learn to wait to have access to a larger reinforcer.

DISCUSSION QUESTIONS

5. What is the meaning of the following sayings? Can you relate them to theory presented in this section?
   a. "Beggars can't be choosers."
   b. "I've saved the best for last."
   c. "Let me sleep on it, and I'll give you my decision tomorrow."
   d. "Never go grocery shopping when you are hungry."
   Are these sayings descriptive of human behavior? What theories help account for their truth?

6. What different food choices might you make from a menu as compared to a cafeteria line? Why?

7. A couple is in love. Compare and contrast their choices either to elope or to have a long engagement.

8. What predictions can you make about the effectiveness of "just say no" campaigns from the two functions expressed in Figure 9.5?

9. What is the difference between a salary and a wage? (Note that the labor supply curve in Figure 9.3 is for *wages* earned.) How do employers' expectations differ for those employees paid wages and those paid salaries? From the employees' perspective, are there different expectations regarding leisure while on the job?

10. Why is impulse control training an important aspect of child rearing in most (all?) of the world's cultures?

CHAPTER SUMMARY

1. Humans and animals engage in decision making throughout their lifetimes. Choices are influenced by feedback from the environment.

2. People and animals decide between two or more alternatives based on the perceived value of alternatives. Value is determined by esthetics, utility, cost, availability, and perception of worth. Together these factors compose the expected utility of an item.

3. Choice behavior can be understood within an adaptive-evolutionary context. Choices among food alternatives are seen as adaptive when they equalize energy attained (food) for energy expended (foraging, work).

4. Bees choose among alternatives in a way that avoids risk and favors consistency. Humans and other animals do likewise.

5. Initially measured in pigeons working on VI-VI concurrent schedules of reinforcement, the matching law describes a form of choice behavior in which responses match the available reinforcement. If one component of the concurrent schedule makes available three times the reinforcement compared to the other, pigeons make three times as many responses, matching the schedule.

6. Undermatching is likely to occur when the passage of time obscures or distorts the reinforcement contingencies of the leanest of the concurrent VI schedules. In undermatching, proportionately more responses are made to the lean schedule. The insertion of *changeover delays* in the concurrent schedules corrects for undermatching.

7. *Overmatching* refers to pigeons on current schedules that by spending a disproportionate amount of time on the rich VI component under-respond on the lean VI component.

8. Theoretical accounts disagree on whether molecular (short-term effects like melioration) or molar (longer-term accounts like maximization) are more important in describing the matching phenomenon

9. When labor supply curves are compared to the matching law, apparent breakdowns in matching occur for the lowest-level wage earner. But leisure has value, and expending energy to work is balanced against the costs of lost leisure. With this understanding, the matching account is still accurate for the low wage earner whether human or nonhuman.

10. Nonhuman animals have been trained to choose between receiving either immediate or delayed reinforcement. Choosing delayed reinforcement demonstrates self-control.

11. The preference of both humans and animals for immediate gratification obtained by choosing small rewards (relative to selecting larger rewards that are delayed) can be accounted for by expected utility theory. Expected utility theory takes into account the relative value of immediate and delayed reinforcers. Expected utility theory predicts that choices between two alternatives will vary as a function of time preceding the experience of the reinforcers.

12. Achieving self-control can be viewed as a defining feature of civilized behavior.

KEY TERMS

CHAPTER 10

Applications of Learning and Behavior Theory

Up to now, we've looked at many empirically-based theories that have been proposed to account for why we behave as we do, and why and how we learn as we do. Among other ideas, these theories have addressed consummatory and species-specific behaviors, excitatory and inhibitory classical conditioning, and how reinforcement and punishment can come to control behavior. We've also seen (Chapter 4) how classical conditioning theory provides a better understanding of both drug tolerance, immune system functioning, and psychosomatic disorders. Here we'll look further at the application of learning and behavior theory to our everyday behavior. Specifically, we'll look at appetite—what controls our eating and drinking behaviors; at sexual behavior; how learning theory helps account for abnormal behavior; and how it is used in psychotherapy.

APPETITE: EATING AND DRINKING BEHAVIORS

> *Man knows that the food he ingests in order to live will become assimilated into his being—will become himself. There must be, therefore, a relationship between the idea he has formed of specific items of food and the image he has of himself and his place in the Universe. There is a link between a people's dietary habits and its perception of the world.* (Soler, 1979)

During the past century, hundreds of researchers have been drawn to the study of ingestive behaviors—that is, to the study of eating and drinking. Why? Because foods and fluids, more tangible than the air we breathe, sustain life. Ingestive behaviors are counted among the ethologists' *consummatory* behaviors—behaviors essential for survival. One doesn't have to be a scientist to recognize that eating and drinking also provide two of life's great pleasures; throughout a lifetime, eating and drinking make us feel good, and help define our social interactions. Indeed, Elizabeth Rozin (1982) has pointed out that patterns of eating and drinking, called cuisines, help define the world's cultures.

Physiology and Behavior of Food Ingestion

Using animal models, nutritionists and dietitians have learned a great deal about the chemical makeup of foods and their ingestional consequences. Of the 942 feeding-related articles that Weingarten (1990) surveyed, only 5% were concerned with the role of environment—that is, of how learning and experience affect appetite. One could get the mistaken impression that eating and drinking behavior are primarily governed by innate factors.

Physiologically-oriented nutritional experts are less concerned with psychological and sociocultural factors—the when, what, and why of food and drink selection. Why, for example, do some people overeat and others undereat to the detriment of their health? Are the determinants of eating disorders better accounted for by learning, or by genes and physiology? A quick comparison of the cuisines of different cultures attest to the idiosyncratic food choices humans *learn* during their lifetimes. In this section, we will approach the study of ingestive behavior from an interdisciplinary perspective that integrates evolutionary considerations with physiology and learning.

Membrane Sensitivity to Foods

The first cellular life forms evolved membranes that separated a cell from its watery environment. These membranes were selectively sensitive to different components of the environment—for example, to edibles, to irritants, and so forth. In meeting the challenge of efficiently securing palatable foods and avoiding toxins, our taste and smell receptors evolved in ways that took advantage of this early cell sensitivity (Young, 1966; Pfaffman, 1959; Beidler, 1982). As a consequence, human infants display innate preferences for sweet and dislike of bitter substances via receptors with membranes that reflect our evolutionary underpinnings.

Receptor-driven Feeding of Simple Animals.   Unlike those receptors found on flies, human receptors do not determine appetite. Earlier in the text (p. 34), we looked at an example of a relatively simple behavioral system that is "receptor driven." Specifically, we saw that a house fly reflexively lowers its proboscis to feed when taste receptors on its legs are stimulated (Dethier, 1978). Other animals also occupy relatively more circumscribed feeding niches than do humans. Carnivores and herbivores are two well known, relatively restricted, feeding niches

Evolution of Eating Behaviors

In addition to taste and olfactory receptors, specific food-related brain structures evolved in humans and other animals. An ability to monitor the nutrient level of a food once it is past the peripheral sensing receptors is also part of our physiology. Homeostatic mechanisms are as much a product of evolution as are bitter and sweet receptors. Next we look at a few examples of how human ingestive behaviors may have evolved. These examples reveal the complexities of what, how, and why we eat, and point out the limitations of a purely physiological approach.

Corn.   The quality of the digestible protein in corn is increased, if, during food preparation, the corn is treated with an alkali solution. Katz (1982) wondered if this was why some American Indian cultures treated their corn with alkali and others did not. He found that those who *did* treat their corn with alkali grew and ate more corn than those not using the alkali treatment. Katz reasoned that the alkali food preparation method increased the nutritional value of the corn, that in turn influenced how corn was incorporated into the diet.

Two points are stressed: First, selecting corn to eat (or other foods) involves more than just the food's taste and smell. Secondly, somehow, for unknown reasons, certain American Indians *learned* to treat corn with alkali. Did they recognize the value of this treatment in the course of a lifetime, and transmit the acquired information to the next generation? It seems so.

Fava Beans, Bitter Manioc, and Soybeans.   Katz (1982) accomplished similar studies of African tribes eating fava beans, bitter manioc, and soybeans. He noted that cultural transformations of foods often enhanced adaptive fitness. For example, when bitter manioc (a tuber) is prepared in a certain way, the food offers increased protection against sickle cell anemia. Food preparation that enhances adaptive fitness often becomes part of the culture, a process that Katz (1975) has called **biocultural evolution.**

Cows' Milk.   Similar work on the relationship of African tribes that historically use cow's milk, and the prevalence or absence of lactose insufficiency was reported by Simoons (1973). Simoons found that those populations that incorporated milk and cheese in their diets had enzymes that aided their digestion, enzymes that were lacking in those that didn't ingest milk and cheese. He theorizes that the consumption of particular types of food and not others over time may have led to divergence of human populations. Katz and Simoons view both the choice of food for consumption and methods of food preparation as an evolutionary interface. Those people who do this more successfully than others enjoy a reproductive advantage. A cultural trend develops as this behavior is successfully passed to the next generation.

Origin of Cuisines.   What humans learn about foods during their lifetimes is important. Learning complements the functioning of taste and smell receptors as well as innately organized homeostatic regulatory processes. Furthermore, the cross-generational transmission of food information is the basis for the origin of the world's various cuisines. Learning, therefore, is an important determinant of culture.

Thought question: What do you know about the origins of food choices within the ethnic cuisine of your subculture?

Specific Hungers

Evolution aside for the moment, individuals survive by eating foods several times each day that are selected from within their local environments. Even with a full complement of evolved food selection mechanisms *and* a supportive culture, the task is not a particularly easy one. Some insight into the complexity of this process can be gained by examining a case history. Box 10.1 illustrates how one particular child, D. W., learned to eat and drink despite faulty physiology. What is remarkable about this example is that it points out the redundant physiological systems we have (a) for recognizing salt and

BOX 10.1   SALT CRAVING AND PERSONALITY DEVELOPMENT: A MYSTERY STORY

A child known to us only by his initials, D.W., was born in the mid-1930s near Baltimore. What happened to him in his short lifetime contains the drama of a good mystery as well as an introduction to complexities of appetite. Sickly from birth, D.W. would drink milk only when mixed with water. He regurgitated most "solid" foods. A watery, salted gruel barely kept him alive. At about 18 months of age, physically and mentally slowed by dietary deficiencies, he began to say a few words—among them were "Mama," "Wa-wa," and "Salt!" His mother described D.W.'s behavior at this time:

> "... as soon as he knew what the word 'water' meant, he would cry for it every time he heard the word mentioned. And when he saw the river or the ocean, he always thought he had to have some to drink. We were finally able to explain to him that it wasn't drinking water."

And then he discovered the salt shaker.

> "He poured some out and ate it by dipping his finger in it. After this he wouldn't eat any food without having the salt, too. . . . He really cried for it and acted like he had to have it . . . practically everything he liked real well was salty, such as crackers, pretzels, potato chips, olives, pickles, fresh fish, salt mackerel, crisp bacon, and most fruits and vegetables if I added more salt."

Between 1 to 3 years old, D.W.'s obsession with salt and water found him searching magazines looking for pictures of lakes. During playtime he liberally "salted" imaginary meals. His parents knew that D.W.'s abnormal cravings were peculiar. But they must have been horrified when the tiny child became *viralized*. (His voice deepened, and he began growing pubic hair and an adult-sized penis.) Referred to Dr. Lawson Wilkins (the founder of pediatric endocrinology at Johns Hopkins School of Medicine), D.W. was admitted to a large children's ward. Placed on a standard hospital diet, he had restricted access to salt and water. He died seven days after admission.

The child's death would be unnoted and unremarkable at the time were it not for Curt Richter, a somewhat reclusive scientist at Johns Hopkins University. Richter had spent the latter part of the 1930s investigating how and why laboratory rats ate and drank. He was particularly interested in why rats with adrenal glands removed died within a few days. However, if he gave them extra salt and unrestricted water, they lived quite normally (Richter, 1936).

Richter heard about the boy in the hospital who had craved salt. He contacted Wilkins and suggested that D.W.'s unusual salt craving might indicate problems with his adrenal glands. Richter and Wilkins performed an autopsy and found an adrenal tumor (Wilkins and Richter, 1940). The tumor had been responsible for two separate disorders. D. W.'s adrenal gland had secreted too much androgen (causing viralization) and too little aldosterone. Aldosterone regulates how much salt is excreted in the urine, and too little of it caused D.W. to excrete too much salt. This child's specific hungers, reflected by his obsession with salt and water, had helped him survive for over three years. The case history serves as a remarkable example of the interplay of physiological regulation and the behavioral selection of essential nutrients in a pre-verbal child.

water in both the internal and external environment, and (b) for regulating their intake. We have **specific hungers** for salt and water. Salt and water are considered as special cases for many reasons, not the least of which is that both are essential to survival in the short term. Animals can survive only a few days without fluid replenishment, and, as we see in the case of D.W., salt is also a critical need.

Special Nature of Salt and Water. Another indication of the "special" nature of salt and water is that every language around the globe has words for these nutrients. By contrast, no language (other than the language of science) has a word for "thiamin," "magnesium," "selenium," and other vitamins and minerals (including the words "vitamins" and "minerals!"). Salt joins sweet, bitter, and sour as one of the "four basic tastes." Along with an innate appetite for water, these tastes are sensed by evolved receptors attuned to foods containing them.

Specific hungers are mediated by peripheral receptors (CNS), neuroendocrine systems, and homeostatic mechanisms of the ANS. These interrelated systems comprise the innate equipment that allows us to regulate calories, electrolytes, minerals, and other specific nutrients. We will not cover these systems here. Rather, we will continue our focus on the role learning plays in modifying and directing our innately organized eating and drinking behaviors.

Carnivores, Herbivores, and Omnivores

As is the case with carnivores, herbivores, and all other living creatures, omnivores must secure from the environment those nutrients essential for survival.

The Omnivore's Paradox. On the surface omnivory appears to be an ideally evolved solution in meeting these needs. If plant sources dry up, eat meat (too bad, herbivores). If rabbits and small rodents disappear, eat plants (sorry, carnivores). The paradox facing the omnivore, however, is that this more open eating strategy increases the risk of making mistakes. If *everything* is fare (sic) game, recognize that *everything* includes toxic plants, *salmonella*, environmentally contaminated shellfish, and so forth. Because it is less specialized, a wide open system contains fewer safeguards. That is why omnivory, beneficial during famine, can also be detrimental to health and well-being. The foregoing cost-benefit analysis has been called the **omnivore's paradox** (Rozin & Kalat, 1971).

Nature and Nurture of Eating. As we saw in a previous chapter, one innately organized behavior that helps us resolve the omnivore's paradox is food neophobia—a wariness concerning new foods. Are there other adaptive behavioral strategies that function to aid in food selection? Box 10.2 examines the eating

BOX 10.2 ... AND THIS IS NORMAL?

Unlike D.W.'s earliest eating experiences (Box 10.2), Jane B. was a perfectly normal infant. She nursed healthily at mama's breast for 1 year and maintained an optimal growth curve. Her physical and psychological development were textbook normal.

"Omnivory" begins with selecting choices from alternative foods as well as learning when, what, and where to eat. For example, at about 10 months Jane B. was offered apple juice from a nursing bottle, and she drank avidly. On her first birthday, she abruptly refused breastmilk and all other animal milk offered her. (Mother was devastated.) Jane B. drank apple juice for the next 8 to 9 years of her life, and then other sweetened drinks. At age 18 she continues to reject milk but still loves her mother.

What did Jane B. learn from her first omnivorous (open) encounter? Did she learn that the sight of a baby bottle (CS) contained a very sweet fluid (US) that she could drink more rapidly than nursing from a breast? That is, was the sweeter, more rapidly attained apple juice a more potent reinforcer that shaped her preference over breast milk? In this particular instance, was the apple flavor and rapid glucose repletion more reinforcing than the overall more nutritious but less sweet, less rapidly digested milk? (These questions are not easily answered. See Weiffenbach, 1977).

During the 2nd year of her life, Jane B. ate bread, fruit, ice cream, jello, some vegetables, and most any-

thing sweet. No meat, poultry, or fish, and rarely cheese. She was avid about her likes and dislikes; she has always seemed to know exactly what and when she wanted to eat, and exactly what and when she did *not* want to eat. Familiar, not novel, foods were the rule. Two examples: From 16 months to about 2 years of age she ate an egg and toast for every breakfast, 7 days a week. One day she abruptly stopped eating eggs, and to the present day does not eat them (she prefers not to eat breakfast). At age 6, she could not get enough of McDonald's "Chicken Nuggets," then as abruptly rejected them. Any food item offered her that is either new, or that she no longer likes, is treated as poison, and the caretaker regarded with extreme caution.

(continued)

BOX 10.2 ... AND THIS IS NORMAL? *(continued)*

Jane B. has always had a wide variety of foods from which she was allowed to choose with few restrictions. In a busy household during her first 4 to 5 years she ate pretty much on her own schedule, with only a nod to that of her family's. While at grandmother's she was allowed to eat in the middle of the night if she woke up and was hungry. Grandmother's philosophy was to let her eat whatever she wanted, in whatever amount, around the clock (in a laboratory setting this is known as an *ad libitum* or *ad lib* feeding schedule—cf. liberty).

Bright, alert, and happy, at age eighteen Jane B.s size/weight ratio is near optimal and she is above average in intellectual achievement. (Apparently her brain *did* manage to get enough protein during development, a constant source of worry for her parents.) Even though her eating patterns have never conformed to eating three squares/day, carefully selected from the food pyramid, her overall physical and mental health are near optimal.

behavior of another child named Jane B. We assume that she has had less opportunity to *learn* to select foods than those humans who have eaten thousands of meals over several years. Her experiences allow us to see what innately predisposed behaviors she brings to this task. Some questions to keep in mind: What is the role of caretakers in Jane's culture? How well could she accomplish her food selection task without the help of adult caretakers?

Open Feeding Systems of Young Humans.   What lessons can we learn from Jane B.'s case history of early omnivory?

1. In large measure choices expressed by very young humans seem to be determined primarily by the *flavors* of food and drink. A reinforcer is not choosy about the behavior it reinforces: Preference for sweet may lead to the selection of (overall) less nutritious foods (see discussion by Pliner, Herman, & Polivy, 1990).

2. Food *neophobia* (translated as finickyness) describes the overall pattern of eating among young humans. Moreover, the highly conservative food selections made by children belies labeling them "omnivorous."

3. Although the foods offered Jane B. were culturally determined, her selections were highly idiosyncratic. She seems to have learned from direct experience that "if it looks like A, then it tastes/smells like B." And, how it tastes and smells, *not* the caretaker's admonitions, guides her ingestive behavior.

4. In her classical *cafeteria feeding studies*, Davis (1928, 1939) concluded that *ad libitum* selections of type and amount of food could be as readily

accomplished by rug rats as by adult caretakers. Selecting one food and eating it nearly exclusively, and then abruptly switching, she described as a "feeding jag" (Davis, 1939). We will discuss a feeding jag as an adaptive specialization of eating in the next section.

5. Advice for new parents: (a) Prepare to worry about your child's nutrition (worrying about your children's nutrition is adaptive and contributes to their fitness); (b) provide many alternative foods (some of them nutritious) from which your child can choose; (c) put the poisons out of reach; (d) get real laid back; and (e) get out of the way.

Learning Appropriate Food Choices

Recall from earlier chapters that taste aversion conditioning is a popular method that is used to study general properties of association formation. By decreasing the preference for certain flavored foods and fluids, conditioned taste aversions influence future food choices. In this section, we shift our focus from general associative processes to the specifics of how learning determines food choices.

Learning to Recognize Nutrients. D.W.'s tragic history underscores the innate regulation of salt and water. Paul Rozin and his colleagues have posed research questions about other adaptive hungers (Rozin, 1967; Rodgers & Rozin, 1966). Identifying, ingesting, and regulating the way animals locate nutrients such as iron and thiamin, for example, must be performed differently than for salt and water. Why? Because animals have *not* evolved taste receptors that are sensitive to approximately 100 other vitamins, minerals, and essential nutrients as they did for salt and water. These other trace elements are typically masked within food complexes, and as such are not consciously recognized as are salt and water.

How is Thiamin Recognized? Rozin and colleagues asked how an animal knows which foods contain thiamin if it cannot be detected by peripheral receptors? Recognize that this is not an academic question. Jane B. somehow seems to have selected the right foods, in the right amounts, and at the right time, from a variety of food sources. The answer to this question would go a long way towards helping us understand how she managed to survive and thrive the first 18 years of life.

Rats eating a diet lacking thiamin become *thiamin deficient*.[1] They lose appetite and weight, their coat does not shine, and they will die unless the thiamin they lack is replaced. When given thiamin in a saccharin-flavored solution, they will avidly drink it, ingest the thiamin, and recover from the deficiency state. They tend to like the saccharin even better than do control

[1]The acute condition of thiamine deficiency in humans is called *Beri Beri*—a continuing problem in Third World countries.

rats, presumably because of the positive association of the flavor with recovery from sickness (Garcia, Ervin, Yorke, & Koelling, 1967). Other experiments have revealed that the analysis of increasing a flavor's preference by its association with recovery from deficiency is more complicated than suggested by Garcia et al. (1967). Zahorik (1977) analyzed the problem as follows, based on research with her colleagues Zahorik, Mair, and Pies (1974):

1. Animals learn to dislike the flavor of a thiamin-deficient diet. When presented with the alternative of a *familiar-safe* diet or a novel one, they prefer the safety of a familiar diet, because novel diets produce neophobic responses. Rats are risk averse and prefer the safety of a familiar diet.

2. Rats that have learned to dislike the flavor of the thiamin-deficient diet, however, will choose a novel diet if it is the only alternative to the *familiar-deficient* (thiamine-deficient) diet. Why? The *familiar-deficient* diet having become aversive, hungry rats overcome their innate *neophobia* and choose the alternative diet.

3. Recovery from deficiency after eating a novel-flavored diet (one that contains thiamin) increases the preference for that novel flavor. This *conditioned preference* is greater than for controls who like the flavor merely because it has become familiar—*preference because of familiarity*.

From Zahorick's analysis we can conclude that thiamin detection differs from salt detection. While we are conscious of salt on our tongue, the taste of thiamin is not recognized in food. Thiamin is "recognized" over the long term by sickness (deficiency) and recovery states. Illness or well-being is attributed to flavored foods that alternatively lack and contain the needed substance, respectively.

Hedonic Conditioning.   What an interesting push-pull system! The possibility is raised that many dozens of nutrients are "unconsciously" regulated by an associative mechanism. Flavors of foods (of which we are conscious) are associated with repletion of nutrients (of which we are unaware). Booth (1982) has called this regulation of nutrient selection by the association of flavored foods with their post-ingestional consequences **hedonic conditioning** (cf. hedonism). In his schema, following every meal flavors of foods consumed during that meal are hedonically adjusted according to their nutritional effects. If the consequences are positive (reinforcing), we increase our preference for the items most recently eaten. If the consequences are negative (i.e., punishing, such as when deficiency states are induced), we are less likely to continue eating those particular flavored foods.

Recall that a child's feeding jags (Davis, 1939) are followed by abrupt switches to new foods. Such switches may reflect the formation of conditioned aversions to a *familiar-deficient* diet. In the case history described in Box 10.2, at age two Jane B. abruptly rejected eggs at breakfast. This may have reflected a shift to other foods to meet nutritional needs. Alternatively, it may be that simple hedonic conditioning can account for the switch. Illness caused by *salmonella* in eggs (undetected by parents) might have caused her to reject them on the subsequent occasions that they were offered.

Conditioned Flavor Preferences. Are changes in preference for flavored foods and beverages restricted to recovery from a thiamin-deficiency state? No. The phenomenon is quite general. Any flavor that is paired with recovery from illness becomes more preferred than normal, a phenomenon called the *medicine effect* (Green & Garcia, 1971; Barker & Weaver, 1991) In one experiment (Barker & Weaver, 1991, Experiment 4), during pretreatment one group of rats drank coffee once per day for fifteen days (Group Familiar), while another did the same on fifteen occasions while recovering from a lithium-induced illness (Group Medicine). A control group drank water on these fifteen days. All were then allowed to drink coffee (the CS) and were poisoned with lithium (the US). Figure 10.1 clearly shows the medicine effect; control rats formed a long-lasting aversion, the familiar group showed a typical latent

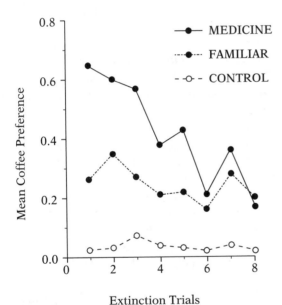

FIGURE 10.1 The Medicine Effect

Eight extinction trials reveal that the preference for coffee following a single coffee-lithium conditioning trial varies as a function of their prior history with coffee; good aversion in a control group that had never before tasted coffee; intermediate aversion in a group that had 15 previous coffee-drinking periods (familiar), and poor aversion (hence preference) in a group that drank coffee on 15 previous occasions while recovering from illness (medicine). (Figure 5, Barker & Weaver, 1991.)

inhibition effect, and the medicine group clearly preferred the coffee even after having an aversion conditioned to it.

Increased preference for flavors has also been associated with *protein replacement* (Baker, Booth, Duggan, & Gibson, 1987), *calories* (Bolles, Hayward, & Crandall, 1981; Mehiel & Bolles, 1984; Capaldi, Campbell, Sheffer, & Bradford, 1987); with *ethanol (beer, spirits, etc.)* (Sherman, Hickis, Rice, Rusiniak, & Garcia, 1983; Deems, Oetting, Sherman, & Garcia, 1986); and with a *repletion of calories following food deprivation* (Capaldi & Myers, 1982; Campbell, Capaldi, & Myers, 1987). Excellent evidence exists, then, to support Booth's notion of *hedonic conditioning*. The reader is referred to Capaldi & Powley (1990) for an overview.

Interim Summary

1. Eating and drinking behaviors are best understood as an interplay of genes and environment, of physiology and behavior.

2. In addition to taste and olfactory receptors that allow the location of foodstuffs in the environment, homeostatic mechanisms have evolved to regulate essential nutrients.

3. Food selection and food preparation processes have evolutionary consequences. This schema is called **biocultural evolution.** Feeding behaviors that are adaptive are selected for because they enhance fitness.

4. What humans learn about foods during their lifetime and transmit to their offspring complements (a) basic taste and smell receptors and (b) innate homeostatic regulatory processes.

5. Salt and water are examples of **specific hungers.** Both peripheral receptors and homeostatic mechanisms have evolved to recognize and regulate these critically essential nutrients.

6. Human are omnivores. The **omnivore's paradox** is that their relatively more open feeding system allows them a diverse range of potential foods, but increases the risks of ingesting toxins.

7. Children often display profound food preferences, food neophobias and prolonged *feeding jags*. They also manage to self-select foods without adverse consequences.

8. General associative mechanisms complement innately organized eating and drinking behavior. Essential nutrients such as thiamin seem to be regulated by learning which flavors produce post-ingestional deficiency or recovery states.

9. The punishing and reinforcing properties of foods experienced post-ingestionally is called **hedonic conditioning.** Such conditioning appears to complement innate flavor preferences in determining food selections.

10. The *medicine effect* is a demonstration that flavors that are experienced while recovering from illness become preferred.

DISCUSSION QUESTIONS

1. Examining your own eating habits, how many of the following ideas can you apply? Biocultural evolution? Specific hungers? Omnivore's paradox? Food neophobia? Feeding jags? Conditioned food aversions? Conditioned food preferences? Hedonic conditioning?

2. Can you relate Katz's (1975) idea of biocultural evolution (corn treated with alkali is an example) to hedonic conditioning?

3. Why should you *not* make your child drink milk (or make them eat anything that they disfavor)? Why might you want to restrict candy? What about salt?

4. Do you agree with the statement that how a food tastes and smells, and *not* a caretakers' or dietitions' admonitions, guides the food and beverage choices of the average person? Why or why not?

5. How might a history of eating chicken soup while recovering from the flu bestow "real" medicinal powers on the soup?

6. *Dorland's Illustrated Medical Dictionary, 25th Edition* (1974; W. B. Saunders Press) defines *pica* as "... a craving for unnatural articles of food; a depraved appetite, as seen in hysteria, pregnancy, and in malnourished children." Can you come up with any reasons for changes in appetite in these three categories of "abnormality?"

LEARNING ABOUT SEX AND LOVE

> ... *abortion, abstinence, adolescent sexuality, aging and sex, anatomy and physiology of sex, animal sexuality, aphrodisiacs, art and dance, attitudes towards sex, autoerotism* ...
>
> (from the Table of Contents,
> *The Encyclopedia of Sexual Behavior*,
> Ellis & Abarbanel, Editors, 1961)

We've seen that both genes and cultures determine our relationship with foods. What is missing in the foregoing analysis is how food is interrelated with other aspects of our lives. Much of the world's political maneuvering, diplomacy and business is conducted in the context of "power breakfasts/lunches/formal dinners." In addition, the phrases "let's do lunch" or "wanna get a cup of coffee?" often play a role in human courtship patterns. Which brings us to sex.

Reason Versus Emotion in Love and Sex?

In their book, *Darwin's Dangerous Idea,* Sagan & Druyan (1992) challenged us to entertain the possibility that a great deal of complex human behavior was biologically predisposed. Emotions rule behavior, they proposed, and "thinking has very little to do with" various aspects of sex and love—such as sexual attraction, falling in love, jealousy, maternal love, and so forth.

Is there anything new in their assertions? We have already discussed issues of biologically predisposed, or instinctive-like human behavior. Without exception, all such behaviors have been shown to be highly sensitive to environmental effects. Can we not also anticipate that expressions of human love and sexual behavior will also be highly determined by the environment in which such behaviors are expressed?

Another assertion of Sagan & Druyan (1992) is that "emotional behavior" is a distinctively different category from "thinking." Certainly different areas of brain and nervous system are involved in Watson's "fear, rage, and sex" relative to specific language areas on the surface of the left temporal lobe of the cerebral cortex. But the convenience of a dichotomous distinction between "emotion" and "reason" belies the integrity of adaptive behavior.

Seldom are we dispassionate in our rationality, and seldom are our emotional behaviors devoid of plans and goals.

Love (Sex) and Love (Taking Care of Others)

Issues of love and sexual behavior cover a lot of ground. To select but a few topics in these realms runs the risk of trivializing themes of central importance in life. Indeed, the argument has repeatedly been made that an organism's behavior can best be understood in terms of *fitness* and *inclusive fitness*: That is, how does behavior contribute to survival and reproduction (fitness) and caretaking of offspring that leads to *their* reproduction (inclusive fitness)?

For humans, issues of love and sex are essential in courting, mating, and care of offspring. There are no more important issues. Where to begin? The table of contents—cited at the beginning of this section—of over 100 chapters in an encyclopedia of sexual behavior (Ellis & Abarbanel, 1961) include only those sexual issues beginning with the letter "A"! The present strategy is to take two behaviors, sexual attraction and maternal love, that Sagan & Druyan (1992) asserted to be "biologically predisposed." Biologically predisposed these behaviors may be, but how does environment shape sexual attraction and maternal love? Both are examples of behavior involving emotion, and both have been investigated in the laboratory. Let us begin by looking at Harry Harlow's interesting research on the development of "maternal love" in rhesus monkeys.

Maternal Love

In a famous series of studies, the Harlows investigated the role of mother-infant feeding in pair bonding (Harlow & Harlow, 1962a; 1962b). In doing so they later found that they had inadvertently studied the effects of isolating infant rhesus monkeys from their mothers. The infant monkeys in question were given surrogate mothers. One was a monkey-shaped wire frame to which a nursing bottle was attached. Next to it was a terry-cloth covered wire frame that didn't contain a bottle. The Harlows measured which of the two surrogates the infants spent the most time with. Not surprisingly, the young monkeys nursed from the wire frame and then clung for hours to the "terry cloth monkey mother." The Harlows speculated that primates had a biological need for "contact comfort" that was *not* met by the life-sustaining but uncomfortable "wire monkey mother."

Effects of Isolation. When these motherless monkeys became adults, the Harlows discovered rather profound differences had occurred because of these deficiencies of early socialization. Neither the males nor females knew how to appropriately court the opposite sex nor how to engage in copulation. Following artificial insemination, a number of the females successfully delivered infant monkeys. But they proved to be ineffective mothers. These surrogate-raised mothers were neither protective of their young, nor effective in nursing them. Some were totally neglectful and physically abusive. Conclusion? Early social isolation can have severe consequences. Primates, undoubtedly including humans, must have supportive environments in which various aspects of sexual and maternal behaviors are learned.

For convenience as well as for control over extraneous variables that might influence experimental outcomes, laboratory animals (mammals) are typically housed in single cages. Social isolation has identifiable effects. Raising young rats in isolation, for example, has been found to influence brain development: Group-housed rats have more cortical development (Bennett, Diamond, Drech, & Rosenzweig, 1964) and more synapses per neuron (Turner & Greenough, 1983). There are concomitant changes in behavior in isolated animals as well, as the Harlows and others have discovered. Harlow and colleagues also found a simple preventative to counteract the pronounced social effects of isolation.

Effects of Social Play. We might suspect that the rhesus monkeys that had surrogate mothers were ineffective because they had not modeled the appropriate behaviors from their real mothers. For example, one might argue that to become an effective nurser, one must first have had the experience of being nursed. The answer is even simpler, but one that raises yet more questions. What Harlow and his collaborators eventually found was that the effects of being raised with a surrogate mother could be mitigated if the isolated infant monkey could play with same age peers for as little as an hour a day (Harlow, 1969). This finding suggests that total isolation per se, and not the specific experience of being mothered, was critical to the development of maladaptive maternal behavior.

Perhaps the recuperative effects of this minimal social contact can be better understood by imagining what a roomful of infant monkeys at play looks and sounds and smells like. Sensory and motor systems, limbic and affective systems, forebrain, midbrain, hindbrain, and spinal cord—all get a workout. As is the case with other primates, monkey play by both sexes involves wrestling, chasing, and aggressive play (Harlow, 1963). Early social interactions influence brain development and adult social behavior in adaptive ways. Likewise, early and profound social isolation is implicated in both maladaptively developed brains and behavior.

Species-specific Factors in Sexual Behavior

Most humans are preoccupied with love and sex. Americans spend billions of dollars yearly, for example—more than is spent on k-12 education—on perfumes, deodorants, and other smell-enhancing attractants. Pick up a newspaper, or a weekly newsmagazine, or novels, movies, or TV shows, and you will likely find a number of the topics relating to sexual behaviors. That these areas of sexual behavior exist in all cultures speaks to their biological predisposition. Before looking at the role of learning in sexual behavior, let's first consider its biological underpinnings.

Male and Female Roles in Reproduction and Parenting.   Sociobiologist Robert Trivers has addressed the issue of biological factors that influence sexual mating patterns (Trivers, 1985). He has proposed that males and females have different stakes in mate selection and in reproduction. Specifically, females invest more time and energy than males in gestation and in maternal care after birth. Because they play less of a role in the care of offspring, males have more free time to seek access to additional females, thereby getting more of their genes into the next generation.

Biological Predispositions of Attraction and Attractiveness.   Physical appearance affects social relationships, including interactions with lovers/significant others. Throughout a lifetime, a physically attractive person has better social relationships than one not as attractive. For example, teachers tend to think that physically attractive boys and girls are smarter and are less likely to be troublemakers. Attractive children are more sought after as friends than are their less attractive peers in the classroom and on the playground. At job interviews, attractive people get the nod over those judged to be less so (Hatfield & Spretcher, 1986).

A review of research concerning the "attractiveness sterotype" found that attractive people are even judged to be happier and more successful than others (Eagly, Ashmore, Makhijani, & Kennedy, 1991). Physical features of the opposite sex contribute to the courtship "dance" that leads to the perpetuation of each species through sexual reproduction. A number of studies have demonstrated that irrespective of age, sex, or skin color, human infants look at attractive faces longer than they do less-attractive ones (Langlois, Ritter, Roggman, & Vaughn, 1991). An infant that prefers to look at attractive faces suggests that it is born with a biased visual system—one that exhibits innate preferences for beauty similar to the infants innate preferences for sweet tastes, warm fluids, and contact comfort.

What Men Find Attractive in Women. Evidence from adolescents and adults also supports the idea that attractiveness might have a biological basis (Cunningham, Druen, & Barbee, 1997; Farrell, 1986). For example, cross-culturally, males prefer females who are younger and who are physically attractive (Buss, 1996, Buss & Schmidt, 1993, Cunningham, 1986). Evolutionary psychologist David Buss and others have speculated that attractiveness (and youth) are predictors of good health. The adaptive-evolutionary logic of Buss and others is that males are both consciously and unconsciously sexually attracted to physically attractive women because mating with a healthy woman will produce more viable offspring than mating with an unhealthy woman. Devandra Singh and colleagues at the University of Texas at Austin have proposed that there is an ideal female body figure to which men are attracted—one with a low waist-to-hip ratio (Singh, 1993; Singh & Luis, 1995; Singh & Young, 1995). (Singh proposes that the optimal waist-to-hip ratio of a woman that men prefer is 5:9.) Why should this be so? Singh agrees with Buss that such ratios predict youth and health, both of which are optimal for high fertility and child bearing.

What Women Find Attractive in Men. Applying this same logic, should females be equally attracted to young, handsome males with optimal shoulder-to-waist ratios? The plot thickens. A male's physical looks are less important to a female than a female's are to a male. Buss reports that cross-culturally, women seek attributes in males that are geared more to promoting the survival and well-being of her offspring. These qualities include social status, financial resources, ambition, and someone who is not afraid of hard work (Buss, 1996). For both males and females, sexual interest is influenced by a host of factors unrelated to physical attractiveness, including personality, values, and affection (Symons, 1979).

Learning Individual Differences in Sexual Behavior

> *. . . beauty, chastity, contraception, coitus, courtship, divorce, extramarital sex, families, femininity, fertility, fetishism, homosexuality, impotence, love, marriage, music and sex, nudism, orgasm, perversions, pornography, premarital sex, prostitution, sexual love, transvestism . . .*
>
> (from the Table of Contents,
> *The Encyclopedia of Sexual Behavior,*
> Ellis & Abarbanel, Editors, 1961)

The wide-ranging scope of sexual topics speaks to a plasticity of sexual behavior. Consider that attitudes towards abortion, contraception and premarital sex, and what is and is not sexually perverse, varies from individual to individual within a culture as well as among cultures. Learning has played a large role in the development of your particular outlook on these issues. There is no reason to expect that you have learned these attitudes and behaviors about sex and love any differently than you have learned other behaviors. Reinforcers and punishers control their very expression.

Within a lifetime, you may learn that too much of the wrong perfume is not sexually attractive (is not reinforced). Some hairstyles are better for you (more reinforcing to other people) than others. You may learn that same sexual practices that were reinforced during your unmarried teen years may be punished following marriage. Next we look at an animal model that demonstrates how sexual attraction can be conditioned.

Conditioning Sexual Attraction

Even animals that we might suspect lead simpler, more reflexive sex lives exhibit unusual plasticity of behavior. Michael Domjan and his colleagues have looked at the role conditioning plays in various aspects of the sexual behavior of the Japanese quail. Domjan's animal model is highly suggestive of the subtle ways in which sexual advances can be conditioned in other animals. For example, male quail make indiscriminate sexual approaches to quail of either sex. They apparently learn to prefer female quail (S^+) after successful copulation and to not prefer males (S^-) because of unsuccessful attempts at copulation (Nash & Domjan, 1991). Successful copulation with a female quail then becomes associated with their distinctively colored feathers: subsequently, males spend more time with a model (a stuffed bird) bearing them (Domjan, 1992).

Among the most interesting of Domjan's studies is his animal model of sexual fetishes. If, in the foregoing studies, artificially colored feathers are associated with successful copulation, male quail preferentially select models with artificially colored feathers over naturally colored female feathers (Domjan, O'vary, & Green, 1988). Their analysis is that non-sexual stimuli may become sexually attractive by their association with sexually reinforcing experiences—which may explain why black leather, for example, can become a turn-on. In recognizing the complexities of quail sexuality—its genetic determinants expressed in the many different environments a quail may encounter—Domjan (1994) cautions against too simplistic Pavlovian conditioning accounts.

Interim Summary

1. Sexual behaviors are best understood as comprising the interplay of genes and environment, and of the interplay of physiology, environment, and behavior.

2. Love and sex are of utmost importance to humans because they bear so directly on each individual's fitness and inclusive fitness.

3. Harlow's research with rhesus monkeys demonstrated that courting, mating, and maternal caretaking behaviors could be severely disrupted

by isolation. Minimal social interactions with same-age peers during early development prevented the sexual deficiencies found in Harlow's early surrogate mother studies.

4. Species-specific factors in humans include genetic predispositions that (a) help determine the physical attractiveness of another; (b) influence different mating strategies in females and males; and (c) influence a male's perception of a female's waist and hips.

5. The variability found within individuals during their lifetime, within a given culture, and cross-culturally attests to the plasticity of many aspects of human sexual behavior.

6. Domjan's animal model of sexual behavior using quail demonstrates that simple conditioning processes, including discrimination learning, provide an account for gender preferences. In addition, visual stimulus characteristics become preferred as a result of sexual reinforcement.

DISCUSSION QUESTIONS

7. Do you agree with the ideas of evolutionary psychologists that some seemingly universal characteristics of a person's attractiveness are predictors of health and fertility? When attractiveness is thought about in this way, is it like the sign-releasing stimulus of an ethologist?

8. Can you come up with some aspects of lovemaking that seem to reflect more of a learning history (or lack of one!) than other aspects of lovemaking?

9. If you like the smell of leather, is it a learned preference, an innately-predisposed preference, or both? Why do you think that black leather is a turn-on for some individuals?

ROLE OF CONDITIONING IN BEHAVIORAL DISORDERS AND IN BEHAVIORAL THERAPY

In earlier chapters, we reviewed evidence attesting to the power of the associative conditioning of immune system responses. We also saw that both the perception of pain and a drug's effectiveness could be markedly influenced by learning experiences. In addition, the open feeding systems of omnivores allow not only ingestional errors such as poisoning and nutritional deficiency, but also the possibility of eating disorders in the form of clinical obesity, anorexia nervosa, and bulimia. Clinical obesity, anorexia nervosa, and bulimia are but three examples of disorders whose etiology and treatment fall within the purview of *behavioral medicine.* At present there exist an abundance of animal models of behavior dysfunction that have the potential to add an important research component to our health-care system (Overmier, 1999).

Pavlov's discovery of a link between a dog's personal experience and its mental health, as seen in his powerful demonstration of experimental neurosis, is an example of the role of conditioning in behavioral medicine. In this section, we will review other conditioning examples that have implications for health, and then turn to treatment strategies based on reinforcement, punishment, extinction, and so forth.

Conditioning Emotional Responses in Humans

Gregory Razran (1971) has pointed out that the most widely used method of investigating associative processes in America, is, sadly, the conditioning of fear responses. Recall in conditioned suppression that when a tone or light (CS) is repeatedly paired with electric shock (US), the neutral stimulus takes on shock-like properties. Rats, dogs, and humans respond fearfully in the presence of the formerly neutral stimulus.

What is the evidence that humans learn to be anxious and fearful, and that phobias and anxiety are conditioned fear responses? Alternatively, perhaps these conditions are innately predisposed behavioral patterns. One line of evidence supporting the role of learning is that both phobias and anxiety are highly idiosyncratic among individuals, and classical conditioning continues to be the best way to account for their origins (Davey, 1992). Let us look at a historical example of conditioned fear.

Watson and "Little Albert."   John B. Watson asserted that human behavior could be controlled by reinforcing and punishing stimuli. His infamous experiments on "Little Albert" bear directly on questions of emotional health and well-being, the etiology of phobias, and related issues in behavioral medicine. Watson assumed that fear, rage, and love were three basic emotions innately shared by all humans. He further proposed that all other emotions (and all emotional behavior) are based on these three. Watson and Rayner (1920) conditioned a fear response in an 11-month-old child named Albert. Watson's point was to demonstrate that innate fears could be arbitrarily attached to any neutral stimulus, the result being a maladaptive phobic response. On numerous occasions in his laboratory, Watson showed Albert a white rat (CS) and paired it with a very loud clanging noise (US). Albert soon responded in the presence of the white rat in the same way he responded to the loud noise; he startled, cried, and initiated escape responses.

Given the wealth of findings from general process learning, it should come as no surprise that Watson's "attachment" of fear responses through conditioning was found to *generalize* to other furry objects presented Albert. These included an inanimate fur coat and a Santa Claus mask. Indeed, the whole gamut of related associative phenomena might have been used to analyze the extent of Albert's emotional conditioning. Perhaps fortunately, Albert was removed from Watson's and Rayner's care before treatment of this phobia could be initiated. These researchers were prepared to present the fear-inducing white rat and stimulate Albert's genitals at the same time so as to attach pleasurable feelings to the rat.

Post-Traumatic Stress Disorder (PTSD)

Ample evidence attests to the positive health outcomes that result from many of life's experiences. In a very real sense, the status of our health "when things go right" provides the control condition by which to gauge compromised health. Often ill health is the result of bad things happening to people. For example, the health we enjoy because of the foods we normally eat may only become appreciated during times of malaise caused by famine or poisoning. Pain makes us appreciate its absence. Likewise, the role that catastrophe, trauma, and Thorndike's annoyers (i.e., loud clangs, mild electric shock, and gastrointestinal distress) play in our health gets our attention precisely because so often the behavioral consequences of these events are unusually unpleasant and long lasting

PTSD (post-traumatic stress disorder) sometimes results in individuals who experience intense aversive stimuli. The human response to overwhelming events that occur during war, and as a result of rape, child abuse, and natural disasters (fires, hurricanes, etc.) is often severe and unique enough to be categorized as a disorder in the DSM-IV (*Diagnostic and Statistical Manual of Mental Disorders, Fourth Edition, American Psychiatric Association*).

The incidence of PTSD in the general population is estimated to be as high as 9.2% (Breslau, Davis, Andreski, & Peterson, 1991) compared to estimates of drug abuse (5.9%) and depression (8.3%) (Solomon, Gerrity, & Muff, 1992). PTSD is not the inevitable result of trauma. Some humans suffer similar trauma and return to high levels of functioning within months. Why, after the passage of many years, do some otherwise talented, intelligent individuals continue to suffer debilitating nightmares, to continue to reexperience the trauma of war or rape via memories and flashbacks?

Some forms of PTSD are considered to be associative; i.e., a special type of conditioned emotional response (Kolb, 1984). The distinctive sounds of a helicopter, for example, may elicit intense conditioned fear responses in Vietnam vets. However, the "conditioned response" may be of such intensity that the person reports reliving, or reexperiencing the original event. No other examples of conditioned responses having this characteristic come to mind. It is an extreme, almost literal instance of Pavlov's theory of *sign-substitution*—when the CS "becomes" the US.

Other features of the disorder (explosive outbursts, atypical dreams, hyper-irritability and startle reflex) seem to be better described in terms of *sensitization*. One prominent researcher (van der Kolk, 1987) invokes Pavlov's notion of an innate reflexive response, or defensive reaction, to environmental threat. Recognizing that flashbacks, nightmares, and intrusive recollections cannot be studied in animals, other researchers have pointed out that both biological and behavioral processes that appear relevant to these problems have been successfully modeled in nonhumans. Both passive avoidance and dissociative symptoms (called numbing in humans) occur in all animals in response to intense stress (Foa, Zinbarg, & Rothbaum, 1992). While reflexes typically are adaptive and promote fitness by contrast, the PTSD response pattern would appear to be maladaptive. The interested reader is referred to van der Kolk (1987) for an in-depth analysis of this fascinating disorder.

PTSD and Learned Helplessness Compared

Is learned helplessness like PTSD? Recall that following learned helplessness treatment, the dogs were described as immobile. In the presence of shock, though unrestrained, they whined and defecated but did not try to escape the shock by moving away. This *reduction* in responsiveness is opposite to some PTSD behavior just described. PTSD patients are characterized by explosive outbursts, hyper-irritability, and startling reflex. For other PTSD patients, however, learned helplessness *is* characteristic of their problem. A victim's response to rape, for example, is sometimes characterized by immobility, passivity, helplessness, and dissociative memory (Burgess & Holstrom, 1979). Why the responses to intense aversive stimuli are so unpredictable is unknown, but some rat models now address this issue (Overmier, Murison, & Johnson, 1997).

Learned Helplessness in Humans.   The learned helplessness research with dogs and rats has been applied to humans (Seligman, 1975). In his earliest formulation, Seligman identified three consequences of learned helpless training in humans; namely, *motivational, cognitive,* and *emotional* deficits. The motivational deficit is characterized by performance changes not unlike that seen in dogs. Whereas dogs will not bother to get off the grid floor to avoid electric shock, a human might not get out of bed for several days. Along with this reduction in a human's behavioral response is his or her *cognitive* interpretation that "responding is futile." Finally, *emotional* distress accompanies both the performance decrements and cognitive ideation. People who perceive themselves as helpless and depressed simply feel bad.

Critics of Seligman's (1975) theory pointed out that not all people who are subjected to uncontrollable events suffer these three deficits (Buchwald, Coyne, & Cole, 1978), and that some research better supports a model of learned irrelevance rather than learned helplessness (Linden, Savage, & Overmier, 1997). For example, some individuals continue to live relatively normal lives even after having found out that they have a terminal illness with only months to live. Nevertheless, learned helplessness theory does fit the response patterns of many individuals, and continues to receive serious attention in psychophysiological theories of stress and other psychosomatic disorders.

For example, withdrawal and concomitant depression is a common response seen in college students who fail the first test, study hard for the second one, and then fail it. In this example, which response(s) are withdrawn in the face of what "uncontrollable events"? (Studying and class attendance, because neither response seems to affect the grades earned on tests.)

Eating Disorders: Anorexia nervosa, Bulimia, and Obesity

Earlier in this chapter evidence was offered supporting two views of human ingestional behavior—that it is both innately organized *and* culturally determined (i.e., learned). The prevalence of eating disorders in our culture is hard evidence for ingestional *plasticity*. Some individuals learn to override the multiple and redundant homeostatic mechanisms that are designed to preclude disorders such as anorexia nervosa and bulimia.

Failure of Primary Reinforcers and Punishers. Because the topic is of high interest, most readers are aware of the prevalence of eating disorders in our culture. The etiology of *anorexia nervosa* and *bulimia* is unknown. Because of a paucity of animal models for these disorders, they will likely remain a mystery for some time. That these disorders are due to maladaptive learned behavior is assumed (Hsu, 1990). However, the sequence of conditioning experiences underlying this learning has never been described. *Secondary reinforcers* seem to maintain both anorexia nervosa and bulimia. Primary reinforcers (i.e., alleviating hunger in anorexia nervosa) and normally punishing stimuli (vomiting in bulimia) no longer function to reinforce and punish behavior, respectively. Another way of saying this is that the normal mechanisms that maintain homeostasis are out of whack. Why a failure of the normal mechanisms? One reason is that the maladaptively learned (mis)perception of thinness serves to act as a reinforcing stimulus that maintains the maladaptive eating behaviors.

Pain as Reinforcement. Under the slogan "no pain, no gain" athletes use the response-produced stimuli of exertion and pain to motivate yet greater pain-producing exertion. Such behavior is not considered maladaptive, unless it so totally dominates all aspects of life that personal and social obligations are not met. Rather, the more bench press repetitions, or miles run, the greater the pleasure of attaining personal goals.

The intense motivation of the anorexic to stay thin appears to be achieved in a similar manner. By *not* responding to the hunger pains (which are normally unpleasant, and simply alleviated), achieving the goal of thinness becomes highly reinforcing. The trick of the masochist is to perceive normally painful stimuli—from a broad spectrum of life—as pleasurable. Then the *law of effect* continues to work as predicted. Though maladaptive, anorexia nervosa and bulimia should not be considered exceptions to the law of effect. Rather, hunger and pain become discriminative stimuli to *not* eat. Furthermore, the ingestion of tasty food sets the occasion for vomiting in the bulimic, and serves as highly effective punishment for the anorexic.

Obesity.   Merely overweight, or obese? Obesity has been defined as being 40% or more above the ideal weight as determined by Metropolitan (standard) weight charts (Bray, 1976). Although classified as an eating disorder, and typically included in the same discussions with anorexia nervosa and bulimia, obesity is both more familiar and better understood than the "thin" disorders. One difference is that being overweight isn't nearly as life-threatening as anorexia nervosa. At 20% above average weight, only very slight increases in morbidity and mortality exist. At 40% above average, however, overweight men are two and a half times more likely to die from all causes (Van Itallie, 1979).

Food as Reinforcer.   Clearly the role of learning in creating obesity is different from the other two eating disorders in that tasty foods *reinforce* the behavior of eating tasty foods. As predicted, reinforcement increases the frequency of the preceding behavior. A simple view of obesity, then, is one in which normal homeostatic control mechanisms are overridden by the reinforcing power of tasty foods. Animal models support this theory. Rats allowed a frequently changing diet of bananas, chocolate, chocolate chip cookies, cheese, fat, marshmallows, peanut butter, sweetened condensed milk, and salami gained 269% more weight than controls eating lab chow (Sclafani & Springer, 1976). Not surprisingly, sugar and fat mixed together produced greater weight gains than diets of sugar, or fat, or lab chow alone (Lucas & Sclafani, 1990). Now, if you just add chocolate . . .

The animal model described above does not begin to account for the individual differences observed among humans. There is some evidence (Jirik-Babb & Katz, 1988) that bulimics and anorexics are *less* sensitive to tastes (and, arguably, are less reinforced for eating tasty food) while flavors are *more* reinforcing for the obese (Schiffman, 1983). An implication of these findings is that these disorders are presumably under more complex stimulus control than merely the taste of foods. Both self-perception and learned social roles are precipitating conditions, and changing maladaptive cognitive and emotional variables are common therapeutic goals in dealing with these disorders.

Behavioral Therapy

Behavioral therapy (and cognitive behavior therapy) is one of the most successful of the various psychotherapies used to effect changes in maladaptive cognitive and emotional behaviors. A **behavioral therapy** is any psychotherapeutic procedure involving the systematic application of reinforcers or punishers, or the implementation of extinction or other classical or operant procedure, known to be effective in effecting behavioral change. The fact that many techniques now used in behavioral therapy were developed using Pavlovian conditioning models is reflected in their earliest descriptions— *conditioned reflex therapy* (Salter, 1949) and the *conditioning therapies* (Wolpe, Salter, & Reyna, 1964). Likewise, one of the more important methodologies used in therapy, *behavior modification,* is a direct application of Skinner's operant conditioning. **Behavior modification** is the systematic application of reinforcers and punishers, and other classical and operant conditioning procedures, to change target behaviors (Allyon & Azrin 1968).

Diverse Applications of Behavioral Therapy. The treatment of phobias and other psychophysiological disorders involving the ANS using behavior modification techniques is highly effective. Outcome studies generally indicate the long-term remediation of symptoms, with little recidivism. That behavioral therapies can be as effective as invasive biomedical therapies (such as drugs and surgery) has been demonstrated for low back pain (Heinrich, Cohen, Naliboff, Collins, & Bonebakker, 1985; Fordyce, Brockway, Bergman, & Spengler, 1986). Figure 10.2 shows a person who exhibits different pain be-

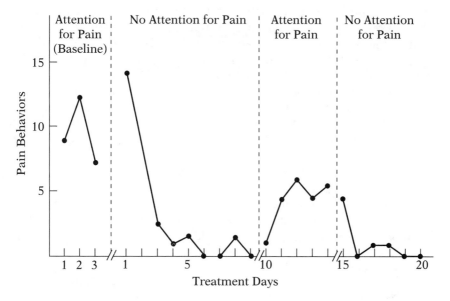

FIGURE 10.2 Paying Attention to Pain: NOT!

A 47-year-old man complains less about chronic lower back pain and moves about more freely and independently if a professional staff ignores his complaints than if they pay attention to him. (Adapted from Fordyce, 1976, p. 89.)

haviors depending on whether they are reinforced (by professional staff paying attention to the patients complaints) or are punished (by not paying attention). Behavioral therapy can also affect survival time in terminal cancer (Grossarth-Maticek & Eysenck, 1989); other aspects of pain management (Turk, Meichenbaum, & Genest, 1983); and enuresis (bed wetting) (Kimmel & Kimmel, 1970). Box 10.3 shows how behavioral therapy can be used as an alternative to biomedical therapy.

Therapy from a Behavioral Viewpoint

Suppose during his 30s Little Albert had presented himself to a psychotherapist for treatment because of an inordinate fear of animals—especially dogs—that interfered with his job as a letter carrier. During an interview with his patient, the therapist attempts to determine the boundaries of Albert's phobia. All animals? Furry animals? Large or small animals? Neither knowing nor especially caring about the reasons underlying the phobia, the behavioral therapist tries to *target* the specific behavior in question, and to get some idea of the extent of the *generalization gradient* around the target behavior.

Systematic Desensitization. Albert's therapist would probably have decided to employ a common behavioral technique called *systematic desensitization*. Systematic desensitization involves first extinguishing fear responses to stimuli far removed from the target. The target behavior is approached in small steps, allowing responses to extinguish at each step. For example, while in a relaxed state the therapist might ask Albert to visualize an elephant sleeping safely behind bars in a zoo. Assuming that Albert showed no fear responses (ANS activity—altered breathing, nausea, sweating) to this image, the therapist might direct Albert to visualize the animal awakening, beginning to move, getting to its feet, and so forth. A next step might be to ask Albert to visualize the cage bars being removed, or having him visually walk to another cage containing a furry animal such as a lion.

The fear responses evoked by these images are allowed to extinguish in the safety of the therapist's office. Assuming that the target response to be alleviated is *fear in the presence of dogs*, the therapist is little by little incorporating more of the distinguishing characteristics of dogs in situations that have caused the patient's past fear responses.

Say the word "dog." (Allow Extinction of Conditioned Fear Response—AECFR).

Imagine a dog barking. (AECFR)

See a stuffed toy dog. (AECFR)

Approach a stuffed toy dog. (AECFR)

Touch a stuffed toy dog. (AECFR)

See a live dog from a distance. (AECFR)

BOX 10.3   BLADDER CONTROL: BEHAVIOR MODIFICATION AS AN ALTERNATIVE TO SURGERY

What was merely an embarrassment to the 5-year-old was perceived as a major problem to mom. Every day, a half-dozen or more of Kris's wet underpants accumulated in the laundry, testimony to a weak external spinctor connecting the child's bladder with her urethra. Her incontinence occurred while running and playing, when excited at her dance competitions, and if she waited too long between voidings.

Surgical intervention is an option, but behavior modification is now recognized as a treatment of choice for this condition (Philips, Fenster, & Samson, 1988). Rather than subject a child to the dangers of general anesthesia and a surgical outcome with decidedly mixed results, Kris's parents initiated a "home" behavior modification program. Her behavioral treatment was both simple and noninvasive. In a busy household, the first two steps in her program were combined and accomplished at the same time; that is, determining how many times each day the 5-year-old urinated (determining her *baseline of bladder voiding*) and simultaneously increasing her sensitivity to the cues attendant with urination. The latter is especially difficult. Even adults suffering from *female urethral syndrome* report few pre-voiding sensations (Bernstein, Philips, Linden, & Fenster, 1992).

Kris was asked to make a mark on "her chart" by the toilet each time she urinated. If she discovered dry underpants, she was asked to place a gold stick-on star on her chart. If she discovered wet underpants, she merely changed herself, and put an "x" on the chart instead of the star. The dependent variables, then, were *frequency of micturition*, and *daily count of wet underpants*. At the end of each day she received a dime for each star, a reasonable reinforcer in the early 1970s.

What are the relevant components of this behavior modification program? Her *baseline*, or *operant level* of micturition was determined by the first day's count of stars and "x's." Discovering wet pants (a) increased her awareness of the target behavior, and

(continued)

BOX 10.3 BLADDER CONTROL: BEHAVIOR MODIFICATION AS AN ALTERNATIVE TO SURGERY (*continued*)

(b) helped focus her attention on subtle pre-voiding sensations. The above intervention consisted of several forms of *reinforced* and *punished* behaviors:

> *Primary reinforcers* (a) parental attention and interest; (b) the absence of parental concern and disappointment, a form of negative reinforcement; (c) the comfort of dry underpants.
>
> *Secondary reinforcers* (a) gold stars, dimes, and words of praise
>
> *Punishers* (a) discomfort of wet pants (b) loss of expected gold stars and dimes

What was the success of the above program? The short-term and long-term outcome was mixed. The frequency of "wet pants" went down rapidly within the first few days. Among the behaviors that had been reinforced was "spending more time on the toilet." In some small part, the decreased frequency of "wet pants" can be attributed to the fact that she wore them less and sat on the toilet more. Increasing her frequency of attempted bladder voidings was a desirable outcome for two reasons: It helped Kris focus on the attendant sensations preceding micturition, and frequent bladder emptying is healthier than prolonged urine retention. In addition, the 5-year-old's successes gave her a sense of personal control. As time passed, she was encouraged to regard occasional incontinence as "accidents." Her parents communicated to her that her self-worth would not be measured by absolute continence, and that more girls than boys had this problem because of different plumbing.

Kris's occasional incontinence persists into her early 30s. She is in good company in that an estimated 10% of all women (and many men) have similar problems, including many of those who choose a surgical alternative. Given the baseline degree of incontinence in this 5-year-old, behavioral therapy was effective in changing her behavior. The secondary gains of enhanced self-esteem and personal control has no counterpart in traditional biomedical approaches. (The interested reader is referred to Philips et al., 1988).

Approach a live dog. (AECFR)
Touch a live dog. (AECFR)
Walk the neighborhood. (AECFR).

Cognitive-Behavioral Therapy. Therapists who self-identify as cognitive-behavioral therapists combine behavioral techniques with traditional talk therapy. A patients who presents with an anxiety disorder is treated by combining specific behavioral interventions with attempts to restructure the way the patient thinks. Consider the treatment of panic. (A panic disorder is one of five types of anxiety disorders identified in the DSM-IV.) A panic attack is a period of intense fear, accompanied by dizziness, heart palpitations, and often a fear of dying or "going crazy."

Panic control treatment (PCT) has proven successful in alleviating panic attacks in 87% of clients (Barlow, Craske, Cerny, & Klosko, 1989). The therapy consists of "cognitive restructuring," exposure to breathing cues associated with panic attacks, and retraining how a person breaths. As part of the treatment, in order to experience what they would normally experience during a panic attack, a patient is trained to induce the disruption of their own breathing. The patient is reinforced by recovering normal breathing in the presence of the anxiety-provoking cues attendant with disrupted breathing.

Biofeedback.   **Biofeedback** refers to a procedure in which a patient (or experimental subject) is provided "feedback" regarding unconscious physiological processes. For example, even though *alpha waves* (8–13 Hz) are frequently produced by the human brain, we are not normally aware of this or any other pattern of brainwaves. Biofeedback equipment can be programmed to monitor a particular waveform, and to signal the subject by beeping when the waveform occurs. When a patients is then asked to "make it beep" by outputting alpha, she or he can do so "voluntarily." "Voluntarily" must be qualified because, when asked, patients typically report ". . . I don't know how I'm doing it." In and of itself, this demonstration indicates that conscious control can be exerted over involuntary processes. From a training perspective, the target brain-waveform can be considered an operant response and, via verbal instructions, the beeper a secondary reinforcer. (A therapist, for example, might say "good" when the patient is successfully producing alpha; the beeper is associated with "good.") That the reinforcement procedure is effective is evidenced by the increased frequency of outputting alpha waves.

In addition to changes in brain waves, muscle tension, skin temperature, blood pressure, heart rate, gastric motility, and skin conductance are other physiological responses that can be manipulated by biofeedback reinforcement procedures. These procedures are easily accomplished in the laboratory, but the usefulness of biofeedback as behavioral therapy is controversial. For example, comparison of biofeedback with relaxation training for headache pain (Blanchard, Andrasik, Ahles, Teders, and O'Keefe, 1980) and for control of blood pressure (Blanchard & Epstein, 1977) has led some researchers to question its practical clinical usefulness. Relaxation training appears to be equally effective, and doesn't require the expensive instrumentation used in biofeedback.

Analysis of Biofeedback Efficiency.   Given that biofeedback training is a form of operant conditioning, and that operant conditioning has proven to be a highly effective way to train instrumental responses, we might ask why biofeedback is not a more effective therapeutic procedure. In the first place, biofeedback uses a rather weak secondary reinforcer to effect permanent psychophysiological changes. Recall that in a biofeedback situation the reinforcement procedure of verbal praise ("good") follows the target psychophysiological response. Pavlov's *second signal system* describes how verbal praise (the word "good") attains its reinforcing value through second-order conditioning. The beeper sound is then paired with "good"; any reinforcing value of the beeper is attained by conditioning of the third-order. Indeed, outside of the biofeedback situation it is unlikely that the beeper would have any reinforcing value at all. Secondly, outside of a twice weekly, 1-h training session, the conditioned change in the target psychophysiological response is "in extinction." Since these target responses are for the most part not consciously experienced, there is no awareness of the response-outcome contingency. The conditioned response can therefore extinguish without the person realizing it. To summarize, it is highly likely that the therapeutic goals of biofeedback are not being realized because of less than optimal operant conditioning methods during acquisition, and due to simple extinction of the conditioned response.

Evaluating Behavioral Therapy.   How effective is behavioral therapy? We saw above that phobias and low back pain, to take two examples, can be successfully treated. Some problem behaviors are more resistant to therapeutic intervention than others, however. For example, programs to change drinking alcohol, smoking tobacco, and weight control behaviors have follow-up success rates of only 20 to 30% (Kaplan, 1984). Extrapolation of laboratory results using short-term behavior change in laboratory animals to lifelong habits of humans is problematic. Adult humans in therapy must overcome literally years of reinforced trials, and neither therapists nor patients should expect 1-h weekly sessions to reverse these lifetime habits. Such cautions, however, are tempered by the observation that both *behavior therapy* and *cognitive behavior therapy* are the most efficacious of the various types of psychotherapy. For example, for treating PTSD, better outcomes result from behavioral techniques than the use of drugs or other forms of therapy (Solomon et al., 1992).

Interim Summary

1. Pavlov and other animal learning psychologists have successfully investigated animal models of neurosis and behavioral dysfunction in laboratory settings.
2. Conditioning emotional responses such as fear and anxiety is easily accomplished in humans and other animals.
3. ***Post-traumatic stress disorder (PTSD)*** and learned helplessness occasionally result from intense aversive stimulation. These disorders can be analyzed from both associative and nonassociative perspectives using animal models.
4. Eating disorders such as anorexia nervosa, bulimia, and obesity are maladaptive but are explainable by the application of the law of effect. In

obesity, the reinforcing effects of palatable foods override homeostatic regulatory mechanisms. In the "thin" disorders, secondary reinforcing effects of "perceived image" override the primary reinforcers of palatable foods.

5. *Behavioral therapies* (or conditioning therapies) are effective, noninvasive methods used in *behavioral medicine*. In *behavior modification*, problem behaviors are identified and modified by the systematic application of reinforcers and punishers, by systematic desensitization, and by biofeedback.

DISCUSSION QUESTIONS

10. To "counter-condition" Little Albert, Watson and Rayner were prepared to present the fear-inducing white rat and to stimulate Albert's genitals at the same time. Can you predict a possible outcome? What would be a more reasonable treatment strategy?

11. Can you relate how a therapist's attempt to accomplish "cognitive restucturing" in a patient invariably involves Pavlov's second signal system?

12. Finding yourself in a biofeedback situation, you are faced with an hour of "making the beeper come on." At the end of the hour, you are informed that you kept the beeper on for a total of 5 minutes out of the 60 you were in the chair. The next session, the therapist reminds you of your previous performance and suggests you try to keep the beeper on for a few more minutes. Now imagine an alternative biofeedback session—one in which you accumulate points that can be traded in for money. (For the sake of the argument, let's say $10 for every minute you keep the beeper on.) Would you perform better the first session? The second and third session? Would you be more likely to output the target response outside of the biofeedback session given money, rather than a beeper sound during training? Before we write off biofeedback as a bad therapeutic procedure, wouldn't you like to see it tried under some conditions other than "keeping the beeper on"?

CHAPTER SUMMARY

1. Animal models of ingestional behavior, some aspects of sexual behavior, of emotional conditioning, learned helplessness and other behavioral dysfunctions provide insight into complex human behavior in these areas.

2. Ingestional behavior reflects evolutionary predispositions in the form of innate flavor receptors, systems of feeding such as carnivory and omnivory, and homeostatic regulatory mechanisms. The latter include innate recognition of certain foodstuffs like salt and water, called specific hungers, and specialized eating behaviors such as "feeding jags" and neophobia.

3. Ingestional behavior also has plastic components, including the conditioning of flavor aversions and flavor preferences. Thiamin and other essential nutrients can be identified in flavored foods by a conditioning process. Conditioning based on application of the law of effect, called hedonic conditioning, is a mechanism that regulates and readjusts food preferences based on each meal's post-ingestive consequences.

4. Both genetic tendencies and environment play crucial roles in the development of various aspects of sexual behavior. Visual stimuli associated with sexual reinforcement have been conditioned in laboratory animals.

5. Behavioral disorders including phobias and other conditioned fear responses are understood in terms of laboratory models initially developed by Pavlov ("experimental neurosis") and John B. Watson (who conditioned "Little Albert").

6. Learned helplessness and PTSD are serious disorders resulting from intense aversive experiences. Laboratory models of these disorders indicate that they are caused by both associative and non-associative components.

7. Disorders of eating behavior (anorexia nervosa, bulimia, and obesity) are also learned. The can be successfully analyzed by application of principles of reinforcement and punishment.

8. Behavioral therapies, including behavior modification, are designed to change behaviors using reinforcement, punishment, and extinction procedures.

9. Behavioral medicine employs a variety of animal-based methodologies as therapeutic alternatives to invasive procedures such as drugs and surgery.

KEY TERMS

behavior modification 357

behavioral therapy 356

biocultural evolution 336

biofeedback 361

hedonic conditioning 342

omnivore's paradox 338

post-traumatic stress disorder (PTSD) 353

specific hungers 338

CHAPTER 11

Conceptual Learning and Thinking

Inquiring human beings of our day have been taught that among the distinctions between humankind and animal life are, first, the ability to use language; second, the ability to make and use tools; third, a sense of consciousness about oneself; and fourth, the ability to transmit culture. Each of these distinctions, as is true of all icons scientific and scriptural, has crumpled and fallen to make dust and detritus. As human beings have come to invest in the study of animal life, they come to understand also that whatever may be thought to be unique and defining about human beings is also characteristic of other animals. The remaining candidates for distinction are metaphysical and spiritual, such as the idea that only human beings are conscious of death or that humankind, alone among animal life, desires to know. These icons may not be as solid as we think.
Candland, *Feral Children and Clever Animals* (1993, p. 3)

ANIMAL COGNITION: AN INTRODUCTION

We have studied common processes of learning in animals, and as a result have achieved a better understanding of human behavior. The organizing theme up to now has been to apply relatively simple models of association formation—both classical and instrumental conditioning—to better account for acquired behaviors in both humans and other animals. Insights attained through the application of conditioning, and through reinforcement and punishment, have enhanced our understanding of emotional behavior, behavioral control, skilled performance, eating and drug behaviors, and dysfunctional behavior and its correction through behavioral therapy.

Nevertheless, when applied to human behavior, this general process view was likely to have frustrated the reader. The reason is that most humans believe that there are qualitative differences between human behavior and the human mind, on the one hand, and animal behavior and animal minds on the other. Unless you are familiar with the evidence of communication, tool making, the transmission of culture, and other alleged behaviors of non-human animals alluded to in Candland's opening statement, you may remain skeptical.[1]

Cognitive Processes. In this and in the following chapter, we turn to the study of animal cognition: conceptual learning, memory, thinking, and language—so-called cognitive processes. Box 11.1 presents a brief history of cognitive psychology and its relationship with behavioral approaches to psychology. The term *animal cognition* typically is used only with reference to

---

[1]A biased sampling of recent contributions to these "big issue" questions include Barkow, Cosmides, and Tooby's (1992) *The Adapted Mind: Evolutionary Psychology and the Generation of Culture*; Candland's (1992) *Feral Children and Clever Animals*; Corballis's (1991) *The Lopsided Ape*; Degler's (1991) *In Search of Human Nature*; Dennett's (1995) *Darwin's Dangerous Idea*; Diamond's (1992) *The Third Chimpanzee*; and Griffin's (1992) *Animal Minds*.

BOX 11.1 A BRIEF HISTORY OF COGNITIVE SCIENCE

Introducing cognitive terms into a textbook on animal learning forces us to acknowledge the historical gap between animal learning and human cognition and memory. Recall that in formulating behaviorism, both John B. Watson and B. F. Skinner were reacting against "soft" conceptions of mind. Confident that the human mind could not be investigated scientifically, they opted for what has become known as experimental analyses of behavior. Rejecting mind properties that could not be operationally defined, they implicitly accepted the Darwinian notion of continuity among animals and adopted instead animal models of behavior. To this behavioral framework, both adaptive/evolutionary theory and the findings of contemporary neuroscience have been incorporated. This textbook is written from within such a perspective.

In the 1950s and 1960s, a different epistemology developed outside the behaviorist framework. Cognitive psychologists focused their study exclusively on humans and developed their own language and methodologies (see Gardner, 1985, for a history and review). During the past 50 years, a very interesting pattern has developed. Cognitive psychologists have conducted research and written books and published articles in journals that dealt with properties of mind that they considered to be exclusively human—memory, attention, language, problem solving, thinking, learning, and intelligence. During the same time period, comparative psychologists and other behavioral scientists conducted research, wrote books, and published articles in journals that dealt with nonhuman learning and behavior. With exceptions (Dennett, 1983; Griffin, 1985; Weiskrantz, 1988, provide examples), few theorists were attempting to bridge the conceptual gaps created by these different philosophical approaches, different research methods, and different terminology.

This issue has not been resolved at present, nor, it seems, will it be in the near future. But the conduct of science is a slow, very human endeavor, and scientists, their thinking constrained by empirical observations, are conservative. Some researchers are bridging the gap by using animals to study parallel problems in human cognition within a comparative cognition framework. (See Zentall & Smeets, 1996; Zental, 1997; Wasserman, 1997; Wasserman & Astley, 1994, for examples and representative thinking on this issue.) At the same time, however, staunch behaviorists continue to decry the cognitive psychologists' plethora of "mind" terms and hypothetical constructs devoid of empirical reference (Malone, 1982; Schlinger, 1993; Wright & Watkins, 1987). Lewontin (1981), for example, argues for "replacing the clockwork mind with something less silly. Updating the metaphor by changing clocks into computers has got us nowhere." Ironically, rapid advances in the study of the central nervous system by behavioral neuroscientists may shape the direction of both cognitivists and behaviorists, forcing all to pay more attention to each other.

non-human animals. But what if concept formation, thinking, language, and complex learning are species-specific behaviors of the adult form of *Homo sapiens*? If so, then animal models become irrelevant, and our study of thinking, language, and complex learning must begin anew. It may be that these are empirical questions. Fortunately, many researchers are interested in pushing the boundaries of comparative cognition, as evidenced by the formation of the *Comparative Cognition Society* in the 1990s.

In keeping with the zoomorphic theme developed earlier, here we'll keep alive the possibility that there may be common processes of "cognition" among humans and non-human animals as there were in other examples of learning and behavior. Therefore, as we examine research in concept formation and other forms of more complex learning, we will continue to extrapolate findings from non-human animals to humans. Let's begin by looking at a laboratory study of concept formation in a chimpanzee.

Concept Formation in Nonhuman Primates: An Example

Earlier we learned that monkeys and chimpanzees make key-pressing responses for food reinforcement. In one experiment (Koestler & Barker, 1965), a display of visual stimuli such as those seen in Table 11.1 were presented sequentially to a chimpanzee. (A picture of the chimpanzee working on the stimulus display panel can be seen in Box 8.2, panel b, on p. 291. The three backlit keys are located in the middle of the panel immediately below two other backlit keys.) Referring to Problem 1 in Table 11.1, a response to the *odd* stimulus—the triangle—was food reinforced. A response to either of the *same* shapes (i.e., either of the circles) displayed in Problem 1 was not reinforced.

All responses, reinforced or not, terminated the visual display for 10 sec. If the chimp responded correctly, on the second training trial (Problem 2 in Table 11.1), a new stimulus array was presented. Note that the formerly correct triangle is now incorrect even though it occupies the same position. The position of the odd stimulus has been altered (i.e., placed on the far right). On Problem 3 in Table 11.1, a new stimulus (square) is correct, and similar patterns repeat throughout the sequence of 18 problems. One way to think about this task is that the odd stimulus is a discriminative stimulus (S^+) and the two same stimuli are S^-s.

With extensive training involving hundreds of trials, eight chimpanzees were able to pick the odd stimulus from these 18 arrays with an average efficiency of 60 to 70% (33% = chance performance). The researchers concluded that the chimpanzees learned the **oddity concept** using these two-dimensional representational stimuli. (This conclusion is probably not warranted, because the chimpanzee's performance would be better than 60 to 70% if they consistently applied a rule of "odd" and/or had an understanding of "same.") Nevertheless, the example is instructive in showing that animals can be asked far more interesting questions than those asked in a standard Skinner box.

Table 11.1   Oddity Problems

The sequence of oddity problems used by Koestler and Barker (1965). Symbols were projected on backlit keys. Each display would terminate if the chimp hit any key or would timeout if the chimp failed to respond within 10 sec. Responding to the correct key was reinforced with a banana-flavored pellet. Correct responses advanced the display to the next problem; incorrect responses re-presented the display until the chimp got it right.

Problem no.	Symbol on display		
	1	2	3
1	○	△	○
2	△	△	○
3	○	○	□
4	△	○	○
5	△	○	△
6	□	□	△
7	○	□	□
8	△	□	□
9	△	△	□
10	□	○	□
11	□	△	△
12	○	□	○
13	○	○	△
14	○	△	△
15	△	□	△
16	□	○	○
17	□	△	□
18	□	□	○

Certainly you would agree that the oddity task requires more complex properties of mind than the task of depressing a lever?

Comparative Cognition

Were these chimpanzees thinking? What constitutes evidence that animals think? Again we can ask, does a human's use of language and other highly developed cognitive abilities require extension and further revision of the simple associative frameworks that we have studied? Some researchers, such as Noam Chomsky (1975) and Steven Pinker (1994), we'll see in the next chapter, think that human language makes us uniquely different from other animals. For Chomsky in particular, learning and simple associative frameworks are irrelevant to understanding the human mind. His analysis, however, begs the question of whether humans alone can form concepts, can think, and can be conscious.

The Question of Animal Consciousness.   The preceding questions are not easy ones, and not everyone agrees on what constitutes evidence bearing on answers to them. Some answers may surprise you. In Focus on Research 11.1, Larry Weiskrantz presents his own research and that of other respected neuroscientists who are of the opinion that even in the absence of language, some animals are every bit as conscious as humans. Their intent is not to make monkeys of us all but to inquire into the rudiments of our human nature.

One reason that we study non-human animals is because we have so little insight into human complexity. It is human nature to talk, and yet the process of acquiring speech and generating language remains an enigma. Possessing analytical skills that far exceed those of other animals, we are puzzled over how we do it and why they can't. Recognizing at the outset that no other animal has even the rudiments of what we humans call culture, nevertheless we shall seek clues to human uniqueness in the behavior of our smaller-brained animal cousins. Sara Shettleworth's (1998) book, *Cognition, Evolution, and Behavior* provides a readable, thoughtful entrée to questions regarding the evolution of mind.

Interim Summary

1. Both human and non-human animals engage in complex behaviors. Some of these complex behaviors are learned.
2. *Cognitive processes* include conceptual learning, memory, thinking, and language. To varying degrees these processes can be studied in non-human animals.

DO ANIMALS THINK?

Dr. Larry Weiskrantz, Department of Experimental Psychology, University of Oxford, Oxford, England

"All multi-cellular animals show changes in behavior as a result of experience—from habituation in the simpler organisms to complex forms of learning and memory in mammals. It cannot be this capacity to learn, per se, that distinguishes animals from humans. The challenging difference concerns the issue of animal thought. Undoubtedly thought is immensely enriched by language, but the question is whether it absolutely requires language. Many philosophers, from Locke in 1690 to Wittgenstein in 1922, have been resolutely unwilling to attribute thinking to nonverbal animals in this regard, largely on a priori grounds. That language is not essential for complex cognitive skills is clear even at the human level: severely aphasic patients can score highly on IQ tests like Raven's Matrices (Kertesz, 1988; Newcombe, 1987), and preverbal infants can segment and categorize their causal world (Leslie, 1988; Spelke, 1988). Therefore, there is no logical necessity to deprive animals of advanced mental skills because they lack language. Many impressive demonstrations have been reported, such as the ability of the chimpanzee to perform arithmetical addition or ratios (Premack, 1988), of rats to show 'intentional' behavior (Dickinson, 1985, 1988), and the spatial cognitive abilities of a number of animals (Thinus-Blanc, 1988). (For examples and a review of 'thought without language' in both animals and humans, cf. Weiskrantz, 1988.)

"But complex cognition, it might be argued, is not the same as having mental imagery. What about animals' images and imaginings? There are a number of approaches to this question. Detailed analysis of S-S classical conditioning suggests a control of behavior by representations of absent events, which have been interpreted as being 'imagined' (cf. review by Holland, 1990). Second, evidence of deception by primates leads to the suggestion that they have 'theories of other minds,' that is, imagine what the consequence of their behavior will be, based on their beliefs about other's belief (Woodruff & Premack, 1979). Finally, human neuropsychology has revealed a large number of residual cognitive capacities caused by brain damage of which the patient is 'unconscious' or 'unaware,' capacities sometimes called implicit processes. One can consider comparable cognitive dissociations in animals based on homologous brain systems. It may be possible to study the difference between 'conscious' (explicit) and 'thoughtless' (implicit) performance in animals (cf. Miller & Rugg, 1992; Weiskrantz, 1986)."

3. Training chimpanzees to perform an oddity task is an example of concept formation in a non-human animal. Animals who form an *oddity concept* are able to apply a rule about same and different.

4. Although such questions are among the most interesting to ask, little agreement exists among scientists concerning comparisons of consciousness, cognition, and language in humans and non-human animals. This text assumes some common processes of "cognition" among humans and non-human animals.

DISCUSSION QUESTIONS

1. Traditional animal learning uses terminology that conveys a descriptive behaviorism. In doing so, the field has kept its focus on developing a science of *behavior*. But this very success may have produced other adverse consequences. Do you agree or disagree that such language may tend to oversimplify the cognitive abilities of humans as well as to underestimate the cognitive processes of non-human animals?

LEARNING ABOUT PATTERNS IN TIME AND SPACE

Learning about concepts and rules involves learning about relationships. Here we begin by analyzing how nonhuman animals learn about simple relationships. Among the simplest of relationships that animals learn are that events are distributed in time and that events occur in patterns.

Timing Behavior in Animals

In previous chapters, we have marveled at the ability of non-human animals to keep track of time. There is no disagreement that rats, dogs, monkeys, and pigeons have the ability to use the passage of time as a discriminative stimulus to control the patterning of their responses. For example, monkeys on DRL schedules of reinforcement can withhold lever-press responding for specified durations of time within margins measured in hundredths of a second (see Box 7.2, p. 251). Their behavior is evidence that monkeys have an excellent sense of timing. Rats and pigeons as well as monkeys and chimpanzees can be trained to make panel-push or lever-press responses within seconds of the onset of a stimulus to avoid an electric shock or to secure food. Indeed, the very basis of conditioning is predicated on the animal's ability to discriminate the time relationships of stimuli and of responses. Only a fraction of a second differentiates forward from trace or backward conditioning; yet as we have seen, such differences are critical in determining both the amount and nature of the resulting association.

Theories of timing behavior abound, some of which have been previously mentioned: that animals have an *internal clock* (Church, 1978, 1984) and that animals use their own behavior to keep track of time (Killeen & Fetterman, 1988). Other theories, that will not be discussed here, reflect different methodologies (e.g., Gibbon & Church, 1984; Roberts, 1981; Rakitin et al., 1997). At present, however, the existence of a central nervous system mechanism (a biological "clock") that would mediate precise timing behaviors is only speculative. All we can say is that an animal's sensitivity to time attests to the precision of sensory and motor nerve conduction velocities measured in fractions of a second and to the overall adaptive functioning of a nervous system whose very survival depends on such exquisite time-keeping functions.

Counting Behavior in Animals

Though related, there is a difference between *timing* and *counting* (Breukelaar, Dalrymple-Alford, 1998; Rakitin et al., 1997; Roberts & Boisvert, 1998; Whalen, Gallistel, & Gelman, 1999). Counting concerns the number of events occuring in a given time period, whereas timing behavior refers to the duration of events (Meck & Church, 1983). Counting behavior in young humans can be considered an example of preconceptual, non-verbal pattern learning, based on perceptual abilities (Whalen, et al, 1999). Children then *learn* to count, initially from 1 to 10, by adding labels (names of numbers). With conceptual training, children then learn to identify odd and even numbers, the multiplication tables, prime numbers, imaginary numbers, and so on. Counting is therefore a precursor to each human's mathematical abilities.

Counting and Rhythmic Timing. That counting and timing behavior are related is evidenced by the musical abilities of humans; the timed beats of varying duration can be considered a form of rhythmic counting. An example of similar behavior in rhesus monkeys has been previously described (see p. 251). These monkeys were reinforced with a sugar pellet for withholding responses for 15 sec before striking a lever. One animal's incredible timing accuracy (responses were repeatedly within hundredths of a second) was apparently achieved by a sequenced pattern resembling rhythmic counting. After making a reinforced response, this seated monkey would (a) rhythmically chew the pellet for a few seconds; (b) then begin to sway from side to side, metronome-like, for the next few seconds; (c) then still swaying, with her left hand she would begin to rhythmically tap the upper-center section of the performance panel positioned in front of her; (d) then, as the end of the 15-sec interval approached, with exaggerated intensity her sway switched from side to side to front to back, and her tapping speeded up to about two taps per second; and (e) finally, with her right hand she deftly slapped the appropriate lever located on the lower left-hand portion of the performance panel. She would then pick up her sucrose pellet and begin the sequenced pattern again, her interresponse latencies not varying by more than a fraction of a second (Barker, 1968).

Who Counts? Was this monkey counting? I think the answer is yes. Counting appears to be one of the simplest possible timed patterns. Timing and/or counting has been demonstrated in rats (Breukelaar & Dalrymple-Alford, 1998; Capaldi & Miller, 1988), chimpanzees (Boysen, Berntson, Hannan, & Cacioppo, 1996), gorillas (MacDonald, 1994), parrots (Pepperberg, 1994), pigeons (Roberts & Boisvert, 1998), 6-month-old infants (Wynn, 1996), and perhaps even honeybees (Chittka & Geiger, 1995).

Counting, Timing, Attention, and Memory

Counting and timing behaviors require the animal to pay attention to what it is doing. The monkey's rhythmic counting and precisely timed lever-pressing response are reflections of the animal's memory for what it has previously learned. In a sense, each timed response matches the monkey's memory for how much time had passed from the previous response. Using the words *attention* and *memory* is a departure from the descriptive language previously used to account for animal learning and animal behavior. Working within the rigorous methodologies afforded by Skinner's descriptive behaviorism, a great deal of learned human and animal behavior has been accounted for without reference to the cognitive processes of paying attention, of remembering, and of memory. However, these cognitive terms and constructs may help us both to explain patterned and other complex animal behavior and to help bridge the gap with human behavior. Therefore, throughout this chapter such terms will be used (with caution) in discussions of complex behavior.

Serial Pattern Learning in Animals

In addition to counting and timing, a good deal of research has been directed toward understanding how sensitive animals are to serial patterns. Again, this research is best understood within the frameworks of both animal memory for patterns and simple rule learning. Given a series of items, can rats and pigeons later recognize (remember) the patterns presented to them and use such patterns to solve problems?

Serial Pattern Methodology. The methodology used by Hulse and his graduate students illustrates how rats can learn serial patterns. Given that hungry rats run faster or slower in a runway depending on whether they receive food, Hulse (1978) measured the running speed of rats rewarded with a monotonic series of reinforcer amounts. Over five successive trial runs, one group of rats found consistently decreasing amounts of pellets of food in the goal box (i.e., 14, 7, 3, 1, and, finally, 0 pellets. This same sequence was repeated (five runs × five sequences of reinforcements each day). Eventually, these rats were found to run more slowly on those trials that ended in an empty goal box. Note that the only way the rats could know that there would be no food in the goal box (as evidenced by their slow rate of running) was that they had learned the sequence of the serial pattern of reinforcement. For this reason, the phenomenon is called **serial pattern learning.**

Cued Counting.   What was the pattern learned in this task? Several analyses are possible. The most parsimonious argument is that these rats may be doing something akin to rhythmic counting (see also Breukelaar & Dalrymple-Alford, 1998). That is, they may have learned the simple rule that they will be reinforced only on every fifth run down the runway. Count to 4, pause, count to 4, pause, cha-cha-cha. If this were the case, then any sequence of four reinforced trials preceding a nonreinforced trial would suffice. Or are some serial patterns more easily learned than others? Hulse (1978) compared the performance of rats on the monotonic series described earlier with another group of rats that successively found 14, 1, 3, 7, and 0 pellets in the goal box. The same training conditions were used; however, notice that the sequence of pellets was not monotonic (amounts did not consistently decrease). After training, however, these rats also learned to slow down on the fifth run, although (a) they took more trials to learn the pattern and (b) they didn't ever slow as much on the fifth, nonreinforced trial as did the group with the monotonic pattern. We can conclude that rats learned the pattern of reinforcement and that the decreasing monotonic series was the more effective cue than the nonmonotonic sequence of 14, 1, 3, 7, and 0 pellets.

Phasing Cues Improve Performance.   What else do we know about serial pattern learning? Other researchers have reported that eliminating the delay between the end of one series (i.e., 0 pellets) and the beginning of the next series (i.e., 14 pellets) makes the pattern unlearnable. Apparently, without the pause in the series, the individual elements of the "pattern" become one long sequence with no discernible elements (to the rat). The time delay between each repeating series is conceptualized as a *phasing cue* that serves to demarcate each series (Fountain, Henne, & Hulse, 1984). These investigators also found that a series longer than five elements can be effectively learned by rats if phasing cues that effectively break the long series into a sequence of shorter elements are introduced. Their finding parallels our understanding of how humans reduce long serial patterns into shorter ones, such as telephone numbers (817/829-1979), social security numbers (571-xx-2260), and the like.[2]

Summary of Serial Pattern Learning in Rats.   Rats are apparently capable of learning to respond to patterns of stimuli grouped together in time. The task is

---

[2]The phenomenon of grouping elements into smaller units is called chunking. The phone number is for the post office in Elm Mott, Texas.

PHOTO 11.1   Liberal Arts Rats in Maze

Frank and Ernest by Bob Thaves. Reprinted by permission of Newspaper Enterprise Association, Inc.

probably best conceptualized as one in which various cues allow the rat to memorize short repeating patterns, separated by discrete periods of time. For reasons that are at present not understood, monotonic series cues (which are orderly for humans) produce better serial learning performance than do non-monotonic cues for rats. Rats are apparently able to detect the pattern of monotonicity and to use it in addition to a serial pattern of reinforcement.

Maze Learning in Animals

The learning of serial patterns as demonstrated by Hulse and his colleagues is in some ways similar to the way a rat learns to find its way through a maze. For example, the running speed of a rat changes as it learns the pattern of the maze in which it is placed. Earlier (Figure 6.2, p. 199), we looked at both the straight runway and T-maze. One of the first mazes (Figure 11.1a) used by a psychologist (Small, 1908) is the most difficult to learn.[3] Tolman & Honzik's latent learning experiment, described previously (see Figure 6.5, p. 213) was conducted in the maze shown in Figure 11.1b.

Rats Learn Mazes in an Associative Fashion

On successive trials, rats typically run faster and make fewer errors at the choice points on their way to food reinforcement in the goal box. For this reason, the rat's performance at these choice points has been analyzed. Did rats make more errors in the first or last part of the maze; did they learn a sequence of left and right turns in an associative manner; did they *memorize* the

---

[3]Small (1901) built a rat-size replica of the high-hedged human maze located in the gardens of Henry VIII's Hampton Court Palace in England. Having been hopelessly lost in the Hampton Court maze on several occasions (trials), I find it incredible that Small's rats ever found their way out. The reader interested in the historical use of mazes in animal experiments is directed to Woodworth and Schlosberg (1954).

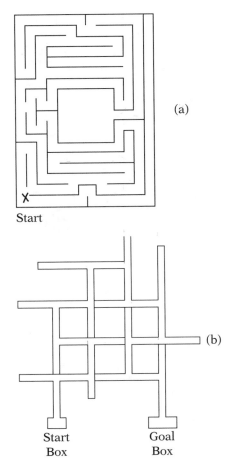

(a)

FIGURE 11.1   Historic Rat Mazes

(a) A miniaturized version of the maze at Hampton Court, England, was first used by Small (1901) to test the mental abilities of rats. At Hampton Court, people enter at point X (by permission of the University of Illinois Press).

(b)

(b) Tolman and Honzik's (1930) multiple-unit T-maze, used in their famous *latent learning* experiments (by permission of the University of California Press).

maze or otherwise learn to *map* it. (The italicized terms refer to cognitive hypotheses.) We'll first consider basic associative theory to account for maze learning, and then look at cognitive alternatives.

In Early Trials, Do Rats Learn the First or Last Part of the Maze?   Hull (1943) hypothesized that rats learn the maze from back to front by a conditioning process. Stimuli encountered on entry *into* the goal box at the end of the runway or maze are paired with food reinforcement. Hull (1932) found that rats first eliminate errors nearest the goal box, and only after many trials do they successfully make appropriate left and right turns in the early part of the maze. He described this in terms of the principle of delay of reinforcement; responses at the end of a series of responses are closest to the reinforcing stimulus.

Do Rats Learn a Sequence of Left and Right Turns in an Associative Fashion?   Hull proposed that "fractional traces" of stimuli encountered earlier in the maze are also conditioned by food found in the goal box. For the earliest responses in the maze these fractional traces of stimuli are secondary, or conditioned reinforcers. In Hull's system of terminology and notation, these stimuli are called **fractional anticipatory goal responses (rGs).** So, to the second question of whether rats learn a sequence of left and right turns, Hull's answer would be a resounding yes. Stimuli at each choice point (the shape, color, smell, vestibular and somesthetic cues, orientation of the maze in the room, etc.) are reinforced by conditioned reinforcement and eventually by primary reinforcement in the goal box.

Role of rGs's in Serial Pattern Learning.   Recall that Hulse's rats learned a serial pattern of reinforcement. After four straight reinforced trials, they learned to run more slowly on a fifth trial that was never food reinforced. One hypothesis is that rats connect the individual elements of this sequence into a pattern. The rat

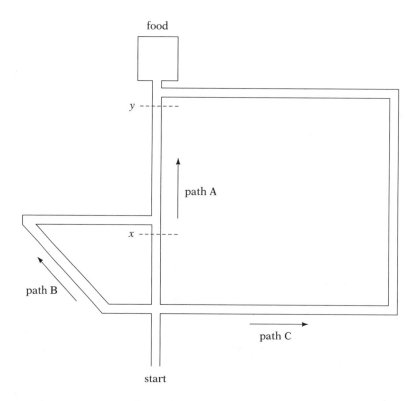

FIGURE 11.2   Insight and Foraging Mazes

(a) Path A is the shortest unless it is blocked at point *x* or point *y*. With both blocks in place, path C, the longest route, is the only way to get to the food in the goal box (Tolman and Honzik, 1930) (by permission of the University of California Press).

uses each reinforced trial as a discriminative stimulus for the next trial. That is, each trial is part of a pattern of trials; each trial has distinctive stimulus properties that signal the rat where it is in the pattern. The patterned sequence of four reinforced trials signals a fifth, nonreinforced trial, in a manner similar to the patterned sequence of left and right turns that signal reinforcement in a goal box. Note that this analysis can likewise be applied to learning where a classroom is located on campus, and the learning of a long musical piece in which one sequence of finger placements and sounds signals the next sequence of finger placements and sounds, and so on. The interested reader is directed to Capaldi and Molina (1979), Capaldi, Verry, Nawrocki, and Miller (1984), and Williams (1994) for further analysis and discussion of this hypothesis.

Rats Form Cognitive Maps of Mazes

A famous maze used by Tolman and Honzik (1930) is shown in Figure 11.2a. Tolman (1932) is credited with providing an alternative hypothesis to the associative account of how rats learn the pattern of mazes. He proposed that rats make a **cognitive map** of the maze. Tolman was well aware that the term *cognitive map* represented a departure from the connectionist model of association formation through a trial and error sequences of reinforced and nonreinforced responses. Tolman assumed that a rat "got the idea" of where, in two-dimensional space, it was located, of where food was located, and of the shortest path connecting it to the food.

Tolman and Honzik's (1930) Experiment. What is the evidence for cognitive maps? Look again at the maze in Figure 11.2a, and notice that points x and y represent blocked passages in the maze. Using mere learning by association, rats encountering these blocked passages could not make the appropriate instrumental responses leading to reinforcement and, therefore, could learn nothing directly about path A (i.e., the straight path from the starting place to the food box). Indeed, with the passage blocked at two places, Tolman's rats had no alternative but to learn to take the long route (path C) through the maze. When the blockades were then removed, however, the rats quickly took the shortcut, path A. They had never before been food reinforced for taking path A, and they had no direct experience with it. How did they know about the shorter path? Tolman argued that the rats could do this only if they had a mental representation of the maze's configuration. The rat's memory for the overall pattern of the maze, apparently attained even in the absence of direct experience, allowed the rat, given the opportunity, to efficiently solve the maze.

Exploration, Investigation, and Spatial Memory

Whether or not one buys into Tolman's mentalistic terminology, his analysis of this problem in terms of the acquisition of spatial memory is probably correct. Bowe (1984) argues that psychologists have long ignored the ability of

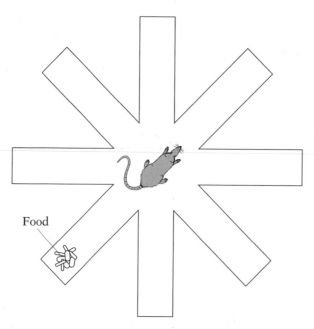

Food

Figure 11.2   Insight and Foraging Mazes

(b) Olton's eight-arm radial maze: Rats are placed in the center and are free to enter any of the eight arms at any time. Several of the eight arms may contain food; hungry rats will systematically forage all eight arms, seldom repeating those previously visited (Olton & Samuelson, 1976).

animals to learn about spatial relationships, focusing instead on time relationships. Rats bring to new environments inborn tendencies to spontaneously explore and to investigate spaces (Renner, 1988; Renner & Seltzer, 1991). In a series of experiments, Renner and his colleagues demonstrated that nonhungry rats systematically explore an experimental space and investigate both new and familiar objects within it. Days following these experiences, they return to previous locations looking for objects that were removed in their absence (Renner & Seltzer, 1991).

Learning in an Eight-Arm Radial Maze.   Renner's work can be thought of as the study of species-specific exploration and investigation patterns, In addition, research with both traditional mazes and the eight-arm maze (Olton et al., 1977; see Figure 11.2b) now lead us to believe that rats are highly expert in the domain of spatial relationships. The eight-arm radial maze has a central start box: Any (or all) of the eight arms can be baited with food and used as goal boxes. Rats actively investigate the maze even when not hungry. When hungry, their search for food in a spatial domain using innately determined **foraging patterns** (Haig, Rawlings, Olton, Mead, & Taylor, 1983).

Rats first become familiar with the eight-arm pattern of this type of maze by finding food placed in one or more of its "arms." After training, when placed in the start box, rats conduct efficient searches of the maze's eight arms. Defining an error as reentry of an arm previously searched for food, under these conditions *rats seldom make errors*. On a given series of trials, they enter each arm once, even if a previously visited arm is rebaited or if shaving lotion is used to mask trail cues (Olton & Samuelson, 1976).

Rebaiting the arm with food provides usable food odor cues. Because rats don't reenter these arms, however, it is clear that the food odor cues do not play a role in their search pattern. If not food odor, what does determine their search pattern? If rats are allowed to visit a few arms and then are removed while the entire maze is rotated 45° (so that the previously visited arms are now in new locations), rats will go to the new locations (even though there is no food). That is, they seem to be responding almost exclusively in terms of spatial cues, not to characteristics of individual arms of the maze.

Foraging Behavior of Other Animals. Rats are not the only animals that bring innately determined patterns of behavior to their task of securing food from the environment. Pigeons (Olson & Maki, 1983), marsh tits (Shettleworth & Krebs, 1982), chimpanzees (Menzel, 1978), and gorillas (MacDonald, 1994) as well as humans join in this ability to conduct efficient searches, the result of which is to rapidly locate and remember where food is located in three-dimensional space. Menzel's (1978) chimpanzee experiment is reminiscent of Tolman and Honzik's (1930) blockaded maze experiment. Chimps were carried around an acre of rough outdoor terrain and were allowed to watch as fruits and vegetables were hidden at 18 different locations. A short time later, they were turned loose from a central location. Not surprising, without hesitation, the chimps went by the shortest paths to their most preferred foods (sweet fruits) and then systematically collected the remaining vegetables from all 18 sites. By making few errors, each acted as if it had memorized the area through which it conducted a patterned search.

Interim Summary

1. Among the simplest of complex behaviors are timing and rhythmic counting.

2. Both human and non-human animals have numbering abilities (can count), and are highly sensitive to the passage of time.

3. One form of counting is evidenced by the fact that rats can learn serial patterns of events distributed in time (***serial pattern learning***) and can break down long serial patterns into shorter ones by the use of phasing cues.

4. Some response tendencies of rats at choice points in mazes can be accounted for by Hull's principle of ***fractional anticipatory goal responses (rGs).***

5. Rats learn not only to negotiate mazes without errors but also to form *cognitive maps* of the areas they are traversing. Tolman thought rats used such cognitive maps to solve mazes in a unique way through "insight."

6. Many animals have been demonstrated to have excellent memories for spatial events. Rats and other animals behave in ways that suggest they *explore* and *investigate* new terrains.

7. The readiness by which different species of animals learn complex spatial patterns is highly suggestive of an innately prepared form of learning. By this analysis, species-specific innate behaviors, called *foraging patterns,* help the animal locate food via patterned searches rather than a random trial-and-error approach.

8. Foraging patterns are influenced by reinforcement contingencies: Locating food both stops the search and reinforces the pattern; searching continues on nonreinforced trials.

DISCUSSION QUESTIONS

2. Many species of animals have a keen sense of time. Recall the rhesus monkeys that were conditioned to time their lever-pressing responses on a DRL schedule of reinforcement. Their reinforcement for correct responses was a tiny sugar pellet-candy as opposed to food. After training for hundreds of sessions, one monkey became so accurate that her interresponse interval never varied by more than a few hundredths of a second. Why do you think these monkeys were able to make such accurately timed responses? Could you do equally well? Your dog and cat?

3. Humans have a great sense of timing, as attested to by such skilled performances as hitting a curve ball or playing the piano. However, could you ever train yourself to do as well as the monkey on her task (i.e., hit a lever every 15 sec for 5 min and never vary the response interval by more than a few hundredths of a second)? Under what conditions could you do this? Would you concentrate or try to "get in a zone"? Would it help or hurt your performance if $100 rode on every response or if you received a rather severe electric shock if your responses varied too much? Is it possible that monkeys are able to do this task so well because they don't think as much, or as well, as you do?

LEARNING ABOUT RULES AND CONCEPTS

This chapter opened by describing the behavior of chimpanzees that apparently had learned a general rule governing the oddity task presented to them (that is, they appeared to learn to select the odd stimulus of three stimuli presented on a display panel, see Table 11.1). In some ways this oddity configuration is similar to the mazes and patterned reinforcement sequences described in the preceding section. Each oddity problem has a pattern, and the problem can therefore be solved by learning what to do for each pattern.

The oddity task and the animal's behavior in a maze differ, however. The "pattern" that the oddity task required involved a set of two-dimensional, visual stimuli that changed from trial to trial. In the other examples, both the maze pattern and Hulse's reinforcement pattern remained fixed from trial to trial over many sessions. And, unlike maze learning, chimpanzees and other animals do not bring innately predisposed foraging strategies to the solution of an oddity problem. Rather, the food hopper is in a fixed position, and animals must learn to solve symbolic problems unrelated to the location of food in space. Symbolic conceptual learning, then, is a different task, presumably a more complex form of learning. Let us take a closer look at the oddity task.

Associative Conditioning, Memorization, or Conceptual Learning?

Table 11.1 shows the various positions that triangles, circles, and squares can assume in this oddity problem. Responding to a square in the center position, for example, was sometimes reinforced and sometimes punished. The same was true for a triangle, circle, or square in any position. Throughout the 18 presentations of stimuli in every session, responding to the triangle (S^+) when it appeared with either two squares or two circles was reinforced on each of six occasions and in each of three positions. During the same session, responding to any of the 12 triangles when they were S^-'s did not produce reinforcement. The animals learned to respond to a particular stimulus only when it was positioned in a particular array with other stimuli.

How did chimpanzees accomplish this task? Is it a case of "simple" differential conditioning of a relatively large number of S^+ and S^- trials? Given the limited number of stimulus arrays (18 in total), following extensive conditioning, perhaps they memorized which response went with each array. (A human analogy would be the rote memorization of the multiplication tables.) Or did the animals truly learn to respond to the odd stimulus in each array? (A human analogy would be using rules to memorize the multiplication tables, such as any odd number multiplied by 5 ends in 5; any number multiplied by an even number ends in an even number; etc.) Recognize that the latter alternative is typically what is meant by conceptual learning; the former can be considered a repertoire of conditioned responses. Presumably both kinds of learning are involved when humans memorize the multiplication tables.

Memory Capacity Versus General Rule Learning? In these specific experiments we cannot decide whether the chimpanzees who were able to solve this oddity task memorized particular stimulus configurations or learned a general rule. Unfortunately, for reasons that soon should become apparent, in these experiments we cannot decide between these two alternatives. We require at least two kinds of information to help us decide: First, we need more information regarding the abilities of nonhuman primates and other animals to memorize (to learn to recognize) a large number of stimulus arrays. Are chimpanzees capable of memorizing the correct response to the 18 stimulus arrays depicted in Table 11.1? If so, they could solve the problem without having developed a concept of oddity. Second, we need a methodology that allows us to test for general rather than specific solutions for the previously learned items. For example, consider a task that requires the animal to select novel (untrained) stimuli using a general rule rather than relying on conditioned responses to particular stimuli that had been reinforced. Let us first look at evidence that chimpanzees can memorize a large number of complex stimulus arrays.

Delayed Match-to-Sample

Figure 11.3 depicts Minnie, a chimpanzee making a conditioned response on a **delayed match-to-sample** task. In this experiment, Farrar (1967) trained Minnie and two other chimpanzees to perform at better than 90% accuracy. A work session consisted of presenting the chimp a sequence of the 24 different problems, each involving a different stimulus array. Table 11.2 shows the sequence of 24 stimulus arrays. Each problem was preceded by the appearance of a single visual stimulus displayed on a backlit key located above four similar side-by-side keys. This stimulus, called the sample, was displayed for 3 sec. The sample was varied in shape and/or color (for example, a blue circle). After the sample terminated, four backlit keys located below the sample were then illuminated, displaying stimuli varying in color and shape. The chimpanzee's task was to survey the four keys, to locate and push the one key with the symbol that matched the previous sample—hence, delayed match-to-sample. For example, Figure 11.3 shows a triangle, horizontal line, square, and circle; the sample, a horizontal line, had been previously presented. If Minnie responded by pressing the horitontal line, she was reinforced by delivery of a banana-flavored pellet. If she selected the wrong stimulus, the display would terminate without food, and the same problem (beginning with the sample) would be presented until a correct response was made.

Learning this task to perfection required hundreds (perhaps thousands) of trials.[4] The three chimpanzees in Farrar's study learned this task and performed at high levels of proficiency. Minnie, for example, achieved perfect scores (144 correct/144 problems per day) on 5 of 10 test days. The occasional "misses" appeared to be because of lack of attention and to problems timing out before responses were made. Minnie and two other chimpanzees' 10-day average accuracy percentage rates were 99.3, 95.4, and 93.7, respectively.

[4]Unfortunately, the training logs no longer exist.

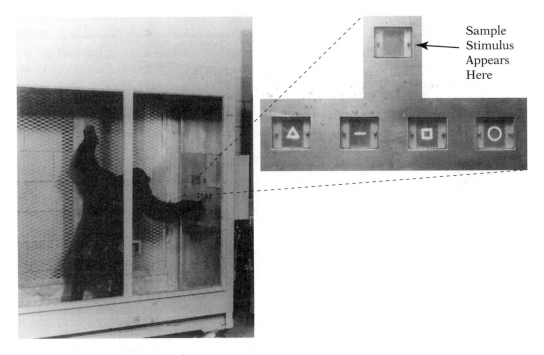

FIGURE 11.3 Minnie and the Story of Picture Memory

The chimpanzee Minnie is seen performing on the delayed match to sample task described in the text. (Minnie continues to live in New Mexico. Now approaching age 40, she has successfully born and raised 15 chimpanzees. A good mother, forever mellow, she remains a joy to all humans who have had the pleasure of working with her.)

Picture Memory.   One day a technician noticed that the light bulb used to illuminate the sample stimulus was burned out. He checked each of the three animal's records for that day and found that none of the three had suffered any performance decrement. Farrar had previously noted that Minnie's lack of attention to the display panel did not seem to impede her performance. On several occasions she did not look at the 3-sec sample stimulus, but when the four-stimulus display was illuminated, she nevertheless made the correct response.[5]

With further testing, Farrar (1967) concluded that each stimulus arrangement composed a picture and that the chimps had memorized each of the 24 different pictures, a phenomenon he called **picture memory.** Each picture, while distinctive, has common elements. For example, a green circle appears on 9 of the 24 pictures in Table 11.2 but is reinforced only on Problem 20. On the seven occasions in which a red circle is part of the picture, it is

[5]Donald Farrar, November 1992, personal communication.

TABLE 11.2   Match-to-Sample Problems

The 24 problems in Farrar's (1967) study of picture memory. Note that Problem 2 (triangle, horizontal line, square, and circle) is displayed on the performance panel in Figure 11.3.

Problem no.	Pictures				Correct position
	Lever no. 1	Lever no. 2	Lever no. 3	Lever no. 4	
1	+	Ⓖ	|	×	4
2	⚠	—	▣	⊙	2
3	Ⓖ	Ⓦ	+	×	3
4	Ⓑ	—	Ⓡ	▣	1
5	Ⓖ	⚠	—	×	2
6	+	×	Ⓡ	Ⓑ	4
7	|	Ⓖ	Ⓦ	⚠	3
8	|	Ⓖ	—	⊙	1
9	+	⊙	ⓄⓇ	×	3
10	△	▣	|	×	2
11	Ⓦ	⊙	Ⓑ	|	4
12	⊙	ⓄⓇ	▣	—	1
13	ⓄⓇ	Ⓦ	—	Ⓖ	1
14	×	▣	ⓄⓇ	Ⓡ	2
15	Ⓡ	—	+	▣	3
16	⚠	Ⓖ	|	Ⓡ	4
17	×	▣	⊙	Ⓑ	3
18	Ⓑ	|	×	—	4
19	Ⓑ	+	▣	—	1
20	+	Ⓖ	|	Ⓑ	2
21	×	Ⓦ	—	Ⓑ	2
22	⚠	×	Ⓖ	Ⓡ	1
23	▣	Ⓑ	×	|	3
24	⚠	—	▣	Ⓡ	4

reinforced twice in position 4 but is not reinforced on five other occasions (including twice in position 4, twice in position 3, and once in the first position). What aspect of each picture, then, is controlling the animal's response?

Randomizing the Serial Position Pattern. Intrigued, Farrar (1967) ran a series of experiments to attempt to determine how these chimpanzees were solving the problem in the absence of a sample. He first randomized the order of the sequence of presentation of the 24 pictures in Table 11.2 and left the sample light off. The chimps' performance did not change. He concluded that the chimps had not solved the problem by responding based on the serial presentation of the 18 pictures. That is, the chimps had apparently not learned the sequence: on trial 1, far right key; on trial 2, second from the left, and so forth.

Removing Elements of Each Picture. In subsequent daily tests (again with the sample light off), Farrar (1967) systematically eliminated one or two of the symbols in each of the 24 pictures in Table 11.2. [The deleted stimulus elements appeared as blank (unlighted) response keys.] Only one of the three chimps suffered any change in performance (i.e., 85% rather than 95% accuracy) even when half the picture (i.e., two of the four distracter stimuli, or S^-s) was eliminated. For example, in Problem 2 (see Figure 11.3), the triangle and the square were removed. Only the circle and the horizontal line appeared. Having never seen this picture before, and in the absence of a sample, the chimps nevertheless picked the horizontal line, the S^+ previously associated with reinforcement. Apparently, Farrar concluded, merely the presence of the S^+ in a particular position and at least one other stimulus element were enough of the composite picture for the animal to solve the problem.

What Is the S+ in "Degraded" Pictures? Farrar then gambled ingeniously. What if the consistently rewarded stimulus in each picture does not by itself constitute the S^+? What would happen if instead of removing two of the three S^-s from each picture, he removed the S^+ and one S^-? How would the animals respond in the absence of the correct stimulus element? On each of the next 2 days, all three chimpanzees were presented with pictures that contained only 50% of the elements with which they originally had been trained. On the first day, one each of 12 S^+s and S^-s were deleted from half the pictures; two S^-s were deleted from each of the other 12 pictures. The second day was like the first except Farrar deleted different S^+s and S^-s. (If the blank key was in the position that an S^+ usually occupied, responding to the blank key would be reinforced.)

The performance of the three chimps deteriorated but, again, far less than one might assume. Assuming that the animals would continue to respond to blank keys (which they did), their chance performance, or guessing, on this problem can be computed as an efficiency of 25%. (Given four keys, the chimps had a one in four chance of being reinforced on each trial.) The three chimps' performance on the first test day with S^+s missing was 49.3, 57.6, and 50.0%, and on the second day, with totally new S^+s missing, was 68.1, 72.9, and 62.5%.

Farrar speculated that the improvement on the second day represented re-learning a new picture, a picture in which the blank keys effectively served as stimulus elements. Unfortunately, training was disrupted at this point, and terminal performance on such highly degraded pictures was not realized.

Learning About Pictures or Learning Concepts?

What have we learned? Or better, what have these animals learned? This rather long section on picture memory was introduced to answer a specific question about the memory capabilities of chimpanzees for this type of problem. Specifically, we wanted to know whether chimpanzees were capable of memorizing which response went with each of the 18 oddity problems displayed in Table 11.1, or whether they learned a general rule (i.e., did they learn to respond to the odd stimulus in each array?). From Farrar's (1967) experiment we know that chimpanzees are capable of memorizing at least 24 pictures, each of which has more pictorial elements than the three-symbol oddity problem. So it is possible that in the previously discussed oddity research, chimpanzees did not learn the concept of oddity; rather, they learned to make specific conditioned responses to 18 different pictures. Although supporting records do not exist, the chimpanzees' performance in Koestler and Barker's (1965) study was low (60 to 70% efficiency) because the chimps consistently missed particular problems: Errors were not randomly distributed throughout the set of 18 problems. Their pattern of performance suggests picture memory rather than a concept of oddity.

Indeed, Farrar's (1967) study of picture memory raises problems for all concept formation methodologies that use a relatively small number of items. Memorization precedes and perhaps precludes rule learning in these tasks. Given the apparently excellent memory of chimpanzees for pictures, we are faced with devising a task that requires an animal to select a novel stimulus using a general rule rather than relying on conditioned responses to particular stimuli. Harlow (1949) showed us how to do just that.

Learning a Win-Stay, Lose-Shift Strategy

Harlow's (1949) task was simpler than the oddity task described earlier. His monkey-training apparatus is depicted in Figure 11.4. The experimenter lowers a screen so the rhesus monkey cannot watch where food is hidden in either of two food cups each covered by one of two objects arranged on a tray. (The stimulus objects were small toys and other novelty items purchased from the local variety store.) One of the items is designated as the correct choice for six consecutive trials (i.e., the reward is hidden beneath it), and the position of the correct item is determined by a randomization scheme. The monkey has a 50% chance of being right on each trial. It can maximize reinforcement by a **win-stay, lose-shift** strategy, as follows.

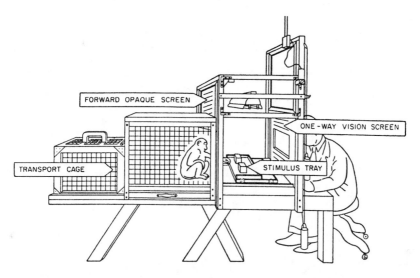

FIGURE 11.4   Wisconsin General Test Apparatus (WGTA)

An apparatus called the Wisconsin General Test Apparatus (WGTA) placed an experimenter across from a monkey. A series of screens could be raised and lowered, allowing the experimenter, out of view of the monkey, to "bait" the correct food cup over which a stimulus object was placed. Once in place, the monkey's screen could be raised, allowing it to respond to the testing situation (see text for further details).

Let a red block be the correct stimulus and a thimble be incorrect. If the monkey selects the red block on the first trial, it will be rewarded (i.e., "win") and on the next trial with the same pair of stimuli, continue to be reinforced by continuing to select the red block (i.e., "stay" with the red block). Selecting the thimble is never reinforced. After these six trials, the monkey has six more trials with two new objects, one of which is reinforced, the other not. Note that the sooner this rule is learned (i.e., "if reinforced, stay with that choice; if not reinforced, shift to the other choice"), the more reinforcements will be attained. Harlow (1949) found that after having six trials with each of eight pairs of objects, monkeys averaged about 75% correct responses on their sixth trial with the eighth pair (see Figure 11.5). He concluded that monkeys were capable of learning a win-stay, lose-shift rule.

Learning Sets or Learning to Learn?

As Harlow's (1949) monkeys continued their training with new objects (i.e., trained beyond the first eight paired objects), another phenomenon emerged. They got better at the task. To perform at only 75% efficiency on the sixth trial of a two-choice task means that during these first eight successive pairs

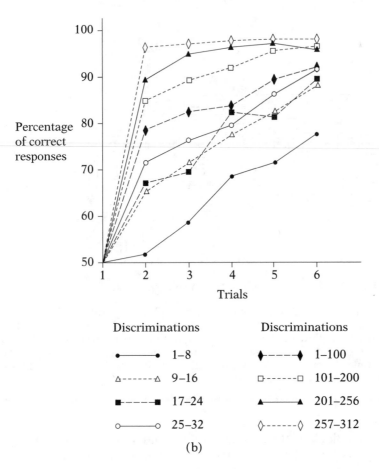

Percentage
of correct
responses

Trials

Discriminations   Discriminations

•———• 1–8   ◆----◆ 1–100

△------△ 9–16   □------□ 101–200

■----■ 17–24   ▲———▲ 201–256

○———○ 25–32   ◇------◇ 257–312

(b)

FIGURE 11.5   Learning to Learn

Harlow's (1949) learning set data that show the acquisition of a win-stay,
lose-shift strategy over several hundred trials. Each learning set consists of
six consecutive trials in which two objects were presented to a monkey, one
of which is arbitrarily and consistently rewarded if the monkey chooses it
rather than the other. Mean percentage correct responses are plotted for the
first eight problems the monkeys encountered, then the next eight (i.e.,
9–16), the next eight (17–24), and so on. The data are then regrouped and
plotted in blocks of 100 problems. Note the performance for problems
257–312; after this number of trials, the win-stay, lose-shift strategy has
been almost perfectly learned as evidenced by 97% correct performance on
the second trial.

of objects, the monkeys required several trials to learn to stay (if reinforced) and several trials to learn to shift (if punished). These monkeys apparently were learning anew the solution to each novel problem within the six training trials. Once each monkey had mastered this concept, however, and had learned a strategy, it no longer needed six trials to learn the correct response. Rather than having to be differentially conditioned to each new S⁺ and S⁻, these monkeys applied a general rule to each new set of paired objects. Harlow described this ability as **learning to learn.**

Our attention, therefore, shifts to the animal's behavior on the second trial. Figure 11.5 shows how these monkeys continued to improve their performance so that after a hundred or so sets of six trials (with two new objects in each set), they began to stay or shift on trial two of the six-trial set. That is, with each new pair, they did not have to learn the strategy anew but had only to implement a strategy (apply a rule) already learned. Harlow called each new task a **learning set.** The monkey, he reasoned, had "learned how to learn" novel learning sets. After 250-plus trials, the monkeys were about 98% accurate on the second through sixth trials with each new learning set.

Comparison of Learning Set Performance Across Species

The simplicity of Harlow's method allowed for the comparison of learning set formation across different species. Figure 11.6 is a composite of studies conducted by different researchers as plotted by Warren (1965). Data on children aged 2 to 5 years reported by Harlow (1949) have been added to Warren's (1965) figure. As can be seen, rats and squirrels seem to be pretty much incapable of learning a win-stay, lose-shift strategy; squirrel monkeys, marmosets, and cats are somewhat better after 1,000 problems (six trials per problem); Harlow's rhesus monkeys do well after several hundred trials; and human children learn the most rapidly of all animals tested. Although some of the children (presumably the older ones) were 85% accurate in fewer than 20 trials, their group means nevertheless showed a typical negatively accelerated learning curve. In this study, then, young humans also had to learn a rule before they could apply it with a high degree of accuracy. The process by which they learned this rule is presumably similar to the process by which rhesus monkeys and other animals learned. The humans, however, were smarter; they learned much more quickly.

New Stimulus Test in Both Match-to-Sample and Oddity Problems

The importance of Harlow's learning-to-learn demonstration is that it clearly shows that animals can learn to apply a rule to solve a novel problem. By contrast, the ability of monkeys and chimpanzees to solve novel problems was not tested using the discrete number of both oddity and match-to-sample problems described earlier. Is there other evidence that monkeys can learn

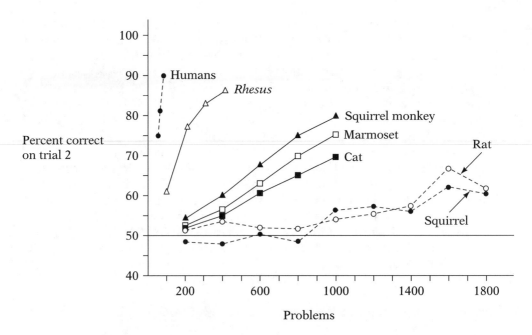

FIGURE 11.6   Learning a Win-Stay, Lose-Shift Strategy:
A Between-Species Comparison

> The percentage of correct responses on trial 2 is plotted as a function of the number of problems encountered in learning set training. Note that after a thousand trials rats and squirrels finally begin to perform slightly better than chance. Rhesus monkeys clearly outperform cats and squirrel monkeys (from Warren, 1965). The data from children aged 2 to 5 years (Harlow, 1949) have been added to Warren's (1965) comparative data.

concepts of match-to-sample and oddity by applying a general rule to novel items? The short answer is yes. After extensive training, capuchin and squirrel monkeys (both New World monkeys) can solve oddity problems with novel items on the first trial (Thomas & Boyd, 1973).

Capuchin monkeys are also capable of learning to apply a rule to solve a simplified version of the match to sample task. In this task, a sample stimulus such as a square is illuminated, and next to it one identical square and one "different" stimulus are presented. The monkey is reinforced for selecting the identical stimulus. After approximately 1,000 to 1,500 trials, monkeys are able to correctly match a novel sample with a high level of efficiency (D'Amato, Salmon, & Colombo, 1985).

Oddness, Sameness, and Familiarity of Stimulus.   Had the chimpanzees who had learned the 18 array oddity task (Table 11.1) and the 24 array match-to-sample task (Table 11.2) been given new stimulus tests, based on these results with monkeys, it is likely they could have performed as well as monkeys. A study by Tanaka (1995) offers another clue as to why repetitive testing for oddity with repetitive stimuli may be such a difficult task. This researcher trained several chimpanzees to place the two similar objects on one tray, and to place the odd object on a separate tray. Using new objects for each trial, they were able to learn the task. However, when he began to mix familiar objects with new objects, their discriminative ability and/or oddness rule broke down: If they were familiar objects the chimps began to treat them as the same, even if they were two odd objects.

Pigeons Can Learn the Concept of Sameness

Figure 11.6 reveals quite marginal performances of rats and squirrels on the learning set problem. Are the above conceptual abilities of rule learning (such as win-stay, lose-shift, oddity, and match-to-sample) restricted to primates? The answer is a decided "no." Pigeons can learn same-different concepts for colors and shapes (Cook, Cavoto, & Cavoto, 1995), and seem to have the ability to generalize same-different from stimuli they were trained on to new classes of visual stimuli (Cook, Katz, & Cavoto, 1997).

In one sameness task, for example, a series of pictures of objects was shown to pigeons. Following this series, a final picture was presented that either was or was not in the series (i.e., same or different). Pigeons were able to remember the series of pictures seen on only one previous occasion. For food reinforcement they solved the same-different problem by responding to one key if a final picture was the same and to another key when the last picture in a series was different from any of the pictures in the preceding series (Wright, Santiago, Sands, & Urcuioli, 1984).

Natural Concepts in Pigeons

Conceptual learning occurs much more rapidly within a pigeon's ecological niche. When required to peck through black & white gravel for food, for example, pigeons learned both matching and oddity in far fewer trials than when pecking at a lighted key (Wright & Delium, 1994).

The ability of pigeons to extract information from complex pictures of natural environments is truly remarkable. In a series of experiments by Herrnstein and his colleagues (reviewed by Herrnstein, 1984), pigeons were trained to respond to photographs in a way that indicated that they recognized such **natural concepts** as trees, people, and other "open-ended" categories. For example, pigeons who pecked at slides of pictures (projected onto keys in the Skinner box) containing trees (S⁺s) were reinforced, but pecking at slides not containing trees (S⁻s) was not reinforced (Herrnstein, Loveland, & Cable, 1976). The pigeons learned this discrimination to a discrete set of stimuli, and the concept generalized to new pictures. Herrnstein et al. (1976)

also were successful in training pigeons to discriminate photos of a particular person (S⁺) from photos of other people (S⁻s). The discrimination was learned even when similar clothing was worn by the target and the distracters. This is surprising. Shouldn't clothing be as discriminative a stimulus as facial features, hair, and whatever other human attributes controlled the pigeon's response?

How Do Pigeons Form Categories?   How are pigeons able to learn this difficult discrimination? Physical dissimilarity of the pictures alone cannot account for what is learned about them. Roitblat (1987, p. 307) argues that pigeons are apparently capable of learning "relatively abstract taxonomic classifications" of objects. Other investigators are trying to understand the rules by which pigeons establish classes of stimuli that are either discriminated or that generalize one to another (see Zentall & Smeets, 1996; Urcuioli, 1996). Another mystery surrounding the pigeon's ability to abstract a rule from highly ambiguous information is that fewer trials are needed relative to the number of trials chimpanzees and monkeys require to learn oddity and match-to-sample tasks. Let us examine this issue more closely.

Number of Trials in Learning Abstract Concepts

In the absence of language, it is apparent that animals learn strategies and rules via basic associative processes. But 1500 trials? Why does it take monkeys and chimpanzees so many trials to learn seemingly simple rules? Learning strategies such as win-stay, lose-shift, and abstract concepts such as oddity and match-to-sample are difficult for chimpanzees, where difficulty is operationally defined as the number of trials to criterion. After many hundreds of consistently reinforced responses to stimuli with specifiable characteristics, they begrudgingly acquire a response strategy that allows them to solve new problems. No Eureka! experience. No A-ha phenomenon. Nothing that resembles what humans typically mean when they use the term insight.

Rather, the cognitive processes that these animals display after extensive training appear to have been learned by differentially reinforced responding. "Rules" governing the selection of specific reinforced choices are learned slowly and appear to be applied to untrained stimulus objects without keen insight. Indeed, it was argued earlier that chimpanzees working oddity and match-to-sample problems seem to prefer to memorize pictures rather than to learn rules.

Pigeons Prepared to Learn Natural Concepts?   In this regard, as noted earlier, pigeons remain something of a mystery. While they learn S⁺ versus S⁻ discriminations in an associative manner, they also seem be prepared (in an adaptive/evolutionary sense) to learn some discriminations more easily than others. They learn concepts better when pecking through gravel than at a disk on the wall. They learn natural concepts in fewer trials than it takes to learn a complex visual discrimination without such taxonomic features. For example, Herrnstein and de Villiers (1980) reported that fish slides are more easily discriminated from nonfish slides than a control condition in which one set of slides is arbitrarily grouped as S⁺ and the other as S⁻. For unknown reasons, pigeons have preferences for some pictures over others and seem to use a taxonomic grouping rule without extensive training.

In addition, after learning a set of fish pictures, a new fish picture also tends to be treated as an S⁺ on the pigeon's first encounter with that picture. Reinforcement of a particular picture is not necessary for it to be included in a category. Pigeons learn faster than monkeys that, after learning either winstay, lose-switch strategies (Harlow, 1949) or an oddity concept (Thomas & Boyd, 1973), are able to respond meaningfully to novel stimuli. The pigeon's task may be easier, however.

Primates Contraprepared to Learn Concepts?

Given that small-brain pigeons can learn natural concepts, what can be said of the pitiful efforts of larger-brain primates who require trials numbering in the thousands? Normally, monkeys and chimpanzees never encounter match-to-sample or oddity problems and other conceptual tasks as presented them in human laboratories. So, from an adaptive-evolutionary perspective, we are asking them to do something other than what their brains were designed to do. Having trained many chimpanzees to attempt to solve such conceptual problems, I have observed that their task-solving behavior often brought to mind that of children—and of mentally retarded and otherwise brain-impaired human adults and of college professors and students—who are confronted with a very difficult problem to solve. Chimpanzees often vocalized their frustration, anger, and sadness when they failed and exhibited happiness when they succeeded. And, like many bright school children I know, on many occasions chimpanzees also expressed disdain and disinterest for the task at hand.

Do All Humans Form Concepts?   The latter point is not unimportant. Conceptual learning does not come easily to all children or, for that matter, to all adults. College-educated students find some concepts easy to understand but others to be impossible. How many trials? After how many years of formal instruction in school do we continue to find "bright, mature adults" who, in the words of Diamond (1988, p. 337), continue to "show the same dumb behaviours seen in infants—that is, failure to show transfer of training, absence of systematic hypothesis testing or planning, rigidity, and perseveration."

An alternative view of the relatively poor performance of primates compared to pigeons on concept-learning tasks is that primates bring to these tasks more hypotheses or strategies that must be discarded. Their poor performance might be viewed as resulting from their relatively greater cognitive resources. Though possible, I find this alternative unlikely. Humans are considered intelligent in no small measure because they rapidly learn response-reinforcement relationships. Why other primates do so poorly is a mystery.

Some forms of conceptual learning, then, seem to be acquired by trial and error rather than by insight. Our association models rather than "insight" provide a better account of conceptual learning.

Transitive Inference Reasoning by Chimpanzees

If *a* is greater than *b*, and *b* is greater than *c*, is *a* greater than *c?* Most (but not all) schoolchildren can answer this riddle. We call the ability of those who can solve this problem **transitive inferential reasoning.** Can chimpanzees reason in this way? If, after having learned that $a > b$ and that $b > c$, a chimp can answer, "Yes, *a* is greater than *c*" without ever having been reinforced for choosing $a > c$, we have evidence of reasoning and have also satisfied the requirement of a new stimulus test.

Sadie, Luvie, and Jessie. Some evidence exists that with difficulty some (but not all) chimpanzees can be trained to solve this problem (Gillan, 1981, 1983; Gillan, Premack, & Woodruff, 1981). Gillan's method was simple. On a given trial, two of five different containers were presented to an animal; choosing the "correct" one was reinforced with a preferred food. The five containers each had a distinctively colored lid by which the chimp could tell one from the other. The rules governing reinforcement were that for every pair, one color was consistently "better than" the other color. For example, in a green versus blue pairing, green was reinforced; in a red versus green pairing, red was reinforced. After extensive training, a novel question could then be asked of the animal: Which do you choose from a red versus blue pairing? Those chimps consistently choosing red over blue provided evidence for transitive inferential reasoning. Gillan reports that after extensive training, Sadie performed at 89% accuracy and Luvie and Jessie were 72% and 69% accurate, respectively (50% = chance performance). Chimpanzees, then, are marginally capable of learning a series of specific relationships taken two at a time and, by extrapolation, of applying these learned rules to construct a larger pattern of relationships. This ability of chimps, albeit halting and puny, resembles the transitive inferential reasoning abilities of many children.

Interim Summary

1. Humans, monkeys, chimpanzees, rats, and pigeons are able to learn simple concepts and form general rules to solve such problems as delayed match-to-sample, sameness, and oddity.

2. After many hundreds of training trials in a ***delayed match-to-sample*** task, chimpanzees are able to form a ***picture memory***. They can pick a "correct" stimulus from each of 24 different stimulus arrays.

3. Chimps with picture memory respond in meaningful ways when the pictures are highly degraded, by dropping out parts of the display, even to the point of continuing to respond in the absence of the S^+.

4. Given a two-choice task, a variety of animals (including children, pigeons, and rats) can learn a ***win-stay, lose-shift rule*** that can then be applied to successfully solve novel problems.

5. Pigeons are capable of extracting a surprising amount of information from pictures presented to them in the laboratory. They can perform match-to-sample, and an odd-same task. They can remember whether they have (or have not) seen a particular picture from a series of pictures presented earlier.

6. Pigeons are also capable of learning so-called ***natural concepts:*** taxonomically grouping trees, fish, humans, and so on, and responding to new examples by including them in the correct categories.

7. The large number of trials required to learn even the simplest of concepts suggests that primates, including humans, are not evolutionarily prepared to think conceptually. The fact remains that most humans can outperform all other animals on every conceptual task devised.

8. Chimpanzees can be trained in ways that show they engage in ***transitive inferential reasoning*** on the conceptual tasks tested.

DISCUSSION QUESTIONS

4. I've often wondered what animals think when you give them a problem that can be solved only by application of a rule. Their bewilderment reminds me of my own at a recent party in which a woman played a game involving mime: She modeled a series of different movements (simple dance steps, pulling her ears, patting her arms, etc.) and asked her audience to find the one thing in common she did on each different occasion. As person after person was able to solve the puzzle by applying the discovered rule, those of us who couldn't figure out the pattern became increasingly uncomfortable. It turned out that the only thing that was common to the series of different movements she made was that she cleared her throat before each one. So easy when you know what the rule is. . . . In your own experience, is rule learning difficult?

5. Can you verbalize rules you memorized in algebra or trigonometry? Were your "A-ha" experiences better characterized as having been attained by trial and error or by insight? (After reading this chapter, do you suspect that these terms are not mutually exclusive?)

6. Related to the preceding question, are you of the opinion that human language so changes the nature of human thought and behavior that simple associative frameworks become irrelevant? Alternatively, can you use the concepts of reinforcement and punishment to help account for your rule learning in Spanish 101, math, computer science, spelling, and so forth?

CHAPTER SUMMARY

1. Conceptual learning, thinking, and language can be studied from within a comparative perspective. Insight can be attained into the human mind by (a) comparing what we can do but other animals can't do and (b) examining the respective roles of genetics and environment as determinants of conceptual learning, and thinking.

2. Evidence from a variety of experiments leads to the conclusion that the categories of conceptual learning, reasoning and thinking (a) can be differentiated from one another and (b) are not exclusive properties of the human mind.

3. Evidence from many sources leads us to the conclusion that animals can think: Rats and other animals can (a) count, (b) keep track of time, (c) solve serial pattern problems, (d) explore and investigate their environments, and (e) memorize complex maze patterns (cf. cognitive maps).

4. A variety of animals have been trained to apply rules and concepts to solve learning-set problems (win-stay, lose-shift strategy) match-to-sample and delayed match-to-sample, oddity, sameness, and so on. Even though they require many hundreds of trials, monkeys and chimpanzees learn these problems better than other nonhumans do. Pigeons learn sameness and natural concepts tasks in surprisingly few trials.

KEY TERMS

cognitive map   379

delayed match-to-sample   384

foraging patterns   380

fractional anticipatory goal responses (rGs)   378

learning set   391

learning to learn   391

natural concepts   393

oddity concept   368

picture memory   385

serial pattern learning   375

transitive inferential reasoning   396

win-stay, lose-shift   388

CHAPTER 12

Communication, Human Language, and Culture

COMMUNICATION, AND NON-HUMAN ANIMAL "LANGUAGE"

In the previous chapter we learned that nonverbal animals are capable of learning simple rules, strategies, and concepts. Together these findings constitute evidence for simple thinking processes. In this chapter we look at communication patterns of non-human animals and at human language. While we are not the only animal that communicates, language is universally recognized as quintessentially human—our hallmark, species-specific capability. We begin by asking how communication is the same and how it differs from language. Another question entertained in this section is what, if anything, communication and language adds to thinking processes. Humans also think abstractly better than other animals; is this because of language ability? Humans think in language, but humans also "think" musically, mathematically, visually, gastronomically, athletically, and so forth.

Framing the Issues.   The strategy for tackling these difficult issues proceeds along several lines. First, we consider whether non-human animals display rudimentary communication skills/language, and second, the success of humans in training animals to communicate using symbol manipulation. Second, we ask what role associative learning plays in both the acquisition and usage of human language? Do simple laws of association help us understand human language, or can language be understood only by reference to specifically human cognitive functioning? Finally, in exploring of the role of language in human behavior, we return to questions of thinking and of human consciousness. What role does language play in the transmission of culture, and in producing civilization?

Animal Communication

Birds sing and snakes hiss, but are they talking? The scientists who study these issues distinguish between animal *communication* and animal *language*. Many animals, including humans, communicate with conspecifics (members of the same species). **Animal communication** involves both the production and reception of signals, typically meaningful only to conspecifics (Bradbury & Vehrencamp, 1998). (Notice that this definition includes human language.) Animals also communicate with each other via pheromones, visual displays, and vocalizations. These types of communication involve both the production and reception of signals, also meaningful only to conspecifics. Such communications seem to have similar functions to those of human language.

Are these signals language? Although modifiable by experience, these animal communications are considered to be reflexively tied to specific eliciting conditions in the environment. By contrast, human language is considered to be less reflexive and more intentional. Modern humans, the argument goes, know what they are talking about, but animals don't. This argument extends to human-like ancestors living 1.5 million years ago who more than likely lacked language (Walker & Shipman, 1996).

Vervet Monkey Calls. Vervet monkeys make what are called *alarm calls* in the presence of predators (Seyfarth, Cheney, & Marler, 1980). These researchers recorded the alarm calls and systematically observed the various reactions of the monkeys when (in the absence of predators) particular calls were replayed from carefully hidden speakers. They found evidence of a primitive form of language; one of the alarm calls caused the monkeys to look up (for predatory eagles), another to look around on the ground (for pythons), and yet another to take to the trees (to escape leopards). Infant vervet monkeys vocalized these alarm calls imperfectly but improved with age and experience.

Intentionality. What are we to make of vervet monkey alarm calls? Are they words? Does a monkey making an alarm call intend to warn others, or is the sight of a predator merely acting as a sign-releasing stimulus that triggers a fixed action pattern (FAP) consisting of both a particular vocalization and attendant movement response? Dennett (1983) argues in favor of intentionality in vervet monkey calls and in other forms of animal communication. He cites Seyfarth et al.'s (1980) observation that when alone (out of hearing range of other monkeys), on seeing a leopard a vervet monkey will silently climb to safety rather than vocalize an alarm call. By this analysis, the vocalization response to seeing a leopard is not reflexive (involuntary). Rather, alarm calls are intended (voluntary) to warn other nearby members of predators.

Origins of Animal Communication. Not all behavioral scientists who study comparative animal cognition agree with Dennett's (1983) analysis. Monkeys may or may not be that smart. Others would like to see evidence of intentionality independent of the monkey's innate vocalization, for example, shaking a branch or throwing an object. What is unarguably clear from this example of vervet monkey behavior, however, is that primates other than humans use vocalized signals to communicate with each other.

Our special interest in asking these questions about primate communication is an acknowledgment of both our genetic relatedness and our curiosity regarding the origins of human language. In the movie *Quest for Fire*, primitive hominids are characterized as having limited language capabilities—simple words and phrases directly related to meeting survival needs. It is assumed that human language evolved (Pinker & Bloom, 1990), presumably from simple to complex, but no evidence of such a transformation exists. Because language does not fossilize, we have no record of the origins of language. When we ask questions about early hominid capabilities, we are restricted to studies of extant primates.

Bridging the Language Gap. No matter how close the brain organization of other primates resembles that of humans, we are left with the fact that humans speak but animals do not. If animals could only talk, we might know more about their intentions as well as other aspects of their psychological experience. The Seyfarth et al. (1980) research strategy was to eavesdrop on what vervet monkeys were saying in their ecological niche and then analyze their behavioral responses to interpret what the vocalizations meant. We leave this area of research in animal communication to look at the results of a different research strategy. What happens when researchers try to teach animals an artificial, symbolic language? Because untrained animals do not understand human language and we likewise struggle with theirs, why not try to develop a common, simplified, symbolic language? In doing this, we remove the animal from its ecological niche and ask it to do the unnatural task of communicating on human terms. We first look at research with porpoises, dolphins, and parrots, and then return to primates.

Porpoises and Dolphins

As was alluded to in the previous section, many animals, porpoises and dolphins included, vocalize among themselves in their natural habitats. Presumably because of these abilities and their apparent eagerness to both interact and possibly communicate with humans (Lilly, 1961), a number of dolphins have been subjected to intensive symbolic language training regimens. Here we concentrate on research by Louis Herman and his associates and a separate research program headed by Ronald Schusterman. Although both use similar training methods and get similar results, their various interpretations of the language capabilities of dolphins differ markedly, along the behavioral-cognitive split alluded to in Box 11.1. The issues raised by either a cognitive or a behavioral interpretation reemerge in a later discussion of what both chimpanzees and humans mean when they use "language."

What Can Dolphins Learn About Symbols?   If you have ever had the good fortune to watch a trained dolphin perform, you might have wondered how it had been trained. Did the porpoise really understand the signaled instructions to fetch the red ball and shoot the ball at the basket on the right-hand side of the pool? Herman, Richards, and Wolz (1984) consider that Ake, a bottlenose dolphin, after being trained to performs such a task, had a "tacit knowledge of syntactic rules." This knowledge allowed the animal to comprehend three- to five-word "sentences." Each "sentence" learned by the dolphin had three essential components, hand-signaled in sequence: the *direct object* (the "basket on the right-hand side of the pool"), the *action* ("fetch"), and the *agent* ("red ball"). Both the color of the objects and the positions (right, left) were modifiers that required Ake to select from alternative responses. Herman et al. (1984) consider the sentence components to be "words" and that "dolphins are sensitive to the semantic and syntactic features of the sentences we construct in those languages, because their responses covary with variations in those features" (Herman, 1989, p. 46).

Language or Rule Learning? While acknowledging the complexity of the tasks that Ake was able to learn, other researchers challenge Herman's (1989) linguistic analysis. For example, Schusterman and Gisner (1988, 1989) have trained both dolphins and sea lions using the same techniques and with the same results reported by Herman. Invoking the law of parsimony, however, they argue that animals are performing conditioned responses, not understanding language. They see the animal's task as a conditional sequential discrimination problem, involving three categories of signs and using two rules:

1. If an OBJECT is designated by one, two, or three signs (an OBJECT sign and up to two modifiers), then perform the designated ACTION to that object.
2. If two OBJECTS are designated (again, by one to three signs each) and the ACTION is FETCH, then take the second designated object to the first. (Schusterman & Gisner, 1988, p. 346)

Analysis of "Language-Trained" Dolphins. Which analysis is correct? In this text, we have consistently taken the position that given two accounts, the more parsimonious explanation is better. In doing so, we run the risk of under-attributing complexity of thought that may in fact accompany the dolphin's performance. Let us here, then, simply emphasize what can be agreed on. There is no disagreement that these dolphins' trained behaviors required many hundreds of trials using both Pavlovian and Skinnerian techniques. Following this elaborate training, we have no window into the dolphin's mind. We do not know (to paraphrase Dennett, 1983, p. 344) what dolphins know, what they want, what they understand, and what they mean. Most researchers agree that nothing emerged from the system that was not put into it.

Other aspects of human language, including such possibilities as irony, metaphor, storytelling, and confabulation (Dennett, p. 347) did not emerge, nor could it, given the primitive language components provided the dolphin. In this regard, the more parsimonious behavioral account is probably closer to the truth of the matter. Rather than language comprehension, their behavior is better construed as an additional example of the ability of animals to learn complex rules. For example, their "If x, then y" rule is similar to the win-stay, lose-shift response strategy described earlier. Indeed, previously considered examples of how S⁺s can come to control behavior of rats and pigeons in multiple and chained schedules of reinforcement approach the complexity of these dolphins' behavior.

Alex, the African Grey Parrot

An African grey parrot named Alex has acquired a considerable vocabulary and language usage by observing and listening to his human trainers (Pepperberg, 1991, 1994). Irene Pepperberg began training Alex in the 1970s to do what parrots are known for—namely, to parrot whatever was said to him. We take for granted what parrots are able to do, yet this is no small feat. According to Pepperberg (1999), Alex's abilities are human-like in that he exhibits "supralaryngeal vocal tract control, anticipatory coarticulation, and sound play" (he talks, alternates listening with making sounds, and like a child does, he "plays" with sounds).

Learning Language Via Social Interaction. Alex also counts and adds the number of objects presented to him, and 80% of the time correctly identifies shapes and colors. Alex learned to correctly say "two blue triangles" when presented with these stimuli by modeling after two human trainers. In his presence, the trainers carried on extended conversations about the colors, numbers, and shapes of objects. One trainer would ask for objects, the other trainer would model correct or incorrect verbal responses to the questions, and would be verbally praised or punished accordingly. They then alternated trials with Alex. Subsequent work with two other grey parrots using audio-tape tutorials rather than a human trainer paying attention to the bird's performance failed to reproduce Alex's abilities. These findings convinced Pepperberg and McLaughlin (1996) that the social interactions, including eye contact and paying attention, are reinforcers as essential for language learning in parrots as they are in humans.

Language Studies with the Common Chimpanzee (*Pan troglodytes*)

Donald, Gua, and Viki. Luella and Winthrop Kellogg's interest in both porpoise and chimpanzee behavior resulted in two classic publications, *Porpoises and Sonar* (1961) and *The Ape and the Child* (Kellogg & Kellogg, 1933). In both books, they addressed questions of comparative cognition: Can these animals communicate with humans, and can we use their vocalizations to better understand the nature of their consciousness? The Kelloggs were among the first of many researchers in this century who systematically attempted to break the communication barrier with chimpanzees (Benjamin & Bruce, 1982). *The Ape and the Child* chronicled Luella and Winthrop Kellogg's 9-month experiment of raising an infant chimp named Gua along with their 10-month-old child, Donald, in their home environment (see Figure 12.1). Among their research objectives, simply stated, was whether humanlike behavior would emerge if a chimp was raised in a human environment. One finding, simply stated, is that not only did Gua remain mute, he seemed to have a retarding effect on Donald's acquisition of language (Benjamin & Bruce, 1982). A several years' effort by other researchers to teach a chimpanzee named Viki to talk proved equally ineffective (Hayes, 1951). Conclusion? The common chimpanzee, *Pan troglodytes*, is unable to talk to us.

FIGURE 12.1   Gua and Donald Kellogg

> Holding hands and walking together served as evidence of a common "understanding" of the command, "Take Gua's hand." At first, when Donald was asked to "take Gua's hand," the chimp responded more quickly and reliably than the child. In a number of other instances, Donald demonstrated that he comprehended commands originally reserved for Gua. (Photo and text from Kellogg & Kellogg, 1933, p. 274.)

Washoe, Nim, and Koko.   Though unquestionably fascinating, the Kelloggs' and Hayes's failure to communicate with their chimps speaks more to these investigators' methodological deficiencies than to the chimpanzees' lack of capacity for language. Both attempted to use the chimpanzees' innate vocalizations, but this species of chimpanzee rarely make humanlike sounds. Allen and Beatrice Gardner provided a solution to this problem by training a chimpanzee named Washoe to sign, using American Sign Language (ASL) (Gardner & Gardner, 1969). Using both food and praise as reinforcers, they reported that Washoe learned well over 100 signed words. Terrace (1979) also trained Nim Chimpsky[1] in ASL; but, contrary to the Gardners' conclusions

---

[1]The name is a take-off on a famous linguist, Noam Chomsky, who is discussed in a later section.

about Washoe's language capabilities, Terrace was struck more by the differences between humans and chimps; in particular he points out (a) the intensity of training effort required of even the simplest of words with his chimp, relative to the little effort expended on humans; (b) the number of signs Nim learned increased at a painstakingly slow pace; (c) the lack of either spontaneity or creativity in language use when not prompted by the experimenter; and (d) evidence that the chimp echoed back the same "multiword" sentences as trained rather than as novel combinations of signs (Terrace, 1979). Although not all primate researchers agree with Terrace, similar criticism has been made of the language skills of a lowland gorilla named Koko following ASL training (Patterson & Linden, 1981). Terrace's (1979) assessment, you might note, is similar to that of Schusterman and Gisner (1989) who concluded that after extensive training, dolphins exhibited conditioned responses rather than "language." This question can be alternatively framed as one of whether animal language is ever proactive (i.e., generative) or merely reactive (elicited after training). Humans definitely exhibit both proactive as well as reactive language.

Sara and Lana. Two other methodological attempts to talk to chimpanzees were independently implemented in the 1970s by David Premack and Duane Rumbaugh and their students. Both trained chimps to associate artificial symbols with actions and objects using food reinforcement. Several of the symbols used by Premack and Premack (1972) are shown in Figure 12.2. Sara was taught to first "read" and then to physically arrange a three-token sequence standing, for example, for "give"–"Sara"–"M&M." After several years of training, the Premacks reported that she had a functional vocabulary of

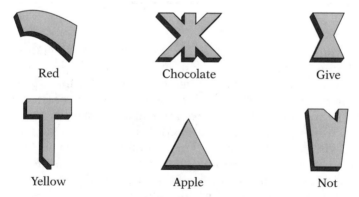

Red   Chocolate   Give

Yellow   Apple   Not

FIGURE 12.2   Communicating with Symbols

A few of the artificial symbols used in David Premack's work with Sarah.

about 130 words. Sara is reported to have learned to use the agent-action-object format to create unique "sentences" that had not previously been reinforced.

It is interesting that the initial association of a symbolic "word" with the meaning of "agent" (or action or object) took Sara thousands of trials.[2] This finding constitutes further evidence that chimpanzees seem to be contraprepared to learn to use the same symbols in a variety of settings (cf. the difficulty in training an oddity problem).

Chimpanzee-Computer Interactions. The method designed by Rumbaugh and colleagues to train Lana (Rumbaugh, 1977; Rumbaugh & Gill, 1976), although not conceptually different from the training of Sara, involved building a chimp-computer-human interface. Lana (and her trainers) interacted with a control panel that contained keys with illuminated symbols called lexigrams. The lexigrams could be activated by the experimenter, either requesting or instructing Lana to respond. Lana in turn could communicate by pressing one or more keys. For example, she could ask for food. If the sequence of lexigrams was correct, she received food reinforcement. A four-lexigram sequence might request "please"–"machine"–"give"–"M&M." A more sophisticated computer-controlled interface continues to be used in modified form at the Language Research Center in Georgia (e.g., Savage-Rumbaugh, McDonald, Sevcik, Hopkins, & Rubert, 1986).

Sherman and Austin. Savage-Rumbaugh and her colleagues trained the chimps Sherman and Austin during the 1970s using a combination of lexigrams, ASL, and real-world objects and reported results that exceeded previous efforts with other chimps. Specifically, Sherman and Austin could (a) sort and categorize both objects and lexigrams on the first trial of a blind test; (b) carry out commands in the absence of seeing the object (i.e., go into a different room and bring back a designated object); (c) make statements (arrange lexigrams) about future actions; and (d) engage in cooperative behavior by sharing reinforcement after using their language to solve a problem (Savage-Rumbaugh, 1987).

Is There a Message in the Medium? A concern of all animal language researchers has been that the various means of communication afforded chimpanzees, be it ASL, plastic tokens, and computer interfaces, are artificial and highly limiting. An analogy would be to take a young child into a laboratory, give her a saxophone, and measure how well she "uses language" by which notes she plays on certain occasions, whether she plays it spontaneously, whether she tries to get other children to play it, and so on. Her language abilities under these conditions would likely be found wanting. Both vocaliza-

---

[2]As it did for Lana, Sherman, and Austin, three other chimps trained by Rumbaugh and his students, to be discussed shortly.

tion and signing are the preferred patterns of language in humans. Is there a preferred pattern of communication in chimpanzees? Let's look at another species of chimpanzee.

Language Studies with the Pygmy Chimpanzee (*Pan paniscus*)

Just when many comparative psychologists thought that the animal language story had become pretty uninteresting, fortuitous observations of the behavior of a young pygmy chimpanzee named Kanzi breathed in new life (Savage-Rumbaugh et al., 1986; see Figure 12.3). Pygmy chimpanzees are known as bonobos; their scientific name is *Pan paniscus*.

FIGURE 12.3

Dr. Sue Savage-Rumbaugh with Kanzi, an adult bonobo chimpanzee (*Pan paniscus*) the Language Research Center, Georgia State University. Notice the portable keyboard in the lower left part of the picture.

Kanzi behaved differently than common chimps had. Without formal training—from merely watching other chimps and humans interact—Kanzi learned more language than any other chimpanzee. And, though his accent is still thick, he also seems to have learned a bit of English. Let's look at the details.

Kanzi's History.   From 6 months of age Kanzi found himself in the artificial language environment of his mother, Matata, as she learned about lexigrams on a keyboard. Within a year, Kanzi began to show interest in the symbols; without prodding or training he quickly learned to respond to the lexigrams. According to Savage-Rumbaugh et al. (1986), at no time was Kanzi food rewarded for the appropriate use of a symbol.

Part of his training took place in a 55-acre forest. At 3 years of age, Kanzi had learned the location of food stashes throughout the forest and was able to "select each location by pointing to either a photograph or a lexigram . . . [and then proceed] to guide the experimenter to the location of the food he had selected." This behavior both confirms previous reports of chimpanzee foraging abilities (i.e., Menzel, 1978) and signals intentionality of a planned behavior (some of the locations were 30 minutes distant from where Kanzi initially signaled).

Kanzi's comprehension of English continued to increase for several years. His language skills were compared with those of a 2-year-old human child (Savage-Rumbaugh et al., 1993). In a test of 660 human-chimp interactions and in comparison with an equal number of human-child interactions (conducted in a manner as similar as possible), Kanzi was found to understand more English than did the child. Language production was a different matter; the child's spoken language was decidedly better than the chimp's attempts.

Having said this, perhaps the most interesting finding of Savage-Rumbaugh's research with Kanzi is his apparent attempt to vocalize/talk to humans. Although both species of chimpanzees are said to lack the ability to form consonants, Savage-Rumbaugh and her colleagues are nevertheless convinced that Kanzi engages in intentional vocal efforts, "answering, disagreeing, or expressing emotion" (Savage-Rumbaugh et al., 1986). This behavior is lacking in the common chimpanzee, *Pan troglodytes*. Kanzi has spoken and used appropriately the English words bunny, good, groom, sweet potato, and tomato and has used appropriately words that "sound like" *lettuce, orange drink, raisins, carrot* (all foods) as well as *yes, there, knife, snake, hot, oil, paint, get it*, and others (Savage-Rumbaugh et al., 1993). Apparently, *Pan promiscus* isn't as disabled in making human-like vocalizations as is *Pan troglodytes*.

Analysis of Kanzi's Language Abilities.   What can be concluded from this study of Kanzi? I believe that Savage-Rumbaugh and her colleagues are correct in their analysis that *Pan paniscus* qualitatively differs in language ability from *Pan troglodytes*. One has more of a propensity for language than the other. Probably these differences are species-specific. The same argument, we see in the next section, is proposed to account for the qualitative differences between human and non-human forms of communication. When Savage-Rumbaugh talks about differences in these chimpanzees' receptive language, she is positing that pygmy chimps "listen" and that common chimps, for the most part, do not. She also suggests that language receptivity precedes language productivity and that "when an ape can, simply by virtue of human rearing, begin to comprehend human speech, the power of culture learning looms very large indeed" (Savage-Rumbaugh et al., 1986, p. 231). I would add the coda that, with the possible exception of Alex, the parrot, a talking chimpanzee far exceeds the language capabilities of any other species. Savage-Rumbaugh's interactions with Kanzi may be considered the most successful attempt yet in establishing contact with another species.

What Can Be Concluded From Studies of Animal "Language"?

We began this section by asking whether non-humans animals (a) can communicate, (b) can be trained to engage in language-like behaviors, and (c) can use an acquired artificial "language" as a human might. The evidence from porpoises, parrots, and chimpanzees allows us to say yes to propositions (a) and (b) but to (c) only with grave reservations. With the possible exception of Kanzi and Alex, animals other than humans seem to have very little to say to humans, and are little interested in making verbal communications among conspecifics as humans do.

Interim Summary

1. **Animal communication** can be meaningfully distinguished from animal "language." Many animals innately vocalize and otherwise signal conspecifics in meaningful ways.

2. Among the issues raised by the question of animal language is the difficult question of intentionality. Vervet monkeys make predator-alerting vocalizations that can be alternately conceived of as involuntary (reflexive, species specific) behavior or as an intentional (voluntary) act.

3. Some animals have been taught to associate artificial symbols with objects and behaviors; they occasionally engage in language-like behavior.

4. Porpoises and dolphins learn to use artificial signals to perform relatively complex acts. Although some theorists talk about their accomplishments in terms of a simple grammar, others view their behavior as conditioned responses and the application of learned rules.

5. Alex, an African grey parrot, has been associatively trained to use English terms to answer questions about the color, number, and shape of

different objects. He alternates listening with making sounds, and plays with sounds much as a child does.

6. The common chimpanzee (*Pan troglodyte*) has been the subject of numerous language investigations during this century. Although these chimpanzees do not vocalize words, they can learn to use American Sign Language (Washoe), plastic tokens (Sara and Nim), and other artificial symbols (Lana, Sherman, and Austin) to engage in meaningful language-like behaviors with their human caregivers.

7. The most promising non-human candidate to exhibit language abilities is *Homo sapiens'* most genetically similar relative, the pygmy chimpanzee (*Pan paniscus*). According to Savage-Rumbaugh, Kanzi's speech comprehension and vocalizations are qualitatively better than the common chimpanzee. Nevertheless, compared to humans, pygmy chimpanzees have meager language abilities.

DISCUSSION QUESTIONS

1. Normally an optimist, for many years I have been profoundly disappointed by our inability to communicate human intentions to non-humans. Assuming that we've approached this research in a meaningful way (a huge assumption; see next question), we've yet to find a non-human animal that shares our curiousity, or our interest in trans-species communication. Are there any lessons learned from these studies that we can carry to possible future encounters with extra-terrestrials?

2. Chimps don't seem any more interested in music or visual representations (such as painting) than they are in symbolic learning, quantification, or "language." What are we doing wrong? Can you come up with an alternative approach to trans-species communication?

HUMAN LANGUAGE

There is a difference between our minds and the minds of other species, a gulf wide enough to make a moral difference. It is—it must be—due to two intermeshed factors, each of which requires a Darwinian explanation: (1) the brains we are born with have features lacking in other brains, features that have evolved under selection pressure over the last six million years or so, and (2) these features make possible an enormous elaboration of powers that accrue from the sharing of Design wealth[3] through cultural transmission. The pivotal phenomenon that unites these two factors is language. We human beings may not be the most admirable species on the planet, or the most likely to survive for another millennium, but we are without a doubt at all the most intelligent. We are the only species with language.

Dan Dennett, *Darwin's Dangerous Idea* (1995, p. 371)

[3]Design wealth refers to the accumulated knowledge—memes—passed from one generation to the next.

Humans are the only species with language. This observation alone has such great import that most humans in most cultures believe we have little to learn about ourselves by studying other animals. Our brief look at non-human language in the previous section serves to reinforce the view that humans "do language" in a qualitatively different way than other animals. Dan Dennett (1995) attributes our species' intelligence to our unique brains (from unique genes) and the language afforded us by these brains that allows for the transmission of knowledge from one generation to the next, and cross-culturally. Dawkins (1976) coined the term meme to refer to such non-genetic transmission of information. Specifically, a **meme** is an element of culture that may be passed on by non-genetic means. Libraries can be thought of as memes. Process of memetic transmission include imitation and language. That humans transmit memes as well as genes make us very special indeed (Blakemore, 1999).

In the next sections we seek an understanding of our human language behavior. Here we hope to answer a number of different, but ultimately related questions. Is language the most important species-specific behavior exhibited by humans? In the study of human language behavior, how does the way that human genes meeting different environments produce language, and individual differences in language? Do we learn to speak? Will we discover that we need unique learning concepts to account for how we speak, read, and write? And finally, what role does language play in allowing humans to become civilized?

Human Language Behavior

My daughter Jane first made the sound "Pup-pee" at 17 months of age when together we turned the pages of her picture book of animals. A "pup-pee" was any picture of a cow, horse, or dog, and, for a while, even an elephant. As she rapidly acquired words during the next year of her life, each incorrect label of "puppy" was replaced by the appropriate word (such as *cow, horse,* and *dog*).[4] During this time she learned to discriminate a rhinoceros from an elephant, and, with apparent ease, correctly applied the verbal label *dog* to both real dogs and pictures of dogs. Puppy ultimately was a word restricted to small, young dogs with puppylike characteristics.

How did Jane learn to do this? Consistent with previous analyses, here it is proposed that humans share associative processes with other animals, and that her language learning can be so characterized. Alternatively, America's foremost linguist Noam Chomsky (1980) proposes that Jane used an innate, species-specific, language-acquisition mechanism. The latter process, Chomsky asserts, does not at all resemble learning. Indeed, for Chomsky, the asso-

[4]This process is called schema extraction by Hintzman (1986). Simple generalization and discrimination processes account equally well for an initial broad umbrella of brown furry animals ultimately becoming discriminable.

ciative processes of learning are meaningless and irrelevant to *all* questions of human language. Is this a conventional nature-nurture argument?

Revisiting the Nature-Nurture Argument

By the late 1950s, in the process of defining a new discipline of language studies called psycholinguistics, Chomsky had adopted a radical nativist position. By contrast, in this and other arguments, we have seen that B. F. Skinner's position was that of an extreme environmentalist. For Chomsky, humans talk the talk, walk the walk, and do both because *that*, without much help from the environment, is what humans are born capable of doing. By contrast, for Skinner, language acquisition and usage only superficially resembled walking: Different environments around the world resulted in the same walk, but the talk was in different languages. In this and in other ways language behavior seemed to reflect both culture and unique reinforcement and punishment histories. How could language not be learned, Skinner argued? Let's look at various aspects of language behavior to see how the nativist and environmentalist arguments were used.

Naming Objects. Learning to *name* objects is an instance of associative conditioning not unlike others you have studied throughout this text. Pavlov's second signal system presented a parsimonious description of how humans are conditioned to apply arbitrary names to objects in the environment; how the sounds of words become CSs for objects; how conditioned responses (such as saying "pup-pee") can generalize along any of a number of stimulus dimensions to similar objects in the environment; and how, with further training, discriminations between words can be learned. Then, following discrimination training, specific responses can become consistently associated with specific stimuli. Adding to Pavlov's account, Skinner pointed out that children who are reinforced for speaking speak more and that those punished for speaking speak less. Mispronunciations of words and misnamed objects are corrected by caregivers. Finally, through conditioning, words acquire the power to both signal and control emotions in different environments.

The problem with a learning analysis, Chomsky countered, is that regardless of environmental differences around the world, humans acquire grammar in a remarkably similar way without consistent intervention by their caregivers. Human language is far more complicated than learning what is, and what is not, a puppy. Human language is not restricted to naming objects; indeed, naming is considered a relatively unimportant component of language by some psycholinguists. And so the issue is joined.

The intensity with which these respective positions on language acquisition are guarded affords us the rare opportunity to declare both sides wrong at the outset. That is, neither of the protagonists, the nativist Chomsky, or the environmentalist Skinner, nor their adherents can alone account for the known facts of human language. This argument has gone on for nearly half a century with both sides asserting the supremacy of their philosophical positions. (The disagreement is due as much to the tenaciousness of both ego and theory in science as it is to the complexity of the phenomenon.) Let us first look at what can be agreed on, and then inquire further into what the argument is about.

First Sounds

Crying As a FAP. Human infants vocalize distress cries at birth, and such crying is adaptive. Vocalizations alert and sensitize caregivers to action, typically to alleviate hunger, pain, temperature changes, and other discomforts. Crying can be characterized as a species-specific behavior with each species having a particular pattern of both sound production and sound reception. More specifically, crying can be analyzed as a fixed action pattern (FAP). (You may want to review the criteria that Moltz (1963) proposed for a behavioral sequence to be considered a FAP, on p. 47).

Crying as an Instrumental Behavior. From Skinner's perspective, crying is an emitted behavior. Infants can cry instrumentally, a behavior that can be reinforced or punished. Caregivers adopt various strategies to deal with instrumental crying behavior. For example, if, after a feeding and a diaper change, the infant continues to cry, a parent might decide to let the baby "cry himself or herself out."[5] In this behavioral contingency, the child is not picked up when he or she cries. Alternatively, at Grandma's the child might be reinforced for instrumental crying by being held and rocked through the night. The frequency of an infant's vocalizations, then, can be manipulated by reinforcement and punishment contingencies in different contexts. Infants cry innately; the environment acts to modify even the earliest of such vocalizations.

Cooing and Babbling

The first noncrying sounds made by infants appear within a few months of being born. Because deaf children make these cooing and babbling sounds, it is assumed that these vocalizations are innately determined. By about one year of age, babies who hear begin to produce "intonal patterns" that resemble the sound characteristics of the caregiver's language—English, Spanish, Chinese, and so forth (Weir, 1966). Once again, this innate behavior is modified by the child's immediate environment.

Parents in different cultures do not act the same way toward their babies. Most caregivers interact with infants, however, by talking back to them as they make their endearing sounds. It is likely, then, that this caregiver behavior also has genetic basis. Language-impoverished environments are those

[5]The author is describing, not prescribing, this approach to parenting.

that provide both less modeling of the target language and less reinforcement (paying attention, smiling, cuddling, etc.) for the babbling behavior. Language will develop in children from language-impoverished environments. But the enormous individual differences seen in adult human language behavior likely have their origins at least in part as a result of these earliest interactions (see following discussion).

First Words

Although infants are highly variable in their time to first word, at about 1 year of age the average child begins to speak the language he or she has been hearing. The first words are usually names for objects encountered in the environment (such as "mama" and "milk") and for actions such as "get" and "go." This is known variously as the **one-word utterance stage** or as holophrastic speech. Adults judge the meaning of these single words by the context in which they are delivered. For example, sitting in a high chair and reaching for her cup, a child might say "wa-wa," short for "I'm thirsty, I want some water." Later, "wa-wa" might be playfully splashed (and drunk) during an evening bath. Parents typically have no problems either understanding or meeting the needs expressed by such utterances. Again, the child learns to use these first words instrumentally. How such words are reinforced (or extinguished or punished) thereafter influences their frequency of usage.

Biological Theory. For Chomsky (1965, 1975), a child's first words reflect the operation of an innate **language acquisition device (LAD)**. For the same reason that children begin to babble, they are evolutionarily prepared to speak their first word.[6] From this perspective, the infant's task is to "map" each new word onto a previously acquired concept (Levine & Carey, 1982). For example, according to this biological/cognitive view, an infant must have entertained a preverbal concept of mama before being able to map the word mama onto her. From this perspective, language acquisition is preceded by and predicated on these innate cognitive categories. Behaviorists disagree with this view.

The Behaviorists' View. It goes without saying that postulating the existence of innate cognitive structures prior to language acquisition was anathema to early behaviorists. For Skinner (1957), first words, like babbling sounds, were described as emitted operants. Skinner was less concerned about where the words come from than in how they could be manipulated—reinforced and punished—once they were spoken.

---

[6]Chomsky conceptualizes LAD as an innate, biological capacity but one that is not necessarily the outcome of a natural selection process. See Pinker (1994) for his analysis of Chomsky's position. Most theorists, including Pinker, have adopted the stronger position that the innate propensity humans have for language production and reception is the end product of a natural selection process.

An offshoot of Skinner's behavioral position that does address the origin of first words is that they appear as a result of "generalized imitation" and subsequently are maintained by conditioned reinforcement (Baer & Sherman, 1964; Kymissis & Poulson, 1990). In this analysis, imitation is itself viewed as an innate behavior that, when combined with reinforcement, produces the first French, Japanese, English, etc., word. Contemporary behaviorists referring to an innate mechanism of imitation? What an interesting development!

Interim Summary

1. Humans are the only species of animal with language.

2. Cross-culturally children seem to learn how to talk without formal instruction.

3. Chomsky's radical nativist position asserts that humans talk and walk because innate programs unfold during development with minimal help from the environment.

4. Skinner's behaviorist position stresses the role of environment in shaping language acquisition and usage through processes of reinforcement and punishment.

5. For Chomsky, language has more to do with the structure of grammar and less with signaling and naming.

6. Crying is the first vocalized, prelanguage communication pattern in humans. Crying can be thought of both as an innate FAP and as one of the first emitted instrumental behaviors that can be reinforced and punished.

7. Cooing and babbling occur during a time when infants begin to hear/discriminate the phonemic sounds of the culture in which they live.

8. A child's first spoken words, the **one-word utterance stage** (also called holophrastic speech) occur cross-culturally at about 1 year of age. The process by which this occurs is unknown.

9. First words that are reinforced continue to be expressed in the vocabulary.

10. Chomsky proposed an innate mechanism—a **language acquisition device (LAD)**—to account for how a child generates its first meaningful utterances. An imitation theory has also been proposed.

DISCUSSION QUESTIONS

3. Given the restricted range of behaviors of human neonates and the necessity of a caregiver (by far the majority of these being mothers), how surprising is it that cross-culturally, children begin to say the same things at the same time?

4. Chapter 5 (p. 146) was introduced with a passage from *The Education of Little Tree*. A sampling of the cultural knowl-

edge of Cherokee Indians in this century illustrates how much can be learned merely from noting the associations between stimuli. Is language necessary to acquire this knowledge? Is language necessary to transmit this knowledge to the next generation?

5. What would John Locke have thought about the assumption of innate cognitive categories?

First Grammar, and Learned Grammar

At about a year and a half, children universally begin to string together two words, called **telegraphic speech** (Bloom, 1970). The word choices are not random, as indicated by the fact that some of the grammatical conventions of the parent language are observed. For example, a child will say in English, "get cookie," not "cookie get."

Receptive and Generative Speech.   As every parent knows, preverbal children understand more than they can say. In other words, the child's receptive language is better at the one- and two-word utterance stage than is the child's productive language. (Recall Savage-Rumbaugh et al.'s (1986) observation that the pygmy chimpanzee named Kanzi had far more receptive than productive language.) Even though some parents on some occasions simplify their language for the child, "normal" language will develop without this help. From the child's perspective, parental language usage extends beyond the child's productive language capability.

As remarkable as the language acquisition process is up to 18 months of age (by which time the average child has about 25 words), a virtual word explosion occurs during the next few years. By age 6, an average child's lexicon contains more than 15,000 words (Medin & Ross, 1990).[7] Long before that, by about age 3½, a child has acquired the grammar and speech patterns (if not the working vocabulary) of the parents' language.

How can this happen? Parents spend less, not more, time eliciting and shaping language behavior after age 3. Can the rapid growth of words and the grammar adopted by the child be considered innate or rather be accounted for by environmental processes of imitated, reinforced, and punished verbal exchanges?

Chomsky's Universal Grammar

In his earliest writings Chomsky was struck by the appearance of the two-word utterance stage in cultures around the world. In no meaningful way, he reasoned, could learning account for this time-locked appearance of pat-

---

[7]This lexicon refers to receptive, not productive language capabilities. The reading and writing vocabulary at age 6 would be far less. What is interesting about this number is that it is identical to the 15,000 distinct words found in all of Shakespeare's written works (according to Pinker, 1994) and the estimated number of words in an average reading vocabulary of a Chinese adult (Holender, 1987, cited in Adams, 1990).

terned communication by 18-month-olds. He postulated the existence of an innate **universal grammar** to account for these observations. As revealed in the following quote, Chomsky's theoretical position resembles a doctrine of innate ideas:

> I'm not . . . convinced that there ever is going to be such a thing as a theory of learning. . . . I see what we call learning as one kind of growth. You know we don't learn to grow arms. We also don't learn to have language in any very interesting sense. What happens is that systems that are sort of pre-formed . . . or pre-adapted to certain consequences will interact with the environment in such a way as to sharpen them by filling in blanks, and you develop a system . . . We can hardly fail to be struck by the fact that so-called "learning theory" has been pursued for seventy or eighty years, and is so limited in its results—very little has come out of it. (Noam Chomsky, in Beckwith & Rispoli, 1986, p. 195)

We can join with Chomsky and proud parents cross-culturally in marveling at the amazing abilities of children who so rapidly acquire language. But let us reserve judgment on his ad hominem attack of all learning theories. What evidence, gathered rather early in the argument, suggested to Chomsky that shaping, reinforcement, and punishment do little to affect the acquisition of grammar?

Home Studies. Researchers Brown & Hanlon (1970) went into homes and recorded parent-child verbal interactions. They concluded that middle-class parents do not consistently reinforce proper grammatical conventions. For example, a toddler whose mother was brushing her hair said, "Her curl my hair" and was immediately reinforced by mom saying, "That's right, darling." By contrast, a grammatically correct comment by this child ("Walt Disney comes on Tuesday") was punished with a parental response, "No it doesn't, it comes on Thursday." Brown and his colleagues concluded that "truth value" of the utterance (i.e., the semantic meaning) rather than grammar was being reinforced. But it is also evident in this example that the parents' "words" shape the child's language behavior. The parents' words have acquired secondary reinforcing and punishing properties by prior associations.

Brown and Hanlon (1970) rediscovered that children apparently grow up in less than optimal language environments. Nevertheless, most children acquire the major grammatical features of their parents' language. Does that mean that Chomsky's theory of universal grammar is correct? Further, is his assertion that learning plays no role in language acquisition a reasonable one?

Associative Learning of the Lexicon

Not everyone agrees with all aspects of Chomsky's theory. Pinker (1991, 1994), for example, divides the "language instinct" into two parts: naming, or attaching arbitrary sounds to their meanings, and grammar, putting words together in meaningful ways. He agrees with Chomsky's position on grammar but disagrees regarding naming. The latter is accomplished by an associative process.

Many other researchers agree with Pinker (1994) that empiricist theories provide a better account for certain parts of the language acquisition process than do biological/cognitive theories. Stemmer (1989) in particular rejects cognitivists' claims that a child innately maps language onto objects in the environment. Mapping, he reasons, is nothing more than what Pavlov described as the pairing of two stimuli. Stemmer reasons that children, like Pavlov's dogs, have an inductive capacity. After pairing neutral stimuli (the sounds of words) with known objects, the child can then meaningfully respond to (i.e., induce) "new" objects as long as they are within the generalization gradient. The (mis)application of the word mama in reference to daddy, for example, can be interpreted as an example of the Pavlovian phenomenon of generalization. With further conditioned discrimination trials, the appropriate response can be consistently paired with the appropriate stimulus (i.e., the word mama becomes associated with mama; papa with papa).

Stemmer's (1989) analysis of language acquisition is a logical extension of Pavlov's second signal system. The role of generalization and the learning of discriminations enable an individual (human or animal) to learn perceptual concepts. An elaboration of this theory can be found in Hall (1991).

Associative Learning of Language Behavior

Parents Simplify Language. In what other way does the environment affect the acquisition and use of language? An adult's speech that is directed to a child is slower, clearly paced, and clearly pronounced. It contains fewer abstract words, and is spoken with exaggerated intonations. This *child-directed speech*, sometimes called *motherese*, holds the child's attention better than adult-directed language (Furrow, Nelson, & Benedict, 1979; Kaplan, Goldstein, Huckeby, Panneton-Cooper, 1995). Presumably, motherese makes it easier for the child to understand what is being communicated. Young children, after all, more often than not do not know what adults are talking about. The fact of the matter is that many children enjoy several years of a structured, hand-tailored interactive language environment before being gradually incorporated into the realm of adult language. Children also speak when no one is around.[8]

Attaching Emotion to Words, and Vice Versa. The most telling deficiency of Chomsky's biological/cognitive theory of language acquisition is his lack of consideration for the psychological and behavioral world of the hearing and speaking child. For the infant, toddler, and child, emotions, objects, and words are embedded in the experience of life. The language structure pro-

---

[8]A conservative estimate is that during the first 5 years of life, 10,000 hours of time are spent "practicing speaking" (Anderson, 1990). (Surely they listen to themselves talk?)

vided by parents includes the attachment of emotion, through conditioning, to words and phrases. To say that the word mama, for example, is associated (or mapped) with the object mama is a gross oversimplification. Mama is a composite of pleasure. Mama is the feel good of our earliest experiences: of food in the stomach, warmth, familiar smells and tastes, and physical contact. Mama is the emotional contract against fear, the dark, the unknown, and Binky's nightmare closet. Mama is symbolic of the lifelong quest for self-understanding that begins with coping when she is not there. Throughout a lifetime, each experience with mama continues the growth of the associative framework of the word, person, and emotional attachment. And then there is papa and other moving animals, including siblings, spouses, and pets.

Language is only a small part of the experience of living. "Experiencing" other living beings includes feeling unique sensations and emotions as well as the attachment of a language that refers to them. Chomsky's LAD totally ignores the reality of humans, especially of children, who learn to use language in their complex cognitive, emotional, and experiential environments.

Unique Emotional Attachments to Words.   Remember D.W., the 3-year-old who survived as long as his mother allowed him to eat salt and drink water around the clock (Box 10.1, p. 337)? Do you suspect that satisfying physiological needs produced emotional attachments to salt and to water and that the words salt and water became conditioned stimuli that gave D.W. pleasure? That the meeting of unusual needs attaches special meaning to some words is not the point. Rather, each of us lives in a unique flux; we share a common language, but the meanings of our own words reflect idiosyncratic learning histories.

Consider another example. A newly married couple find themselves arguing about each other's families. One says, "I don't want anything to do with family." The other says, "Family is very important to me." They are both using the same word, but their experience with the meaning of that word and the emotions attached to it are very different. To one, negative emotions, possibly from bad experiences with family, are attached to the word. The same word, even the same sentences, can mean different things to both speakers and listeners.

The Role of Context in Language Meaning

Do all of us learn the same meaning of even simple words such as yes and no? Or do we learn conditional yes's and no's? Arguments for a universal grammar ignore the subtleties and idiosyncrasies of language learning and language usage experienced by everyone who learns to speak.

Many demonstrations of classical and operant conditioning of language meaning have been reported (see Cicero & Tryon, 1989). For example, strict parents attach strong emotions to *yes* and *no*, to *right* and *wrong*. Less strict parents use *yes* and *no* in a looser fashion. Recall the verbal interchanges of Joey and his mother in the grocery store (summarized in Table 7.1, p. 268). *No* never meant more than *maybe*. Joey had learned that with enough verbal persistence (a behavior that had been consistently reinforced), the "No, you can't" would soon become "Oh, all right, but this is the last time."

Few linguists question that the meaning of words is associatively conditioned, and for clinical psychologists, reconditioning the meaning of words is one goal of psychotherapy (Staats & Staats, 1957). In summary, postulating a universal grammar doesn't tell us much at all about what will be verbalized when, what such verbalizations mean, or why the same words mean different things to different people. Language is embedded in behavior and culture as much as in biology.

Language "Growth" or Language "Learning"?

Chomsky (1980) conceptualizes the environment as a triggering and shaping instrument that determines the manner in which language grows. An analogy is that acorns do not learn to be oaks but grow into oaks; likewise, language growth is viewed as a genetic unfolding shaped by environment (Pateman, 1985). Perhaps, then, in seeking to understand language behavior, we are merely arguing over the relative importance of environment and genetics. Each plays a key role, as we have discovered for each topic covered in this next.

But surely Chomsky underestimates the role of environment. In the first place, as Skinner (1957) pointed out, language behavior is not synonymous with linguistic structure. Postulating a universal grammar and noting similarities across the world's different languages accounts more for the form than the function of language. Where do we see the influence of environment? Examples abound. Chinese isn't French, and the differences between these and hundreds of other languages are environmentally determined. In addition, language fails to develop in language-deficient environments (Candland, 1993; Curtiss, 1977).[9]

Environment and Individual Differences in Language

Listen to speaking humans in your particular subculture. Do some have more to say than others? Is it likely that Chomsky's universal grammar affords us all a "lowest common denominator" of verbal expression? Isn't it just as likely that unique environments produce the vast range of expressed human lan-

---

[9]In addition to Genie, the language-deficient child who was raised in a closet in Los Angeles (Curtiss, 1977), other well-documented cases of nonspeaking "wild children" raised without language givers include Peter (found in Germany in 1724); Victor (found in France in 1799); and Kamala and Amala (found in India in 1920). Their stories are recounted in a highly readable book by Candland (1993).

guage, from perfunctory utterances to finely crafted storytelling? The tremendous variation in language acquisition and usage both within and across cultures can be tied directly to unique environmental experiences.

Postulating a universal grammar doesn't address the enormous individual differences we find in spoken vocabulary, estimates of which range from a few thousand words in some individuals to tens of thousands of words in others. Nor does postulating a universal grammar address other than spoken language; reading and writing are two examples. Not surprisingly, those environments that support reading and writing are responsible for the profound individual differences in thought and consciousness that accompany differences in word usage. In the next section we look to the beginnings of something we are less biologically prepared to do, reading and writing.

Speaking and Learning (But Not Yet Reading)

> *Since [John] was six weeks old, we have spent 30–45 minutes reading to him each day. By the time he reaches first grade at age six and a quarter, that will amount to 1000 to 1700 hours of storybook reading—one on one, with his face in the books. He will also have spent at least as many hours fooling around with magnetic letters on the refrigerator, writing, participating in reading/writing/language activities in preschool, playing word and "spelling" games in the car, on the computer, with us, with his sister, with his friends, and by himself, and so on. [Furthermore] to account for such variation [within households], we may therefore add or subtract a thousand hours from John's total.*
>
> Marilyn Adams, *Beginning to Read: Thinking and Learning About Print* (1990, p. 85)

We have seen that the nativist position focuses on the ease of language acquisition. Chomsky's analysis is that, like walking, grammatical speech requires no training. By contrast, hundreds of hours are required for a toddler to make "basic" letter-sound correspondences (Adams, 1990). The child spends these hours in more structured environments than one in which speech is merely heard. A "reading environment" minimally requires printed text and, at least part of the time, a literate caregiver to direct the child's interaction with the text.

What Is the Reading Environment?   Parents who read with their toddlers do more than "teach them their letters." As a secondary gain the child benefits from the transmission of values, lifestyle, and the positive affect that accompanies reading and learning (Wigfield & Asher, 1984). From the child's perspective, these moments are among the most intense and most personally directed of all their interactions with caregivers. Children identified by Teale (1986) who had highly limited interactions with reading parents—an estimated 4 hours per year—are not only poor readers, but also miss out on the secondary social benefits. Four hours per year is a qualitatively different environment than the estimated thousands of hours per year in middle-class homes.

By contrast with learning to talk, learning to read is so painfully slow and difficult that after 12 years of formal schooling, high school illiteracy estimates remain as high as 25% (Weaver, 1994). Children who will become the best readers have, prior to formal schooling, several thousand hours or more of exposure to print. Such effort is reminiscent of our primate relatives who also require thousands of trials to learn to use artificial symbols both to communicate and to solve problems.

Associative Theory and Reading. Both Pavlovian and instrumental versions of associative theory account very well for how a child (or an adult) learns to read. From a Pavlovian perspective, both letters and their sounds are CSs. The visual letters signal the associated sound: The symbolic visual letter *D* is pronounced (and heard as) *dee*. The child's learning task is to make discriminated sight-sound associations—a process obviously more complex than this simple associative analysis suggests. (The kinesthetic cues of vocal cords, tongues, and air passage also become associated with the sight and sound of the letter.) Caregivers correctly vocalize and thereby model each letter. Correct vocalizations by the child are reinforced and/or shaped by successive approximation.

Conditioning Performance Factors. In reading to the child, parents direct attention to visual features of letters (and colors and pictures) in special children's books. (In doing this, parents are presenting the CSs in the form of discrete trials.) With reinforced practice, the mechanics of holding the book and of turning pages become automatic. As longer reading periods are demanded of children, attention spans are systematically lengthened (shaped). The child develops expectations about the amount of information per unit time that can be processed. By contrast, television programmers condition shorter attention spans by changing images in fractions of seconds.

Also, while reading (but not while watching television), the child controls the pace of behavioral engagement and, hence, the flow of information. The value of books and of reading is further conditioned by parental attention, physical contact, pleasing sights, sounds, odors, and so on.[10] Such early conditioning might account for lifelong emotional attachment to books by some people, such as librarians and others who love both libraries and the smell of books and who consider books to be best friends. These positive preverbal, prereading conditioning factors occur prior to the additional reinforcing properties of being entertained by stories and the reinforcement that occurs when concepts and ideas contained in the print are understood.

---

[10]A Jewish custom is to give candy to children during their first encounters with books. In an even older custom, infants were allowed to taste a drop of honey from a book cover, thereby conditioning a love of books by their pleasurable association with a sweet taste.

Preparing to Read: Cognitive or S-R Mechanism?

We have seen how easy it is for children to begin to speak. How do children learn to read? Can performance of this task be explained by the associative methods discussed in the preceding chapters, or do we need to invoke a specially human "cognitive" mechanism? There is now enough research to come to some tentative answers regarding this issue (Adams, 1990), but let us first take a closer look at the demands of reading.

Letter Recognition.   English-speaking readers have forgotten how foreign (and how similar) the letters H and F once looked. Lowercase p, b, and d not only look alike but also sound similar. Learning letters in English requires perhaps at least 52 sight-sound associations (26 lower- and 26 uppercase letters). These must be memorized before any reading takes place. The "empiricist principles—contiguity, recency, frequency, and similarity" provide the best account of how this procedure occurs (Adams, 1990, p. 202).

The facility with language has led one neuroscientist to proclaim humans as the "symbolic species" (Deacon, 1997). However, compared to the evolutionarily prepared "no training" acquisition of speaking, the fact is that learning to make sight-sound associations requires hundreds (thousands?) of trials over many hundreds of hours. This large number of training trials suggests that a human learning these rudimentary prereading tasks is as contraprepared as a chimp learning a symbolic oddity task. Indeed, Figure 1.1 (p. 15) points out the difficulty of learning symbols of different fonts, sizes, and colors. It is safe to conclude that no special cognitive mechanism facilitates the learning of the elements of printed language.

Phoneme Recognition.   What other prereading experiences prepare a 6-year-old child to read? Although letter knowledge has been found to be the strongest predictor of those who will be reading at the end of the first year of school, the ability to discriminate phonemes (syllable and letter sounds) was the second most important variable (Bond & Dykstra, 1967). These are not mutually exclusive skills. If the letters b and p are to be learned, the child has to hear the difference between these two sounds as well as recognize the differences in their letter shapes.

Interim Summary

1. One-word utterances merge into a two-word utterance stage during the second year. Cross-culturally, rules of syntax appear to govern how words are used. Chomsky proposed an innate ***universal grammar*** mechanism.

2. Observation of parent-child interactions in homes does not support the proposition that parents are instrumental in shaping a child's grammar by reward and punishment.

3. The role of environment can be seen in the specifics of phoneme production and receptivity, in the associative learning of the lexicon, in the role parents play in simplifying language, and in the unique ways in which words acquire emotional meanings.

4. The meaning of words is conditioned as the child interacts with his or her verbal environment. Likewise, the context, or environment, in which words are used helps to determine their meaning.

5. During these first few years, receptive language capacity far exceeds productive language.

6. The range of spoken language and language comprehension is enormous. Individual differences are better accounted for by reference to environment rather than an innate language mechanism.

7. Language acquisition is best conceptualized as being determined by the interaction of biology, behavior, and culture.

8. Middle-class parents spend a few thousand hours teaching children their letters and helping them sound out simple words before, often about age 6, the child encounters formal reading instruction.

9. The child's prereading preparation in English involves many hundreds of hours memorizing the sound-sight associations of over 52 (upper- and lowercase) letters, not counting different fonts and colors. The process is best described as simple associative conditioning involving contiguity of the stimulus elements and frequency of presentation.

10. Individual differences in a child's prereading preparation are enormous, ranging from a few hours to thousands of hours per year. Parent-child reading interactions also provide optimal settings for learning other tasks and for the transmission of cultural values.

11. Before becoming a reader, the child must learn to discriminate the phonemic sounds of the language being learned (probably preceding and during the time they learn their letters).

12. Letters and their sounds are CSs that are paired in an associative manner.

13. Among the performance factors conditioned during early training are attention spans, holding books, and turning pages.

DISCUSSION QUESTIONS

6. Brown and his colleagues studied how parents reinforced and punished their children's language behavior. Their conclusion was that correct grammar was less important to parents than how well the child's language accurately reflected what was going on around them. These researchers pointed out the irony of all children being consistently reinforced for telling the truth but who then lie so much as adults. Can you identify the contingencies of reinforcement and punishment that maintain confabulation, lying, and other deceptive language practices? That is, under what conditions is lying reinforced and when is it punished? What are "white lies"? Does a universal grammar predict white lies?

7. Tamil says, "I love to read!" Roberto says, "I hate to read!" Does their lan-guage reflect unique conditioning histories?

8. Recall that "no" meant "maybe" for Joey (p. 264). Now accused of rape, Joey's defense attorney has argued that his 18-year conditioning history absolves him of his behavior. You are the prosecuting attorney . . .

LANGUAGE, LITERACY, AND INTELLIGENCE

Humans have been compared to other animals throughout this text. We have seen that non-human animals can think but cannot talk. Non-human animals are conscious but arguably not in the same way as humans. Monkeys and chimpanzees can learn relatively complex rules and concepts more easily than other mammals, and humans require fewer trials to learn even higher-order concepts. No surprises here.

What makes us so different from other animals? Certainly, language defines us, but the activities of yet other areas of our brain also make us different. No other animal composes music, records it symbolically, builds the instruments on which to play it, or invests the time and effort necessary to accomplish a virtuoso performance. (Nor would any animal—except a human—attend the performance if it were to be given.)

No other animal behavior comes anywhere near the accomplishments of humans in the arts, home construction, mathematics, cooking, literature, fashion design, athletics, editorial cartoons, science, or technology. So it is easy to agree with Dennett's comparisons of humans with other animals (p. 411): Humans are the only ones that use language, and we are smarter than all other animals. Given this observation, it is not unreasonable to inquire into the relationship of language to intelligence.

Lastly, humans with written language are the only animals to have developed culture and, among some groups of humans, civilization.[11] Here we entertain some of the complex relationships that exist among language, literacy, and intelligence.

Literacy and Cognitive Processes

A delay in learning to read has behavioral and motivational consequences as well as cognitive ones, in no small part because the growth of a child's cognitive processes correspond to his or her ability to read. The longer this devel-

[11]Chimpanzees also develop basic features of culture (Whiten, et al, 1999). See http://chimp.st-and.ac.uk/cultures/variation.htm

opmental delay is allowed to continue, the more generalized the deficits will become, seeping into yet more areas of cognition and behavior. Or to put it more simply—and sadly— in the words of a tearful 9-year-old, already falling frustratingly far behind his peers in reading progress, "reading affects everything you do." (Stanovich, 1986, p. 390). The implication is that literacy is a building stone on which some aspects of thought and intelligence are based.

Vocabulary Growth and Print Exposure. Consider the following facts: An excellent reader in the fifth grade is encountering 6 million printed words each year in out-of-school reading while the average student sees only 650,00 words (Anderson, Wilson, & Fielding, 1988; Fielding, Wilson, & Anderson, 1987).[12] Furthermore, the amount of print exposure for fifth-graders reading at the 90th percentile is 200 times greater than for those reading at the 10th percentile. That is, for every 100 words a person at the 10th percentile reads, his or her counterpart at the 90th percentile is reading 20,000 words. First conclusion: Profound individual differences exist in time spent reading. Those who have spent more time reading know more words. The process is associative.

Next, consider vocabulary growth. An average school-age child is acquiring an English vocabulary at a rate of about 8 words per day, or about 3,000 words per year (Miller & Gildea, 1987; Nagy & Anderson, 1984). Vocabulary growth appears to be determined largely by the frequency with which words are encountered in print. For example, as you are well aware, a college environment is a reading environment. The average high school graduate in the United States has a reading familiarity with approximately 45,000 words, while, on average, the college graduate has nearly twice as many words (Miller, 1991). Second conclusion: Those children who are exposed to more print (who read more) ultimately acquire a larger vocabulary. The process is associative.

Print Exposure and IQ

The most important point to be gleaned from these data concerns the size of the differences in both print exposure and vocabulary by about age 11. Not only does reading affect everything you do, as the 9-year-old says in the quote from Stanovich (1986), the effects of these differences on the development of intellectual life are profound. Another important finding in the print exposure study cited is that the quality of reading material is a less important factor than is the quantity of reading. In college-age students, the single best predictor of IQ is the amount of print exposure. Conclusion? We should encourage our children to read whatever interests them. The evidence indicates that

---

[12]I doubted this statistic the first time I encountered it. Since my daughter Jane was then an avid reader in the fifth grade, she and I used two different methods to compute her print exposure for the year. Our estimates from both methods were 5 and 9 million words per year.

their overall cognitive abilities will be enhanced. One outcome of thousands of hours of exposure to the printed word is that it allows them to use language better than those who don't read as much. But does it make them smarter? Let us look next at the relationship of language and intelligence.

Literacy and Intelligence

The development of written language during the past several thousand years has allowed some human cultures to develop new ways of thinking about what it means to be human and about the universe. Western culture, as an example, is the product of cumulatively written as well as orally transmitted knowledge. Now, since all living humans have ancestors that could not read or write, literacy is neither a necessary nor sufficient condition to survive and reproduce the next generation.[13] Intelligence as a collection of behaviors that enhance inclusive fitness can be defined without reference to either oral or written language. But intelligence at a higher level is tied to language, especially to written language.

Language Acquisition and Intelligence. Among the questions that can be asked about language and intelligence is whether more intelligent children read sooner and better than less intelligent children. The answer is a mixed one, depending on one's definition of intelligence (Adams, 1990). Some studies show no relationship of early reading ability and tests of nonverbal intelligence. What does seem to be the case, however, is that the better readers (those who have more print exposure) soon begin to score higher on IQ tests (also, see pp. 426, the quote from Stanovich, 1986). Even after controlling for differences in nonverbal cognitive ability (differences that are considerable), a recent study reports that mere exposure to large numbers of words enhances the verbal intelligence of college students (Stanovich & Cunningham, 1992).

Literacy and the Brain

About 7000 to 10,000 years ago some cultures developed reading and writing. As a result, they produced sophisticated civilizations. Why is it that literate humans seemed to make a qualitative leap over other animals, including nonliterate humans? This question has occupied scholars for centuries and will not be adequately answered here. Steven Pinker and others have pointed to a unique human brain organization that supports language. Reading and writing add to these language areas of the human brain by incorporating the visual cortex and other areas of neocortex into the language loop. According to one theory, known as the Wernicke-Geschwind model, when a person reads a

---

[13]All other animals do just fine without language.

printed word, visual areas of the brain are involved in addition to the so-called "language areas" (the angular gyrus, Wernicke's area, and Broca's area) (Geschwind, 1970). Figure 12.4 shows the extent of reading-associated brain areas using functional magnetic resonance imaging (fMRI) (Bavelier, et al, 1997). One can see that reading causes increases in a large portion of the frontal, temporal, and parietal cortex (the darkened areas in Figure 12.4). Prior to reading (and in the illiterate) these areas of the brain would not be concurrently activated. This increased computational power of the brain underlies the intellectual achievements that define civilization.

Language, Literacy, and Culture

People in all cultures acquire spoken language in the same way (i.e., as described by Chomsky), but not all cultures enjoy literacy. In an earlier chapter, for example, a young Cherokee Indian named Little Tree learned survival skills from his grandfather, who told him and showed him how to walk on a hillside, how to catch fish with his hands, and so forth. But neither the Cherokees nor any other native American Indian developed written language. It is likely that for literate cultures the oral transmission of cultural knowledge preceded writing by tens of thousands of years.

Left Hemisphere

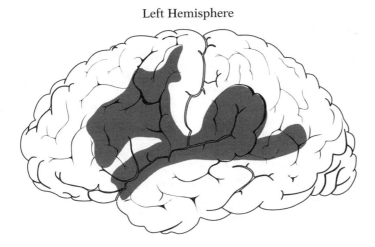

FIGURE 12.4   Brain Areas Involved in Literacy

A new technology, functional magnetic resonance imaging (fMRI) allows researchers to look at brain activity as a human behaves. The darkened areas of the left hemisphere show increased neural activity in the frontal, temporal, and parietal lobes when a person reads passages. (Modified from Bavelier et al., 1997.)

Human culture differentiates us from other animals because of our unique brains and behavior, including language behavior, and, through literacy, by the transmission of one generation's accomplishments to the next. A working assumption is that written history has allowed the tremendous explosion in knowledge and culture humans have entertained during the past few thousand years. Finally, among humans with written language, civilization emerged.[14]

Language Doesn't Guarantee Civilization. Language by itself, however, does not guarantee either civilization or even cultural development much beyond that of other primates. The Tasmanians, a race destroyed by European settlers several hundred years ago, had been isolated from other humans for so long that they had not shared the accumulated "Design wealth" alluded to by Dennett in the opening quotation. Isolated from other humans, they suffered a lack of the cross-cultural transmission of memes from other cultures (Diamond, 1997). The consequences of isolation were dire: As discussed in Box 12.1, the last Tasmanian died in 1876.

Written Language and Human Culture

From a comparative perspective, then, it is reasonable to assume that human language preceded and allowed the development of important aspects of human thought. Language as a species-specific behavior that enhances inclusive fitness remains the most important difference separating humans from other animals. Moreover, with the development of written language we see opening an enormous gap among members of the human species—those who learn to read and write, and those who do not. Consider, for example, the following devastating effects of illiteracy on success in our culture:

Illiterate adults account for 75% of the unemployed, one-third of the mothers receiving Aid to Families with Dependent Children, 85% of the juveniles who appear in court, 60% of prison inmates, and nearly 40% of minority youth; of people in the work force, 15% are functionally illiterate, including 11% of professional and managerial workers, and 30% of semiskilled and unskilled workers. Fortune magazine reports that "of the 3.8 million 18-year-old Americans in 1988, fully 700,000 had dropped out of school, and another 700,000 could not read their high school diplomas." (Adams, 1990, p. 27)

With few exceptions, someone who cannot read or write is a beneficiary of, but not a major contributor to, civilization.

---

[14]The Incas of Peru are an exception: They developed a relatively sophisticated civilization without the benefit of a written language.

BOX 12.1   THE LAST OF THE TASMANIANS

Anthropologists make the distinction between human culture and human civilization. The former is defined by humans living in groups, the latter by the growth of walled cities, a division of labor, and typically, the development of writing. Jarod Diamond (1997) has provided a highly informative account of the growth of civilization (or not) in various parts of the world.

One example is the story of cultural clash that began in the 1600s when Europeans began to settle in Tasmania (Diamond, 1992). Tasmania is a large island 200 miles south of the Australian continent, populated with people that had been separated from their aboriginal ancestors for an estimated 10,000 years. About 5,000 Tasmanians lived in hunter-gatherer societies when discovered by Europeans. Their lifestyles were primitive by most standards:

> *Like the mainland Aborigines, they lacked metal tools, agriculture, livestock, pottery, and bows and arrows. Unlike the mainlanders, they also lacked boomerangs, dogs, nets, knowl-*

> *edge of sewing, and the ability to start a fire.* (Diamond, p. 278)

Their European discoverers enslaved, imprisoned, and slaughtered these indigenous people over the next few hundred years until the last Tasmanian, named Truganini, died over a century ago. The Tasmanians had language (Chomsky's universal grammar) but lacked written language.

Language is common to all *Homo sapiens*. Language alone, however, does not guarantee the sophisticated culture that modern humans associate with civilization. You may argue that there was nothing "civilized" about a European culture that committed genocide on the Tasmanians. Unfortunately, neither language nor written language can completely insulate humans from those parts of their genetically determined brain that will always be capable of generating uncivilized behavior. Conclusion: Human language is a necessary but not sufficient condition for civilization.

Human Learning and Culture

We began this chapter seeking an understanding of our most unique behavior, human language. We have found that all humans speak and that this is best understood as the most important species-specific behavior in our repertoire. We have also found that learning plays an enormous role in how we use language and whether or not we become literate. We have determined that it is learning to read and write, and not language per se, that best accounts for the role a person will play in our culture. It is for these reasons that Chomsky's assertion to the effect that learning plays no meaningful role in human behavior is so baffling.

What is the counterpoint? First, language behavior affords humans the opportunity to occupy a unique place among other animals on this planet.

Second, reading and writing allow some fortunate humans (and cultures) to achieve a qualitatively higher level of discourse—of conceptual thinking, of realized consciousness, and of intelligence—than that enjoyed by speaking but illiterate humans. Human culture is not synonymous with human civilization. The Tasmanians were uncivilized, and had they survived without being influenced by other cultures, would probably still not be able to start a fire. Unfortunately, the culture of the civilized Europeans they encountered allowed for their destruction. But a variety of that same European culture allowed humans to land on the moon several hundred years later.

Contrary to Chomsky's message, literacy is learned and learned only by tremendous effort within a supportive environment. Literacy is much like the other things you have learned as a human, be it dancing or ice skating, or playing soccer, the guitar, or the piano. The role of learning and environment is of critical importance. We are not the only animals who learn, but because of our unique genetic makeup, we certainly learn and behave in interesting ways.

Interim Summary

1. The development of reading skills leads to the development of other cognitive skills. Developmentally delayed readers fall behind in other areas of school performance.
2. Print exposure differences measured in thousands of hours separate good from poor readers and people with large vocabularies from those with small ones. Exposure to print is the single best predictor of verbal intelligence measures of IQ.
3. Literacy is learned in an associative manner.
4. Literate individuals score higher on nonverbal intelligence tests than do the illiterate.
5. Reading uses areas of the cerebral cortex that would not otherwise be used in oral language.
6. Illiterate individuals do not do well in our culture. Illiteracy is associated with unemployment, crime, and other societal problems.
7. Humans are the only animals that enjoy language and the only animals to have developed culture. Civilization depends on literacy.

DISCUSSION QUESTIONS

9. Given the finding that children who have their noses in books most of the time do better in school, score higher on intelligence tests, and are generally smarter and have more successful careers than their less scholarly contemporaries throughout a lifetime, how are you going to raise your own children?

CHAPTER SUMMARY

1. Although a number of animals show communication patterns in the real world (some even resembling primitive language), the results of having animals learn symbolic language in laboratories have been discouraging.

2. Among the issues related to animal "language" are questions of intentionality, spontaneity (proactive rather than reactive language), and cost benefit (few demonstrations of even minimal animal language following intensive training efforts by different experimenters).

3. Despite numerous efforts to engage porpoises and chimpanzees in symbolic conversation throughout this century, in the realm of language humans remain in a class by themselves.

4. The most encouraging findings have come from work with Alex, a parrot, and Kanzi, a pygmy chimpanzee (*Pan paniscus*).

5. Kanzi differs from other chimpanzees (a) in voluntarily entering the conversation as opposed to being trained into it, (b) attempting to vocalize language as humans do.

6. Children start to to talk without formal instruction, a phenomenon that is best accounted for by a nativist position.

7. Language is readily modifiable by environment. Individual differences in language, best accounted for by traditional theories of learning, include which language is spoken, the unique meanings and emotions conditioned to words, and the role of environmental context.

8. Crying is an FAP and can be modified by reinforcement and punishment.

9. Two extreme theories propose to account for how children acquire language; represented by Noam Chomsky's nativist position, and by B. F. Skinner's behaviorist position.

10. At 6 to 12 months human infants begin to discriminate the phonemic sounds of the language they hear. First words (*holophrastic speech*) occur at about 1 year of age, via what Chomsky called a *language acquisition device*.

11. Chomsky's innate *universal grammar* mechanism mediates a two-word utterance stage during the second year. Syntax is similar cross-culturally. The child's spoken grammar is little affected by traditional learning processes.

12. Environments vary markedly with respect to how much language a child hears. Children do not learn to speak in language-less environments. The meaning of some words is conditioned by association of word sound with objects and actions.

13. Reading skills are acquired much more slowly than speaking. Reading is best understood from within a framework of learning by association (i.e., of sight of printed text with the sound of the spoken language).

14. Other behaviors are conditioned while a middle-class child learns to "read" during the several thousands of hours of preschool instruction. These include attachment of positive emotions to caregivers, books, and the reading process itself.

15. The child's prereading preparation involves memorizing (by simple associative conditioning) the sound-sight associations of 52 (upper- and lowercase) letters and by learning to discriminate their phonemic differences.

16. Reading skill development allows for further cognitive development. Poor readers fall behind in other areas of school performance.

17. Print exposure differences among readers are enormous. Amount of print exposure is a predictor of verbal intelligence scores.

18. Readers score higher than non-readers on nonverbal tests of intelligence.

19. Language skills, including literacy, differentiate humans from other animals and make civilization possible.

20. Language behavior, not unlike other behavior, is best understood as the interaction of biology, behavior, and culture.

KEY TERMS

GLOSSARY

adaptation Any characteristic that improves an organism's chances of transmitting its genes to the next generation.

animal communication The production and reception of signals, typically meaningful only to conspecifics.

animal model The use of animals in research that bears on the human condition. Example: an animal model of alcohol addiction.

annoyers (Thorndike) Unpleasant, or aversive stimuli. (Cf. *punisher.*)

anthropomorphism The attribution of human characteristics to animals, deities, and others.

appetitive conditioning (Pavlov) Foodbased Pavlovian conditioning. (Cf. *appetite.*)

association theory The relationship (connection, union) of two or more stimuli when they are paired together in time.

automaintenance Maintenance of key-pecking behavior in the absence of a response contingency due to the contiguity between response and reinforcement.

autoshaping Occurrence of key-pecking responses in the absence of a reinforcement contingency. (Also called *signtracking.*)

aversive conditioning Conditioning experiments using aversive stimuli.

avoidance procedure Any procedure in which an animal's instrumental response prevents an aversive consequence. Example: a lever press prevents, or avoids, delivery of electric shock.

backward conditioning (Pavlov) Pairings of the CS and US in which the onset of the unconditioned stimulus precedes the onset of the conditioned stimulus.

baseline The preexperimental, or normal, level of a measured response.

behavior The way in which an animal acts or responds within the environment.

behavior modification The systematic application of reinforcers and punishers, and other classical and operant conditioning procedures, to change target behaviors.

behavior theory An analysis of the way in which animals act or respond with environments as encompassing the interplay of genes and environment.

behavioral contrast Reinforcement effects determined by an animal's prior comparison and contrast with other reinforcers. (See *negative contrast*).

behavioral control The past and present reinforcement and punishment contingencies that determine the expression of a behavior.

behavioral therapy Any psychotherapeutic procedure involving the systematic application of reinforcers or punishers, or the implementation of extinction or other classical or operant procedure, known to be effective in effecting behavioral change.

behavioral tolerance The portion of total drug tolerance that can be attributed to learned or environmental variables.

behaviorism A philosophical position of environmental determinism, that behavior is determined and controlled by reinforcing and punishing contingencies.

between-groups design The design of an experiment in which the effect of manipulating an independent variable (i.e., the treatment group) is compared to a control group not having the independent variable. (Cf. *within-groups design*.)

biocultural evolution (S. Katz) The process by which the selection, preparation, and consumption of particular types of food by some individuals provided a reproductive advantage, one that contributed to the divergence of human populations.

biofeedback A procedure by which a subject can become aware of and can gain voluntary control over brain waves, heart rate, skin conductance, and so forth.

biological determinism The philosophical position that behavior is caused by the immutable action of genes. (Cf. *environmental determinism.*)

blocking A procedure in which prior conditioning to CS_1 blocks the conditioning to CS_2 when CS_1 and CS_2 are conditioned in compound.

chained operant A behavioral sequence analyzed in terms of a succession of discriminative stimuli that set the occasions for a series of operant responses, eventually ending with a reinforcer. (cf., *stimulus-response chains*)

changeover delay (COD) A brief period of time during which reinforcement is not available immediately following a switch, or changeover, from one reinforcement schedule to the other, in a concurrent schedule procedure.

classical conditioning See *Pavlovian conditioning.*

classical eyeblink conditioning A conditioning procedure in which a light or tone CS is paired with an airpuff to the eye, and presenting the CS causes an eyeblink response.

cognitive map (Tolman) The proposal that some animals (including rats) can form memories of where they are located relative to a food source and, even without direct experience of the route, "know" the shortest path connecting them with the food.

cognitive processes Psychological processes of perceiving, thinking, knowing, remembering, and so on.

concurrent schedules A training procedure in which a subject can respond on either of two reinforcement schedules that run simultaneously and independently of each other.

conditioned compensatory responses Learned physiological responses that reduce the effectiveness of the drugs that are taken in familiar environments; the stimuli from these environments trigger the compensatory responses.

conditioned discrimination A procedure used to train an animal to respond differently to two stimuli.

conditioned emotional response The outcome of an experimental treatment in which a CS is paired with an aversive US.

conditioned excitor A descriptive term for the CS after it has been conditioned in a forward, or excitatory, manner. The CS acquires excitatory properties.

conditioned facilitation Conditioning the immune system as demonstrated by an increase in antibody production in the presence of a conditioned stimulus.

conditioned immunosuppression Conditioning the immune system as demonstrated by a decrease in antibody production in the presence of a conditioned stimulus.

conditioned inhibition An inhibitory process that in many ways is the opposite of conditioned excitation.

conditioned inhibitor A descriptive term for the CS after it has been conditioned in a backward, or otherwise inhibitory, manner. The CS acquires inhibitory properties.

conditioned response (CR) (Pavlov) A new response, learned to the CS, following pairings of a neutral stimulus (i.e., the CS) with an unconditioned stimulus.

conditioned stimulus (CS) (Pavlov) A stimulus that comes to control a reflexive response following pairings with an unconditioned stimulus.

conditioned suppression A conditioning procedure in which a tone CS is paired with an electric shock US, and presenting the CS suppresses an animal's lever-pressing response for food.

conditioned taste aversion A conditioning procedure in which an animal drinks a flavored solution (the CS) and is then made sick by a toxin (the US).

consummatory behaviors (ethology) Innate, genetically determined "survival" behaviors, including fixed action patterns, which determine species-specific patterns of feeding, courting, reproduction, social interactions, and so on.

context The background stimulus conditions of a learning experiment.

contiguity theory of association The theory that stimulus-stimulus associations occur when two stimuli are perceived close together in time.

contingency theory of association The theory that stimulus-stimulus associations occur when one stimulus reliably precedes and signals the occurrence of a second stimulus.

contraprepared The opposite of a prepared, or easily conditioned, response.

control group A comparison group for a treatment group.

critical period (ethology) A specific time period (usually early in an animal's development) when an animal is particularly sensitive to certain features in the environment. Exposure to such sign stimuli "releases" genetically determined behavioral responses. (Cf. *imprinting; sign stimulus*)

CS preexposure effect A reduction in conditioning due to familiarity of the conditioned stimulus. (also known as *latent inhibition*.)

CS-US interval A time interval measured from the onset of the conditioned stimulus to the onset of the unconditioned stimulus.

delayed match-to-sample A task measuring learning and memory processes that involves briefly presenting a target stimulus (i.e., the stimulus to be remembered) and, after a delay, again presenting the target with a number of distractor stimuli. The animal is reinforced for selecting the target from the distractors. (See also *picture memory*.)

dependent variable In an experiment, the treatment effect of an independent variable is assessed by measuring changes in the dependent variable.

differential reinforcement of high rates (DRH) A schedule of reinforcement that reinforces bursts of operant responses.

differential reinforcement of low rates (DRL) A schedule of reinforcement that reinforces timed pauses between operant responses.

discrete avoidance A procedure in which a stimulus sets the occasion for an avoidance response, that, when emitted, delays or prevents an aversive stimulus.

discriminated operant A particular operant response under stimulus control.

discriminative stimulus (S⁺) (*pronounced S-plus*) A stimulus that signals that a particular response-reinforcement contingency is in effect, therefore setting occasions during which operant responses become highly probable.

disinhibition (Pavlov) The process by which an extraneous stimulus disrupts the ongoing effects of an inhibitory stimulus, typically allowing a release of excitation. The stimulus involved is called a *disinhibiting stimulus*.

drive reduction theory (Hull) The theory that physiological needs instill drives, and that reinforcement occurs when specific needs are met (or reduced), restoring an animal to homeostatic balance.

drive theory (see *drive reduction theory*.)

drive-stimulus reduction The theory that stimulus properties of incentives, and not the necessity of meeting physiological needs, are sufficient to reduce drive states.

electrical stimulation of the brain (ESB) The reinforcing effects of passing minute amounts of electric current through an implanted electrode to specific areas of the brain.

elicited behavior Reflexive or otherwise innately organized behavior, sometimes characterized as *involuntary* behavior. (Cf. Skinner's distinction between *elicited* and *emitted* behavior.)

embedded conditioning A variation of simultaneous conditioning in which the onset and offset of either the CS or US occurs during the other element.

emitted behavior Instrumental responses, sometimes characterized as *voluntary* behavior, that are not readily tied to specific eliciting stimuli. (Cf. Skinner's distinction between *elicited* and *emitted* behavior.)

environmental determinism The philosophical position that behavior is caused (determined) by environmental influences. (Cf. *behaviorism; biological determinism.*)

escape procedure A procedure in which an animal makes an instrumental response that has the effect of terminating an aversive stimulus.

evolution Charles Darwin's theory that existing species of life on Earth are the end result of a process of natural selection; descent with modification.

expected utility The expected gain from a decision made about a wager or transaction involving money or other tangible valuable.

extinction (experimental extinction) (Pavlov) A reduction of the CR in the presence of the CS.

FI (See *fixed interval*.)

fitness The measure of an animal's success in producing viable offspring.

fixed action pattern (FAP) (ethology) An orderly, relatively fixed series of movements, triggered by a biologically meaningful stimulus.

fixed interval (FI) A schedule of reinforcement in which an animal is reinforced for its first response following a specified time interval from the preceding reinforcer.

fixed ratio (FR) A schedule of reinforcement in which reinforcement is contingent upon the completion of a fixed number of operants responses.

foraging patterns Innately disposed behavior that results in the conduct of patterned searches and remembering where food is located in three-dimensional space.

FR See *fixed ratio*.

fractional anticipatory goal responses (rGs) (Hull) The theory that self-generated stimuli occur during the run down the pathway prior to entry into the goal box, are reinforced, and in turn become secondary reinforcers for even earlier responses in the maze. This theory allows a single reinforcer to connect complex sequences of behavior.

free operant An easy, repeatable operant response, such as a lever press.

frustration theory (Amsel) The theory that following a history of continuous reinforcement, an extinction procedure produces a state of negative emotions such as frustration.

general process learning theory The theory that animals have common learning processes. General process learning is contrasted with species-specific learning.

generalization The tendency of animals to both perceive (stimulus generalization) and respond (response generalization) in a similar manner to stimuli that share common properties.

genetics The study of patterns of heredity and variations in plants and animals.

habituation The reduced responsiveness of an organism to repeated stimulation.

habituation control group A nonassociative control group that is presented the CS but not the US during conditioning.

hedonic conditioning Changes in food selected based on the positive or negative post-ingestional consequences of previous selections.

hedonism The proposal that humans and other animals are innately motivated to seek pleasure and to avoid pain.

heredity The genetic transmission of characteristics from one generation to the next.

higher-order conditioning (Pavlov) The conditioning process by which a CS acquires unconditioned stimulus properties.

hypothetical construct The psychological terms used to label alleged processes of the mind, such as personality, learning, memory, motivation, perception, and intelligence. (Cf. *intervening variable.*)

imprinting (Ethology) The is a type of learning characterized by the rapid development of a genetically-programmed response to a specific stimulus at a particular stage of development. (Cf. *critical period; innate releasing mechanism.*)

incentive motivation (Hull) Motivation to behave that can be attributed to the quality and amount of a reinforcer. The reinforcer is said to act as an incentive.

independent variable In an experiment, the variable that is manipulated to see how it affects the dependent variable.

induction method A procedure used to condition an inhibitory response by pairing an excitor with a neutral stimulus, not followed by food.

inhibition of delay (Pavlov) The effect of an inhibitory process caused by the passage of time, measured as a suppressed responding in the early part of an interval of responding.

innate releasing mechanism (IRM) (Ethology) A postulated neural mechanism that, when stimulated by a sign-releasing stimulus, triggers an innately organized motor program. (Cf. critical period; sign stimulus.)

instinct Genetically predisposed, innately organized behavior.

instinctive drift The theory that arbitrarily established responses erode (drift) in the face of more innately organized (instinctive) behavior (Breland).

instrumental conditioning See *instrumental learning.*

instrumental learning Acquiring and modifying "voluntary," emitted, or otherwise nonreflexive behavior by the application of reinforcers or punishers.

intermittent reinforcement (See *partial reinforcement.*)

intertrial interval The elapsed time between conditioning trials in a conditioning experiment.

intervening variable Processes of the mind, such as learning, memory, and motivation that are operationally defined, and that bridge the gap between measurable stimulus and response variables. (Cf. *hypothetical construct.*)

labor supply curve A backward-bending curve that shows increased amount of work produced as rate of pay declines, up to a point. From that point, a decreased amount of work is produced for further declines in rate of pay.

Lamarckian evolution The theory that genetic changes in populations (i.e., evolution) can occur through the inheritance of characters acquired during a lifetime.

language acquisition device (LAD)　(Chomsky) A proposed species-specific brain mechanism (or series of mechanisms) that allows a human child to rapidly acquire language, once triggered by a minimal language environment.

latent inhibition　A reduction in conditioning due to familiarity of the conditioned stimulus. (Also known as the *CS preexposure effect* and *US preexposure effect*.)

latent learning　(Tolman) Learning that is alleged to occur in the absence of a specific food reward.

law of effect　(Thorndike) A response followed by a pleasant consequence (satisfier) will tend to be repeated and a response followed by an unpleasant consequence (annoyer) will tend to decrease in frequency.

law of strength　(Pavlov) Three interrelated factors that account for the strength (or magnitude) of a conditioned response: the intensity of the CS, the intensity of the US, and a close interstimulus interval between the CS and US.

learning　A relatively permanent change in observable behavior that results from experience within the environment.

learning set　(Harlow) A learning procedure in which two stimuli are presented to an animal for a set of six consecutive trials. Selecting one, arbitrarily designated as the "correct" choice, is reinforced. After completing many sets of such problems, animals learn a win-stay, lose-shift strategy and are able to consistently respond correctly on the first opportunity.

learning theory　The proposition that a limited number of general principles of learning can account for much of the observed variability in animal behavior.

learning to learn　(Harlow) The term that describes the ability of animals to slowly learn a general rule that they could then apply to rapidly solve new problem sets. (See *win-stay, lose-shift strategy; learning set*.)

learning-performance distinction　The difference between what is measured (performance) and what is inferred from the measurement (learning).

long-term depression (LTD)　Decreased responsiveness of certain neurons stimulated rapidly and repeatedly that may last for days and even weeks. LTD may mediate associative effects between neurons.

long-term potentiation (LTP)　Increased responsiveness of certain neurons stimulated rapidly and repeatedly that may last for days and even weeks. LTP may mediate associative effects between neurons.

magazine training　An initial stage of operant conditioning in which the sound of the food delivery mechanism becomes associated with food delivery.

matching law　A monotonic direct functional relationship typically found between the rate of responding and available reinforcement (Herrnstein).

melioration　Equalization of obtained reinforcement for two alternatives.

meme　An element of culture that is passed on by non-genetic means.

Morgan's canon　Morgan's (1894) position that scientists should not attribute complex psychological processes to animals if their behavior could be understood from the perspective of lower (simpler) psychological processes.

natural concepts　A term used to describe the ability of pigeons to extract information from complex pictures of natural environments and to respond in a way that indicates that they recognize trees, people, and other "open-ended" categories.

natural selection　(Darwin) Plants and animals better adapted to their environment (i.e., nature) produce more offspring. Animals not able to overcome selection pressures have fewer to no offspring.

negative contrast　Following the contrasting experience of small and large reinforcers, the smaller one is less reinforcing. (See also *Behavioral Contrast*.)

negative reinforcement　The process by which a response that prevents or avoids an aversive stimulus increases in frequency.

neophobia A behavioral tendency to approach new objects cautiously (literally, *fear of the new*).

nonassociative learning Relatively permanent changes in behavior that result from an animal experiencing a single stimulus. Sensitization and habituation are two examples. (Cf. *association theory*.)

null hypothesis In an experiment, the hypothesis that no differences exist between a treatment condition with a control group.

occasion setting A procedure in which a stimulus or context signals that a following stimulus will be a discriminative stimulus.

oddity concept Learning to select the odd stimulus from a three-stimulus display containing two that are identical and one that is different.

omnivore's paradox The paradox that eating from a wide variety of food sources enhances an omnivore's fitness during famine but decreases fitness by increasing the risk of poisoning. (Paul Rozin).

one-word utterance stage The first words spoken in any language, typically referring to names for objects encountered in their environment, such as mama and milk and for actions such as get and go. (Also known as *holophrastic speech*.)

operant (*or* **operant response**) (Skinner) A designated response, such as a lever press, that effectively *operates* upon the environment (Cf. *instrumental response*.)

operant conditioning (Skinner) A variant of instrumental conditioning. (See *instrumental conditioning*.)

operant level (Skinner) An existing baseline rate of a response as measured prior to the administration of reinforcement and punishment contingencies. (Cf. *baseline* or *free-operant level*.)

operational definition A definition of a term or concept that refers to the operations that measure the presumptive process.

overmatching Responding *more* than predicted for available reinforcement.

overshadowing A procedure in which two CSs are conditioned simultaneously and one of them acquires more associative strength than another. The CS that conditions best is said to *overshadow* the other CS.

partial reinforcement Any reinforcement schedule other than continuous reinforcement. (Also called *intermittent reinforcement*.)

partial reinforcement effect The tendency for animals maintained on partial reinforcement schedules to be highly resistant to extinction.

Pavlovian conditioning An experimental procedure in which a basic reflex, consisting of an unconditioned stimulus (US) and an unconditioned response (UR) is paired in time with a neutral stimulus (the conditioned stimulus, CS). After several pairings, the CS by itself can elicit components of the original reflex, called the conditioned response (CR). (Also called *conditioning* and *classical conditioning*.)

peak shift The observation that following S^+/S^- discrimination training of two wavelengths, the peak response of the generalization gradient to S^+ is shifted in a direction opposite to (away from) the S^- wavelength.

pharmacological tolerance The portion of total drug tolerance that can be attributed to pharmacological properties of drugs.

phenotype A genotype expressed in an environment; defining an organism by its appearance, and not by its genetic constitution or hereditary potential.

picture memory (Farrar) The term used to describe the performance of chimpanzees that memorized 24 pictures with common elements.

placebo effect A conditioned response that mimics the effects of a drug treatment (the unconditioned stimulus); in humans, via the second signal system, the expectation of drug or other treatment effects.

plasticity Modification of brain physiology due to experience.

positive reinforcement The process by which the application of a reinforcer contingent on a desired response increases the frequency of that response.

positive reinforcer Any stimulus (such as food) delivered to an animal immediately following a designated response that leads to an increase in the frequency of that response. (Cf. Thorndike's *satisfiers*.)

post-reinforcement pause A break in responding following delivery of a reinforcer.

post-traumatic stress disorder (PTSD) A disorder characterized by one or more of the following symptoms: Intense fear, feelings of helplessness, and recurrent intrusive memories/dreams, whose etiology is thought to be caused by an unusual, markedly distressing event such as rape, battle fatigue, etc.

potentiation The finding that a CS conditions better when it is simultaneously paired with a flavor stimulus. The flavor stimulus is said to *potentiate* the conditioning of the CS.

Premack principle David Premack's proposal that the more probable of two responses will reinforce the less probable response.

preparedness The argument that animals are (evolutionarily) prepared to readily make associations between certain stimuli and between some stimuli and certain responses because such rapid learning enhances fitness.

primary punisher A stimulus that is inherently aversive.

psychic secretion (Pavlov) Pavlov's term for salivation attributable to psychological factors—the dog's thoughts, memories, expectations, prior learning—rather than a physiological reflex.

psychoneuroimmunology The field of research attempting to describe and integrate the interconnectedness of the immune system, central and autonomic nervous systems, neuroendocrine system, and behavior.

psychosomatic disorder A disorder of anatomy and/or physiology that can be attributed in part to psychological or behavioral variables.

punisher See primary punisher; secondary punisher.

punishment The process by which an aversive stimulus acts to decrease the rate of the response to which it is applied.

reductionism Explaining a phenomenon by reference to a more molecular process (i.e., a biochemical level). Reductionism is the primary means of scientific explanation.

reflex Innate, involuntary response to specific stimuli in the environment. Example: Iris closure in response to sudden bright light.

reinforcement See *positive reinforcement* and *negative reinforcement*.

resistance-to-extinction A measure of the strength of conditioning or learning based on a the number of extinction trials it takes to extinguish a conditioned response.

retardation test A procedure in which a stimulus is first made a conditioned inhibitor and is then conditioned as an excitor. The acquisition of conditioned excitation is retarded, relative to a neutral stimulus.

R-S conditioning Response-stimulus, or instrumental conditioning. (Cf. *S-S Conditioning.*)

S⁻ (*prounounced S-minus*) A stimulus that signals that response-food contingencies are *not* in effect; responding in the presence of this stimulus is not reinforced.

S⁺ (See discriminative stimulus)

salience A descriptive (not explanatory) term that refers to the relative associability of a stimulus. More *salient* stimuli are more easily conditioned.

satisfiers (Thorndike) Pleasant, or positive stimuli. (Cf. *positive reinforcer.*)

schedule of reinforcement A schedule or rule that determines how and when an animal's response will produce a reinforcer.

second signal system Pavlov's theory that words are signals that are associated with real-world sensory impressions. Words are the signal of signals, hence, the second signal system.

secondary punisher Stimuli that acquire punishing properties through a conditioning procedure. Example: The word "no." (Cf. *secondary reinforcer*)

secondary reinforcer A neutral stimulus that acquires reinforcing properties via the process of higher-order conditioning; also called *conditioned reinforcer*.

selective pressure Any feature of an environment that allows one phenotype to have reproductive advantage over another.

self-control The ability to delay immediate gratification, usually with the goal of attaining a larger reinforcer at a later time.

sensitization Increased responsiveness following presentation of a stimulus. Sensitization is an example of nonassociative learning.

sensitization control group A nonassociative control group (also referred to as a pseudoconditioning control) that is exposed only to the US during conditioning.

sensory preconditioning A method used to measure the association of two CSs that have been presented together by conditioning CS_1 and measuring a CR to CS_2.

serial pattern learning A learning task in which rats are exposed to and learn a sequence of patterns of reinforcement (or nonreinforcement) in the goal box over a succession of trials.

shaping by successive approximation The selective reinforcement of responses that approximate the target behavior.

Sherringtonian reflexes Reflexes characterized by identifiable sensory neurons synapsing upon identifiable interneurons and motor neurons (named for British physiologist Sir Charles Sherrington).

sign stimulus (ethology) A specific environmental stimulus that triggers innately organized behaviors. (Cf. *FAP; IRM.*)

sign tracking See *autoshaping.*

simultaneous conditioning (Pavlov) Paired CSs and USs that have identical onsets, durations, and offsets.

single-stimulus effect (*association theory*) Behavioral change due to the action of a single stimulus, as opposed to the association of two or more stimuli. (See *habituation; nonassociative learning; sensitization.*)

Skinner box An experimental environment consisting of a small box containing one or more (a) levers or response keys, (b) lights/speakers, and (c) feeding/watering devices used in animal learning experiments (named for B. F. Skinner).

social reinforcement theory (Bandura) A theory that human learning is accomplished primarily by imitation and modeling of observed behavior that is reinforced by social reinforcers.

S-O-R theory (Hull) S-R theory in which intervening variables, specifically organismic variables such as thirst and hunger mediate the functional relationship between stimulus and response variables.

species A group of animals with common genetic material and common behavior patterns that are reproductively isolated from other animals.

species-specific behaviors Innate perceptual and response patterns typical of a species.

species-specific defense reaction (SSDR) An innately organized hierarchy of defense behaviors elicited by signals indicating potential danger.

specific hungers Innate cravings for salt and water.

spontaneous recovery (Pavlov) The reappearance of a higher level of conditioned response following a delay in the extinction process.

S-S conditioning Stimulus-stimulus, or classical conditioning. (Cf. *R-S conditioning.*)

stimulus control The condition in which an animal reliably makes an operant response in the presence of an S⁺ and do not respond in the presence of S⁻.

stimulus generalization gradient A pattern of responses to similar stimuli made following training to a target stimulus.

stimulus specificity The idea that certain stimuli more or less easily enter into association depending on the species of animal.

stimulus substitution (Pavlov) The theory that through conditioning the conditioned stimulus comes to be a "substitute" for the unconditioned stimulus.

successive approximation See *shaping by successive approximation.*

summation test A procedure that shows the effect of combining a conditioned inhibitor and conditioned excitor, with each stimulus affecting the response to the other stimulus.

target response The instrumental or operant response that, when executed, is reinforced.

telegraphic speech The term used to define a stage of language when, at the age of about 1½ years, children begin to string together two words in a grammatically meaningful fashion.

temporal conditioning (Pavlov) Conditioning that results from regularly spaced food presentations.

Thorndikean conditioning See *Instrumental Learning.*

trace conditioning (Pavlov) Pairings of the CS and US in which the CS onset and offset precede the US onset.

transitive inferential reasoning A problem of the following type: If *a* is greater than *b*, and *b* is greater than *c*, is *a* greater than *c*? Its solution indicates reasoning ability and a knowledge of relationships that extend beyond immediate experience.

treatment group In an experiment, the group of subjects that receives the independent variable.

trial (Pavlov) A CS-US pairing.

two-factor theory (Mowrer) A theory proposing that two factors underlying avoidance behavior are Pavlovian-conditioned emotional behavior and instrumentally conditioned motor (muscle) responses.

two-factor theory of punishment A theory that punishment learning is accomplished in two stages; i.e., a fear response is first conditioned classically, and then an avoidance response reduces the fear response.

two-stage theory of association Stage 1: two stimuli are perceived as being temporally contiguous and correlated. Stage 2: S₂ is perceived as being contingent upon, and caused by, S₁.

unconditioned response (UR) (Pavlov) The reflexive response to an unconditioned stimulus (the US). Salivation is the unconditioned response to food.

unconditioned stimulus (US) (Pavlov) A stimulus that innately and involuntarily elicits a reflexive response (i.e., the UR). Example: Food is an unconditioned stimulus that elicits reflexive salivation.

undermatching Responding *less* than predicted for available reinforcement.

universal grammar (Chomsky) A theoretical position that postulates the existence of innate structures underlying the rapid acquisition and output of grammatically correct language and that denies any role for Pavlovian and instrumental conditioning processes.

unprepared Conditioning that requires an intermediate number of trials. Such conditioning is neither *prepared* (learned in one or a few trials) and nor *contraprepared* (many trials to learn).

US preexposure effect A reduction in conditioning due to familiarity of the unconditioned stimulus. (Cf. *CS Preexposure Effect.*)

value The relative worth, merit, or importance of an object or activity, based on *esthetics, cost, availability, perceived utility,* and other properties.

variability (Darwin) An aspect of the theory of evolution that describes the role played by the wide range of genetic variation (i.e., variability) within a species. Genetic variance is the raw material upon which natural selection works.

variable interval schedule (VI)   A schedule of reinforcement in which an animal is reinforced for its first response following a variable interval of time from the preceding reinforcer.

variable ratio schedule (VR)   A schedule of reinforcement in which delivery of a reinforcer is contingent upon the completion of a variable number of operant responses since the preceding reinforcement.

vertebrate plan   The observed similarities in brain structure among all vertebrates characterized by their common bilaterality, cranial nerves, thalamus, medulla, and other structures.

VI   See *variable interval schedule.*

VR   See *variable ratio schedule.*

win-stay, lose-shift   (Harlow) A strategy that animals are capable of learning. When presented with repeated opportunities to solve a two-choice discrimination problem in which one of the choices is consistently rewarded, reinforcement can be maximized by adopting the two-part rule: (a) to continue selecting the reinforced choice (i.e., win-stay) and (b) to shift to the alternative when a choice is not reinforced (i.e., lose-shift).

within-subjects design   The design of an experiment in which a pretreatment measure of the dependent variable is compared with a post treatment measure in the same subjects.

zoomorphism   The attribution of animal qualities to humans.

REFERENCES

Abramson, C. I. (1994). *A primer of invertebrate learning*. Washington, DC: American Psychological Association.

Ackil, J. K., Carman, H. M., Bakner, C. L., & Riccio, D. C. (1992). Reinstatement of latent inhibition following a reminder treatment in a conditioned taste aversion paradigm. *Behavioral and Neural Biology, 58*, 232–235.

Adams, M. J. (1990). *Beginning to read: Thinking and learning about print*. Cambridge, MA: MIT Press.

Ader, R. (1985). Conditioned taste aversions and immunopharmacology. *Annals of the New York Academy of Sciences, 443*, 293–307.

Ader, R. (1993). Conditioned responses. In B. Moyers (Ed.), *Healing and the mind*. New York: Doubleday.

Ader, R., & Cohen, N. (1982). Behaviorally conditioned immunosuppression and murine systemic lupus erythematosus. *Science, 215*, 1534–1536.

Ader, R., Cohen, N., & Bovbjerg, D. (1982). Conditioned suppression of humoral immunity in the rat. *Journal of Comparative and Physiological Psychology, 96*, 517–521.

Ader, R., Weiner, H., & Baum, A. (Eds.). (1988). *Experimental foundations of behavioral medicine: Conditioning approaches*. Hillsdale, NJ: Erlbaum.

Albert, M., & Ayres, J. J. B. (1989). With number of preexposures constant latent inhibition increases with preexposure CS duration or total CS exposure. *Learning and Motivation, 20*, 278–294.

Amsel, A. (1958). The role of frustrative nonreward in partial reinforcement and discrimination learning. *Psychological Review, 69*, 306–328.

Amsel, A. (1992). *Frustration theory: An analysis of dispositional learning and memory*. Cambridge: Cambridge University Press.

Anastasia, D., & LoLordo, V. M. (1994). Evidence for simultaneous excitatory and inhibitory associations in the explicitly unpaired procedure. *Learning and Motivation, 25*, 1–25.

Anderson, C. D., Ferland, R. J., & Williams, M. D. (1992). Negative contrast associated with reinforcing stimulation of the brain. *Society for Neuroscience Abstracts, 18*, 874.

Anderson, J. R. (1990). *Cognitive psychology and its implications*. New York: W. H. Freeman.

Anderson, R. C., Wilson, P. T., & Fielding, L. G. (1988). Growth in reading and how children spend their time outside of school. *Reading Research Quarterly, 23*, 285–303.

Annau, Z., & Kamin, L. J. (1961). The conditioned emotional response as a function of intensity of the US. *Journal of Comparative and Physiological Psychology, 54*, 428–432.

Archer, T., & Sjoden, P. O. (1982). Higher-order conditioning and sensory preconditioning of a taste aversion with an exteroceptive CS1. *Quarterly Journal of Experimental Psychology, 34B*, 1–17.

Ayllon, T., & Azrin, N. (1968). *The token-economy: A motivational system for therapy and rehabilitation*. New York: Appleton-Century-Crofts.

Ayres, J. J., Philbin, D., Cassidy, S., & Bellino, L. (1992). Some parameters of latent inhibition. *Learning & Motivation, 23*, 269–287.

Azrin, N. H. (1966). Sequential effects of punishment. In Verhave, T. (Ed.), *The experimental analysis of behavior: Selected readings*. New York: Appleton-Century-Crofts.

Azrin, N. H., & Holz, W. C. (1966). Punishment. In W. K. Honig (Ed.), *Operant behavior: Areas of research and application*. New York: Appleton-Century-Crofts.

Azrin, N. H., Holz, W. C., & Hake, D. F. (1963). Fixed-ratio punishment. *Journal of the Experimental Analysis of Behavior, 6*, 141–148.

Baddeley, A. (1998). *Working memory*. Needham Heights, MA: Allyn & Bacon.

Baer, D. M., & Sherman, J. A. (1964). Reinforcement control of generalized imitation in young children. *Journal of Experimental Child Psychology, 1*, 37–49.

Baer, D. M., Peterson, R. F., & Sherman, J. A. (1967). The development of imitation by reinforcing behavioral similarity to a model. *Journal of the Experimental Analysis of Behavior, 1967*, 10, 405–416.

Baker, A. G., & Baker, P. A. (1985). Does inhibition differ from excitation: Proactive interference, contextual conditioning, and extinction. In R. R. Miller & N. E. Spear (Eds.), *Information processing in animals: Conditioned inhibition*. Hillsdale, NJ: Erlbaum.

Baker, A. G., & Mackintosh, N. J. (1977). Excitatory and inhibitory conditioning following uncorrelated presentations of CS and UCS. *Animal Learning & Behavior, 5*, 315–319.

Baker, A. G., & Mercier, P. (1982). Extinction of the context and latent inhibition. *Learning and Motivation, 13*, 391–416.

Baker, A. G., Mercier, P., Gabel, J., & Baker, P. A. (1981). Contextual conditioning and the US preexposure effect in conditioned fear. *Journal of Experimental Psychology: Animal Behavior Processes, 7*, 109–128.

Baker, A. G., Singh, M., & Bindra, D. (1985). Some effects of contextual conditioning and US predictability on Pavlovian conditioning. In P. Balsam & A. Tomie (Eds.), *Context and learning*. Hillsdale, NJ: Erlbaum.

Baker, B. J., Booth, D. A., Duggan, J. P., & Gibson, E. L. (1987). Protein appetite demonstrated: Learned specificity of protein-cue preference to protein need in adult rats. *Nutrition Research, 7*, 481–487.

Baker, T. B., & Tiffany, S. T. (1985). Morphine tolerance as habituation. *Psychological Review, 92*, 78–108.

Balsom, P. D., & Tomie, A. (Eds.). (1985). *Context and learning*. Hillsdale, NJ: Erlbaum.

Bandura, A. (1962). Social learning through imitation. In M. R. Jones (Ed.), *Nebraska symposium on motivation*. Lincoln: University of Nebraska Press.

Bandura, A. (1971). *Social learning theory*. Englewood Cliffs, NJ: Prentice Hall.

Bandura, A., & Walters, R. H. (1963). *Social learning and personality development*. New York: Holt, Rinehart, & Winston.

Barker, L. M. (1968). *Effects of (classified drug) on aversive and appetitively motivated behavior of Rhesus monkeys in aeronautical simulation studies*. Unpublished USAF Technical Report.

Barker, L. M. (1982). Building memories for foods. In L. Barker (Ed.), *The psychobiol-*

ogy of human food selection. Westport, CT: AVI Publishing.

Barker, L. M., & Smith, J. C. (1974). A comparison of taste aversions induced by radiation and lithium chloride in CS-US and US-CS paradigms. *Journal of Comparative and Physiological Psychology, 87,* 644–654.

Barker, L., Smith, J. C., & Suarez, E. M. (1977). "Sickness" and the backward conditioning of taste aversions. In Barker, L., M. R. Best, & M. Domjan (Eds.). *Learning Mechanisms in Food Selection,* Baylor University Press, Waco, Texas. (pp. 533—553)

Barker, L. M., & Weaver, C. A. (1991). Conditioning flavor preferences in rats: Dissecting the "medicine effect." *Learning and Motivation, 22,* 311–328.

Barker, L. M., Best, M. R., & Domjan, M. (Eds.). (1977). *Learning mechanisms in food selection.* Waco, TX: Baylor University Press.

Barkow, J. H., Cosmides, L., & Tooby, J. (1992). *The adapted mind: Evolutionary psychology and the generation of culture.* New York: Oxford University Press.

Barlow, D. H., Craske, M. G., Cerny, J. A., & Klosko, J. S. (1989). Behavioral treatment of panic disorder. *Behavior Therapy, 20,* 261–282.

Barnett, S. A. (1963). *The rat. A study in behavior.* Chicago: Aldine Publishing Co.

Barnett, S. A. (1981). *Modern ethology.* New York: Oxford University Press.

Batsell, W. R. Jr., & Batson, J. D. (1999). Augmentation of taste conditioning by a preconditioned odor. *Journal of Experimental Psychology: Animal Behavior Processes, 25,* 374–388.

Batson, J. D., & Batsell, W. R. Jr. (in press). Augmentation, not blocking, in an A+/AX+ flavor-conditioning procedure. *Psychological Bulletin & Review.*

Batson, J. D., Hoban, J. S., & Bitterman, M. E. (1992). Simultaneous conditioning in honeybees (*Apis mellifera*). *Journal of Comparative Psychology, 106,* 114–119.

Baum, W. M. (1974). On two types of deviation from the matching law: Bias and undermatching. *Journal of the Experimental Analysis of Behavior, 22,* 231–242.

Baum, W. M. (1979). Matching, undermatching, and overmatching in studies of

choice. *Journal of the Experimental Analysis of Behavior, 32,* 269–281.

Baum, W. M. (1981). Optimization and the matching law as accounts of instrumental behavior. *Journal of the Experimental Analysis of Behavior, 36,* 387–403.

Bavelier, D., Corina, D., Jessard, P., Padmanabhan, S., Clark, V. P., Karni, A., Prinster, A., Braun, A., Lalwani, A., Rauchecker, J. P., Turner, R., & Neville, H. (1997). Sentence reading: A functional MRI study at 4 Telsa. *Journal of Cognitive Neuroscience, 9,* 664–686.

Beckwith, R., & Rispoli, M. (1986). Aspects of a theory of mind: An interview with Noam Chomsky. *New Ideas in Psychology, 4,* 187–202.

Beidler, L. M. (1982). Biological basis of food selection. In L. M. Barker (Ed.), *The psychobiology of human food selection.* Westport, CT: AVI Publishing.

Benjamin, L. T., & Bruce, D. (1982). From bottle-fed chimp to bottlenose dolphin: A contemporary appraisal of Winthrop Kellogg. *The Psychological Record, 32,* 461–482.

Bennett, E. L., Diamond, M., Krech, D., & Rosenzweig, M. R. (1964). Chemical and anatomical plasticity of the brain. *Science, 146,* 610–619.

Bernstein, A. M., Philips, H. C., Linden, W., & Fenster, H. A. (1992). Psychophysiological evaluation of female urethral syndrome: Evidence for a muscular abnormality. *Journal of Behavioral Medicine, 15,* 299–312.

Bernstein, I. L., & Webster, M. M. (1980). Learned taste aversions in humans. *Physiology and Behavior, 25,* 363–366.

Best, M. R., & Gemberling, G. A. (1977). The role of short-term processes in the CS preexposure effect and the delay of reinforcement gradient in long-delay taste-aversion learning. *Journal of Experimental Psychology: Animal Behavior Processes, 3,* 253–263.

Best, M. R., Brown, E. R., & Sowell, M. K. (1984). Taste mediated potentiation of non-ingestional stimuli in rats. *Learning & Motivation, 15,* 244–258.

Best, P. J., Best, M. R., & Mickley, G. A. (1973). Conditioned aversion to distinct environmental stimuli resulting from gastrointestinal distress. *Journal of Compara-*

tive and Physiological Psychology, 85, 250–257.

Bitterman, M. E., Menzel, R., Fietz, A., & Schäfer, S. (1983). Classical conditioning of proboscis extension in honeybees (*Apis mellifera*). *Journal of Comparative Psychology, 97,* 107–119.

Blakemore, S. (1999). *The meme machine.* New York, NY: Oxford University Press.

Blanchard, E. B., & Epstein, L. H. (1977). The clinical usefulness of biofeedback. In M. Hersen, R. M. Eisler, & P. M. Miller (Eds.), *Progress in behavior modification* (Vol. 4). New York: Academic Press.

Blanchard, E. B., Andrasik, F., Ahles, T. A., Teders, S. J., & O'Keefe, D. (1980). Migraine and tension headache: A meta-analytic review. *Behavior Therapy, 11,* 613–631.

Bliss, T. V. P., & Lomo, T. (1973). Long-lasting potentiation of synaptic transmission in the dentate area of the anaesthetized rabbit following stimulation of the perforant path. *Journal of Physiology* (London), *232,* 331–356.

Bloom, L. (1970). *Language development: Form and function in emerging grammars.* Cambridge, MA: MIT Press.

Boice, R. (1973). Domestication. *Psychological Bulletin, 80,* 215–230.

Boice, R. (1977). Burrows of wild and albino rats: Effects of domestication, outdoor raising, age, experience, and maternal state. *Journal of Comparative and Physiological Psychology, 91,* 649–661.

Boice, R. (1981). Behavioral comparability of wild and domesticated rats. *Behavior Genetics, 11,* 545–553.

Bolles, R. C. (1970). Species-specific defense reactions and avoidance learning. *Psychological Review, 71,* 32–48.

Bolles, R. C. (1971). Species-specific defense reactions. In F. R. Brush (Ed.), *Aversive conditioning and learning.* New York: Academic Press.

Bolles, R. C. (1972). The avoidance learning problem. In G. H. Bower (Ed.), *The psychology of learning and motivation* (Vol. 6). New York: Academic Press.

Bolles, R. C., Hayward, L., & Crandall, C. (1981). Conditioned taste preferences based on caloric density. *Journal of Ex-* *perimental Psychology: Animal Behavior Processes, 7,* 59–69.

Bond, G. L., & Dykstra, R. (1967). The cooperative research program in first grade reading instruction. *Reading Research Quarterly, 2,* 5–142.

Booth, D. A. (1982). How nutritional effects of foods can influence people's dietary choices. In L. M. Barker (Ed.), *The psychobiology of human food selection.* Westport, CT: AVI Publishing.

Booth, R. J., and Ashbridge, K. R. (1992). Implications of psychoimmunology for models of the immune system. In A. J. Husband (Ed.), *Behavior and Immunity.* London: CRC Press.

Bousfield, W. A. (1955). Lope de Vega on early conditioning. *American Psychologist, 10,* 828.

Bouton, M. E. (1993). Context, time, and memory retrieval in the interference paradigms of pavlovian learning. *Psychological Bulletin, 114,* 80–99.

Bouton, M. E. (1994). Context, ambiguity, and classical conditioning. *Current Directions in Psychological Science, 3,* 49–53.

Bouton, M. E. (1984). Differential control by context in the inflation and reinstatement paradigms. *Journal of Experimental Psychology: Animal Behavior Processes, 10,* 56–74.

Bouton, M. E. (1991). Context and retrieval in extinction and in other examples of interference in simple associative learning. In L. Dachowski & C. F. Flaherty (Eds.), *Current topics in animal learning.* Hillsdale, NJ: Erlbaum.

Bouton, M. E., & Bolles, R. C. (1979a). Contextual control of the extinction of conditioned fear. *Learning and Motivation, 10,* 455–466.

Bouton, M. E., & Bolles, R. C. (1979b). Role of conditioned contextual stimuli in reinstatement of extinguished fear. *Journal of Experimental Psychology: Animal Behavior Processes, 5,* 368–378.

Bouton, M. E., & Swartzentruber, D. (1986). Analysis of the associative and occasion-setting properties of contexts participating in a Pavlovian discrimination. *Journal of Experimental Psychology: Animal Behavior Processes, 12,* 333–350.

Bouton, M. E., Dunlap, C. M., & Swartzentruber, D. (1987). Potentiation of taste by another taste during compound aversion learning. *Animal Learning & Behavior, 15,* 433–438.

Bovbjerg, D., Cohen, N., & Ader, R. (1987). Behaviorally conditioned enhancement of delayed-type hypersensitivity in the mouse. *Brain Behavior Immunology, 1,* 64.

Bowe, C. A. (1984). Spatial relations in animal learning and behavior. *The Psychological Record, 34,* 181–209.

Boysen, S. T., Berntson, G. G., Hannan, M. B., & Cacioppo, J. T. (1996). Quantity-based interference and symbolic representations in chimpanzees (*Pan troglodytes*). *Journal of Experimental Psychology: Animal Behavior Processes, 22,* 76–86.

Bradbury, J. W., & Vehrencamp, S. L. (1998). *Principles of Animal Communication.* Sunderland, MA: Sinauer.

Bray, G. A. (1976). *The obese patient.* Philadelphia: W. B. Saunders.

Breland, K., & Breland, M. (1961). The misbehavior of organisms. *American Psychologist, 16,* 681–684.

Breslau, N., Davis, G. C., Andreski, P., & Peterson, E. (1991). Traumatic events and posttraumatic stress disorder in an urban population of young adults. *Archives of General Psychiatry, 40,* 216–222.

Brett, L. P., Hankins, W. G., & Garcia, J. (1976). Prey-lithium aversions III: Buteo hawks. *Behavioral Biology, 17,* 87–98.

Breukelaar, J. W., C. Dalrymple-Alford, J. C. (1998). Timing ability and numerical competence in rats. *Journal of Experimental Psychology: Animal Behavior Processes, 24,* 84–97.

Breznitz, S., Ben-Zur, H., Berzon, Y.,W., David, W., Levitan, G., Tarcic, N., Lischinsky, S., Greenberg, A., Levi, N., & Zinder, O. (1998). Experimental induction and termination of acute psychological stress in human volunteers: Effects on immunological, neuroendocrine, cardiovascular, and psychological parameters. *Brain, Behavior and Immunity, 12,* 34–52.

Brown, J. S., & Cunningham, C. L. (1981). The paradox of persisting self-punitive behavior. *Neuroscience & Biobehavioral Reviews, 5,* 343–354.

Brown, P. L., & Jenkins, H. M. (1968). Autoshaping of the pigeon's key peck. *Journal of the Experimental Analysis of Behavior, 11,* 1–8.

Brown, R., & Hanlon, C. (1970). Derivational complexity and the order of acquisition of speech. In R. Brown (Ed.), *Psycholinguistics.* New York: Free Press.

Buchwald, A. M., Coyne, J. C., & Cole, C. S. (1978). A critical evaluation of the learned helplessness model of depression. *Journal of Abnormal Psychology, 87,* 180–193.

Buckley, K. W. (1989). *Mechanical man: John Broadus Watson and the beginnings of behaviorism.* New York: Guilford Press.

Bull, D. F., Brown, R., King, M. G., & Husband, A. J. (1991). Modulation of body temperature through taste aversion conditioning. *Physiology and Behavior, 49,* 1229–1233.

Bull, D. F., Brown, R., King, M. G., Husband, A. J., & Pfister, H. P. (1992). Thermoregulation: Modulation of body temperature through behavioral conditioning. In A. J. Husband (Ed.), *Behavior and immunity.* London: CRC Press.

Bull, J. A. III, & Overmier, J. B. (1968). Additive and subtractive properties of excitation and inhibition. *Journal of Comparative and Physiological Psychology, 66,* 511–514.

Bus, A. G., & van IJzendoorn, M. H. (1999). Phonological awareness and early reading: A meta-analysis of experimental training studies. *Journal of Educational Psychology, 91,* 403–414.

Bush, R. R., & Mosteller, F. (1951). A model for stimulus generalization and discrimination. *Psychological Review, 58,* 413–423.

Buss, D. M. (1996). The evolutionary psychology of human social strategies. In E. T. Higgins & A. W. Kruglanski (Eds.), *Social psychology: Handbook of basic principles.* New York: Guilford Press, 1996.

Buss, D. M., & Schmidt, D. P. (1993). Sexual strategies theory: An evolutionary perspective on human mating. *Psychological Review, 100,* 204–232.

Caggiula, A. R., & Hoebel, B. G. (1966). "Copulation-reward" site in the posterior hypothalamus. *Science, 153,* 1284–1285.

Camp, D. S., Raymond, G. A., & Church, R. M. (1962). Response suppression as a function of the schedule of punishment. *Psychonomic Science, 5,* 23–24.

Campbell, D. H., Capaldi, E. D., & Myers, D. E. (1987). Conditioned flavor preferences as a function of deprivation level: Preferences or aversions? *Animal Learning and Behavior, 15,* 193–200.

Candland, D. K. (1993). *Feral children and clever animals.* Oxford: Oxford University Press.

Capaldi, E. D., & Myers, D. E. (1982). Taste preferences as a function of food deprivation during original taste exposure. *Animal Learning and Behavior, 10,* 211–219.

Capaldi, E. D., & Powley, T. L. (Eds.). (1990). *Taste, experience, and feeding.* Washington, DC: American Psychological Society.

Capaldi, E. D., Campbell, D. H., Sheffer, J. D., & Bradford, J. P. (1987). Conditioned flavor preferences based on delayed caloric consequences. *Journal of Experimental Psychology: Animal Behavior Processes, 13,* 150–155.

Capaldi, E. J., & Miller, D. J. (1988). Counting in rats: Its functional significance and the independent cognitive processes that constitute it. *Journal of Experimental Psychology: Animal Behavior Processes, 14,* 3–17.

Capaldi, E. J., & Molina, P. (1979). Element discriminability as a determinant of serial pattern learning. *Animal Learning & Behavior, 7,* 318–322.

Capaldi, E. J., Verry, D. R., Nawrocki, T. M., & Miller, D. J. (1984). Serial learning, interim association, phrasing cues, interference, overshadowing, chunking, memory, and extinction. *Animal Learning & Behavior, 12,* 7–20.

Carew, T. J., Hawkins, R. D., & Kandel, E. (1983). Differential classical conditioning of a defensive withdrawal reflex in *Aplysia californica. Science, 219,* 397–400.

Carlson, N. R. (1992). *Foundations of physiological psychology* (2nd ed.). Boston: Allyn & Bacon.

Carter, Forrest. (1976). *The education of Little Tree.* Albuquerque: University of New Mexico Press.

Chambers, K. C. (1990). A neural model for conditioned taste aversions. *Annual Review of Neuroscience, 13,* 373–385.

Chittka, L., & Geiger, K. (1995). Can honey bees count landmarks? *Animal Behaviour, 49,* 159–164.

Chomsky, N. (1965). *Aspects of the theory of syntax.* Cambridge, MA: MIT Press.

Chomsky, N. (1972). *Language and mind.* New York: Harcourt Brace Jovanovich.

Chomsky, N. (1975). *Reflections on language.* New York: Pantheon.

Chomsky, N. (1980). *Rules and representations.* New York: Columbia University Press.

Church, R. M. (1978). The internal clock. In S. H. Hulse, H. Fowler, & W. W. Honig (Eds.), *Cognitive processes in animal behavior.* Hillsdale, NJ: Erlbaum.

Church, R. M. (1984). Properties of the internal clock. In J. Gibbon & L. Allen (Eds.), *Timing and time perception.* New York: Annals of the New York Academy of Sciences, Vol. 438.

Cicero, S. D., & Tryon, W. W. (1989). Classical conditioning of meaning—II. A replication of triplet associative extension. *Journal of Behavioral Therapy and Experimental Psychiatry, 20,* 197–202.

Clark, R. C., & Squire, L. R. (1998). Classical conditioning and brain systems: The role of awareness. *Science, 280,* 77–81.

Clark, R. C., & Squire, L. R. (1999). Human eyeblink classical conditioning: Effects of manipulating awareness of the stimulus contingencies. *Psychological Science, 10,* 14–18.

Clay, A. (2000, January). Psychotherapy is cost effective. *Monitor on Psychology, 31,* 1–2.

Collier, G. (1983). Life in a closed economy: The ecology of learning and motivation. In M. D. Zeiler & P. Harzem (Eds.), *Advances in analysis of behavior: Vol. 3: Biological factors in learning.* Chichester, UK: Wiley.

Collier, G., Hirsch, E., & Hamlin, P. H. (1972). The ecological determinants of reinforcement in the rat. *Physiology & Behavior, 9,* 705–716.

Collier, G., Johnson, D. F., Borin, G., & Mathis, C. E. (1994). Drinking in a patchy environment: The effect of the price of water. *Journal of the Experimental Analysis of Behavior, 62,* 169–184.

Conger, R., & Killeen, P. (1976). Use of concurrent operants in small group research. *Pacific Sociological Review, 17,* 399–416.

Cook, R. G., Cavoto, K., & Cavoto, B. R. (1995). Same-different texture discrimination and concept formation learning by pigeons. *Journal of Experimental Psychology: Animal Behavior Processes, 21,* 253–260.

Cook, R. G., Katz, J., & Cavoto, B. R. (1997). Pigeons same-different concept learning with multiple stimulus classes. *Journal of Experimental Psychology: Animal Behavior Processes, 23,* 417–433.

Corballis, M. C. (1989). Laterality and human evolution. *Psychological Review, 96,* 494–505.

Corballis, M. C. (1991). *The lopsided ape.* Oxford: Oxford University Press.

Cunningham, M. R., Druen, P. B., & Barbee, A. P. (1997). Angels, mentors, and friends: Tradeoffs among evolutionary, social, and individual variables in physical appearance. In J. A. Simpson & D. T. Kenrick (Eds.), *Evolutionary social psychology.* Mahwah, NJ: Erlbaum.

Curtiss, S. (1977). *Genie: A psycholinguistic study of a modern day wild child.* New York: Academic Press.

D'Amato, M. R., Salmon, D. P., & Colombo, M. (1985). Extent and limits of the matching concept in monkeys *(Cebus apella). Journal of Experimental Psychology: Animal Behavior Processes, 11,* 35–51.

D'Amato, M. R., & Schiff, E. (1964). Further studies of overlearning and position reversal learning. *Psychological Reports, 14,* 380–382.

Dantzer, R., & Kelley, K. W. (1989). Stress and immunity: An integrated view of relationships between the brain and the immune system. *Life Sciences, 44,* 1995–2008.

Dantzer, R., Arnone, M., & Mormede, P. (1980). Effect of frustration on behavior and plasma corticosteroid levels in pigs. *Physiology & Behavior, 24,* 1–4.

Darwin, C. (1859/1962). *The origin of species.* New York: Collier Books.

Darwin, C. (1871). *The descent of man and selection in relation to sex.* London: John Murray.

Darwin, C. (1872/1965). *The expression of emotions in man and animals.* Chicago: University of Chicago Press.

Davey, G. C. L. (1992). Classical conditioning and the acquisition of human fears and phobias: A review and synthesis of the literature. *Advances in Behavior Research & Therapy, 14,* 29–66.

Davis, C. M. (1928). Self-selection of diet by newly weaned infants. *American Journal of Diseases of Children, 36,* 651–659.

Davis, C. M. (1939). The results of self-selection of diets by young children. *The Canadian Medical Association Journal, 41,* 257–261.

Davis, M. (1974). Sensitization of the rat startle response by noise. *Journal of Comparative and Physiological Psychology, 87,* 571–581.

Davis, M., & File, S. E. (1984). Intrinsic and extrinsic mechanisms of habituation and sensitization: Implications for the design and analysis of experiments. In H. V. S. Peeke & L. Petrinovich (Eds.), *Habituation, sensitization, and behavior.* New York: Academic Press.

Davison, M. (1991). Choice, changeover, and travel: A quantitative model. *Journal of the Experimental Analysis of Behavior, 55,* 47–61.

Dawkins, R. (1976). *The selfish gene.* London: Oxford University Press.

Dawkins, R. (1995). *River out of Eden: A Darwinian view of life.* New York: Basic Books.

Dawkins, R. (1995). The evolved imagination. *Natural History, 104,* 12–24.

Deacon, T. (1997). *The symbolic species: The co-evolution of language and the human brain.* London, Penguin.

Deems, D. A., Oetting, R. L., Sherman, J. E., & Garcia, J. (1986). Hungry, but not thirsty, rats prefer flavors paired with ethanol. *Physiology and Behavior, 36,* 141–144.

Degler, C. N. (1991). *In search of human nature.* New York: Oxford University Press.

Dennett, D. C. (1975). Why the law of effect will not go away. *Journal of the Theory of Social Behavior, 5,* 169–187.

Dennett, D. C. (1983). Intentional systems in cognitive ethology: The "Panglossian paradigm" defended. *The Behavioral and Brain Sciences, 6,* 343–355.

Dennett, D. C. (1995). *Darwin's dangerous idea.* New York: Simon & Schuster.

Dess, N. K., & Chapman, C. D. (1998) Humans and animals: On saying what we mean. *Psychological Science, 9,* 156–157.

Dethier, V. G. (1978). Other tastes, other worlds. *Science, 201,* 224–228.

Dews, P. B. (1958). Studies on behavior. IV: Stimulant actions of methamphetamine. *Journal of Pharmacology and Experimental Therapeutics, 122,* 137–147.

Diamond, A. (1988). Differences between adult and infant cognition: Is the crucial variable presence or absence of language? In L. Weiskrantz (Ed.), *Thought without language.* Oxford, UK: Clarendon Press.

Diamond, J. (1992). *The third chimpanzee: The evolution and future of the human animal.* New York: HarperCollins.

Diamond, J. (1997). *Guns, germs, and steel: The fates of human societies.* New York: Norton.

Dickinson, A. (1985). Actions and habits: The development of behavioural autonomy. *Philosophical Transactions of the Royal Society (London), B308,* 67–78.

Dickinson, A. (1988). Intentionality in animal conditioning. In L. Weiskrantz (Ed.), *Thought without language.* Oxford, UK: Clarendon Press.

Dinsmore, J. A. (1954). Punishment I. The avoidance hypothesis. *Psychological Review, 61,* 34–46.

Dinsmore, J. A. (1977). Escape, avoidance, punishment: Where do we stand? *Journal of the Experimental Analysis of Behavior, 28,* 83–95.

Domjan, M. (1977). Attenuation and enhancement of neophobia for edible substances. In L. M. Barker, M. R. Best, & M. Domjan (Eds.), *Learning mechanisms in food selection.* Waco, TX: Baylor University Press.

Domjan, M. (1983). Biological constraints on instrumental and classical conditioning: Implications for general process theory. In G. H. Bower (Ed.), *The pyschology of learning and motivation* (Vol. 17). New York: Academic Press.

Domjan, M. (1987a). Animal learning comes of age. *American Psychologist, 42,* 556–564.

Domjan, M. (1987b). Comparative psychology and the study of animal learning. *Journal of comparative psychology, 101,* 237–241.

Domjan, M. (1994). Formulation of a behavior system for sexual conditioning. *Psychonomic Bulletin & Review, 1,* 421–428.

Domjan, M., & Wilson, N. E. (1972). Specificity of cue to consequence in aversion learning in the rat. *Psychonomic Science, 26,* 143–145.

Domjan, M., O'Vary, D., & Greene, P. (1988). Conditioning of appetitive and consummatory behavior in male Japanese quail *(Coturnix coturnix japonica). Journal of Comparative Psychology, 105,* 157–164.

Dorland's Illustrated Medical Dictionary, 25th Edition (1974). Philadelphia: W. B. Saunders Press.

Dougan, V. A. F., & Dougan, J. D. (1999). The man who listens to behavior: Folk wisdom and behavior analysis from a real horse whisperer. *Journal of the Experimental Analysis of Behavior, 72,* 139–149.

Eagly, A. H., Ashmore, R. D., Makhijani, M. G., & Kennedy, L. C. (1991). What is beautiful is good, but . . .: A meta-analytic review of research on the physical attractiveness stereotype. *Psychological Bulletin, 100,* 109–128.

Eibl-Eibesfeldt, I. (1970). *Ethology: The biology of behavior.* New York: Holt, Rinehart and Winston.

Ellis, A., & Abarbanel, A. (Eds.). (1961). *The encyclopedia of sexual behavior.* New York: Hawthorn Books.

Estes, W. K., & Skinner, B. F. (1941). Some quantitative properties of anxiety. *Journal of Experimental Psychology, 29,* 390–400.

Farrar, D. (1967). Picture memory in the chimpanzee. *Perceptual and Motor Skills, 25,* 305–315.

Felten, D. (1993). *The brain and the immune system.* In B. Moyers (Ed.), *Healing and the mind.* New York: Doubleday.

Ferster, C. B., & Skinner, B. F. (1957). *Schedules of reinforcement.* New York: Appleton-Century-Crofts.

Fielding, L., Wilson, P., & Anderson, R. (1987). A new focus on free reading: The role of trade books in reading. In T. E. Raphael & R. Reynolds (Eds.), *Contexts of literacy.* New York: Longman.

Fiori, L., Barnet, R., & Miller, R. (1994). Renewal of Pavlovian conditioned inhibition. *Animal Learning and Behavior, 22,* 47–52.

Fisher, J., & Hinde, R. A. (1949). The opening of milk bottles by birds. *British Birds, 42,* 347–358.

Flaherty, C. F. (1982). Incentive contrast: A review of behavioral changes following shifts in reward. *Animal Learning and Behavior, 10,* 409–440.

Flaherty, C. F. (1991). Incentive contrast and selected models of anxiety. In L. Dachowski & C. F. Flaherty (Eds.), *Current topics in animal learning.* Hillsdale, NJ: Erlbaum.

Flynn, J. C. (1991). *Cocaine.* New York: Birch Lane Press.

Foa, E. B., Zinbarg, R., & Rothbaum, B. O. (1992). Uncontrollability and unpredictability in post-traumatic stress disorder: An animal model. *Psychological Bulletin, 112,* 218–238.

Fordyce, W. (1976). *Behavioral methods for chronic pain and illness.* St. Louis: Mosby.

Fordyce, W. E., Brockway, J. A., Bergman, J. A., & Spengler, D. (1986). Acute back pain: A control group comparison of behavioral vs. traditional management methods. *Journal of Behavioral Medicine, 9,* 127–140.

Fountain, S. B., Henne, D. R., & Hulse, S. H. (1984). Phasing cues and hierarchical organization in serial pattern learning by rats. *Journal of Experimental Psychology: Animal Behavior Processes, 10,* 30–45.

French, S. (1986). *Decision theory.* New York: Halstead Press.

Freud, S. (1930/1961). *Civilization and its discontents.* New York: Norton.

Furrow, D., Nelson, K., & Benedict, H. (1979). Mothers' speech to İchildren and syntactic development: Some simple relationships. *Journal of Child Language, 6,* 423–442.

Furumoto, L., & Scarborough, E. S. (1987). Placing women in the history of comparative psychology: Margaret Floy Washburn and Margaret Morse Nice. In E. Tobach, (Ed.), *Historical perspectives and the international status of comparative psychology.* Hillsdale, NJ: Erlbaum.

Galef, B. G. (1984). Reciprocal heuristics: A discussion of the relationship of the study of learned behavior in laboratory and field. *Learning and Motivation, 15,* 479–493.

Gamzu, E. (1977). The multifaceted nature of taste-aversion-inducing agents: Is there a single common factor? In L. M. Barker, M. R. Best, & M. Domjan (Eds.), *Learning mechanisms in food selection.* Waco, TX: Baylor University Press.

Gamzu, E., & Schwartz, B. (1973). The maintenance of key pecking by stimulus contingent and response-independent food presentation. *Journal of the Experimental Analysis of Behavior, 19,* 65–72.

Gamzu, E., & Williams, D. R. (1971). Classical conditioning of a complex skeletal act. *Science, 171,* 923–925.

Gamzu, E., & Williams, D. R. (1973). Associative factors underlying the pigeon's key pecking in autoshaping procedures *Journal of the Experimental Analysis of Behavior, 19,* 225–232.

Garb, J. J., & Stunkard, A. J. (1974). Taste aversions in man. *American Journal of Psychiatry, 131,* 1204–1207.

Garcia, J., & Koelling, R. A. (1966). Relation of cue to consequence in avoidance learning. *Psychonomic Science, 4,* 123–124.

Garcia, J., Ervin, F. R., & Koelling, R. A. (1966). Learning with prolonged delay of reinforcement. *Psychonomic Science, 5,* 121–122.

Garcia, J., Ervin, F. R., Yorke, C. H., & Koelling, R. A. (1967). Conditioning with delayed vitamin injections. *Science, 155,* 716–718.

Garcia, J., Hankins, W. G., & Rusiniak, K. W. (1974). Behavioral regulation of the milieu interne in man and rat. *Science, 185,* 824–831.

Garcia, J., Kimeldorf, D. J., & Koelling, R. A. (1955). Conditioned aversion to saccharin resulting from exposure to gamma radiation. *Science, 122,* 157–158.

Gardner, H. (1985). *The minds new science: A history of the cognitive revolution.* New York: Basic Books.

Gardner, R. A., & Gardner, B. T. (1969). Teaching sign language to a chimpanzee. *Science, 165,* 664–672.

Gauci, M., Husband, A. J., & King, M. G. (1992). Conditioned allergic rhinitis: A model for central nervous system and immune system interaction in IgE-mediated allergic reactions. In A. J. Husband (Ed.), *Behavior and immunity.* London: CRC Press.

Geshwind, N. (1970). The organization of language and the brain. *Science, 170,* 94–944.

Gibbon, J., & Church, R. M. (1984). Sources of variance in information processing theory of timing. In H. L. Roitblat, T. G. Bever, & H. S. Terrace (Eds.), *Animal cognition*. Hillsdale, NJ: Erlbaum.

Gillan, D. J. (1981). Reasoning in the chimpanzee: II. Transitive inference. *Journal of Experimental Psychology: Animal Behavior Processes, 7*, 150–164.

Gillan, D. J. (1983). Inferences and the acquisition of knowledge by chimpanzees. In M. L. Commons, R. J. Herrnstein, & A. R. Wagner (Eds.), *Quantitative analyses of behavior: Vol. 4; Discrimination processes*. Cambridge, MA: Ballinger.

Gillan, D. J., Premack, D., & Woodruff, G. (1981). Reasoning in the chimpanzee: I. Analogical reasoning. *Journal of Experimental Psychology: Animal Behavior Processes, 7*, 1–17.

Gorczynski, R. M., Macrae, S., & Kennedy, M. (1982). Conditioned immune response associated with allogeneic skin grafts in mice. *Journal of Immunology, 129*, 704.

Gormezano, I., Kehoe, E. J., & Marshall, B. S. (1983). Twenty years of classical conditioning research with the rabbit. In J. M. Prague & A. N. Epstein (Eds.), *Progress in psychobiology and physiological psychology* (Vol. 10). New York: Academic Press.

Gottlieb, G. (1984). Evolutionary trends and evolutionary origins: Relevance to theory in comparative psychology. *Psychological Review, 91*, 448–456.

Gould, S. J. (1989). *Wonderful life: The burgess shale and the nature of history*. New York: W. W. Norton.

Grahame, N. J., Barnet, R. C., Gunther, L. M., & Miller, R. R. (1994). Latent inhibition as a performance deficit resulting from CS-context associations. *Animal Learning & Behavior, 22*, 395–408.

Gray, J. A. B. (1964). *Pavlov's typology*. New York: Pergammon Press.

Green, J. T., Ivry, R. B., & Woodruff-Pak, D. S. (1999). Timing in eyeblink classical conditioning and timed-interval tapping. *Psychological Science, 10*, 19–23.

Green, K. F., & Garcia, J. (1971). Recuperation from illness: Flavor enhancement for rats. *Science, 173*, 749–751.

Green, L., Kagel, J. H., & Battalio, R. C. (1987). Consumption-leisure tradeoffs in pigeons: Effects of changing marginal wage rates by varying amount of reinforcement. *Journal of the Experimental Analysis of Behavior, 47*, 17–28.

Greenberg, G. (1987). Historical review of the use of captive animals in comparative psychology. In E. Tobach (Ed.), *Historical perspectives and the international status of comparative psychology*. Hillsdale, NJ: Erlbaum.

Griffin, D. R. (1978). Prospects for a cognitive ethology. *Behavioral and Brain Sciences, 4*, 527–538.

Griffin, D. R. (1985). Animal consciousness. *Neuroscience and Biobehavioral Reviews, 9*, 615–622.

Griffin, D. R. (1992). *Animal minds*. Chicago: University of Chicago Press.

Grossarth-Maticek, R., & Eysenck, H. J. (1989). Length of survival and lymphocyte percentage in women with mammary cancer as a function of psychotherapy. *Psychological Reports, 65*, 315–321.

Grundel, R. (1992). How the mountain chickadee procures more food in less time for its nestlings. *Behavioral Ecology and Sociobiology, 31*, 291–300.

Guttman, N., & Kalish, H. I. (1956). Discriminability and stimulus generalization. *Journal of Experimental Psychology, 51*, 79–88.

Haig, K. A., Rawlins, J. N. P., Olton, D. S., Mead, A., & Taylor, B. (1983). Food searching strategies of rats: Variables affecting the relative strength of stay and shift strategies. *Journal of Experimental Psychology: Animal Behavior Processes, 9*, 337–348.

Hake, D. F., & Azrin, N. H. (1965). Conditioned punishment. *Journal of the Experimental Analysis of Behavior, 8*, 279–293.

Hall, G. (1991). *Perceptual and associative learning*. Oxford, UK: Clarendon Press.

Halliday, T. R., & Slater, P. J. B. (Eds.). (1983). *Animal behavior: Vol. 3. Genes, development, and learning*. New York: W. H. Freeman.

Hanson, H. M. (1959). Effects of discrimination training on stimulus generalization. *Journal of Experimental Psychology, 58*, 321–333.

Harder, L. D., & Real, L. A. (1987). Why are bumble bees risk averse? *Ecology, 68(4)*, 1104–1108.

Harlow, H. F. (1949). The formation of learning sets. *Psychological Review, 56,* 51–65.

Harlow, H. F. (1963). Basic social capacity of primates. In C. H. Southwick (Ed.), *Primate social behavior.* Princeton, NJ: Van Nostrand.

Harlow, H. F. (1969). Age-mate or peer affectional system. In D. S. Lehrman, R. H. Hinde, & E. Shaw (Eds.), *Advances in the study of behavior* (Vol. 2). New York: Academic Press.

Harlow, H. F., & Harlow, M. K. (1962a). The effect of rearing conditions on behavior. *Bulletin of the Menninger Clinic, 26,* 213–224.

Harlow, H. F., & Harlow, M. K. (1962b). Social deprivation in monkeys. *Scientific American, 207,* 137–146.

Hartman, T. F., & Grant, D. A. (1960). Effect of intermittent reinforcement on acquisition, extinction, and spontaneous recovery of the conditioned eyelid response. *Journal of Experimental Psychology, 60,* 89–96.

Hatfield, E., & Spretcher, S. (1986). *Mirror, mirror…The importance of looks in everyday life.* Albany, NY: State University of New York Press.

Hayes, C. (1951). *The ape in our house.* New York: Harper & Row.

Hearst, E. (1972). Some persistent problems in the analysis of conditioned inhibition. In R. A. Boakes & M. S. Halliday (Eds.), *Inhibition and learning.* London: Academic Press.

Heath, R. G. (1963). Electrical self-stimulation of the brain in man. *American Journal of Psychiatry, 120,* 571–577.

Hedges, S. B., Kuman, S., Tamura, K., & Stoneking, M. (1991). Human origins and analysis of mitochondrial DNA sequences. *Science, 255,* 737–739.

Heinrich, R. L., Cohen, M. J., Naliboff, B. C., Collins, G. A., & Bonebakker, A. D. (1985). Comparing physical and behavioral therapy for chronic low back pain on phy ical abilities, psychological distress, and patients' perceptions. *Journal of Behavioral Medicine, 8,* 61–78.

Herman, L. M. (1989). In which procrustean bed does the sea lion sleep tonight? *Psychological Record, 39,* 19–50.

Herman, L. M., Richards, D. G., & Wolz, J. P. (1984). Comprehension of sentences by bottlenosed dolphins. *Cognition, 16,* 129–219.

Herrick, C. J. (1948). *The brain of the tiger salamander.* Chicago: University of Chicago Press.

Herrnstein, R. J. (1961). Relative and absolute strength of response as a function of frequency of reinforcement. *Journal of the Experimental Analysis of Behavior, 4,* 267–272.

Herrnstein, R. J. (1969). Method and theory in the study of avoidance. *Psychological Review, 76,* 49–69.

Herrnstein, R. J. (1984). Objects, categories, and discriminative stimuli. In H. L. Roitblat, T. G. Bever, & H. S. Terrace (Eds.), *Animal cognition.* Hillsdale, NJ: Erlbaum.

Herrnstein, R. J., & deVilliers, P. A. (1980). Fish as a natural category for people and pigeons. In G. H. Bower (Ed.), *The psychology of learning and motivation* (Vol. 14, pp. 60–97. New York: Academic Press.

Herrnstein, R. J., & Hineline, P. N. (1966). Negative reinforcement as shock frequency reduction. *Journal of the Experimental Analysis of Behavior, 9,* 421–430.

Herrnstein, R. J., & Vaughan, W., Jr. (1980). Melioration and behavioral allocation. In J. E. R. Staddon (Ed.), *Limits to action.* New York: Academic Press.

Herrnstein, R. J., Loveland, D. H., & Cable, C. (1976). Natural concepts in pigeons. *Journal of Experimental Psychology: Animal Behavior Processes, 2,* 285–301.

Heth, C. D. (1976). Simultaneous and backward fear conditioning as a function of number of CS-UCS pairings. *Journal of Experimental Psychology: Animal Behavior Processes, 2,* 117–129.

Hilgard, J. R. (1979). *Personality and hypnosis: A study of imaginative involvement* (2nd ed.). Chicago: University of Chicago Press.

Hintzman, D. L. (1986). Schema extraction in a multiple trace memory model. *Psychological Review, 93,* 411–428.

Hodos, W., & Campbell, C. B. G. (1969). *Scala Naturae:* Why there is no theory in comparative psychology. *Psychological Review, 76,* 337–350.

Hogan, J. (1973). How young chicks learn to recognize food. In R. A. Hinde & J. Stevenson-Hinde (Eds.), *Constraints on learning*. London: Academic Press.

Hogan, J. (1977). The ontogeny of food preferences in chicks and other animals. In L. M. Barker, M. R. Best, & M. Domjan (Eds.), *Learning mechanisms in food selection*. Waco, TX: Baylor University Press.

Holender, D. (1987). Synchronic description of present-day writing systems: Some implications for reading research. In J. K. O'Regan & A. Levy-Schoen (Eds.), *Eye movements: From physiology to cognition*. Amsterdam: Elsevier North Holland.

Holland, P. C. (1986). Temporal determinants of occasion setting in feature-positive discriminations. *Animal Learning and Behavior, 14,* 111–120.

Holz, W. C., & Azrin, N. H. (1961). Discriminative properties of punishment. *Journal of the Experimental Analysis of Behavior, 4,* 225–232.

Honig, W. K., Boneau, C. A., Burstein, K. R., & Pennypacker, H. S. (1963). Positive and negative generalization gradients obtained under equivalent training conditions. *Journal of Comparative and Physiological Psychology, 56,* 111–115.

Hsu, L. K. G. (1990). *Eating disorders*. New York: Guilford Press.

Hull, C. L. (1932). The goal gradient hypothesis and maze learning. *Psychological Review, 39,* 25–43.

Hull, C. L. (1943). *Principles of behavior*. New York: Appleton.

Hull, C. L. (1952). *A behavior system*. New Haven: Yale University Press.

Hulse, S. H. (1978). Cognitive structure and serial pattern learning by animals. In S. H. Hulse, H. F. Fowler, & W. K. Honig (Eds.), *Cognitive processes in animal behavior*. Hillsdale, NJ: Erlbaum.

Husband, A. J. (Ed.). (1992). *Behavior and immunity*. London: CRC Press.

Jahnke, J. C., & Nowaczyk, R. H. (1998). *Cognition*. Upper Saddle River, NJ: Prentice-Hall.

Jaynes, J. (1969). The historical origins of "ethology" and "comparative psychology." *Animal Behavior, 17,* 601–606.

Jemmott, J. B., III, & Magloire, K. (1988). Academic stress, social support, and secretory immunoglobulin A. *Journal of Personality and Social Psychology, 55,* 803–810.

Jemmott, J. B. III, Hellman, C., McClelland, D. C., Locke, S. E., Kraus, L., Williams, R. M., & Valeri, C. R. (1990). Motivational syndromes associated with natural killer cell activity. *Journal of Behavioral Medicine, 13,* 53–73.

Jenkins, H. M., & Moore, B. R. (1973). The form of the autoshaped response with food or water reinforcers. *Journal of the Experimental Analysis of Behavior, 20,* 163–181.

Jirik-Babb, P., & Katz, J. L. (1988). Impairment of taste perception in anorexia nervosa and bulimia. *International Journal of Eating Disorders, 7,* 353–360.

Justesen, D. R., Braun, E. W., Garrison, R. G., & Pendleton, R. B. (1970). Pharmacological differentiation of allergic and classically conditioned asthma in the guinea pig. *Science, 170,* 864–866.

Kahneman, D., & Tversky, A. (1979). Prospect theory: An analysis of decision under risk. *Econometrica, 47,* 263–291.

Kalat, J. (1977). Status of "learned-safety" or "learned noncorrelation" as a mechanism in taste-aversion learning. In L. M. Barker, M. R. Best, & M. Domjan (Eds.), *Learning mechanisms in food selection*. Waco, TX: Baylor University Press.

Kalat, J. (1984, 1994). *Biological psychology*. Belmont, CA: Wadsworth.

Kalat, J., & Rozin, P. (1973). "Learned safety" as a mechanism in long-delay taste-aversion learning in rats. *Journal of Comparative and Physiological Psychology, 83,* 198–207.

Kamin, L. J. (1965). Temporal and intensity characteristics of the conditioned stimulus. In W. F. Prodasy (Ed.), *Classical conditioning*. New York: Appleton-Century-Crofts.

Kamin, L. J. (1968). "Attention-like" processes in classical conditioning. In M. R. Jones (Ed.), *Miami symposium on the prediction of behavior: Aversive stimulation*. Miami: University of Miami Press.

Kamin, L. J. (1969). Predictability, surprise, attention, and conditioning. In B. A.

Campbell & R. M. Church (Eds.), *Punishment and aversive behavior.* New York: Appleton-Century-Crofts.

Kamin, L. J., & Brimer, C. J. (1963). The effects of intensity of conditioned and unconditioned stimuli on a conditioned emotional response. *Canadian Journal of Psychology, 17,* 194–200.

Kamin, L. J., Brimer, C. J., & Black, A. H. (1963). Conditioned suppression as a monitor of fear of the CS in the course of avoidance training. *Journal of Comparative and Physiological Psychology, 56,* 497–501.

Kandel, E. R., & Schwartz, J. H. (1982). Molecular biology of learning: Modulation of transmitter release. *Science, 218,* 433–443.

Kaplan, P. S., Goldstein, M. H., Huckeby, E. R., Panneton-Cooper, R. (1995). Habituation, sensitization, and infants' re sponses to motherese speech. *Developmental Psychobiology, 28,* 45-57.

Kaplan, R. M. (1984). The connection between clinical health promotion and health status. *American Psychologist, 39,* 755–765.

Karsh, E. B. (1962). Effects of number of rewarded trials and intensity of punishment on running speed. *Journal of Comparative and Physiological Psychology, 55,* 44–51.

Kassel, J. D., & Shiffman, S. (1992). What can hunger teach us about drug craving? A comparative analysis of the two constructs. *Advances in Behavioral Research and Therapy, 14,* 141–167.

Katz, S. (1982). Food, behavior, and biocultural evolution. In L. M. Barker (Ed.), *The psychobiology of human food selection.* Westport, CT: AVI Publishing.

Katz, S. (Ed.). (1975). *Biological anthropology: Selected readings from Scientific American.* San Francisco: W. H. Freeman.

Kellogg, W. N. (1961). *Porpoises and sonar.* Chicago: University of Chicago Press.

Kellogg, W. N., & Kellogg, L. A. (1933). *The ape and the child.* New York: Whittlesey House.

Kelsey, J. E., & Allison, J. (1976). Fixed-ratio lever pressing by VMH rats: Work vs. accessibility of sucrose reward. *Physiology and Behavior, 17,* 749–754.

Kelso, S. R., Ganong, A. H., & Brown, T. H. (1986). Hebbian synapses in hippocampus. *Proceedings of the National Academy of Sciences USA, 83,* 5326–5330.

Kemperman, G., Kuhn, H. G., & Gage, F. H. (1998). Experience-induced neurogenesis in the senescent dentate gyrus. *Journal of Neuroscience, 18 (9),* 3206–3212.

Kertesz, A. (1988). Cognitive function in severe aphasia. In L. Weiskrantz (Ed.), *Thought without language.* Oxford, UK: Clarendon Press.

Kiecolt-Glaser, J. K., Page, G. G., Marucha, P. T., MacCallum, R. C., & Glaser, R. (1998). Psychological influences on surgical recovery: Perspectives from psychoneuroimmunology. *American Psychologist, 53,* 1209–1218.

Killeen, P. R., & Bizo, L. A. (1998). The mechanics of reinforcement. *Psychonomic Bulletin & Review, 5,* 221–238.

Killeen, P. R., & Fetterman, J. G. (1988). A behavioral theory of timing. *Psychological Review, 95,* 274–295.

Killeen, P. R. (1975). On the temporal control of behavior. *Psychological Review, 82,* 89–115.

Kimble, G. A. (1992). *A modest proposal for a minor revolution in the language of psychology.* Paper presented at the 4th Annual Meeting of the American Psychological Society, San Diego, CA.

Kimmel, H. D., & Kimmel, E. (1970). An instrumental conditioning method for the treatment of enuresis. *Journal of Behavior Therapy and Experimental Psychiatry, 1,* 121–123.

Klopf, A. H. (1988). A neuronal model of classical conditioning. *Psychobiology, 16,* 85–125.

Knowles, J. H. (1977). The responsibility of the individual. In J. H. Knowles (Ed.), *Doing better and feeling worse: Health in the United States.* New York: W. W. Norton.

Koestler, F. G., & Barker, L. M. (1965). *The effect on the chimpanzee of rapid decompression to a near vacuum* (Contractor Report No. NASA CR-329). Washington, DC: NASA.

Kolb, L. (1984). The posttraumatic stress disorders of combat: A subgroup with a conditional emotional response. *Military Medicine, 149,* 237–243. (As cited in van der Kolk, B. S. [1987]. *Psychological trauma*. Washington, DC: American Psychiatric Press.)

Konorski, J. (1948). *Conditioned reflexes and neuron organisation*. Cambridge, UK: Cambridge University Press.

Krane, R. V., & Wagner, A. R. (1975). Taste aversion learning with a delayed shock US: Implications for the "generality of the laws of learning." *Journal of Comparative and Physiological Psychology, 88*, 882–889.

Krank, M. D., & MacQueen, G. M. (1988). Conditioned compensatory responses elicited by environmental signals for cyclophosphamide-induced suppression of antibody production in mice. *Psychobiology, 16*, 229–235.

Kymissis, E. & Poulson, C. L. (1990). The history of imitation in learning theory: The language acquisition process. *Journal of the Experimental Analysis of Behavior, 54*, 113–127.

Langlois, J. H., Ritter, J. M., Roggman, L. A., and Vaughn, L. S. (1991). Facial diversity and infant preferences for attractive faces. *Developmental Psychology, 27*, 79–84.

Laudenslager, M. L., Ryan, S. M., Drugan, R. C., Hyson, R. L., & Maier, S. E. (1983). Coping and immunosuppression: Inescapable but not escapable shock suppresses lymphocyte proliferation. *Science, 221*, 568–570.

Lavond, D. G., Kim, J. J., & Thompson, R. F. (1993). Mammalian brain substrates of aversive classical conditioning. *Annual Review of Psychology, 44*, 317–342.

Le, A. D., Poulos, C. X., & Cappell, H. (1979). Conditioned tolerance to the hypothermic effect of ethyl alcohol. *Science, 206*, 1109–1110.

Lehner, G. F. J. (1941). A study of the extinction of unconditioned reflexes. *Journal of Experimental Psychology, 29*, 435–456.

Lennartz, R. C., & Weinberger, N. M. (1992). Analysis of response systems in Pavlovian conditioning reveals rapidly versus slowly acquired conditioned responses: Support for two factors, implications for behavior and neurobiology. *Psychobiology, 20*, 93–119.

Leslie, A. L. (1988). The necessity of illusion: Perception and thought in infancy. In L. Weiskrantz (Ed.), *Thought without language*. Oxford, UK: Clarendon Press.

Levine, S. C., & Carey, S. (1982). Up front: The acquisition of a concept and a word. *Journal of Child Language, 9*, 645–657.

Lewontin, R. (1981). [Review of Gould's *The mismeasure of man.*] *New York Times* pp. 12–16. (As quoted in D. C. Dennett [1983]. Intentional systems in cognitive ethology: The "Panglossian paradigm" defended [p. 355]. *The Behavioral and Brain Sciences, 6*, 343–390.)

Lewontin, R. C. (1983). Gene, organism, and environment. In D. S. Bendell (Ed.), *Evolution from molecules to men*. Cambridge, UK: Cambridge University Press.

Linden, D. R., Savage, L. M., & Overmier, J. B. (1997). General learned irrelevance: A Pavlovian analog to learned helplessness. *Learning & Motivation, 28*, 230–248.

Locke, J. (1690). An essay concerning human understanding. Reprinted in E. Sprague & P. W. Taylor (Eds.) (1959). *Knowledge and value*. New York: Harcourt, Brace.

Logue, A. W. (1979). Taste aversion and the generality of the laws of learning. *Psychological Bulletin, 86*, 276–296.

Lorenz, K. (1935). Der Kumpan in der Umwelt des Vogels; die Artgenosse als auslosende Moment sozialer Verhaltungswiesen. *Journal für Ornithologie, 83*, 137–213. (As cited in Hess, E. H. [1973]. *Imprinting*. New York: Van Nostrand.)

Lorenz, K., & Tinbergen, N. (1938). Taxis und instinkthandlung in der eirollbewegung der graugans. *Zeitschrift fur Tierpsychologie, 2*, 1–29. (As cited in Eibl-Eibesfeldt, I. [1975]. *Ethology, the biology of behavior* [2nd ed.]. New York: Holt, Rinehart, & Winston.)

Lubow, R. E. (1989). *Latent inhibition and conditioned attention theory*. Cambridge, UK: Cambridge University Press.

Lubow, R. E., & Moore, A. U. (1959). Latent inhibition: The effect of nonreinforced preexposure to the conditioned stimulus. *Journal of Comparative and Physiological Psychology, 52*, 415–419.

Lucas, F., & Sclafani, A. (1990). Hyperphagia in rats produced by a mixture of fats and sugar. *Physiology and Behavior, 47*, 51–55.

MacDonald, S. E. (1994). Gorillas' (*Gorilla gorilla gorilla*) spatial memory in a foraging task. *Journal of Comparative Psychology, 108*, 107–113.

MacLean, P. D. (1970). The limbic brain in relation to the psychoses. In P. Black (Ed.), *Physiological correlates of emotion.* New York: Academic Press.

MacLean, P. D. (1977). The triune brain in conflict. *Psychotherapy & Psychosomatics, 18*, 207–220.

Maier, S. F., & Seligman, M. E. P. (1976). Learned helplessness: Theory and evidence. *Journal of Experimental Psychology: General, 105*, 3–46.

Malone, J. C. (1982). The second offspring of general process learning theory: Overt behavior as the ambassador of the mind. *Journal of the Experimental Analysis of Behavior, 38*, 205–209.

Mayr, E. (1991). *One long argument: Charles Darwin and the genesis of modern evolutionary theory.* Cambridge, MA: Harvard University Press.

McCarthy, Cormac. (1992). *All the pretty horses.* New York: Vintage International.

McCormick, D. A., & Thompson, R. F. (1984). Cerebellum: Essential involvement in the classically conditioned eyelid response. *Science, 223*, 296–299.

Meck, W. H., & Church, R. M. (1983). A mode control model of counting and timing processes. *Journal of Experimental Psychology: Animal Behavior Processes, 9*, 320–334.

Medin, D. L., & Ross, B. H. (1990). *Cognitive psychology.* Fort Worth, TX: Harcourt Brace Jovanovich.

Mehiel, R., & Bolles, R. C. (1984). Learned flavor preferences based on caloric outcome. *Animal Learning and Behavior, 12*, 421–427.

Melchior, C. L., & Tabakoff, B. (1984). A conditioning model of alcohol tolerance. In M. Galanter (Ed.), *Recent developments in alcoholism* (Vol. 2). New York: Plenum Press.

Melzac, R. (1990, February). The tragedy of needless pain. *Scientific American, 262*, 27–33.

Menzel, E. W. (1978). Cognitive mapping in chimpanzees. In S. H. Hulse, H. F. Fowler, & W. K. Honig (Eds.), *Cognitive processes in animal behavior.* Hillsdale, NJ: Erlbaum.

Metsala, J. L. (1999). Young children's phonological awareness and nonword repetition as a function of vocabulary development. *Journal of Educational Psychology, 91*, 3–19.

Miller, A. D., & Rugg, M. D. (Eds.). (1992). *The neuro-psychology of consciousness.* London: Academic Press.

Miller, D. J., & Kotses, D. J. (1995). Classical conditioning of total respiratory resistance in humans. *Psychosomatic Medicine, 57*, 148–153.

Miller, G. (1991). *The science of words.* New York: Freeman.

Miller, G. A., & Gildea, P. M. (1987). How children learn words. *Scientific American, 257*, 94–99.

Miller, N. (1985). The value of behavioral research on animals. *American Psychologist, 40*, 423–440.

Miller, R. R., & Schactman, T. R. (1985a). The several roles of context at the time of retrieval. In P. D. Balsam & A. Tomie (Eds.), *Context and learning.* Hillsdale, NJ: Erlbaum.

Miller, R. R., & Schactman, T. R. (1985b). Conditioning context as an associative baseline: Implications for response generation and the nature of conditioned inhibition. In R. R. Miller & N. E. Spear (Eds.), *Information processing in animals: Conditioned inhibition.* Hillsdale, NJ: Erlbaum.

Milner, P. M. (1976). Theories of reinforcement, drive, and motivation. In L. L. Iverson & S. H. Snyder (Eds.), *Handbook of psychopharmacology* (Vol. 7). New York: Plenum Press.

Mineka, S. (1979). The role of fear in theories of avoidance learning, flooding, and extinction. *Psychological Bulletin, 86*, 985–1010.

Minor, T. R., Dess, N. K., & Overmeir, J. B. (1991). Inverting the traditional view of "learned helplessness." In M. R. Denny (Ed.), *Fear, avoidance, and phobias.* Hillsdale, NJ: Erlbaum.

Mischel, W. (1966). Theory and research on the antecedents of self-imposed delay of reward. *Progress in Experimental Personality Research, 3*, 85–132.

Mitchell, D. (1976). Experiments on neophobia in wild and laboratory rats: A reevaluation. *Journal of Comparative and Physiological Psychology, 90,* 190–197.

Moltz, H. (1963). Imprinting: An epigenetic approach. *Psychological Review, 70,* 123–138.

Monroe, B., & Barker, L. M. (1979). A contingency analysis of taste aversion conditioning. *Animal Learning and Behavior, 7,* 141–143.

Montague, P. R., Dayan, P., & Sejnowski, P. J. (1993). Foraging in an uncertain world using predictive Hebbian learning. *Society for Neuroscience, 19,* 1609.

Moore, T. (1994). *Soul mates.* New York: HarperCollins.

Morgan, C. L. (1894). *Introduction to comparative psychology.* London

Mowrer, O. H. (1947). On the dual nature of learning: A reinterpretation of "conditioning" and "problem solving." *Harvard Educational Review, 17,* 102–148.

Mowrer, O. H. (1960). *Learning theory and behavior.* New York: Wiley.

Mowrer, O. H., & Lamoreaux, R. R. (1942). Avoidance behavior and signal duration: A study of secondary motivation and reward. *Psychological Monographs, 54* (Whole No. 247).

Moyers, B. *Healing and the mind.* New York: Doubleday.

Myers, D. L., & Myers, L. E. (1977). Undermatching: A reappraisal of performance on concurrent variable-interval schedules of reinforcement. *Journal of the Experimental Analysis of Behavior, 25,* 203–214.

Nagy, W. E., & Anderson, R. C. (1984). How many words are there in printed school English? *Reading Research Quarterly, 19,* 304–330.

Nash, S., & Domjan, M. (1991). Learning to discriminate the sex of conspecifics in male Japanese quail (*Coturnix coturnix japonica*): Tests of "biological constraints." *Journal of Experimental Psychology: Animal Behavior Processes, 17,* 342–353.

Newcombe, F. (1987). Psychometric and behavioral evidence: Scope, limitations, and ecological validity. In H. S. Levin, J. Grafman, & H. M. Eisenberg (Eds.), *Neurobehavioral recovery from head injury.* Oxford, UK: Oxford University Press.

O'Brien, C. P. (1975). Experimental analysis of conditioning factors in human narcotic addiction. *Pharmacological Reviews, 27,* 533–543.

O'Brien, C. P., Testa, T., Ternes, J. W., & Greenstein, R. (1978). Conditioning effects of narcotics in humans. In *Behavioral Tolerance* (NIDA Research Monograph no. 18, pp. 67–71). Washington, DC: NIDA.

Olds, J., & Milner, P. (1954). Positive reinforcement produced by electrical stimulation of septal area and other regions of the rat brain. *Journal of Comparative and Physiological Psychology, 47,* 419–427

Olson, D. J., & Maki, W. S. (1983). Characteristics of spatial memory in pigeons. *Journal of Experimental Psychology: Animal Behavior Processes, 9,* 266–280.

Olton, D. S., & Samuelson, R. J. (1976). Remembrance of places passed: Spatial memory in rats. *Journal of Experimental Psychology: Animal Behavior Processes, 2,* 97–116.

Olton, D. S., Collision, C., & Werz, M. A. (1977). Spatial memory and radial arm maze performance of rats. *Learning and Motivation, 8,* 289–314.

Overmier, B., & Seligman, M. (1967). Effects of inescapable shock upon subsequent escape and avoidance responding. *Journal of Comparative and Physiological Psychology, 63,* 28–33.

Overmier, J. B. (1999). On the nature of animal models of human behavioral dysfunction. In M. Haug & R. E. Whalen, (Eds.), *Animal models of human emotion and cognition.* Washington, DC: American Psychological Association.

Overmier, J. B. Murison, R., & Johnson, T. B. (1997). Prediction of individual variability to stress-induced gastric ulcerations in rats: A factor analysis of selected behavioral and biological indices. *Physiology & Behavior, 61,* 555–562.

Palya, W. L. (1993). Bipolar control in fixed interfood intervals. *Journal of the Experimental Analysis of Behavior, 60,* 345–359.

Pateman, T. (1985). From nativism to sociolinguistics: Integrating a theory of language growth with a theory of speech practices. *Journal of the Theory of Social Behavior, 15,* 38–58.

Patterson, F., & Linden, E. (1981). *The education of Koko.* New York: Holt, Rinehart and Winston.

Pavlov, I. (1927/1960). *Conditioned reflexes.* New York: Dover. (First published 1927, Oxford University Press.)

Peeke, H. V. S., & Petrinovich, L. (Eds.). (1984). *Habituation, sensitization, and behavior.* New York: Academic Press.

Pepperberg, I. M. (1991). A communicative approach to animal cognition. A study of the conceptual abilities of an African grey parrot. In C. A. Ristau (Ed.), *Cognitive ethology: The minds of other animals.* Hillsdale, NJ: Erlbaum.

Pepperberg, I. M. (1994). Numerical competence in an African gray parrot (*Psittacus erithacus*). *Journal of Comparative Psychology, 108,* 36–44.

Pepperberg, I. M. (1999). Rethinking syntax: A commentary on E. Kako's "Elements of syntax in the systems of three language-trained animals." *Animal Learning and Behavior, 27,* 15–17.

Pepperberg, I. M. & McLaughlin, M. A. (1996) Effect of avian-human joint attention in allospecific vocal learning by grey parrots (*Psittacus erithacus*). *Journal of Comparative Psychology, 110,* 286–297.

Pfaffman, C. (1959). The sense of taste. In J. Field (Ed.), *Handbook of physiology. Neurophysiology* (Vol. 1). Washington, DC: American Physiological Society.

Pfaffman, C. (1960). The pleasures of sensation. *Psychological Review, 67,* 253–268.

Philips, H. C., Fenster, H., & Samson, D. (1988). An effective treatment for voiding dysfunction: A control treatment trial. *Journal of Behavioral Modification, 15,* 45–63.

Phillips, A. G., & Fibiger, H. C. (1989). Neuroanatomical bases of intracranial self-stimulation: Untangling the Gordian knot. In J. M. Liebman & S. J. Cooper (Eds.), *The neuropharmacological basis of reward* (pp. 66–105). Oxford, UK: Clarendon Press.

Pinel, J. P. J. (2000). *Biopsychology,* 4e. Boston: Allyn & Bacon.

Pinker, S. & Bloom, P. (1990). Natural language and natural selection. *Behavioral and Brain Sciences, 13,* 707–784.

Pinker, S. (1991). Rules of language. *Science, 253,* 530–535.

Pinker, S., (1994). *The learning instinct.* London: Penguin Press.

Pliner, P., Herman, P. C., & Polivy, J. (1990). Palatability as a determinant of eating: Finickiness as a function of taste, hunger, and the prospect of good food. In E. D. Capaldi & T. L. Powley (Eds.), *Taste, experience, and feeding.* Washington, DC: American Psychological Society.

Plomin, R. (1990). The role of inheritance in behavior. *Science, 248,* 223–228.

Powell, J., & Azrin, N. (1968). The effects of shock as a punisher for cigarette smoking. *Journal of Applied Behavior Analysis, 1,* 63–71.

Premack, A. J., & Premack, D. (1972). Teaching language to an ape. *Scientific American, 227,* 92–99.

Premack, D. (1962). Reversibility of the reinforcement relation. *Science, 136,* 255–257.

Premack, D. (1988). Minds with and without language. In L. Weiskrantz (Ed.), *Thought without language.* Oxford, UK: Clarendon Press.

Rachlin, H. C. (1974). Self-control. *Behaviorism, 2,* 94–107.

Rachlin, H. C., & Green, L. (1972). Commitment, choice, and self-control. *Journal of the Experimental Analysis of Behavior, 17,* 15–22.

Rakitin, B. C., Gibbon, J., Penney, T. B., Malapani, C., Hinton, S. C., & Meck, W. H. (1997). Scalar expectancy theory and peak interval timing in humans. *Journal of Experimental Psychology: Animal Behavior Processes, 24,* 15–33.

Randich, A., & LoLordo, V. M. (1979). Preconditioning exposure to the unconditioned stimulus affects the acquisition of the conditioned emotional response. *Learning and Motivation, 10,* 245–275.

Razran, G. (1971) *Mind in evolution.* Boston: Houghton Mifflin.

Real, L. A. (1991). Animal choice behavior and the evolution of cognitive architecture. *Science, 253,* 980–986.

Renner, M. J. (1988). Learning during exploration: The role of behavioral topography during exploration in determining subsequent adaptive behavior. *The International Journal of Comparative Psychology, 2*, 43–56.

Renner, M. J., & Seltzer, C. P. (1991). Molar characteristics of exploratory and investigative behavior in the rat (*Rattas morregicus*). *Journal of Comparative Psychology, 105*, 326–339.

Rescorla, R. A. (1967). Pavlovian conditioning and its proper control procedures. *Psychological Review, 74*, 71–80.

Rescorla, R. A. (1968). Probability of shock in the presence and absence of CS in fear conditioning. *Journal of Comparative and Physiological Psychology, 66*, 1–5.

Rescorla, R. A. (1969). Pavlovian conditioned inhibition. *Psychological Bulletin, 72*, 77–94.

Rescorla, R. A. (1971). Summation and retardation tests of latent inhibition. *Journal of Comparative and Physiological Psychology, 75*, 77–81.

Rescorla, R. A. (1985). Conditioned inhibition and facilitation. In R. R. Miller & N. E. Spear (Eds.), *Information processing in animals: Conditioned inhibition*. Hillsdale, NJ: Erlbaum.

Rescorla, R. A., & Wagner, A. R. (1972). A theory of Pavlovian conditioning: Variations in the effectiveness of reinforcement and nonreinforcement. In A. H. Black & W. F. Prokasy (Eds.), *Classical conditioning II: Current research and theory*. New York: Appleton-Century-Crofts.

Reynolds, G. S. (1968). *A primer of operant conditioning*. Glenview, IL: Scott, Foresman.

Richter, C. P. (1936). Increased salt appetite in adrenalectomized rats. *American Journal of Physiology, 115*, 155–161.

Richter, C. P. (1942). Total self-regulatory functions in animals and human beings. *Harvey Lectures, 38*, 63–103.

Richter, C. P. (1958). Rats, man, and the welfare state. *American Psychologist, 13*, 1–17.

Riley, A., & Tuck, D. L. (1985). Conditioned taste aversions: A behavioral index of toxicity. *Annals of the New York Academy of Sciences, 443*, 272–292.

Roberts, S. (1981). Isolation of an internal clock. *Journal of Experimental Psychology: Animal Behavior Processes, 7*, 242–268.

Roberts, W. A., & Boisvert, M. J. (1998). Using the peak procedure to measure timing and counting in pigeons. *Journal of Experimental Psychology: Animal Behavior Processes, 24*, 416–430.

Rodgers, W., & Rozin, P. (1966). Novel food preferences in thiamine deficient rats. *Journal of Comparative and Physiological Psychology, 61*, 1–4.

Rohles, F. H., Grunzke, M. E., & Reynolds, H. H. (1963). Chimpanzee performance during the ballistic and orbital Project Mercury flights. *Journal of Comparative and Physiological Psychology, 56*, 202–210.

Roitblat, H. L. (1987). *Introduction to comparative cognition*. New York: W. H. Freeman.

Rolls, B, J., Rolls, E. T., and Rowe, E. A. (1982). The influence of variety on human food selection and intake. In L. M. Barker (Ed.), *The psychobiology of human food selection*. Westport, CT: AVI Publishing.

Romanes, G. (1884). *Animal intelligence*. New York: Appleton.

Rosas, J. M. & Bouton, M. E. (1997). Additivity of the effects of retention interval and context change on latent inhibition: Toward resolution of the context forgetting paradox. *Journal of Experimental Psychology: Animal Behavior Processes, 23*, 283–294.

Rosensweig, M. R., Krech, D., Bennett, E. L., & Diamond, M. C. (1962). Effects of environmental complexity and training on brain chemistry and anatomy: A replication and extension. *Journal of Comparative and Physiological Psychology, 55*, 427–429.

Rosenzweig, M. R., Leiman, A. L., & Breedlove, M. S. (1999). *Biological psychology: An introduction to behavioral, cognitive, and clinical neuroscience*. Sunderland, MA: Sinauer Associates, Inc.

Ross, R. T., & Holland, P. C. (1981). Conditioning of simultaneous and serial feature-positive discriminations. *Animal Learning and Behavior, 9*, 293–303.

Routtenberg A., & Lindy, J. (1965). Effects of the availability of rewarding septal and hypothalamic stimulation on bar pressing for food under conditions of deprivation. *Journal of Comparative and Physiological Psychology, 60*, 158–161.

Rozin, E. (1982). The structure of cuisine. In L. Barker (Ed.), *The psychobiology of human food selection*. Westport, CT: AVI Publishing.

Rozin, P. (1967). Thiamine specific hunger. In C. F. Code (Ed.), *Handbook of physiology (Section 6): Alimentary canal (Vol. 1): Control of food and water intake*. Washington, DC: American Physiological Society.

Rozin, P., & Kalat, J. W. (1971). Specific hungers and poison avoidance as adaptive specializations of learning. *Psychological Review, 78*, 459–486.

Rudy, J. W. (1994). Ontogeny of context-specific latent inhibition of conditioned fear: Implications for configural associations theory and hippocampal formation development. *Developmental Psychobiology, 27*, 367–379.

Rumbaugh, D. M. (Ed.). (1977). *Language learning by a chimpanzee: The LANA project*. New York: Academic Press.

Rumbaugh, D. M., & Gill, R. V. (1976). The mastery of language-type skills by the chimpanzee (*Pan*). *Annals of the New York Academy of Sciences, 280*, 562–578.

Rzoska, J. (1953). Bait-shyness: A study in rat behavior. *The British Journal of Animal Behavior, 1*, 128–135.

Sagan, C., & Druyan, A. (1992) *Shadows of forgotten ancestors*. New York: Ballantine Books.

Salter, A. (1949). *Conditioned reflex therapy*. New York: Farrar, Straus.

Sampson, H. A., Mendelson, L., & Rosen, J. P. (1992). Fatal and near fatal anaphylaxis reactions to food in children and adolescents. *Journal of the American Medical Association, 327*, 380–384.

Savage-Rumbaugh, S. (1987). Communication, symbolic communication, and language: Reply to Seidenberg and Petitto. *Journal of Experimental Psychology: General, 116*, 288–292.

Savage-Rumbaugh, S., McDonald, K., Sevcik, R. A., Hopkins, W. D., & Rubert, E. (1986). Spontaneous symbol acquisition and communicative use by pygmy chimpanzees (*Pan paniscus*). *Journal of Experimental Psychology: General, 115*, 211–235.

Savage-Rumbaugh, S., Murphy, J., Sevcik, R. A., Brakke, K. E., Williams, S. L., &

Rumbaugh, D. M. (1993). Language comprehension in ape and child. *Monographs of the Society for Research in Child Development*, Serial No. 233, Vol. 58 (3–4), pp. 30–170. Chicago: Society for Research in Child Development.

Schiffman, S. S. (1983). Taste and smell in disease. *New England Journal of Medicine, 308*, 1337–1342.

Schlinger, H. D. (1993). Learned expectancies are not adequate scientific explanations. *American Psychologist, 48*, 1155–1156.

Schmajuk, N. A., & Christiansen, B. A. (1990). Eyeblink conditioning in rats. *Physiology and Behavior, 48*, 755–758.

Schusterman, R. J., & Gisner, R. (1988). Artificial language comprehension in dolphins and sea lions: The essential cognitive skills. *Psychological Record, 38*, 311–348.

Schusterman, R. J., & Gisner, R. (1989). Please parse the sentence: Animal cognition in the procrustean bed of linguistics. *Psychological Record, 39*, 3–18.

Schwitzer, J. B., & Sulzer-Azaroff, B. (1988). Self-control: Teaching tolerance for delay in impulsive children. *Journal of the Experimental Analysis of Behavior, 50*, 173–186.

Sejnowski, T. J., & Churchland, P. S. (1992a). *The computational brain*. Cambridge, MA: MIT Press.

Sejnowski, T. J., & Churchland, P S. (1992b). Silicon brains. *BYTE, 17* (10), 137–146.

Seligman, M. E. P. (1970). On the generality of the laws of learning. *Psychological Review, 77*, 406–418.

Seligman, M. E. P. (1975). *Helplessness: On depression, development, and death*. San Francisco: W. H. Freeman.

Seligman, M. E. P., & Maier, S. F. (1967). Failure to escape traumatic shock. *Journal of Experimental Psychology, 74*, 1–9.

Seyfarth, R. M., Cheney, D. L., & Marler, P. (1980). Vervet monkey responses to three different alarm calls. Evidence of predator classification and semantic communication. *Science, 210*, 801–803.

Sheffield, F. D., & Roby, T. B. (1950). Reward value of a non-nutritive sweet taste. *Journal of Comparative and Physiological Psychology, 43*, 471–481.

Sheffield, F. D., Roby, T. B., Campbell, B. A. (1954). Drive reduction versus consummatory behavior as determinants of reinforcement. *Journal of Comparative and Physiological Psychology, 47,* 349–354.

Sheffield, F. D., Wulff, J. J., & Backer, R. (1951). Reward value of copulation without sex-drive reduction. *Journal of Comparative and Physiological Psychology, 44,* 3–8.

Sherman, J. E., Hickis, C. F., Rice, A. G., Rusiniak, K. W., & Garcia, J. (1983). Preferences and aversions for stimuli paired with ethanol in hungry rats. *Animal Learning and Behavior, 11,* 101–106.

Sherrington, C. S. (1906). *Integrative action of the nervous system.* New York: Scribner.

Shettleworth, S. (1998). *Cognition, evolution, and behavior.* New York: Oxford University Press.

Shettleworth, S. J. (1975). Reinforcement and the organization of behavior in golden hamsters: Hunger, environment, and food reinforcement. *Journal of Experimental Psychology: Animal Behavior Processes, 1,* 56–87.

Shettleworth, S. J., & Krebs, J. R. (1982). How marsh tits find their hoards: The roles of site preference and spatial memory. *Journal of Experimental Psychology: Animal Behavior Processes, 8,* 342–353.

Shumake, S. A., Thompson, R. D., & Caudill, C. J. (1971). Taste preference behavior of laboratory versus wild Norway rats. *Journal of Comparative and Physiological Psychology, 77,* 480–494.

Sibley, C. G., Comstock, J. A., & Ahlquist, J. E. (1990). DNA hybridization evidence of hominoid phylogeny: A reanalysis of the data. *Journal of Molecular Evolution, 30,* 202–206.

Sidman, M. (1953). Avoidance conditioning with brief shock and no exteroceptive warning signal. *Science, 118,* 157–158.

Siegel, S. (1975). Evidence from rats that morphine tolerance is a learned response. *Journal of Comparative and Physiological Psychology, 89,* 498–506.

Siegel, S. (1977). Morphine tolerance acquisition as an associative process. *Journal of Experimental Psychology: Animal Behavior Processes, 3,* 1–13.

Siegel, S., Hinson, R. E., Krank, M. D., & McCully, J. (1982). Heroin "overdose" death: Contribution of drug-associated environment cues. *Science, 216,* 436–437.

Simoons, F. J. (1973). New light on ethnic differences in adult lactose intolerance. *American Journal of Digestive Disorders, 18,* 595–611.

Singh, D., & Luis, S. (1995). Ethnic and gender consensus for the effect of waist-to hip ratio on judgment of women's attractiveness. *Human Nature, 6,* 51–65.

Singh, D., & Young, R. K. (1995). Body weight, waist-to-hip ratio, breasts, and hips: Role in judgments of female attractiveness and desirability for relationships. *Ethology and Sociobiology, 16,* 483–507.

Skinner, B. F. (1938). *The behavior of organisms.* Englewood Cliffs, NJ: Prentice Hall.

Skinner, B. F. (1948). *Walden two.* New York: Macmillan.

Skinner, B. F. (1950). Are theories of learning necessary? *Psychological Review, 57,* 193–216.

Skinner, B. F. (1953). *Science and human behavior.* New York: Macmillan.

Skinner, B. F. (1957). *Verbal behavior.* New York: Appleton.

Skinner, B. F. (1959). A case history in scientific method. In S. Koch (Ed.), *Psychology: A study of a science.* New York: McGraw Hill.

Skinner, B. F. (1960, January). Pigeons in a pelican. *American Psychologist, 14,* 5–23.

Skinner, B. F. (1963). Behaviorism at fifty. *Science, 140,* 951–958.

Skinner, B. F. (1966). The phylogeny and ontogeny of behavior. *Science, 153,* 1204–1213.

Skinner, B. F. (1971). *Beyond freedom and dignity.* New York: Knopf.

Skinner, B. F. (1989). The origins of cognitive thought. *American Psychologist, 44,* 13–18.

Slameka, N. J. (Ed.) (1967). *Human learning and memory.* New York: Oxford University Press.

Small, W. S. (1901). An experimental study of the mental processes of the rat. *American Journal of Psychology, 12,* 206–239.

Smith, J. C., & Roll, D. L. (1967). Trace conditioning with x-rays as the unconditioned stimulus. *Psychonomic Science, 9,* 11–12.

Snow, C. E., Burns, M. S., & Griffin, P. (Eds.). (1998). *Preventing reading difficulties in young children*. Washington, DC: National Academy Press.

Soler, J. (1979, June 14). The dietary prohibitions of the Hebrews. *The New York Review of Books*, p. 24.

Solomon, P. R., Brennan, G., & Moore, J. W. (1974). Latent inhibition of rabbits' nictitating membrane response as a function of CS intensity. *Bulletin of the Psychonomic Society, 4*, 445.

Solomon, R. L., & Wynne, L. C. (1953). Traumatic avoidance learning: Acquisition in normal dogs. *Psychological Monographs, 67* (Whole No. 354).

Solomon, S. D., Gerrity, E. T., & Muff, A. M. (1992). Efficacy of treatments for post-traumatic stress disorder: An empirical review. *Journal of the American Medical Association, 268*, 633–638.

Sonuga-Barke, E. J. S., Lea, S. E. G., & Webley, P. (1989). The development of adaptive choice in a self-control paradigm. *Journal of the Experimental Analysis of Behavior, 51*, 77–85.

Spanos, N. P., & Chaves, J. F. (Eds.). (1989). *Hypnosis: The cognitive-behavioral perspective*. Buffalo, NY: Prometheus Books.

Spelke, E. S. (1988). The origins of physical knowledge. In L. Weiskrantz (Ed.), *Thought without language*. Oxford, UK: Clarendon Press.

Stanovich, K. E. (1986). Mathew effects in reading: Some consequences of individual differences in the acquisition of literacy. *Reading Research Quarterly, 21*, 360–406.

Stanovich, K. E., & Cunningham, A. E. (1992). Studying the consequences of literacy within a literate society: The cognitive correlates of print exposure. *Memory & Cognition, 20*, 51–68.

Steinmetz, J. (1996). The brain substrates of classical eyeblink conditioning in rabbits. In J. R. Bloedel, T. J. Ebner, & S. P. Wise (Eds.), *The acquisition of motor behavior in vertebrates*. Cambridge, MA: MIT Press.

Stemmer, N. (1989). The acquisition of the ostensive lexicon: The superiority of empiricist over cognitive theories. *Behaviorism, 17*, 41–61.

Stoddart, D. M. (1990). *The scented ape: The biology and culture of human odour*. Cambridge, UK: Cambridge University Press.

Storms, L. H., Boroczi, G., & Broen, W. E. (1962). Punishment inhibits an instrumental response in hooded rats. *Science, 135*, 1133–1134.

Suarez, E. M., & Barker, L. M. (1976). Effects of water deprivation and prior lithium chloride exposure in conditioning taste aversions. *Physiology & Behavior, 17*, 555–559.

Symons, D. (1979). *The evolution of human sexuality*. New York: Oxford University Press.

Tanaka, M. (1995). Object sorting in chimpanzees *(Pan troglodytes)*: Classification based on physical identity, complementarity, and familiarity. *Journal of Comparative Psychology, 109*, 151–161.

Teale, W. H. (1986). Home background and young children's literacy development. In W. H. Teale & E. Sulzby (Eds.), *Emergent literacy*. Norwood, NJ: Ablex Publishing.

Ternes, J. W., O'Brien, C. P., Grabowski, J., Wellerstein, J., & Jordan-Hays, J. (1980). Conditioning drug responses to naturalistic stimuli. In *Problems of drug dependence, 1979*. (Research Monograph no. 27, pp. 67–71. Washington, DC: NIDA.)

Terrace, H. S. (1979). *Nim*. New York: Alfred A. Knopf.

Theios, J., Lynch, A. D., & Lowe, W. F. (1966). Differential effects of shock intensity on one-way and shuttle-avoidance conditioning. *Journal of Experimental Psychology, 72*, 294–299.

Thinus-Blanc, C. (1988). Animal spatial cognition. In L. Weiskrantz (Ed.), *Thought without language*. Oxford, UK: Clarendon Press.

Thomas, R. K., & Boyd, M. G. (1973). A comparison of *Cebus albifrons* and *Saimiri sciureus* on oddity performance. *Animal Learning and Behavior, 5*, 151–153.

Thompson, R. F. (1986). The neurobiology of learning and memory. *Science, 233*, 941–947.

Thompson, R. F., & Spencer, W. A. (1966). Habituation: A model phenomenon for the study of neuronal substrates of behavior. *Psychological Review, 73*, 16–43.

Thorndike, E. L. (1898). Animal intelligence: An experimental study of the associative processes in animals. *Psychological Review Monograph Supplement, 2*, 1–109.

Thorndike, E. L. (1911). *Animal intelligence: Experimental studies.* New York: Macmillan.

Thorndike, E. L. (1932). *Fundamentals of learning.* New York: Teachers College, Columbia University.

Tiffany, S. T. (1990). A cognitive model of drug urges and drug use behavior: The role of automatic and non-automatic processes. *Psychological Review, 97,* 147–168.

Timberlake, W. (1993). Animal behavior: A continuing synthesis. *Annual Review of Psychology, 44,* 675–708.

Timberlake, W. (1994). Behavior systems, associationism, and Pavlovian conditioning. *Psychonomic Bulletin and Review, 1,* 405–420.

Timberlake, W., & Grant, D. S. (1975). Autoshaping in rats to the presentation of another rat predicting food. *Science, 190,* 690–692.

Timberlake, W., Wahl, G., & King, D. (1982). Stimulus and response contingencies in the misbehavior of rats. *Journal of Experimental Psychology: Animal Behavior Processes, 8,* 62–85.

Tinbergen, N. (1950). The hierarchical organization of nervous mechanisms underlying instinctive behaviour. *Symposium of the Society for Experimental Biology, 4,* Cambridge, UK: Cambridge University Press.

Tinbergen, N. (1951). *The study of instinct.* Oxford, UK: Clarendon Press.

Tolman, E. C., & Honzik, C. H. (1930b). "Insight" in rats. *University of California Publications in Psychology, 4,* 215–232.

Tolman, E. C. (1932). *Purposive behavior in animals and men.* New York: Appleton-Century-Crofts.

Tolman, E. C. (1938). The determiners of behavior at a choice point. *Psychological Review, 45,* 1–41.

Tolman, E. C., & Honzik, C. H. (1930a). Degrees of hunger; reward and non-reward; and maze learning in rats. *University of California Publications in Psychology, 4,* 241–256.

Trivers, R. (1985). *Social evolution.* Menlo Park, CA: Benjamin/Cummings Publishing Co.

Turk, D. C., Meichenbaum, D., & Genest, M. (1983). *Pain and behavioral medicine: A cognitive behavioral perspective.* New York: Guilford Press.

Turner, A. M., & Greenough, W. T. (1983). Synapses per neuron and synaptic dimensions in occipital cortex in rats reared in complex, social, or isolation housing. *Acta Stereologica, 2,* 239–244.

Twitmyer, E. B. (1974). A study of the knee jerk. *Journal of Experimental Psychology, 103,* 1047–1066.

Urcuioli, P. (1996). Acquired equivalences and mediated generalization in pigeon's matching to sample. In T. R. Zentall & P. M. Smeets (Eds), *Stimulus class formation in humans and animals. (Advances in Psychology, No. 117).* Amsterdam, Netherlands: Elsevier.

Vaccarino, F. J., Schiff, B. B., & Glickman, S. E. (1989). Biological view of reinforcement. In S. B. Klein & R. R. Mowrer (Eds.), *Contemporary learning theories: Instrumental conditioning and the impact of biological constraints on learning.* Hillsdale, NJ: Erlbaum.

Valenstein, E. S., Cox, V. C., & Kakolewski, J. W. (1967). Polydipsia elicited by the synergistic action of a saccharin and glucose solution. *Science, 157,* 552–554.

van der Kolk, B. S. (1987). *Psychological trauma.* Washington, DC: American Psychiatric Press.

Van Itallie, T. B. (1979). Adverse effects on health and longevity. *American Journal of Clinical Nutrition, 32,* 2723–2733.

Vaughan, W., Jr. (1981). Melioration, matching, and maximizing. *Journal of the Experimental Analysis of Behavior, 36,* 141–149.

Vaughan, W., Jr. (1985). Choice: A local analysis. *Journal of the Experimental Analysis of Behavior, 43,* 383–405.

Vega, L. de. (1615). El Capellan de la Vergen [*The Chaplain of the Virgin*]. In W. A. Bousfield. *American Psychologist, 10,* 828.

Verhave, T. (Ed.) (1966). *The experimental analysis of behavior: Selected readings.* New York: Appleton-Century-Crofts.

Vigilant, L., Stoneking, M., Harpending, H., Hawkes, K., & Wilson, A. C. (1991). African populations and the evolution of human mitochondrial DNA. *Science, 253,* 1503–1507.

von Neuman, J., & Morganstern, O. (1944). *Theory of games and economic behavior.*

Princeton, NJ: Princeton University Press.

Wagner, A., R. (1976). Priming in STM: An information processing mechanism for self-generated and retrieval-generated depression in performance. In T. J. Tighe & R. N. Leaton (Eds.), *Habituation: Perspectives from child development, animal behavior, and neurophysiology.* Hillsdale, NJ: Erlbaum.

Walker, A., & Shipman, P. (1996). *The wisdom of bones: In search of human origins.* London: Weidenfeld & Nicolson.

Warren, J. M. (1965). Primate learning in comparative perspective. In A. M. Schrier, H. F. Harlow, & F. Stollnitz (Eds.), *Behavior of non-human primates (Vol. 1).* New York: Academic Press.

Washburn, M. F. (1908). *The animal mind: A textbook of comparative psychology.* New York: Macmillan.

Wasserman, E. A., & Astley, S. L. (1994). A behavioral analysis of concepts: Its application to pigeons and children. In D. E. Medin (Ed.), *The psychology of learning and motivation: Advances in research and theory, Vol. 31.* San Diego, CA: Academic Press.

Wasserman, E. A. (1997). The science of animal cognition: Past present and future. *Journal of Experimental Psychology: Animal Behavior Processes, 23,* 123–135.

Watson, J. B. (1924). *Behaviorism.* New York: Norton.

Watson, J. B., & Rayner, R. (1920). Conditioned emotional reactions. *Journal of Experimental Psychology, 3,* 1–14.

Weaver, C. A. (1994). The psychology of reading. In *The encyclopedia of human behavior.* San Diego: Academic Press.

Weingarten, H. P. (1990). Learning, homeostasis, and the control of feeding behavior. In E. D. Capaldi & T. L. Powley (Eds.), *Taste, experience, and feeding.* Washington, DC: American Psychological Society.

Weir, R. H. (1966). Some questions on the child's learning of phonology. In F. Smith & G. A. Miller (Eds.), *The genesis of language.* Cambridge, MA: MIT Press.

Weiskrantz, L. (Ed.). (1988). *Thought without language.* Oxford, UK: Clarendon Press.

Wenger, J. R., Tiffany, T. M., Bombardier, C., Nicholls, K., & Woods, S. C. (1981).

Ethanol tolerance in the rat is learned. *Science, 213,* 575–577.

Whalen, J., Gallistel, C. R., & Gelman, R. (1999). Nonverbal counting in humans: The psychophysics of number representation. *Psychological Science, 10,* 130–137.

Whiten, A., Goodall, J., McGrew, W. C., Nishida, T., Reynolds, V., Sugiyama, Y., Tutin, C. E. G., Wrangham, R. W., & Boesch, C. (1999). Culture in chimpanzees. *Nature, 399,* 682–685.

Wickler, W. (1973). Ethological analysis of convergent adaptation. *Annals of the New York Academy of Science, 223,* 65–82.

Wigfield, A., & Asher, S. R. (1984). Social and motivational influences on reading. In P. D. Pearson, R. Barr, M. L. Kamill, & P. Mosenthal (Eds.), *Handbook of research and reading.* New York: Longman.

Wilcoxson, H. C., Dragoin, W. B., & Kral, P. A. (1971). Illness-induced aversions in rats and quail: Relative salience of visual and gustatory cues. *Science, 171,* 826–828.

Wilkins, L. & Richter, C. P. (1940). A great craving for salt by a child with a cortico-adrenal insufficiency. *Journal of the American Medical Association, 114,* 866–868.

Williams, B. A. (1988). Reinforcement, choice, and response strength. In R. C. Atkinson, R. J. Herrnstein, G. Lindzey, & R. D. Luce (Eds.), *Stevens' handbook of experimental psychology* (2nd ed.). New York: Wiley.

Williams, B. A. (1994). Conditioned reinforcement: Neglected or outmoded explanatory construct. *Psychonomic Bulletin and Review, 1,* 457–475.

Williams, D. A., Overmier, J. B., & LoLordo, V. M. (1992). A reevaluation of Rescorla's early dictums about Pavlovian conditioned inhibition. *Psychological Bulletin, 111,* 275–290.

Williams, D. R., & Williams, H. (1969). Automaintenance in the pigeon: Sustained pecking despite contingent non-reinforcement. *Journal of the Experimental Analysis of Behavior, 12,* 511–520.

Wilson, E. O. (1975). *Sociobiology: The new synthesis.* Cambridge, MA: Harvard University Press.

Wise, R. A., Bauco, P., Carlezon, W. A. Jr., & Trojniar, W. (1992). Self-stimulation and drug reward mechanisms. *Annals of the New York Academy of Sciences, 654,* 192–198.

Wolpe, J., Salter, A., & Reyna, L. J. (1964). *The conditioning therapies.* New York: Holt, Rinehart and Winston.

Woodruff, G., & Premack, D. (1979). Intentional communication in the chimpanzee: The development of deception. *Cognition, 7,* 333–362.

Woodruff-Pak, D. S. (1999). New directions for a classical paradigm: Human eyeblink conditioning. *Psychological Science, 10,* 1–3.

Woodworth, R. S., & Schlosberg, H. (1954). *Experimental psychology.* New York: Holt, Rinehart and Winston.

World Book Encyclopedia. (1991). Chicago: World Book.

Wright, A. A., & Delius, J. D. (1994) Scratch and match: Pigeons learn matching and oddity with gravel stimuli. *Journal of Experimental Psychology: Animal Behavior Processes, 20,* 108–112.

Wright, A. A., & Watkins, M. J. (1987). Animal learning and memory and their relation to human learning and memory. *Learning and Motivation, 18,* 131–146.

Wright, A. A., Santiago, H. C., Sands, S. F., & Urcuioli, P. J. (1984). Pigeon and monkey serial probe recognition: Acquisition, strategies, and serial position effects. In H. L. Roitblat, T. G. Bever, & H. S. Terrace (Eds.), *Animal cognition.* Hillsdale, NJ: Erlbaum.

Wynn, K. (1996). Infants' individuation and enumeration of actions. *Psychological Science, 7,* 164–169.

Xie, X., Berger, T. W., & Barrionuevo, G. (1992). Isolated NMDA receptor-mediated synaptic responses express both LTP and LTD. *Journal of Neurophysiology, 67,* 1009–1013.

Yin, H., Barnet, R., & Miller, R. (1994). Second-order conditioning and Pavlovian conditioned inhibition: Operational similarities and differences. *Journal of Experimental Psychology: Animal Behavior Processes, 20,* 419–428.

Young, P. T. (1966). Hedonic organization and regulation of behavior. *Psychological Review, 73,* 59–86.

Zahorik, D. (1977). Associative and non-associative factors in learned food preferences. In L. M. Barker, M. R. Best, & M. Domjan (Eds.), *Learning mechanisms in food selection.* Waco, TX: Baylor University Press.

Zahorik, D., Mair, S. F., & Pies, R. W. (1974). Preferences for tastes paired with recovery from thiamine deficiency in rats. *Journal of Comparative and Physiological Psychology, 87,* 1083–1091.

Zentall, T. R., & Smeets, P. M. (Eds.) (1996). *Stimulus class formation in humans and animals. (Advances in Psychology, No. 117).* Amsterdam, Netherlands: Elsevier.

Zentall, T. R. (1997). Animal memory: The role of "instruction." *Learning and Motivation, 28,* 280–308.

ACKNOWLEDGMENTS

P. 39 Figure 2.1 Figure 19.2 from EVOLUTION 2nd ed. by Monroe W. Stuckberger. Copyright © 1995 by Jones and Bartlett Publishers, Inc. Reprinted by permission of Jones and Bartlett Publishers, Sudbury, MA. *WWW.jbpub.com*.

P. 38 Box 2.1 Figure 2.1 from THE THIRD CHIMPANZEE: The Evolution and Future of the Human Animal by J. Diamond. Copyright © 1992 by HarperCollins Publishers, Inc. Reprinted by permission of HarperCollins Publishers, Inc.

P. 48 Box 2.3 Figure 3.1 from ETHOLOGY: The Biology of Behavior by I. Eibl-Eibesfeld. Copyright © 1967 by R. Piper & Co., Verlag, Munich. Reprinted by permission from the English translation by the author. Grundrib der vergleichenden Verhaltensforschung: Ethologie by permission of R. Piper & Co., Verlag.

P. 106 Figure 4.1 (upper three figures) From "The Conditioned Emotional Response as a Function of Intensity of the US" by Z. Annau & L. J. Kamin, *Journal of Comparative and Physiological Physiology*, 54, 1961.

P. 106 Figure 4.1 (lower figure) From "Temporal and Intensity Characteristics of the Conditioned Stimulus" by L. J. Kamin in CLASSICAL CONDITIONING ed. by W. F. Prodasy. (1965) Appleton-Century-Crofts.

P. 108 Figure 4.2a Graph from "Twenty Years of Classical Conditioning Research with the Rabbit" by I. Gormezano, E. J. Kehoe, & B. S. Marshall in PROGRESS IN PSYCHOBIOLOGY AND PHYSIOLOGICAL PSYCHOLOGY ed. by J. M. Prague and A. N. Epstein, Volume 10. Copyright © 1983 by Academic Press. Reproduced by permission of the publisher.

P. 108 Figure 4.2b From "Effect of Intermittent Reinforcement on Acquisition, Extinction, and Spontaneous Recovery of the Conditioned Eyelid Response" by T. F. Hartman and D. A. Grant in *Journal of Experimental Psychology*, 60, 1960.

P. 108 Figure 4.2c Graph from "New Directions for a Classical Paradigm: Human Eyeblink Conditioning" by D. S. Woodruf-Pak in *Psychological Science*, 10, 1999. Copyright © 1999 by D. S. Woodruf-Pak.

Reprinted by permission of Blackwell Publishers.

P. 110 Figure 4.3 Figure 5.3 from "Building Memories for Foods" by Lewis M. Barker in THE PSYCHOBIOLOGY OF HUMAN FOOD SELECTION ed. by Lewis M. Barker. Copyright © 1982 by Lewis M. Barker. Reprinted by permission of the author.

P. 139 Figure 4.8 Figures 2 and 3 from "Morphine Tolerance Acquisition as an Associative Process" by S. Siegel in *Journal of Experimental Psychology: Animal Behavior Processes*, 3, 1977.

P. 213 Figure 6.5 Graph from INTRODUCTION AND REMOVAL OF REWARD AND MAZE PERFORMANCE IN RATS by E. C. Tolman and C. H. Honzik. Copyright 1930 by The Regents of the University of California. Reprinted by permission of University of California Press.

P. 247 Figure 7.4 Figure 1 from "The Mechanics of Reinforcement" by P. R. Killeen and L. A. Bizo in *Psychonomic Bulletin & Review*, 5, 1998. Copyright © 1998 by P. R. Killeen and L. A. Bizo. Reprinted by permission of Psychonomic Society, Inc.

P. 260 Figure 7.6 Reprinted courtesy of Dr. Clint D. Anderson.

P. 283 Figure 8.2 Figure 1 from "Sequential Effects of Punishment" by N. H. Azrin in THE EXPERIMENTAL ANALYSIS OF BEHAVIOR: Selected Readings edited by T. Verhave, 1966. Appleton-Century-Crofts.

P. 290 Figure 8.4 Figure 6 from "An Introduction to the Experimental Analysis of Behavior" by T. Verhave in THE EXPERIMENTAL ANALYSIS OF BEHAVIOR: Selected Readings edited by T. Verhave, 1966. Appleton-Century-Crofts.

P. 285 Box 8.1 From "Response Suppression as a Function of the Schedule of Punishment" by D. S. Camp, G. A. Raymond, & R. M. Church in *Psychonomic Science*, 5, 1962. Reprinted by permission of Psychonomic Society, Inc.

P. 313 Figure 9.1 From "Animal Choice Behavior and the Evolution of Cognitive Architecture" by L. A. Real in *Science*, 253, 1991. Copyright © 1991 by the American Association for the Advance-ment of Science. Reprinted by permission.

P. 318 Figure 9.2 From "Relative and Absolute Strength of Response as a Function of Frequency of Reinforcement" by R. J. Hernnstein in *Journal of the Experimental Analysis of Behavior*, 4, 1961. Copyright © 1961 by the Society for the Experimental Analysis of Behavior, Inc. Reprinted with permission.

P. 343 Figure 10.1 Graph from "Conditioning Flavor Preferences in Rats: Dissecting the 'Medicine Effect'" by L. M. Barker and C. A. Weaver in *Learning and Motivation*, 22, 1991. Copyright © 1991 by Academic Press. Reproduced by permission of the publisher.

P. 357 Figure 10.2 From Fig. 6.5, p. 89 in BEHAVIORAL METHODS FOR CHRONIC PAIN AND ILLNESS by W. Fordyce. Copyright © 1976 by W. Fordyce. Reprinted by permission of Mosby, a division of W. B. Saunders Company.

P. 377 Figure 11.1a Figure 1 from "An Experimental Study of the Mental Processes of the Rat" by W. S. Small in *American Journal of Psychology*, 12, 1901.

P. 377, 378 Figures 11-1b, 11-2a From INTRODUCTION AND REMOVAL OF REWARD AND MAZE PERFORMANCE IN RATS by E. C. Tolman and C. H. Honzik. Copyright 1930 by The Regents of the University of California. Reprinted by permission of University of California Press.

P. 380 Figure 11.2b Adapted from Figure 1 in "Remembrance of Places Past: Spatial Memory in Rats" by D. S. Olton and R. J. Samuelson in *Journal of Experimental Psychology: Animal Behavior Processes*, 2, 1976. Copyright © 1976 by American Psychological Association. Reprinted by permission of American Psychological Association.

P. 392 Figure 11.6 Figure 4 from "Primate Learning in Comparative Perspective" by J. M. Warren in BEHAVIOR OF NONHUMAN PRIMATES ed. by A. M. Schrier, H. F. Harlow and F. Stollnitz. Copyright © 1965 by J. M. Warren. Reprinted by permission of Academic Press.

P. 386 Table 11.2 Table from "Picture Memory in the Chimpanzee" by Donald

N. Farrar in *Perceptual and Motor Skills,* 25, 1967. Copyright © 1967 by Southern Universities Press. Reprinted by permission of the author and publisher.
P. 429 Figure 12.4 Figure 3 from "Sentence Reading: A Functional MRI Study at 4 Telsa" by D. Bavelier, D. Corina, P. Jessard, S. Padmanabhan, V. P. Clark, A. Karni, A. Prinster, A. Braun, A. Lalwani, J. P. Rauchecker, R. Turner and H. Neville in *Journal of Cognitive Neuroscience*, 9, 1997.

Photo Credits

p. 7 John Markham/ Bruce Coleman Inc. **p. 46** Thomas McAvoy/ Life Magazine, © Time Warner; **p. 85, and 198** Bettmann Archive; **pp. 104, 291,** and **385** courtesy of United States Air Force; **p. 130** Justesen, D. R., Braun, E. W., Garrison, R. G., & Pendleton, R. B. (1970). Pharmacological differentiation of allergic and classically conditioned asthma in the guinea pig. *Science, 170,* 864–866. **pp. 158, 195, 339,** and **359** courtesy of the author; **p. 164** courtesy of Dr. John Batson and Dr. Bob Batsell; **p. 203** Box 6.3, courtesy of Dr. Charles Brewer and Furman University; **p. 207** Nina Leen/Life Magazine, © Time Warner; **p. 217** Fig. 6.6, photos of pigeons from H. M. Jenkins and B. R. Moore (1973), The form of the autoshaped response with food or water reinforcers. *Journal of the Experimental Analysis of Behavior, 20,* 163–181. Copyright 1973 by the Society for the Experimental Analysis of Behavior, Inc., and reprinted by permission of Dr. Herbert Jenkins; **p. 371** courtesy of Dr. Larry Weiskrantz; **p. 405** © McGraw-Hill; and **p. 408** courtesy of Dr. Sue Savage-Rumbaugh.

Cartoons

p. 82 Zamorano; **p. 151** "The Far Side" by Gary Larson. Copyright © 1992 by Farworks, Inc. Reprinted by permission of Universal Press Syndicate; **p. 243** "Oh, not bad..." by Tom Cheney. Copyright © The New Yorker Magazine. Reprinted by permission of The Cartoon Bank. **p. 285** "Harold! The dog's trying..." from THE FAR SIDE by Gary Larson. Copyright © 1984 by Farworks, Inc. Reprinted by permission of Universal Press Syndicate; **p. 376** "Oh, I can solve mazes..." from FRANK & ERNEST by Bob Thaves. Reprinted by permission of Newspaper Enterprise Association, Inc.

AUTHOR INDEX

SUBJECT INDEX